the
# Unofficial
# Guide® to
# Windows®
# XP

*Michael S. Toot*
*Derek Torres*

WILEY

Wiley Publishing, Inc.

Published by
**Wiley Publishing, Inc.**
111 River Street
Hoboken, NJ 07030-5774

Copyright © 2006 by Wiley Publishing, Inc., Indianapolis, Indiana

Published simultaneously in Canada

For general information on our other products and services, please contact our Customer Care Department within the U.S. at (800) 762-2974, outside the U.S. at (317) 572-3993, or fax (317) 572-4002.

For technical support please visit www.wiley.com/techsupport.

Wiley also publishes its books in a variety of electronic formats. Some content that appears in print may not be available in electronic books. For more information about Wiley products, please visit our Web site at www.wiley.com.

Library of Congress Control Number: 2005936635

**ISBN-13:** 978-0-471-76320-8

**ISBN-10:** 0-471-76320-9

10 9 8 7 6 5 4 3 2 1

Book design by Lissa Auciello-Brogan

Cover design by Anthony Bunyan

Page creation by Wiley Publishing, Inc. Composition Services

*To my beautiful bride, Victoria*
*and*
*In loving memory of Simone LaPlume*
*—Michael S. Toot*

*To Celine and our two lads,*
*Pablo and Victor-Emmanuel*
*and*
*In loving memory of Eugene P. Gray*
*—Derek Torres*

# Acknowledgements

**Mike Toot**

Many thanks to Derek Torres, my co-author and all-around good guy, who pitched in and wrote four chapters for this book and made the whole thing possible. Thank you to acquisitions editor Jody Lefevere, technical editor Jim Kelly, copy editor Scott Tullis, and project editor Sarah Hellert, who put all the pieces together and gently pointed out where I was being a block-head. Thanks also to the heroes in production who made the Unofficial Guide format work so effortlessly. My wife Victoria kept me sane throughout the project, including my back surgery and the death of our beloved pet. She is the living embodiment of care and support and I owe her more than I can ever express.

**Derek Torres**

Many thanks and much respect to Mike Toot for giving me this opportunity to work with him on this book. Thanks to the great folks at Wiley — Jody, Sarah, Scott, and Jim in particular — who were not only great to work with, but also very patient and always there to steer me back on track when necessary. I can never repay my wife, Celine, for her support during the book — from putting up with my bad moods during late night writing to taking care of the children when it was my turn — she has always supported my career, for which I am eternally grateful. Finally, to my parents, who still do not understand what I do, but do not question why I do it.

# Credits

**Acquisitions Editor**
Jody Lefevere

**Project Editor**
Sarah Hellert

**Technical Editor**
James F. Kelly

**Copy Editor**
Scott Tullis

**Editorial Manager**
Robyn Siesky

**Vice President & Group Executive Publisher**
Richard Swadley

**Vice President & Publisher**
Barry Pruett

**Director of Composition Services**
Debbie Stailey

**Project Coordinator**
Maridee V. Ennis

**Graphics & Production Specialists**
Sean Decker
Denny Hager
Lynsey Osborn
Amanda Spagnuolo

**Quality Control Technicians**
David Faust
John Greenough
Joe Niesen

**Proofreader**
Vicki Broyles

**Indexer**
Steve Rath

**Cover Design**
Anthony Bunyan

# Contents

C hances are you are reading this book because Windows XP has come into your life, whether on a new computer, as part of an upgrade at work, or because an older version of Windows lacks the tools to get things done. Whether it was forced upon you or you installed it willingly, the first question many people ask is, "Okay, so what can it do?" After playing with Windows XP a while, the second question is usually, "Why does it do things that way?" This book is written to help answer both questions: It shows you how to do things in a new or more efficient way, and shows you how to change some of the odd or inefficient ways to ones that suit your work habits better.

Even though Windows is the 800-pound gorilla of desktop operating systems, there are many things that Microsoft does wrong. For example, Microsoft would have you believe that the spread of viruses and spyware is the fault of uneducated end users, rather than due to key design flaws in the operating system. To me, when you use a product as it was designed to be used and that causes harm, the problem lies with the designer, not the user. I will point out these flaws throughout the book and make you rethink some of the ideas you may have had about Windows XP's suitability for the desktop.

For all its vaunted user-friendliness, Windows XP also has many eyebrow-raising ways of doing things that frustrate users as often as they help. This blend of design oddities didn't happen overnight; Windows XP comes from a long history of programming and interface design that perpetuates as many poor decisions as it improves upon old ones. I call this "throwing good code after bad," and it is a corollary to an adage that bit me more than once as a product manager: Nothing is more permanent than a temporary fix.

In all fairness to Microsoft, Windows is an incredibly complex piece of software. Windows XP contains an estimated 45 to 50 million lines of code, more code than any one person could possibly understand or maintain. Even Bill Gates in his role as Microsoft's Chief Software Architect doesn't have working familiarity with every line of code in Windows. Microsoft's developers have sweat blood and tears to make Windows XP the go-to environment for desktops everywhere. When Microsoft gets something right, it really, *really* works.

The rest of this introduction goes into the good and the not-so-good parts of Windows, the main differences between the two versions of Windows XP you are likely to encounter on your computer, and a quick recap of the other Windows operating systems that are available in the marketplace.

## What Microsoft did right

Stability has greatly improved for all features across the board. Windows XP joined together the two different philosophies present in earlier Windows versions, yet made the program more stable than either Windows Me or Windows 2000. The improved stability is due to a number of changes: some from re-architecting key Windows functions, some with cleaning up problem areas of code, and some by good old-fashioned smart development and testing. If you are going to run Windows, Windows XP is the one to run. Get rid of your old Windows 95 machine, buy a new one, and run XP. It's one of the smartest things you can do.

As mentioned earlier, when Microsoft does something right, it really nails it down. One of the best features of Windows XP is hardware device support, including the newcomer to the scene, USB. Plug and Play has been a concept that Microsoft heavily promoted, correctly deciding that people want computers and associated hardware to just work, without a lot of installing, changing settings, rebooting, and troubleshooting. The early history of Windows showed Microsoft that device driver problems were one of the most frustrating things for users and IT support staff to solve, with most problems ending in finger-pointing matches between hardware manufacturers, Microsoft, and end users. By designing and building solid device driver support and driver-handling features, Microsoft has made "DLL Hell" shrink almost into obscurity.

The user interface has been tweaked and adjusted so that more settings are easily configurable without having to manually edit the Registry; Start Menu behavior has been cleaned up; and enough nips and tucks have been built in to make it easier to figure out for new users and easier to strip down to basics for power users.

Windows is also smarter about handling multimedia and is much less likely to encounter problems when viewing a DVD or playing a game. Some of this is due to the beefier hardware requirements needed to run Windows XP, but much of it has to do with the elimination of DOS and direct hardware access by applications and device drivers. It's now possible to watch a movie coast-to-coast on your laptop without having to reboot along the way. Now *that's* progress!

# What Microsoft got wrong

There are entire books and Web sites dedicated to railing against the bugs, flaws, and "What were they thinking?" design decisions that are a part of Windows XP. One of the biggest flaws, without a doubt, is security. Despite pouring thousands of hours of developer and test time into finding and fixing vulnerabilities, Microsoft is still perceived as being less secure than other operating systems on the market. This insecurity arises out of fundamental design decisions that provided fertile ground for virus writers and "script kiddies" to take advantage of these poor decisions.

For example, in previous versions of Windows, Microsoft shipped the software with many services enabled by default, thinking that they might be useful. Unfortunately, this presented a larger attack surface when these machines were connected to the Internet, and the bad guys took advantage of flaws and loopholes in these services. Windows XP turns off many of these services, but some are still enabled by default.

Another example is that of running applications in a "least privileged" context. Microsoft wanted to bring the Internet experience with all its multimedia and presentation effects directly onto the desktop, linking local data and applications with those found on the Internet. The problem is that applications such as Word and Outlook had powerful scripting engines that had full access to the hard drive and control over much of the operating system. It didn't take long for people to figure out how to write scripts that would run in the scripting engine and wreak havoc. If Windows had been designed to grant only the access needed to perform an application's duties, most viruses and malicious scripts would not run. By bringing the Internet directly to the desktop, Microsoft gave the Internet full access to the desktop.

Less serious but highly frustrating is product activation. In an attempt to circumvent software pirates, Microsoft requires that anyone who installs a retail copy of Windows activate the product within thirty days of installation, otherwise the system is inaccessible until Windows is activated. In essence, this generates mistrust with home and casual users; corporate users have volume licenses that do not require activation, so theoretically unlimited corporate copies could be installed at a large institution (far exceeding the licenses paid for) and Microsoft would never know about it. If you change hardware, such as installing a new video card or hard drive, you may trigger the activation sequence again — and if you exceed three activations on a single product key, the software will not activate and you must call Microsoft to explain just what you are up to before they will "release" your system back to you. In short, this is not a good way to engender trust with customers.

Lastly, there are numerous quirks, glitches, and just plain bad design decisions still lurking about in Windows. Settings are remembered — except when they're not. Window sizes and positions are remembered — unless it's Internet Explorer, which will randomly resize and reposition itself. Some windows insist on always appearing in the same place every time (Task Manager), while other windows refuse to stay where they're told (Windows Explorer). This book will cover these quirks and let you know when something won't behave the way you'd expect it to, and in the long run help prevent frustration from rearing its ugly head.

## Differences between Home and Professional Editions

There are several technologies present in Windows XP Professional Edition that are not found in the Home Edition. Nearly all of these technologies are ones that are more useful — or at least more in demand — in corporate environments and would be considered overkill (overhead?) for home use. The additional technologies are:

- **Dual processor support.** Windows XP Professional contains kernels that will run on dual-processor motherboards which are most often found on high-end workstations, such as ones doing video editing or advanced graphical manipulation. Interesting note: Most applications are not written to take advantage of multiple processors, so Windows handles the scheduling chores. This means that you aren't able to have one processor work only on your video application while the other processor handles everything else.

- **Remote Desktop.** This feature allows you to remotely access your Windows XP Professional computer from another Windows XP computer so you can work with all of your data and applications while away from your office. It uses the Terminal Services service to work this magic. While this may be useful for small offices, larger organizations have more efficient and secure ways of granting remote access to applications and data.

- **Offline Files and Folders.** This useful feature allows you to designate any folder on a server as containing Offline Files. Your computer caches a local copy, and when you disconnect from the network, the files are still available for you to work on. If you make any changes, the changes are synchronized when you connect back up to the network. This is most helpful for road warriors who travel with an office on a laptop. No more remembering to drag and drop folders or run backup programs before hitting the road.

- **Encrypting File System.** This advanced feature of NTFS allows you to encrypt and decrypt data on the fly from designated folders on your hard drive. Sounds great, but if you somehow lose the encryption key diskette and you forget the password, your data is gone forever. Not even Microsoft can recover it once it's gone.

- **Access Control.** There are all kinds of advanced settings that you can apply to your files and folders, providing extremely granular (and sometimes conflicting) control over who can see them and what can be done with your files. If you are not an IT manager in a large corporate environment, you are not likely to explore the labyrinth of access control, nor will you ever need to.

- **Centralized Administration.** This is a civilized reference to Active Directory, the centralized command-and-control backbone introduced in Windows 2000 Server and greatly expanded in Windows Server 2003. You can join an Active Directory domain and partake of all kinds of benefits that an all-Windows network provides. The downside is that you need to buy Windows Server 2003, Client Access Licenses, and spend a lot of time getting up to speed on the nuances and quirks of yet another operating system. The easiest way to get the benefits of centralized administration without the headaches is by purchasing Microsoft Small Business Server 2003 which has much-simplified management tools that even a small-business CEO can operate.

- **Group Policy.** This is one of the management tools that has been improved in Windows Server 2003. With Group Policy a network administrator can exert fine control over a computer, the desktop, visible menus and icons, and even whether applications can be installed by the user. This is too much control for home use, but a lifesaver for overworked IT administrators who keep getting calls from users who download and install a shareware screensaver containing pictures of cute cats and now the logon password doesn't work.

- **Software Installation and Maintenance.** Formerly known as IntelliMirror, this service provides a way to publish what applications are available for installation, or automatically install a set of applications if they are not present at logon. Again, this is too much for a home network, or even a small business network.

- **Roaming User Profiles.** The idea here is that, no matter which computer you log on to, your desktop, applications, documents, and interface settings travel with you. It is a great idea in theory. But it is more useful when there is a standard desktop for workers (for example, Accounting) with minimal changes that need to be moved around the network from desktop to desktop.

- **Remote Installation Services.** With this service, you can plug a bare computer into the network, boot up, and in perhaps half an hour a full, working version of Windows, your applications, and your files is available for work. The downsides are the amount of preparation and setup required and the network traffic generated by shipping an entire OS plus applications across the wire. More sophisticated than running Norton DriveImage Ghost, but more complex due to its integration with Active Directory.

- **Multi-lingual User Interface (MUI) Add-on.** This add-on lets you change the user interface language to get localized dialog boxes, menus, help files, dictionaries, and proofing tools. It is purchased separately from Microsoft and is most useful in countries that have multi-lingual users logging into the same machine at different times throughout the day.

At home I run Windows XP Professional Edition because I work with many Microsoft products and sometimes need things like Active Directory support for my testing and writing. My laptop also has Windows XP Professional as I sometimes contract for Microsoft and need to log on to the network when I am on campus. My wife runs Windows XP Home on her laptop. We don't need anything more advanced and so don't run Windows Server or any of the enterprise-grade technologies.

If you are buying a new computer and are in doubt as to which version to purchase, go with Professional. You could always upgrade from Home to Professional if you need to at a later date, but why pay twice for the operating system if you don't have to?

# Other members of the Windows XP family

Microsoft, never one to miss a market opportunity when it sees one, has released other versions built from the core Windows XP code base. These versions are targeted at hardware-specific opportunities, helping ensure that some version of Windows will be on almost any device you buy. The additional versions are:

## Windows XP Tablet PC Edition

Are Tablet PCs the Next Big Thing? Some people think so, and several vendors have developed specialized hardware that acts like an electronic version of a paper tablet. Tablet PC Edition extends pen and speech capabilities so you can write directly on the screen and control your computer with a stylus. You can also enter text into any application by using your own handwriting. When used with Microsoft OneNote, users get a versatile, flexible, and portable computer, making laptops look like yesterday's news. Tablet PC Edition is only available when you purchase a Tablet PC from authorized hardware vendors; it can not be purchased separately.

## Windows XP Media Center Edition

Computers running Windows XP Media Center Edition let you experience video, audio, pictures, and TV through a convenient user interface that makes it easier than ever to enjoy digital media. You can use the "ten foot view" to comfortably enjoy video, audio, pictures, and television on your computer monitor or TV display using a custom Media Center remote control. You can also switch to the "two foot view" and turn your TV into a computer monitor, allowing you to surf the Internet, use Windows applications, and do everything that you normally do with your computer. Media Center Edition is only available as part of a Media Center computer purchased from authorized hardware vendors and cannot be purchased separately. If you want to know more about Media Center Edition, check out the Media Center enthusiast Web site at www.thegreenbutton.com.

## Windows XP Professional x64 Edition

Windows XP Professional x64 Edition is essentially recompiled from the 32-bit version so that it will run natively on 64-bit processors such as Intel Pentium 4 and AMD Athlon 64. It is designed to provide faster performance, increased reliability, and flexibility, and enables users to run memory- and calculation-intensive applications and processes more efficiently. This new technology arms technical workstation users and cutting-edge home PC enthusiasts with a secure platform that can run new 64-bit applications as well as most existing 32-bit applications for maximum flexibility on a single PC.

Two downsides to this edition are first, that it requires 64-bit device drivers for all hardware, meaning many hardware devices will not be supported until drivers are available; and second, no upgrade path is available from the 32-bit version of Windows. Users must perform a new install on their system. Note also there are few native 64-bit applications available, so as of this writing, if you move to 64 bits, you are living on the cutting edge.

Windows XP Professional x64 should be available for separate purchase at retail outlets or from your original computer's manufacturer.

## Other lesser-known editions

There are a couple other editions built off the Windows XP code base, but these will not be commonly available to most users. They are:

- **Windows XP Starter Edition.** It is similar to Windows XP Home, but has some features removed and some limitations added: display resolution can only be up to 800x600 pixels, only three applications may be run at the same time, any application may have no more than three windows open, PC-to-PC home networking and printer sharing is not available and only a single user account is allowed. Added to the operating system are localized help features, country-specific wallpapers and screensavers and certain pre-configured settings to make it easier for novices to use. According to a Microsoft press release, Windows XP Starter Edition is "a low-cost introduction to the Microsoft Windows XP operating system designed for first-time desktop PC users in developing countries." It is seen as an effort to fight unauthorized copying of Windows XP, and also to counter the spread of the open source Linux operating system which has been gaining popularity in Asia and South America.

- **Windows XP Home Edition N.** In March 2004, the European Commission fined Microsoft €497 million and ordered the company to provide a version of Windows without Windows Media Player, claiming Microsoft "broke European Union competition law by leveraging its near monopoly in the market for PC operating systems onto the markets for work group server operating systems and for media players." Microsoft is currently appealing the ruling. In the meantime, the company plans to offer a court-compliant version of its flagship operating system under the name Windows XP Home Edition N, and at the same price as the full version.

# Making the most of this book

Every book in the Unofficial Guide series offers sidebars that are devised to help you get things done cheaply, efficiently, and smartly. Each takes a different approach to providing you with useful information about the material in the chapters. Use them to educate, inform, and guide your way through the sometimes conflicting or confusing information provided by Microsoft.

1. **Hacks:** If you are comfortable with advanced techniques, the Hacks sidebars will show you ways to get things done using more efficient techniques, or by using techniques that take you into the expert's realm.

2. **Watch Out!:** There are times when the route to success is flanked with traps for the unwary. The Watch Out! sidebars warn you when you need to be open-eyed and sure-footed and provide you with guidance so you avoid potentially harmful results.

3. **Bright Idea:** If Watch Out! sidebars point you away from danger, Bright Idea sidebars point you towards time-, effort-, or money-saving techniques. You don't have to use these tips but they will reward you if you do.

4. **Inside Scoop:** These sidebars give you real-world perspective and lift the material from the theoretical to the practical. Use them to guide your own approach and choose which path is best for you.

# Installation, Configuration, and Customization

**GET THE SCOOP ON...**
Different ways you can install Windows XP ▪ Upgrading your
hardware versus buying a new system ▪ Determining if your
existing system is compatible, or needs upgrades ▪
Preserving your existing files and settings

# PART I

# Preparing for Installation

Chapter 1

**T**hank goodness for advancements in technology. The early days of Windows were fraught with nightmares, and with hours spent trying to determine which hardware would work with the operating system, which drivers were needed, and in what order everything should be hooked together. If you ever tried to perform an upgrade over the weekend and discovered that your system wouldn't boot because you didn't have the correct drivers, you understand the frustration that many people felt during the early days of Windows.

Today, the technology works with you rather than against you. For nearly all users, installing Windows XP is easier and nearly trouble-free compared to earlier versions. Microsoft has built a lot of technology into the setup and installation process so that you will have as smooth a procedure as possible.

It is still a good idea to understand what types of installation are available, what your options are, and what precautions you can take to help ensure a smooth ride.

## Windows XP installation options

There is more to installing Windows XP than just clicking Setup. Depending on the type of installation you choose, you can bring additional functionality to your existing computer. The different types of installation available reflect the different needs of users: an upgrade of an existing installation with the latest bug fixes and features; installation on a brand-new computer; an upgrade of an older version of Windows; a dual-boot between versions of Windows; installation on computers across a network; a scripted installation that takes place automatically without user intervention.

Your choice of installation depends on what your role is. If you are a home user, you are most likely to use either a Service Pack installation or an upgrade installation. If you are a small office/home office (SOHO), or a networking professional supporting many computers, you may use any of these methods for varying reasons.

For the most part, Microsoft made it fairly easy for you to get Windows XP up and running, no matter how you plan to install it. The different installation types vary only in the first steps. Once the system has booted into graphical mode, the rest of the installation takes place normally.

## New installation

A new installation is performed on "bare metal," a hard drive with no other operating system on it. This is most often performed when you want to wipe out everything and start over, or if you've backed up your previous operating system's contents and data files and want to learn about XP from the ground up. If you choose this path, you will need to reinstall your applications, such as Microsoft Office, before you can use them again. For more information about keeping your settings and minimizing the reinstallation process, see "Transfer files and settings from another installation," later in this chapter.

## Upgrade installation

An upgrade installation is used when you want to install Windows XP on top of an earlier version of Windows, such as Windows 2000 or Windows Me. An upgrade preserves your existing applications and settings so that you can be up and running more quickly than if you performed a new installation. This installation method is frequently used by people who purchase an upgrade version of Windows XP, which costs much less than a full install version. Compatibility can be an issue, so see "Use the Upgrade Compatibility Wizard," later in this chapter, for information on running the Upgrade Advisor prior to starting your upgrade.

---

**Watch Out!**

If you purchase the Windows upgrade version, you are required to have your existing Windows installation disk and will be asked for it during install. Without that disk, the upgrade verison will not install, and you will have to buy a full version of Windows instead.

## Dual boot installation

A dual boot installation differs from a new installation and is most often used when you have a spare partition on your hard drive. Each partition contains its own operating system; you can then choose which operating system to run at boot time, allowing you to preserve the old OS with its applications and settings but giving you a new OS to test, work with, or educate yourself. This is most often used for compatibility reasons or when the installation disks for older software are no longer available and you cannot install the application onto a new OS. You will need to reinstall your applications into the new partition, rather than use the copy in the existing partition; otherwise, you will run into problems with conflicting program settings and possibly corrupted files.

## Service Pack only installation

If you already have Windows XP installed, with or without Service Pack 1, you can install Service Pack 2 over your existing operating system. This brings you all the bug fixes and feature updates you need without disturbing the underlying OS or requiring you to engage in a lengthy new OS installation. You do not need to reinstall any applications when you do this.

Service Pack 2 is available as a download from Microsoft, as a CD you can purchase, and as part of a TechNet or MSDN subscription. It is also available "slipstreamed" into retail versions of Microsoft Windows XP that you can find at various retail and online outlets. If you have Automatic Updates turned on in Windows XP, the new service pack will be downloaded in the background for installation onto your computer.

## Network installation

Network installations are used when you have more than a few computers that you need to install Windows XP on. With a network installation, the source files are stored on a network share and the setup program is invoked over the network. You can perform either a new installation or an upgrade installation using this method. One of the chief benefits of this method is having the installation files centrally located, rather than requiring you to take the CD to every desktop. The Network Install section in this chapter will

---

**Bright Idea**

It is extremely helpful to have Service Pack 2 available for offline installation. Download the "Windows XP Service Pack 2 Network Installation Package for IT Professionals and Developers" version from Microsoft and burn it onto a CD, or purchase the Service Pack 2 CD for a nominal fee.

show you how to "slipstream" Service Pack 2 into the original Windows XP installation files so you can perform a one-step installation process.

## Other installation methods

There are other methods that can be used to install Windows XP onto a computer, including cloning (using either Microsoft's Sysprep utility or a commercial program like Symantec's Ghost) and Remote Installation Services (RIS). Both methods are more likely to be used in larger enterprises, though they can sometimes be used in SOHO environments. Although these are not covered in this book, you can find out more information in the online help files and the release notes for Windows XP and Service Pack 2, as well as the Microsoft Web site.

# Buy a new computer, get XP free!

When you buy a new computer — whether from an online giant, a big box store, or a local white box computer dealer — it almost always arrives with Windows XP with Service Pack 2 installed on it. This is one of the fastest, albeit more expensive, ways to obtain Windows XP. The best thing about this method is that you can get systems that are "optimized" for your particular needs: running your business, gaming, doing homework, or watching and listening to multimedia. Most vendors are more than happy to customize your system with any features you want, though this will probably negate any advertised specials that brought you to their doorstep in the first place.

One of the downsides to buying a new computer is that most of the larger vendors install all kinds of applications onto a system, many of them trial versions that require you to pay more money to activate all the features. You will also find lots of icons in the notification area, indicating that various helper applications are loaded and waiting, whether you need them or not. Fortunately these can be removed with little to no effect, other than speeding up the boot time and making your desktop performance livelier. See Chapter 3 for more information on removing these annoyances.

Another downside is that getting high quality, post-sale customer support can be difficult. You may have paid money for that extended support warranty

**Watch Out!**

Your new computer may not come with a Windows XP CD, only a "restore CD" that wipes your hard drive clean, including your files and settings, and reinstalls a factory image. Ask your vendor for a Windows XP CD; otherwise, keep frequent backups of your files and settings.

only to find the contract was subbed out to a company in a different time zone. Of course, if you're in a corporation with an IT department, you already know the person and extension to dial, so support is not as vital an issue. As a general rule, local stores will provide better support than online vendors, so if you have business-critical work that you do on your system, you may want to purchase your new system from a local store and take advantage of the better support.

# Upgrade your existing computer for XP

It's misleading to rely on the Windows XP minimum requirements list when determining what hardware should be upgraded. Microsoft uses the term "minimum" for the bare bones needed to run only an operating system, without any applications. However, even though you can install Windows XP on a minimum configuration, system performance is glacially slow, especially if you run any applications that take significant amounts of memory or processing power. The Microsoft "recommended" system configuration should be considered the bare minimum for minimally tolerable performance. Installation blocking issues reported by the Upgrade Wizard are based on the minimum hardware requirements, not the recommended ones. See Table 1.1 for the rundown on Windows XP requirements.

One good thing about the minimum and recommended requirements list is that it hasn't changed since Windows XP first came out in 2001. Since then, capacity and capability have skyrocketed while prices have plummeted. If your current computer doesn't meet the recommended specifications, upgrading key components is an inexpensive way to support Windows XP without buying a new system. Upgrade complexity varies in scale from

**Table 1.1.** Windows XP minimum, recommended, and realistic Hardware Requirements

| Component | Minimum | Recommended | Realistic |
|---|---|---|---|
| Processor | 233 MHz | 300 MHz | 1 GHz |
| RAM | 64MB | 128MB | 256MB |
| Hard drive | 1.5GB | 2.5GB* | 8GB |
| Video card | 800x600 | 1024×768 | 1024×768 |
| Network | 14.4 Kbps modem | "Network Adapter" | 10/100 Mbps |

* Although Microsoft says actual size varies, experience has shown that 2.5GB is the lower usable limit for a full Windows installation.

simple ones (installing new RAM) to challenging ones (swapping mother-board and CPU). Either you can do it yourself, which in most cases is fairly easy to do and is a great way to learn about your own system, or you can have a local shop perform the upgrades. Local stores usually have an installation special when you buy hardware; just bring in your old system and let some-one else crack the case for you.

There are also numerous online resources and books that walk you through the procedures needed to add or remove any hardware component. When in doubt, read the manufacturer's instructions and follow those over any that you may find on the Internet.

**WARNING!** Turn off your computer and disconnect the plug from the wall before opening any computer case. Computers contain high voltage that can injure or even kill you. If you are not sure you know what you are doing, have a professional service the computer for you.

**CAUTION!** You can generate static electricity that can damage or destroy delicate electronic components such as memory or the CPU. A stray shock can ruin that CPU you just bought, turning it into a lovely and very expensive high-tech paperweight. Always ground yourself by touching part of the computer case before handling computer components, or use a grounding strap attached to an anti-static work pad. Again, if you have any concerns, have a professional do the work.

## Use your existing hardware for XP

If your current computer is capable of running Windows XP, you should run the Upgrade Compatibility Wizard anyway to see if any of your other periph-erals need updating. Older but common hardware may have updated drivers available as part of Windows XP; very old or obscure hardware may not have XP-compatible device drivers available, and you may need to remove the hardware from your computer before upgrading. If the hardware isn't sup-ported but you still must have the hardware available, consider dual-booting with your current version of Windows. You won't be able to use the hardware under Windows XP but you will have access to it with your older version of Windows.

## Collect information about your existing computer

Microsoft has made great advances in making installation and configuration simpler for end users and system administrators alike. For the most part, the process can be done with little to no intervention. However, there is still no sub-stitute for knowing the details of what hardware, firmware, and connectivity are

**Inside Scoop**

If you have a number of computers that you maintain, collect the necessary information for each computer and keep it on a CD-ROM with updated drivers and service packs.

being configured on the system. Not only does Windows ask for some of this information during different phases of configuration, but if there are problems with installing new hardware, software, or driver updates, having this information at hand will go a long way to helping solve the problem.

## SysInfo collects — you guessed it! — system information

The SysInfo program displays and prints out the details of your system's hardware and software. It shows useful information about your existing system, though some of the information is needed only for technical troubleshooting. The report is exhaustive and may cover several printed pages. To collect your system's information, click Start, All Programs, and then Accessories (see Figure 1.1). From the Accessories menu, click System Tools and then System Information. This will launch the Sysinfo application (see Figure 1.2); it will take a few moments to collect all the necessary data from your computer.

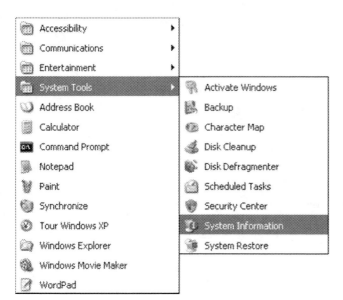

**Figure 1.1.** Access SysInfo from the System Tools menu.

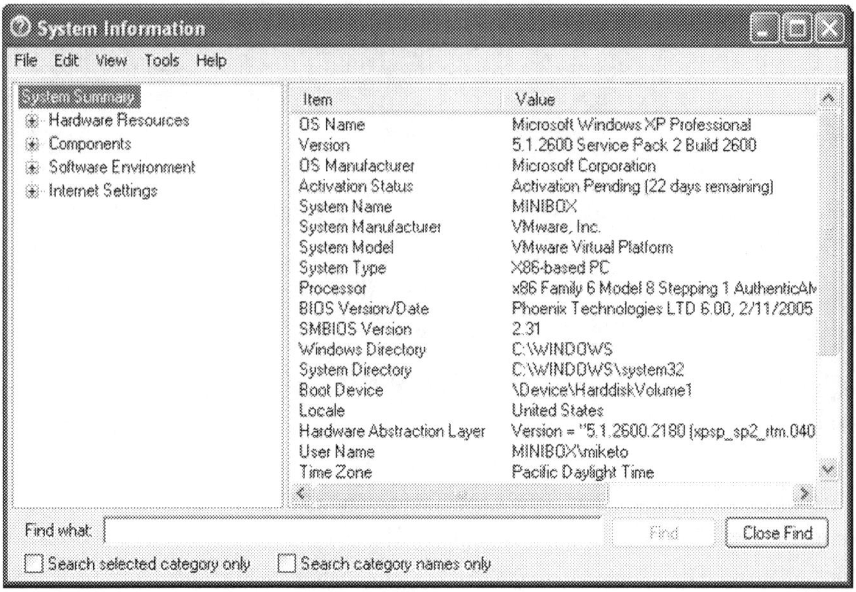

**Figure 1.2.** The SysInfo screen presents you with more detail than you thought possible about your computer and operating system.

If you are using Windows 98 or Windows Me, the same information is available in a slightly different location. Right-click My Computer, click Properties, and then click the Device Manager tab.

Once SysInfo has collected your system's information, click File and then Print to print out a list of the hardware components, driver information, and other useful details.

## Number, please: Obtain hardware model numbers

If you have purchased a computer from a hardware vendor, make sure you have a list of the model numbers for all the components in your system: motherboard, video card, hard drives, CD or DVD drive, and network card. You will need this information if you have to find and install updated device drivers for your system, or if known incompatibilities exist between some of the devices. In some cases the only way to find out the particular model number is to open the computer case and look at the component in question.

## My hardware has firmware!

Some hardware devices have device-specific code called firmware embedded in them. Firmware enables features and functions so that operating systems can make the best use of the hardware. Devices that often have firmware are motherboards (the BIOS, or basic input-output operating system, is the "brain" of the motherboard), CD or DVD drives, and network cards. Sometimes video cards have firmware as well. Check with each device's manufacturer to see if updated firmware is available for your device.

**CAUTION!** You can completely disable hardware if you overwrite it with the wrong firmware, such as the wrong BIOS for your motherboard. If you download new firmware for your hardware, follow the manufacturer's instructions exactly on how to install it. Do not skip steps or guess how to use a firmware installer. If the potential for rendering your hardware inert and unusable makes you nervous, have a computer professional help you.

## Determine device driver versions

Device drivers are hardware-specific code used by the operating system so that it can interact, manage, and control the hardware's functions. Windows XP ships with device drivers for a large number of hardware devices on the market, and new ones are sometimes made available on the Windows Update site. (See Chapter 6 for information on the Windows Update service.) You should check with the device manufacturer to see if new drivers have been made available that are compatible with Windows XP.

## What's your file system type?

If you are performing an upgrade from an earlier version of Windows, you should determine the file system type currently in use on your hard drive: FAT, FAT32, or NTFS. The first two are more likely found on Windows 9x or Windows Me machines, while NTFS is found on Windows NT, Windows 2000, or Windows XP machines. The file system type is relevant, because NTFS features such as access control, encryption, and compression are not available in FAT or FAT32 file systems. If you have multiple drives or partitions, note the file system types for each. Chapter 2 discusses the pros and cons of keeping your existing file system type versus using or converting to NTFS during installation.

## Internet settings

Internet connectivity is perhaps the single most important function of any computer today. Whether you are connected to a nationwide service provider, a local ISP, or connected through your company's network, you should have the necessary connection information so that you can set up your new computer properly. This information may already be available on your computer, or you may need to get it from your system administrator. On existing Windows systems, click Start, Control Panel, and then Network and Internet Connections. From the dialog box, click Network Connections, right-click Local Area Connection, and then click Properties. Scroll down the list and then select the Internet Protocol (TCP/IP) item if it is not already selected (see Figure 1.3). Make sure the checkbox stays selected; otherwise, you will disable the Internet connection itself. Click Properties.

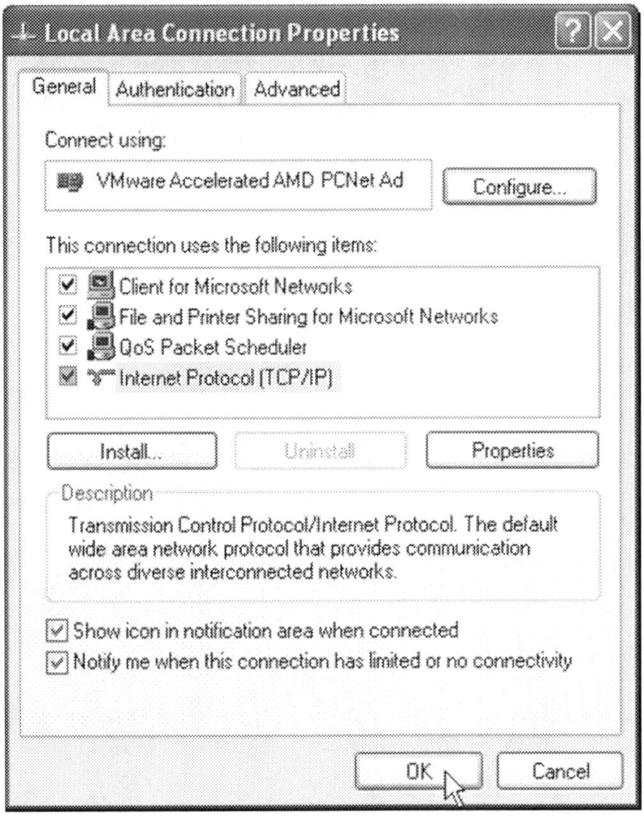

**Figure 1.3.** The Local Area Connection Properties dialog box is the entry point to configure your adapter's network settings.

Write down all the information in the Internet Protocol (TCP/IP) Properties dialog box (see Figure 1.4). This may not be all the information you need. Dialup users need the dialup access information, including account name, password, and server settings. Cable modem users may require PPPoE (Point-to-Point Protocol over Ethernet) modem and account logon settings. If you have any questions, call your Internet service provider or refer to the ISP's Web site support section for help in collecting this information.

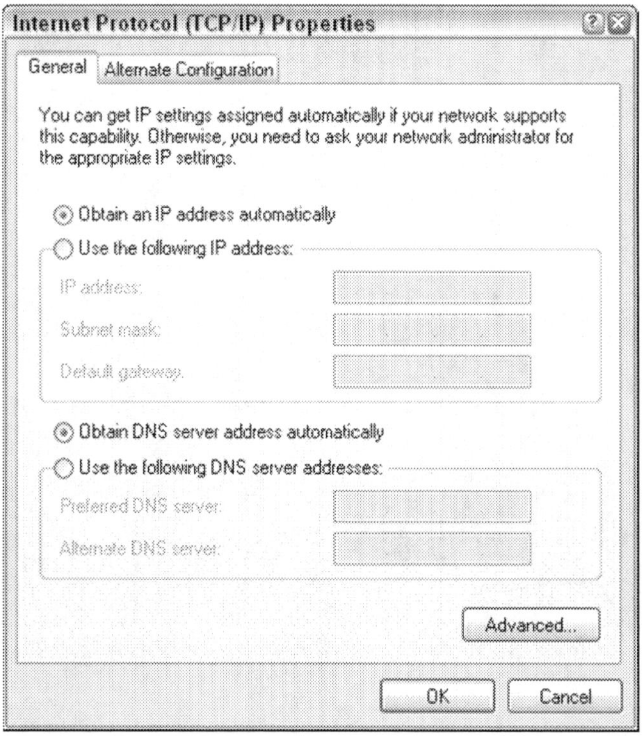

**Figure 1.4.** Most users will enter their connection information in the Internet Properties dialog box.

# Use the Upgrade Compatibility Wizard

The Upgrade Compatibility Wizard (see Figure 1.5) is one of the most useful tools for upgrading an older version of Windows to Windows XP. The wizard takes a survey of system hardware, software, and device drivers, compares the results against a component database, and presents a report of its findings. The Upgrade Wizard bases its findings on the Windows Catalog (see sidebar), which is a list of hardware and software tested by Microsoft and confirmed to work with Windows.

The Upgrade Wizard generates two types of errors: blocking errors and incompatibility warnings. Blocking errors, such as insufficient disk space or RAM, prevent you from running the installation program at all. Incompatibility warnings are generated either for hardware that may need additional files (red Do Not Enter symbol), or for software that does not support Windows XP (yellow warning triangle). Incompatibility warnings will not stop the upgrade process, but the hardware and software may not function properly, or at all, after the upgrade.

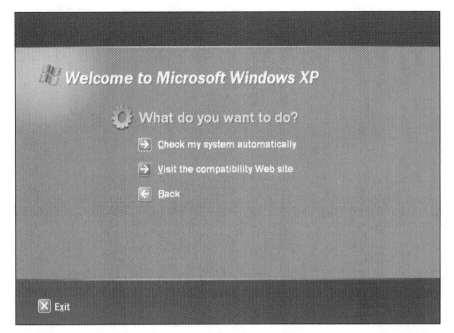

**Figure 1.5.** The Upgrade Wizard is the best starting point to see if your system meets the minimum requirements for Windows XP.

Although the wizard does not guarantee it will find all known problems or system incompatibilities, it helps you avoid ones that have previously been reported to Microsoft and provides suggestions on how to avoid the problems (install more memory, obtain upgraded device drivers, make more room on a hard drive). You should check the hardware and software manufacturer's Web site to see if known problems exist, or if updated components are available. This helps you approach an upgrade forewarned and forearmed, better able to correct any potential pitfalls or shortcomings before installation.

The wizard can be run on most versions of Windows, but it will provide the best results on Windows 2000 or Windows XP-based systems. The wizard will not work with Windows 95 or Windows NT 3.5x. You need to upgrade Windows 95 to Windows 98 or later, and upgrade Windows NT 3.5x to Windows NT 4.0 or later. If you are running those earlier versions of

**Hack**

You can also launch the wizard from a command box. Browse to i386 and run winnt32.exe /checkupgradeonly. This method is particularly useful if the source files are stored on a network share and you don't want to carry the installation CD with you.

## Windows Catalog and your computer

The Windows Catalog, found at www.microsoft.com/windows/catalog/, lists all hardware and software that has passed testing in Microsoft's labs. This testing ensures that the hardware or software follows Microsoft's design recommendations and performs within specified limits. When you run the Upgrade Compatibility Wizard, it checks your existing hardware and device drivers against information found in the Windows Catalog. If your hardware is not found on the list, you are notified that you should either obtain better drivers, or risk the device not working properly under Windows.

The Windows Catalog is not just about hardware and software passing some tests; it's also tied in with Microsoft's branding and the Windows Logo program. The original Hardware Compatibility List, or HCL, was used to provide a listing of hardware and its device drivers that would function within the Windows NT environment. Windows NT changed the rules as to how device drivers should be written and how they would function; manufacturers would submit their hardware and drivers to Microsoft, who would test them to see if they performed as requested.

Microsoft also tied a logo program into the HCL, so that vendors who passed the tests would be able to put a "Designed for Windows NT" logo on the package. Microsoft 9x and Windows 2000 also had specific logo programs, as did Office and BackOffice. Microsoft eventually consolidated many of its desktop-related logo programs and renamed the HCL to Windows Catalog to support the "Designed for Microsoft Windows XP" logo program.

Today, almost all hardware on the market is capable of passing the HCL tests. But because of testing and logo fees, some vendors elect not to go through the process. If you try installing drivers for hardware not on the list, Windows XP will alert you that the drivers have not passed the tests and Microsoft can't be responsible if you install them and bad things happen.

In the real world mainstream vendors issue updated drivers all the time. The Windows Catalog testing and logo verification process takes time, and vendors need to get new bug fixes or feature updates into the hands of users. If you are installing drivers from a mainstream, reputable company, don't worry about the lack of logo or presence on the Windows Catalog list. You may need to keep an eye on performance, and roll back the installation if the system is more unstable than before, but otherwise you can most likely take the risk.

Windows, it will be easier to upgrade your hardware and then perform a new install, rather than take your system through multiple OS upgrades.

1. Insert the Windows XP CD. The Welcome to Microsoft Windows XP dialog box appears. You can also browse to the CD drive and click Setup to launch the CD.

2. Click Check system compatibility. The What do you want to do? dialog box appears.

3. Click the option to check your system automatically. The Microsoft Windows Upgrade Advisor dialog box appears.

4. Click Yes, download the upgraded Setup files (recommended).

5. Click Next. The wizard downloads additional files needed to check your system and then checks your system for potential incompatibilities. The wizard creates a summary report, showing you problems or potential problems that may occur (see Figure 1.6).

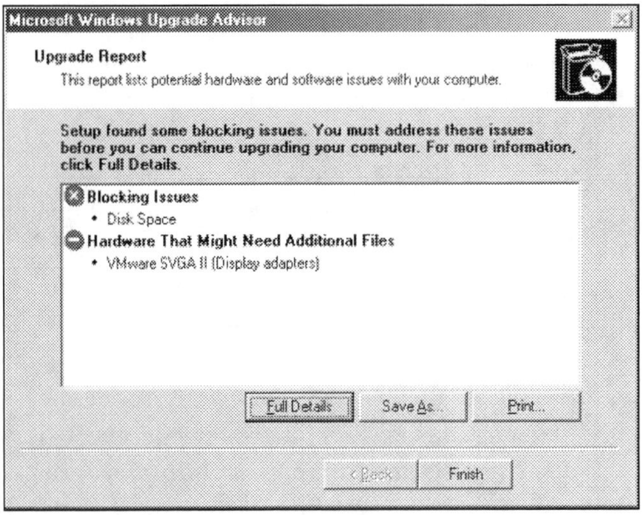

**Figure 1.6.** You cannot install Windows XP until you address any blocking issues that arise.

6. Click Full Details to review details about the blocking issues or potential problems, in the form of a detailed report. Click Summary to return to the summary report.

7. Click Finish. The wizard will report if there are no problems or potential pitfalls for your upgrade.

Microsoft also provides a downloadable version of the wizard, called the Upgrade Advisor. It lets you check your system for incompatibilities before buying Windows XP; this way you don't need to buy the software, open the box, and then decide you'd rather not make the move to XP. You can download the Advisor (all 50MB worth) at www.microsoft.com/windowsxp/home/upgrading/advisor.mspx.

# Transfer files and settings from another installation

If you are performing a new install rather than an upgrade, you can use a wizard to transfer existing files and settings to Windows XP. This timesaving wizard restores personal desktop settings and menu options that you have set up previously in other versions of Windows, including your Internet Explorer security settings, bookmarks, and cookies.

The Files and Settings Transfer Wizard moves a large number of files and settings by default. It can also be used to move additional files and folders that you select when you run the wizard. You can point the wizard at any folder and move its contents, or you can select files by file type and have those moved to the new system. The wizard is designed to transfer settings for Windows, some Windows applications, and user files. The default settings include:

- Hardware Settings
- Mouse, keyboard, regional settings, network, dialup, and printer driver settings
- Desktop Settings
- Wallpaper, colors, screen saver, menu and taskbar options, folder settings, audio settings
- Software Settings
- Internet Explorer bookmarks and cookies, Microsoft Office settings, Outlook and Outlook Express settings, mail folders and address books, some third-party application settings
- Files and Folders
- Desktop, My Documents, My Pictures, My Favorites, Shared desktop, fonts

Moving only Windows settings does not take up much room. Moving files, especially if you have selected additional files and folders, takes up much more room. Plan on anywhere from 5MB to 600MB of room needed on the target system — more if you choose to move movie, multimedia, or music files such as MP3s.

**Inside Scoop**

Before running the wizard, run Disk Cleanup to remove temporary files and Internet Explorer cached files. This can shave tens or hundreds of megabytes from the files to be transferred.

You may be able to save only your settings to a single floppy disk; you will not be able to save your additional selected files onto a floppy disk. If you will not be deleting or reformatting a partition during the install process, you can save all your files to that partition. You can also connect to a network share or burn your settings and files to a CD or DVD. Finally, you can copy the settings across a network to a new computer. You will need to set up the necessary shares and permissions before you do so.

To run the Files and Settings Transfer Wizard:

1. Insert the Windows XP CD. The Welcome to Microsoft Windows XP dialog box appears. You can also browse to the CD drive and click Setup to launch the CD.

2. Click Perform Additional Tasks. The What do you want to do? dialog box appears.

3. Click Transfer files and settings. The Files and Settings Transfer Wizard dialog box appears.

4. Click Next. The Select a transfer method dialog box appears.

5. Click the transfer method you want to use.

6. Click Next. The What do you want to transfer? dialog box appears (see Figure 1.7).

7. Select the option for what you want to transfer: settings, files, or both. Click the checkbox to select a custom list of files.

8. Click Next. The Select custom files and settings dialog box appears.

9. Click a button to add settings, folders, files, or file types.

10. Click Next. The wizard collects the selected files and settings.

11. Click Finish.

Although the wizard is good about picking up your settings, there are a few caveats for the target system. First, the wizard moves only settings, not entire applications. Second, the specific application should be installed on the target system first and then the settings imported. Third, the wizard supports only some third-party applications or may only support later versions. A list of supported applications can be found at http://support.microsoft.com/default.aspx?scid=kb;en-us;304903.

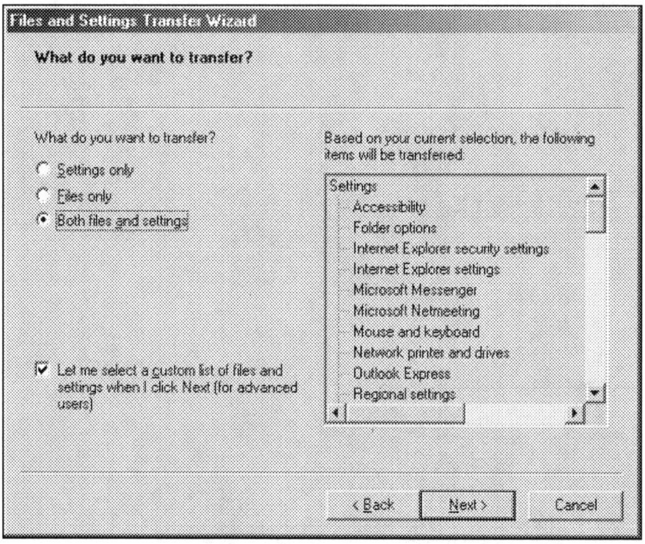

**Figure 1.7.** Select settings, files, or both to transfer to your new computer.

# Restore your files and settings

Once you have collected your files and settings from the source computer, you can import and install them onto the target computer running Windows XP. Only Windows XP natively ships the Files and Settings Transfer Wizard as part of the operating system, giving you easy access to the wizard for any new installations you may be creating.

The Files and Settings Transfer Wizard contains a "safety valve": If you are running the wizard from within Windows XP, it gives you the opportunity to create a Wizard Disk that you can run on the source machine without requiring the Windows XP install disk. This is an extremely handy shortcut and gives you the ability to create another tool for your support toolbox so that you don't have to carry around the Windows XP install disk everywhere. (The install disk is worth its weight in gold and causes much frustration when it can't be found).

The following instructions assume you have already run the wizard to collect settings on the source computer.

1. Click Start.

2. Click All Programs.

3. Click Accessories.

4. Click System Tools.

5. Click Files and Settings Transfer Wizard. The Files and Settings Transfer Wizard dialog box appears.

6. Click Next.

7. Click New Computer (see Figure 1.8).

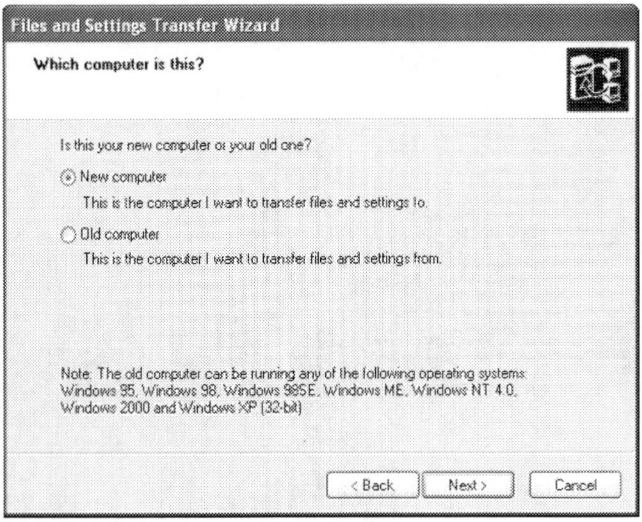

**Figure 1.8.** Import your settings to your new installation.

8. Click Next. If the Windows Security Alert dialog box appears, click Unblock.

9. Click I don't need the Wizard Disk.

10. Click Next. The Where are the files and settings dialog box appears.

11. Click Other.

12. Click Browse to browse to the previously collected settings (see Figure 1.9).

13. Click Next. The source files and settings are applied to the new system.

14. Click Finish. After applying the settings, you will need to log off and log on again for the new settings to take effect.

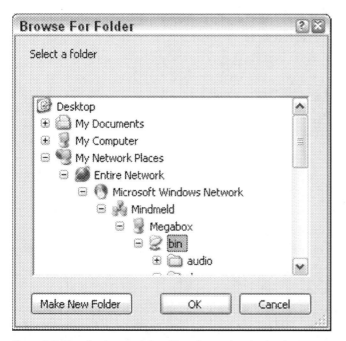

**Figure 1.9.** The wizard can restore settings from a shared network resource.

# All about registration and activation

Windows XP includes two "features" as part of the Windows XP installation process. One, registration, has been around since the early days of Windows 95. Other than putting your name and personal information into the Microsoft marketing machine, registration has no benefit to you other than getting more junk mail in your mailbox. You can choose to register or not register your copy of Windows; it's up to you.

Product activation is a different story. Windows Product Activation (WPA) was created to help curb software piracy and protect Microsoft's revenue stream being generated by sales of Windows XP. With WPA you have 30 days after installation to activate Windows; otherwise, Windows will not let you log onto the system. WPA uses a combination of the 25-character product key and information about your system's hardware to generate a code that is sent to Microsoft (over the Internet or via phone call). A forty-two-digit confirmation key is then input into Windows, which disables the 30-day time bomb.

There are significant gotchas that are part of the WPA experience.

- WPA is most often encountered in retail copies of Windows. Corporate licensing versions and versions that are preinstalled by large computer vendors commonly do not use WPA. Cynical translation: Microsoft believes that you as an individual are more likely to install a copy of Windows that you haven't paid for than a large corporation with uncounted thousands of desktops.

- The WPA creates a software "hash" based on your computer's hardware. If you change some of the following items, you may need to re-activate Windows: CPU, motherboard, RAM, hard drive, hard drive controller card, video card, network card, and CD or DVD drive. In real-world terms, this means that if you ever upgrade your hardware, you may need to contact Microsoft over the phone and explain why you need to activate Windows again. Microsoft does not qualify how many of these components you can change before you must re-activate Windows.

Microsoft assures customers that no personal information is sent back to Microsoft as part of the activation process. You can read Microsoft's view on WPA at www.microsoft.com/technet/prodtechnol/winxppro/evaluate/xpactiv.mspx. A somewhat more objective analysis can be found at http://aumha.org/win5/a/wpa.php.

There is a saying that goes something like, "The law forbids rich and poor equally from sleeping under bridges." This is another way of saying that WPA disproportionately punishes home and SOHO users who may not know all the ins and outs of computer upgrades, modifications, and how they interact with retail versions of Windows. If you never tangle with WPA, count yourself among the fortunate.

## Most important: Make a backup of your system!

Even with all the advisories, settings, and transfers, Things Can Still Go Wrong. Make a backup of all your important files, whether it means copying them to a different machine or burning them onto a CD. If you have software that creates hard drive images, make one before you launch Windows XP's setup. It seems that there's always a file that is needed but is now gone, thanks to an aggressive installation. Always create a backup, unless you don't mind spending the time to re-create the necessary data later on.

# Just the facts

- To run Windows XP, you can use your existing computer, upgrade your existing computer, or buy a new computer.

- If you use your existing computer or install new hardware, collect information about the hardware and drivers before you upgrade.

- Use the Upgrade Compatibility Wizard to make sure you have both compatible hardware and the latest software available for Windows XP.

- You can transfer your files and settings from an old computer to a new one, or save the settings prior to upgrading your hardware and installing XP.

- Finally, and most importantly, *make a backup* of your existing system!

# Installing Windows XP

Installing Windows XP is one of the best ways to learn the basics of how your computer is configured and how the pieces work together. A new installation wipes everything clean, starts fresh, and puts a crisp new copy of the software on your hard drive. An upgrade installation copies Windows XP over your older Windows version, keeping your existing settings and application information intact.

If all you are looking to do is bring your existing Windows XP up to date, then a Service Pack 2 installation is what you need. For more sophisticated installations, you can use dual booting, network installations, and automated installs to give you more flexibility as to how you want to deploy Windows XP.

Before you jump in you should know a few things about what Windows XP will ask you during the setup process. A checklist is provided to help you collect the information and have it available when you install Windows onto your system.

## Hard drives, partitions, and XP

Most new desktop computers come with a single hard drive for storing all the applications, data, and files that you will use. If you have an older computer or have modified your existing computer, you may have two or more hard drives in your PC. Many times it's easier to add another hard drive than it is to buy a single hard drive and then migrate from the old drive to the new.

**Watch Out!**

During setup, Windows uses "destructive partitioning" to edit a drive's partition table. If you make a change, you have *irretrievably* lost your old partitions and all the data on them. Consider using Symantec's PartitionMagic or VCOM's Partition Commander to nondestructively create, resize, merge, or remove old partitions before you install.

One thing that can be confusing about a Windows installation is the difference between a drive and a partition. The Windows installation program doesn't tell you what the differences are, yet it asks you key questions about where you want to install the software.

A hard drive is like a filing cabinet, while a partition is like a file drawer in that cabinet. When you run setup, you tell Windows which "file cabinet" and which "drawer" should be the new home for the operating system. The Windows setup program has a rudimentary set of tools to create and delete partitions on your hard drives, so you can create a partition with the right size for your files.

New computers often have the entire hard drive formatted as a single partition. This isn't necessarily a bad thing; there are a lot of services built into Windows that assume everything is kept within the same partition, and by allocating an entire drive as a single partition it keeps things simple for Windows. However, it is not always the best way to work or the most convenient for other applications.

Most people who work with computers will tell you that it's a good idea to create two partitions on a single hard drive: one for your operating systems and applications, and one for your data and user files. It's easier to back up user data when it resides on a separate partition than when it is intermingled with system and application files on a single partition.

If you are performing a new installation, a good rule of thumb is to allocate a third of a hard drive for your operating system and applications and two thirds for your data files, with the numbers adjusted in favor of the OS and application files. For a 40GB hard drive, this translates to about 15GB and 25GB, respectively.

An upgrade installation has fewer options available; usually you install into the same partition as your older Windows installation. This is necessary to preserve your existing application and settings information. Dual boot installations require installing XP into a different partition than other operating systems.

---

### Keep it simple!

Windows XP contains many ways to configure hard drives, partitions, and file systems. These tools were built in for different technologies that are required in different situations.

Windows is designed to be run on diskless workstations, as a session within Terminal Services, as a platform for legacy application support, and as a remotely manageable system in a large corporation. Individually, the options sound like great ideas. Things like setting up RAID (Redundant Array of Inexpensive Disks), creating mount points, and dynamic disks all have different benefits that can make your computer faster or provide features like roaming profiles across the network. You can read more about advanced drive, disk, and partition management technologies in Chapters 5 and 12.

But with this flexibility comes complexity. The benefits quickly disappear if the options have been configured in ways that are confusing and difficult to work with or troubleshoot. Most home users will not need to work with any of these advanced options, while corporate users may have some of the options already configured.

If this is your first time working with the Windows XP installation process, it's best to keep things simple. After you have spent some time with XP, and after reading the chapters mentioned above, feel free to branch out into different disk and partition configurations. For now, keep it simple.

---

# Choosing a file system: FAT32 or NTFS

If you are performing an upgrade from an earlier version of Windows, you should find out the file system type in use: FAT, FAT32, or NTFS. The first two are more likely found on Windows 9x or Windows Me machines, while NTFS is found on Windows NT or Windows 2000 machines. The file system type is highly relevant because NTFS features such as access control, encryption, and compression are not available in FAT or FAT32 file systems. Use Windows Explorer to right-click on the drive letter and then click Properties. The file system type is shown on the properties dialog box.

Unless you have an application that requires FAT32, you should select NTFS for a new installation. You gain the benefits of access control, encryption and compression, event auditing, and the use of dynamic disks. The

> **Inside Scoop**
>
> Converting FAT to NTFS requires some additional space on your hard drive. The size varies depending on a number of factors; allow up to 500 additional megabytes for conversion.

only reason to use FAT32 is if you are dual booting with Linux or DOS and need access to files on your Windows partition; even then, there are Linux drivers you can use to gain access to native NTFS partitions.

For upgrade installations, you can choose to convert an existing FAT partition to NTFS during the install process. This adds an additional reboot to the system, but otherwise does not affect setup.

## Old terms, new meanings: Workgroups and domains

The setup process will ask you if you want to join a workgroup or domain. The difference between the two revolves around the centralized authentication, access, and security provided by a Windows domain controller.

Workgroups are an ad hoc network structure commonly used with Windows 9x or Me networks. Each computer is a peer of every other computer, and things such as file shares and passwords are managed separately on each computer. With networks of more than just a few computers, this quickly becomes unmanageable.

Domains were initially used with Windows NT. Special servers were designated as domain controllers and were responsible for managing users, passwords, printer and server shares, and other network services. It was a flat hierarchical model where you could have multiple domains and domain controllers interconnected with each other, but no one server was the "top dog."

Windows 2000 Server introduced a new domain model called Active Directory, or AD. AD is a flexible, powerful, and hierarchical management model that offers much greater control over nearly every aspect of the network, other servers, desktop computers, and users. It was designed to interoperate with the Internet and use Internet naming conventions within the domain.

But like many things in life, with increased power came increased complexity. AD is not for the faint of heart. If you are not already using Windows NT or Windows Server domains on your network, you should stick with workgroups. But if you have more than ten computers in a workgroup, you should think about installing a Windows Server and using Active Directory to make management tasks easier. AD is relatively straightforward for a SOHO, but for larger departments and divisions in a corporation, you should find

> **Bright Idea**
>
> In addition to the server and workstation licenses, you must buy a Client Access License (CAL) for every computer that will connect to a Windows server. Small businesses can save significant costs by purchasing Microsoft Small Business Server 2003. See www.microsoft.com/windowsserver2003/sbs/default.mspx for more information.

an expert who has deployed AD in a similarly sized business rather than attempt it on your own.

In order to join a domain, you must have a domain controller running on your network and you need the name and password of an account with rights to add a computer to a domain. Most commonly this will be someone who is a member of the Domain Admins account, but it can be any group that has been given rights to join computers to a domain.

If your computer cannot find the domain server, either because you specified an incorrect domain or lack the rights to join the computer to a domain, setup will ask if you want to try joining a domain later. Chapter 10 has more information on working with Active Directory and how to integrate Windows XP into domains.

When you are asked for a computer name, you can use up to 63 characters. However, older versions of Windows you may have running on your network, such as Windows 98 or Windows NT, recognize computer names of only 15 characters. If this is the case, you should use 15 characters or less. Do not use spaces, periods, or other punctuation marks (dashes are okay) because these cause problems not only with Windows but with other operating systems on your network.

# Networks: Making the connection

Once you've worked with computers on a network, it's difficult to imagine working any other way. Windows XP was designed for working on a network from the ground up. It even has enough powerful tools and utilities built into it that it can act as a small-scale Web server or a modestly-powered file and print server.

Setup includes numerous tools to detect your networking capabilities. However, the Networking portion of setup can be a mixed blessing. You can accept the Typical installation, which installs the Microsoft Network client, TCP/IP protocol, file and printer sharing, and quality-of-service (QoS) management. The Typical installation uses DHCP for retrieving IP addresses and DNS information, which is convenient for most home users and SOHO environments that use DHCP.

**Watch Out!**

Do not connect your network adapter to the network until *after* your desktop's firewall is enabled and anti-virus software installed. Get your computer protected first, and *then* expose it to the Internet. If you don't, in the short time it is unprotected your new system can be infected by worms and viruses.

However, if you are connected to an ISP or are in an environment that uses static IP addresses, you will need to select the Custom installation process and fill in the necessary information that you obtained from your ISP or system administrator. This may include your IP address, the subnet mask, gateway address, and DNS server name or address. All of this information is necessary to make connections to other computers on the Internet.

You can always change this information later by clicking Control Panel and then Network Connections. If you have troubles connecting despite using the correct information, you can use the network troubleshooting techniques described in Chapter 8 to help isolate the problem.

## Installation checklist

To help you with your next installation, here is a list of information and questions you will need to answer. If you have this in hand, your installation process should be smoother.

- Determine the type of installation — new install, upgrade, dual boot, or network.

- Run the Upgrade Compatibility Wizard on your existing system.

- Correct any problems reported by the Upgrade Compatibility Wizard.

- Obtain the latest Windows XP-compatible device drivers for your hardware.

- Obtain the latest Windows XP-compatible application updates, if needed.

- Upgrade your hardware if needed.

- Determine which hard drive and which partition you will use for the installation. If you will be using a hardware-based RAID array for any of your disks (see Chapter 12), create the array according to the manufacturer instructions. Make sure you have the latest Windows XP-compatible SCSI or RAID drivers for your RAID card.

- Determine which file system types you currently have and which types you will be using.

- If you need regional support for things like currency types or regionalized keyboards, write down the ones you need. This does not include localized (that is, language-specific) menus or dialog boxes.

- Make sure you have the appropriate name and organization information available, as well as a Windows XP 25-digit product key.

- Pick a name for your computer that is descriptive or easily remembered; if possible, keep it to 15 characters or less. If you are in a company, ask if there are computer-naming requirements or guidelines that your networking group would like you to use.

- Collect your TCP/IP networking information. This should include whether your address is dynamic (DHCP) or static, your gateway address, your DNS server addresses, and any special connection or logon information from your network provider.

- If multiple people will be using your computer, ask them what user names they want to use. If you are connecting to a domain, make sure the names are listed in Active Directory.

- If you are adding this computer to an existing domain, make sure you have the name and password of an account with this privilege, or you add the computer to the domain beforehand.

# Install Windows XP: New installation

A new installation will take anywhere from one hour to a couple hours, depending on the speed of your computer, the number of hard drives and drive space you have, and whether you sit by and baby-sit the computer, ready to click Next or fill in parameters when asked.

Retail boxes of Windows XP ship with Service Pack 2 already included, a practice referred to as "slipstreaming." Pre-SP2 retail versions may still be for sale, so you should check to ensure that Service Pack 2 is a part of the product. Otherwise you will need to download or purchase separately Service Pack 2 from Microsoft.

Once you have run through a new installation a few times, you may want to examine scripting your installation so that user intervention is not required. See the task "Automate the installation process" later in this chapter for more information.

In some cases you may not be able to perform a new installation on your computer. For example, most systems from computer manufacturers ship with "restore disks." These are CDs or DVDs that contain an image of your operating system and applications that were pre-selected and pre-installed by

## When "free" isn't always free

New computers are often advertised as being "Loaded with EVERY-THING you need for the home!" The computer indeed comes loaded with applications for everything, from writing letters to watching movies to playing games.

It sounds like a great deal, but oftentimes it's not what you think. Most pre-loaded applications come in two flavors: trial versions or stripped-down versions. The trial versions require you to purchase the full version after a certain number of days, and if you don't, they stop working. "Express" or "lite" versions are ones that have been stripped down, with key product features removed or disabled. In both cases you must contact the software manufacturer and either purchase and download a full version or purchase a license key that unlocks the features or turns off the time bomb. Time bomb software is found in most anti-virus and firewall products, while stripped-down product versions are found nearly everywhere else.

Some people may be perfectly satisfied with the stripped-down versions; for example, there are people who truly believe that Microsoft Works is a great program. But don't feel you are locked into using the programs that came with your computer. If you would rather use software that has the features you need and works the way you work, expect to spend some time and money over and above what you spent on your "loaded" new system.

the manufacturer. When you run the setup program for the restore disk, it copies the image, OS, applications and all, onto your hard drive. This may not always be what you want, especially if there are applications that are incompatible with the ones you want to install.

For example, you may want to use Trend Micro's PC-cillin antivirus product but your laptop came with an evaluation copy of Symantec's Norton AntiVirus installed instead. If this is the case, you can't customize your restore disk. The only solution is to uninstall Norton and install PC-cillin. You can also purchase a retail copy of Windows XP, wipe your hard drive, and build up your system the way you want it, not the way your computer's manufacturer wants it. But be warned that if you do this, you may void your customer support agreement with your manufacturer.

The following instructions assume you are installing a retail edition of Windows XP Professional with Service Pack 2. To perform a new installation:

1. Insert your Windows XP CD and reboot the computer. The text-mode setup program launches. If you have a third-party driver for a RAID array, press F6 when prompted by setup and follow the instructions.

2. Press Enter. The Welcome to Setup screen appears. Press Enter again. The Windows XP license screen appears. Press the PageDown key to read the license agreement and then press F8. The disk partitioning screen appears.

3. You can choose to format your entire drive as a single partition; you can also create and format additional partitions. Press Enter to use the entire disk as a single partition, or press C to create more than one partition and follow the instructions on the screen (see Figure 2.1).

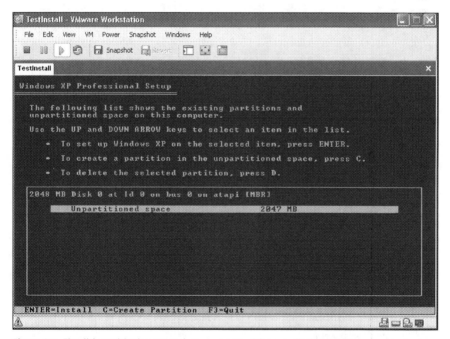

**Figure 2.1.** The disk partitioning screen lets you create, delete, or display partitions on your hard drives.

4. Use the arrow keys to move the highlight to the file system type you want to use and then press Enter. The partition is then formatted with the appropriate type, and files are copied onto your hard drive. After the files are copied, press Enter to reboot or wait for Windows to

**Hack**

You can change the user and company name in Windows without re-running setup. Using Regedit, browse to HKEY_LOCAL_MACHINE\SOFTWARE\Microsoft\Windows NT\ CurrentVersion, double-click the RegisteredOwner or RegisteredOrganization key, and type in the new value. This is useful if you change company names or the key technical contact at your company.

reboot automatically. Do not remove the CD from the disk drive, because more files are needed during the graphical setup phase.

5. The Regional Settings and Language Options dialog box appears. The Regional Settings and Language Options change only some aspects of Windows XP: the date, time, currency formats, and the kinds of input devices that are different depending on the country. In order to change the menus, dialog boxes, and help files, you need to install the Multi-Language User Interface add-on. You can purchase it separately from Microsoft. Click Next. The Personalize Your Software dialog box appears.

6. Type in your name and, optionally, your organization. Click Next. The Your Product Key dialog box appears.

7. Type in the 25-digit Windows XP serial number, found on either your CD jewel case or on a separate license sticker. If you work for a company that has a Windows XP site license, use the site license key instead. When you are done, click Next. The Computer Name and Administrator Password dialog box appears.

8. Type a name for your computer. Windows has generated one for you, but unless you like alphabet soup, you will want to choose one that has more meaning for you. The computer name should be different than an existing user's name; Active Directory gets a headache if unique identifiers aren't used. Type an administrator password in both boxes (the passwords must match). Remember or write down the administrator password and keep it in a safe place. Click Next. The Date and Time Settings box appears.

9. Make any adjustments to the date and time, including your time zone and whether Daylight Savings Time is observed. Click Next. The Networking Settings dialog box appears.

10. The Typical setting instructs Windows to get its network information from a DHCP (Dynamic Host Configuration Protocol) server. Many

networks, including home or SOHO networks using a router or hardware firewall use DHCP addressing. If you need to enter a static IP address or add a specific network protocol, click Custom. The Networking Components dialog box shown in Figure 2.2 will let you configure the necessary settings. In general, you can click Typical and then Next with no ill effects, because you can always enter network and configuration information later. If Windows setup detected a modem, you will see the Modem Dialing Information screen immediately after the Date and Time screen. Enter your country or region, your area code, whether you dial a number to get an outside line, and whether you use tone or pulse dialing. Click Next to continue.

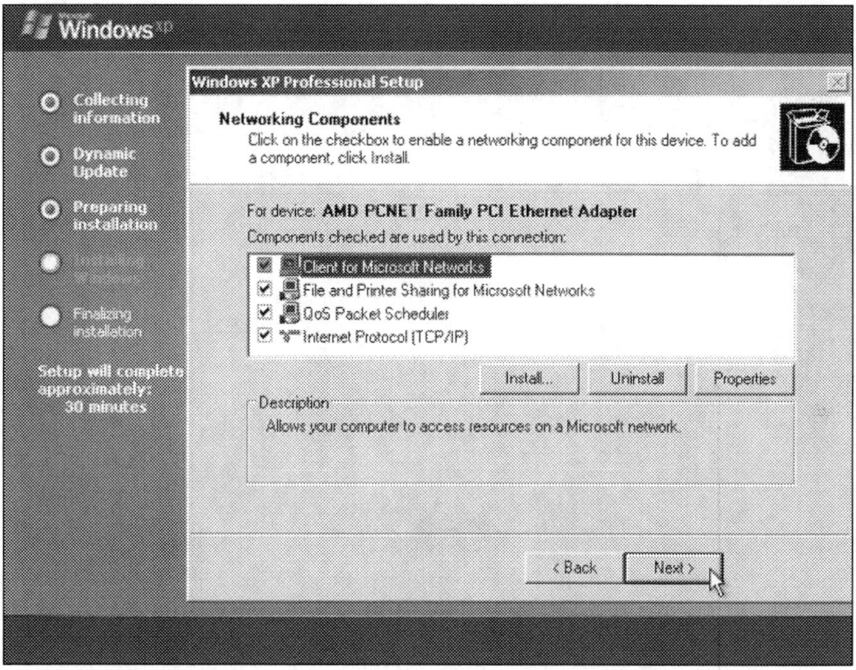

**Figure 2.2.** You can select, add, or remove components and services to your network adapter. For now, keep it simple.

---

### Inside Scoop

Don't be in a rush to install all needed network protocols and settings. Once Windows is installed, test your bare-bones networking; then add additional protocols or services one at a time and test them too.

11. The Workgroup or Computer Domain dialog box appears, as shown in Figure 2.3. Select whether you want to join a workgroup or domain, and then type the name of the workgroup or domain you wish to join. As with machine names, your workgroup name should be 15 characters or less. Click Next. Windows finishes copying files and settings, and then automatically restarts your computer. If a message appears stating that Windows wants to automatically adjust the screen resolution, click OK when prompted.

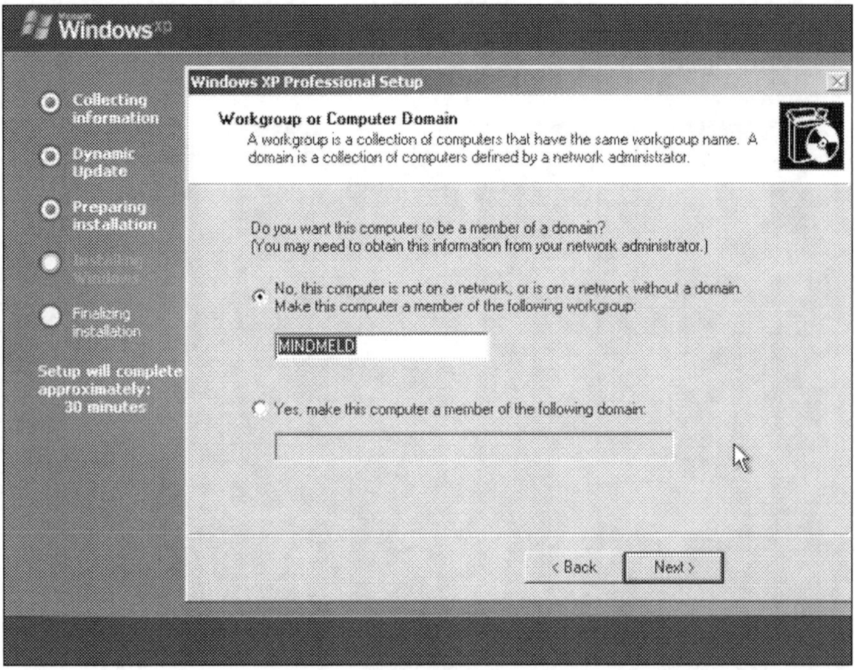

**Figure 2.3.** Enter the name of an existing workgroup or domain in the appropriate box.

12. The Welcome to Microsoft Windows screen appears. Click Next. The Help Protect Your PC dialog box appears. Click the option to help protect your PC by turning on Automatic Updates now. Click Next.

13. The network connection dialog box appears as in Figure 2.4. Microsoft doesn't explain it for you, but the primary difference between connecting directly or through a network is whether you need hard-coded connection information (direct connection) or need DHCP (LAN connection) to gain access to the Internet. If you use a dialup modem or a broadband modem inside your computer, you should select the

direct option. If in doubt, check with your ISP or system administrator to see which will work. This selection isn't crucial because all your network settings can be changed later. Select the network option that applies to your computer. Click Next.

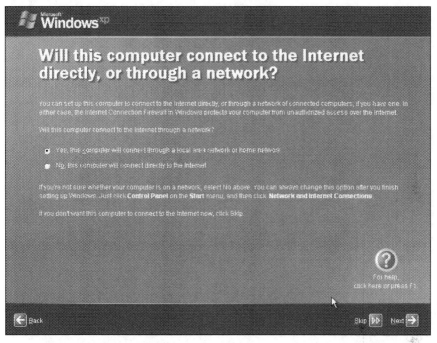

**Figure 2.4.** If you use static internet addresses, choose direct connection. If you use DHCP, choose LAN connection.

14. The Windows Product Activation dialog box appears. Click No to be reminded every few days. Click Next.

15. The next dialog box (Figure 2.5) asks who will use the computer. At least one name must be entered; type in the names of those who will be using your computer and then click Next. The Thank You dialog box appears. Click Finish.

---

**Bright Idea**

Don't activate your copy of Windows until you test your applications and especially your hardware. If you find your brand new video card doesn't work well with XP, you can start a new installation with a new card and not use up one of your activations.

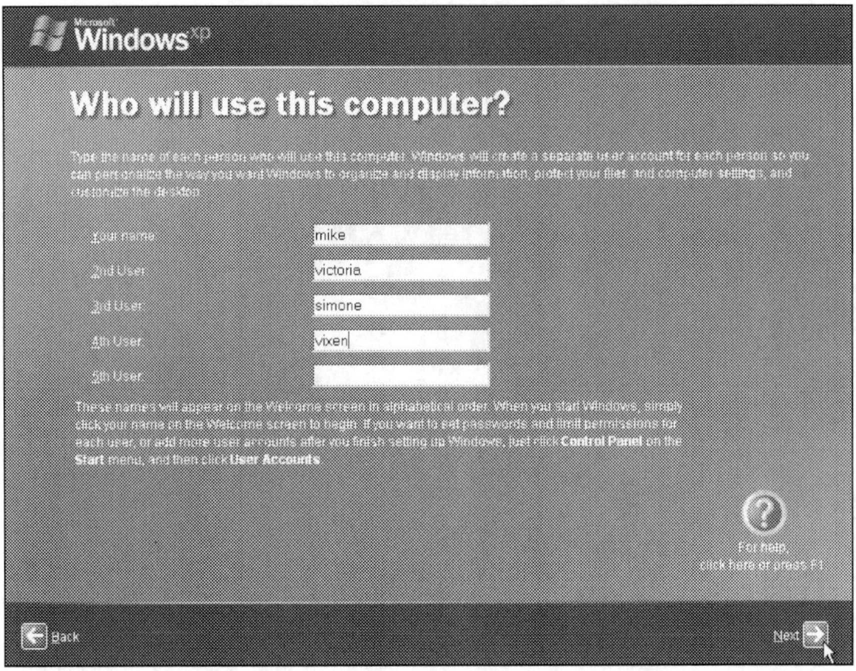

**Figure 2.5.** Add the names of individuals who will use this computer.

If you've entered only one user name, the Windows XP desktop appears. If you've joined a workgroup and entered more than one user name, the logon desktop appears. If you've joined a domain, the Windows logon dialog box appears.

# Install Windows XP: Upgrade installation

An upgrade installation occurs when you move from an earlier version of Windows such as Windows Me or Windows 2000 to Windows XP. You can perform an upgrade with either the retail or the upgrade version of Windows, using either the Home or Professional editions.

The upgrade depends on which operating system you are upgrading from. Table 2.1 lists the upgrade options for older versions of Windows. Older applications that may have run on Windows 98, such as DOS games or applications that wrote directly to the video adapter, may not natively run on Windows XP. You will need to create a custom environment for those applications. See Chapter 3 for information on application compatibility.

If you are upgrading from consumer editions of Windows, such as Windows 98 or Windows Me, you are moving to a true 32-bit operating system

**Table 2.1.** Windows XP upgrade compatibility

| Previous Version | Windows XP Home | Windows XP Pro |
|---|---|---|
| Windows 3.1 | No | No |
| Windows 95 | No | No |
| Windows 98 / 98 SE | Yes | Yes |
| Windows Me | Yes | Yes |
| Windows NT Workstation 3.51 | No | No |
| Windows NT Workstation 4.0 | No | Yes |
| Windows 2000 Professional | No | Yes |
| Windows XP Home Edition | --- | Yes |
| Windows XP Professional | No | --- |

and gaining the protection of an enterprise-grade kernel and memory manager. Earlier versions had 16-bit components that were used throughout the product, including the core parts of the operating system, and this caused problems with hardware and applications that tried to write directly to hardware. This resulted in hard locks or sudden reboots.

With Windows XP, the kernel and memory manager are written so that applications cannot write directly to hardware, but must go through managers that keep track of application access and memory management. Hard locks and crashes are drastically reduced and uptime is increased. When you install certified device drivers written specifically for Windows XP, you ensure that those devices will not bring your work or desktop to a crashing halt.

If you are upgrading from Windows NT or Windows 2000, you are gaining improved performance, reliability, and a much-improved interface that makes your work more streamlined and seamless.

Note that you cannot "upgrade" from a server edition of Windows. This is done to preserve the domain, security, and services information that is only available to server editions of Windows. If for some reason you need to move from a server edition to a workstation edition, your choices are to either perform a new Windows XP installation in the same partition, losing all your server information, or perform a dual boot installation to a different partition so you can boot into the different operating systems as needed.

Before you upgrade, run the Files and Settings Transfer Wizard to capture your existing Windows desktop settings and important data files. This acts as a safety net in case some settings do not transfer cleanly. Make sure to back up your data files to removable media or to a network drive so you can restore them in case the upgrade doesn't go smoothly.

Plug in and turn on any hardware, such as scanners, PDAs, printers, or USB devices, that you want to use with your Windows XP upgrade. Finally, turn off anti-virus software and shut down all background applications such as file sharing utilities or PDA synchronization utilities. See Chapter 1 for more information on checking upgrade compatibility and obtaining any necessary updates so Windows can install smoothly.

1. Insert the Windows XP CD in your computer. The Welcome to Windows XP dialog box appears. Click Install Windows XP.

2. The Windows Setup dialog box appears. Click the drop-down arrow and then click Upgrade (recommended). Click Next (see Figure 2.6).

**Figure 2.6.** The Upgrade option lets you preserve your existing settings.

3. The License Agreement dialog box appears. Click the option to accept this agreement. Click Next.

4. The Your Product Key dialog box appears. Type the 25-digit Windows XP serial number, found on either your CD jewel case or a separate license sticker. If you work for a company that has a site license for Windows XP, use the site license key instead. Click Next.

>  **Hack**
>
> If your existing Windows partition is FAT or FAT32, the upgrade will offer you the option to convert it to NTFS. You can also convert it manually after Windows XP is installed by opening a command prompt and typing convert / ? for a list of commands and command syntax.

5. The Get Updated Setup Files dialog box appears. This step is not criti-cal, because it only gathers Windows Catalog data from Microsoft (see Chapter 1 for more information). Click Yes if you are currently con-nected to a network and the connection is active; otherwise, click No.

6. Setup updates the local files, copies the graphical installation files onto your computer before rebooting, and then runs the graphical install portion of Windows. The rest of setup proceeds as in the New Installation task.

# Install Windows XP: Service-pack-only installation

Service-pack-only installation is available for anyone running Windows XP, with or without Service Pack 1. The Windows XP Service Pack 2 is cumulative, meaning it contains all the fixes and features found in Service Pack 1 and most of the interim fixes issued by the Windows Update Service. One of the key features in Service Pack 2 is the Security Advisor, which turns on the Windows Firewall by default, monitors your anti-virus software, and turns on the Windows Update Service. For home and SOHO users, this "hands off" management and monitoring capability is a blessing, because it no longer requires users or system administrators to visit each PC and make sure the necessary security protections and virus definitions are installed and working.

Service Pack 2 also includes major upgrades to Internet Explorer. Older versions of Internet Explorer were lax when it came to security; by default, Web page scripting and ActiveX controls were allowed to operate without restriction. It took manual intervention by users to define secure zones, restrict Web sites, and block pop-ups or unwanted cookies. This was cumber-some and often difficult to figure out, and the bad guys out on the Internet took advantage of the patchwork approach to security.

In Service Pack 2, there are updates to Internet Explorer that address a number of these issues. For example, scripting and ActiveX are turned off by default, and Web site pop-ups are blocked. This fixes two of the most annoy-ing (and insecure) aspects of Internet Explorer: reducing the exposure to

## How to obtain Service Pack 2

Service Pack 2 is available to anyone running Windows XP or Windows XP with Service Pack 1. Microsoft provides three ways for end users to obtain SP2:

- Turn on Automatic Updates. This allows your computer to automatically download SP2 in the background and notify you when it's ready to be installed. You can read more about Automatic Update settings in Chapter 6.

- Download SP2 directly from Microsoft. This method stores the executable on your computer but does not run it until you want to upgrade your computer. If you have several computers you want to upgrade, this is the fastest way to do it — download the file once, then upgrade multiple computers later. One caveat: The file is over 272MB in size. Do a search for Knowledge Base article 322389 at Microsoft.com to find the download location.

- Order the SP2 CD free of charge. Yes, Microsoft actually pays for the shipping for once, at least in North America. You can find the order form and plenty of SP2 information and supplemental resources at www.microsoft.com/windowsxp/sp2/default.mspx.

malicious scripting bugs, and shutting down the ability for Web sites to generate seemingly endless pop-ups and referral windows without user permission.

An additional security feature includes an Attachment Manager that is used by Internet Explorer, Windows Messenger, and Outlook Express. It acts as an intermediary during file downloads and pops up a warning dialog box, identifying attachments such as .exe or .pif files that could contain malicious code. The Attachment Manager goes a long way to help stop the accidental opening of attachments that may contain viruses.

 **Inside Scoop**

I highly recommend getting the SP2 CD because it comes with supplemental documents and administrator tools that make your job easier. It's a great disk to have in your administrator toolbox.

Microsoft also includes upgrades to Windows Media Player 9, with support for additional codecs; upgrades to DirectX 9, with additional support for the most recent video rendering functions and 3D graphical applications; and additional networking support and compatibility add-ons for Tablet PCs and Media Center Editions.

On the less serious side, Service Pack 2 also includes Movie Maker 2, an upgrade to the multimedia editing program that shipped in Windows XP, so that you can edit your movies and pictures on your own computer. See Chapter 7 for more information on Movie Maker 2.

Before you run the Service Pack setup program, close all programs, back up your data, and turn off any antivirus software you may be running. The Service Pack install that follows is done using the official Microsoft Windows XP Service Pack 2 CD. The standalone download and Windows Update procedures differ slightly, but not enough to be confusing.

1. Insert the Windows XP Service Pack 2 CD in your disk drive. The Welcome to the Service Pack 2 Setup Wizard dialog box appears (see Figure 2.7). Click Continue.

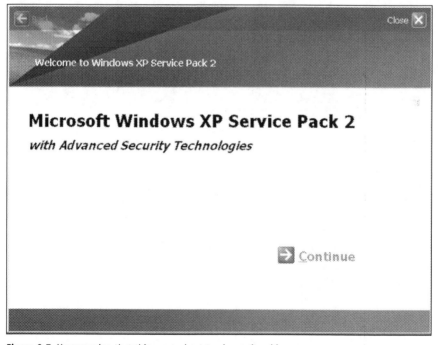

**Figure 2.7.** Your warning that things are about to change in a big way.

2. The Service Pack 2 Security Features dialog box appears. For more information on the installation process, select the option to find out what to know before installing Service Pack 2. Otherwise, click Install Now. The service pack files are decompressed and copied to your computer.

3. The Welcome to the Service Pack 2 Setup Wizard dialog box appears. Click Next. You can read the license agreement by scrolling through the window. Click Print to print a copy of the license agreement. When you have read the license agreement, select the option to accept the agreement and then click Next (see Figure 2.8).

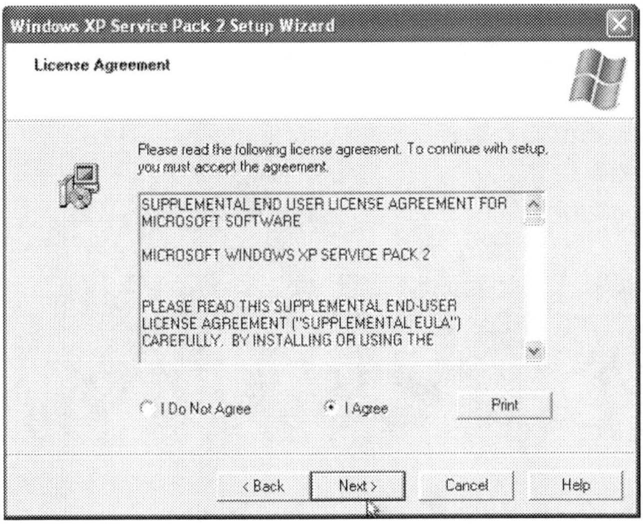

**Figure 2.8.** If you have questions about the license, now is the time to read it.

4. The Select Options dialog box appears. You can click Browse to change to another directory to store the backup files, but for most people the default is fine. Click Next.

5. The wizard updates your system. When it is done, you can choose not to reboot, but otherwise go ahead and click Finish. Windows reboots, and the Help protect your PC dialog box appears.

6. Click Help protect my PC by turning on Automatic Updates now (see Figure 2.9). Click Next. Your desktop reappears, with the Security Center visible. See Chapter 6 for information about the Security Center and its available options.

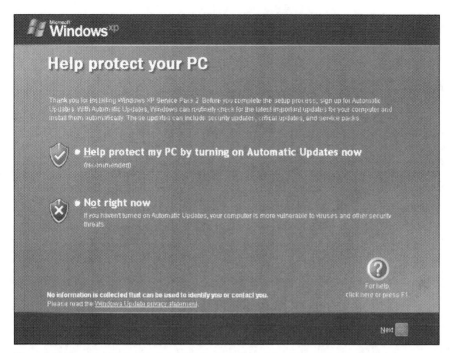

**Figure 2.9.** If you don't intend to immediately check for updates, turn on Automatic Updates now.

# Install Windows XP: Network installation

A network install uses a share on the network to store the Windows XP setup and installation files. If you are managing several computers you can save time by having the files centrally located on a share rather than carrying the Windows XP and Service Pack 2 CDs from one computer to another.

With a network installation, the setup program is executed across the network and the files are copied to the local computer. This method requires user or administrator input, such as the 25-digit license key, to select options or complete information during setup.

A network installation differs from using cloning (such as Norton Ghost) or Microsoft's RIS (Remote Installation Services, part of Windows Server 2003) to install a new operating system. With cloning or RIS, an exact copy of an existing operating system and its applications is created, stored centrally, and then imaged onto networked computers. This image contains the necessary drivers and hardware details for a specific desktop or laptop configuration, so it cannot be imaged onto any machine on the network, only ones with similar hardware. (You cannot use an image from a Pentium machine on an AMD machine, for example.) With a network install, the

## The hidden gotcha of network installs

On the surface, a standard network installation is useful only for upgrade scenarios. The reason is straightforward: You need network drivers and a Microsoft network client in order to connect to a shared folder containing the installation files. When you are running Windows 9x or Me, or Windows NT, 2000, or XP, you already have the drivers and client installed and are able to connect to a share.

With a bare-metal PC, however, you do not have any of this support installed. This makes it pretty tough to connect across a network to a share when networking is not loaded.

However, there is a free utility available that creates a "universal" TCP/IP boot floppy for connecting to Microsoft network shares. Visit www.netbootdisk.com for the download and instructions on how to put this disk together. It assumes you have a healthy familiarity with DOS and network card drivers, so you may need to get your hands dirty to create a boot disk that works with an off brand of network adapter. The site also includes instructions on how to make a boot CD for machines (like laptops) that do not use legacy devices such as floppy drives.

Note that Windows Server 2003 uses a different security model and so the boot disk will not connect directly. See the netbootdisk Web site for instructions on how to access a share on this server.

---

entire setup program is run on each machine, so it automatically configures the operating system to match the hardware it's running on.

But just because you can copy the installation files to a network share does not mean you are free to install Windows XP on every computer you own. Retail, upgrade, or OEM licenses are good for a single installation on a single computer. Even if you create a network installation, you are required to have a valid license for every copy of Windows XP you run on your network.

If you have more than a couple of machines, you should contact a reseller for information on purchasing additional licenses. You may also need to purchase Client Access Licenses (CALs), which are required for connections to Windows Servers. This is most often a scenario in larger companies or corporate environments. Microsoft volume licensing programs do not apply if you have fewer than five computers to manage, so many home or SOHO users must rely on standard pricing for their copies of Windows XP.

**Watch Out!**

The service pack installation program is very picky about where files are installed. It appears to work best if the \i386 folder is located at the root of a drive.

The following instructions show you how to copy the Windows XP installation files to a network drive and then "slipstream" (integrate) Service Pack 2 into the original files. This saves you the step of installing XP and then separately running the service pack setup to bring a computer up to date.

1. Copy the contents of the \i386 directory on your Windows XP CD to a shared folder.

2. Create a temporary folder on the share, such as \tmp. Copy the Windows XP Service Pack 2 executable to the temporary folder.

3. Open a command window and change to the temporary folder. Type xpsp2.exe /integrate:<path\sharename>. The service pack is integrated into Windows XP.

# Install Windows XP: Dual booting with Windows

You can install Windows XP in a dual boot or side-by-side installation so that you can choose which operating system you want to run at boot time. This gives you the ability to test Windows XP with your hardware and software without damaging a working installation. It also lets you keep your old installation in case compatibility issues preclude your moving to Windows XP with all your hardware and software.

There are three ways to create a dual boot system, two of which are recommended; one is not. The first two are to either install Windows XP onto a second hard drive in your system, or to install Windows XP into an empty partition on an existing hard drive.

The third way that is *not* recommended is to install Windows XP into the same partition as your existing Windows installation. This is not recommended: You will end up altering application files within the same partition when you boot between the two systems. This will cause the applications and the operating system to become unstable and eventually unusable. The only reason to use this method is for troubleshooting purposes; typically the other operating system is so corrupted that the machine will no longer boot. The same-partition install lets you boot back into the machine and commence data recovery measures.

To create a dual boot installation:

1. Follow the steps in the section "Install Windows XP: New installation" through Step 2. The disk partitioning screen appears (see Figure 2.10). You can install into an unpartitioned space or create a new partition from this screen. Create a partition for your Windows XP installation. Use the arrow keys to highlight your new installation partition. Press Enter.

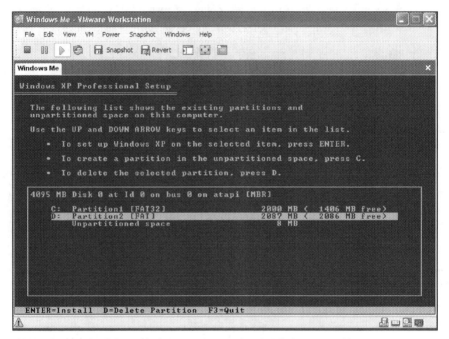

**Figure 2.10.** Use the disk partitioning screen to create a new Windows XP partition.

2. The Format Partition screen appears. Use the arrow keys to highlight the type of formatting you want applied to your new partition. Press Enter. If you've chosen a destructive format, press F to confirm the format procedure.

3. Follow the rest of the steps in the section "Install Windows XP: New installation" from Step 4 onwards. The next time you reboot you can select either operating system.

## Give your system the (multi-) boot

Some people want to multi-boot a computer with numerous versions of Windows. This can be for various reasons: testing new applications, supporting legacy applications, training or education, or good old-fashioned hobbyist fiddling and twiddling. If you fall into one of these categories, there are three ways you can set up a multi-boot system: the cheap way, the moderately cheap way, and the "it'll-cost-you-a-bit" way.

The cheap way is free. In essence, you start off with a bare hard drive and sequentially install your Windows operating systems, from oldest to newest. Use a different partition for each and let Windows XP's boot manager detect the different operating systems and create an entry in the boot.ini file. (More on the boot process can be found in Chapter 11.) Before you format your drives, read the Microsoft Knowledge Base article 306559, "How to create a multiple-boot system in Windows XP" and Knowledge Base article 217210, "How to Multiple Boot Windows XP, Windows 2000, [other OS names omitted]." These will give you an idea of what to watch for and the best way to approach multi-booting with Windows.

The moderately cheap way is to invest in a program specifically designed to be a standalone boot manager. Products to look for include Symantec's PartitionMagic (which includes the BootMagic boot manager) at www.symantec.com; OSL2000 at www.osloader.com; Masterbooter at www.masterbooter.com; and Boot-US at www.boot-us.com. Prices range from free to $69.95 retail for PartitionMagic.

The high-end way is to use virtual machine software that lets you run each operating system within its own sandbox on your existing version of Windows XP. Two popular choices for virtual machine software are VMWare's VMWare Workstation (retail $189) or Microsoft's Virtual PC (retail $129). Each of these lets you keep a snapshot of an OS so you can easily roll back any changes and return your virtual machine to a known, stable state. If you plan on doing a lot of testing, debugging, or writing books about software, this is the best option.

# Install Windows XP: Dual booting with Linux

Many people from businesses to regular folks are adopting Linux as a free desktop replacement. It has plenty of features that appeal to users: the ability to configure just about every aspect of the operating system, the free, high-quality applications available for it, lack of susceptibility to viruses and worms that target Microsoft products, and the desire to avoid the "Microsoft Tax." Because of this, you may find that you'd like to kick the tires on Linux and see if switching over is a good idea.

Often the term "Linux" is used generically to mean a complete package of programs, including the core operating system and applications. However Linux is just the kernel that makes the whole operating system work. What most people really mean when they say Linux is a distribution (or "distro") configured to meet various goals. There are hundreds of distros available and new ones built every day. Some focus on security, some focus on gaming, and some try to be a better Microsoft than Microsoft. To see what distros are available, browse the www.distrowatch.com Web site which lists some distros you may have heard of and a lot you probably haven't.

Dual booting with a Linux distro can sometimes be an exercise in frustration. The difficulty arises due to the Microsoft boot manager's deliberate design to recognize only operating systems that come from Microsoft. If you install a Linux distro followed by Windows XP, you will find that the boot.ini file does not list the Linux distro — and you now have no way to boot into Linux. Both Linux boot managers (GRUB and LILO) recognize Windows and will provide a way to boot into it, but if you then boot into Windows XP and install Service Pack 2, it clobbers your Linux boot manager and you're back to fiddling with Linux boot manager settings.

You can still set up your computer for dual booting with a complete version of Linux on a partition on your hard drive. Most Linux distros come with HOWTO files that explain how to set up a dual boot environment with Windows, though the HOWTOs can vary in quality and comprehension. Microsoft, of course, does not provide any instructions on how to do this. In fact, the Microsoft Knowledge Base includes articles only on how to *remove* Linux. Clearly Microsoft doesn't want you receiving other suitors for your

---

**Bright Idea**

When you purchase a new computer, you can ask for one that does not have an operating system on it. This allows you to save some money by not paying licensing fees for the operating system or all those other pre-installed applications you'll never use (Microsoft Works, anyone?).

attention; whether you appreciate Redmond's concern for your computer's choice of operating system is for you to decide.

Because the dual boot procedures differ from distro to distro, a step-by-step dual boot or multi-boot guide won't be provided here. The Linux community, on the other hand, hasn't taken the dual boot challenge lying down. Several major distros have created live CDs that you can boot from and that load a preconfigured version of Linux into RAM — no partitions or files on your hard drive are ever touched. If you have a broadband or DSL connection, you can download and burn a distro to a CD or DVD and run Linux from your CD or DVD drive. You can also order a live CD or DVD from various vendors at a nominal cost.

The most popular live versions are Knoppix at www.knoppix.org, Mandriva Move (formerly Mandrake LiveCD) at www.mandriva.com/products/move, and the Novell SUSE (pronounced "SOO-suh") Professional Live DVD at www.novell.com/products/linuxprofessional/index.html. The Knoppix version shown in Figure 2.11 is particularly adept at detecting your hardware and presenting you with a working desktop at boot time, courtesy of sophisticated installation scripts.

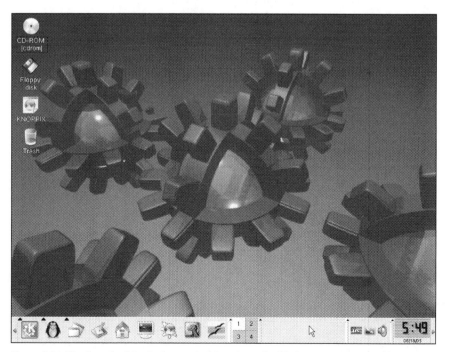

**Figure 2.11.** The Knoppix distro is clean, colorful, and easy for Windows users to work with.

Live CDs are a fantastic way to "dual boot" with Linux, see what all the excitement is about, and leave your existing operating system untouched. With Knoppix, if you like what you see you can issue commands that will install the live CD onto your computer into a dual boot configuration (or, if you're willing, as the *only* operating system). Because Linux is so flexible and configurable, you may find yourself running Linux more often than Windows.

## Automate the installation process

Ever get tired of babysitting a new Windows installation, keeping an eye out for the next pause in the process just so you can click "Next"? Fortunately, you do not need to keep repeating the same behavior. Windows XP includes tools to create an answer file that setup uses to fill in boxes, make selections, and click Next where appropriate.

This is possible through the use of extensive and powerful command-line switches for the setup programs, winnt32.exe for 32-bit platforms like Windows 2000 and Windows NT, and winnt.exe for mixed platforms like Windows 9x and Windows Me. The command-line switches help control nearly every aspect of installing Windows XP, including location of source files, programs to run after setup completes, and which answer files to use during the setup process.

You can use the automation process to install Windows XP Home Edition, Windows XP Professional Edition, and Windows Server 2003 Standard, Enterprise, and Data Center editions.

This section shows you how to use setupmgr.exe to create answer files and how to use those files with winnt32. Because there are many options available, and many things you can do with option files, this task will not try to cover them all. Instead, it will use the integrated install created in the Network Install task as the source files to be used with the answer file.

---

**Inside Scoop**

The Service Pack 2 CD and the Microsoft Web site have updates and bug fixes to the tools that originally shipped with Windows XP, so it is worth your time to obtain the newer versions.

## Licensing and installing multiple copies

Licensing is an issue that you must consider when you use automated installation, no matter which product you are installing. You can create an automated installation file that contains a separate license key for each copy of Windows you want to install.

A UDF, or Uniqueness Database File, is a text file that is used when you have large numbers of computers that you want to automatically upgrade. Because there are often several unique configuration items for each computer, such as its name on the network, its license file number, and membership in a domain, the UDF allows system administrators to specify the unique entries for each machine.

You cannot and should not use the same license for multiple machines on your network. This practice is known as *cheating*. Given that Microsoft employs product activation codes in Windows XP Home and Professional Editions and in Windows Server 2003, it becomes difficult to sneak around the license agreements. Make sure your licenses are in compliance and you will have no problems.

You can use the support files from the Windows XP CD, the ones from the Service Pack 2 CD, or you can download xpsp1DeployTools_en.cab from Microsoft.

1. Insert the Service Pack 2 CD from Microsoft into your computer. Copy the file \support\tools\deploy.cab to a new folder. Double-click deploy.cab, double-click setupmgr.exe, choose an extraction folder, and then click OK.

2. Double-click setupmgr.exe. The Windows Setup Manager Wizard starts. Click Next.

3. The New or Existing Answer File dialog box appears. Click Create a new answer file. Click Next. The Type of Setup dialog box appears. Click Unattended setup. Click Next.

4. The Product dialog box appears, as shown in Figure 2.12. Select Windows XP Professional and then click Next. The User Interaction dialog box appears. Click Fully automated. Click Next.

5. The Distribution Share dialog box appears. Click Create a new distribution share. Click Next. The Location of Setup Files dialog box appears. Click In the following folder. Type the location of the i386 folder created in the previous task, or click Browse to browse to it instead. Click Next.

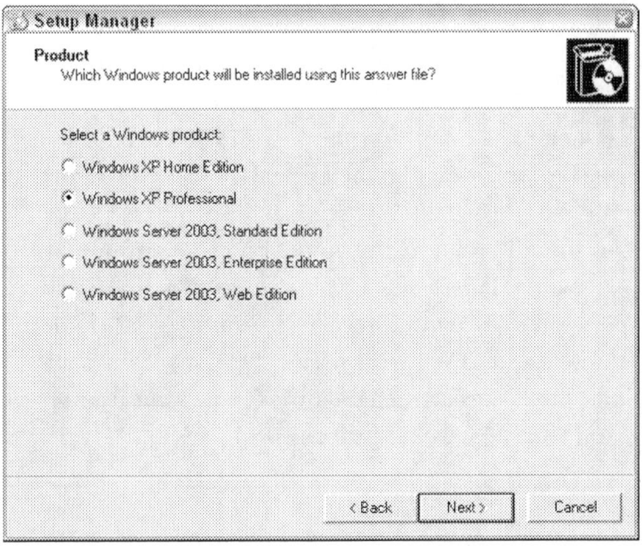

**Figure 2.12.** You can create answer files for all current Microsoft operating systems.

6. The Distribution Share Location dialog box appears. Type the location where you want to place the Windows files and configuration files. You can also browse to a different location than the one suggested by the wizard. Type a share name for the distribution. Click Next.

7. The License Agreement dialog box appears. Click the option to accept the terms of the license agreement. Click Next.

8. The Customize the Software dialog box appears. Type your name and organization (see Figure 2.13). Click Next to move through each item in the tree sequentially. You can also click each item to move between dialog boxes to change or edit your answers. When the wizard is done, click Finish.

9. The Windows Setup Manager dialog box appears. It will prompt you for a location for your answer file. For now, click OK. The wizard copies your files to the new distribution share. The Setup Manager Complete

dialog box appears. Click File and then Exit to close the wizard. You can view the answers created by the wizard by viewing the unattend.txt file, located in the new distribution share.

10. To run the unattended install, copy unattend.bat and unattend.txt to the new machine and run unattend.bat.

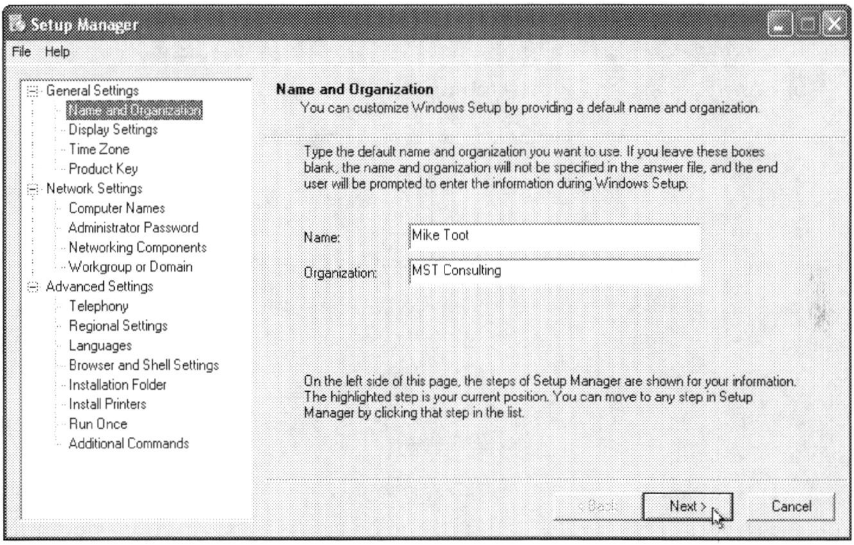

**Figure 2.13.** The Name and Organization screen lets you "brand" your copies of Windows XP.

You will need to have sharing enabled on the distribution folder. If you are using Active Directory, make sure that you log in with an account that has read and execute permissions on that folder. If you are attempting to upgrade a Windows 98 or Windows Me installation, you will need to create a separate unattend.bat file that uses winnt.exe. Type winnt.exe /? at a command prompt to see the available switches.

# Uninstall Windows XP

You can uninstall Windows XP only if you have performed an upgrade installation to Windows 98 or Windows Me. The upgrade process leaves many of the core 16-bit Windows files available on the hard drive for restoring back to the original operating system. This is convenient if you have compatibility issues with your existing applications and need to regain any lost features or functionality. You *cannot* uninstall Windows XP if you upgraded from a 32-bit version of Windows such as Windows NT or Windows 2000.

## Uninstalling Service Pack 2

Older versions of Windows service packs let you select whether to back up the updated files so you could uninstall the service pack. With Service Pack 2 the backup is mandatory and the older files are kept by default in the Windows directory. You can uninstall the service pack by going to Control Panel, clicking Add or Remove programs, Windows XP Service Pack 2, and then Remove. You cannot uninstall Service Pack 2 if it is part of a slipstream install.

Note that you need your uninstall files in order to revert back to an earlier version. Sadly, the Windows XP Disk Cleanup Wizard prompts you to delete these files 30 days after you upgrade. If you deleted those files and then decide later to uninstall Windows XP, you cannot go back. You have to reinstall your earlier version of Windows. Not only that, but if you revert to your earlier version of Windows, your applications won't work. Windows XP makes too many changes to the Registry, which means you must reinstall your applications.

Microsoft clearly wants to encourage you to move to Windows XP, which in many cases is a great idea. But if you need access to your older operating system and applications, Microsoft makes it very difficult to take a step back to the past. For all these reasons, if you must keep your older version of Windows around, a dual boot is preferable than an upgrade or even a brand-new installation.

To uninstall Windows XP, open the Control Panel and click Add/Remove Programs. Click Windows XP Uninstall and then click Change/Remove.

The Uninstall Windows XP dialog box appears. Click Uninstall Windows XP and then click Continue (see Figure 2.14). The confirmation dialog box appears, asking if you are sure you want to remove Windows XP. Click Yes. The Windows XP Upgrade is then uninstalled from your system.

**Figure 2.14.** The Uninstall Windows XP dialog box lets you revert to your other operating system or remove the reversion files from your hard drive.

## Just the facts

- Get all the details of your installation nailed down before you start.

- Use the checklist to help guide you through the process.

- Make a backup of your data.

- Installing Windows XP is generally a great thing to do, just don't expect to go back to your old OS easily.

- Dual boot scenarios can sometimes have gotchas in them; make sure you know what they are before you start.

GET THE SCOOP ON...
Configuring the basic desktop ▪ Making the Start menu and
taskbar work for you ▪ Enhancing Windows with PowerToys ▪
Managing applications ▪ Improving performance

# Managing the Windows Desktop

**"Y**ou don't get a second chance to make a good first impression." This saying has never been truer than with an operating system. People make snap judgments about an OS based on how it looks — are the colors crisp and clean, with enough variation to be pleasing to the eye? Does it look comfortable to work with? And is it flexible, so that it can be changed if boredom sets in?

Out of the box, Windows XP is the most flexible and colorful version that Microsoft has released to date. It has mixed together a new design, an upgrade to some old components, and some much-needed tweaking to give the Windows desktop a fresh new look. It's an improvement over the Windows 9x and Me series, and not as industrial as the Windows NT or Windows 2000 flavors.

The graphical parts of the XP desktop include the overall screen resolution (which determines how much information you can pack onto a monitor's real estate), icons, desktop wallpaper, graphical schemes (a collection of settings that determines how windows, menu text, and other items appear), and themes or global changes that create order out of configuration chaos — hopefully in a pleasant and useful way.

# Resolution, icons, wallpaper, screen savers, and themes

Personalizing a desktop is a fun way to make a computer "yours." You can change nearly everything you see on the desktop, including the wallpaper, icons, and desktop resolution. If you don't like something you see, odds are you can change it with a few judicious clicks.

## Desktop resolution

Desktop resolution is a combination of what modes your video adapter is capable of and what resolutions your monitor can display. Most new video adapters today have no problem running at 1600 (horizontal) × 1200 (vertical) resolution at 32-bit color. Older cards lack the onboard horsepower and memory to render all the computations needed at that rate.

Monitors vary and will play a role in what resolutions to use from your video card. Older monitors will not be able to display high resolutions; even newer LCD monitors will not clearly display higher resolutions.

Resolution is changed by right-clicking the desktop, clicking Properties, and then clicking the Settings tab (see Figure 3.1). You can select the screen resolution and color quality in this dialog box; feel free to play with the settings until you find one you like. If the screen appears to "paint" more slowly than you like, such as with noticeably jerky movements of your mouse cursor when you move it, try lowering the color quality from 32-bit to 24- or 16-bit. This exponentially reduces the number of calculations the graphics card has to perform and will help with slow redraw rates.

LCD monitors are the coolest thing to hit computing in years. You can ditch your bulky, power-gobbling CRT and switch over to a svelte, energy-efficient LCD monitor, incidentally reclaiming a lot of your real-life desktop's real estate. There are a few things to watch out for when you go shopping for one, however.

First, you have to be sure your video card and LCD monitor can talk to each another. Either your LCD monitor should support an analog connection or your video card should have a digital output connection (most commonly a DVI connector). Most LCDs support analog input, though there are some that do not. Check to see that you have the necessary connections available and buy the necessary cable to connect them if you don't have one in the LCD box.

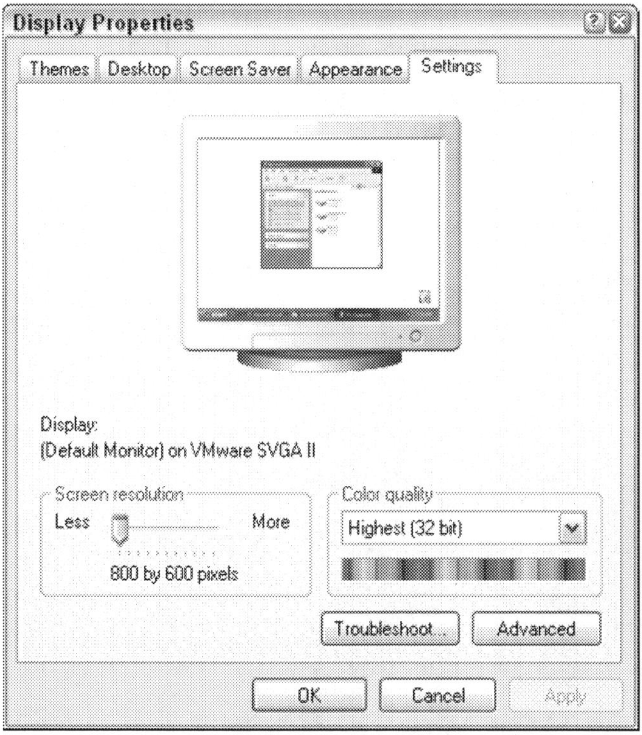

**Figure 3.1.** The most common desktop resolution settings are readily accessible in the Display Properties dialog box.

Next, your LCD will look its best at its native resolution which should be listed on the box or at the manufacturer's Web site. Though your LCD monitor can perform scaling (taking an input at one resolution and changing it to another), you're better off passing it a signal that doesn't require additional calculations and incur dithering and jaggies in the process.

Third, pixel response time is typically slower than CRTs. If you plan on playing high-speed games with intense graphical changes, LCDs will blur and look messy, because the crystals can't change as fast as CRT pixels in response to the video signal. There are some expensive LCD monitors with response times of approximately 8 milliseconds, but most are in the 18–25ms range.

Finally, Windows XP has a feature made initially for laptops called ClearType. This is a font dithering algorithm that can make screen fonts look cleaner. You can try using it on your LCD monitor to see if it helps with

## Video cards, drivers, and management applications

Most new video cards come with comprehensive drivers and management programs that can adjust nearly every aspect of a card's performance. Frequently, they install tabs in place of the standard Windows ones that change desktop resolution, color quality, and monitor refresh rates for you.

If you have one of these programs installed you should use it to fiddle with your adapter's settings. Although you can still use the default Windows dialog boxes, you're better off playing the game the way the video card manufacturer intended. Because the interfaces vary dramatically among adapters, an in-depth discussion of specifics is beyond this chapter. But here are a few tips on getting the best out of your card:

- Make sure your drivers and management applications are up-to-date. Even though the screamingly newest drivers may have bugs, any drivers that are more than a couple weeks old are probably safe to use. And, as with many things in software, the older the hardware, the more likely the bugs have been pretty well squashed.

- Most video card help files and user guides are hopelessly obscure. Find an official or unofficial forum or message board for your video card, lurk there for a while, and learn from the mistakes of others.

- If you work in a profession such as graphics design or video editing, hang out on profession-specific forums. You will find a lot of advice about specific adapter settings for particular projects, including tweaks to make the card faster.

visibility. From the Display Properties dialog box, click the Appearance tab and then click Effects. Select the Use the following method to smooth screen fonts check box, and then select ClearType from the drop-down list (see Figure 3.2).

The other setting that affects your viewing quality is off the beaten path, for reasons known only to Microsoft. From the Settings tab, click Advanced and then click the Monitor tab (see Figure 3.3). From here you can change the screen refresh rate. Set the screen resolution and color quality first, and then set the refresh rate to the highest your monitor supports.

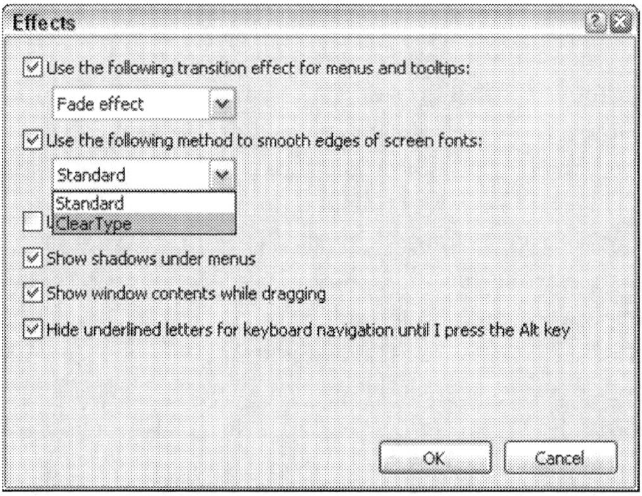

**Figure 3.2.** ClearType can help you see text better on LCD screens.

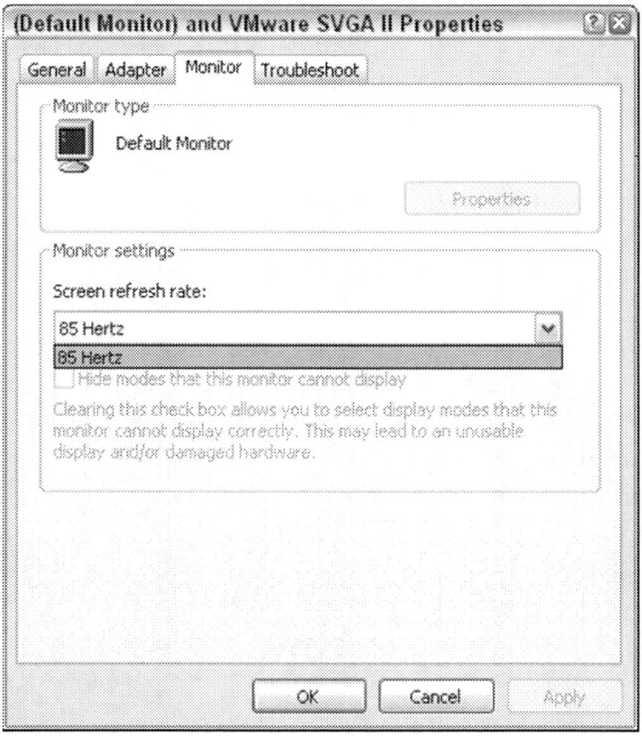

**Figure 3.3.** Increasing your monitor refresh rate reduces eyestrain and fuzzy screen objects.

# Icons

The Windows XP icon set is colorful and sometimes fun to watch. Most people will never change the icons that are applied to any application, file, or shortcut on the desktop. However, like many things in software, the default icons are ones that a developer thought would look good with an application, not necessarily what is informative or helpful to you.

Windows and Windows applications use four sizes of icons. Two of these are used on the desktop, while the other two are used by the system in Windows Explorer folder views and window title bars. For desktop tweaking, there are two icon sizes (see Figure 3.4) to know about: large (32 × 32 pixels) and extra large (48 × 48 pixels). Large is displayed by default; extra large requires changing a setting. From the Display Properties dialog box, click the Appearance tab and then Effects. Select the option to use large icons, click OK, and then click Apply.

Size isn't all that you can change with your desktop icons. There is nothing that requires you to use the default icon for an application shortcut. If you are an inveterate tweaker, you can change around the icons themselves to suit your pleasure. Icons can be found in three primary places: Windows system files, such as shell32.dll, application executables, and icon files with the extension .ico.

The cheap although not easy way to switch your desktop icons is by changing every program's shortcut from its default to another one more to your liking. From the Start menu or the desktop icon, right-click an icon, click Properties, and then click Change Icon. A dialog box appears, listing the currently available icons for the shortcut. These icons are the ones embedded within the application's executable; some programs have only one icon; others offer several or even dozens of icons to choose from. Select an icon and then click OK twice. Your icon changes to your selection.

Large                    Extra large

**Figure 3.4.** You can switch to larger icons when you use higher desktop resolutions.

---

**Bright Idea**

If you are using the large icon set, you can also switch to using larger fonts. From the Display Properties dialog box, click the Appearance tab. From the Font size drop-down list, select Normal (10 pt.), Large (14 pt.), or Extra large (17 pt.) and then click OK.

**Inside Scoop**

Some system icons can be changed only through Display Properties. Click the Desktop tab and then click Customize Desktop. You can also choose which of these icons you want displayed (or not) on the desktop from this dialog box.

If you don't like the limited selection of icons, you can browse to other applications or even Windows system libraries. From the Change Icon dialog box, click Browse and then go hunt down icons that are more to your liking. Shell32.dll holds many of the Windows system icons, some of which you may have never seen (see Figure 3.5). Take a look in other executables, too; you may find something that is more appealing. The Internet also has icon libraries available if you want to add some pizzazz without having to do the heavy lifting yourself. Do a search for "free XP icons" in your favorite search engine and start browsing!

The easier way to change your icons is to use a program designed to collect all icon files from your computer, create icon libraries, and then point your shortcut to a library. There are a number of freeware and shareware programs available to extract icons, create static or animated icons, and do just about anything you could ever want with icons. Popular icon manager choices include Microangelo (www.microangelo.us), IconCool Manager (www.iconcool.com), and AZ Icon Editor (www.hermancompute.com).

After a while your desktop may get cluttered with icons, especially when programs install lots of links to affiliate Web sites or trial software that shipped on the CD. Some people like the casual disorder that comes with acres of icons; other people get tired of dragging icons to the Recycle Bin in an attempt to clear some space on the desktop. Windows XP has the Desktop Cleanup Wizard that cleans up unused icons and puts them into a folder on your desktop. By default it runs every 60 days, but you can run it on demand. From the Display Properties dialog box, click

**Figure 3.5.** Shell32.dll contains most of the standard Windows system icons found in menus, windows, and on the desktop.

the Desktop tab and then Customize Desktop (see Figure 3.6). Click Clean Desktop Now, and Windows sweeps the icons away for you.

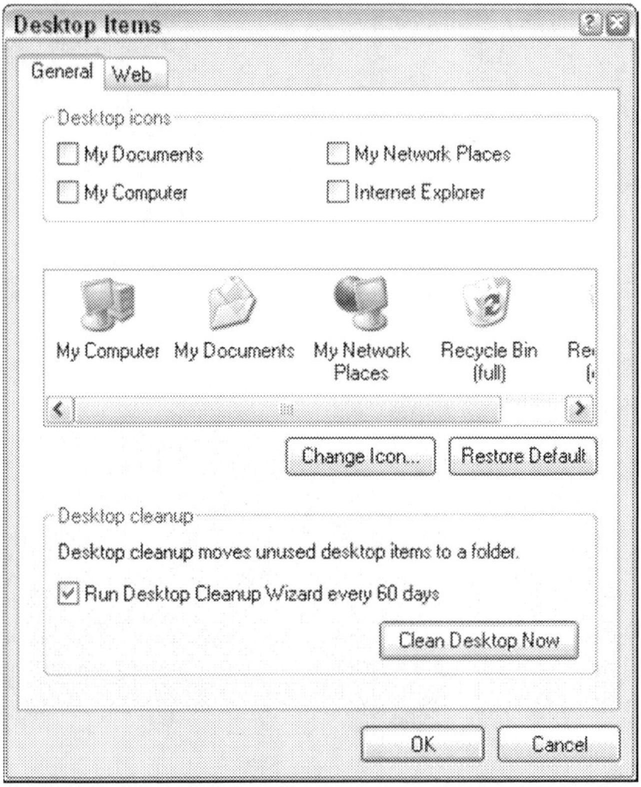

**Figure 3.6.** Use the Clean Desktop Now feature instead of dragging all those icons to the Recycle Bin.

Be warned: The wizard scans and removes icons that apply to single users as well as all users of a computer. If no one in your family has used a common icon in a while, it could disappear into the Unused Desktop Shortcuts folder.

## Wallpaper and screen savers

Most people need no introduction to desktop wallpaper. It's one of the few things in Windows that can be changed easily, and many people like to

---

**Hack**

To change the cleanup interval, open Regedit and browse to HKEY_CURRENT_USER\ Software\Microsoft\Windows\CurrentVersion\Explorer\Desktop\CleanupWiz. Double-click Days Between Clean Up, change the base to Decimal, and then type the number of days you prefer.

personalize their desktop with pictures of family, pets, travel destinations, hobbies, or inspiring artwork.

You can access the basic wallpaper settings by right-clicking the desktop, clicking Properties, and then clicking the eponymous Desktop tab. You can choose which wallpaper to display, and the mini-monitor gives you a preview of what it will look like. For images that are smaller than the screen resolution, you can use the drop-down list box to stretch the image to fill the screen, tile the images, or display it normal size with a color background that you pick from the color list box.

Windows XP comes with several wallpapers that you can use and some of them are quite well done. By default, the wallpapers are stored at Windows\ Web\Wallpaper. You can copy personal images to this directory, or you can use the Browse button to go to a separate location. If you are practicing safe computing, you have a separate folder on a non-Windows partition with your personal data on it, including desktop wallpaper. See Chapter 2 for additional information on using one partition for your programs and one for your data.

You can use Internet Explorer's "Set as background" feature to copy an image to your desktop. Windows saves this image at Documents and Settings\ %username%\Application Data\Microsoft\Internet Explorer\Internet Explorer Wallpaper.bmp. However, this clobbers any other image previously saved at this location. You are better off saving the image to a different folder and then pointing your desktop to that image.

Another way to change your desktop with minimal hassle is by using a wallpaper rotation program that can automatically switch your desktop image without relying on Active Desktop to do it for you. These programs fill a nice little niche between static desktops and dynamic screensavers. One of the best (and free!) programs is WinWall, available at www.desktopchanger. com. It is small, flexible, and unobtrusive. The Web page features links to wallpaper sites where you can easily spend days sorting through images for your desktop.

Screen savers are another popular and easy desktop modification. Screen savers were initially developed for monitors built in the '80s and '90s that ran the risk of having an image burned onto the screen. A screen saver blanked the screen or drew random images over the monitor, reducing the likelihood of burning in any one image. Berkeley Systems marketed the "After Dark" product that contained the near-legendary "Flying Toasters" screen saver. Today there are hundreds of screen saver programs available for every interest and hobby. With today's monitors the risk of burn-in is low to non-existent, but the fun factor remains.

## (In)Active Desktop

When Windows 95 first shipped, someone had the bright idea of creating the "Active Desktop." The concept was to bring Internet content directly to the desktop so that users could have an ever-changing stream of information that connected people with things that were useful or helpful to them.

The concept didn't work, in part because people wanted images and information from multiple sources aggregated into a single location, in part because other applications and services did a better job, and in part because Active Desktop was inflexible. Web content could be synchronized to the desktop only once per day, so other than connecting to "Picture of the Day" sites, Active Desktop was not useful for pulling down news sites or frequently-changing information.

Despite these drawbacks Active Desktop is still lurking in the background and you must have it enabled in order to use themes or to view the new Windows XP interface. If you want to explore its settings, open the Display Properties dialog box, click the Desktop tab, click Customize Desktop, and then click the Web tab.

The Windows XP screen saver has 11 built-in effects you can use. It will also lock your desktop so that no one can access your computer — you must log on again to clear the screen saver. You can access these settings on the Screen Saver tab on the Display Properties dialog box. When you select a screen saver and then click the Settings button, you can change things like transitions, effects, colors, and other options depending on the specific saver chosen (see Figure 3.7).

If you want a free screensaver rotation program, choose the My Pictures Slideshow option from the drop-down list box. You can point it at any folder with pictures or images and display them after a certain amount of desktop inactivity.

**Watch Out!**

Sometimes the nastiest things are contained in the most innocent-looking packages. Screen saver programs are notorious for containing adware, spyware, and viruses. Before downloading one, do a search to see if it's been reported as a malicious program. Also, scan the program with antivirus software before clicking "setup."

**Figure 3.7.** The "Mystify" screen saver uses few computer cycles but still looks good.

# Themes

Themes affect nearly every aspect of the desktop, including wallpaper, icons, audio events, transitions, effects, and other glitz and sizzle that give you the feeling of looking at a completely different version of Windows.

Themes are where artistry and creativity can truly soar; there are thousands of themes available on the Internet and new ones are being created every day. Most first-run blockbuster movies have desktop themes available, and of course there are plenty of fan-built themes for everything from aardvarks to zeppelins (air and Led).

Unfortunately Windows comes with only two themes in the box: the Windows XP theme and the Windows 2000 theme. You can experience the raw excitement of changing between these two by right-clicking the desktop and then clicking Properties. The Display Properties dialog box defaults to opening on the Themes tab. The drop-down list includes Windows XP and Windows Classic (see Figure 3.8); if you have installed other themes you will find them listed here. The mini-monitor shows you what your new theme will look like; click OK if you want to keep the new theme.

You can also save your current settings as a theme so that you can switch between themes without losing your custom settings. Click the Save as button. Windows defaults to saving a .theme file in the My Documents folder, which is normally a great place to save personalized information. However, the themes listed in the drop-down list box are found in the Windows\Resources\Themes folder, so you should browse to that folder and save your .theme files there.

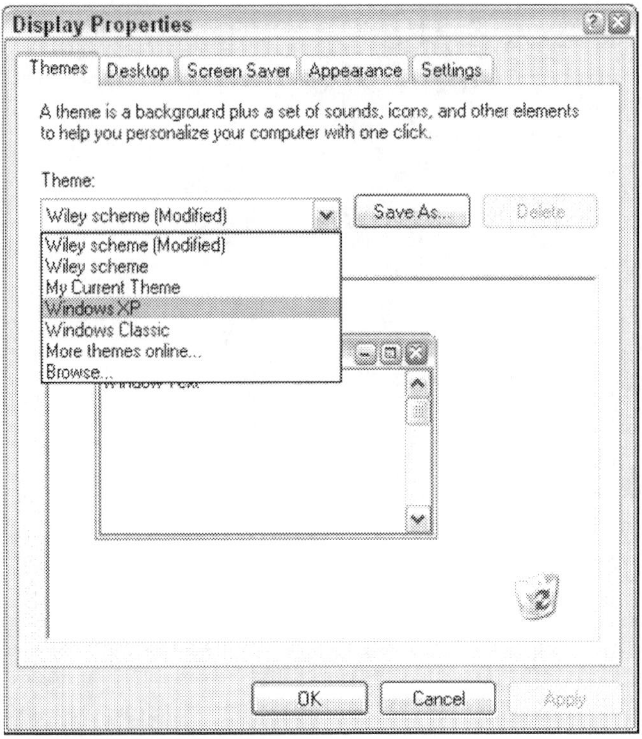

**Figure 3.8.** You can switch between Windows themes or third-party themes if you have them installed.

Oddly, Microsoft has stashed several color schemes that were found in earlier incarnations of Windows 9x. From the Display Properties dialog box, click Appearance. You can switch the window and button styles between Windows XP and Windows Classic; when you do this, the contents of the Color Scheme list box change and you have access to several of the eye-blinding schemes from Windows 9x (see Figure 3.9). The primary difference is that windows and buttons have a 3-D appearance in XP while the Classic is strictly 2-D.

Even odder, if you choose the Windows XP style and click the Advanced button, many of the settings you can change have no effect on the current theme, such as Active Title Bar. Try changing the Active Title Bar to fade from bright red to dark blue; the default XP theme won't change. (Interestingly, when you minimize or maximize a window, you will see the modified title bar colors flash by; however, when the window comes to a rest it displays the default colors.)

## Themes, schemes, and styles

Someone at Microsoft was aiming for job security when the design specifications for themes, schemes, and styles were created. The technologies are interrelated, affect each other, and cause customer confusion rather than clarity. Quick — where do you change title bar colors? Answer: any or all three will do the trick. Here is an attempt to explain the difference.

- **Themes** cover the most desktop territory, affecting anything that generates a common look and feel. When you create or install new themes, you are affecting nearly every aspect of the desktop. Theme information is stored in a text file with a .theme suffix.

- **Schemes** are collections of settings that affect specific sets of operating system components. For the desktop, this means such elements as title bar colors and text, window background color, and icon spacing, among other window-specific elements. Scheme information is stored in the Registry.

- **Styles** are a middle ground, specifying the look and feel of common Windows controls, such as windows, buttons, and title bar colors and shading effects. Styles are accessed using APIs, and specific style information is stored either in the Registry or in a custom configuration file read by a program's library.

If you must dive into the wild world of the Windows desktop, stick to working with Themes. Your life will be simpler and happier for it.

Because of the maddening design choices built into Windows XP, if you are into themes you are better off not wasting your time wrestling with obscure and undocumented quirks. Your best bets are either to download themes from the Web or to invest in a theme management program. For the first option, visit www.themexp.org or www.wincustomize.com or any theme site that grabs your interest after a quick Google search.

 **Inside Scoop**

If you install a theme and it doesn't work, you need to enable the Themes service. Click Start, Run, and then type services.msc. Scroll down to Themes, double-click it, change the startup type to Automatic, click Start, and then click OK.

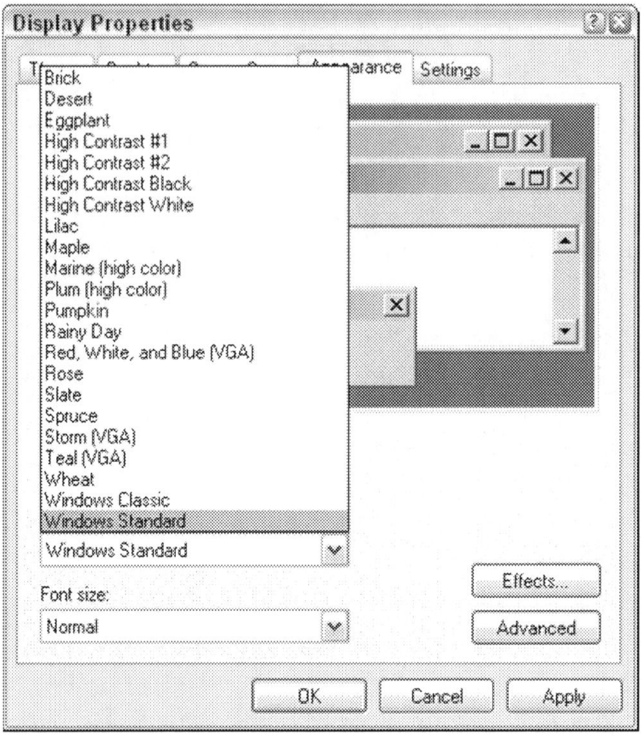

**Figure 3.9.** Switch to the Windows Classic style and you unlock Windows color schemes that can charitably be described as "blinding."

# Themes, schemes, and skins

Microsoft uses the terms *themes* and *schemes* to mean different subsets of technology, though to most end users the difference is academic. In the rest of the software world, anything that changes the look and feel of an application is called a skin. Many programs are "skinnable," including MSN Messenger and Windows Media Player.

Although you'd think that skins apply to applications, and themes apply to entire operating systems, it doesn't always work that way — WindowBlinds applies skins to Windows, according to the Web site. Rather than get wound up about proper use of terminology, just pretend that it all means the same thing: the changing of the interface to look the way you want it to.

Highly regarded theme management programs include WindowBlinds at www.stardock.com and StyleXP at www.tgtsoft.com. Both are shareware, cost $19.95, and occasionally have the odd operational discontinuity (bug) to work around; but the sites also have libraries of themes that you can browse and download for free.

Finally, if you want additional themes, Microsoft encourages you to give them more money for the privilege. You can purchase the Microsoft Plus! SuperPack for Windows XP. For only $29.95, you can get four "astounding" new themes and eight "stunning" screen savers, according to the Microsoft Web site. There are also some additional games and multimedia add-ons, some of which may be useful to you, others that are available elsewhere (Movie Maker 2 is a free download, so you don't need to buy the SuperPack to get it).

# The hidden powers of the Start button

The Start button is the place where everything can be done to your computer. By clicking Start, you can work your way through stacks of menus in order to launch applications, run system programs, and access frequently-used documents.

The Start button was introduced in Windows 95 and ever since then has undergone modification. The latest version separates the menu into four areas: the pinned applications area, the most-recently-used area, an area for common Windows-related functions, and a menu structure for everything else (see Figure 3.10).

Like many things with Microsoft software, there are numerous access points that lead you to settings you can change, and some of the more important settings are hidden where you wouldn't expect them. The Start button is a prime example. It contains a number of settings that change how it behaves and how your desktop looks.

You can access the hidden powers of the Start button by right-clicking it and then clicking Properties.

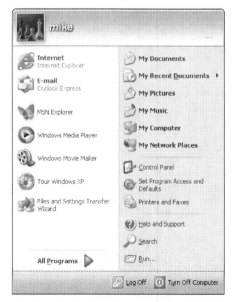

**Figure 3.10.** The four Start button areas present you with different ways to launch applications or open documents.

The Taskbar and Start Menu Properties dialog box appears, with the Start Menu tab selected (see Figure 3.11).

**Figure 3.11.** The Start menu can display the new look or the classic look.

## New look or old look?

Your first choice available is to switch between the Windows XP menu system and the Windows 2000 menu system. Some people find the Windows XP look a real mess; others find it useful. If you prefer the pre-XP menu structure, without a lot of distractions, you can switch between the two by clicking the appropriate button. The mini-monitor shows you what the two will look like. Notice also that several icons are added to the desktop with the Classic look (see Figure 3.12) — My Documents, My Computer, My Network Places, and Internet Explorer. These can be added to the Windows XP desktop by using the PowerToy Tweak UI covered later in this chapter.

You can customize either menu by clicking the Customize button. Most of the settings differ between the standard and classic menus; those that occur on both, such as Display the Run command, are not persistent between the dialog boxes, so if you change a setting in one it will "mysteriously" change when you switch between them.

The Start menu's basic customization (see Figure 3.13) includes viewing large or small icons in the menu, setting the number of most-recently-used (MRU) applications visible in the menu, and choosing which Internet and e-mail applications to "pin" to the upper left section of the Start menu. There is also a button that clears the MRU area so you can get rid of menu clutter.

Now click the Advanced tab. This dialog box (see Figure 3.14) lets you change what items are visible and how the Start menu behaves. Some of the more annoy-

**Figure 3.12.** If you long for the days of Windows 2000, Windows XP lets you quickly switch back to its look.

ing features you can turn off, including the "Open submenus" and "Highlight new programs" options. You can also configure whether some of the common menu options, like the Control Panel, open up a new window (link) or list all the window's contents (menu). If you want to work with the more advanced options of Windows XP, you need to make the Administrator Tools visible. Although it's understandable why Microsoft wouldn't want just anyone poking around in there, it's one of the rare cases where something should be enabled by default, not hidden by default.

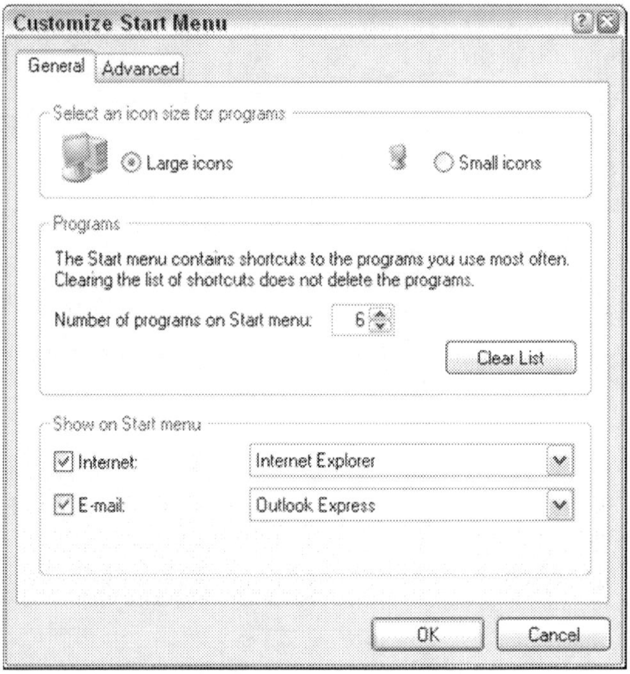

**Figure 3.13.** Use the Customize Start Menu dialog box to change your basic menu options, such as icon size and number of most-recently-used items.

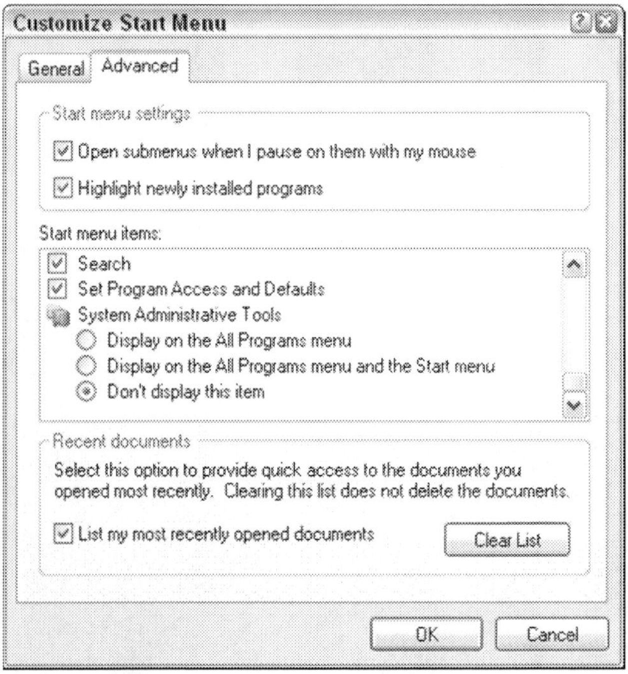

**Figure 3.14.** Save yourself some clicks and enable the Administrative Tools menu items.

**Bright Idea**

You can pin any program to the top-left part of the Start menu by dragging it onto the Start button, or by right-clicking a shortcut and clicking Pin to Start menu. Right-click the icon and click Unpin from Start menu or right-click it in the menu and click Remove from this list.

The Classic Start menu's Customize button has fewer options than the Windows XP one (see Figure 3.15), and some of the options are not as clear as to what they do. The option to "expand" a menu option such as Control Panel means to display its contents as menu items rather than open up a window displaying the contents.

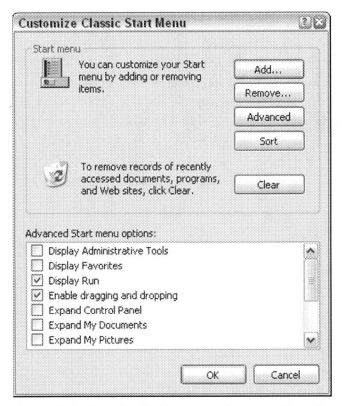

**Figure 3.15.** The Classic Menu is a bit more confusing to work with but it performs the same functions as the one for the new Start menu.

---

### Minimalist at work

As a writer I make my living writing books about software. I launch and close applications, flip between windows, and in general put the desktop through a solid workout every day. Anything that gets in the way or slows down a train of thought is dispensed with. So nearly all of the ooh-ahh things that Microsoft built into the operating system are banished immediately.

I turn off all animations and video effects except dropped shadows on the cursor and desktop icons (see the section "Windows, applications, and performance," later in this chapter). Sound effects are turned off (click Start, Control Panel, Sounds, Speech, and Audio Devices, and then Change the sound scheme). Any applications I use on a regular basis are placed on the Quick Start toolbar — no need to have them on the desktop, too (see the section "Customize your toolbars," later in this chapter). I get rid of all "helper" applications in the notification area, except for a few key ones like antivirus and firewall (see the section "Improve startup with MSCONFIG," later in this chapter).

The net result is a faster, cleaner desktop that doesn't get in my way or slow me down when I work.

---

One annoying feature of the Classic view is the Personalized Menus command. This feature changes the contents of the Programs window depending on how often you use the various programs. The rest are hidden, waiting to be rediscovered behind a downward-facing arrow. Unless you like interfaces that hide themselves from you, you're better off deselecting this option.

## Mucking about with menus

One of the big annoyances with Windows is that it quickly becomes cluttered with programs, icons, shortcuts, and other debris. Start menu items are found in the Documents and Settings folder and come from two primary places: the All Users folder and the logged-on user's folder. Windows looks in both places to see which icons should be displayed and then creates a Start menu from those items. When software is installed it may end up in one or the other folder depending on how the software's designers intended it to be used.

**Hack**

The best way to clean up clutter is to prevent it. When asked for a folder for the program icons during Setup you can type in any location, such as \Programs\Fun Stuff\.
This makes it easier to categorize your applications to match the way you work.

Some menu items can be turned off or disabled as shown in the previous section, but most of the annoyances can be resolved only through judicious pruning of the Start menu. There are two main ways to do this: dragging items around the Start menu one at a time, or using Windows Explorer to work with multiple items at the same time.

Click and drag an icon to a different location on the Start menu. Windows displays a black horizontal bar showing you where the item will land when you release the mouse button. Using this method, you can quickly pin a frequently-used application to the Start menu.

If you are using the standard Windows XP menus and want an easier way to reorganize your menus, you have to do a little digging with Windows Explorer. Click Start, All Programs, Accessories, and then Windows Explorer. By default it opens to My Documents. In the folders pane, browse to Documents and Settings\All Users\Start Menu\Programs (see Figure 3.16). From this point you can follow the rest of the Start menu hierarchy and use the multiple-selection and drag-and-drop capabilities of Windows Explorer to create and delete fold-ers, move icons and folders around, and in general make the organization more to your liking. For applications that install to a specific user's directory, browse to Documents and Settings\%username%\Start Menu\Programs.

One incomprehensible Windows design decision is the non-alphabetization of menus by default. In other words, when you move menu items around, they are tacked on at the end of the current menu structure, rather than put in alphabetical order automatically like in any other folder. To remedy this decision Microsoft included a sorting option that you must invoke each time you want the menu structure cleaned up. Right-click anywhere in the All Programs menu and then click Sort by name. Folders are moved to the top of the menu and sorted, followed by individual menu items. You need to do this for each subsequent level of the Start menu; sadly the sort feature isn't recursive, so it won't work its way through the levels of the Start menu orga-nizing your icons for you.

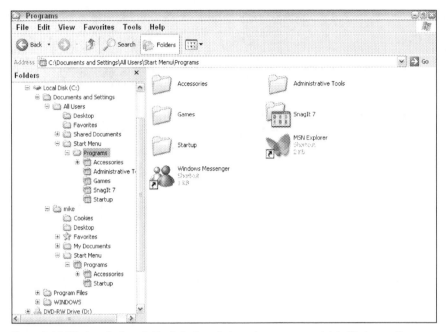

**Figure 3.16.** Windows Explorer is the fastest, easiest way to rearrange or delete Start menu items.

With the Classic view, you are given a wizard to create or remove new folders and shortcuts. In the Classic view, right-click Start, click Properties, and then click the Customize button. At the top of the Customize dialog box are the Add and Remove buttons that walk you through the steps needed to, well, add or remove items in the Start menu. This wizard works its magic only on the logged-on user's own folders, not the All Users folder. To do that, or to move things around, click the Advanced button. This launches Windows Explorer, focused on the user's folders, but you can browse up and down the folder list and work with menu items normally.

Note that Windows places the Sort function on this menu, rather than as a right-click menu option (see Figure 3.17). This button also sorts the Start menu recursively. There's probably a reason Microsoft flip-flopped the sorting behavior between the menu versions, but it seems counterintuitive to take away functionality that was perfectly decent in a previous release.

---

**Watch Out!**

If you shuffle icons around, you may make some programs go "invisible" to other users. Feel free to move icons within a particular user's directory, including the All Users one, but be careful moving icons from a user to All Users and from All Users to a specific user.

# It's our policy to say no

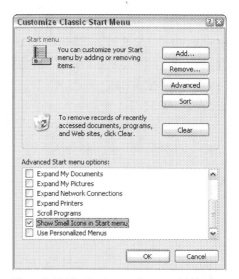

Group policies are used by Windows-centric environments to define and control just about every aspect of the operating system and related software. The Group Policy Editor (GPE) is the tool used to define and apply policies to computers and users and is especially helpful in locking down unneeded services or restricting the damage that end users can accidentally do. These settings override those created by users, which makes it a powerful tool to help keep a computer stable and running. To read more

**Figure 3.17.** The Classic menu lets you alphabetically sort your menu with only a single button click.

about the GPE and user settings, see Chapter 4; to find out how to create and apply security profiles, see Chapter 6.

Although the GPE is most often used in larger businesses, you can still use it to configure settings related to the Start menu, rather than manually adjusting the settings. Launch the GPE by clicking Start and then Run, typing gpedit.msc, and then clicking OK. Browse to User Configuration\Administrative Templates\Start Menu and Taskbar (see Figure 3.18).

The far right pane lists a number of settings that can be applied to all users that log onto the computer, including the removal of various Start menu items, locking the taskbar, and clearing out any "tracking" items such as Recent Documents. When you have the Extended View tab selected, you can click an item and see an explanation of what the item does and the operating system requirements, if any. To change one of these settings, double-click the item. Select the appropriate radio button and then click OK.

---

**Hack**

The GPE isn't available in Windows XP Home Edition, because it creates policy files that apply registry keys at startup, rather than edit the registry directly. You can still edit the appropriate registry values in XP Home Edition, but it would be simpler (and less error-prone) to purchase XP Pro.

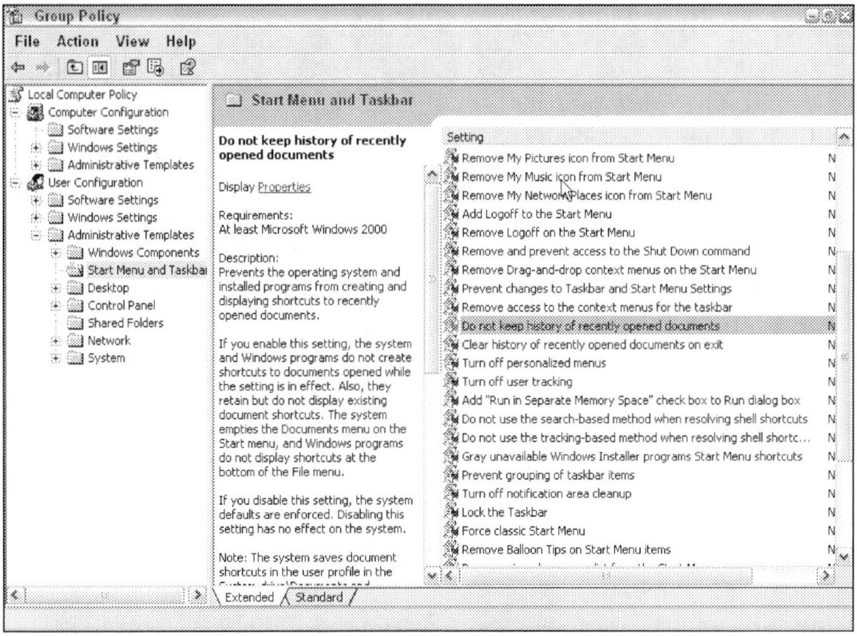

**Figure 3.18.** The Group Policy Editor is the industrial-strength Windows settings editor.

A cautionary note to the casual hacker: Sometimes the language in the GPE uses double negatives, which means that "enabling" a setting doesn't always do what you think it might. For example, when you *enable* a Remove option, it means you remove the object. If you select *disable*, that means the Remove item will be present on the menu. Yes, it's counterintuitive. Just get into the habit of reading the GPE items and the explanations closely before making changes.

But you're not done yet. The GPE has written the changes to the necessary files but Windows hasn't been told to apply them yet. You can do this in two ways. You can log off and log back on again, or click Start, Run, type cmd, and then click OK. In the command window, type gpupdate and press Enter. This instructs Windows to read the local policies file and apply any changes that have been made.

Additionally, if you browse around the Administrative Templates folder, you will see that you can change *a lot* of settings related to Windows XP's basic operation. Browse to Control Panel\Display and you can hide many of the options that have been covered in this chapter. Feel free to experiment, but remember that it's possible to lock down Windows so tightly that you cannot gain access to any administrator tools, the GPE, or Regedit. There are ways around this but they can be painful and complicated. The moral of the story: Change only a few things at a time, and don't be in a rush to make your system impenetrable. You just may lock yourself out of your own house.

---

## Run! Run!

Unless you have really good reasons to hide the Run command from users (pesky inquisitive children, for example), you should think twice before disabling it with either the Group Policy Editor or Tweak UI. The Run command is like a bridge between the GUI world and the command line, capable not only of saving you time but opening up powers you didn't know you had.

Any application that is in Windows' application path can be launched by typing the executable name, such as winword. Most Windows-specific applications, such as Regedit, are in this path and can be launched in this manner.

Many management functions can be launched directly from the Run command, such as the Group Policy Editor (gpedit.msc) and the Local User Manager (lusrmgr.msc). For some of these, such as mscorcfg.msc (.NET configuration), using the Run command is the only way to gain access to them.

You can also open shares across the network without browsing through My Network Places. Type \\computername\sharename and then click OK. The share opens up in a new window.

Finally, you can open up Control Panel components without the seemingly endless drill-down. To open the Add or Remove Programs component, type appwiz.cpl, or open the Network Connections component with ncpa.cpl.

So keep the Run command around. You will find yourself using it with increasing frequency.

---

## The antitrust icon

The United States Department of Justice filed an antitrust lawsuit against Microsoft, saying that Microsoft was using unfair business practices to prevent competition. They presented evidence that Microsoft ignored or clobbered other programs' settings when those programs were installed, specifically Web browsers, e-mail clients, instant messaging clients, media players, and Java interpreters. The courts agreed and ordered Microsoft to play well with others.

Microsoft's response was to create the Set Program Access and Defaults option in the Add or Remove Programs dialog box (see Figure 3.19); this option appears in Service Pack 1 and Service Pack 2. Shortcut icons are added directly beneath the Control Panel icon in the Start menu and at the top of the All Programs menu. Click one of these icons or open the Control Panel and click the icon in the left-hand column.

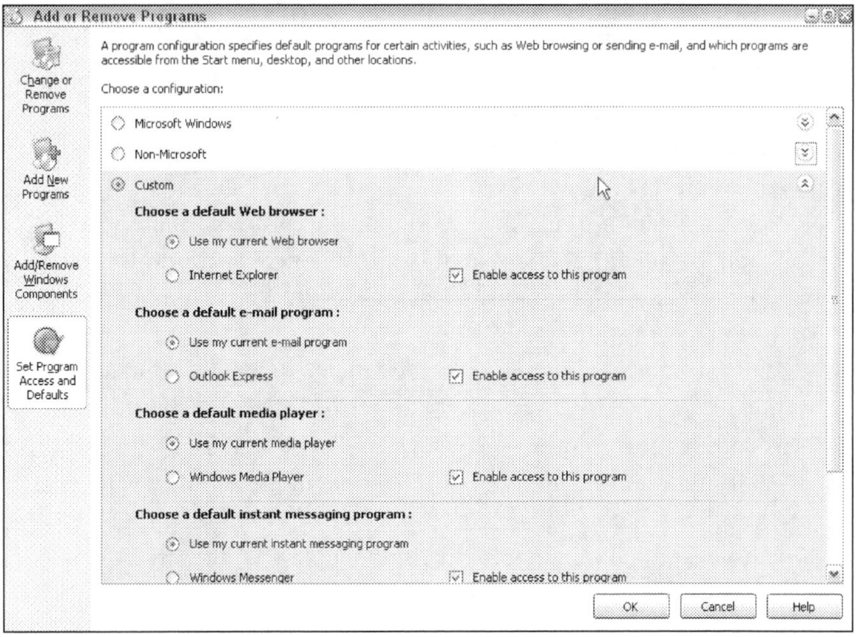

**Figure 3.19.** The Set Program Access and Defaults dialog box lets you specify non-Microsoft programs to use for key Internet functions.

There are three configuration radio buttons listed. The first is the nothing-but-Microsoft option. In essence, you tell Windows that, no matter what else is installed on your machine, you want to use only Microsoft products. Your other programs are still available, but the related program associations remain with Microsoft applications, and the pinned applications on the Start menu belong to Microsoft.

The second option is the anything-but-Microsoft option, where you tell Windows that you want to use your non-Microsoft browsers, media players, and instant messengers. However, this is a "scorched earth" option; all references to Microsoft applications in the Start menu (and program associations) are removed. The applications are still on disk, and can be restored by coming back to this dialog box, but otherwise it's as if they were never on your system.

The Custom option lets you mix and match between the two. For example, you can choose a non-Microsoft browser as your default but still allow access to Internet Explorer. If you choose not to allow access to a program, it may not work, even if you click on the program's executable. Be careful if you decide to lock out a program using this method. Besides, if it's a non-Microsoft program and you don't want access to it, why not just uninstall it?

One interesting behavior is that the Start menu icons reappear every time you install or reinstall a service pack. If it bothers you, use Tweak UI or the Group Policy Editor to get rid of them.

# All about the taskbar and the notification area

Along with the Start menu, the taskbar and the System Tray are two areas you can optimize for the way you work. They present a limited area to work with, and so you need to determine the best balance between having plenty of information and preserving screen real estate.

## Taming the taskbar

By default the taskbar appears at the bottom of the screen, but you can move it to any edge. Right-click the taskbar and deselect the option to lock the taskbar. Click and drag the taskbar to any edge of the screen you prefer (see Figure 3.20). One benefit of moving the taskbar to the sides is that you can reduce "button crunch," the condition where you have many windows open and the buttons get smaller, making it impossible to tell what a particular button's content is.

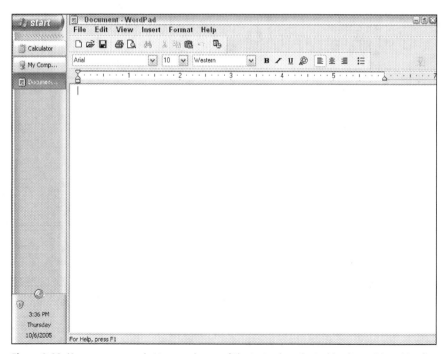

**Figure 3.20.** You can see more buttons, and more of the text, when the taskbar is to either side of the desktop.

With the taskbar unlocked, you can also resize it. Click and drag the edge to resize it to show as much or as little information as you like. This tends to have better results when the taskbar is at the sides of your screen, rather than the top or bottom, but it's a matter of personal preference. When you have it resized, you can re-lock the taskbar so that it keeps its size and location.

There are several other behavior and appearance settings you can change for the taskbar. Right-click the taskbar and then click Properties, or right-click the Start button, click Properties, and then click the taskbar tab (see Figure 3.21).

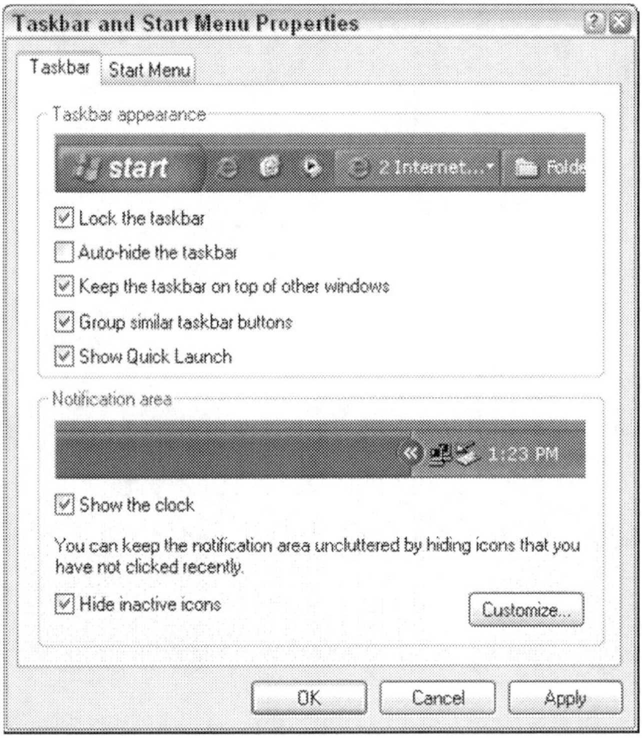

**Figure 3.21.** Change key taskbar behavior using the Taskbar Properties dialog box.

Most of the settings are self-explanatory, but the two that you may want to change are Group similar taskbar buttons and Show Quick Launch. The grouping feature is an attempt to save button space in the taskbar. When you open more than one window using the same application, such as Word or Internet Explorer, Windows will collect the windows into a single taskbar button. The button is then modified to show the number of collected windows and a down-pointing arrowhead. When you click the button, a document list appears, and you can click on the necessary document to jump to it. Turn this option off and you go back to the Windows 2000 default behavior, where "button crunch" is the normal state of being.

The other setting is to show the Quick Launch toolbar (see Figure 3.22). The next section covers custom toolbars in depth, but the Quick Launch toolbar was turned on by default in Windows 2000, and then turned off in Windows XP. I find the Quick Launch toolbar to be one of the most helpful features of the desktop and I rely on it extensively; I don't need to sort through multiple layers of menus on the Start Menu in order to launch a commonly-used application. And, because I prefer not to have my desktop cluttered with icons, the Quick Launch is where I put short-cuts to my most frequently used applications.

**Figure 3.22.** The Quick Launch toolbar, shown undocked, is the perfect place to launch frequently-used programs.

## Customize your toolbars

Windows XP comes with a few toolbars that you may find useful. When you first activate them, the toolbars appear on the existing taskbar; you can click and drag them onto your existing desktop, creating separate windows. You may also need to increase the taskbar's size to accommodate the additional toolbars.

To display the new toolbars, right-click the taskbar and then click Toolbars. The menu (see Figure 3.23) shows four toolbars that you can add to your desktop:

- **Address.** The Address toolbar is, next to Quick Launch, the most useful of the bunch. It displays a dockable toolbar that lets you type in or copy and paste a URL. This will launch your default browser and navigate to the link. It's very handy and saves you a click or two.

- **Links.** The Links toolbar shows you the contents of Internet Explorer's Favorites\Links folder. This is only partially useful — you may not put all your favorites into this folder, and you may not even use Internet Explorer as your browser.

- **Desktop.** This toolbar may be useful to someone, but it's not clear whom it's meant for. It contains a subset of buttons that you can reach in other and better ways. Maybe you'll discover the use that Microsoft thought of when they included it in Windows XP.

- **Quick Launch.** The single most useful toolbar in the bunch. This lets you add any program, document, or URL onto it that you want. If you are always opening budget.xls, for example, you can put a shortcut to it here so that you are never more than one click away.

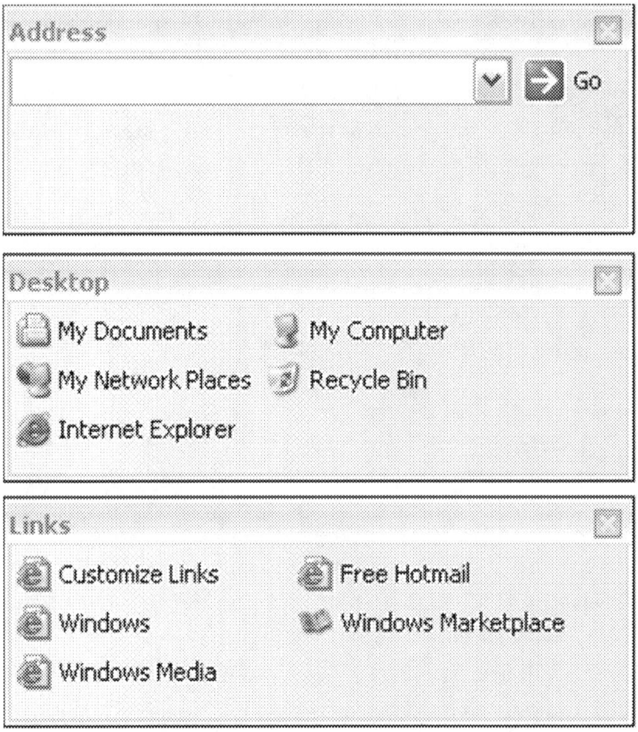

**Figure 3.23.** Revealed at last: the "hidden" toolbars of Windows XP.

If you have installed Windows Media Player 10, you will have a Windows Media Player toolbar listed. When WMP is launched and then minimized, a control toolbar appears in the taskbar with the necessary media controls. This is handy for when you are listening to music but don't need the screen real estate consumed with the player's interface.

**Inside Scoop**

Microsoft applications such as Windows Media Player and Outlook have an annoying habit of installing shortcuts onto the Quick Launch toolbar for you without asking first. Don't hesitate to delete these shortcuts if you find them annoying.

You add items to all toolbars but the Address toolbar by dragging and dropping an icon onto them. The easiest way is to open the toolbar, click Start, browse to the icon you want to add, and then drag the icon onto the appropriate toolbar. Left-clicking and dragging automatically creates a shortcut; if you right-click and drag, a menu appears, giving you the option to move the icon to the toolbar rather than just copying it.

Drag-and-drop is also used to re-order items in a toolbar. Left-click and drag the icons to new locations. Windows displays a black vertical bar showing you where the icon will land when you release the mouse button.

If you get tired of any of these toolbars, you can get rid of them by right-clicking the toolbar and then clicking Close Toolbar (see Figure 3.24), or you can right-click the taskbar, click Toolbars, and then deselect the specific toolbar. If you have the toolbar visible as a window, just click the Close button.

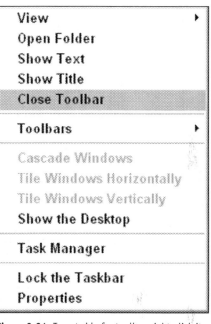

**Figure 3.24.** To get rid of a toolbar, right-click it and then click Close.

## All systems are go: The notification area

The notification area is at the far right of the taskbar (see Figure 3.25). This area is also known as the system tray, because it is where many system-related icons appear. Microsoft calls it the notification area on the theory that when something happens with your system that you should know about, a widget will notify you about it.

**Figure 3.25.** The Notification Area can contain many icons, only some of which actually notify you of important events.

The reality is that many applications, system-related or user-related, put icons here. Many of them are spawned by applets loaded at startup; others are here instead of minimizing to the taskbar, which helps save real estate.

Whether you prefer lots of notification icons or few, there are two basic settings you can control regarding overall appearance. You can manage the settings by right-clicking the taskbar and then clicking Properties. The two settings are to display the clock (or not), and to hide inactive icons.

To hide or unhide icons, or to hide only inactive icons, click the Customize button. You are presented with a list of icons that have made an appearance at one time or another in the notification area. Click an entry and then click the drop-down list and change its status to whichever one suits your needs (see Figure 3.26).

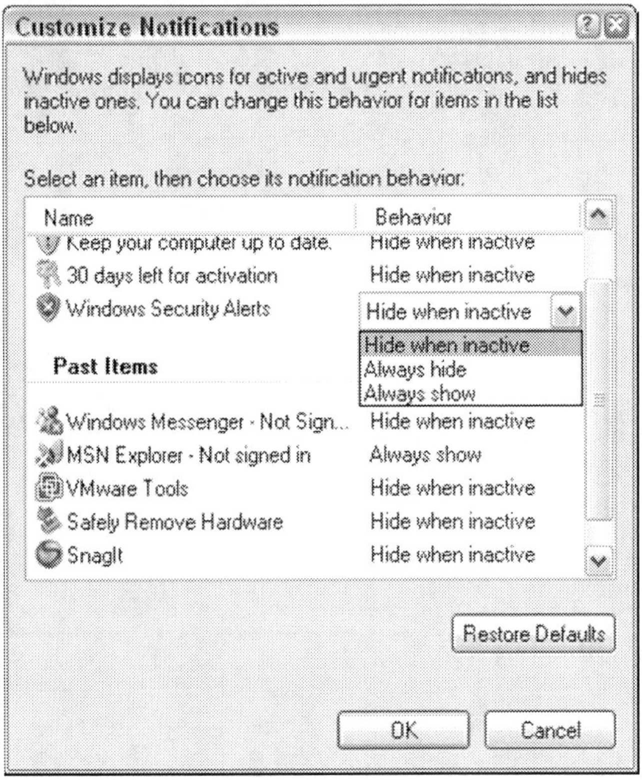

**Figure 3.26.** You can change the way icons appear in the notification area.

A few words about the Hide when inactive option: When this box is selected, any icons that have not been active for a while will "disappear" and be replaced by a left-facing chevron in the notification area. You can see the chevron in the preview box above the check boxes. Your inactive icons can be briefly redisplayed by clicking the chevron, which scoots to the left and shows you all the icons again. If you want to click an icon, click quick; the chevron gives you only a few seconds' time before concealing the icons again.

**Hack**

Want to get rid of the notification area completely? Open gpedit.msc and browse to User Configuration\Administrative Templates\Start Menu and Taskbar. Change the policy in the Hide the notification area to Enabled and reboot.

Two other ways of reducing the number of icons are to tell applications not to use the notification area (either when minimizing or when just plain running), and to reduce the number of applets that load at startup. Some programs like media players let you choose whether to minimize to the notification area or to minimize to the taskbar; others, like MSN Messenger, don't give you an option. For the latter applications you can change the visibility status as recommended above.

For dealing with applets that load at startup, see the section "Improve startup with MSCONFIG," later in this chapter.

# Edit desktop settings with Tweak UI

Despite all the improvements in the Windows interface, and new usability enhancements, there are many aspects of Windows that are odd, get in the way, or just plain don't work the way you expect them to. Microsoft developers found this was true for them as well, so some unsung geniuses developed the PowerToys.

The PowerToys collection started out as only an interface configuration application, using checkboxes and tabbed dialog boxes to make changes to obscure Registry settings. The changes would turn off animated menus, for example, or clear all search dialog boxes at logoff. The recent batch of PowerToys has been expanded to include useful utilities, not just for the user interface, but for other Windows applications including the command line. Not everyone will need all of them, but if you find that Windows out of the box is a little too inflexible, the PowerToys are a good first place to look for opening up Windows.

Tweak UI configures many of the Windows behaviors that are otherwise difficult to control. If you are acting as the system administrator and you want the changes to be global, use the Group Policy Editor to make the necessary edits. Otherwise, if you are changing things on a per-user basis only, Tweak UI is the PowerToy of choice.

Once you have installed Tweak UI, click Start, click All Programs, click PowerToys for Windows XP, and then click Tweak UI. The window (see

**Watch Out!**

Although PowerToys are written by Microsoft and available from Microsoft, Microsoft lets you know in no uncertain terms that all PowerToys are unofficial and unsupported. If you install one and Windows breaks, you're on your own.

Figure 3.27) displays a tree in the left pane, a collection of settings related to tree items in the upper right, and the lower right contains explanations — sometimes very brief — of what each setting accomplishes. Most settings are per user, some are global, and some require a log off and a log on to change the desktop.

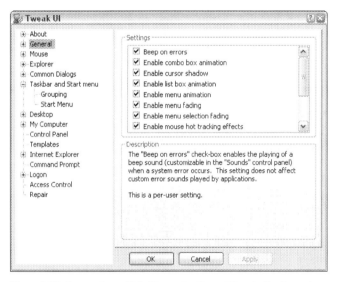

**Figure 3.27.** You can turn off desktop animation settings in the General category.

You can spend quite a bit of time exploring all the settings that Tweak UI makes available to you; here are a few favorites.

- **General.** This collection of settings configures many of the animation "features" of Windows XP. With the exception of the cursor shadow, all of these get turned off.

- **Explorer.** Use this section to show or hide various Windows XP folders, such as ones labeled "My" or options you never use such as Links.

- **Taskbar and Start menu\Start menu.** This section allows you to choose which applications will stick around in the most-recently-used section of the Start menu. You can eliminate little-used applications and keep the clutter minimized. Double-check this section every now and again, as new options are added as you install and use additional programs.

- **Logon.** You can choose which accounts are visible in the workgroup's logon screen. This is nice for those occasions when you don't want your kids attempting to hack the Administrator account (hidden by default).

One setting you should be careful with is the Logon\Autologon setting. In general you should always log on with a user name and password, even if you're the only person in your home. To save time, you can have Windows log on with any user's account automatically, but because this setting bypasses the normal log on process, anyone can get access to your personal information or masquerade as you online. This setting is most useful for testing and troubleshooting, when you never leave the computer. It is a high security risk and should be disabled once you have finished your testing.

Lastly, there is another setting that can be a huge help. Occasionally Windows gets confused about resource information and mixes up icons on the desktop and in Windows Explorer. In the Repair section (see Figure 3.28), the first item in the drop-down list allows you to rebuild icon resource information, and nine times out of ten it will restore the mixed-up icons to their normal programs and files.

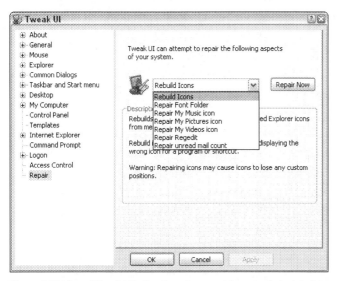

**Figure 3.28.** One of Tweak UI's Repair options reset icons to their default appearance.

# A grab bag of PowerToys

PowerToys are additional programs that Microsoft developers worked on after Windows XP was released to manufacturing. They add missing functionality to Windows, and even make Windows fun in some cases.

The PowerToys collection is updated from time to time as new applets are built, or as existing PowerToys gain some features or bug fixes. Here is a list of PowerToys currently available:

- **RAW Image Thumbnailer and Viewer.** The RAW format is considered the most flexible and true-to-life file format (unlike lossy formats such as JPG). With this PowerToy, you can organize and work with digital RAW files in Windows Explorer (much as you can with JPEG images). It also provides thumbnails, previews, printing, and metadata display for RAW images.

- **ClearType Tuner.** This PowerToy lets you use ClearType technology to make it easier to read text on your screen, and installs in the Control Panel for easy access. It is a definite boon for LCD or laptop users, since ClearType was initially either on or off, with no easy means of control.

- **HTML Slide Show Wizard.** This wizard helps you create an HTML slide show of your digital pictures, ready to place on your Web site.

- **Open Command Window Here.** This PowerToy adds an Open Command Window Here context menu option on file system folders, giving you a quick way to open a command window (cmd.exe) pointing at the selected folder. Incredibly handy for users who enjoy a command-line interface.

- **Alt-Tab Replacement.** With this PowerToy, in addition to seeing the icon of the application window you are switching to, you will also see a preview of the page. This helps particularly when multiple sessions of an application are open. The page preview size is configurable, which is a big help for people with limited vision.

- **Power Calculator.** With this PowerToy you can graph and evaluate functions as well as perform many different types of conversions. It won't replace your HP scientific calculator but it's handy nonetheless.

**Bright Idea**

You can download all the PowerToys for Windows XP at www.microsoft.com/windowsxp/downloads/powertoys/xppowertoys.mspx.

- **Image Resizer.** This PowerToy enables you to resize one or many image files with a right-click. This is a fast and easy way to resize images for Web pages, or to reduce the size of image attachments in e-mail (such as when you send your newest pictures of the kids to the grandparents).

- **CD Slide Show Generator.** With this PowerToy you can view images burned to a CD as a slide show. Doing a proper job of mastering a slide show produces better results (and requires more effort), but if you just want a quick and dirty way to display images from a disk, this is it.

- **Virtual Desktop Manager.** Manage up to four desktops from the Windows taskbar with this PowerToy. Microsoft attempts to do what Linux has done for years — increase the size of the virtual desktop. You can switch between desktops and have each desktop focused on a particular task or application.

- **Taskbar Magnifier.** Use this PowerToy to magnify part of the screen from the taskbar. Similar to the Magnifier function in the Accessibility folder, but more focused (pun intended).

- **Webcam Timershot.** This PowerToy lets you take pictures at specified time intervals from a Webcam connected to your computer and save them to a location that you designate. You may have a feature like this already in your Webcam software; if so, use the software that came with your Webcam instead.

If you decide you don't like a PowerToy, you can uninstall it from the Add or Remove Programs window in Control Panel.

# Add, remove, and change Windows components

You can add, remove, and change most of the components that are available in Windows. These run the gamut from accessibility tools, to applets like Calc and WordPad, to services like Internet Information Server (IIS) or Distributed Transaction Coordinator.

Some components, such as additional mouse pointers, are just for fun or add to the things you can do with Windows. Others, like IIS, are meant for heavy duty use or more extensive use of Windows than as an ordinary desktop PC.

Because many of these components and services are really meant for development usage there are limits on what you can do with some of them. For example, the version of IIS that ships with Windows XP has a limit of ten concurrent connections. So, although you can run a Web server on your desktop, it's more for development efforts than for actual serving of content on the Internet.

It all starts with the Add or Remove Programs dialog box. Click Start, click Control Panel, and then click Add or Remove Programs (see Figure 3.29). The default view shows you which applications and software updates you have installed on your computer. You can remove (or change the program's installation, if that option is available) by clicking a program and then clicking Remove.

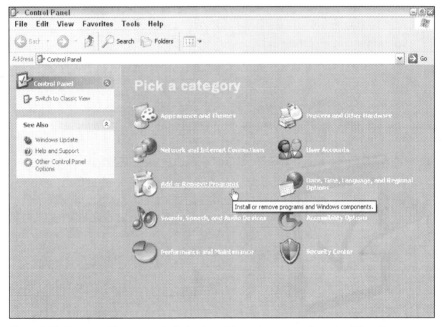

**Figure 3.29.** You can add or remove just about anything on your computer using this option.

To remove Windows components, click the Add/Remove Windows Components button on the left side of the dialog box. The Windows Components Wizard appears (see Figure 3.30), showing you a list of Windows components that you can install or remove. Scroll through the list to find the components you want to add or remove; you can click Details to get a list of subcomponents that can be added or removed. Select a component to add or remove and then click Next. Windows adds or removes the selected component. Close the wizard by clicking Finish. Depending on the component, you may need to reboot your system.

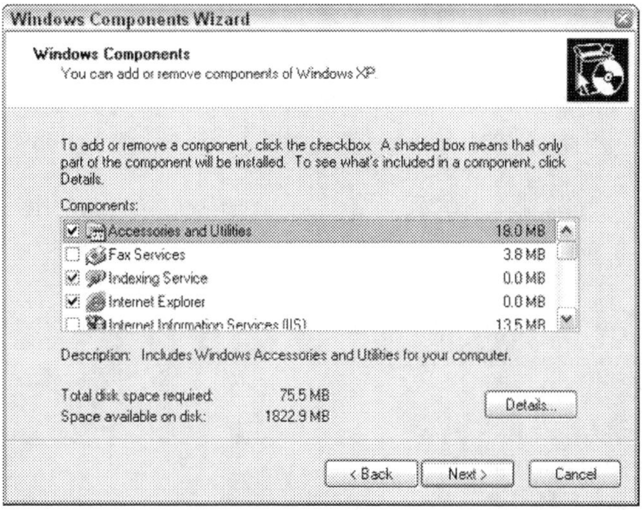

**Figure 3.30.** The wizard shows you a list of Windows components to install or remove.

## Removing hidden Windows components

Older versions of Windows allowed you to select components such as games, the Briefcase, and WinTV (remember that one?) at installation time. Windows XP sped up the installation process by removing the component selection process. Instead, it installs many components without asking you for permission, some of which look like they can't be uninstalled. You won't find a way to uninstall Pinball, for example, even though it takes up a lot of space on your hard drive.

But there is a way to list those hidden components in the Add/Remove Components dialog box. Using Windows Explorer, browse to the Windows\inf folder and use Notepad to open the file SYSOC.INF. (If you can't see the folder, change Explorer's settings to show you hidden and system files.) You will see a number of line entries like this one:

```
Games=ocgen.dll,OcEntry,games.inf,HIDE,7
```

Delete the word HIDE from the component you want to appear in Add/Remove Components and then save the file. Go to the Add/Remove Components dialog box, and you will see the components, ready to be deleted.

# Manage applications with Task Manager

Task Manager is a jack-of-all-trades application that provides a wealth of information about the overall health of Windows. Most frequently it is used to kill applications and processes that have crashed and are no longer responding.

You can launch Task Manager (see Figure 3.31) in three different ways: Right-click on the taskbar and then click Task Manager; press Ctrl+Shift+Esc; or press Ctrl+Alt+Del. The latter will either bring up Task Manager, if you are in a workgroup, or bring up the Windows Security dialog box if you are in a domain, where you can then click the Task Manager button.

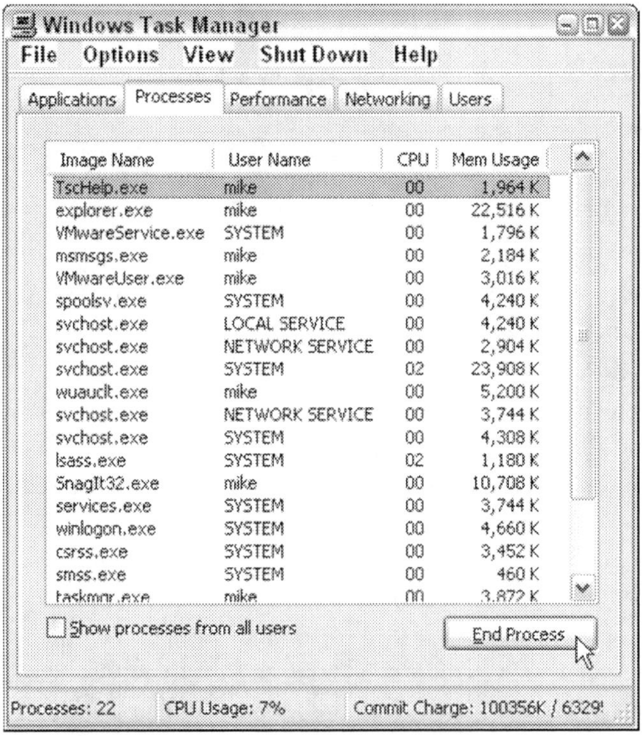

**Figure 3.31.** Task Manager displays a list of what is running on your computer.

Click the Applications tab and you will see a list of all running applications on your system and each application's status. If the program has crashed and has stopped responding — your mouse cursor moves but you cannot open menus or click the close button — Task Manager shows you the helpful message "Not Responding." Click the unresponsive application in

**Inside Scoop**

Because Task Manager displays CPU usage and helps identify misbehaving applications, I put a shortcut to taskmgr.exe in my Startup folder. That way information about my system and misbehaving applications is just one click away.

Task Manager and then click End Task. The application may close right away, or you may receive a system notification that "This program is not responding." Click End Now, or wait for Windows to lose patience and close the application for you.

Sometimes it's not an application that goes awry but a system process. This often happens with poorly-written device drivers or services related to hardware that are running around, listening for a response, but not smart enough to figure out that the hardware isn't responding. Usually when this happens, the CPU usage (found on the Performance tab) rockets up to 100%. Click the Processes tab and find the process that is consuming all or nearly all of the CPU cycles. Click the process and then click End Process; most of the time, this is sufficient to put down the misbehaving process.

There are times, however, when the process won't be or can't be killed. Unlike UNIX-based systems, there is no way to log on as root and have ultimate control over what happens with the system; Windows protects some processes even if you think they should be ended. A third-party program called Process Explorer works much like Task Manager but provides far more detail about running processes (such as file system handles) than average users would ever need. But it does one thing that Task Manager doesn't: It lets you end processes, any processes, even ones that Windows thinks you shouldn't. For this reason it's a great tool to have in your toolbox, and is a worthy replacement for, or addition to, Task Manager. Best of all, it's freeware. You can find Process Explorer at www.sysinternals.com.

# Improve startup with MSCONFIG

When Windows XP boots it starts a number of services and applications so that the Windows environment is configured for your use. These services and applets may or may not be needed; many of them are enabled out of the box, while others are added by applications or device managers you install.

Microsoft provides a program called the System Configuration Utility, or MSCONFIG that lets you determine which services and applications run at startup. You can see which programs are starting, where they reside on your system, and enable or disable them by clicking a check box. This makes it easy to determine if a particular service or application is needed, and lets you undo any changes if you find your system is less stable or less functional without the applets.

You can also control these services and applets using the Services Manager and RegEdit (see Chapter 11 for more information on these applications). However, if you are experimenting with the boot time and application startup, MSCONFIG is easier to use than the other applications.

Click Start, click Run, type MSCONFIG, and then click OK. Click the Startup tab (see Figure 3.32). You will see a list of the applets that are loaded at boot time: the name of the applet, the applet's location and any command-line options, and the registry key that contains the information.

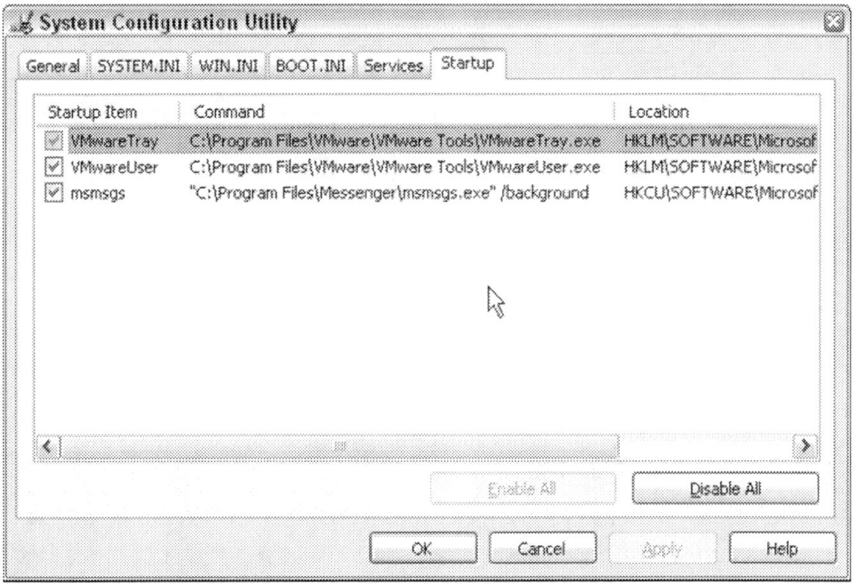

**Figure 3.32.** MSCONFIG lets you select which applets to load at boot time.

From this dialog box you can select and deselect which applets you want loaded at boot time. This is a great way to determine which applets are needed and which are just consuming CPU cycles. For example, I never used my video card's control panel, which was so generously installed into the notification area for me. Using MSCONFIG, I determined that my system worked just fine without it, so I launched Regedit and removed the registry key that loaded the applet.

**Hack**

Want a fast way to bypass loading all those applets at boot time? Hold down the Shift key when your computer is booting.

MSCONFIG's other tabs go into detail on legacy startup files, services, and boot configurations. It is best to leave these alone unless you have some experience with legacy applications, hacking boot files, and working with startup diagnostics. Services are covered in more detail in Chapter 11, and it's better to use the Services management panel (services.msc) to control how services are launched.

# Windows, applications, and performance

There are other ways to tune Windows XP for optimal performance, ones that do not require diving deeply into the registry or hacking away at applications. Surprisingly for Windows some of these settings are accessible *and* understandable.

The first two settings are usually set for you, but depending on your needs you can change them around. They tell Windows, on a macro scale, how to allocate its cycles: best performance for applications, or best performance for services.

Click Start, right-click My Computer, and then click Properties. (You can also right-click the My Computer icon if it is on your desktop, click Start, Run, and then type sysdm.cpl, or access the dialog box through Control Panel ⇨ System.) The System Properties dialog box appears; click the Advanced tab and then in the Performance section click Settings. The Performance Option dialog box appears. Click the Advanced tab. This tab contains two primary settings: one for processor scheduling and one for memory usage (see Figure 3.33).

By default, on a Windows XP desktop, both are set to optimize for Programs, so you should not have to change these options. If you are doing development or testing Web server programs, you can change these settings so that background services and the system cache receive the majority of the available computer cycles.

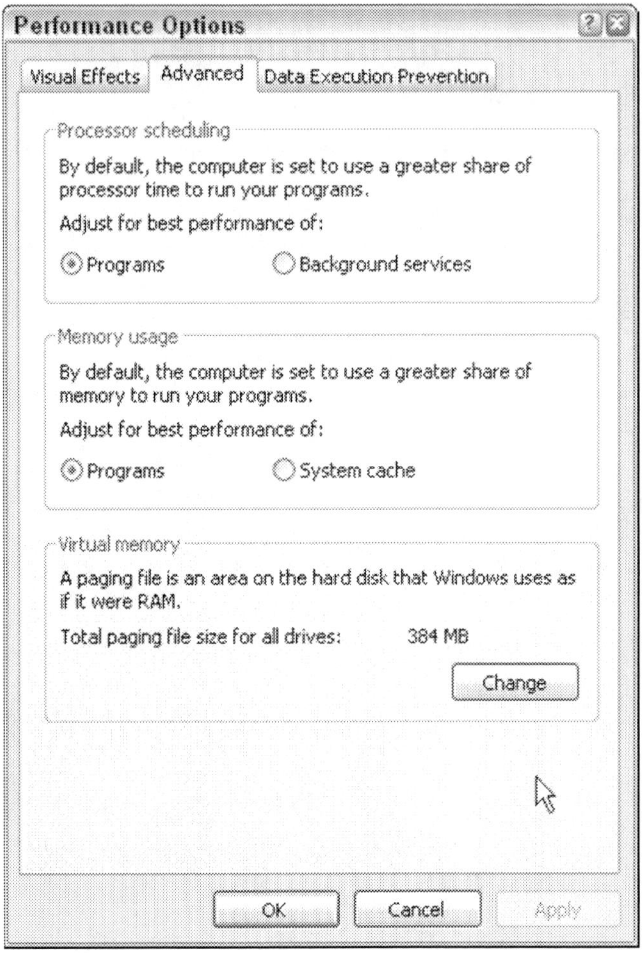

**Figure 3.33.** You can instruct Windows how to optimize its performance: for applications or for services.

The next group of settings is in the same general area but pertain to video performance. From the Performance Options dialog box, click the Visual Effects tab (see Figure 3.34). Here you can fine-tune the amount of eye candy you want when you use Windows. The first two radio button options are all-or-nothing switches; they select all or none of the items listed in the Custom list box. The Custom radio button lets you pick and choose which animation elements you want Windows to spend time computing and displaying for you.

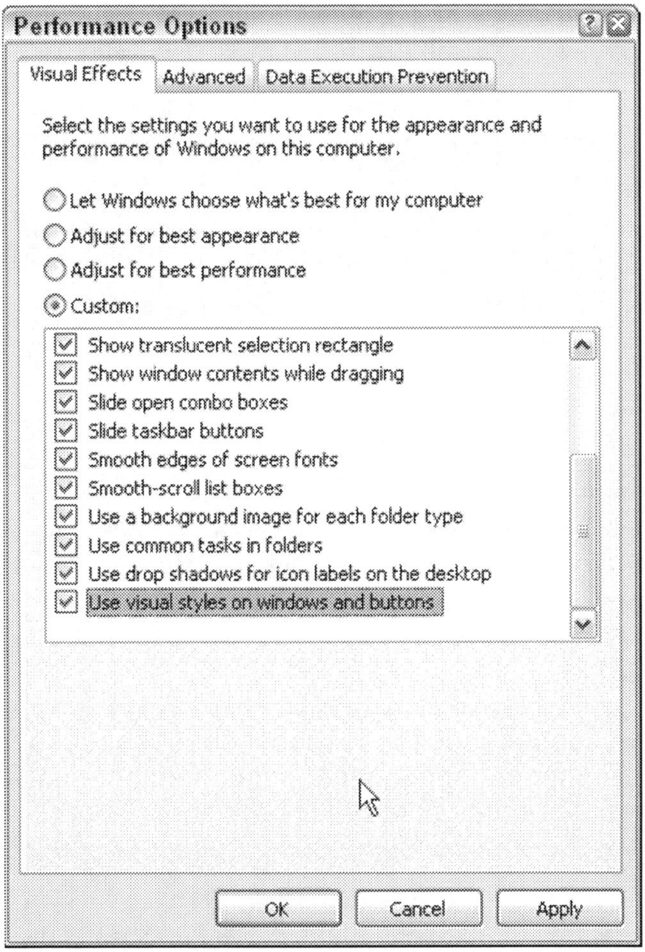

**Performance Options**

Visual Effects | Advanced | Data Execution Prevention

Select the settings you want to use for the appearance and performance of Windows on this computer.

○ Let Windows choose what's best for my computer
○ Adjust for best appearance
○ Adjust for best performance
◉ Custom:

- ☑ Show translucent selection rectangle
- ☑ Show window contents while dragging
- ☑ Slide open combo boxes
- ☑ Slide taskbar buttons
- ☑ Smooth edges of screen fonts
- ☑ Smooth-scroll list boxes
- ☑ Use a background image for each folder type
- ☑ Use common tasks in folders
- ☑ Use drop shadows for icon labels on the desktop
- ☑ Use visual styles on windows and buttons

[ OK ] [ Cancel ] [ Apply ]

**Figure 3.34.** Select the visual effects you want displayed.

If you play computer games, there are two additional changes you can make that will help with performance, especially if your system is on the borderline for the game's hardware requirements. Most games suggest turning off anti-aliasing and anisotropic filtering, both of which ask your video card to spend precious cycles calculating features that probably won't be missed in fast-action, first-person-shooter games.

**Watch Out!**

The last item in the list, Use visual styles on windows and buttons, turns on and off the Windows XP style. If you deselect this item, the interface reverts to the Windows 2000 style, though it keeps the Windows XP Start menu structure.

These settings are found in your video card's management applet or on a special tab in the Display Properties dialog box. Deselect these options and you will gain some additional cycles without drastically reducing image quality.

# Running old DOS or Windows applications

With Windows 2000, Microsoft removed the support for older DOS and 16-bit Windows applications that was in Windows 9x and Windows Me. This code, though well-written, allowed applications and device drivers to write directly to hardware, causing hard locks, system-level crashes, and the infamous "blue screen of death." Removing this code drastically reduced the number of crashes, but also made backwards compatibility trickier, especially for custom software that relied on legacy applications or gamers with several years of older games they wanted to play.

However, with Windows 2000 and Windows XP, Microsoft included Compatibility Mode, a set of software services and database collection of application information that provides limited DOS emulation for these older applications. For example, some Windows 16-bit applications query Windows to find out what version it is, and the application will not run if the answer is not recognized. Compatibility mode provides the necessary information to the application, allowing it to run. Compatibility mode also includes re-creating registry structures and other OS-specific variables found in Windows 9x, which differed in significant ways from the structure currently used by Windows XP.

Compatibility mode isn't an instant cure-all. There are numerous applications that *should not* be run using compatibility mode. These include ones that interact directly with hardware, such as older antivirus software, disk defragmentation programs, registry editors, and rescue utilities like Norton Utilities. If you try to run an application that directly manages hardware or the operating system using compatibility mode, you stand an excellent chance of corrupting your system and making it unbootable.

The easiest way to configure compatibility mode is by using a wizard.

1. Click Start, click All Programs, click Accessories, and then click Program Compatibility Wizard. Click Next. The Program Compatibility Wizard appears. Click Next.

2. The Program Compatibility Wizard offers you a choice of how to locate your program: choosing from a list, running a program on CD, or manually browsing to a location. If you select the first option, the wizard searches the Program Files and Windows folders for applications that

you have already installed. This option is best for older Windows applications. The second option is for programs on a CD that are not yet installed, whether Windows or older DOS applications. The third option is for programs not installed but present on your hard drive; this is the best option for all older DOS applications. Assuming you're working with an older Windows application, choose the first option and then click Next.

3. A list of programs is presented (see Figure 3.35). Select the program you want to configure from the list and then click Next.

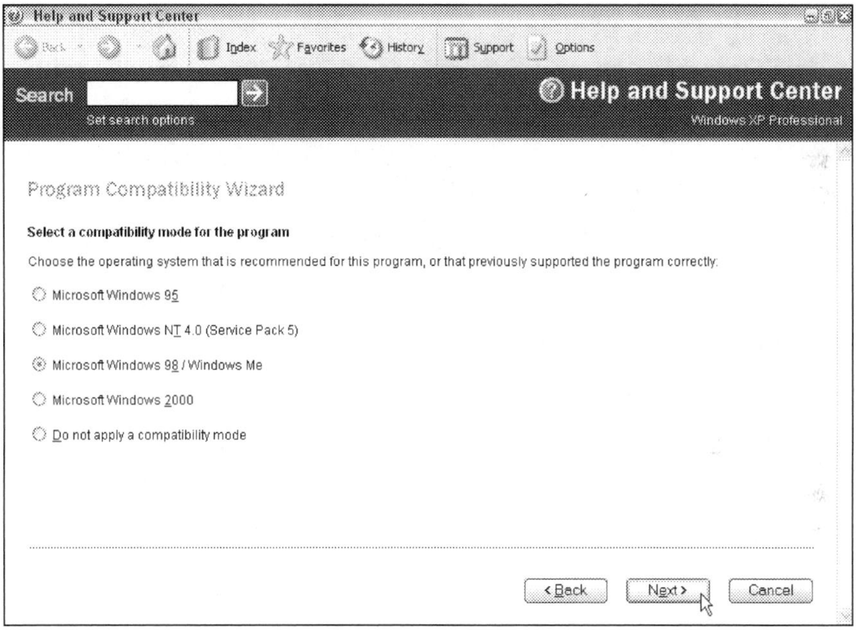

**Figure 3.35.** Select the compatibility mode you want to use for your program.

4. Select the operating system compatibility mode and then click Next. Select optional display modes for your application if needed, and then click Next.

5. To test the compatibility settings, click Next.

6. Click which result applies to your compatibility tests, and then click Next. The wizard collects Windows system information based on your responses, and you can voluntarily choose whether to send your custom configuration information to Microsoft. Click Yes or No, and then click Next. Click Finish to exit the wizard.

You can configure compatibility for any application without using the wizard. Right-click on an executable or a shortcut that launches it and then click Properties. Click the Compatibility tab (see Figure 3.36) to show the compatibility mode options on a single dialog box page, make the necessary selections, and then click OK. Clicking the executable or the shortcut will launch your application using the compatibility mode settings.

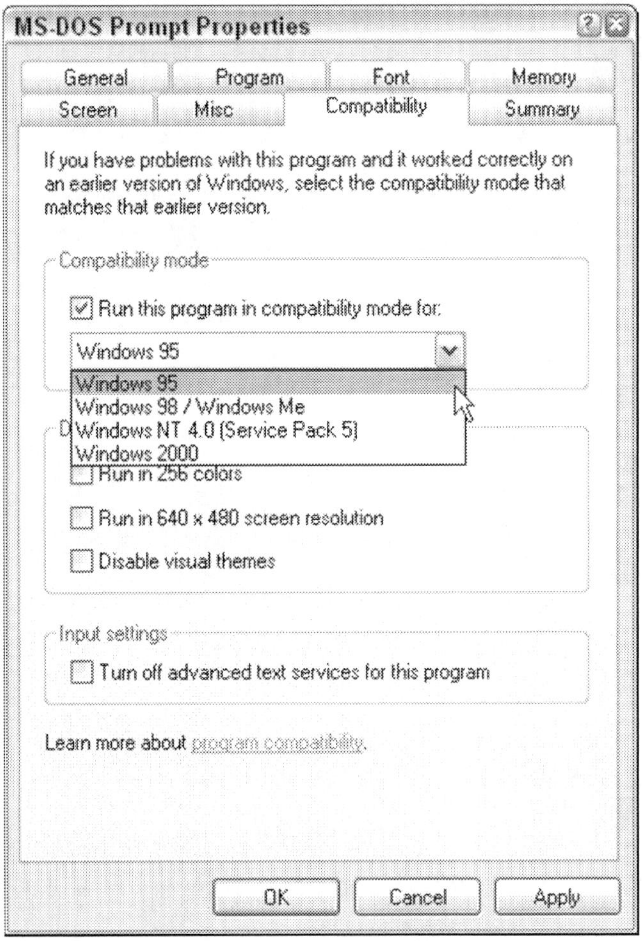

**Figure 3.36.** Select the compatibility mode you want to use for your program.

## Application Compatibility Toolkit

If you don't want to spend your time adjusting settings repeatedly in order to find what works, there may be an easier way to create a compatible environment for your older applications.

Microsoft offers an advanced set of tools, intended for system administrators, called the Application Compatibility Toolkit. Its core application, the Compatibility Administrator, contains a number of settings and fixes for many applications. They are settings that have worked in other environments and may in yours. You can download the toolkit at http://msdn.microsoft.com/library/default.asp?url=/downloads/list/appcomp.asp.

If you want to run MS-DOS applications on Windows XP, your course of action is a little trickier. You can run applications in the standard command-line virtual machine, cmd.exe. Or you can run your application in a DOS emulation environment, command.com. Both are managed by NTVDM, or NT Virtual DOS Machine, which sets environment variables needed by DOS programs when you run them.

Environment variables can be set by modifying or creating custom AUTOEXEC.NT and CONFIG.NT files that are run when the virtual machine starts. The AUTOEXEC.NT and CONFIG.NT files can be found in the Windows\system32 directory. If you were comfortable modifying their analogues in DOS, you can do the same in Windows XP.

Very old MS-DOS applications relied on the CPU clock speed to determine how fast the application ran. Even if you configure the environment correctly, there's no easy way under Windows XP to slow down the emulation environment. Your best bet is to download a third-party "slowdown" applet that you can run prior to launching your older application. This can provide some relief for impossibly fast applications. However, this is not guaranteed, and the environment may not be stable, so use slowdown applications at your own risk. Mo'slo is a popular slowdown utility available in several different versions at www.hpaa.com/moslo.

## Just the facts

- Nearly every aspect of the Windows basic look and feel can be configured.

- Additional wallpapers, themes, and icons can be added to further customize Windows.

- With the addition of a few PowerToys you can tweak the last 10 percent of the Windows settings.

- It is easy to take control of applications and system applets so that Windows works the way you want it to.

- With a little luck, older applications can run on XP.

# Manage the XP Environment

# PART II

# Managing Users

**W**indows XP, more so than previous versions of Windows, puts heavy emphasis on the concept of users. More than in any other release (with the exception of NT), Windows XP puts roles and responsibilities in the hands of the user.

In addition to users, Windows XP continues to use the Microsoft Management Console to keep on top of your computer's various tasks and components.

## Users and Windows XP

Microsoft emphasizes the notion of "user accounts" in the Windows XP release. In addition to your standard "administrator" or "computer owner" accounts, you can also create highly customized user accounts on your computer so that everyone in the family has a tailor-made Windows experience. In other words, as the administrator, you can assign permissions to allow certain users to access only those programs or features you assign.

Separate user accounts for different users is a good idea. First, there is the privacy; for example, user1 cannot see the active desktop of user2. If a user decides to store personal files on the desktop, these files are not visible to other users. The same goes for application icons if they were installed only for a given user and not for everyone. This is a helpful feature if you share a computer with others — it allows you to "hide" programs from other users. (However, the application itself is

111

actually installed — if a user wants to use that particular application, he can launch it manually.) Besides having a customized desktop (not to mention individual wallpapers and screensavers), each user also has the luxury of his own My Documents folder. This is an invaluable benefit, especially if one user stores business/work files in his My Documents folder and another user stores school files in his. Finally, each user can personalize his Windows XP experience — each can set his own folder options, Internet Explorer Favorites, and Start menu settings. See Chapter 3 for more about these options.

To set up separate user accounts on a home machine, you create a local user name or group that is stored locally on your machine in a local security database. Things become a little more complicated if you're working with domains or workgroups. In these cases, to set up separate user accounts you'll need a domain user account and not a local user account for domains and, for accounts for workgroups, you'll need to install the same user account on any machine that you will want to access.

When you create an account, a list of advantages or permissions for both administrator and limited accounts appears (mouse over the corresponding radio button for a description). As you can see, there are some clear differences between the two accounts. If you decide to create a limited account and you are logged on to this account, you will be able to change/set your password, change your picture, set up a .NET passport, work with network passwords, and use the Forgotten Password Wizard. It is clearly better for you to log on as an administrator for any dealing with user accounts for the simple reason that you have full authority over all accounts. As a limited user, you have very limited leverage over your account.

## Add users

Adding users is a very easy, routine task that can be performed from any administrator account; you cannot add users while logged onto a limited account. You can add users through the Windows XP Control Panel; simply select User Accounts (in either the Classic or Category views). The User Accounts page (see Figure 4.1) lets you perform a number of user-oriented tasks. Select Create a new account from the Pick a task menu. Enter your

---

**Watch Out!**

If you plan on adding new users/accounts, make sure you are logged on as an administrator (or "computer administrator," as Windows XP likes to say); otherwise adding users will just be a distant dream. Limited user accounts are unable to add or change users (other than updating their own account).

desired name for the account and click Next (see Figure 4.2). Keep in mind that this is the name that will appear when you start up Windows.

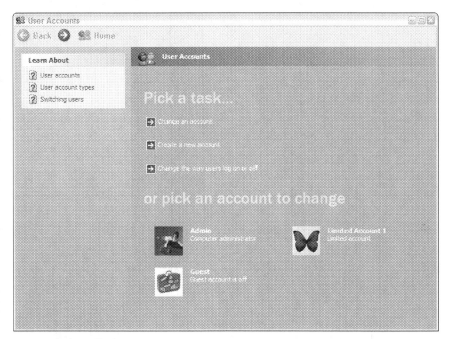

**Figure 4.1.** The User Accounts window.

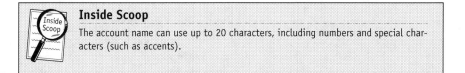

**Figure 4.2.** Name your new account.

> **Inside Scoop**
>
> The account name can use up to 20 characters, including numbers and special characters (such as accents).

**Watch Out!**

Some applications can only be installed if the current user has administrator access. If you are unable to install your application, log out and then log on as the administrator.

If you are logged on as an administrator and you click the Create a new account option, Windows XP gives you the option of selecting whether to give the account administrator access or limited access in the Add User Wizard that appears. Administrator access essentially allows full control of the machine; as administrator, you can install applications, make system-wide changes, modify accounts, and so on. Limited accounts, on the other hands, do not have as much leeway in terms of machine access and administration tasks — they can simply change account pictures and their account password.

Both account types are designed to allow software installation. However, some software may require administrator access simply so the administrator can choose whether to make the software package available to all users. Limited accounts cannot make this decision. There are some known compatibility issues between software developed prior to the release of Windows XP and limited access accounts. If your software application is not certified for use with Windows XP (but is still Windows compatible), it is best to use the administrator account.

This ends the account creation process in Windows XP. The new account appears at the bottom of the User Accounts page with a randomly assigned picture, the account name, and its type (see Figure 4.3).

While the account creation process is simple enough, administrators still don't have total control of limited access accounts from the User Accounts menu. This is left to the Group accounts, which I will discuss later in this chapter, in the section "Create Group Policies."

The last option in the Pick a task menu of the User Accounts page provides two different ways of logging on and off. The Use the Welcome Screen option allows you to simply click your name to start your Windows session. For security purposes you can turn this off (it is enabled by default) and use the classic logon/password prompt. The second option, Use Fast User

**Hack**

There is also a third account type, Guest, which is ideal for people who will be temporarily using your machine but not enough to justify the creation of an account. You cannot create this account — it exists by default in the administrator's User Accounts window with the other accounts. By default, it is inactive. Click Guest to activate it.

Switching, allows you to toggle between accounts without having to close programs. This will help you save time by quickly getting back to your work when the other user finishes.

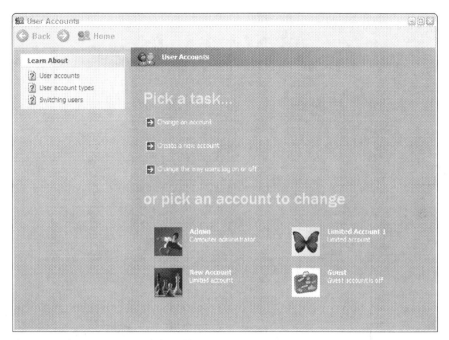

**Figure 4.3.** The User Accounts window with new account.

# Modify accounts

Users with administrator access can modify existing user accounts (including their own) from the User Accounts page from the Control Panel.

There are two ways of editing an account from this window. Frankly, one would suffice because there is no real advantage of having two here! You can select Change an account from the Pick a task menu, or you can click the account name or icon listed in the "or pick an account to change" menu.

If you select a limited account, the Edit Account menu presents five options for the account (see Figure 4.4):

- Change the name
- Create a password
- Change the picture
- Change the account type
- Delete the account

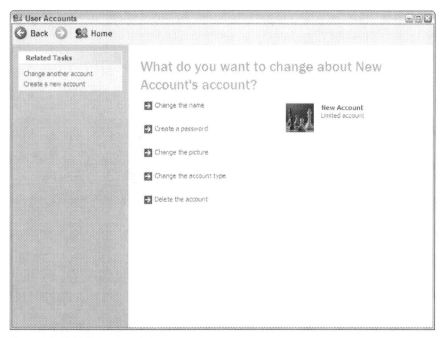

**Figure 4.4.** The Edit Account window.

On the Edit Account page, you will notice a set of Related Tasks in the left panel. These tasks will change dramatically depending on if you are editing an administrator or a limited access account. A limited access account has two options: Change another account and Create a new account, as shown in Figure 4.4. (The Administrator account also has the Manage my network passwords and Prevent a forgotten password options, which will discussed later in this chapter.)

## Change the account name

If you select the Change the name option, the same window that appeared when you created the account appears asking you to provide an account name (see Figure 4.5).

**Watch Out!**

Remember, you must have administrator privileges to change user accounts. If you're currently logged on as a limited access user, simply click Start and then Log Off. You can then quickly re-log on as a computer administrator.

> **Inside Scoop**
>
> The account name can use up to 20 characters, including numbers and special characters (such as accents).

**Figure 4.5.** Name your new account.

Once you change the name, you will automatically return to the Edit Account window. Should you decide that you do not want to change your name for whatever reason, you can either use the Cancel button or the back arrow at the top left of the New Account name window. If you select Home, you will return to the main page of the User Account window.

# Create a password

Windows XP allows you to protect your account, and by extension, your computer, using a unique password. Once you select the Create a password option from the Edit Account window (see Figure 4.4), a new window appears that allows you to create a new password, confirm the new password, and then provide a password hint (should you forget it).

Once the new password is created, you automatically return to the Edit Account page. This page will have slightly changed because a new menu option is available: Remove the password. If you select this option, you remove the password currently set for the account. This does not require you to re-enter the password for validation.

It is important to note that if you have stored any passwords or certificates from Web sites on your machine (while logged on to your account) and then you decide to add a password for your account that previously did not have

---

### Losing your password

If you are using Windows XP over a network, the number of incorrect password attempts you can make before your account is locked depends on how your system administrator configured your Windows server. For home users, this feature is disabled by default. However, it can be set to prevent password hacking.

If you forget your password as a limited access account, you can use the Forgotten Password Wizard, or you can ask the administrator to remove or reset your password. Administrators should use the Forgotten Password Wizard to reset their password. I will discuss the use of the Forgotten Password Wizard later in this chapter.

---

one, you will lose this data. To avoid this problem in the future, you can create a password reset floppy disk, which I will discuss later in this chapter.

Creating a reasonably secure password is essential; while no password is 100 percent safe, you can take steps to make your password as secure as is reasonably possible. For example, use at least eight characters in your password using a mix of uppercase, lowercase, numbers, or symbols. It is said that no part of your password should be a real word, but let's be realistic: If you have a bad memory, use a word, a part of a word, or a number that you can recall but isn't easily attributed to you. For example, it is not a good idea to use the names of your children or of a pet. A password must be something that only you would think to put — perhaps a first love, your favorite poet, your favorite lottery numbers, and so on. Passwords are case-sensitive, so do remember where you put those uppercase and lowercase letters!

## Change the picture

Windows XP lets you change the default image that was associated with your account when it was created. This image will appear at the welcome screen. Click Change the picture from the Edit Account window (see Figure 4.4).

---

### Inside Scoop

If you forgot your password (even as administrator), reboot your machine and hold down the F8 key to enter the Boot Mode menu. Launch Windows in Safe Mode, which logs you on as administrator without a password. Reset passwords as needed. This workaround should be used as a last resort because it is a potential security risk.

Windows XP offers 23 pre-installed pictures (see Figure 4.6) that you can use. Of course, you can browse for any other pictures on your machine that are in BMP, GIF, JPG, or PNG format. Simply click the icon and then click the Change Picture button. You can also click the Browse for more pictures link and select your desired picture. Once you select the image, you will return to the Edit Account page.

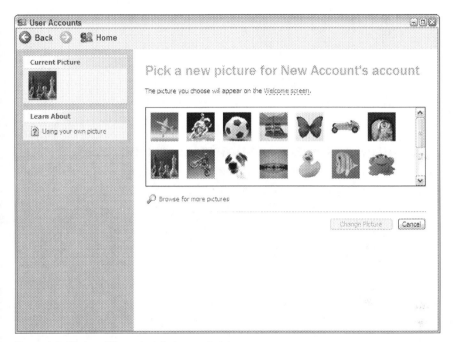

**Figure 4.6.** Windows XP's pre-installed account pictures.

# Change the account type

Windows XP also allows you the option of changing your account from a limited access account to an administrator account. If you click the Change the account type option from the User Accounts window, the same window (Pick a new account type) that appears during account creation asking you to designate the account type appears. Accounts can be changed to limited access or to administrator access as many times as desired; the access privileges are instantaneous. Any administrator account can be deleted, on the condition that there is another administrator account on the machine. If you have a single administrator account, you cannot delete it.

## Delete the account

Administrators can easily delete any account by selecting the Delete the account option from the Edit Account window (see Figure 4.4). Once you select this option, you have the option of keeping or deleting the corresponding account files. If you keep the files, Windows XP will store the deleted account's My Documents folder and Desktop in a folder that has the same name as the deleted account to the administrator's desktop. Limited users, however, can only delete their own account.

Once you decide whether to keep or delete the files, Windows XP asks you to confirm the deletion before going forward. Unfortunately, Windows XP does not provide a gentle reminder that once the account is gone, it's gone (unless you have a backup). Like the other options, once you execute this command, you return automatically to the Edit Account window.

## Editing the computer administrator account

Everything changes if you're working with the computer administrator account. Having this role means more responsibilities, which in turn means more options! As I mentioned earlier, if you create another administrator account (you can have more than one machine administrator), this account can eventually be deleted. However, there must always be at least one administrator account on the machine. If you have two administrator accounts, one will have the same options as the limited access accounts (purely optional accounts) while the other has a different Edit Account page with different options (see Figure 4.7).

The first four options on the Edit Account window are the same for computer administrator or limited access accounts. Unlike the limited access accounts, all computer administrator accounts cannot be deleted. However, there are three unique options for the original computer administrator on this page.

One option is that you can set up your administrator account to be used as a .NET passport. This would provide a single sign-on to any of Microsoft's .NET Web sites, including Hotmail. If you decide to use this option, you will need an active Internet connection.

**Watch Out!**

Despite Windows XP's generously saving My Documents and Desktop for the deleted user account, it is unable to save other vital information such as e-mails, Internet Explorer bookmarks, or system settings.

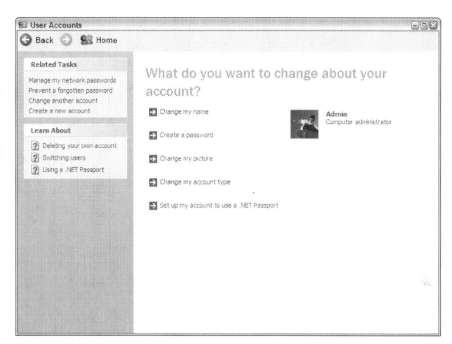

**Figure 4.7.** The options available for the administrator account.

You can also manage any network passwords from the Edit Account window by clicking Manage my network passwords, which opens the Stored User Names and Passwords window (see Figure 4.8).

## Microsoft's .NET Passport

What exactly is the .NET Passport? If you thought it was going to make that trip to France easier, think again. However, if you were hoping that it would make navigating Microsoft Corporation's various Web sites easier, you're on the right track.

The Passport program was created as a way to provide a single sign-on for Microsoft users. With your "passport," you could use the same logon and password for various Microsoft services and sites, such as MSN Messenger, MSN Hotmail, and MSN Music, among others.

However, the Passport concept seems to be slowing fading away and Microsoft has not really done much to revive it.

Click Add to open the Logon Information Properties window (see Figure 4.9). In this window, you can set server and logon properties for a site. For example, perhaps there is a Web site that you visit frequently that requires a logon and password. If you save your logon credentials (the logon dialog box has a checkbox asking if you want to save your logon for future use), they would be stored here. This also applies if you log on to any FTP sites or if you connect to your office remotely and you decide to store your logon details. Using this option, you can view details about a given entry or remove it.

The final difference for administrator accounts is the Forgotten Password Wizard, which I will discuss later in the chapter.

**Figure 4.8.** The Stored User Names and Passwords window.

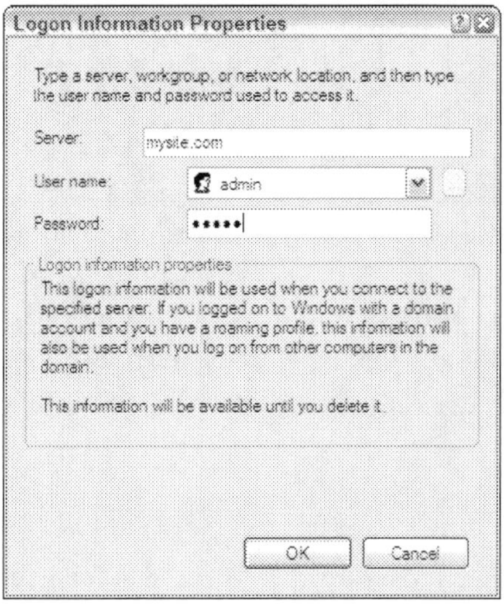

**Figure 4.9.** The Logon Information Properties dialog box.

## Change group membership

Changing group membership for a user account can only be done if you are using Windows XP Professional. In fact, your computer must be logged on to a domain and you must also be logged on as a computer administrator and have the necessary network permissions to perform this task. Please see your network administrator should you have any questions about your access level. You will not be able to perform this procedure without the necessary permission.

Group accounts are similar to local user accounts, except that they are used to assign rights to a group of users instead of a single user. This makes life much easier for administrators, since they can add groups of users to a single category and apply similar properties across the board.

To change group membership for a user account, you will work with the User Accounts window from the Control Panel. If you are working on a domain, you will find a User tab at the top of the User Accounts window. Click the name of the desired user account under the Users for this computer menu and click Properties. Select the new group for the user and click OK.

Windows offers nine default groups from which to choose:

- **Administrators.** Administrators have full access to the machine.

- **Backup Operators.** This group can override security settings only in order to back up or restore files.

- **Guests.** This group is similar to the Users group; the Guest account has additional restrictions.

- **Network Configuration Operators.** This group can have limited administrator rights in order to manage network configurations.

- **Power Users.** This group has many of the rights as the administrators, but still has certain restrictions.

- **Remote Desktop Users.** This group can log on to the domain remotely.

- **Users.** This group can run certified applications, but not legacy applications (unlike Power Users). They cannot make system-wide changes.

- **Debugger Users.** This group can debug processes locally and remotely, if necessary.

- **HelpServicesGroup.** Group for Help and Support service center.

You can also add new groups in the Computer Management window.

Keep in mind that this section does not apply to you if you are using Microsoft Windows XP Home or if you are not on a domain.

## Use the Forgotten Password Wizard

Windows XP (both Home and Professional!) offer a way for both administrators and limited access accounts to retrieve their passwords. Of course, there is the F8 reboot workaround (see the section "Create a password"), but let's look at the official Microsoft way.

When you select a specific user from the User Accounts window (see Figure 4.7), there is a Related Task in the upper left corner of the screen entitled Prevent a forgotten password.

---

**Watch Out!**

Before you start the Forgotten Password Wizard, make sure that you have some sort of external devices, like a floppy drive, a USB thumb drive, or an external drive that you can write to. If you aren't using one of these, you aren't using this feature.

---

The Forgotten Password Wizard offers two pieces of important advice in the opening window (see Figure 4.10):

1. This disk only needs to be created once, no matter how many times you forget your password. It wouldn't hurt to keep this disk/media alongside your rescue disk or boot disk (and Windows XP installation CD).

2. That said, anyone can access this disk/media and use it to reset your password, so you'd do well to mind where you leave it.

**Figure 4.10.** The Forgotten Password Wizard.

The next screen of the wizard asks you to insert a blank, formatted disk into drive A. (The drive letter may change depending on your local drive configuration, but it must represent a removable drive). The next screen of the wizard (see Figure 4.11) asks for the current password; type it, click Next, and the wizard creates the necessary files and copies them to your media.

**Figure 4.11.** The Current User Account Password screen.

There are two unusual things about this wizard; first, the Forgotten Password Wizard is based on preventive action. Follow the steps in the wizard before you lose your password. The wizard will not help you retrieve a lost password; it helps you prepare for the future. Second, the wizard will still function if you have not set a password for your account but decide that you'd like to add one! Simply leave the password text box blank in the third wizard screen and click Next. The wizard will generate the necessary files and copy them to your media.

# Configure fast user switching

Windows XP has a cool feature that lets you toggle user accounts in the blink of an eye. You do not even have to save your work (though it would still be a good idea to do so) or shut anything down to do it. Your current user account will "freeze" while you work in the new session and defreeze when you log out of the second session and bring it back.

This is a useful feature, say, if you are working on a file and another household member needs to log on quickly to send an important e-mail.

**Watch Out!**

You may notice a marked difference in your machine's performance when you load a second user session, especially in the time to load the desktop. This second session also eats up available memory. Of course, if you've maxed out your machine in terms of memory, you should be fine! Otherwise, shut down any applications that you do not need before you switch accounts (especially ones that use lots of memory).

To switch users, simply select Log Off from the Start menu and select Switch User (see Figure 4.12).

Windows then takes you to the Welcome screen (just like when you boot up your machine) and you can select any of the available user accounts. Once you are done with the second session, repeat this process and return to the first ses-

**Figure 4.12.** The Switch User screen.

sion. If you shut down the machine from the second session, Windows will remind you that a user is still logged on and you may lose any unsaved data if you continue to shut down without logging off the other user.

# Switching users via the Run as command

Windows XP provides a special command that allows you to use an application with a different user account or permissions than what is currently set in your active Windows session. In other words, you can open an application as a different user instead of as yourself. This command is both Windows-based — in other words, accessible from the Windows XP interface — and command-line based — accessed from the command prompt or Run menu.

You do not need to be an administrator to access or use this feature. It can be used for a number of reasons; for example, if you wanted to create a desktop shortcut for another user account. It is helpful for times when you need to perform actions on an account but you do not want to switch users or log off to do so. It can also be helpful if you are an administrator logged on to a more restrictive account and want to perform some tasks that are not authorized using your account, but you do not wish to log off.

## Use Run as from the interface

If you are working within the Windows XP interface, you can access the Run as command from any application icon or shortcut found in Windows Explorer, the Start menu, or My Computer. If you right-click the icon, the Run as command appears second from the top. Select the command and a Run As dialog box appears (see Figure 4.13).

The dialog box asks you which user account should run the selected application. By default, the current user (you) is selected. There is an option (also checked by default) that protects your machine (programs and data) from any unauthorized activity. The problem with this option is that it puts you

square in the middle of a Catch-22:
Keeping the option does protect
your machine from potential virus
attacks; on the other hand, disabling may cause some programs
not to work. When in doubt, stick
with the default option until
another option proves necessary.

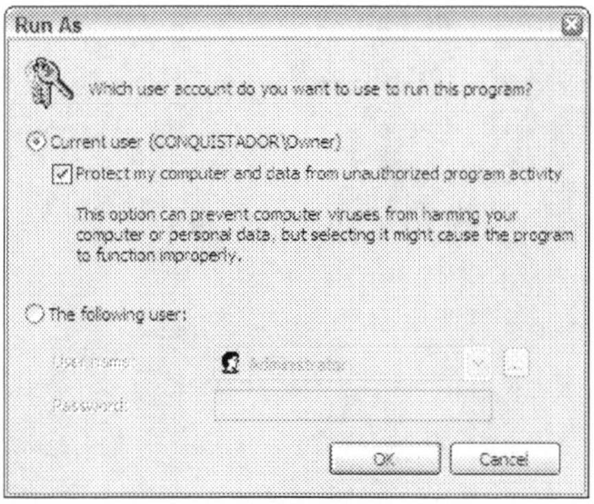

Of course, if you are planning
on using this command, you will
select a different user account. In
The following user area of the Run

**Figure 4.13.** The Run As dialog box.

As dialog box, you can select another available account. Once you select the
account, you must enter the corresponding password. Once validated, the
program or folder will open using the permissions set for this other user
account.

## Use Run as from the command line

The command-line version of the Run as command is slightly more complicated than from the interface or contextual menus. You can access the command prompt in several ways. From
the Start menu, click Start and then
Run. Type cmd and click OK. Also
from the Start menu, you can click
All Programs, Accessories, and then
Command Prompt. You can also
access the command by creating a
shortcut on the desktop and then
typing cmd in the Create Shortcut
dialog box (see Figure 4.14).

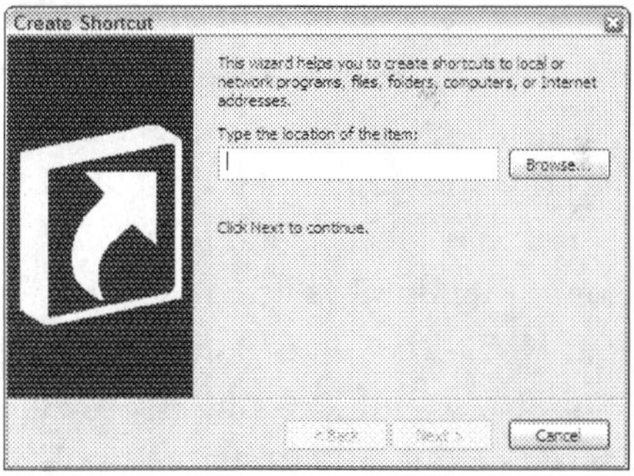

**Figure 4.14.** The Create Shortcut dialog box.

The runas command accepts a
number of parameters, or settings, which are shown below. For information
on each of these parameters, please see the Windows XP Help and Support

---

**Watch Out!**

Another big difference between the command line and interface commands is that
the command line command is runas while the interface command is Run as. Using
Run as at the command prompt will return an error.

Center. Or, you can simply type runas at the command prompt and press Enter — the definition for each parameter will appear.

The proper syntax for the runas command is:

```
RUNAS  [  [/noprofile  |  /profile]  [/env]  [/netonly]  ]/
smartcard [/user:<UserName>] program
```

Some examples that Windows offers of the runas command syntax are as follows:

- `runas /noprofile /user:mymachine\administrator cmd`

  No profile will be loaded; the user's environment will be used, and it will open the .cmd file.

- `runas /profile /env /user:mydomain\admin "mmc %windir%\system32\dsa.msc"`

  The user's profile will be loaded using the current environment; the user will open the .msc file

- `runas /env /user:user@domain.microsoft.com "notepad \"my file.txt\""`

  The current environment will be used; the user will open the designated file with Notepad.

## Create custom Management Consoles

Windows XP uses consoles, which list administrative tools, folders, Web pages, and other items to manage your Windows experience. The console is the framework that holds these items together.

You can create your own Microsoft Management Console (MMC) to monitor hardware, software applications, or networking devices on your system. MMC creation is done by adding wizards, snap-ins, tasks, documentation, and so on. You can also view and use a number of pre-configured consoles in the Administrative Tools menu in the Control Panel. This menu includes familiar consoles, such as Computer Management and Data Sources (ODBC).

The MMC is easily accessible from the Run command in the Start menu. Simply type mmc and click OK. You can also add extensions, such as /a (to open in author mode), /32 (to open in 32-bit mode), or /64 (to open in 64 bit mode, however, this requires a 64-bit processor). A blank Console Root window appears inside the Console box (see Figure 4.15), unless you added a path after mmc at the command-line, in which case the desired existing console will appear, Computer Management, for example (see Figure 4.16).

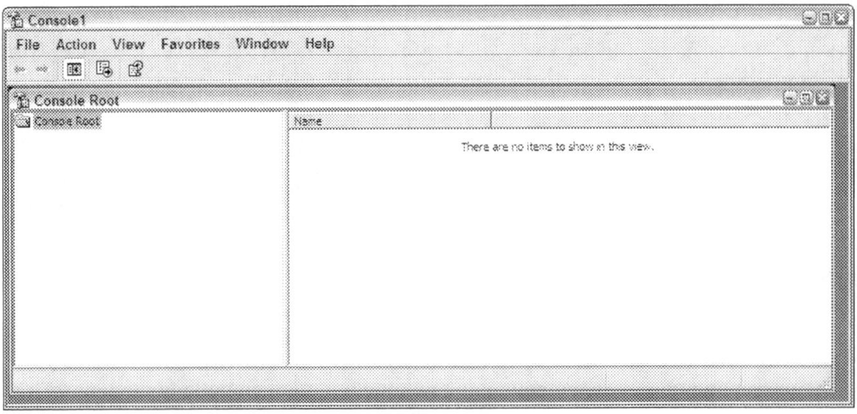

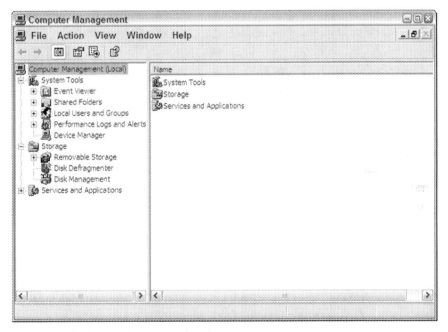

**Figure 4.15.** The blank Console window.

**Figure 4.16.** The Computer Management Console.

The Console Root window is split into two parts: the console tree and the details pane. The console tree, which shows the available components in your console, is the left pane of the window. The right pane, the details pane, lists any information relating to the selected component in the console tree.

There are two different ways of viewing the consoles, either in user mode or author mode. You view pre-configured consoles in user mode. Author mode is the mode required for editing or creating new consoles. These modes can be selected in the File ⇨ Options menu of the Console menu (see Figure 4.17).

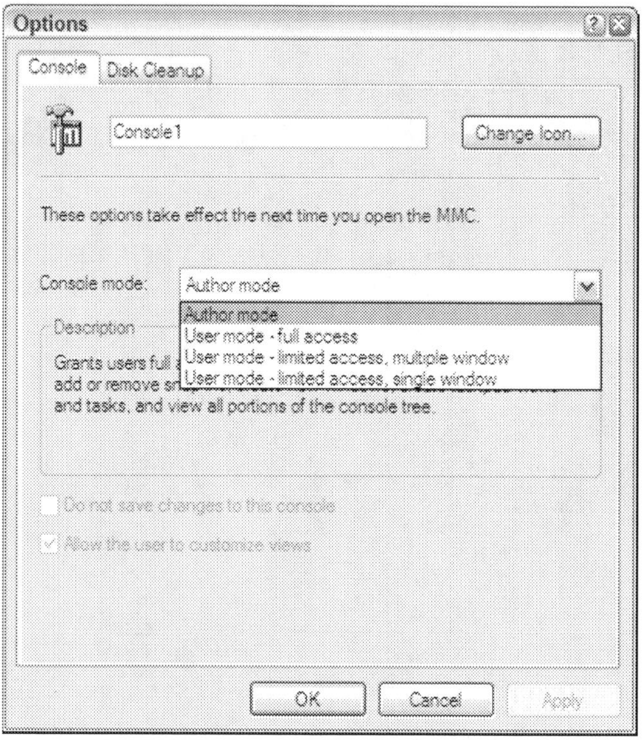

**Options**

Console | Disk Cleanup

Console 1      Change Icon...

These options take effect the next time you open the MMC.

Console mode:   Author mode

> Author mode
> User mode - full access
> User mode - limited access, multiple window
> User mode - limited access, single window

Description

Grants users full
add or remove s
and tasks, and view all portions of the console tree.

Do not save changes to this console

Allow the user to customize views

OK        Cancel        Apply

**Figure 4.17.** Available modes in the Options dialog box.

## Create a new console

Now that the Console window is up and running, it's time to get started on the console. Creating the console "shell" is the first step in creating a custom MMC. Before we begin, verify in the Options menu that you are set to author mode. You could potentially create a console that monitors computer management, IP security, and local users and groups.

**Watch Out!**

You should only use author mode when you need to create or update a console. Otherwise, use one of the three user modes — full access; limited access, multiple window; or limited access, single window.

From the File menu, use the Add/Remove Snap-in command to add or remove snap-ins. The Add/Remove Snap-in dialog box appears. If you are adding a snap-in to your console, this dialog box lets you select from among 24 snap-ins provided by Microsoft. For more information on your snap-in, simply click it, and a brief description will appear at the bottom of the dialog box. Once you select a snap-in and validate your selection, either it will appear in the Add Standalone Snap-in dialog box (see Figure 4.18), or a wizard will appear requiring you to configure the snap-in before it is added. If you are removing a snap-in from the list, simply select the snap-in and click Remove. Some snap-ins, as I will discuss below, require extra configuration; for example, you may need to select a machine, or set an ActiveX control.

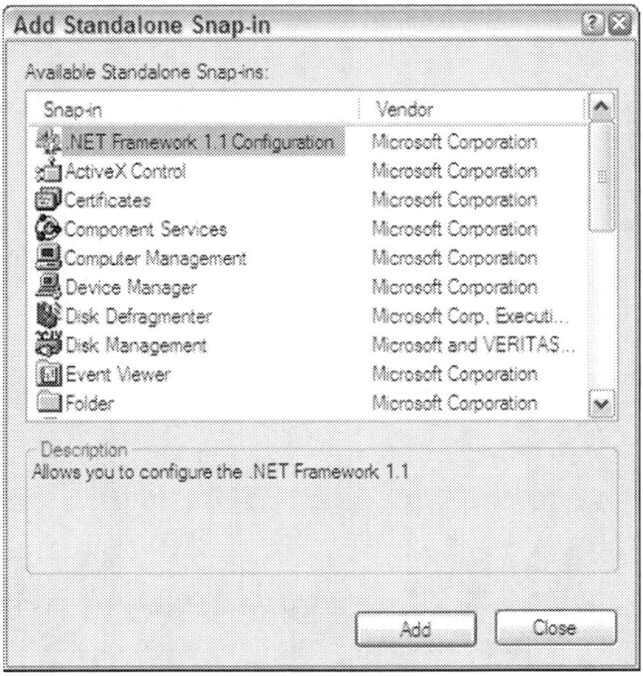

**Figure 4.18.** The Add Standalone Snap-in dialog box.

Snap-ins are nothing more than tools or components that are designed to monitor or achieve a certain task and are stored in your console. There is no need to be confused by their presence because of the unusual name afforded them by Microsoft. There are two types of snap-ins. The first is the snap-in that we saw in the list of 24 back in the Add/Remove Snap-in dialog box; these are called "standalones." The second kind of snap-in is called an extension; this is a sub-snap-in that can only be added to an existing snap-in to enhance its functions.

In the dialog box, you will notice that there is a second tab called Extensions (see Figure 4.19). Click this tab to view the list of extensions for your snap-ins and to configure them.

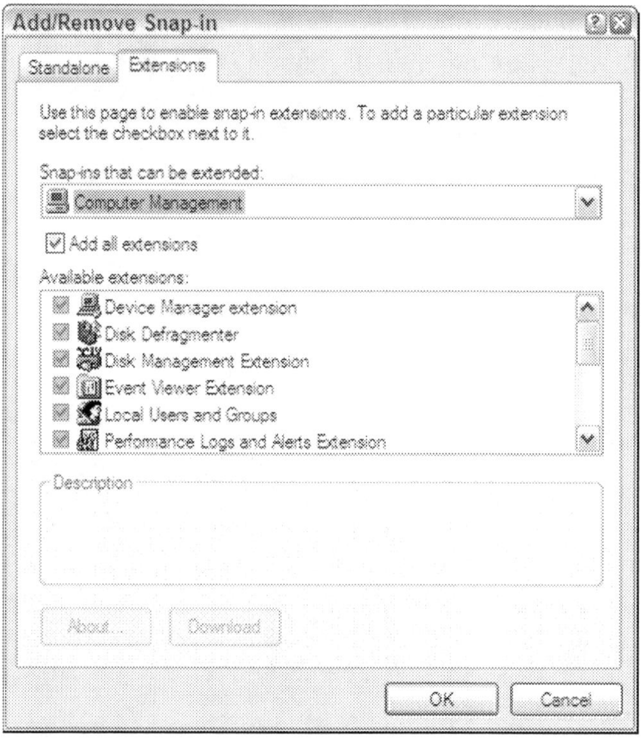

---

**Add/Remove Snap-in**

| Standalone | Extensions |

Use this page to enable snap-in extensions. To add a particular extension select the checkbox next to it.

Snap-ins that can be extended:

☑ Computer Management ▼

☑ Add all extensions

Available extensions:

☑ Device Manager extension
☑ Disk Defragmenter
☑ Disk Management Extension
☑ Event Viewer Extension
☑ Local Users and Groups
☑ Performance Logs and Alerts Extension

Description

About...    Download

OK    Cancel

---

**Figure 4.19.** The Extensions tab of the Add/Remove Snap-in dialog box.

If you click on the extension name, a brief description appears at the bottom of the dialog box. If your snap-in has more than one extension available, there is a checkbox that allows you to select them all.

Once you've validated your selection, your console looks just like one of the pre-configured consoles that you're used to seeing! The snap-ins appear

**Watch Out!**

Not every snap-in has an extension! If the Extensions tab is dimmed, that means that none of your snap-ins have extensions.

under the Console Root in the console tree and the relevant information for your snap-in appears in the details pane (see Figure 4.16). Remember, you must click the snap-in in the console tree in order for it to appear in the details pane. By default, the Console Root is selected and the names of all the installed snap-ins appear in the details pane.

Simply save the console in the File menu and your new MCC will appear alongside the other pre-configured consoles provided by Microsoft.

## Use your console

Now that you've created the console, it's time to put it to work for you. Admittedly, consoles are something that the average user probably won't use. Consoles aren't an overly complex component in Windows XP, but many people simply won't use them. At best, the average user may use one of the pre-configured Microsoft Management Consoles to troubleshoot a problem. Let's go back to a console you could create that monitors computer management, IP security, and local users and groups (see Figure 4.20). If you decide that you want to create or edit a user, you can do so by opening your console in the MMC and then right-clicking the appropriate snap-in, Local Users and Groups. You can create a new user or right-click an existing user that appears in the Details pane and establish settings, for example, that prevent users from changing their passwords, or you can disable or lock a user's account.

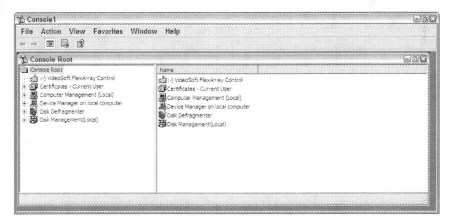

**Figure 4.20.** A customized console.

Snap-ins can be used or configured from the Console dialog box. To do this, in the console tree, click the name of the desired snap-in.

As you click the snap-in, you'll notice the details pane change. There are two other more subtle changes in the Action and View menus, although you may not notice those right away. These are the associated actions and commands in these menus that change.

The Action menu lets you perform any associated actions for a snap-in from a single toolbar menu. You can also achieve this by right-clicking the snap-in name in the console tree. The View menu, quite simply, lets you select how you wish to view the snap-in. Some View menus are more robust than others; for Device Manager on local computer, you can select to view Devices or Resources by type of connection while other snap-ins may only allow you to select large or small icons.

If there is a particular snap-in that you find you use more than others, the Microsoft Management Console allows you to store favorites in the same way you would save a Web site as a favorite in Internet Explorer. You can even create Favorite folders to better organize your snap-ins.

# Create Taskpad views

The Microsoft Management Console also features Taskpad views. These views appear in the details pane of a console and feature shortcuts to other commands. Like many other procedures in Windows XP, this, too, is facilitated through the use of a wizard.

The New Taskpad View Wizard is a rare commonality in the MMC Action menu (it is actually available for all snap-ins); you can find it by clicking the New Taskpad View menu item. Right-click the snap-in to be changed — for example, the IP Security snap-in from our earlier example — and click New Taskpad View from the menu that appears (see Figure 4.21).

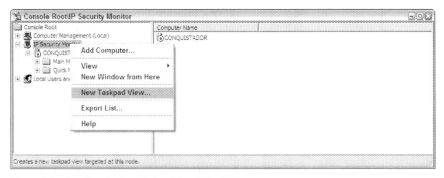

**Figure 4.21.** Opening the New Taskpad View Wizard.

The New Taskpad View Wizard (see Figure 4.22) starts off like most wizards. It provides a quick overview of what the wizard will achieve and what it will do for you.

**Figure 4.22.** The New Taskpad View Wizard.

The first screen in the wizard walks you through the Taskpad display. In other words, you set up how the details pane will appear for a selected snap-in. The wizard provides three different styles for you to choose from: Vertical list, Horizontal list, and No list. If you're confused on which one to use, each style tells where it is most applicable if you select it. A sample picture appears real-time next to the style options. You can also opt to hide the standard tab, which is a list of controls.

You may also choose between displaying task descriptions as text (they will appear below the task names) or as an InfoTip, where they will appear in a pop-up window. Finally, this screen lets you decide if you want the list size set to small, medium, or large. This is simply a question of how large you want the details pane to be. By default, medium is selected (see Figure 4.23).

The next wizard page lets you decide where to apply the new Taskpad view.

**Watch Out!**

Make sure you clicked on the desired snap-in in the console tree before you launch the New Taskpad View Wizard. The wizard takes into account the selected snap-in, so if it's not the one you want, you'll have to cancel and start over.

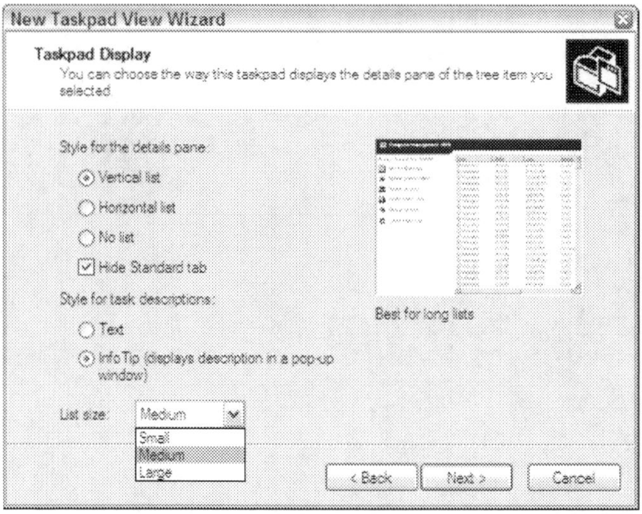

**Figure 4.23.** Taskpad display options.

You can either apply the Taskpad view to the currently selected item or you can apply it to all occurrences of the item. In other words, if you have two instances of the Disk Defragmenter snap-in, you can apply the new Taskpad view to both instances (as well as make this view the default display for both instances of the snap-in).

The next screen of the wizard allows you give a name to the new Taskpad view. By default, it takes the name of the selected snap-in. You can also add a brief description of the Taskpad view if you like.

The final step is to validate your work by clicking Finish. Your new Taskpad view appears (see Figure 4.24).

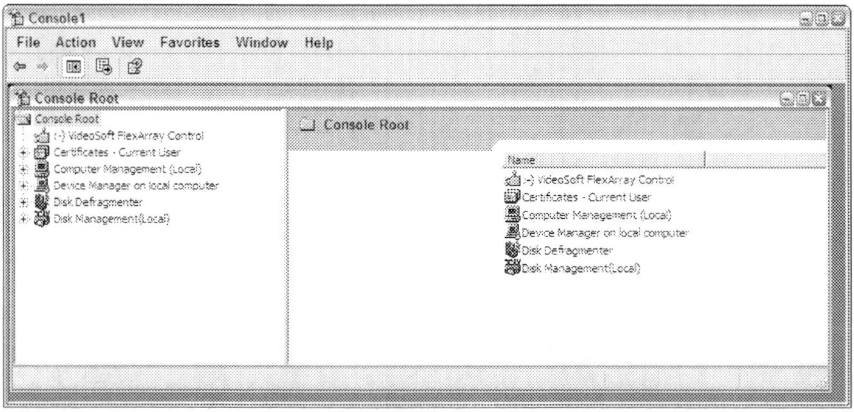

**Figure 4.24.** The new Taskpad view.

You have the option of adding new tasks to your new Taskpad view by selecting the New Task Wizard. The New Task Wizard allows you to create a task for the Taskpad you created above. You can launch the New Task Wizard immediately after you complete the new Taskpad view. Once you launch it, you can select the type of command you will use:

- **Menu command** allows you to run commands from a menu.

- **Shell command** allows you to run scripts, launch a program, or open a Web page.

- **Navigation** allows you to navigate to a view chosen from your Favorites.

The next page is the Shortcut Menu Command page. This page lets you select a menu command from an item on your tree or from the list in the Details pane. Start by selecting a command source from the drop-down menu, List in details pane, or Tree item task (see Figure 4.25). The console tree and available commands illustrated at the bottom of the window will switch depending on which command source you choose.

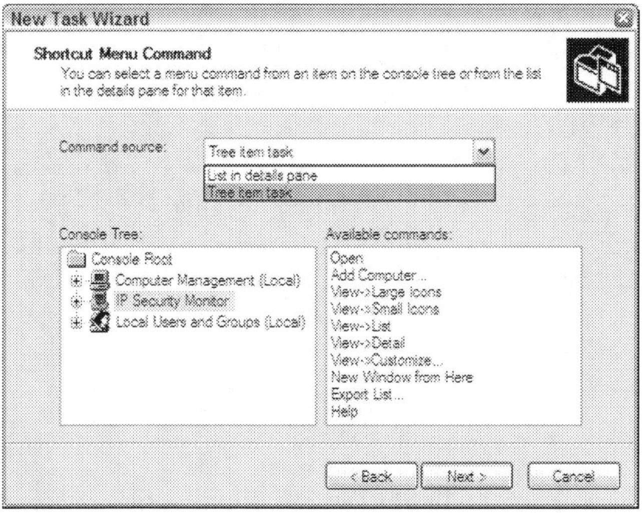

**Figure 4.25.** The Shortcut Menu Command page of the New Task Wizard.

The following page lets you enter a description for the Task name you selected on the previous page. The description features a default description for the task name.

The Task Icon page lets you select an icon for your task. By default, the MMC provides a number of icons that you can select simply by clicking. Also, you can select a custom icon by clicking that option and using the Browse button to locate and select it (see Figure 4.26).

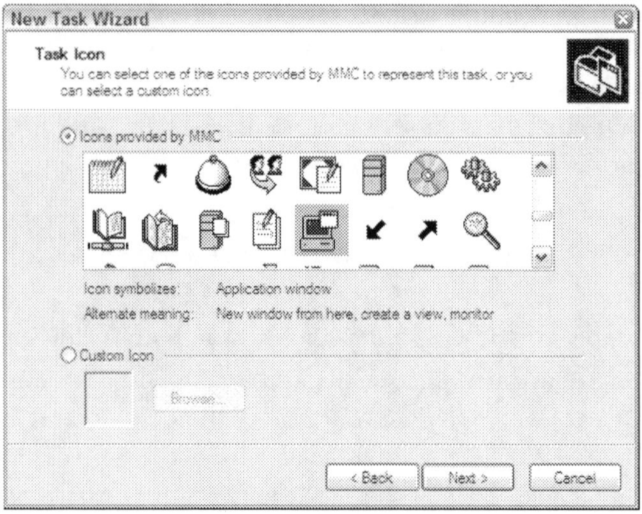

**Figure 4.26.** The Task Icon page of the New Task Wizard.

Click Next and then Finish to complete the procedure. There is always the option of running the wizard again by checking the corresponding box on the last page.

# Create Group Policies

There are a number of places where you would create or use group policies. These could include your local machine, another computer on your network, a Web site, a domain, or an organizational unit, such as accounting, documentation, and so on. Group Policies let you control the user environment. Examples of Group Policies include managing wallpapers, scripts, security settings, or software deployment.

Group Policies are essentially group policy settings set using the Group Policy Objects snap-in from the Microsoft Management Console. These are stored locally on your machine; however, if you are working over a domain, the Group Policy is stored at the domain level (in addition to your local group policy). In previous versions of Windows (notably Windows 2000), this was primarily designed for use with Active Directory or a network. However, Windows XP Professional shows that it is also great for use for stand-alone machines because you can completely control your machine's environment without having to be on a network.

**Watch Out!**

Group Policies and the Group Policy Object Editor snap-in are only available with Windows XP Professional. This section does not apply to XP Home users.

You can view the current Group Policy on your machine in the following directory: C:\WINDOWS\system32\GroupPolicy. The Group Policy folder is an invisible folder, so make sure you are able to view them. If you cannot see this folder, open My Computer, click the Tools menu and then Folder Options. In the Folder Options dialog box, click the View tab and then select Show hidden files and folders, which follows Hidden files and folders (see Figure 4.27).

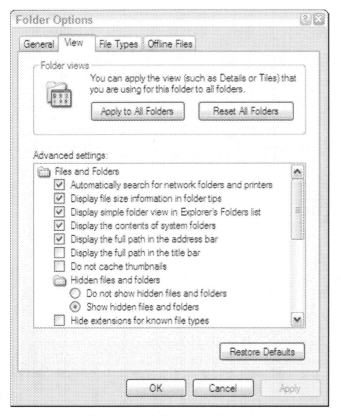

**Figure 4.27.** The View tab of the Folder Options dialog box.

The contents of the Group Policy folder may differ depending on the policies set, but there are a minimum of four items in the folder:

- **Adm folder.** This folder contains .adm files (Administrative template files) used for the group policy as well as the admfiles.ini configuration file.

- **User folder.** This folder contains a list of registry settings and Logon/Logoff scripts (if any were created).

- **Machine folder.** This folder contains a list of registry settings and a Scripts folder containing Startup/Shutdown scripts (if any were created).

- **Gpt.ini file.** This file details any extension modification settings.

Let's take a look at creating a Group Policy locally on your machine. To do this, you'll want to access the Microsoft Management Console (MMC) window as discussed in the section "Create custom Management Consoles." Working with either a console you created or a brand new console, add a Group Policy Object Editor snap-in from the Add Standalone Snap-in menu.

Once you select the Group Policy Object Editor, the Group Policy Wizard appears in a separate window. These objects are stored in the Active Directory or locally.

The wizard gives you the opportunity to select a Group Policy Object on your machine or on another machine on the domain. If you opt to browse the objects on another machine, the wizard lets you pick the type of objects as well as the location. There is a set of advanced options that looks similar to your standard Find menu.

Once you finish the Group Policy Wizard, go back to the Add/Remove Snap-in dialog box and click the Extensions tab. Extensions are used to extend the functionality of the snap-in. The Group Policy Object Editor snap-in features a number of available extensions. Once you validate your selections, the Console dialog box will appear again.

---

**Hack**

If you are looking to access the existing Group Policy, type gpedit.msc at the command window, or in the Run dialog box.

**Watch Out!**

Before you modify any Group Policy settings, make sure you have a recent backup of your machine as well as a bootable disk handy. Changes to Group Policy settings can make your system unstable or even crash it.

# Determine Group Policy settings

Now that we know a little bit about Group Policy, it's time to work with the settings and how to change them. For example, you may want to add or remove a user or change security settings. However, it's extremely important to note that any changes made to Group Policy settings could have profound affects on your system and how it performs or behaves.

You can use either the console you created in the MMC discussed above or use the gpedit.msc file to make changes to your Group Policy settings locally.

Using the console tree on the left (see Figure 4.28), you can expand and collapse the various menus. Once you find the desired policy to change, click it in the details pane. A detailed overview of the policy appears on the left side of the details pane (see Figure 4.29).

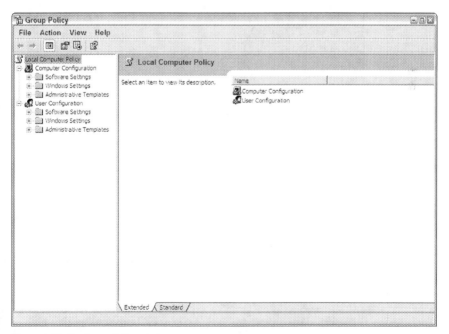

**Figure 4.28.** The Group Policy window.

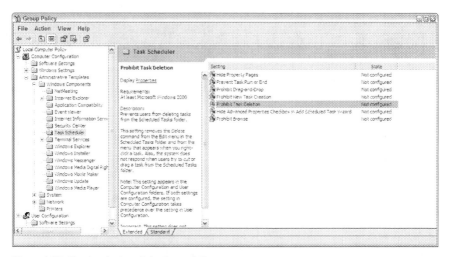

**Figure 4.29.** The description of the Group Policy.

Double-clicking the setting in the details pane opens a task properties dialog box (see Figure 4.30) where you can apply a new setting with a simple mouse-click. If you click the Explain tab, Microsoft provides a detailed explanation of the setting and its purpose and behavior.

Back in the original Setting tab, once you've made your change, you can either validate the setting by clicking OK or you can move on to the next setting or previous setting by clicking the corresponding button. However, none of these changes are permanently made until you validate them as detailed above.

**Figure 4.30.** The Task Properties window.

**Watch Out!**

You may have noticed that the MMC or the Group Policy console had both Computer Configuration and User Configuration. Please note that the Computer Configuration setting always takes precedent over the User Configuration. By default, these settings have the same setting for both configurations.

# Just the facts

- Windows XP features three types of user accounts: Administrator, Limited, and Guest. Each account has varying levels of access and rights.

- Using Fast User Switching, you can quickly toggle between multiple user accounts without having to shut down your session or having to log off.

- Switch users when launching an application from a particular account using the Run as command.

- Create customized consoles using the Microsoft Management Console to analyze and stay on top of your machine's activities.

- Create Group Policies to manage and control your user environment.

GET THE SCOOP ON...
Adding files and folders to the Start menu ▪ Customizing
just about every aspect of a folder's appearance ▪
Compressing or encrypting files and folders on your hard
drive ▪ Configuring both of XP's file sharing methods ▪
Working with the Search and Index features

# Managing Files and Folders

The Start menu, despite its shiny interface, tends to interfere more than help when it comes to working with files as files, rather than as things created or used by applications. For example, most people don't want to use Word to move a report from the Draft folder to the Final folder. It's much easier to use a tool specifically designed for working with files.

Enter Windows Explorer. Called "Explorer" back in the Windows 3.x days, Windows Explorer has undergone a number of feature and interface changes since its creation. In Windows 2000, you could find Windows Explorer at Start\Programs; in Windows XP, it's down another level at Start\All Programs\Accessories.

It keeps getting moved deeper into the Start menu, as if Microsoft doesn't quite know what to do with it, or as if Microsoft doesn't want people to know about the cool things it can do.

In essence, Windows Explorer is the go-to application for nearly all folder- and file-related activity, from working with the Start menu to sharing files with others. It is worth getting to know Windows Explorer.

## Add files and folders to the Start menu

Most people save files directly to the My Documents folder, in part because Windows forces this location as the default for almost every application. You can change the default within each application, so you can store images in one folder, word processing documents in another, and your financial files in a third. But if you have files or folders that you refer to frequently, whether on the local computer or on the network, you can add them to the Start menu in order to gain quick access to the necessary files.

When you add a file or folder to the Start menu, you are adding a short-cut only, not the actual folder contents. This is important because you can change the underlying document and the shortcut will point to your changed document. If the document was part of the Start menu, then differ-ent versions of the document might exist and you would quickly lose track of which document was the last version you worked on.

If you look at a shortcut in Explorer, you will see that it is a small file. Your desktop and Start menu are a collection of shortcuts and documents; if you stored your actual documents in the Start menu, or on the desktop, your desktop file size would grow to an alarmingly large size. Some administrators use administrator roaming profiles on the network, where your desktop and its settings are kept on a server and copied to your computer when you log in. If your actual files are part of your desktop, the log on time can be very slow if tens of megabytes of files must be copied across the network.

Click Start, All Programs, Accessories, and then Windows Explorer (see Figure 5.1). Browse to the folder that contains the file or folder you want to add to the Start menu. Click and drag the folder to the Start button. The Start menu appears. Browse to the place where you want the folder to appear. Release the folder. A shortcut to the folder appears on the Start menu.

You can use this same method to add shortcuts to most of the Windows toolbars. See Chapter 3 for information on working with Taskbar toolbars.

When you drag items onto the Start menu, you can either wait for the menu to open, or you can drop the item directly onto the Start

**Figure 5.1.** One of the most useful programs, Windows Explorer, is buried rather deeply in the Start menu.

button. When you drop an item directly onto the Start button, you "pin" the item, and it appears in the upper right of the Start menu.

**Watch Out!**
If you drag a folder or file to My Documents or My Pictures, you move the item instead of copying it. To copy it, hold the Ctrl key while you drag it to the appropriate folder.

When you are adding shortcuts to the Start menu, there are times when you're not sure what file to point to. Even with Microsoft you have to guess sometimes; Microsoft Word's executable isn't word.exe but winword.exe. Instead of guessing, use the Search function to locate the necessary file. See the task on the Search function later in this chapter.

If you want more control over the appearance of the Start menu, you can use Windows Explorer to move or consolidate items so that they reflect how you work. See the section "Mucking About with Menus" in Chapter 3 for information on reorganizing the Start menu with Windows Explorer.

# Get more information from folders

Whenever you open a folder in Windows XP, you get a default view of the files, some big icons, and a list of tasks that change depending on what is selected in the file window (see Figure 5.2). It's a nice simple interface, but after a while it feels like there should be something more.

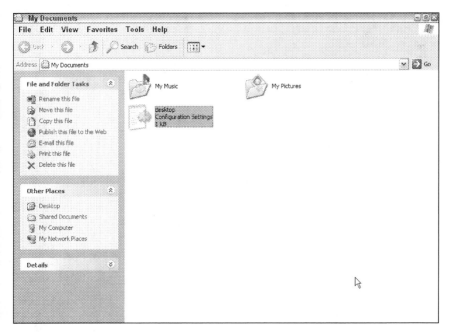

**Figure 5.2.** The default Folder View interface is useful for seeing what file types are present, but not much else.

Fortunately you can change the default view in order to show you more information. Folders are accessed either through a default folder view (such as My Documents) or by using Windows Explorer.

## Change folder views

The default Windows XP folder view contains some information about your files and related folders. If you hover your mouse over an icon, you will get information such as the name and file type, the date it was last modified, and the file size. This is helpful for when you would rather see pretty icons than useful information. But if you want to see information without having to move your mouse over an icon, you can change the default view to provide you with more information about a file or folder.

You can change the amount of information by clicking the Views icon on the far right of the toolbar (see Figure 5.3).

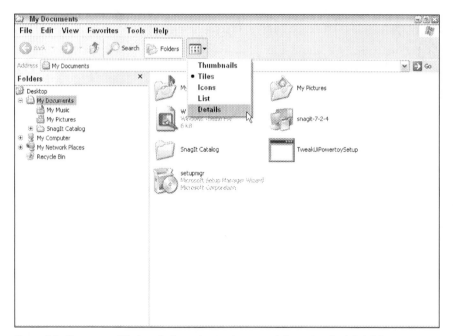

**Figure 5.3.** Change your Windows Explorer view to show more information that's helpful to you.

Then using the following list as a reference, select one of the following:

▪ **Thumbnails** view displays the images a folder contains on a folder icon so you can quickly identify the contents of the folder. For example, if you store pictures in several different folders, in Thumbnails view you can tell at a glance which folder contains the pictures you want.

Windows displays up to four images on a folder background, by default. Or, you can choose one picture to identify a folder in Thumbnails view. The complete folder name is displayed under the thumbnail.

■ **Tiles** view displays your files and folders as icons. The icons are larger than those in Icon view, and the sort information you select is displayed under the file or folder name. For example, if you sort your files by type, "Microsoft Word document" appears under the filename for a Microsoft Word document.

■ **Icons** view displays your files and folders as icons. The filename is displayed under the icon; however, sort information is not displayed. In this view you can display your files and folders in groups.

■ **List** view displays the contents of a folder as a list of file or folder names preceded by small icons. This view is useful if your folder contains many files and you want to scan the list for a filename. You can sort your files and folders in this view; however, you cannot display your files in groups.

■ In **Details** view, Windows lists the contents of the open folder and provides detailed information about your files, including name, type, size, and date modified. In Details view you can also show your files in groups. To choose the details you want to display, click the View menu and then click Choose Details.

■ **Filmstrip** view is available in picture folders. Your pictures appear in a single row of thumbnail images. You can scroll through your pictures using the left and right arrow buttons. If you click a picture, it is displayed as a larger image above the other pictures. To edit, print, or save the image to another folder, double-click the picture.

■ **Show in Groups** allows you to group your files by any detail of the file, such as name, size, type, or date modified. For example, if you group by file type, image files appear in one group, Microsoft Word files appear in another group, and Excel files in another. Show in Groups is available in the Thumbnails, Tiles, Icons, and Details views. To show your files in groups, click the View menu, point to Arrange Icons by, and then click Show in Groups.

The view is modified on a per-folder basis. If you change the look of a particular folder, Windows remembers the settings and will use those settings the next time you browse to that folder.

You also can change the look of the folder, not just the way it displays contents. A quick way to change a folder's appearance is to right-click the toolbar, deselect Lock the toolbars, and then click Customize (see Figure 5.4). You can add or remove buttons to the toolbar, as well as use large or small icons, with or without text. This is very helpful for saving space on your desktop; after a while, you know what a button does and you don't need a large graphic or text to tell you what you're clicking on.

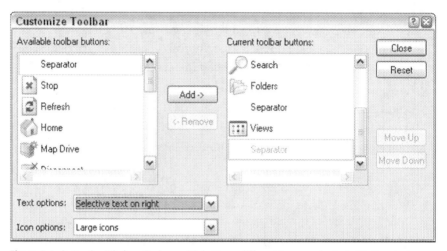

**Figure 5.4.** Customize Windows Explorer with buttons, different icons, and selected button text.

Finally, you can use a folder as a sneaky way to launch a Web browser. The Address bar isn't just for folders: It's also a place where you can type in a URL and go to the Web resource directly.

Folder views can also be changed on a global basis, rather than folder-by-folder. For example, the default view chooses to hide system files and folders from the user. If you are an intermediate-to-advanced user, you probably want to work with many of those files.

The easiest way to globally change the default folder view is through Windows Explorer. You can still set different views for individual folders and have those remembered; for example, you may prefer large icons for Control Panel rather than a detail list.

**Inside Scoop**

Microsoft gives you seemingly endless ways to connect to the Internet. Rather than using a folder's Address bar to browse the Internet, try using the Address toolbar instead.

Click Start, click All Programs, click Accessories, and then click Windows Explorer. Select any folder. Click Tools and then click Folder Options (see Figure 5.5). The Folder Options dialog box that appears contains numerous advanced settings that change the information presented to you.

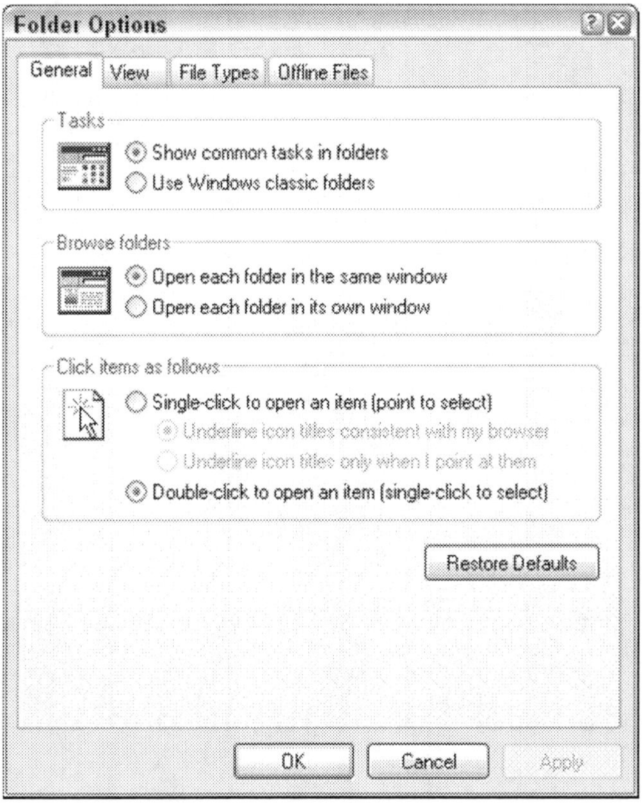

**Figure 5.5.** If you want Windows Explorer to be more browser-like, select Single-click to open an item.

The General tab controls Windows Explorer behavior. You can view folders or tasks in the left pane, and change how links are displayed and how many clicks it takes to open an icon or a link. There is a "panic button" (also known as Restore Defaults) that changes this tab's options back to the Windows out-of-the-box default.

The View tab (see Figure 5.6) is where you can toggle the "secret settings" and hidden-by-default information. It also has a panic button to get you back to a known state. Here are some options you may want to change from the defaults:

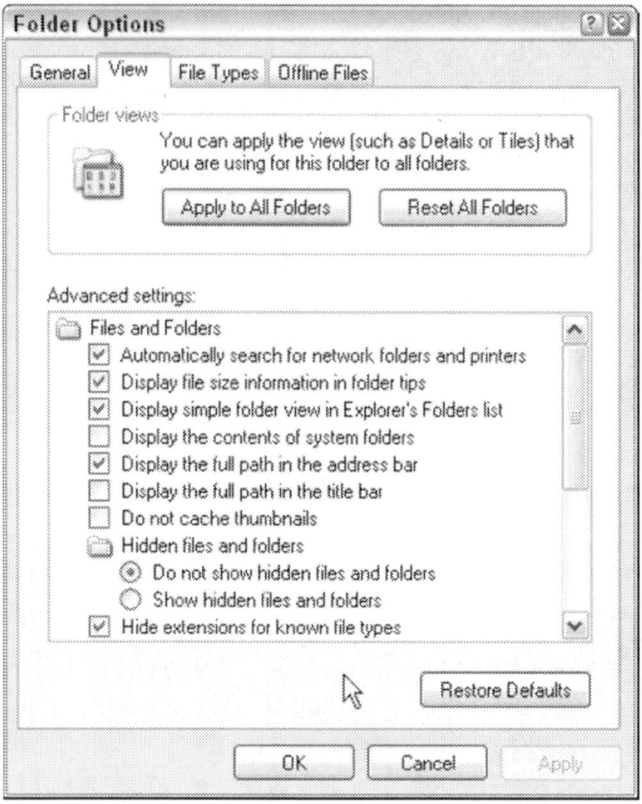

**Figure 5.6.** The View tab changes a folder's appearance and contents.

- **Automatically search for network folders and printers.** This introduces pauses while Windows queries your network for available shares every time you open a folder. Realistically, you don't need Windows to do this for you; you can disable this option.

- **Display the contents of system folders.** By default this is turned off; if you browse to a system folder, Windows presents a nice blue "do not enter" screen. Turn this on so you can see all of the folders, such as Program Files.

- **Do not cache thumbnails.** The cache is re-created automatically whenever you view a folder in thumbnail view. If you have a folder with many images, a cache speeds up the thumbnail display; you can enable caching for that folder only.

- **Hidden files and folders.** These are folders such as Documents and Settings\%username%\Application Data. It's a good idea to hide these from your six-year-old. But you may need to get at these for various reasons. Click the radio button to Show hidden files and folders.

- **Hide extensions for known file types.** Early virus writers used this feature to make viruses look like innocuous text files. Though this is not as dangerous as it once was, it's far better to see the full filename and extension than to hide part of it.

- **Hide protected operating system files.** This is similar to displaying system folders but works on an individual file basis. This hides files such as boot.ini, which is used to load Windows at boot time and normally should not be messed with unless you know what you are doing. Naturally, if you're reading this book, you'll probably want to show these files, not hide them.

- **Remember each folder's view setting.** This option is a mixed bag. By default, Windows remembers your changes on a per-window basis; this includes such things as window size and position, column sizes, and which view you prefer. The downside is that any changes you make, even if incidental (such as resizing a window) are remembered the next time the window is opened.

This tab also has the Apply to All Folders and Reset Folders buttons. The first button takes all changes made *anywhere* on the folder you are viewing, not just on the Folder Options View tab, and applies them as the default to all other folders, even ones you haven't edited yet. The Reset Folders is a panic button for resetting all the changes made to all folder views and restoring the default Windows settings. The other panic button resets only the advanced options listed on the tab.

The File Types tab (see Figure 5.7) shows you a list of which file extensions are associated with which programs. For the most part you will not have to worry about editing or maintaining this list. When you install applications, they register their file types with Windows, which allows Windows to take care of the housekeeping related to file types.

---

**Bright Idea**

Determine how you want most of your folders to look, apply those changes globally, and then rely on the Remember each folder's settings option to remember your exceptions. This saves you from configuring each folder separately.

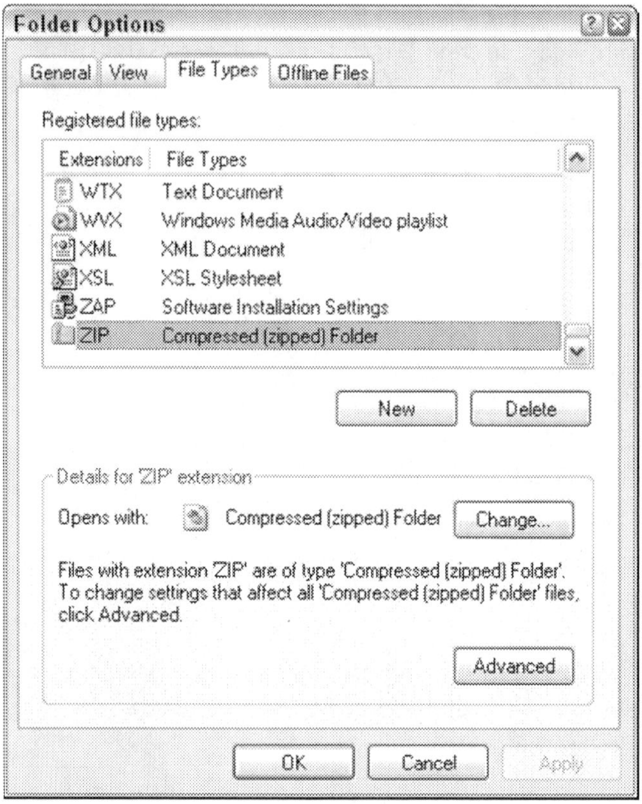

**Figure 5.7.** File extensions determine what type of file it is and what application will be used to handle it.

This can become annoying when you have different applications that can both register to handle particular file types and they clobber each other's settings. Although the Antitrust icon takes care of some of these conflicting settings (see Chapter 3), other applications such as image editors or multimedia programs can change around file associations when you don't want them to.

The first and best way to manage the tug-of-war for file associations is to check and see if your favorite file type handler has options that allow it to set itself as the default. This lets the application make the necessary registration changes in Windows.

The other way is to edit the associations in the File Types tab. Scroll through the list until you find the file type you want to change. Highlight the extension and then click the Change button. The Open With dialog box appears (see Figure 5.8), presenting you with a list of applications Windows thinks may be able to handle the file type. You can also click the Browse button to select a specific application as the file handler. If you want this to be a permanent change, click Always use the selected program to open this kind of file.

**Figure 5.8.** If you have an application you prefer using to handle files, you can change the application associations here.

This method is also available as a context menu shortcut. Right-click a file, click Open with, and then either pick an application from the menu or click Choose program to bring you to the Open With dialog box (see Figure 5.9). This is a very handy shortcut, especially when you have a choice between a full-featured or lightweight program. For example, you don't always need to use Photoshop to view a photograph when the Windows Picture and Fax Viewer will do just as well.

The final tab, Offline Files, is useful primarily for laptop users. Chapter 13 goes into greater detail about configuring and using Offline Files.

**Figure 5.9.** Context-menu shortcuts let you open a document with a different application on the fly.

## Launch custom Windows Explorer views

Windows Explorer is like the Master Folder Browser. Anything you've configured in an individual folder, you can access, configure, manage, and rearrange in Windows Explorer. One thing that's not as well known is that you can start up Windows Explorer in a folder of your choosing, not just at the default My Documents folder.

First, create a shortcut to Windows Explorer using any of the methods described in Chapter 3. Right-click the shortcut click Properties, and then click the Shortcut tab (see Figure 5.10).

In the Target text box, you can add several command-line options that tell Explorer where to start and how to display information. Two useful examples are:

```
explorer.exe /e,c:
explorer.exe /e,/root,d:\bookprojects
```

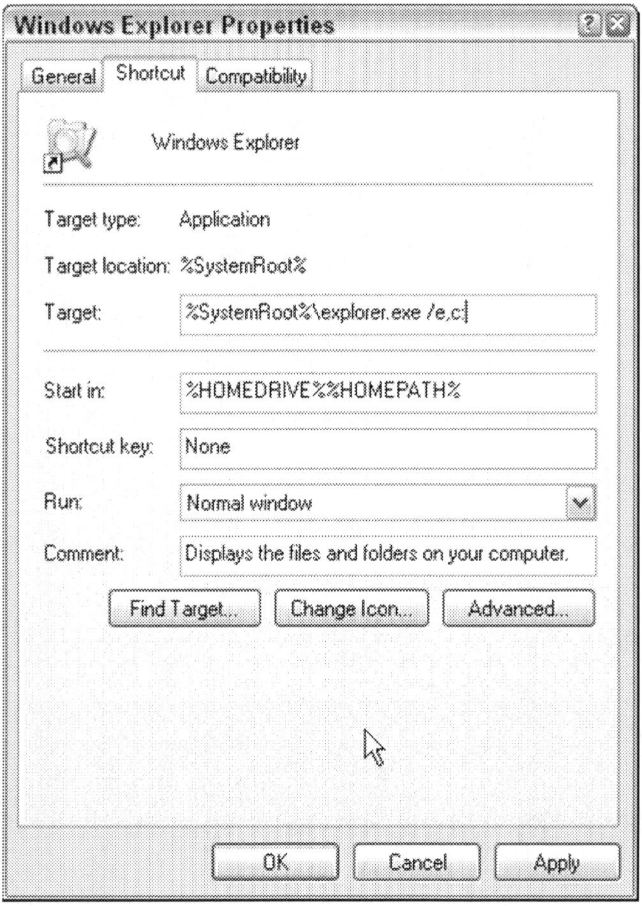

**Figure 5.10.** Start Explorer in a desired folder.

The first example opens Windows Explorer in folder view at the root of the C: drive. The second one (see Figure 5.11) opens in folder view, with bookprojects as the root folder. In both examples, the syntax is crucial: Use forward slashes, and don't forget the commas.

When you click the Windows Explorer shortcut, it opens in the specific folder. This is one of the best ways to save time and mouse clicks; you can custom-build your own shortcuts and folder structure, giving you access to your frequently used files with just one click.

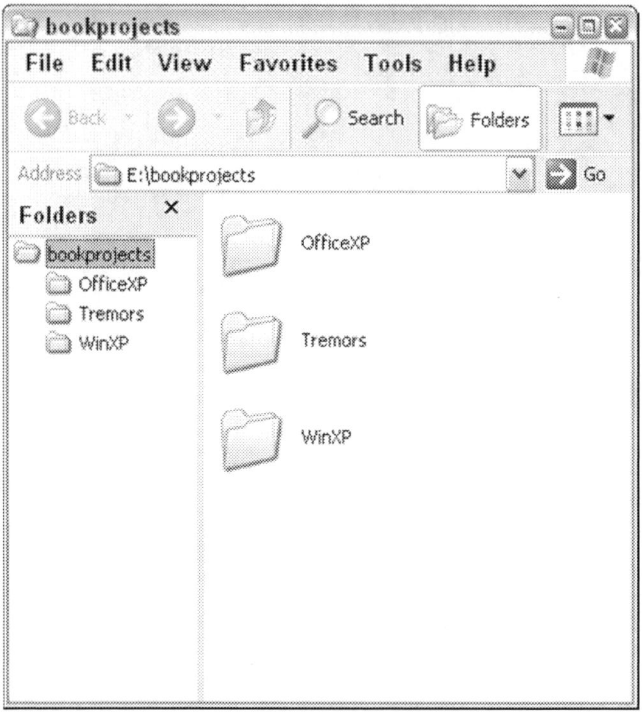

**Figure 5.11.** Start Explorer at a "root" folder.

# Customize folder details

By default, Windows displays every folder in Tiles view, which shows large icons for each object in the details pane. For more advanced users this is not particularly helpful. Information such as file extensions, file attributes, and date last modified is more useful because it presents more clues about a file's purpose and use elsewhere on the computer.

You can customize the folder details, and the order in which they appear, through any folder interface, or by using Windows Explorer and setting a default view for all folders. You can include such details as those mentioned previously, or you can add more specialized details depending on the folder contents. There are fields for audio and video information as well as document and copyright information. Nearly any information you wish stored about your files can be displayed in the Details view.

This is one case where the partition format matters (see Chapter 2); FAT32 has only the basic file details available: Archive, System, Read Only, and Hidden. NTFS has far more details available that you can display in a folder view. If you select which file details to show, the information will be displayed in the files pane — but only if the information was stored as part of the filename.

To view this supplemental information in Windows Explorer, click View and then click Choose Details. The Choose Details dialog box appears (see Figure 5.12). You can then select any information that you want to appear in the Details view, and a category for that information will be available in Windows Explorer. Click OK when you have finished.

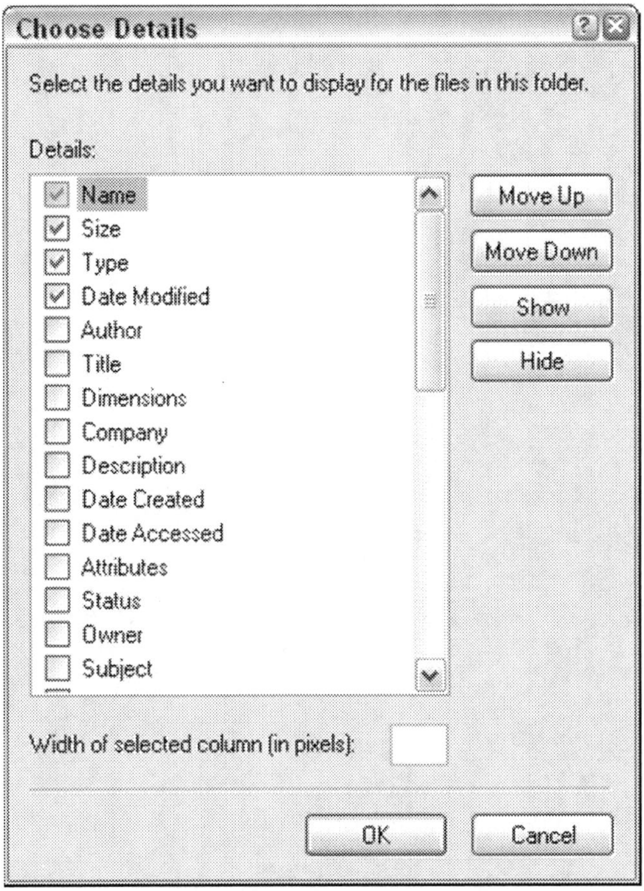

**Figure 5.12.** There is a wealth of file detail stored on an NTFS partition.

You can reorder the columns or set column size, but for most people it's easier to click and drag a column heading to change placement or to click and drag a divider between columns to change column size.

**Inside Scoop**

Usually the best way to edit information details is to use software that works with the application. Music management apps can edit tags or other information whole-sale, so you don't have to open each file and edit it by hand.

If you want to view a file's information directly, you can view it by right-clicking the file and then clicking Properties. You can edit file information on this tab, or click the Advanced button to view and edit supplemental information about the file (see Figure 5.13).

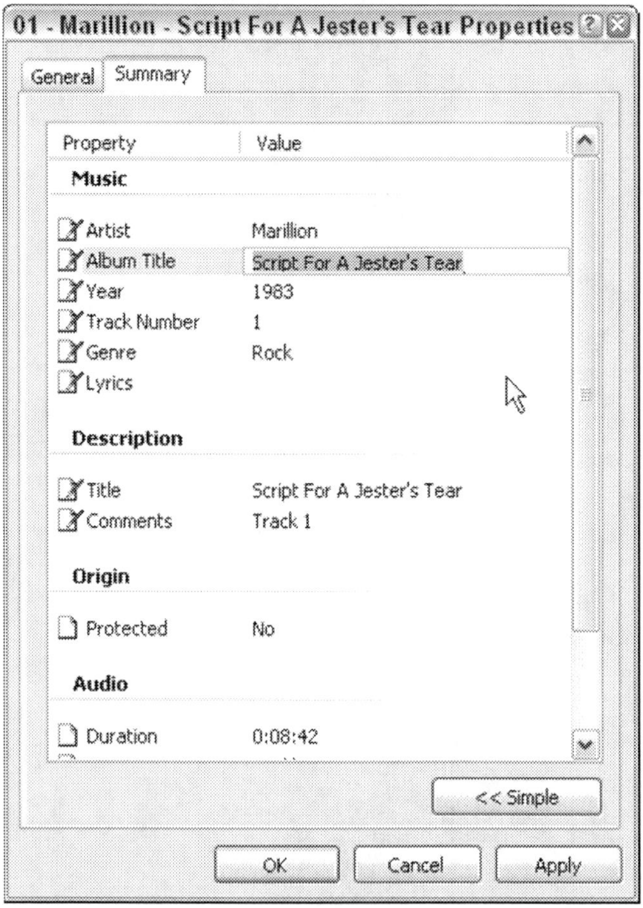

| 01 - Marillion - Script For A Jester's Tear Properties |
|---|
| General  Summary |

| Property | Value |
|---|---|
| **Music** | |
| Artist | Marillion |
| Album Title | Script For A Jester's Tear |
| Year | 1983 |
| Track Number | 1 |
| Genre | Rock |
| Lyrics | |
| **Description** | |
| Title | Script For A Jester's Tear |
| Comments | Track 1 |
| **Origin** | |
| Protected | No |
| **Audio** | |
| Duration | 0:08:42 |

<< Simple

OK     Cancel     Apply

**Figure 5.13.** Advanced file details will depend on the type of file; you won't see multimedia details in a Word document.

# Customize folder templates

The generic manila folder has been around since the days of filing cabinets, and they are uniformly considered boring. Even real-world school subject folders were "improved" by generations of student artwork in an attempt to add some zing to a blah background.

Previous versions of Windows folders were also boring, doing nothing more than holding other folders or files. With Windows XP you can customize a folder with a folder template that modifies the look and behavior of files within that folder. This gives you the ability to have a set of tasks and tools readily available for working with the files in question.

The Explorer bar (see Figure 5.14) shows you a list of common tasks for working with that particular type of media. When you right-click within a folder modified by a template, the context-sensitive menu contains other tasks that you might use with those files. In some cases the visual appearance is modified as well, usually showing thumbnails of visual media and large icons for audio media. In other cases, such as with pictures, you can view a filmstrip or a slideshow of the images contained in that folder.

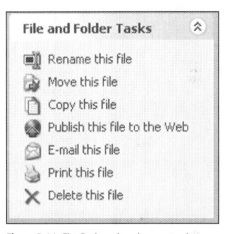

**Figure 5.14.** The Explorer bar changes to show you tasks appropriate to the folder type.

To modify a folder, right-click within the details pane and then click Customize this folder. You can also right-click the pane, click Properties, and then click the Customize tab (see Figure 5.15). From here you can choose the type of documents that will reside in this folder, and change the list of tasks accordingly. Most of the customizations weigh heavily in favor of multimedia; the available categories and tasks are:

- **Documents.** Tasks include Make a new folder, Publish this folder to the Web, and Share this folder. View defaults to Tiles.

- **Pictures.** Tasks include View as a slide show, Order prints online, Print pictures, and Copy all items to CD. View defaults to Thumbnails.

- **Photo album.** Same tasks as for Pictures, but defaults to Filmstrip view.

- **Music.** Tasks include Play all and Shop for music online. View defaults to Tiles.

- **Music artist.** Same tasks as Music, but view defaults to Thumbnails.

- **Music album.** Same tasks as the Music category.

- **Videos.** Tasks include Play all and Copy all items to CD. Uses Thumbnail view.

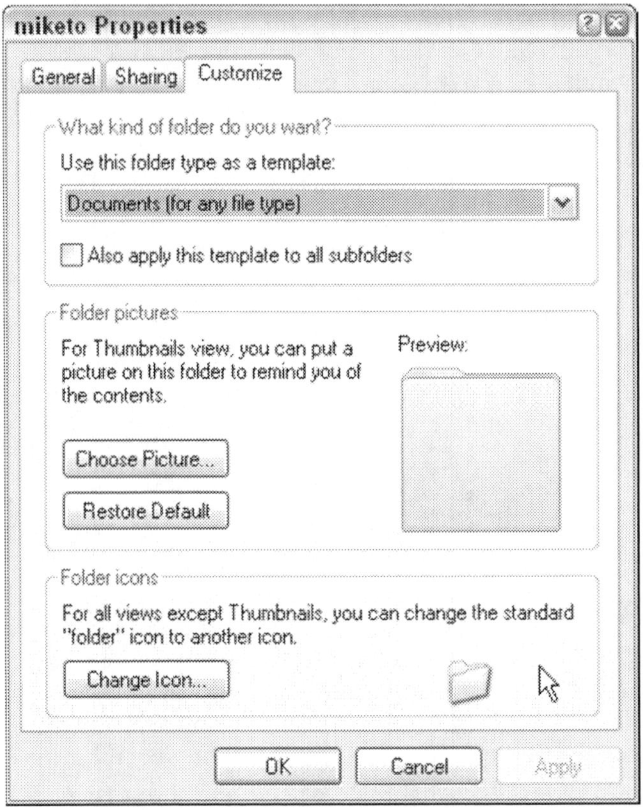

**Figure 5.15.** Choose your favorite template for your folders.

If you want to apply the same template style to all subfolders (especially helpful for Music or Pictures), select Also apply this template to all subfolders.

Some folders can't be changed. Certain Windows folders, most of them starting with "My," have special uses to applications and functions within Windows itself. For example, the My Music folder has the task to burn all folder contents to a CD. These folders already use a template that is useful for the type of media you want to store in them, and Windows doesn't want you changing things around. If you want to mix and match your media but use a template that fits your needs better, just create a new folder and apply the desired template to it.

The Folder Properties dialog box also lets you change around the normally boring folder icons. For any folder you can apply a specific image or picture to remind you of its contents. On the folder's Properties page, click the Change Icon button to edit the default icon (see Figure 5.16); you can use icons from shell32.dll or browse to custom ones of your own. To change the image, click Choose Picture and browse to an image or picture you want to use for that specific folder.

**Figure 5.16.** You can change the folder icon to another one more to your liking.

# Edit context-sensitive menus

Context-sensitive menus are the menus that appear when you right-click an item in Windows. They are context-sensitive because the contents change depending on which application is open when you click an object. The menus present you with the most likely actions you want to perform at that location or with that object. These menus are great when they show you the options you use the most; you don't have to go hunting for menu options or application-specific tasks — they are there for you to use, just a single click away.

However, this feature is sometimes a curse. Microsoft required application developers to develop context-sensitive menus so that this ease-of-use feature would be available. Some applications will ask you during setup whether you want to install context-sensitive menus, commonly called "shell extensions"; others blast right along and place their menu options everywhere. This is primarily apparent with applications that work with the Windows environment, such as archiving programs, but standalone applications will do this too (by default, WinAmp adds *eight items* that you can select).

> **Watch Out!**
>
> Editing the registry is always a tricky job. Because this particular task affects how both Windows and applications behave, you should create a system restore point (Chapter 12) or export registry keys (Chapter 11) before hacking the registry.

Very rarely these applications allow you to remove the context-sensitive menus, usually by rerunning the setup program and deselecting the "install context-sensitive menus" option. More often, you need to uninstall the application completely to remove the menu options.

There is another way, but it requires some delicate surgery in the registry to remove specific context menu entries. Sometimes context menu entries apply throughout Windows; other times they are scattered throughout other registry keys. You will need to understand what programs are associated with what entries and which specific entries you need to remove or change.

## Remove global menu items

Click Start, Run, and type regedit. Click OK. Regedit starts. The first registry hive, or collection of keys, is HKEY_CLASSES_ROOT (see Figure 5.17). When you expand the hive you will see a listing of all extension types and "handlers" for those extensions. If a particular context-sensitive menu item is available globally, you will find it under the first list item, the "*."

Browse to HKEY_CLASSES_ROOT\*\shellex\ContextMenuHanddlers. You will see a list of globally available menu items. Right-click the item you want to remove and then click Delete. This change takes place immediately.

Some items are cryptic, such as the one in Figure 5.17. It doesn't have a name, just a string of alphabet soup. You can sometimes determine what this is by right-clicking the value, selecting Copy Key Name, clicking Edit, Find, and then clicking Ctrl+V to paste the full key name into the text box. Use the Delete key and the backspace key to remove all but the alphabet-soup part of the name, and then click Find Next to find other occurrences of the key in the registry. These other occurrences may give you an idea of what the key is related to. If in doubt, leave it alone!

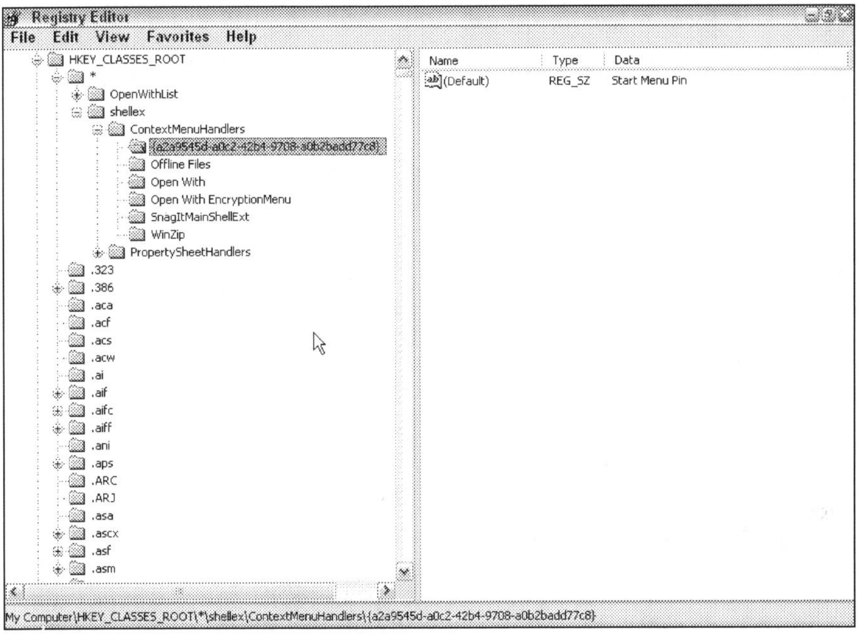

**Figure 5.17.** Edit the global context menu items using Regedit.

# Remove specific menu items

When a menu item is local, not global (the "context" part of the phrase context-sensitive), it is either listed under a specific file extension type, such as .mp3, or it is associated with a program and with events generated by that program. Instead of hacking the registry to chase these down, there is a simpler way to remove these menu items.

From any window or from Windows Explorer, click Tools, Folder Options, and then the File Types tab. Scroll through the list to the specific file extension, select it, and then click Advanced.

You will see a listing of actions that are available for that particular file type (see Figure 5.18). To pare down the context-sensitive menu, select an action and then click Remove. This takes effect immediately. Note that programs can have multiple file types associated with them, so you may need to browse through the list of registered file types and make edits as needed. If it's an obscure file association, you should probably leave it alone so that when it pops up you have some idea of which application can work with it.

**Figure 5.18.** The dialog box for a file type changes the actions associated with it.

# Create compressed files and folders

File compression has been around since before the Internet. In the prehistoric days of dialup, transmission times were measured in hundreds of bits per second, and even small files could take a long time to transfer if the phone line conditions were sketchy. File compression was invented as a way of reducing file size, allowing files to be crunched down before transmission and then expanded back to normal after transmission. It was an inexpensive way to speed up file transfer without spending exorbitant amounts of money to upgrade modem hardware.

File compression was also helpful because in those same dark days, disk space was costly. Disk sizes were measured in tens of megabytes, and people frequently archived programs off onto floppy disks or tape backup systems as a way of saving precious disk space for programs or program-related files like databases.

**Bright Idea**

You can sort the listing of registered file types by clicking the File Types column heading. This gives you a speedy way of seeing all the associations to a particular application at one time.

---

### Squeezing the myth out of compression

Compression uses mathematical algorithms to reduce file sizes. There are several mechanisms that are used; one of the commonest is through the use of *tokens* or small symbols that in turn represent larger quantities of information. For example, if you use the phrase "Unofficial Guide to Windows XP" many times in a single page, a compression algorithm would replace that phrase with perhaps a two-letter token. This reduces the file size, and the more tokens that can be used, the smaller the file.

Some file types are more amenable to compression than others. Picture files such as TIFF or BMP that contain digital descriptors for each pixel compress nicely; a big stretch of blue sky, like on the default Windows desktop, can be crunched down to a fraction of the size — a single token can be used to describe large chunks of data. JPG files, on the other hand, cannot be compressed because the JPG standard already uses compression to create the file. There is little additional benefit to running a file through a compression algorithm multiple times.

The Windows compression algorithm mechanism is okay, but it's not intended to be a replacement for full-featured applications like PKWare's PKZip or WinZip Computing's WinZip. In Windows, support for file compression is used more for compatibility than as a full-fledged power tool. If you move files across the Internet frequently, you should invest in one of those applications for your industrial-strength compression needs.

---

Many compression programs were written, but one has become the de facto standard in the Windows world: the Zip format. The original PKZip program wasn't the fastest and it didn't make the smallest archives, but it was pretty darn good at both, and had enough compression options to make it a popular choice for file compression.

Today file compression is built into Windows in order to help manage file sizes, and Windows gives you the ability to set and forget folder compression. You can also create your own compressed archives for when you want to send files to friends but their mail system accepts attachments of only a certain size.

There is a price you pay for this convenience: You must be using NTFS in the partition that will contain compressed folders or files. FAT32 does not have the necessary compression capabilities built into it, so you cannot use this feature on a FAT32 drive, or on a drive you upgraded from the Windows 9x or Me operating system. You can always convert an existing FAT32 partition to NTFS; see Chapter 12 for details.

## Turn on folder compression

Folder compression allows you to select folders on an NTFS partition and reduce the size that the folder and its files consume on the hard drive. It is only somewhat useful in Windows XP, not because of technology drawbacks but because today's hard drives are large enough that saving space is not as much of a concern as it was five or more years ago.

Once you compress a folder, Windows XP compresses and decompresses files in the background for you. This results in a slight performance drop, so if you are running on a system that barely meets the minimum CPU specification, you may decide not to use compression on any folders.

Browse to the file or folder you want to compress. Right-click the file or folder and then click Properties. Click Advanced. In the Advanced Attributes dialog box (see Figure 5.19) select Compress contents to save disk space, click OK, and then click OK again.

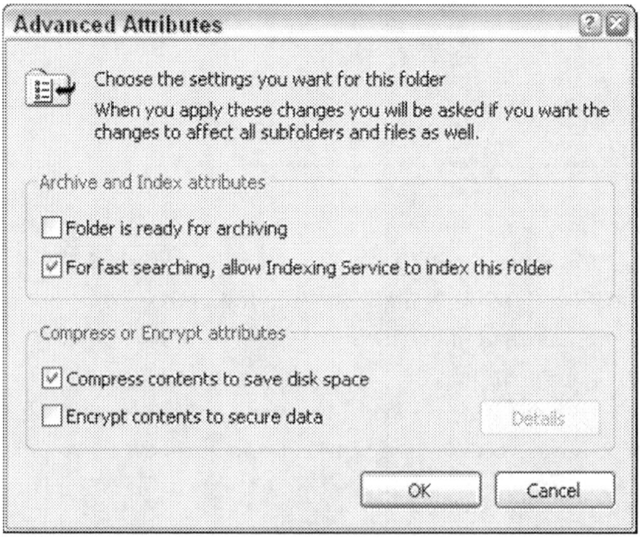

**Figure 5.19.** You can select compression and encryption attributes on a folder's Advanced dialog box.

**Inside Scoop**

When you *copy* files from uncompressed to compressed folders, Windows automatically compresses the file for you. If you *move* the file, the file retains its original compression attribute.

The Confirm Attribute Changes dialog box appears. You can choose whether to apply compression only to files in that particular folder, or to apply compression to all files and subfolders. The latter is useful if you are compressing files that are all of a single, compressible type. Select how you want the compression applied. Click OK. Compression is applied to your folders and files.

Once the compression process is complete, the compressed files are displayed in a different color than uncompressed files, both in folder views and in Windows Explorer. You can reverse the process to decompress your files and folders.

You can compress an entire drive using the same method. In Windows Explorer, right-click the drive, click the General tab, and select or deselect the compression check box. It may take a while to compress your entire drive, depending on how many documents are on it.

File compression is lurking in one other place within Windows XP. The Disk Cleanup program (see Figure 5.20) has an option to compress files that have not been modified for a certain length of time. Note that you cannot select which files to compress within Disk Cleanup; it's an all-or-nothing switch. You can learn more about Disk Cleanup in Chapter 12.

One last note on compressed folders and hard drives: You cannot use both compression and encryption (discussed later in this chapter) at the same time. The two methods are not compatible and use different algorithms. If you need greater security for your files, use encryption. If you need more room on your hard drive, choose compression.

## Create compressed archives

Compressed archives are special files within a folder that contain compressed files. They are used most frequently for transferring a number of files between one computer and another, or are used as part of an installation program.

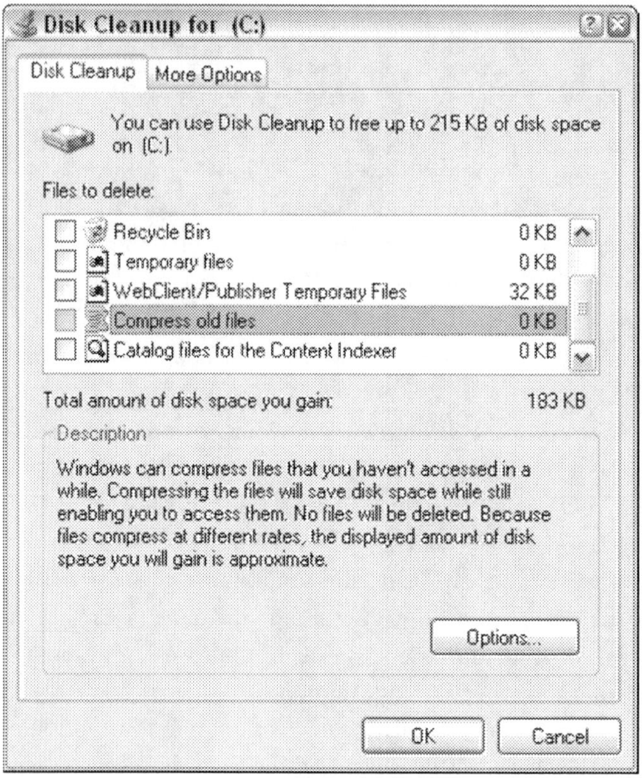

**Figure 5.20.** Windows will compress little-used files for you when you want to reclaim some disk space.

In a folder view or in Windows Explorer, compressed archives look like a standard folder icon with a vertical zipper on it (see Figure 5.21). It's a good reminder that the contents are compressed and may require special handling before you can use them.

**Figure 5.21.** Compressed archives are easy to spot in Windows.

To create a new archive, right-click anywhere in a folder or within the details pane, click New, and then click Compressed (zipped) Folder. The zippered folder appears; type in the name you want to use and then press Enter. The folder is created and you can add files to it.

**Watch Out!**

Although Windows compresses and decompresses files and folders automatically, it doesn't do it for files within compressed archives. This means that applications cannot see those files unless you extract them from the archive first. Click File and then Save As to save an editable uncompressed copy onto your hard drive.

**Hack**

Even if you install a third-party Zip program, Windows sometimes thinks it knows best how to handle Zip archives. Before you install the new handler, disable Windows' busybody attitude by typing this at the Run prompt: regsvr32 /u %windir% \system32\zipfldr.dll. To re-enable it, type regsvr32 %windir%\system32\zipfldr.dll.

You can *copy* a file into the archive (which keeps an uncompressed copy on your hard drive) by clicking and dragging the file onto the archive icon. The file is automatically compressed for you. If you want to *move* the file so that the only version is within the archive, hold down the Shift key and then click and drag the file onto the archive.

You can also one-step the process, creating an archive and copying files or folders into it. Select a group of files, icons, or folders, right-click the selection, click Send to, and then click Compressed (zipped) Folder. The archive will take the name of the first object in the selection and use that as the default archive name.

If you are snooping around the Windows system folders, you will find a special form of compressed files called "cabinet" files that end in the .cab extension, and whose icon resembles an actual file cabinet (see Figure 5.22). Setup programs use these special files for all kinds of software, including Windows. If for some reason you find a particular file is corrupted or missing, you can extract a pristine copy from a CAB file or make a copy to a new location.

**Figure 5.22.** Cabinet files are a special archive used by setup programs and by the operating system.

You cannot add any files to the existing cabinets or make new ones, so unless you move or delete the CAB files (not a good idea), you can't do much harm to them. The best bet is to know that they're there, and leave them alone.

# Encrypt files and folders

File and folder encryption is used to keep unauthorized persons from viewing or changing private files. Although file and folder permissions prevent people from gaining access to your My Documents folder (see Chapter 6 for more on permissions), you can still add another layer of protection by encrypting a folder or the documents within it.

The Encrypted File System (EFS) is a feature of NTFS, so it is not available for use on FAT32 partitions. If you bought a computer with Windows XP Home Edition on it, EFS is not available; it's a feature of Windows XP Professional only. This exclusion seems counterintuitive, because thefts of home computers can be equally as damaging to one's private information as would theft of a company computer. But Microsoft had to justify the cost difference, and this is one feature that was considered "advanced" enough to include only in XP Pro.

In theory, encryption can be used on any hard disk or folder. In the real world, encryption is most often used on specific folders on a laptop, so that in case the laptop is stolen the data will not be readable to thieves. If you are going to use encryption, get in the habit of encrypting entire folders rather than individual files. This makes it much easier for you to remember which files are protected — folder views show encrypted files in a different color (see Figure 5.23), but programs such as Word don't, and it's easy to forget whether your file is encrypted or not.

The encryption key is stored as part of your Windows credentials, so whenever you open or close an encrypted file, Windows makes the

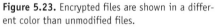

**Figure 5.23.** Encrypted files are shown in a different color than unmodified files.

appropriate checks to determine if you can read the file. This means that others who use your computer will not be able to read the contents of the encrypted files unless you expressly grant them permission to do so.

Encryption and decryption methods change depending on what you are doing with your files.

- If you move or copy an unencrypted file into an encrypted folder, Windows encrypts the file.

- If you move or copy an encrypted file from an encrypted to an unencrypted folder, the file stays encrypted.

- If you move or copy an encrypted file to a FAT32 (or other non-NTFS file system), you are given a warning that Windows is about to decrypt the file for you.

To encrypt a file or folder, browse to the file or folder you want to encrypt. Right-click the file or folder and then click Properties. On the properties dialog box, click Advanced.

---

**Watch Out!**

Encryption creates a security certificate that is used as the key to open your files. If you ever lose your certificate — for example, if you must reinstall Windows — you *cannot* recover your files. They're gone. They're really gone. Find out how to save certificates and recover encrypted information in Chapter 6.

In the Advanced Attributes dialog box (see Figure 5.24), select Encrypt contents to secure data. Click OK, and then click OK again. The Confirm Attribute Changes dialog box appears; you can choose whether to encrypt just the file, or all the files and parent folder. Select how you want the compression applied and then click OK. Encryption is applied to your folders and files.

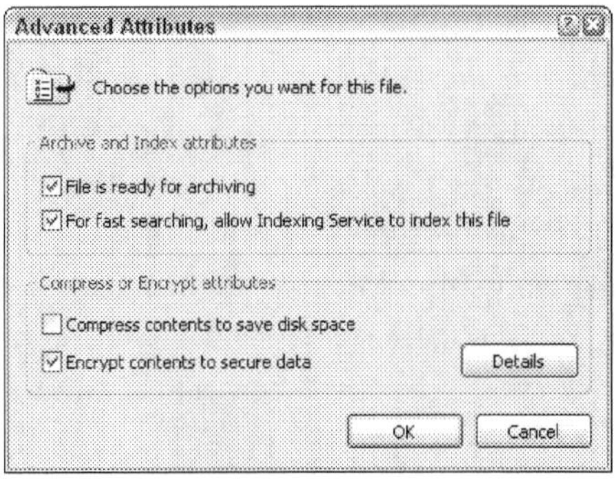

**Figure 5.24.** You can select encryption or compression in the same dialog box; make sure you choose the correct one.

You can share an encrypted file with some people without giving out the password or decrypting all your files and folders. Right-click the file, click Properties, and then click Details. Click the Add button (see Figure 5.25) and add users on the local computer that you want to view your files. Windows XP will take care of the permissions behind the scene. However, if you want to share the file with others across the network, you will probably need to decrypt it and set up a share where you and they have access.

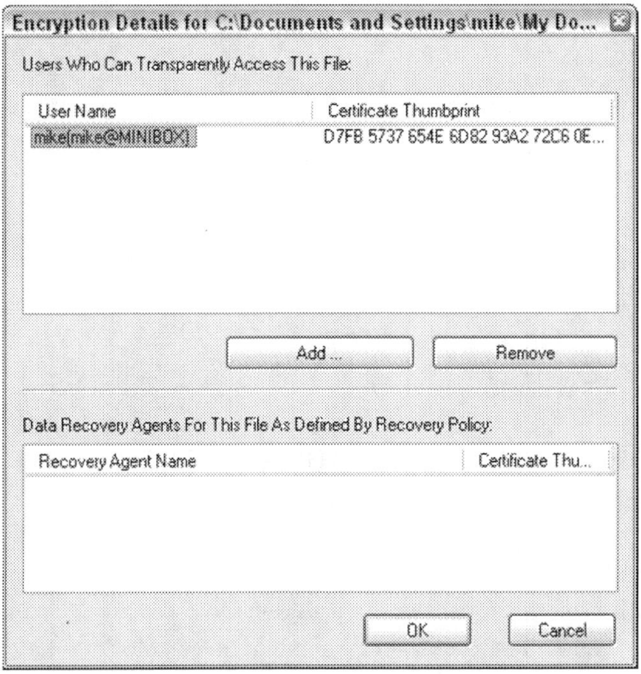

**Figure 5.25.** If other users have security certificates on your computer, you can add their certificate to the file to grant them access.

If you want to view your encrypted files or folders from other computers on your network, it gets a bit trickier. You must save a copy of your certificate file onto a floppy disk and take it with you to decrypt your files. Open Internet Explorer, click Tools, click Internet Options, click the Content tab, and then click the Certificates button (see Figure 5.26). Encrypting a file, any file, automatically generates a certificate for you. Click the certificate and then click Export. Follow the rest of the dialog boxes to copy the certificate to a floppy disk. Take the disk to another computer and log on with the same user name as on your computer. From the Certificates dialog box, click Import and then follow the rest of the dialog boxes. With your certificate installed, you can now view your encrypted materials from another computer.

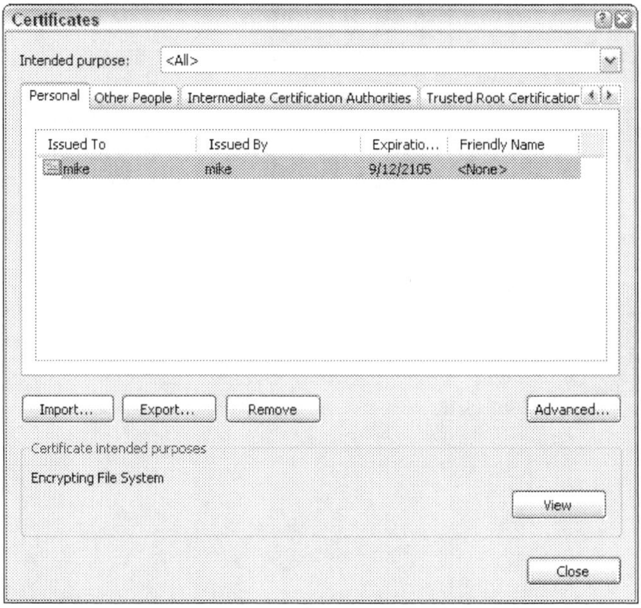

**Figure 5.26.** Internet Explorer's Content tab is where certificate management takes place.

# Redirect the My Documents folder

The My Documents folder is intended to be the central location for users to store any documents they create or work with on the local machine. This folder is the default storage area for Microsoft Office applications and applications of a certain data type; for example, pictures or images default to the My Pictures folder, and movies created with Movie Maker 2 default to the My Movies folder.

Most versions of Windows store user folders on the local machine. This made sense when peer-to-peer sharing was the norm. With Windows 2000,

Microsoft built in the ability to redirect a user's My Documents folders and contents to a server. This gave administrators the ability to automatically create a central storage location, provide backup and recovery services, and provide access to roaming or remote users.

You can redirect your My Documents folder from its default location at c:\Documents and Settings\%username% to another drive on the local computer or a server. This makes it much easier to back up important data without impairing the functionality of Windows and other programs.

Click Start, right-click My Documents, and then click Properties. The My Documents dialog box appears; click Move. The Select a destination dialog box appears. Browse to the location where you want to redirect the folder, such as another partition on the same hard drive or another hard drive entirely. The My Documents Properties dialog box appears (see Figure 5.27). Click OK. The confirmation dialog box appears. Click Yes. The My Documents folder is moved and redirected to the new location.

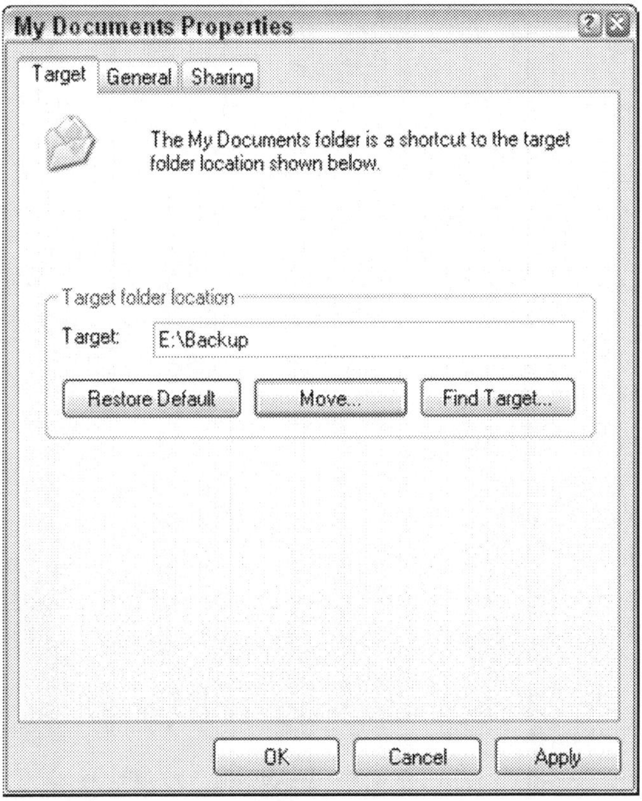

**Figure 5.27.** You can redirect your personal folders to another partition.

If you are an administrator you can define a home folder for users on the local computer or who are members in your domain. Go to Administrative Tools, open Local Users and Groups, and then browse to the Users folder. Open a user and click the Profile tab (see Figure 5.28). You can define a home directory either on the local computer or on a network share on this tab. It will be applied the next time the user logs on.

**Figure 5.28.** Home folders can be either on the local computer or on a server share.

If you need to restore the default setting, Windows XP gives you a one-button click to restore your My Documents folder to the local C: drive. In the My Documents Properties dialog box, click Restore Default and then click Apply. You will be asked if you want to move your files back to the local drive; click Yes.

## Enable file sharing

Sharing information is the key reason for having computers linked together on a network. However, setting up and managing shares became difficult as the number of users on a network increased. Windows 9x file sharing was insecure, allowing nearly anyone to connect to a share without a password. Windows 2000's file sharing relied on NTFS permissions, which was much more secure but too complex for the average home user to deploy on a trusted network. Users requested an easier but more secure way to share documents on a workgroup without indulging in the intricacies of NTFS.

The compromise, Simple File Sharing (SFS), is available only to standalone computers or computers participating in a workgroup. The goal of simple file sharing is to provide the ability to share files without requiring users or administrators to manage a web of users, permissions, and folders. Most of the file sharing settings are locked down, are not changeable, and are activated by checking or clearing a couple boxes for a folder. If you are managing a home or small office network without a domain and where everyone is a trusted participant, SFS is probably all you need.

## Manually configure file sharing

One of the first things to do is ensure that your computer is able to share files across the network. There are two places where the file sharing service can be turned on or off: the network card, and the Windows Firewall. The network card setting determines whether the necessary file and printer sharing services are available, and the Windows Firewall setting determines whether you can share files with computers on your local subnet. You can read more about networking in Chapter 8 and more about Windows Firewall in Chapter 6.

In a default Windows XP installation, the network adapter's File and Printer Sharing is installed and enabled. However, you may have turned this off, or if you upgraded from an earlier version of Windows you may have kept your older settings. To confirm if it is enabled, click Start, click Run, type ncpa.cpl, and then press Enter. Right-click the Local Area Connection icon and then click Properties.

You should see an entry called "File and Printer Sharing for Microsoft Networks," and it should have a check mark in the check box (see Figure 5.29). If the check box is empty, click it and then click OK. If the File and Printer Sharing driver isn't present, click the Install button, click Service, select File and Printer Sharing, and then click Add. You may need your Windows or Service Pack 2 CD to install the files, and you will need to reboot your computer. Return to this dialog box after the reboot to ensure the service is available and active.

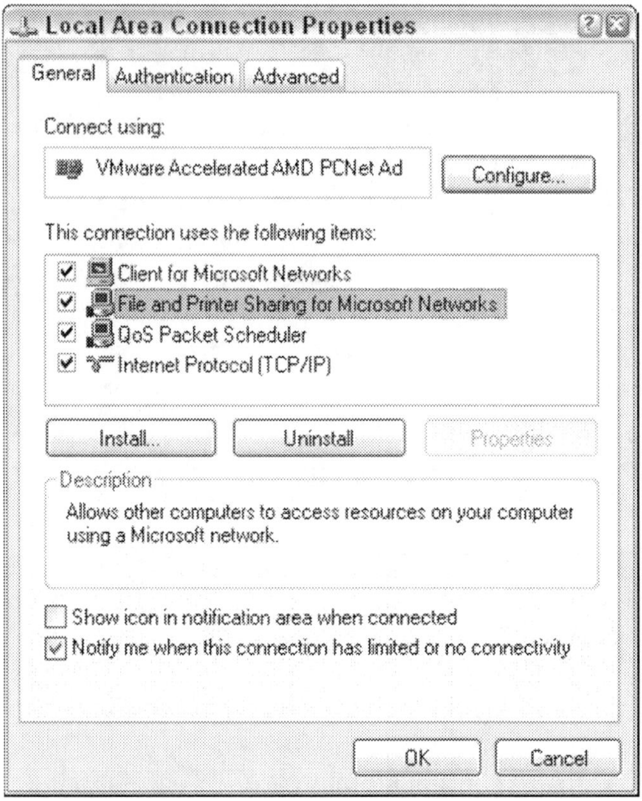

**Figure 5.29.** File and Printer Sharing is enabled by default on each network adapter.

Windows Firewall, part of Service Pack 2 and formerly called Internet Connection Firewall, blocks anyone from getting to your computer unless you expressly allow them to. File sharing is automatically turned off when you install Service Pack 2. To enable file sharing on your local subnet, click Start, click Run, type firewall.cpl, and then press Enter. The Windows Firewall dialog box appears (see Figure 5.30). Click the Exceptions tab.

In Windows Firewall the File and Printer Sharing service is a collection of specific settings that can be turned on and off, but not changed or removed. This ensures that Windows networks can communicate effectively, without requiring additional network administration. By default the service is turned off. Select it and then click OK. The new settings take effect immediately.

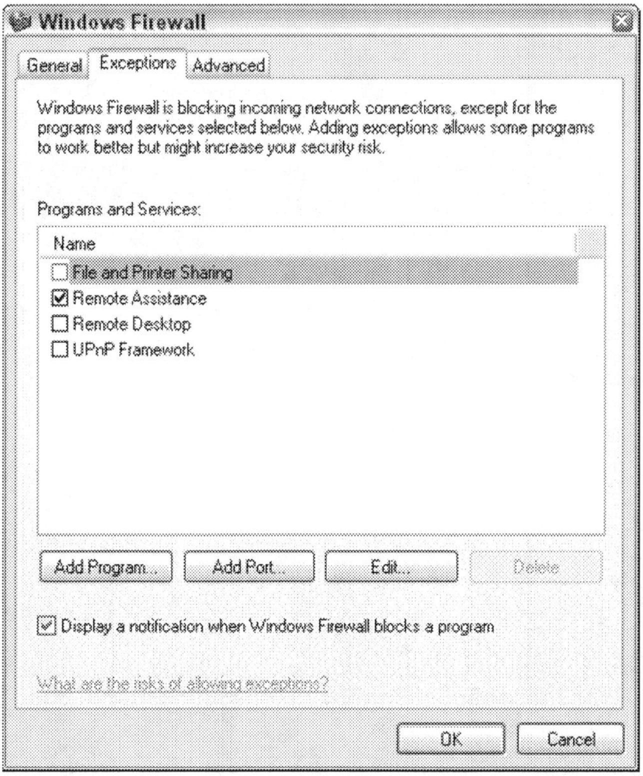

**Figure 5.30.** File sharing is disabled by default in Windows Firewall.

# Enable file sharing using the Network Setup Wizard

The Network Setup Wizard is new to Windows XP, though earlier versions were present in Windows 9x. Its purpose is to enable networking on home or SOHO computers. An administrator runs through the wizard once, creating a working configuration for one computer, and then the wizard makes a copy of that network configuration information so it can be installed on other computers.

There are benefits to running the Network Setup Wizard, even if you have already configured your Internet connection. For one, you let Windows handle the undercover details of enabling SFS. For another, you are given multiple opportunities to read additional information and consult help files about what you are seeing and doing. Even for hardened system administrators, a refresher course like this can be a big help.

To run the Network Setup Wizard, click Start, Control Panel, Network and Internet Connections, and then Network Setup Wizard. When the wizard starts, click Next. You can review the network checklist if you want; otherwise, click Next. The wizard may detect an existing connection (see Figure 5.31). Select Yes, use the existing shared connection, and then click Next. If you see an option you don't recognize, you can click No and be taken to a dialog box where you can get information on different types of connections and make the appropriate choice from there.

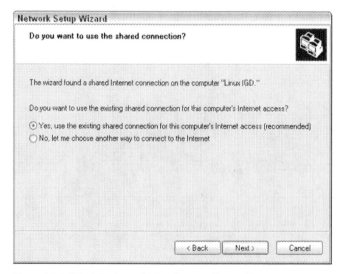

**Figure 5.31.** Select the type of network connection you'll use.

The computer description and name dialog box appears. You should already have a computer name from when you installed Windows XP, but you can change it here if you want to. See Chapter 2 for restrictions for computer names. The description text box is entirely optional: It is a way of making computers more human — the text shows up when you browse the Network Neighborhood. Click Next.

You are asked for the workgroup name. A default Windows installation uses the name WORKGROUP or MSHOME (depending on the version of Windows); type in the actual name of your workgroup here, or if you're creating a new one, use that name here as well. See Chapter 2 for restrictions on workgroup names. Finally, the dialog box you've been waiting for: Configure File and Print Sharing (see Figure 5.32). It's a yes-or-no choice. Select Turn on file and printer sharing and then click Next. A confirmation dialog box appears, reiterating the choices you've made. If you want to change any of them, click the Back button and make the necessary changes. When you're satisfied, click Next. The wizard makes the necessary configuration changes for you.

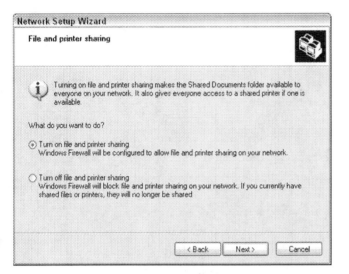

**Figure 5.32.** Select the first option to enable file and printer sharing.

As its last task, it asks if you want to create a Network Setup Disk. Select Just finish the wizard and then click Next. Click Finish. Your computer is now enabled to share files across the network.

# Share folders using simple file sharing

When you share a folder using simple file sharing, you are making the information available to anyone in the Administrator or Power User group on the local computer. Simple file sharing sets read access only on shared folders. You can change this on a per-folder basis, though if you're using simple file sharing it's best to keep your folders at read-only access for users on your network.

You can share any folder on the local computer except Windows and Program Files. You should restrict sharing to folders and not entire drives. The one exception would be a CD or DVD drive for when you may want all users to have read access to all of a CD's files (such as archived data or other information).

If you want to share folders that reside on a FAT32 partition, you can still use SFS to do so; however, this is not safe. FAT does not support any security mechanisms that keep people from reading, writing, or deleting files, or keep unauthorized people from gaining access. You should convert the partition to NTFS, or move files to a folder on an NTFS partition and then share it.

## Shared Documents versus Shared Folders

The Shared Documents folder is a special folder set up by Windows XP for users on the local computer only. If you want to share documents between people who log onto the same computer, you can drag documents to the Shared Folders folder so that anyone who logs on to the computer can access them. The Shared Documents folder is not visible to anyone across the network, and it is not available to computers that participate in a domain.

Shared Documents is most useful in single-computer households where everyone shares the computer. You can exchange documents, music, or multimedia files without setting up simple file sharing.

It can get confusing, especially if everyone is a local administrator. Under My Computer, you'll see the Shared Documents folder, followed by an entry for every account on the local computer. The best way to alleviate this is to be cautious about whom you make an administrator on the local machine; see Chapter 4 for information on using group membership to change privileges.

Also, if your computer is connected directly to the Internet, simple file sharing is not a safe way to share files on your home network. You should either route your network through a single computer using Internet Connection Sharing (ICS), or have a hardware-based firewall using network address translation (NAT) between your network and the Internet. See Chapter 6 for more on security.

To enable SFS on a folder, browse to the folder you wish to share. Right-click the folder and then click Sharing and Security. The folder properties dialog box appears (see Figure 5.33).

If you have not run the Network Setup Wizard but you have manually enabled file sharing services, click the "security risks" link and then select Just enable file sharing. If you have run the Network Setup Wizard, you can select the Share this folder on the network option. By default Windows uses the folder name as the share name; you can change the share name without changing the folder name by typing a new share name in the text box.

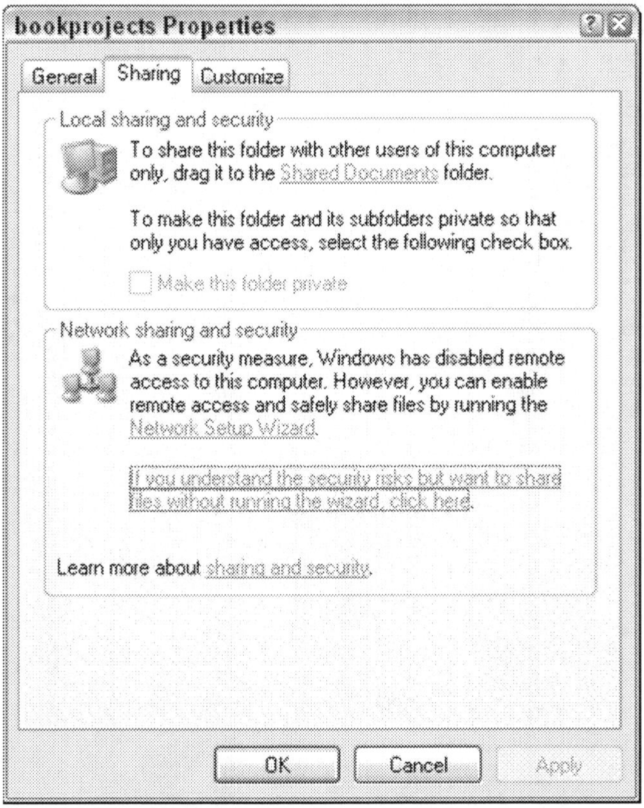

**bookprojects Properties**

General | Sharing | Customize

Local sharing and security

To share this folder with other users of this computer only, drag it to the Shared Documents folder.

To make this folder and its subfolders private so that only you have access, select the following check box.

☐ Make this folder private

Network sharing and security

As a security measure, Windows has disabled remote access to this computer. However, you can enable remote access and safely share files by running the Network Setup Wizard.

If you understand the security risks but want to share files without running the wizard, click here.

Learn more about sharing and security.

[ OK ] [ Cancel ] [ Apply ]

**Figure 5.33.** Windows warns you about the security risks of file sharing.

SFS also sets network shares as read only, so that network users can copy or look at files but cannot save files or copy new files to your folder. If you want to enable write privileges for network users, select Allow network users to change my files (see Figure 5.34). Click OK when you are done. The new shared folder is effective immediately.

**Hack**

You can "hide" a share from other computers by putting a dollar sign ($) at the end of the share name: "SECRET$" will not appear in the Network Neighborhood, but if anyone knows the name they can still connect directly to it.

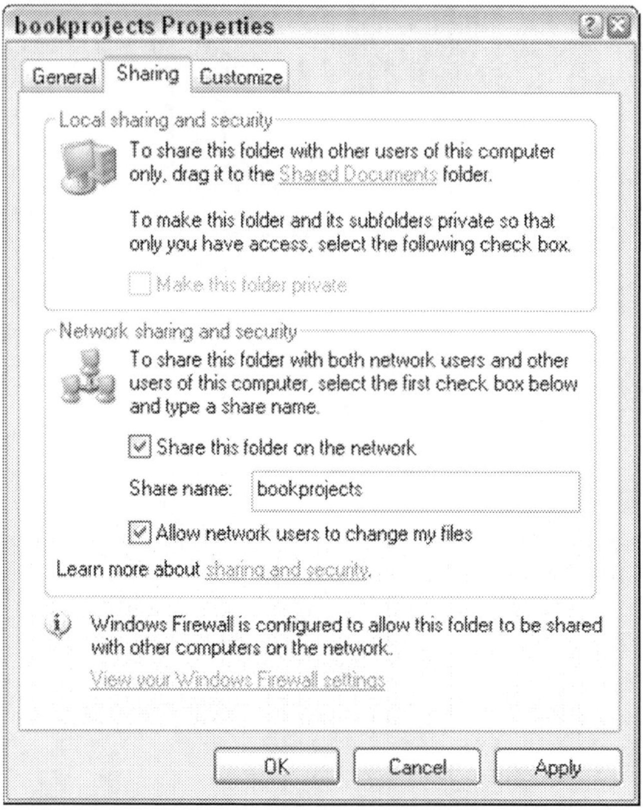

**Figure 5.34.** Type a new share name, and decide if you want others to save files to your share.

For the most part SFS is a painless and maintenance-free way to share files with others in your workgroup. There are some caveats and gotchas that go along with using SFS.

- You must be the member of the Administrator's Group in order to change file sharing settings. This also means that any other computer administrator can turn on and off *your* file settings, or gain access to your files.

- When you turn on SFS, you enable the Guest account. Though this account has limited privileges, it allows anyone on your network access to your files, which could be a security risk depending on your setup.

- The "Make this folder private" option in SFS applies only to files and folders in My Documents. If an application stores its data anywhere outside of the My Documents folder, you can't make that data private (unless you move the data file). Your kids can discover your credit card account info if they're snooping around. Not a fun concept, is it?

- The "Make this folder private" option applies at a folder level, not a file level. It marks as private all files within a folder and the folder itself. You can't pick and choose which files within a folder to make private.

If you can live with these restrictions, continue using SFS. If you want more flexibility, you need to move up to NTFS.

## Configure NTFS file sharing

NTFS file sharing is more complex than simple file sharing for several reasons. First, when your computer is part of a domain, NTFS derives its security information and credentials from Active Directory. Second, NTFS uses far more granular levels of permissions, controlling aspects of file ownership and file management that can be difficult to understand, much less apply. Finally, managing NTFS permissions requires an understanding of how remote and local permissions interact over a network and when to use such permissions.

Domains have two different sets of permissions that apply to file sharing: NTFS permissions and share permissions; they work together to create NTFS file sharing. NTFS permissions apply to users who log on to the local computer. Share permissions apply to anyone accessing a folder from across a network. When Windows is considering whether to grant someone access to a file, Windows merges both sets of permissions, and as a rule of thumb the most restrictive set of rules applies. When you configure a folder for network access, you are typically setting share permissions, deciding who has access to the share and what rights they have. NTFS permissions go one step further and protect specific files within a share.

On a home or SOHO network, setting share permissions will be all you need to protect your documents. Larger businesses need to understand NTFS permissions and the interactions with share permissions. A discussion of all the nuances of permissions is beyond the scope of this book, but a good resource to consider is *Windows XP for Power Users* by Curt Simmons, Wiley Publishing, ISBN 0-7645-4998-7.

---

 **Inside Scoop**

Turn off SFS in Windows Explorer at Tools, Folder Options, View; this lets you use NTFS file sharing even if you are in a workgroup. Oddly, if you are in a domain, you can still check and uncheck the box, but Windows still uses NTFS file sharing.

To configure NTFS sharing, browse to the folder you want to share, right-click the folder, and then click Sharing and Security. The folder properties dialog box appears. Select Share this folder, and then type a name for the share on the network (see Figure 5.35).

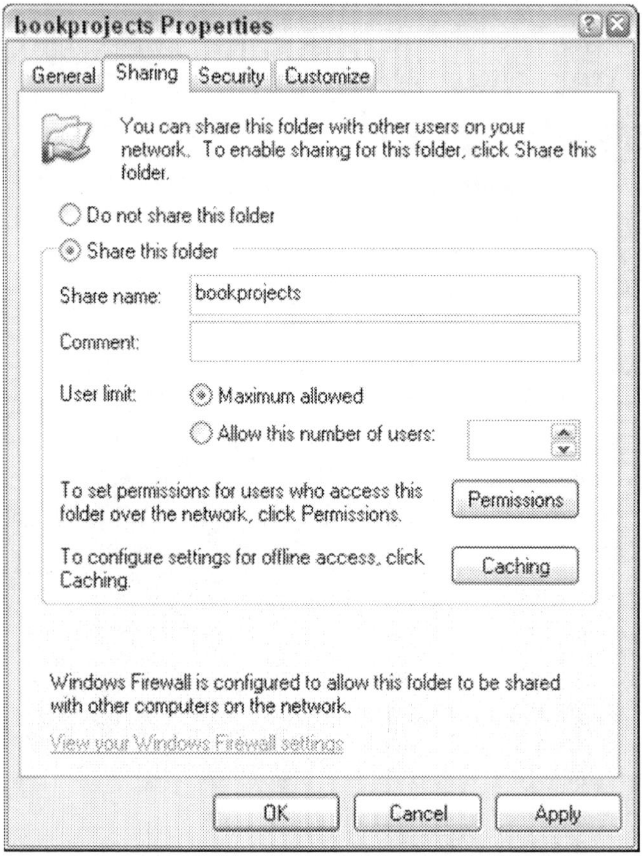

**Figure 5.35.** NTFS sharing options allow for more complexity than with simple file sharing.

Next, click Permissions to determine who can access the share. Select the group you want to set permissions for (see Figure 5.36); you can add or remove domain groups by clicking Add or Remove and then selecting the necessary group. Select the permissions you want to apply for the group in this folder. Click OK twice, and the folder is shared on the network.

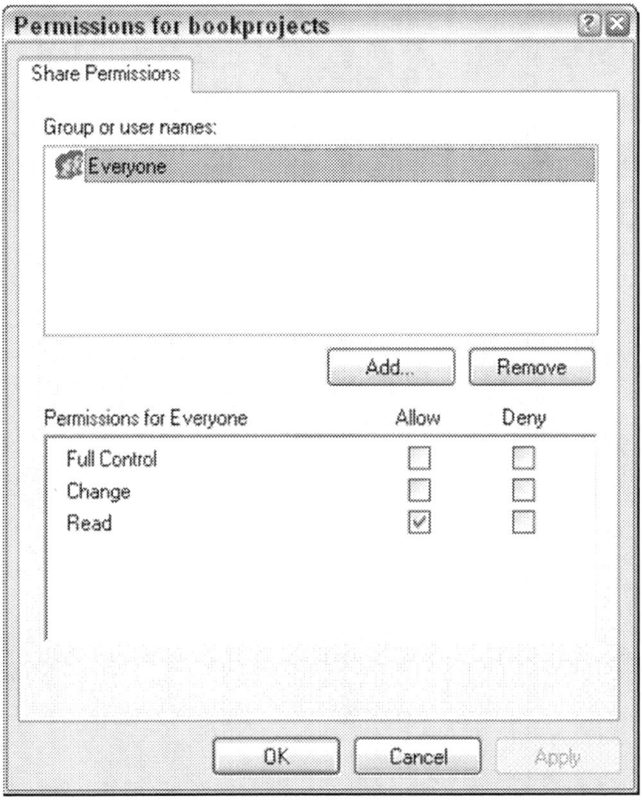

**Figure 5.36.** Set read, write, and execute permissions for specific groups, or explicitly deny access to groups.

The Deny option is a powerful one; it is like the trump card of permissions. Windows rightfully assumes that if you explicitly tell it not to grant access to a specific person or group, then that will take precedence over any explicit granting of access.

You may have noticed a Security tab at the top of the folder properties dialog box (see Figure 5.37). The Security tab allows you to set share-level permissions for users, groups, and organizational units throughout an enterprise. A thorough discussion of the functions and options on this tab and its related dialog boxes is beyond the scope of this book; however, see Chapter 7 and Chapter 11 for more discussion about permissions and how to use them.

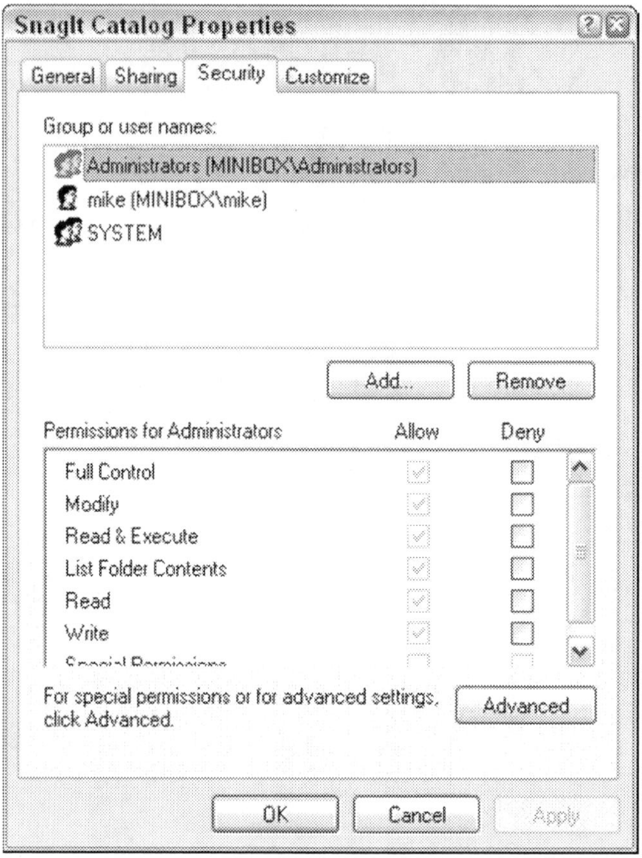

**Figure 5.37.** You can be very specific about who can access shared information, and what type of access they will have.

After you configure file sharing, you may find that your shares are still not available on the network. One setting that is frequently overlooked is the Server service — you may have it set to Manual or Disabled. Look in Administrative Tools ⇨ Services and start the service if it is stopped.

## Managing the Recycle Bin

The Recycle Bin is the place where old files go to die. It's a relatively overlooked place, but you can make it do a few tricks to help it perform better on your desktop.

Right-click the Recycle Bin and then click Properties. Depending on the partitions you have, you will see tabs across the top for each drive (see Figure 5.38). The Recycle Bin appears to allocate a percentage of your hard drive's size for deleted files. This is misleading; it really allocates a percentage of *free space* on your drive. As your drive fills with files, correspondingly less space is available for deleted files.

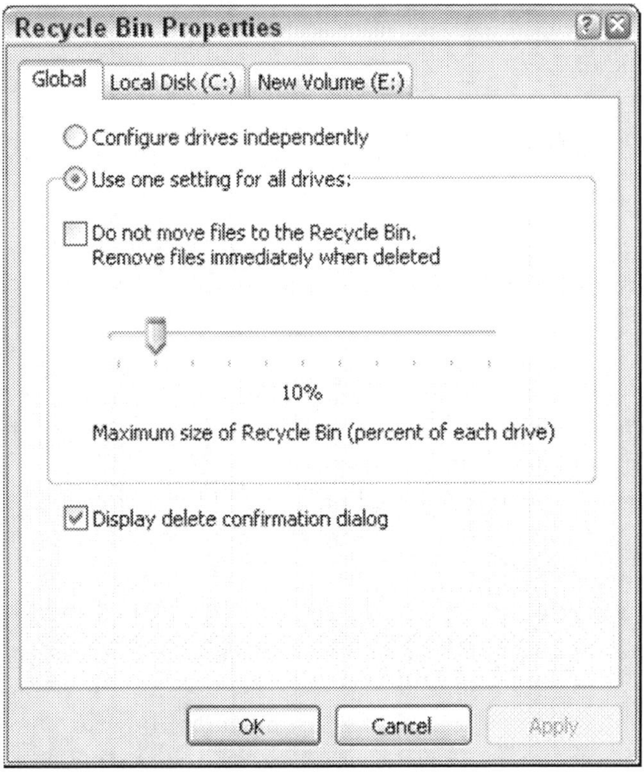

**Figure 5.38.** Recycle Bin properties are few but easily managed.

To make management easy, don't change the default configuration setting; let Windows use one free-space setting for all drives. If your hard drive isn't large to begin with, you can adjust the slider control to reserve less or more space than the Windows default of 10 percent. You can move between the tabs to see how much space Windows is allocating on each drive.

If you get tired of seeing "Are you sure you want to send <filename> to the Recycle Bin?" messages from Windows, deselect the Display delete confirmation dialog box option. Because the Recycle Bin acts as a fail-safe, giving you the opportunity to restore a file if you decide later you want it back, the deletion message seems like a little too much micromanagement.

One case where the delete dialog box may be appropriate is if you select the Do not move files to the Recycle Bin option. When this option is selected, files are automatically deleted, without the safety net of the Recycle

**Hack**

Change the name of the Recycle Bin by browsing to HKEY_CURRENT_USER\Software\
Microsoft\Windows\CurrentVersion\Explorer\CLSID\{645FF040-5081-101B-9F08-
00AA002F954E}. Double-click the (Default) value, type the new name, and click OK.
Press F5 to refresh your desktop and show the new name.

Bin to catch you if you make a serious mistake. Although you could check this box and send all deleted files to a better, happier place, a smarter method is to use the Shift+Delete keystroke to permanently delete files. That way you have to make a conscious decision to make the file go away for good; and, while it's not foolproof, at least it helps keep you from erring in the other direction.

## Working with the Search Companion

Windows XP's Search function is one of the most annoying features in the entire desktop. To start with, it's officially called the Search Companion, as if it's going to be as good to you as your significant other. It has cartoon characters, hidden options, and forces you to open a new instance of Windows Explorer if you want to do anything useful with the results. It's difficult to imagine that the Microsoft Usability Labs came back with test results showing that ordinary people preferred an obtrusive, obscure, and cartoony interface.

In spite of that it has become a modestly capable utility, one that can look for anything, anywhere it might be located. You can use it to find multimedia, application documents, files, folders, computers, and people. Given the scope alone, it's head and shoulders above the previous version (called Find) in Windows 9x. You can start the Search Companion by either clicking Start and then Search, or by clicking the Search button in any folder.

One of the first things you may want to do is to send the animated Search dog to the pound (see Figure 5.39). It has no effect on your searches except to sit there and consume CPU cycles. You can switch to another animated character, or just bag the whole concept. Click Turn off animated character to get rid of the mutt. Or, click Change preferences and you can choose a new animation, turn it off completely, or change other Search Companion behavior to better fit the way you like to work.

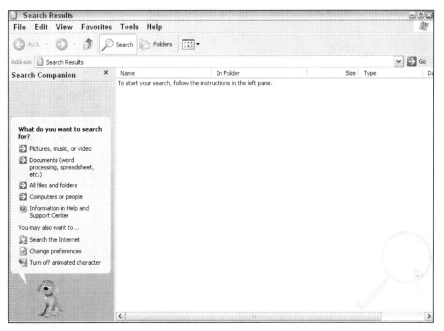

**Figure 5.39.** Rover the Retriever awaits your search command.

For the most part the Search process is self-explanatory. You enter search terms into a field, select any properties you think may help Windows find the items you're looking for, and then click Search. One of the most frequently used search types is the All Files and Folders search. Unless you know exactly what type of file you are looking for (is a PowerPoint slide a document or a picture?), the All Files option covers the broadest territory and can return the most results. If you are in the habit of storing your personal data and files on a separate partition, either through redirecting the My Documents folder or by setting your applications to store data on that partition, you can narrow down the physical locations the Search Companion must search. Note that you can browse to network drives, enabling you to search for information on shares across your network.

**Watch Out!**

Sometimes you will get "duplicate" files as part of your search results: The Search engine treats files in My Documents and %username%\My Documents as being in two different locations, when they are really the same file. Maybe Microsoft will fix this in a future release.

Searching by date modified and file size may be useful, but they probably aren't the ones you will use most often. Instead, click the More advanced options link (see Figure 5.40) and select the Search system folders, Search hidden files and folders, and Search subfolders options. This tells Windows to look in all the odd byways and temporary subdirectories that are lurking about, in hopes that your information may be found there.

The Search Companion is not picky about what you enter into the search criteria boxes. Capitalization doesn't matter, nor does position; if you type "one" and do a search, you will get the word *one* as well as words like *Simone* and *onerous*. Searching for filenames is much faster than searching for content because the Search engine must scan the contents of every file, including Zip archives, and this will take a very long time unless you are using the Indexing Service.

**Figure 5.40.** Select More advanced options to narrow your search parameters.

## A few words about the Indexing Service

The Indexing Service was first introduced to the desktop in Windows 2000 Professional. Originally part of the Windows NT 4.0 Option Pack, Index Server was designed to provide content indexing services primarily for Internet Information Server, but also for early versions of Microsoft's Commerce Server products. As disk sizes grew and information expanded rapidly, putting indexing services on the desktop sounded like a great idea, and so the service has been available on desktops ever since.

The Indexing Service (see Figure 5.41) not only indexes contents of data files and their attributes but provides a powerful query language that can be accessed through the Search Companion.

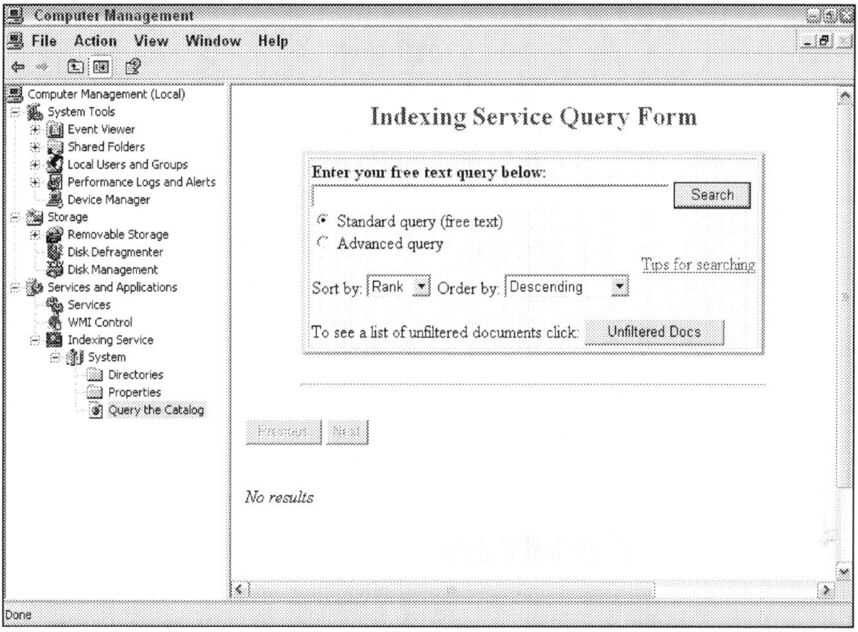

**Figure 5.41.** Index Services manager can be accessed through the Computer Management snap-in.

You can start the Indexing Service in two ways. Open the Search Companion, click Change preferences, and then click With Indexing Service (for faster local searches). Or you can start the service by clicking Start, Run, typing services.msc, and then pressing Enter. Scroll down the list to Indexing Service and then click the Start Service button in the toolbar.

At any time you can also configure which folders you want indexed. By default, Indexing Service will index all disks and all files and folders. To limit the service, browse to a folder, right-click the folder, and then click Properties. Click the Advanced button, and check or uncheck the For fast searching, allow Indexing Service to index this folder option.

When it's done, the service will have generated a catalog file that takes up approximately 25 percent of the space as the indexed files themselves. Fortunately, by default the service indexes only Microsoft Office files, text files, HTML files, and files for which a proper filter has been installed.

---

**Bright Idea**

If you have a hard drive of any size, with any decent amount of content, the service will take a long time to generate the master index. Leave your computer on overnight to complete its housekeeping chores.

---

### Do you speak Query?

The Search Companion is powerful but it is still pretty simple about what it looks for. The Index Service allows you to search by file attributes, file metadata (such as which program created the file), and by using Boolean logic and relational operators.

If you want to see what the engine is capable of and want to experiment with the query language, click Start, Run, type compmgmt.msc, and then click Enter. Browse to Services and Applications\Indexing Service\System\Query the Catalog. Click Tips for Searching and then click Query Syntax. You can also find up-to-date query language documentation at msdn.microsoft.com/library/default.asp?url=/library/en-us/indexsrv/html/ixqlang_92xx.asp.

---

Your queries can be typed into the A word or phrase in the file: text box. The Search Companion will return the results much faster than if the Indexing Service wasn't enabled.

## Just the facts

- Desktop folders and Windows Explorer can be enhanced with performance and cosmetic changes.

- File compression saves space; file encryption protects data.

- You can't use both compression and encryption on files.

- File and folder sharing can be simple, with SFS, or complex, with NTFS file sharing.

- The Search engine, in combination with the Indexing Service, is a powerful data management tool.

**GET THE SCOOP ON...**
Monitoring the Security Center ▪ Configuring firewalls,
antivirus, and anti-spyware programs ▪ Analyzing your
computer's security exposure ▪ Securing Internet
Explorer and Outlook Express

# Managing Security

T he Internet is everywhere, from libraries to corner cafés to your parent's house. It's a great era to live in: Ready access to information makes formerly burdensome tasks much easier to accomplish.

At the same time, ever-present access also brings with it ever-present risks from people who have less-than-honorable motivations for gaining access to your computer and its contents. Security, once thought to be required only around banks and gold repositories, is now mandatory for any computer that connects to the Internet.

This chapter helps you understand what the risks and concerns are, walks you through the new security features in Windows XP, and informs you about other programs that enhance the security features in XP.

## Configure the Security Center

The Security Center is new in Service Pack 2 and it is one of the biggest upgrades since Windows XP was released. The Security Center provides a one-stop resource for monitoring and managing basic security functions within XP and for monitoring third-party programs that you can use to enhance security.

### Easy Hacking 101: The short history of Windows security

Even when the Security Center arrived, some people said it was too little, too late. Microsoft does not have a good track record when it comes to security; in fact, nearly every month

## Security is a many-layered thing

People banter the word "security" around as if it is a concrete, absolute thing. But as any IT professional will tell you, security is an ongoing process that must be strengthened at several layers. No one system is absolutely secure; the best that anyone can do is to erect enough barriers so that the bad guys eventually get discouraged and go look for easier, softer targets.

Security is sometimes separated into five conceptual layers: authentication (you are who you say you are), authorization (you have permission to see things and do things), encryption (ensuring others cannot see information), integrity (ensuring the data doesn't change along the way), and auditing (keeping track of who does what). A comprehensive security model puts barriers at each layer, so that the failure of one barrier doesn't compromise the entire system. While this approach does not guarantee a system is secure, it makes it much tougher to compromise a computer. Many professionals mentally add a sixth layer, that of physical access. If anyone can get unrestricted access to your computer, the bad guys' hard work is 90 percent done.

Sometimes the security layers are sliced a bit differently: physical security, operating system security, application security, data security, and network security. As long as you understand that there is no "magic bullet" for making your systems secure but that you must engage in protection at several levels, it doesn't matter how you classify your security exposure.

Microsoft releases hot fixes and security patches to help shore up the attack surface presented by most Windows installations. To be fair, with a 90 percent+ market share on the desktop, Windows is the default target of bad guys everywhere — very few people are writing viruses attacking the BeOS platform, for example.

Yet there has always been a bit of the "closing the barn door after the horse has escaped" cachet about Microsoft's strategy with regards to security. It took Windows XP's release in 2001 for Microsoft to disable various services by default, services that were enabled (and buggy) in earlier versions of Windows. This was long after worms and viruses had already wreaked millions of dollars in lost productivity and stolen data at corporations worldwide.

At the time, Microsoft security bulletins took the attitude of, "Don't open attachments from people you don't recognize." Which wouldn't have been a problem, except that most virus writers had long ago figured out how to mine a person's address book for e-mail addresses and make e-mail look like it came from someone the recipient knew. After the havoc, Microsoft changed its tune to "Don't open attachments you don't recognize." That didn't work either, because bosses and co-workers often sent documents the recipient had never seen before. So Microsoft took the draconian step of preventing users from opening any e-mail attachments. Most IT professionals and nearly everyone in the security community snorted in derision at this ineffective attempt to improve Windows security.

Meanwhile third-party vendors got busy making antivirus software for both the desktop and for e-mail servers, software and hardware vendors cranked out firewalls for homes and small businesses, and wireless connectivity (Wi-Fi) opened up a whole new avenue for attack and security countermeasures.

Belatedly, Bill Gates figured out that people were increasingly unhappy with Microsoft's combined "we know best" and laissez-faire attitude toward security, and he issued the infamous "Trustworthy Computing" memo on January 15, 2002, three months after Windows XP rolled out the door.

Microsoft put the brakes on further product development until all umpty-million lines of Windows Server 2003 and Windows XP code were reviewed for security-related bugs and design flaws. Monthly updates were issued, and word came down of a Security Center in Service Pack 2 that would finally bring the spaghetti-like security of Windows under control.

## View Security Center monitoring

As it turns out, the Security Center isn't really much more than a health monitor for other services that deal with security issues directly, such as antivirus software. The Security Center alerts you to various conditions that arise with the Windows Firewall, antivirus software if you have it installed, and the Automatic Updates service. It's very much like middle management: It reports on what front-line employees are doing without doing anything of value itself with the information.

**Inside Scoop**

The initial Bill Gates memo is available at www.wired.com/news/business/ 0,1367,49826,00.html, while a follow-up Trustworthy Computing Executive Summary is at www.microsoft.com/mscorp/execmail/2002/07-18twc.asp.

## "Would you confirm your password, please?"

Security experts agree: *You* are the single weakest point in security. It is far too easy to obtain passwords from unsuspecting people, and passwords are the most common and least secure authentication method used. In security parlance, authentication proves that you are who you say you are. This typically consists of your user name or logon ID plus something you know (password), something you have (smart card), or something you are (fingerprint or other biometric). Because smart cards and biometric scanners are expensive, most everyone uses passwords for authentication.

While bad guys can use brute force attacks to guess passwords one after the other, the easier approach is to use methods that trick you into revealing your password. The euphemism for this is "social engineering." Falsified e-mails, phishing (Web sites or e-mail that look official but are fake), searching your desk or office area for passwords that are written down, and phone calls purporting to be from your bank or company's IT department are all methods the bad guys use to get this information from you, hopefully without your knowing just who you're dealing with and why they want your information.

My advice? Never, ever give out your password or Social Security number over the phone. Do not e-mail them to anyone, or click on links in an e-mail that asks you to confirm your security credentials, even if it is from a bank you do business with. Even if the friendly woman from the cubicle next door offers to help you with your computer problems, don't give her your password. Once she has your password, she can log on as you — and for all you know she's looking to fund her retirement plan and point to you as the culprit.

You can always check Security Center's status yourself. Click Start, Run, type wscui.cpl, and then press Enter. You can also click Start, Control Panel, and then double-click the Security Center icon.

Figure 6.1 shows all three monitored services, and all three potential status conditions.

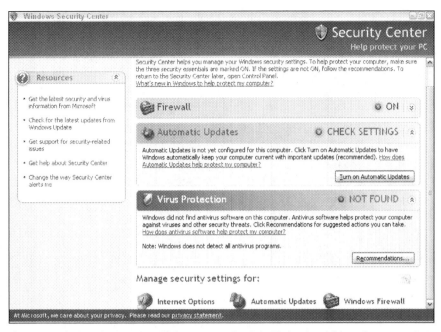

**Figure 6.1.** The Security Center provides a one-stop view into Windows' security services.

- If a service is active and is providing adequate protection, it displays a green light.

- If a service is active but may not be providing adequate protection, it displays a yellow banner and a yellow light, indicating you should check the settings and perhaps take action.

- If a service is not active, it displays red. You should check the settings immediately as your computer is at risk.

Security Center displays status alerts in the notification area of the taskbar (also known as the system tray). These shield-shaped alerts, seen in Figure 6.2, will take you to the Security Center or to a configuration dialog box so that you can enable any settings needed to make your computer safer.

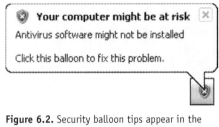

**Figure 6.2.** Security balloon tips appear in the notification area and alert you to a condition that needs attention.

The notification icons also generate balloon tip messages (see Figure 6.2) that, in effect, alert you to the alerts. The balloons usually say, "Click this balloon to do something!" and have the same effect as if you clicked a shield icon.

There's nothing quite like a little belt-and-suspenders notification support from Security Center.

To disable balloon alerts for any or all of the services, on the Security Center, click Change the way Security Center alerts me (see Figure 6.3). The Alert Settings dialog box appears and you can select or deselect any of the alerts you want to receive. You can also turn off the monitoring functions of Security Center completely and rely on the underlying services to do their jobs. If you do this, it will be up to your software's own update services and your own diligence to manage security services.

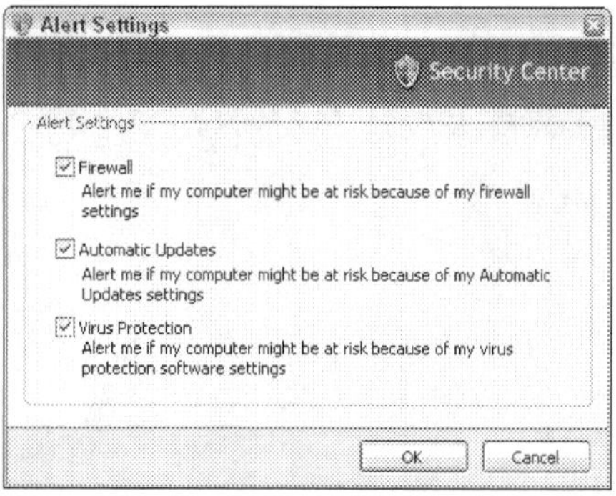

**Figure 6.3.** Select which balloon tips you want to appear.

If you choose to monitor security yourself, you can disable the Security Center service itself so it doesn't spin idly, waiting for notifications that will never happen. To turn off the service, click Start, Run, type services.msc, and then press Enter. Scroll down the list to Security Center, double-click it, change the startup type to Disabled, click Stop, and then click OK. The service is stopped and will not start at the next boot. If you want to restart the service, change the startup type to Automatic, click start, and then click OK.

As one final note, Security Center uses Windows Management Instrumentation (WMI) to monitor the three services and trigger alerts when needed. If you install a third-party program for antivirus or firewall services, only ones that support WMI can be monitored by Security Center. For example, if you have an antivirus program on your computer and you've installed Service Pack 2, and now Windows reports that you don't have any antivirus protection, it is probably caused by your software not supporting WMI. This isn't necessarily a bad thing: It indicates that you rely on the software to properly schedule updates and notify you of security problems. Your software vendor may have a WMI-compatible release available, or you can be content with monitoring your software yourself.

### Hardware firewalls: They should be mandatory

A hardware firewall is a device whose function is dedicated to network connectivity and packet inspection. Because it is such a narrowly-focused device, there is a very small "attack surface" and it is difficult to compromise. Many residential and SOHO routers or gateways come with firewall capabilities built in. This gives you a much more flexible and configurable solution than putting two network cards into your computer and then using the computer as a gateway. With a dedicated firewall you can protect other Internet devices such as your TiVo or Playstation without having to turn on your computer every time.

In contrast, running only a software firewall leaves you susceptible to far more attacks; if the firewall is compromised, it is quite possible that your entire computer becomes available to the bad guys. So even if you are running Windows Firewall to protect your direct Internet connection, you should invest in a hardware firewall *and* run a software firewall on every computer on your network. Remember that security is enhanced with layers, and by reducing or eliminating a single point of failure you increase the security of your overall network.

## Configure and manage firewalls

A firewall helps protect your computer by preventing unauthorized users from gaining access to it through a network or through the Internet. It stops unauthorized traffic from getting into your local network, and allows authorized traffic to pass to the Internet from inside your local network. It works by checking each data packet, and if the data packets match the "VIP Guest List," it allows the data to pass. Otherwise, the packets are not allowed to pass and are simply discarded.

When you install Service Pack 2, Windows checks to see if you have a firewall installed, and if not, it activates Windows Firewall for you. Windows Firewall is an improvement over the previous version, called Internet Connection Firewall (ICF) in Windows XP, because it's more configurable and more flexible than its earlier iteration. You should always have a software firewall enabled on your computer, even if you already have a hardware firewall on your network.

For example, if you use a laptop for your work, you probably connect to the Internet from multiple locations. If you go on the road and use either a Wi-Fi hotspot or a hotel's network, there could be bad guys on the local network waiting for an unprotected computer to appear. Don't rely on luck or a false sense of security; make sure you have a software firewall running on your computer.

## Configure Windows Firewall

Windows Firewall is one of the most basic firewalls available, but it works for the average user. It blocks most inbound traffic, will automatically configure exceptions for you, and will let you know if someone is actively attacking your computer.

The three fastest ways to open Windows Firewall are:

- In the Security Center, click the Windows Firewall link at the bottom of the page.
- Click Start, Control Panel, and then double-click Windows Firewall.
- Click Start, Run, type firewall.cpl, and then click OK.

The firewall's General tab (see Figure 6.4) has two simple settings: On and Off. When first installed Windows XP turns the firewall on, but if you are opening the firewall settings for the first time and see it set Off, don't panic; you may still be protected. Service Pack 2-compatible firewalls such as ZoneAlarm turn off Windows Firewall automatically so they can do their job. You should double-check your other software to make sure it's running. If you don't have any, turn On your Windows Firewall. The change in settings takes effect immediately.

If you have more than one way to access the Internet, such as a network card and a dialup connection, you can enable or disable the firewall independently for each connection. Go to the Control Panel, click Network Connections, right-click the connection you want to modify, and then click Properties (see Figure 6.5). Click the Advanced tab and then click Settings. You are taken to the Windows Firewall dialog box for that connection, and you can change the settings as needed. Note that if you turn off Windows Firewall for one connection, the banner at the top of the Settings dialog box (and Security Center) reports that the firewall is off, even though other connections may have the firewall active.

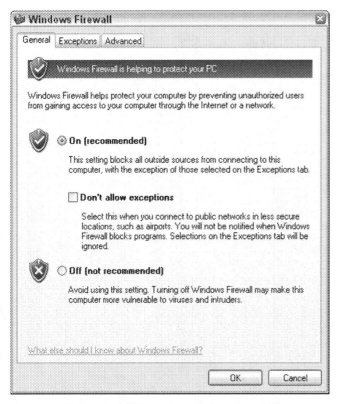

**Figure 6.4.** Windows Firewall has two basic settings: On and Off.

The Don't allow exceptions option shuts down all incoming traffic, regardless of any exceptions you have configured. If you are at a public Wi-Fi hotspot, you may want to check this box so you are protected from all incoming traffic or possible hack attacks. The firewall still allows outbound traffic that originates from your computer, but inbound won't work. Forget trying to instant message when this checkbox is enabled — you can shout out but no one can shout back at you.

But with the default setting of denying all inbound connections, there will be times when you want to allow others access to your computer across the Internet. Applications such as instant messaging, Web servers, or online gaming may require contact from beyond your firewall. When that happens you must create an exception for the firewall that lets only that traffic in.

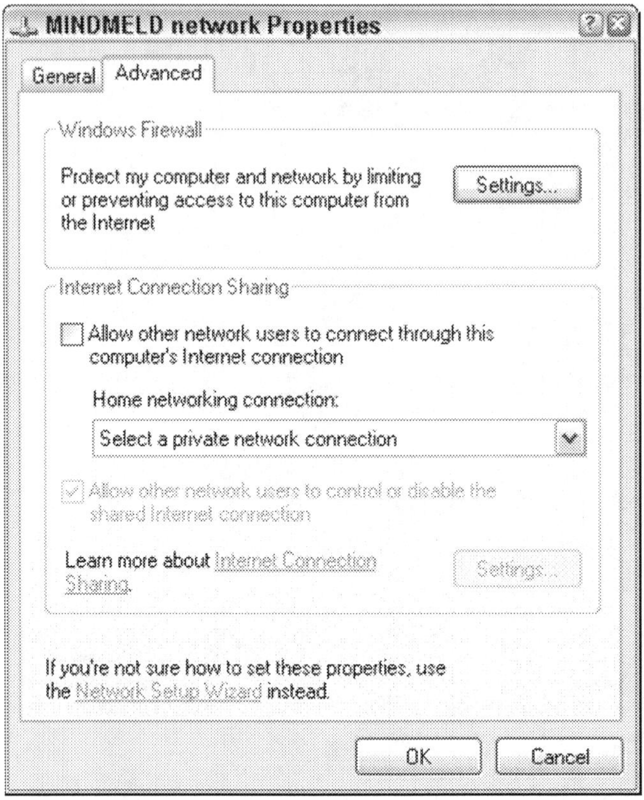

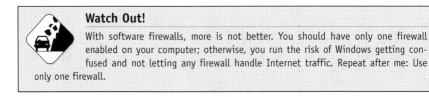

Figure 6.5. You can configure Windows Firewall for each network connection.

Click the Exceptions tab (see Figure 6.6). It shows you some preconfigured exceptions that have been added by Microsoft such as File and Printer
Sharing and Remote Assistance that are enabled by default. You can turn off
an exception by deselecting it. You can also remove an exception if you are
positive you will no longer need it by selecting it and then clicking Delete.
(Microsoft won't let you delete its preconfigured exceptions including the
two mentioned above plus UPnP Framework and Remote Desktop.)

---

**Watch Out!**

With software firewalls, more is not better. You should have only one firewall
enabled on your computer; otherwise, you run the risk of Windows getting confused and not letting any firewall handle Internet traffic. Repeat after me: Use
only one firewall.

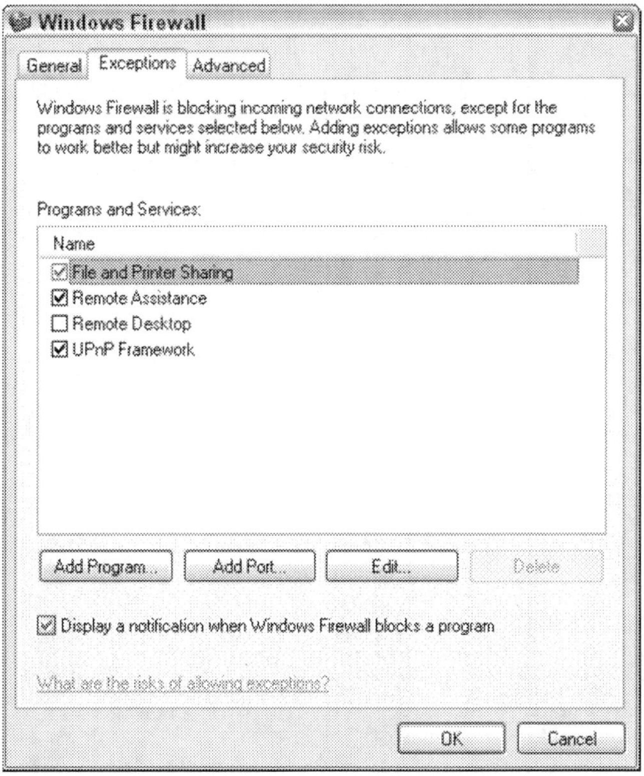

**Figure 6.6.** Exceptions are added and modified for applications that require access.

There are three ways to create your own exceptions for the list. The first is when Windows detects an incoming connection. It blocks the connection and warns you that a program is trying to make a connection with your computer (such as an instant messaging program). The alert dialog box gives you three choices:

- **Keep blocking.** No exception is created.

- **Unblock.** An exception is created and it is enabled, allowing traffic through to your machine.

- **Ask Me Later.** Creates an exception in the list but does not enable it, so the connection is blocked for now.

Your choice takes effect immediately, so if you grant an application access, it will begin communicating with your computer.

The second method is by creating an exception for a particular application that requires inbound connections. Click Add Program. Scroll down the list and select an application or click Browse to find the specific application.

Now click Change Scope. This lets you specify which other computers can get access to yours (see Figure 6.7). Your choices are Any computer, My network subnet, or Custom (enter the specific IP addresses to allow). Click OK and then click OK again. Your exception is enabled and entered into the list.

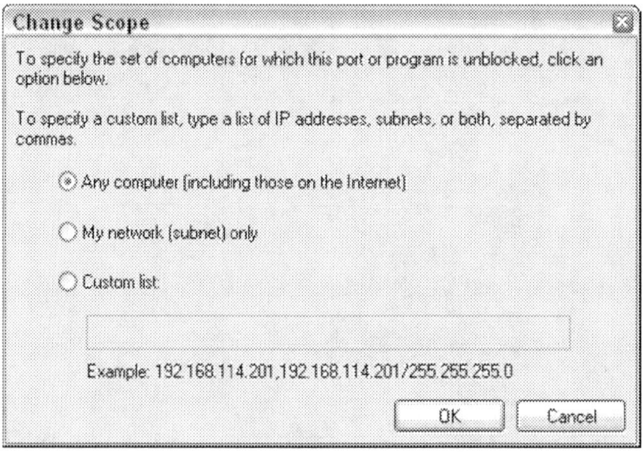

**Change Scope**

To specify the set of computers for which this port or program is unblocked, click an option below.

To specify a custom list, type a list of IP addresses, subnets, or both, separated by commas.

◉ Any computer (including those on the Internet)

○ My network (subnet) only

○ Custom list:

[                                              ]

Example: 192.168.114.201,192.168.114.201/255.255.255.0

[ OK ]  [ Cancel ]

**Figure 6.7.** The Change Scope dialog box lets you determine which computers can gain access to your computer.

The third method is by creating an exception based on a port, which is required if an application always uses a specific port for traffic. Some applications use more than one port, so an application exception by itself would not work. For this you will need to know the port numbers needed by your application as well as the type of communication, TCP (transmission control protocol), or UDP (user datagram protocol). Click Add Port. In the Add a Port dialog box (see Figure 6.8), type in a descriptive name for the port that will appear in the firewall exception list; type in the port number; and select the type of service. Click change scope, and make the appropriate selection

**Inside Scoop**

You've set up exceptions, and still can't connect? You must open ports in your hardware firewall as well. Some firewalls do this automatically for outbound traffic but require you to open ports for inbound traffic. Check your router instructions for more information.

the same way you did for an application exception. Click OK twice,
and the new port is enabled and
added to the firewall list.

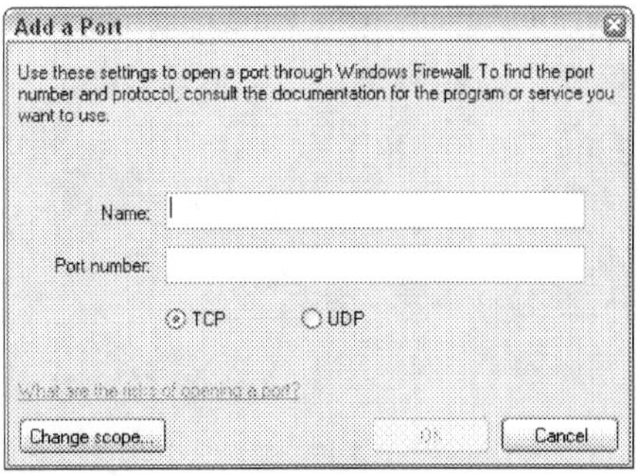

Servers are a special exception
to how Windows Firewall behaves.
If you want to run a Web server
or other Windows service, there
is another method for allowing
inbound connections. In the
Windows Firewall dialog box, click

**Add a Port**

Use these settings to open a port through Windows Firewall. To find the port
number and protocol, consult the documentation for the program or service you
want to use.

Name:

Port number:

⦿ TCP          ○ UDP

What are the risks of opening a port?

Change scope...          OK          Cancel

**Figure 6.8.** If you know the technical details of a
service, you can create a port-based exception.

the Advanced tab. In the Network Connection Settings box (see Figure 6.9),
select the connection that will provide the service and then click Settings.

**Windows Firewall**

General | Exceptions | Advanced

Network Connection Settings

Windows Firewall is enabled for the connections selected below. To add
exceptions for an individual connection, select it, and then click Settings:

☑ Local Area Connection          Settings...

Security Logging

You can create a log file for troubleshooting purposes.          Settings...

ICMP

With Internet Control Message Protocol (ICMP), the
computers on a network can share error and status
information.          Settings...

Default Settings

To restore all Windows Firewall settings to a default state,          Restore Defaults
click Restore Defaults.

OK          Cancel

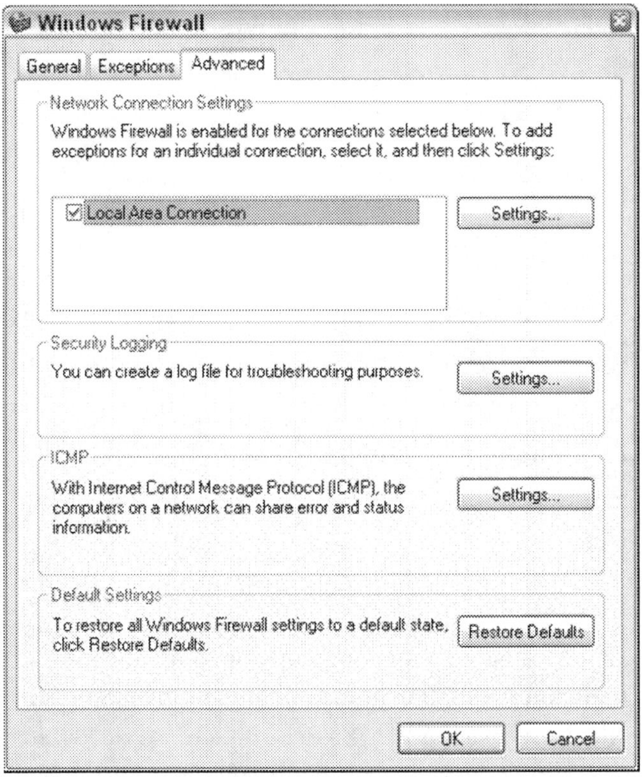

**Figure 6.9.** Setting up server access is deeply hidden within network settings.

The Advanced Settings dialog box (see Figure 6.10) lets you select which servers you want to make available through the Windows Firewall. This applies only to programs that register as a server, not for applications that let others connect to them, like game servers.

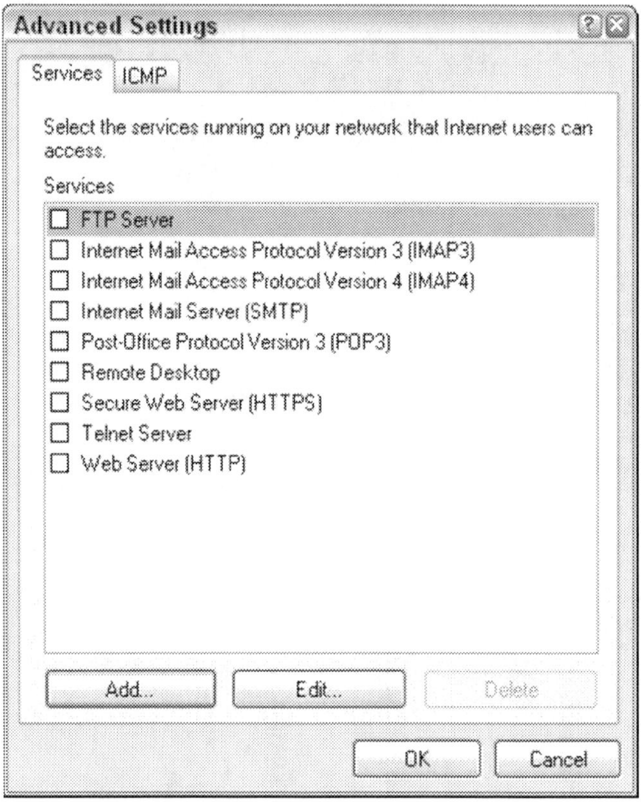

**Figure 6.10.** Any server registered with Windows can be made available to others.

If your computer is acting as a router for the rest of your home network by using one network adapter for the Internet and one for your local network, you can also use the Advanced Settings dialog box to grant access to a server residing elsewhere on your local network. This is an uncommon configuration but it can be done. Click Add. The Service Settings dialog box appears (see Figure 6.11), and it looks similar to the Add a Port dialog box, with entries for the service name, the IP address of the computer hosting the server, and a selection for TCP or UDP.

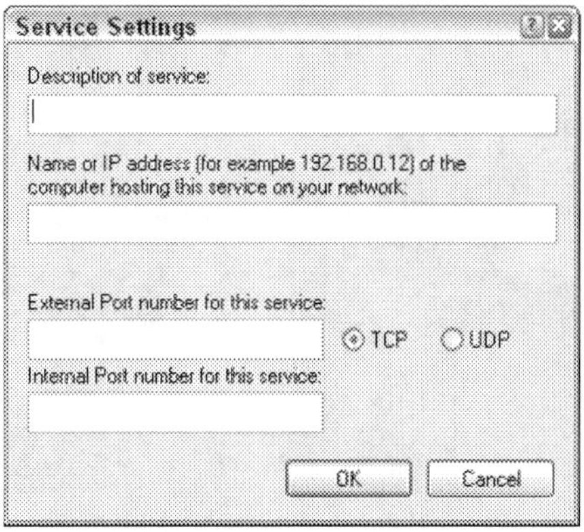

If you find that things have gotten out of control and you're not sure what is enabled, disabled, or providing you alerts, Windows Firewall has a "panic button." On any connection's firewall page, click the Advanced tab. At the bottom of the page is the Default Settings button, which restores the firewall's out-of-the-box settings for you.

The Windows Firewall settings are on a per-computer basis, not per-user, so the settings apply to

**Service Settings**

Description of service:

Name or IP address (for example 192.168.0.12) of the computer hosting this service on your network:

External Port number for this service:

⊙ TCP  ○ UDP

Internal Port number for this service:

OK    Cancel

**Figure 6.11.** You can hand-configure service parameters for applications you want to run as servers.

anyone who logs on to your computer. As a practical matter, this means you only have to configure the settings once. However, if you administer a domain, the Group Policy Editor (GPE) comes to the rescue again. You can set policies for the firewall settings depending on whether the computer is connected to a domain. Open the GPE by clicking Start, Run, typing gpedit.msc, and then pressing Enter. Browse to Computer Configuration\ Administrative Templates\Network\Network Connections\Windows Firewall (see Figure 6.12). The Domain Profile is used when the computer is connected to a domain, while the Standard Profile is used all other times. This gives you flexibility in setting up which applications are granted exceptions depending on where the computer is connected.

## Test your firewall

You have your firewall turned on, but how do you know it is doing the job? Are all ports closed, or are some open that you don't know about?

An independent Web site provides a port scan that checks to see if your computer is stealthy. Gibson Research Corporation runs the Shields UP! service at www.grc.com that will initiate a port scan against your computer and report back on what it finds. While there are other ways to check your computer's attack surface (usually using intrusion-oriented software), Shields UP! does it quickly and easily.

**Hack**

To show all open ports plus the process ID of which application opened the port, open a command prompt and type netstat /a /o. Most of these are harmless or required, but you should check this list occasionally for mystery entries.

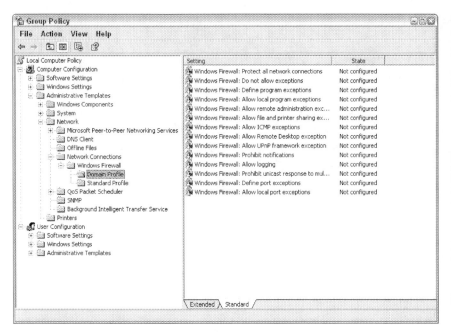

**Figure 6.12.** You can define separate firewall parameters depending on whether you are connected to a domain or not.

If you decide to run the check, consider this: Most hardware firewalls at businesses and corporations respond actively and aggressively to port scans — as they should. If you start a scan while behind the corporate firewall, you may receive a visit from several people in your IT department, wanting to know why you are triggering an all-out assault on the firewall. Get permission first before running the test.

You can usually run these tests from home without too much worry from your ISP (they have to leave most ports open because they don't know what services are needed by their clients), but you can always e-mail tech support and double-check to see if it's okay.

If a scan shows you have open ports you didn't know about, remove the exceptions from Windows Firewall or your third-party software and re-run the tests.

## Log firewall activity

Auditing is a key part of security; it is a record of activity that you want to track, such as dropped packets that indicate you may be under attack. Windows Firewall doesn't tell you when it blocks a potential attacker from connecting to your computer, but it does offer a logging function so you can audit the activity to see if the bad guys are actively attacking your computer.

To turn on logging, click the Advanced tab and then in the Security Logging section click Settings. The Log Setting dialog box appears (see Figure 6.13).

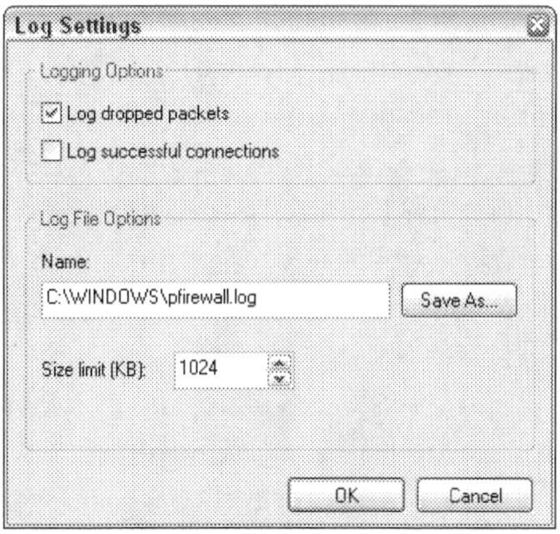

You can log dropped packets, ones that Windows Firewall thought may be harmful, and successful connections, any connection you or anyone else completes. Enable only the dropped packets log: A successful connections log will fill quickly and provide too much "static" to search through.

**Figure 6.13.** Selecting either check box turns on firewall logging.

You can also set the log file location and the log file size. The default location is not ideal, because most people don't check the contents of the Windows directory with any frequency. You are better off saving it to a location that you frequently browse so you are nudged to look through it every time you see it. The log file size can be up to a maximum of 32MB, though unless you are running a server you probably won't want it that large. One or two megabytes are manageable.

Auditing doesn't do any good if you don't review the audits. Windows Firewall generates logs using W3C Extended Log Format, which can be parsed and read by third-party utilities. You can also import it into Excel as a space-delimited file and use Excel's searching, sorting, and analyzing features to help you detect patterns in the dropped packets. If you detect a pattern, contact your IT department or ISP with the information so they can use more sophisticated techniques to find the attacker.

## Improve your firewall's protection

Windows Firewall does a decent, basic job of protecting your computer from inbound attacks. But it is not intended to be a full-featured program; others on the market stop outbound connections, provide more information about potential intruders and their attacks, or include antivirus protection, spyware detection and removal, and pop-up blockers.

**Bright Idea**

Microsoft has a decent article on interpreting the log file data. You can read it at http://support.microsoft.com/default.aspx?scid=kb;en-us;875357.

One of the best software-based firewalls is Zone Labs' ZoneAlarm, (www. zonealarm.com). The basic firewall, which is free, provides a high degree of configurability, stops outbound traffic, is easy to use, and provides plenty of information about programs that are attempting to gain access to your computer. The Security Suite also provides centralized alert monitoring and auditing, which is a huge help if you maintain your family or business's network. If you haven't tried it, you should.

Lastly, you can find an informative comparison and review of various firewall products at www.firewallguide.com/software.htm. There are a number of firewalls available, with different features, strengths, and price points. At least one of them would be a good replacement for Windows Firewall.

# Update your Windows installation

As time marches on, the busy programmers at Microsoft release software updates for Windows and Windows applications. Most often these are security updates intended to patch holes or strengthen known weaknesses. Some take the form of feature updates or driver fixes that are not considered as critical.

You should make sure that you are checking for updates on a regular basis. Microsoft provides three ways for you to keep your system up to date. One is done automatically for you using the Automatic Update service. One requires you to manually check for updates using the Windows Update Web site. The third is a new Web site from Microsoft that expands the Windows Update concept to include all Microsoft software on your computer, including the Office family of products. You can choose any or all of these services to keep your Windows installation up to date.

## Configure Automatic Updates

Automatic Updates is the Windows service that provides bug fixes, patches, and optional features that you can install on Windows. Automatic Updates finds all important updates for your computer, including security updates, critical updates, and service packs, and installs them automatically, so that you don't have to search for them or worry that some might be missing. These updates, which include critical updates and security updates, should be installed on your computer as soon as they are released, so that they can help protect your computer against viruses and other security threats.

**Watch Out!**

The update service replaces system files, so in order to install updates you must have local administrator rights.

You can still manually check for available updates, or disable Automatic Updates if you prefer to have more control over what your PC does in the background. Automatic Updates can still be reached from the Start Menu, but it is also part of the Security Center.

For most users, setting Automatic Updates to download and install high priority fixes is the easiest way to keep computers up-to-date. This allows users to help defend against hacker attempts and rogue programs that can corrupt or steal data from your computer.

You can view the Automatic Update settings two ways: click Start, click Control Panel, and then double-click Automatic Updates. Or you can click Start, click Run, type wscui.cpl, and then click OK. In the Manage security settings section, click Automatic Updates.

The Automatic Updates dialog box appears (see Figure 6.14), and there are only a few settings you can change.

- **Automatic.** Microsoft wants you to pick this, and for most people it is a decent choice. You can set a day and time for when Automatic Updates phones home to Microsoft to see if updates are available. If you leave your computer on all the time, you can pick a time in the early morning so that your normal work day isn't disrupted. Security Center displays a green light when you choose this option.

- **Download updates for me, but let me choose when to install them.** A self-explanatory option. However, I've noticed that Automatic Updates will alert you every ten minutes that you have updates ready to install. This gets annoying, especially when you're rushing to meet a deadline. It's a good choice if your computer is on but you're away from your desk frequently. A yellow light appears and you will see a yellow shield in the notification area, asking you to check your settings.

- **Notify me but don't automatically download or install them.** This is the Junior Power User option. Automatic Updates phones home and lets you know if anything is available,

**Figure 6.14.** Configure automatic update frequency to search for fixes on a regular basis.

and then it's up to you to manually download the necessary fixes at a time of your choosing. A yellow light appears and you will see a yellow shield in the notification area, asking you to check your settings.

▪ **Turn off automatic updates.** This is the Super Power User setting. Microsoft doesn't trust you to check for downloads regularly or to install them, and so you get a red light in the Security Center and a red shield in the notification area.

Select the level of updating you want to use and click OK.

## Manually update Windows

If you choose to monitor updates yourself, you can go to the Windows Update Web site and choose which updates you want to install. There are three ways you can connect to the Windows Update Web site. You can click Start, All Programs, and then Windows Update. Or you can open Security Center and click Check for the latest updates from Windows Update on the left-hand menu. Lastly, you can open Internet Explorer, click Tools, and then click Windows Update.

### Using the Windows Software Update Service

If you have just a few computers to manage, the Automatic Update service works fine, especially over a shared DSL or broadband connection. But once there are more than twenty-five computers updating themselves, it puts a strain on the network connection if all the computers are downloading the same fixes at the same time. It was also difficult for organizations that used a "standard desktop": The sudden influx of new code sometimes broke a carefully crafted operating environment.

Because of this, Microsoft developed the Windows Software Update Service. With this service, updates are downloaded to a server in the organization and then desktops receive their updates from that server. This meant that the fixes are downloaded only once, and IT departments can test the code and then schedule a time for the fixes to be rolled out across the organization.

If you are managing a significant number of desktops, it is worth your time to look into WSUS. You can find more information at www.microsoft.com/windowsserversystem/updateservices/downloads/ WSUS.mspx.

**Watch Out!**

The Windows Update Web site uses an ActiveX control that must be installed into Internet Explorer before the site will work. If you already installed SP2, you will get a security warning about the control. For this once, it's okay to install. Right-click the information bar and then click Install ActiveX control.

The site (see Figure 6.15) provides updates for the operating system and Windows-based hardware. It also has settings you can choose to affect which software packages are made available to you, and it also includes a helpful Automatic Updates reminder that lets you know if you're not configured to automatically download and install updates.

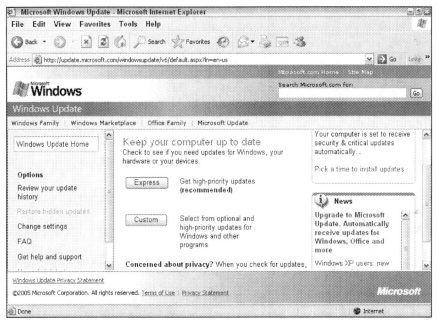

**Figure 6.15.** The Windows Update site lets you manually install updates to your computer.

The Windows Update packages address known issues and help protect against security threats. The download categories available are:

- **High priority.** These include critical updates, security updates, service packs, and update rollups that should be installed as soon as they become available and before you install any other updates.

- **Software, optional.** These include non-critical fixes for Windows programs, such as Windows Media Player and Windows Journal Viewer.

- **Hardware, optional.** These are non-critical fixes for drivers and other hardware devices, such as video cards, sound cards, scanners, printers, and cameras. Typically, these are drivers that have passed hardware testing (see the section on the Windows Catalog in Chapter 1) but are not necessarily the latest drivers from your hardware vendor. This does not include any updates for software packages that came with your hardware, such as DVD burning or music-playing software.

- **Beta software.** You can download and install pre-released "beta" versions of products as they become available. As usual, use beta software at your own risk; it is intended for testing and evaluation purposes only. Do not install beta software on your primary computer or production environment. The beta software category is not shown by default; to enable it, click Change settings in the left-hand menu and select Show beta products and related updates.

When you click the Express button, Windows Update prepares a list of all high-priority fixes. These are the same fixes that are downloaded by the Automatic Update service. The Custom button displays the high priority updates and the other update categories for your computer. You review and select the updates that you want to install.

One of the key benefits of visiting the Windows Update Web site is that updates Microsoft doesn't consider important are often found in the Software, Optional section. While fixes or product enhancements may not be high priority in terms of security, they may be important to you and your work. Check the Software, Optional category on a regular basis. The Automatic Update service only notifies you of high-priority fixes, and not the other categories, so you aren't notified of any driver fixes to your network adapter; you have to go digging for those on your own.

Lastly, if you are not the only person with local administrator rights on your computer, there may be "hidden updates" that were tucked away by someone else and are just waiting to be rediscovered. In every category but the high priority one, each software update's description has a checkbox at the end that reads, "Do not show this update again." There are various reasons why you

**Inside Scoop**

Unless it's a crisis-response update requiring immediate patching, Microsoft releases its high-priority fixes on or about the second Tuesday of each month. Various news sites have rumblings of the fixes, so you may have a few days' notice before the fixes are available.

would hide an update; for example, you will be removing an existing network card and replacing it with a new one, and updating the drivers for the old one is not needed. In that case, hiding the update is perfectly acceptable.

To show the updates again, under Options click Restore hidden updates. If there were any hidden ones they are back in full view, and you can select and install them.

# View or remove updates

Sometimes you may find that your system is less stable after you update a component. While this is not a frequent occurrence, given the complexity of Windows and the interlocking nature of many of its subsystems, it happens often enough that you may want to back out a "fix" that causes more trouble than it's worth.

You can view the update history on your local computer; you may find that the "fix" causing the problem failed its install.

On the Windows Update Web site, under Options click Review your update history. The site (see Figure 6.16) presents you with a table showing you each update, when it was installed, and its status. You can print out the entire table or just the current page for reference, which is helpful when you are searching the Microsoft Knowledge Base for other reports of headache-causing fixes.

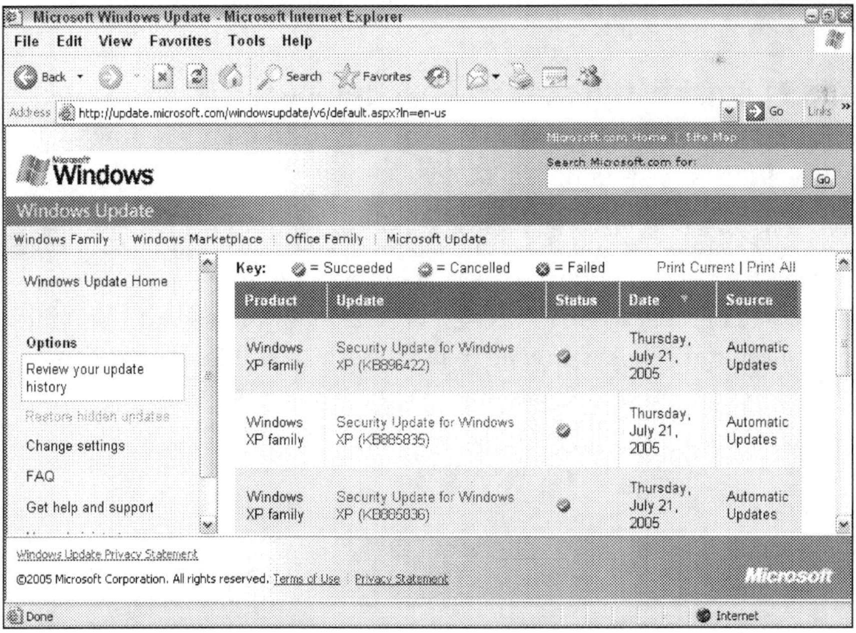

**Figure 6.16.** You can review your system's updates and status, such as a failed update.

**Hack**

Even if someone has local administrator rights over his computer, you can limit or disable the various update services. Click Start, Run, type gpedit.msc, and then click OK. Browse to Computer Configuration\Administrative Templates\WindowsComponents\ Windows Update and browse the options available to you.

From this list you can get the name of the fix and often the Knowledge Base article number that discusses the fix. With the fix's name, you often can use Add / Remove Programs to remove the specific fix that is causing problems. With the Knowledge Base article (the KB number you may see in the fix's name), you can go to http://support.microsoft.com and do a search using the number as a search term. You can then research to see if there are any specific requirements for using the fix, or any subsequent articles that suggest workarounds or repair strategies if the fix was "broken" on delivery.

However, there are some updates that cannot be uninstalled. These are most often specific security updates or updates to core system services. For example, Windows Media Player 10 cannot be uninstalled once you install it on a system. At that point you have only the brute force method of using the System Restore to roll your entire system back to a point before you installed the update. This means that any applications you installed after the fix will have to be reinstalled.

## Add Microsoft Updates to your computer

Microsoft ran two separate "update" sites for its users: Windows Update and Office Update. The only connection between the two was a link from Windows Update to the Office Update Web site, but otherwise they did not coexist or share information, until recently.

Microsoft created a "Microsoft Update" Web site that is used to update Windows, Office, and other Microsoft applications. It looks and feels much the same as the Windows Update Web site (see Figure 6.17), with the exception of adding Office products into the mix. (If you don't have Microsoft Office installed, you will not see any Office updates available.)

The Web site also adds a shortcut to the Start menu. To check for future updates, click Start, All Programs, and then Microsoft Update.

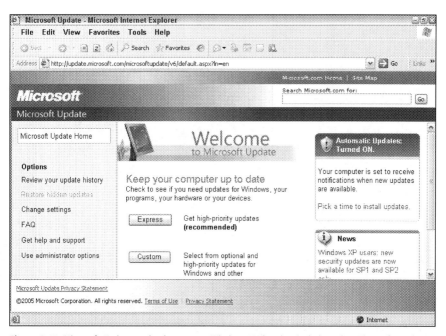

**Figure 6.17.** Microsoft Update works the same as Windows Update but includes other Microsoft products.

# Add antivirus protection

Antivirus protection is a requirement for every computer that participates on a network. Viruses, worms, and Trojan horse applications can wreak havoc with your computer by spamming all the addresses in your e-mail address book or turning your PC into a "zombie" that is under the control of someone else on the Internet. Antivirus applications run scans on e-mail coming into your computer and scan each application as it starts, looking for telltale signatures that identify some code as containing a virus.

One of the saddest things about Security Center is that, of the three "pillars of security" that Microsoft emphasizes, antivirus software is not present anywhere in Windows. And with viruses being the most common form of attack, getting warnings from Security Center is almost humorous: "You're not protected, but we can't do anything about it."

So as part of its security strategy Microsoft relies on third-party vendors to provide protection for the core operating system components as well as e-mail applications. The Security Center monitors third-party virus protection tools and notifies you if the virus definition files are out-of-date, or if the software itself is not functioning correctly, such as an expired virus definition subscription.

If you haven't installed antivirus software, the question isn't whether you'll be attacked, but *when*. Run, don't walk, to the nearest Web site that sells antivirus software and install it *now*. You will be smiling with glee when that first alert pops up, telling you it snagged a dangerous payload on your incoming e-mail, or that it stopped an innocuous-looking Web site from running a nasty applet on your computer.

Microsoft isn't completely ignorant of the danger from an unprotected computer. They recently purchased an antivirus company, so someday soon there may be a Microsoft-branded antivirus product available on the market. If you don't know what product to install, Microsoft gives you a list of vendors that sell antivirus software (see Figure 6.18). Open the Security Center and then click the Recommendations button. You can find a list of Microsoft partners that provide antivirus software by clicking Get another antivirus program. The list is also available at www.microsoft.com/athome/security/ viruses/wsc/en-us/default.mspx.

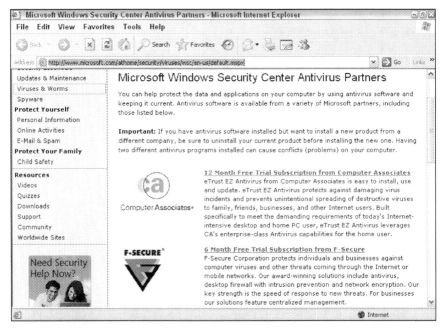

**Figure 6.18.** Microsoft is pleased to recommend you to "antivirus partners" should you wish to protect your computer.

## One author's antivirus experience

In my quest for antivirus software, I have tried some of the market leaders and a few of the second-tier vendors. Here are my impressions, which are neither scientific nor comprehensive, but feel free to use them as data points in your own market research.

Trend Micro's PC-cillin is my favorite to date. It's lightweight, fast, and updated aggressively. It has a yearly subscription fee but given the updates and product quality, it's worth it. This company started out building server-side virus scanners, and that experience carries over to the desktop. Highly recommended.

Norton Antivirus was on my machine for a long time. Its positives are that it's a robust scanner and it's easy to configure and use. Negatives are that it's *very* slow, eats up a lot of system resources, it has a yearly subscription, and my experience with Symantec's tech support was dismal. If you have it, stick with it; if you don't, look elsewhere.

McAfee's Virus Scan was on my computer and then off it inside of a month. I found it very slow, awkward to configure and use, and it has a yearly subscription fee. I can't recommend it.

Other antivirus applications I have had experience with are ZoneAlarm, F-Secure, F-Prot, and Panda. None of them impressed me enough to recommend or downcheck any of them, and they have their advocates for different reasons, such as speed, system resources consumed, or update frequency.

All of these companies offer downloadable trial versions. Don't feel you have to stick with one; download several, install them one at a time, see how you like a particular program, then uninstall it and try a different one. Check various comparative Web sites for reviews that run the scanners against live viruses to see how they perform. Then buy one, and rest a little easier knowing your computer is quite a bit safer.

You can find more objective evaluations of antivirus products at www. software-antivirus.com and antivirus software certifications at www.icsalabs. com. PC Magazine is also a pretty good source of information, though the Web site at www.pcmag.com is cluttered and difficult to navigate, and the search function is more likely to link to advertisements than to product reviews. This is one of the rare times that I recommend checking out the print edition from a local library rather than digging through layers of links on a Web site.

**Bright Idea!**

Most antivirus companies offer a real-time virus scan from their Web site, allowing you to see if you are currently infected. Most also offer scans for spyware. Run the scans; you may be surprised at what they find lurking on your computer.

When installing antivirus software you should follow its directions to the letter. This includes shutting down all applications before running setup. All software runs a preliminary scan to determine if you have any boot sector viruses and then will install itself and retrieve updated virus definition files (if needed). An antivirus software program typically offers to do a full system scan; click Yes and go get some lunch. By the time you get back your computer should have a clean bill of health.

# Add anti-spyware

Spyware is often used to mean just about everything bad that can be put onto a computer. Technically, it is software that is designed to capture user behavior or personal information and report it back to a central location. Spyware is often found in other software programs or is downloaded as part of a Windows enhancement. The most common types of spyware track your Web surfing habits and report it to another site, usually one involved in advertising, that then delivers "customized" ads and pop-ups to your computer based on your surfing habits.

The worst types of spyware actually spy on you: called key loggers, they record every keystroke in hopes of catching you type something useful, like your password to a financial Web site or private correspondence related to litigation.

Spyware is often disguised as a payload within another program, such as peer-to-peer software or Windows interface enhancements like screen savers or custom cursor packages. You can download and install something that is fun and entertaining, while in the background the spyware is watching you. It sounds like paranoia, but it can be a real problem, especially when the spyware targets your personal information.

## Install Microsoft Windows AntiSpyware

For a long time, Microsoft took little notice of spyware as a threat. No mention of it was made anywhere in Security Center, and even the Microsoft Web site was silent on the topic — other than reciting the mantra, "Don't install software you don't trust," Microsoft acted as if the fault lay with the user, not weaknesses in the operating system.

## How to avoid spyware

Spyware, by definition, is sneaky. You will not see a pop-up that announces, "I'm spyware! Want to install me?" Instead it comes in either as a tracking cookie that gets past Internet Explorer's "security" zones, or it is installed as part of another program's setup procedure. To avoid spyware, short of disconnecting your computer from the Internet forever, there are a few precautions you can take.

- Don't install dubious software that does dubious things. People will readily install a file-sharing application that is designed to circumvent copyright and security measures, and then wonder why the computer suddenly is slower, spawns pop-ups, or hijacks the browser's home page.

- Don't install cute icons, screensavers, search toolbars from oddball Web sites, or other interface enhancements. Leave well enough alone.

- Don't install hacked or cracked software. If someone broke the copy protection, they can bundle in anything else if they have a mind to. Besides, you should be a good net citizen and pay for software you use.

- Don't run Internet Explorer. Use another browser, such as Firefox, Mozilla, or Opera. Even with SP2 enhancements, IE is the target of most bad guys, and the bad guys can crank out nasty code faster than Microsoft can issue patches.

Microsoft finally broke radio silence in December 2004 with the purchase of a company that manufactured anti-spyware software. In conjunction with the purchase Microsoft issued a strategy document stating the problem and setting out Microsoft's approach to helping remove spyware from the desktop.

**Bright Idea**

Read the Microsoft spyware strategy document at www.microsoft.com/athome/ security/spyware/strategy.mspx. It provides a good outline of what spyware is, what it does, and what to look for. The parent Web site, www.microsoft.com/ spyware, goes into more detail about Microsoft's spyware strategy.

As of this writing Microsoft has a free download of Microsoft Windows AntiSpyware in beta form (see Figure 6.19). You can download and install the software on your computer and use it to find and remove spyware.

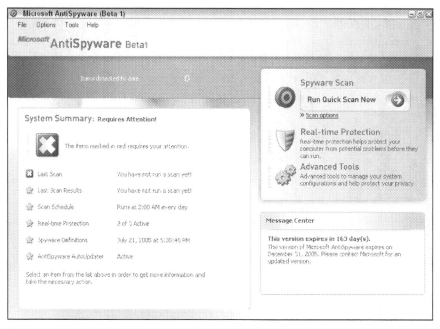

**Figure 6.19.** Microsoft's AntiSpyware beta software helps remove spyware from your computer.

As with most Microsoft programs, there are some gotchas. But because these are based on beta software, they may be fixed by the time the software is released in full form.

First, Microsoft requires that you install an ActiveX control that validates you are running "genuine Microsoft Windows" (see Figure 6.20). Microsoft has always had concerns about hacked or pirated copies of Windows floating around in the market (see Chapter 1 for a discussion of product activation), and this is another way of checking to see if you've been bad or good. While the validation process won't keep you from downloading the software, it does place another registry key on your computer that in theory enables faster downloads. It is also not a far reach to conclude that at some point you will not be able to download fixes or updates if you are not running "genuine Microsoft software."

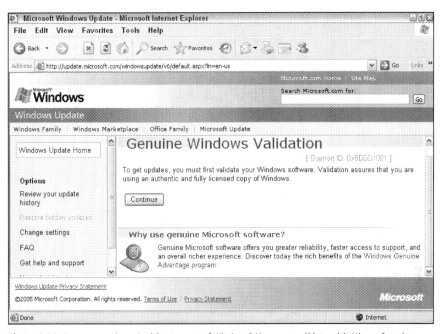

**Figure 6.20.** Are you running a legitimate copy of Windows? You must validate with Microsoft to be sure.

Next, Giant Antispyware (the software's original name) was a subscription-only product, requiring a yearly fee. Microsoft has not said whether it will continue to require a subscription fee for its spyware, or whether it will be free for personal use. The beta software is a time bomb version that ends on December 31, 2005. This implies that Microsoft intends to charge for spyware removal, but as noted above this may change with the final release.

Lastly, as of this writing, Microsoft had changed the detection profile for Claria (formerly Gator) from "quarantine" to "ignore," meaning that the software would not take action if any of Claria's spyware was found on the system. Claria, the rebranded name for Gator, is one of the most notorious and prevalent of the spyware manufacturers. Microsoft responded that it made the change at the request of Claria because Microsoft felt the software met the less stringent definitions for ignoring rather than quarantining. Sadly, buyout talks between Microsoft and Claria were in progress at the time the spyware reclassification was made (the buyout talks have since been canceled), leading many in the industry to recommend removing Microsoft Windows AntiSpyware and using other software instead.

**Bright Idea**

Well-respected columnist Brian Livingston explains why Microsoft blew its chance for industry leadership with its bonehead partnership with the industry's most notorious spyware maker. Read the details at www.windowssecrets.com/comp/ 050714/#baseli and determine if you want to continue using Microsoft's anti-spyware software.

You can keep up to date on spyware and the attempts by the bad guys to hijack your computer at www.netrn.net/spywareblog.

## Install other anti-spyware software

Other companies have rushed to fill the void left by Microsoft, and several companies have made excellent products that detect and remove spyware. Many of them have spyware detection tools on their Web sites that will scan your computer and let you know if any spyware is found.

One of the highest-rated products is Sunbelt Software's CounterSpy at www.sunbelt-software.com. For $19.95 per year you get award-winning anti-spyware and real-time threat protection. Though the Web site has too much hyperbole (usually indicative of marketing fluff over substance), the awards and reviews from various industry magazines praise CounterSpy for its features and power.

If free anti-spyware products that are almost as good sound like a deal, take a look at Lavasoft's Ad-Aware SE (see Figure 6.21) at www.lavasoft.com and Spybot Search & Destroy at www.safer-networking.org. Both have fared very well over the years, and both sell "pro" versions that have real-time threat protection and enhanced monitoring capabilities.

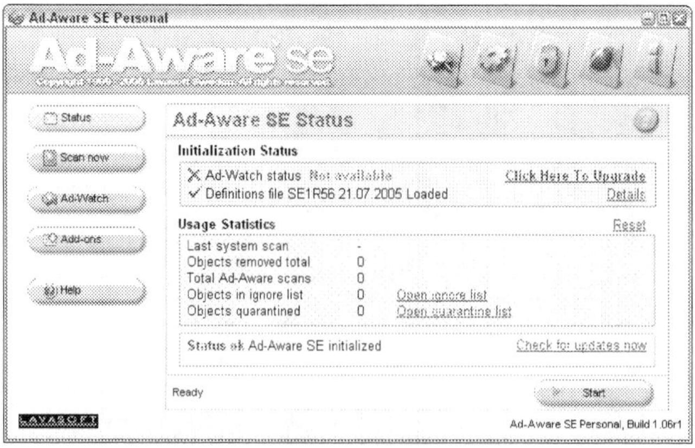

**Figure 6.21.** Lavasoft's Ad-Aware SE offers thorough spyware scanning – for free!

## Spy versus Spy

With any software that provides real-time scanning and prevention, like firewalls or antivirus software, you should have only one installed and running on your computer at a time. With spyware scanners, if you aren't running a real-time scan, you can install one or more of them and run scans on a regular basis.

For several years now I have had both Ad-Aware and Spybot Search & Destroy installed, and I flip-flop which one I run first. Every now and again one of them will catch something the other missed, so while it may seem like a "belt and suspenders" setup, I sleep better at night knowing that they have caught all the oddball spyware that was placed on my computer despite my best efforts to prevent it.

As with antivirus software, the lead as to which product is considered "the best" changes on a monthly basis as new versions leapfrog over competitors. Recent reviews of the most popular anti-spyware products, including ease of use and scanning efficiency, can be found at www.pcworld.com/reviews/article/0,aid,119572,pg,1,00.asp. Most vendors offer trial versions so you can download, install, and see which ones work the best for you.

# Add a logon warning

The Welcome screen in Windows XP is generic and non-threatening. Most people don't think twice about it, and will try to log on to any machine on the assumption that if it's in the open it must be available to anyone.

With Windows 2000, clever administrators could make registry hacks that added a logon warning and a logon notification in the title bar. In essence, it acted kind of like a EULA (enterprise universal licensing agreement): If you had to click through it, it was tough to argue later that you hadn't been presented with a warning.

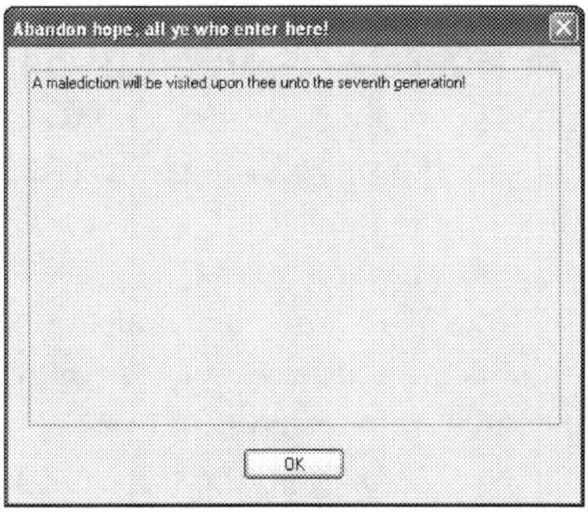

This fun trick is also available in Windows XP (see Figure 6.22), though it's more useful for business and corporate users than for the

**Figure 6.22.** Logon warnings give notice that people should not mess with your computer.

average home user. Yes, you can threaten your family with the flames of perdition, but is that really necessary?

It is also much easier to manage as it is now part of the Security Policy editor and does not require rolling out registry hacks to domain computers. In fact, with domains, you can change the logon warning. The procedure varies depending on whether you are editing the property for a domain, organizational unit, or computer.

## Configuring a logon message for a domain

On the domain controller, start the Active Directory Users and Computers snap-in. Right-click the domain object in the left pane, and then click Properties. Click the Group Policy tab. Click Default Domain Policy, and then click Edit. Browse to Configuration\Windows Settings\Security Settings\ Local Policies\Security Options.

In the right pane, double-click Policies, and then follow these steps to create the message text:

- On a Windows Server 2003-based domain controller, click Interactive log on: Message title for users attempting to log on, and then type the text that you want to appear in the title bar of the message dialog box. Then click Interactive log on: Message text for users attempting to log on, and then type the text of the message that you want to appear in the message dialog box.

- On a Windows 2000-based domain controller, click Message title for users attempting to log on, and then type the text that you want to appear in the title bar of the message dialog box. Click Message text for users attempting to log on, and then type the text of the message that you want to appear in the message dialog box.

## Configure a logon message for an organizational unit

On the domain controller, start the Active Directory Users and Computers snap-in. Right-click the organizational unit object in the left pane, and then click Properties. Click the Group Policy tab, and then click New. Type a name for the Group Policy Object (GPO), and then press Enter. Click Edit.

Browse to Computer Configuration\Windows Settings \Security Settings\ Local Policies\Security Options. In the right pane, double-click Policies, and then follow these steps to create the message text:

- On a Windows Server 2003-based domain controller, click Interactive log on: Message title for users attempting to log on, and then type the text that you want to appear in the title bar of the message dialog box. Then click Interactive log on: Message text for users attempting to log on, and then type the text of the message that you want to appear in the message dialog box.

■ On a Windows 2000-based domain controller, click Message title for users attempting to log on, and then type the text that you want to appear in the title bar of the message dialog box. Then click Message text for users attempting to log on, and then type the text of the message that you want to appear in the message dialog box.

## Configure a logon message for Windows XP

With Windows XP, either a standalone computer or a member of a workgroup, the process is a little simpler. Click Start, click Run, type secpol.msc, and then press Enter. The Local Security Policy Editor appears. Browse to Local Policies\Security Options (see Figure 6.23). Click Interactive log on: Message title for users attempting to log on, and then type the text that you want to appear in the title bar of the message dialog box. Then click Interactive log on: Message text for users attempting to log on, and then type the text of the message that you want to appear in the message dialog box.

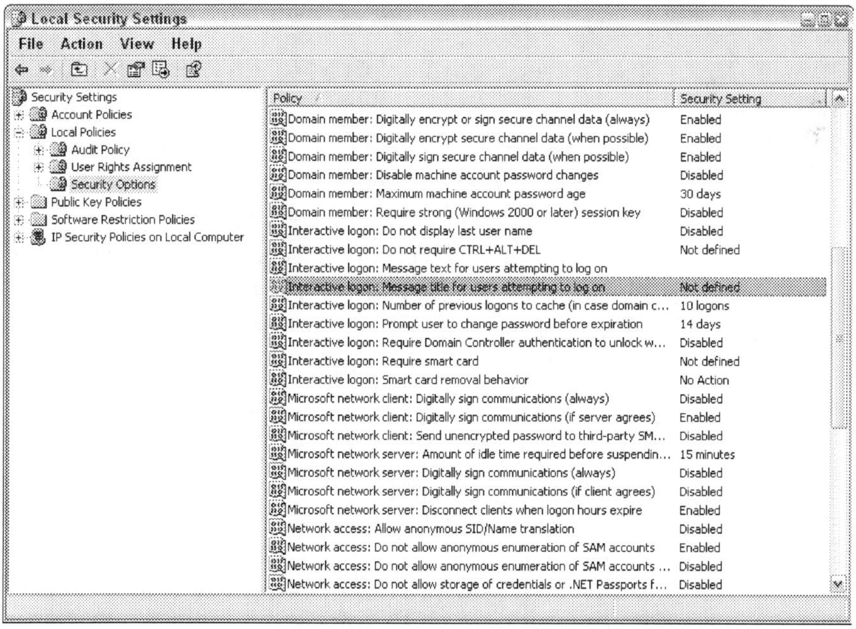

**Figure 6.23.** The Security Policy Editor lets you configure custom logon warning messages.

> **Hack**
>
> You can hide the last user's name in the Log On dialog box. Click Start, Run, type secpol.msc, and then press Enter. Browse to Local Policies\Security Options and then enable Interactive log on: Do not display last user name. This takes away one piece of the authentication puzzle from bad guys: the user ID.

# Analyze your computer's security

Microsoft Windows XP is a complex operating system, capable of working as a standalone desktop and as a node on a multi-national network. The Security Center provides you with the status of the external-facing "attack surfaces," but there are plenty of other ways that bad guys can attack the system. These are most commonly associated with misconfigured systems, where particular security features are disabled and allow the bad guys to circumvent security.

The complexity and out-of-the-box settings on Microsoft products led many security experts to complain about the openness of the operating system. There were far too many security checklists and best-practices documents that required users to change the default settings to improve security. While the changes may have been applied in a large corporate setting, most home or SOHO users either didn't know or didn't take advantage of the checklists to help secure the desktop.

Finally, Microsoft heard the complaints of the experts and the cries of the desperate and created a program to check your system's security. The download, which suggests you "validate" that you are running a "genuine Microsoft Windows" program, can be found at www.microsoft.com/mbsa (see Figure 6.24).

The Microsoft Baseline Security Analyzer (MBSA) 2.0 is an easy-to-use tool that helps small and medium businesses determine their security state in accordance with Microsoft security recommendations and offers specific remediation guidance. It allows you to improve your security management process by using MBSA to detect common security misconfigurations and missing security updates on your computer systems.

One of the cool things about MBSA is that it does not have to be installed on every computer; it can remotely scan computers in your network or in your domain for security vulnerabilities. If you administer any size network, this is a good way to find out if any of your computers at home or in a small office have any potential holes in them.

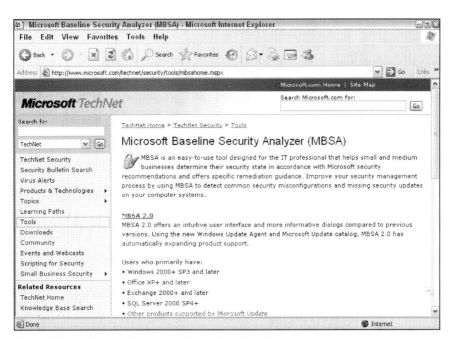

**Figure 6.24.** The Microsoft Security Baseline Analyzer Web site gives you access to a handy security tool.

## MBSA 2.0 versus MBSA 1.2

When you visit the Microsoft Baseline Security Analyzer Web site, you can choose between version 1.2 and 2.0. The primary differences between the two versions are the earlier version supports scanning Windows NT machines, plus older versions of SQL Server, IIS, and Microsoft Office. Version 2.0 supports only Windows 2000, Windows XP (32- and 64-bit), and Windows Server 2003, plus the newest versions of SQL Server, IIS, and Office XP.

You can see a list of supported software at http://support. microsoft.com/?scid=kb;en-us;895660. If you have older software on your network, you can run both MBSA versions to determine security holes on machines in your network.

MBSA assigns severity ratings to the problems it finds and provides you with information on how to close the holes or how to find software updates that patch any known vulnerabilities. MBSA also scans Office XP products, so if you are a true-blue Microsoft shop, you can find and fix holes in your Office applications, especially for Outlook's virus definition files or the macro engine in Office.

To install MBSA 2.0, download it from the link and then double-click the .msi file. Click Next (see Figure 6.25). Select I accept the license agreement and then click Next. Choose the folder where you want to install MBSA. Click Next and then click Install. When setup has completed, click OK.

**Figure 6.25.** The Microsoft Security Baseline Analyzer installation program only needs to be run on one machine.

To run MBSA, click Start, All Programs, and then Microsoft Baseline Security Analyzer 2.0. You can select a scan of one or more computers, and you can scan by domain or by IP range. Click Scan a computer, select the options to scan for (see Figure 6.26), and then click Start scan. You can deselect the IIS and SQL Server scans if you know those services are not

**Watch Out!**

If you install MBSA on a Windows XP machine that is using simple file sharing, you can only run scans on that machine. To run on other machines you need local administrator rights on each machine, and you need to be running NTFS file sharing.

installed on your computer, but it doesn't hurt to run the scan anyway, so leave them enabled. The scan may take several minutes as MBSA downloads security update information from Microsoft, and then scans the computers you selected.

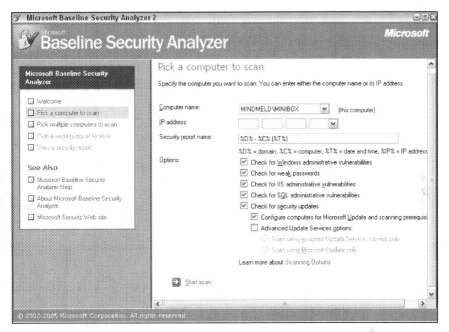

**Figure 6.26.** You can run thorough scans with the security analyzer or focus only on specific areas.

When the scan is complete, you will see a report of each computer you have scanned and, in many cases, be provided links to descriptions of what was scanned, result details, and suggestions for how to fix the problem (see Figure 6.27). Some of the negative findings may be acceptable risks for your computer, for example if any drives are running FAT32 instead of NTFS.

You can print out a hard copy of the results and include it in a network notebook for your computers, or you can copy the results to an Excel or Word document for further filtering and sorting.

**Inside Scoop**

While you can run MBSA manually, smart administrators use scripts to perform the scans. This is much faster, much easier, and makes you look smart. You can find MBSA scripts at www.microsoft.com/technet/security/tools/mbsa2/default.mspx.

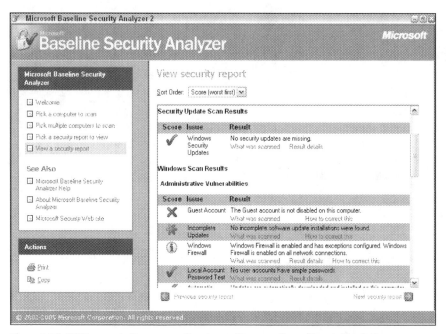

**Figure 6.27.** MBSA presents the scan results, along with suggestions of how to repair them.

# Analyze and apply security templates

Most home and SOHO computers are installed with the out-of-the-box settings intact. As noted in the previous section this is not always a good idea,
especially if your computer has its settings less secure than they could be.
With Security Templates, you can create a security policy for your computer.
The templates are a single point of entry where the full range of system security can be taken into account. Security Templates do not introduce new
security parameters; they simply organize all existing security attributes into
one place to ease security administration.

One tool that Microsoft provides users of Windows XP (and Windows
2000) is the Security Configuration and Analysis (SCA) snap-in. The snap-in
is not normally installed with any of the Administrative Tools, but users can
add the snap-in to the Microsoft Management Console and run an analysis
of any computer on their network.

The analysis shows you which Group Policy settings are applied and
which should be changed to improve security. In addition, Microsoft provides security templates that you can apply depending on the role your

computer plays. If it's a publicly-visible server, security should be locked down as tightly as possible to reduce the attack surface. If it's a standalone computer in a home office, less stringent security is needed to protect the computer.

The SCA snap-in differs from the Microsoft Baseline Security Analyzer (MBSA) in that it analyzes your computer based on its role in the organization. The MBSA is a much broader tool, determining whether basic global security precautions are in place, such as the most recent security patches. SCA runs over your computer and user settings with a fine-tooth comb.

# Install and run the Security and Configuration Analysis snap-in

To install the SCA snap-in, click Start, Run, type mmc, and then press Enter. The Microsoft Management Console appears. Click File and then Add/Remove Snap-in. Click Add, scroll down the list to Security Configuration and Analysis, select it (see Figure 6.28), and then click Add. Click Close and then click OK. The snap-in appears in the management console.

To run an analysis against the local computer, right-click the SCA snap-in and then click Open Database. Type a name for your

**Figure 6.28.** MBSA presents the scan results, along with suggestions of how to repair them.

machine's database and then click Open. You are presented with a choice of seven templates that you can compare your existing settings against (see Figure 6.29). The available templates include:

- Reapplying default settings. (Setup security.inf)
- Implementing a highly secure environment. (Hisecws.inf)
- Implementing a less secure but more compatible environment. (Compatws.inf)
- Securing the system root. (Rootsec.inf)

## About the Microsoft Management Console

The Microsoft Management Console, or MMC, is a generic framework for computer and network management components called snap-ins. The snap-ins can be added into the framework in any combination and then saved as "views" on the desktop (or distributed to others on the network). This flexibility lets IT administrators mix and match and assign administrative rights to others, such as the ability to reset user passwords but not change a user's group membership.

Windows XP ships with a number of pre-built views including the Administrator Tools\Computer Management console. Others are included in the Windows\system32 directory that end with the file extension .msc. You launch these consoles by typing the name and .msc extension in the Start, Run box.

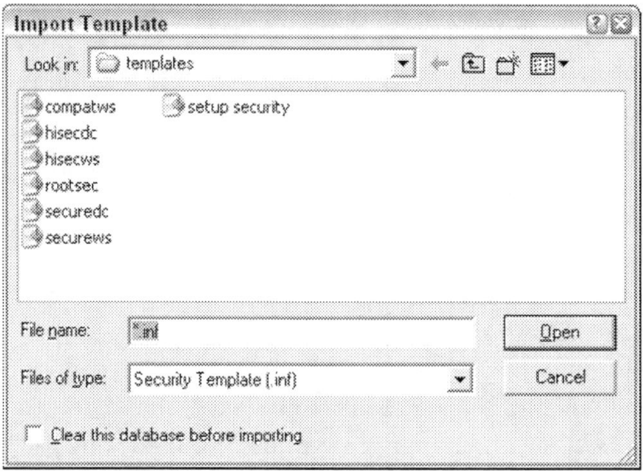

**Figure 6.29.** Select a security template to compare your computer against.

You can find excellent descriptions of these templates and any warnings or system requirements before applying them in the Help and Support Center. Do a search for "predefined security templates" and click on the link entitled, aptly enough, "Predefined Security Templates."

**Bright Idea**

You can add the Security Templates snap-in to MMC and examine all the security templates' settings at the same time. This lets you see which one would be easiest to modify for your own needs.

Select the template you wish to use and click Open. The database is created. Right-click the SCA snap-in and then click Analyze Computer Now (see Figure 6.30). Type a path for the log file or accept the default which is located in Documents and Settings\%username%\My Documents\Security\Logs. Click OK to perform the analysis.

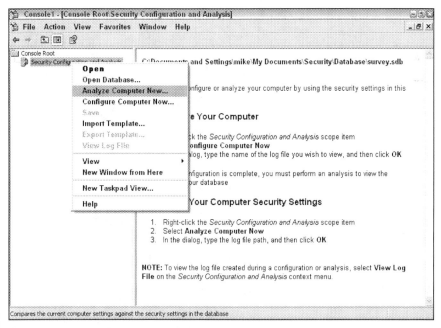

**Figure 6.30.** Select Analyze Computer Now to compare your settings against a template.

When the analysis is complete, you can view the results in the snap-in (see Figure 6.31). Depending on which template you used to compare recommended settings versus what is configured on your computer, you will see red Xs on settings that do not match the recommended ones, and green check marks that do match the recommended ones.

| Policy | Database Setting | Computer Setting |
|---|---|---|
| Accounts: Administrator account status | Not defined | Enabled |
| Accounts: Guest account status | Disabled | Disabled |
| Accounts: Limit local account use of blank passwords to console... | Enabled | Enabled |
| Accounts: Rename administrator account | Not Analyzed | Administrator |
| Accounts: Rename guest account | Not Analyzed | Guest |
| Audit: Audit the access of global system objects | Disabled | Disabled |
| Audit: Audit the use of Backup and Restore privilege | Disabled | Disabled |
| Audit: Shut down system immediately if unable to log security a... | Disabled | Disabled |
| DCOM: Machine Access Restrictions in Security Descriptor Defin... | Not Analyzed | Not Analyzed |
| DCOM: Machine Launch Restrictions in Security Descriptor Defi... | Not Analyzed | Not Analyzed |
| Devices: Allow undock without having to log on | Disabled | Disabled |
| Devices: Allowed to format and eject removable media | Administrators | Administrators |
| Devices: Prevent users from installing printer drivers | Enabled | Enabled |
| Devices: Restrict CD-ROM access to locally logged-on user only | Disabled | Disabled |
| Devices: Restrict floppy access to locally logged-on user only | Disabled | Disabled |
| Devices: Unsigned driver installation behavior | Warn but allow inst... | Warn but allow inst... |
| Domain controller: Allow server operators to schedule tasks | Not Analyzed | Not Analyzed |
| Domain controller: LDAP server signing requirements | Not Analyzed | Not Analyzed |
| Domain controller: Refuse machine account password changes | Not Analyzed | Not Analyzed |
| Domain member: Digitally encrypt or sign secure channel data (... | Disabled | Disabled |
| Domain member: Digitally encrypt secure channel data (when p... | Enabled | Enabled |
| Domain member: Digitally sign secure channel data (when possi... | Enabled | Enabled |
| Domain member: Disable machine account password changes | Disabled | Disabled |
| Domain member: Maximum machine account password age | 30 days | 30 days |
| Domain member: Require strong (Windows 2000 or later) sessi... | Disabled | Disabled |
| Interactive logon: Do not display last user name | Disabled | Disabled |
| Interactive logon: Do not require CTRL+ALT+DEL | Disabled | Disabled |

**Figure 6.31.** Your computer's settings are compared to the ones in the security template.

The log file is in text format, so you can review the files in any text editor. The files can be rather lengthy, so you're better off letting the snap-in do all the work.

When you are done reviewing the settings, you can close the MMC. You will be asked to save the view you have created. If you thought it was handy, feel free to save the changes. The MMC defaults to saving the views in the Administrator Tools folder, which is a good place for them.

## Apply security templates

Now that you have a report on the potential shortcomings of your computer's settings, you can choose to apply a template to your computer and change the settings to the ones recommended for your desired security level. You can also choose to edit the imported template's settings so that they match your company's policies. For example, the maximum password age of forty-two days may be too few; you can double-click the setting, change it to ninety days, and then re-run the analysis if you want.

---

**Watch Out!**

If you have made any changes to the template you should export the changes to a new template instead of overwriting the old one. Right-click the SCA snap-in and select Export Template.

To apply the template to your computer, right-click the Security and Configuration Analysis snap-in and then click Configure Computer Now (see Figure 6.32). Type or browse to a location for the error log and then click OK. The SCA snap-in applies all the template settings to your computer. Some of the settings may not take effect until the next time you log out and back on again.

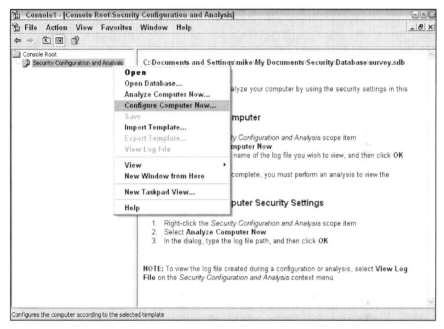

**Figure 6.32.** Select Configure Computer Now to apply the template settings to your computer.

# Change Data Execution Prevention settings

Data Execution Prevention, or DEP, is a technology designed to stop exploitation of buffer overrun hacks. A buffer overrun occurs when a particular piece of code is flawed and a malicious software program deliberately stuffs more data into the buffer than it can handle. Rather than just toss away the extra code, most applications will attempt to run the additional code. A cleverly crafted malicious program knows exactly how much data it takes to overrun the buffer, and the executable code begins immediately after that point in memory.

DEP attempts to stop this by locking memory and marking it as not executable. That way, if data overruns a buffer, unless it overruns into an area specifically marked as executable by a program, the excess code will not run.

The program may still crash but at least it won't spawn something nasty that takes over your computer as it dies.

As you might expect, there is a catch to using DEP. There are two components to DEP: software code that Windows XP monitors and manages, and hardware support in your computer's CPU. The latter is only found in the newer 64-bit processors that contain the necessary checks to prevent code from being executed after a buffer overrun.

The software portion can be run on any computer that has Windows XP Service Pack 2. By default DEP is enabled only for essential Windows programs and services and not for all applications running on your computer. This is a mixed blessing; common sense says that DEP should be enabled for all applications. However, Microsoft states applications that use dynamic code generation ("just-in-time code generation" — in other words, Java) and applications that do not mark generated code with execute permission may have compatibility issues on computers that use DEP. Thus it leaves Windows applications vulnerable.

Fortunately DEP is not an all-or-nothing configuration. You can set DEP to apply for all applications, and then place specific applications in an exception list, essentially opting out of the DEP protections, if you have compatibility problems that arise.

To view and configure DEP, click Start, right-click My Computer, and then click Properties. You can also click Control Panel and then System to get to the same dialog box. Click the Advanced tab and then under Performance click Settings. Click Data Execution Prevention (see Figure 6.33).

If your processor does not have hardware DEP support, you will see a notice to this effect at the bottom of the dialog box. You can still use software DEP, and by default software DEP is enabled for "essential Windows programs and services only." A casual search at MSDN does not uncover a list of what these might be, so at this point you have to take Microsoft's word that it's protecting *something* for you.

You can choose Turn on DEP for all programs and services except those I select and in theory gain more protection from buffer overruns. However, the Help and Security Center reports problems with some Windows programs. If you enable the global setting, you should watch to see which programs inexplicably crash, and then add them to the exception list. That is, if you trust the program hasn't been hacked and is crashing because of a buffer overrun exploit.

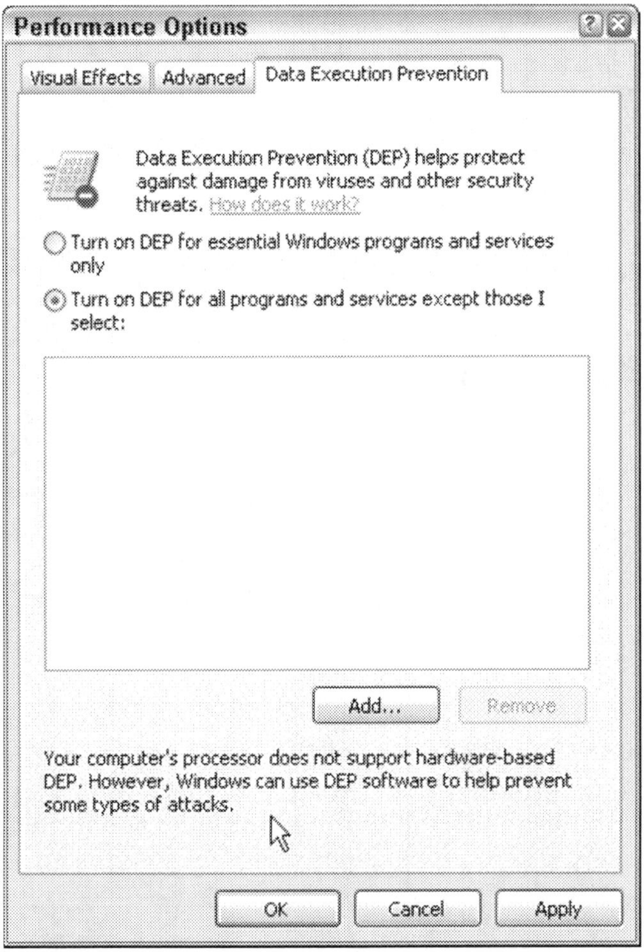

**Figure 6.33.** The DEP configuration dialog box lets you determine how much protection is running on your system.

Performance may also be a concern, though at this writing there has not been anything definite as to the effect of DEP when turned on for Windows processes or all processes. Most of the Internet discussion is anecdotal with no surveys concluding anything about a performance hit. If you have a system slowdown after enabling DEP (more likely on software-only systems), try disabling it except for Windows programs and services, or try adding only trusted applications to the exception list.

**Hack**

You can configure DEP at boot time, rather than switching it off in Windows. Edit the boot.ini file with execution options: "/NoExecute=OptIn" (system binaries only), OptOut (all binaries, process exception list), AlwaysOn (all binaries, no exceptions), and AlwaysOff (DEP fully disabled).

If you have more interest in how DEP works, you can read a fairly technical but detailed discussion of DEP at http://support.microsoft.com/default.aspx?scid=kb;en-us;875352.

# Determine effective Group Policies

If you or your computer is the member of a domain, policies can be applied at different levels: domain, organizational unit, computer, user, and local computer. In especially large domains it's possible to have different groups assigning policies without knowing which others are in effect. The net result at your level can be confusing or conflicting policies, such that you think you should have the ability to do something on your computer but you don't. Note that this is different from the situation where you want to do something that the company policy explicitly excludes, such as running peer-to-peer applications from behind the company firewall.

Microsoft realized that sorting through multiple policy layers can be difficult, so they provide two tools with which to determine which policies are effective when you log on. The first provides a quick summary of your effective policies. The second is a more comprehensive tool that lets you see which group policies are affecting the specific policy in question.

The first tool is available through the Help and Support Center. Click Start and then Help and Support. Under Pick a Task, click Use Tools to view your computer information and diagnose problems (see Figure 6.34). Click Advanced System Information, and then click View Group Policy settings applied.

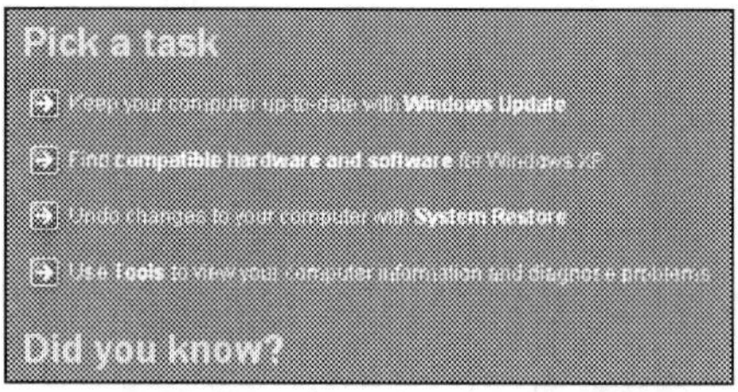

**Figure 6.34.** The Help and Support Center gives you links to advanced tools such as determining effective policies.

The tool (see Figure 6.35) reports on the Group Policy Objects that are applied to the computer and to the user. It lists specific policies as well as the source GPO for the policy. This provides an easy way to trace where a particular policy is coming from and how it is being applied (or not applied, in some cases) to you or your computer.

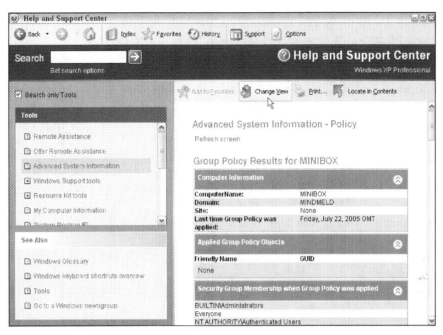

**Figure 6.35.** View the applicable Group Policies using the Help and Support Center tool.

The other tool is an MMC snap-in. The Resultant Set of Policy snap-in provides a more extensive look at which policies are being applied and where they came from.

To install the snap-in, click Start, Run, type mmc, and then press Enter. The Microsoft Management Console appears. Click File and then Add/Remove Snap-in. Click Add, scroll down the list to Resultant Set of Policy, select it (see Figure 6.36), and then click Add. Click Close and then click OK. The snap-in appears in the management console.

To run the snap-in, right-click the snap-in and select Generate RSoP data. The Resultant Set of Policy Wizard appears. Click Next. Select Logging mode and then click Next. Select This computer and then click Next. Select Current user and then click Next. Review the selection summary and then click Next. When the wizard is done, click Finish.

**Inside Scoop**

Both tools are most helpful when you or your computer connect to a domain. Workgroups or standalone computers use only local policies, so determining where a policy came from or how to change it isn't as difficult as sorting through domains, trees, and forests for the appropriate GPO.

The RSoP snap-in (see Figure 6.37) shows a view similar to the Group Policy editor. The computer is listed in the left pane, while the details pane shows policies, how the computer in question is configured, and which Group Policy Object (GPO) is the source for the setting.

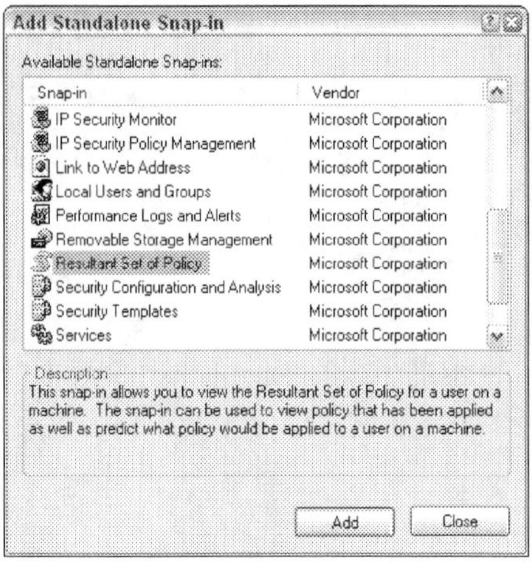

This tool has greater flexibility because it can be run against other computers in a domain, run against other users on the local computer, and can be used in "planning mode" to see how additional GPOs will affect computer or user policies.

**Figure 6.36.** The Resultant Set of Policy tool is usable for domain and workgroup computers.

The two downsides to the RSoP tool is that you must add the snap-in again to re-run the tool against the local computer, rather than refreshing the existing snap-in, and you can't print out the policy descriptions. However, you can export the policies and then import them into other applications such as Excel or Word for further massaging.

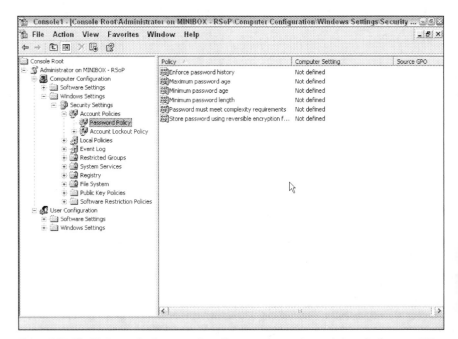

**Figure 6.37.** The RSoP snap-in shows you the policy, computer setting, and the policy's source GPO.

# Determine file permissions

Determining file permissions can be trickier than determining the resultant set of policies. NTFS file sharing has a mind-boggling array of file permissions that can be assigned, some of which interact in unexpected ways. When many permissions are assigned to multiple objects in a domain, the eventual file permissions for a user can be downright confusing.

Windows XP provides a tool to help determine what permissions are being applied to a file or folder, for a user, on a specific computer. The tool is not available for users running simple file sharing, so most default installations of Windows XP won't have the tool immediately available. Domain members automatically use NTFS permissions; you cannot use simple file sharing even if you wanted to.

To turn off simple file sharing, from any folder window (such as My Documents) click Tools and then Folder Options. Click the View tab, scroll down the Advanced Settings list to the bottom, and deselect Use simple file sharing (see Figure 6.38). Click OK; the settings will not be applied until you close and re-open the window.

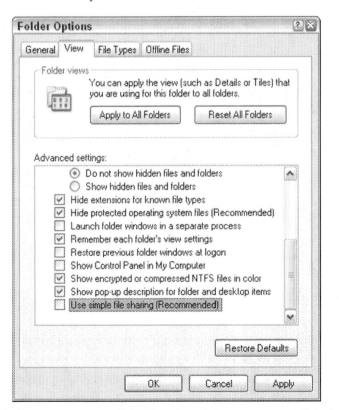

**Figure 6.38.** In order to work with NTFS permissions you must turn off simple file sharing.

Viewing effective permissions for a file or folder is relatively simple, with a slight detour at the end. Log on as a user with local administrator privileges. Right-click the file or folder and then click Properties. Click the Security tab (see Figure 6.39) and then click the Advanced button. Click the Effective Permissions tab.

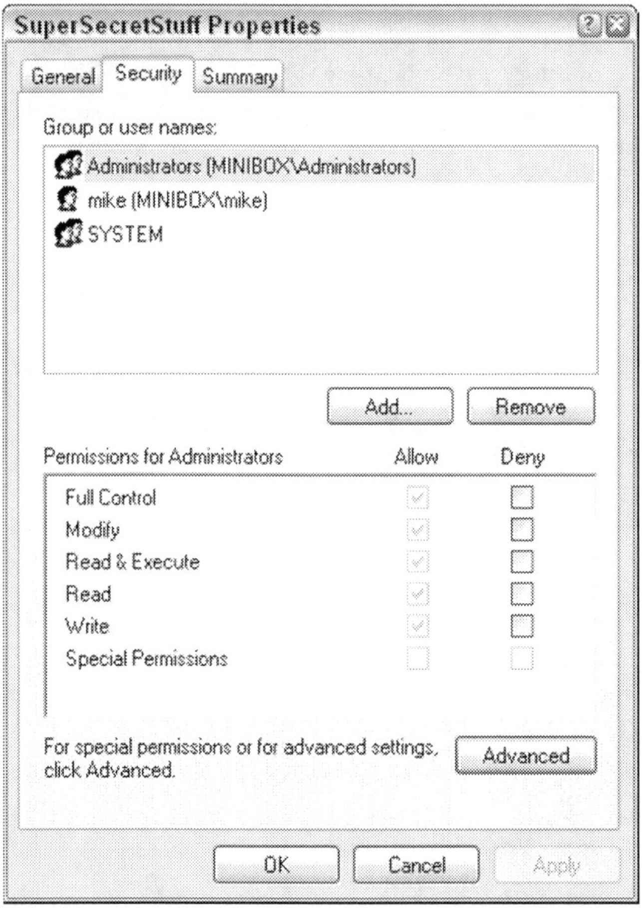

**Figure 6.39.** The Security tab is the initial access point for determining permissions for a folder or file.

Here's where the detour comes in. The Group or user name field looks like you can type into it, but you can't. Click the Select button. The defaults of User, group, or security principal and the local machine name are fine, though you can change any of these if you want to view only users on a different machine, for example. Type an object name into the field that you want to check file permissions for (see Figure 6.40). You can see appropriate syntax by clicking the examples link. Click Check Names to see if the object is valid for the computer you are examining. If everything is go, the object name will be underlined.

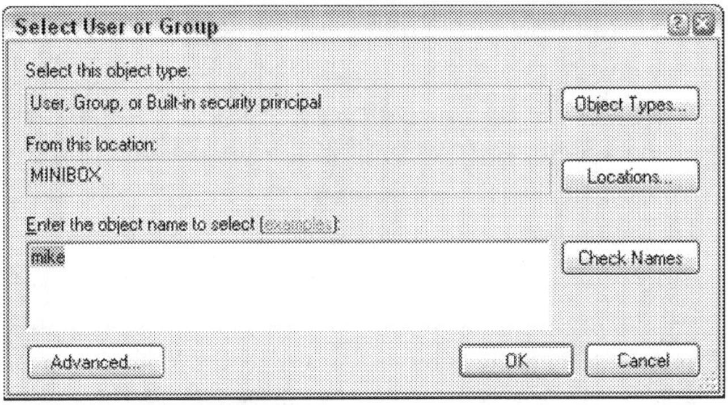

**Figure 6.40.** Enter the name of the person or computer that you want to set permissions for.

Click OK, and you are returned to the Effective Permissions tab (see Figure 6.41), showing the permissions applied to the file or folder (those with a check mark) and those that are not applied (those without a check mark).

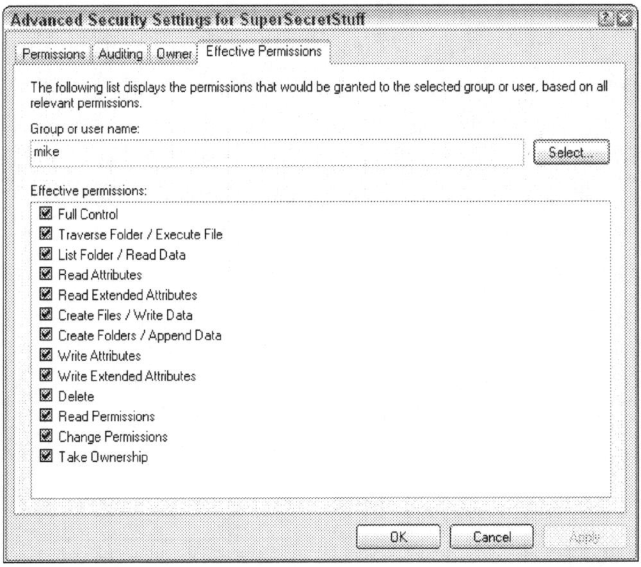

**Figure 6.41.** Effective permissions show you what a user can and can't do with a specific folder or file.

You cannot change any of the permissions on this tab, only view the effective ones. What makes it so useful is that you can go back, select or deselect permissions, and before clicking Apply or OK, visit the Effective Permissions tab to see what the resulting permissions will be. A full discussion of permissions and their interrelationship is beyond the scope of this book.

If things get so confusing that they seemingly can't be undone, there is a panic button of sorts that is available. As an administrator you can Take Ownership of a file, regardless of who else owns it or what permissions are set on it. Once you have ownership you can then assign or re-assign permissions so that the file's access is properly set again.

To take ownership, log on as a user with local administrator privileges. Right-click the file or folder and then click Properties. Click the Security tab. Click Add, type Administrator (individual) or Administrators (group) into the list, click Check Names, and then click OK. From the Security tab, click Advanced. Select Administrator or Administrators from the list and then click Edit (see Figure 6.42). Select Full Control which applies all the permissions for you, and then click OK twice. You now have ownership and can assign permissions as necessary to restore the situation to normal.

## Audit computer and security events

As one of the main pillars of security, auditing is perhaps the least known and most overlooked. When a system crashes, most people reboot, hoping the problem will be cleared up. (This technique nearly always worked with earlier versions of Windows.) What isn't as well known is that Windows can be configured to audit nearly everything that happens within its boundaries, from performance issues to potential security breaches. This gives you some idea of what went wrong, and in the case of audit events, it provides a warning that unauthorized activity is afoot.

Auditing can be done for many things, but the two most connected to security are auditing access policies and auditing file usage. To audit access policies you need to change some settings to the local computer's policies. This can be done using the Local Security Policy snap-in for standalone or workgroup computers, or using the Group Policy Editor for computers attached to a domain.

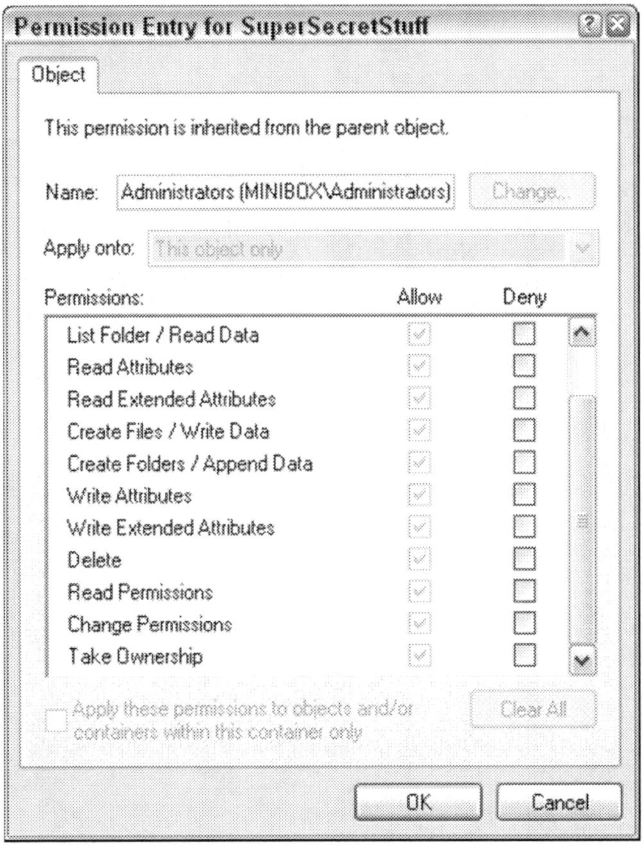

**Figure 6.42.** When you take ownership of a file as an administrator, you can then set appropriate permissions for anyone else.

## Audit access policies

To audit access policies on the local computer, click Start, Run, type secpol.msc, and then press Enter. You can also launch the snap-in (see Figure 6.43) by clicking Start, Administrative Tools, and then Local Security Policy. Browse to Local Polices\Audit Policy.

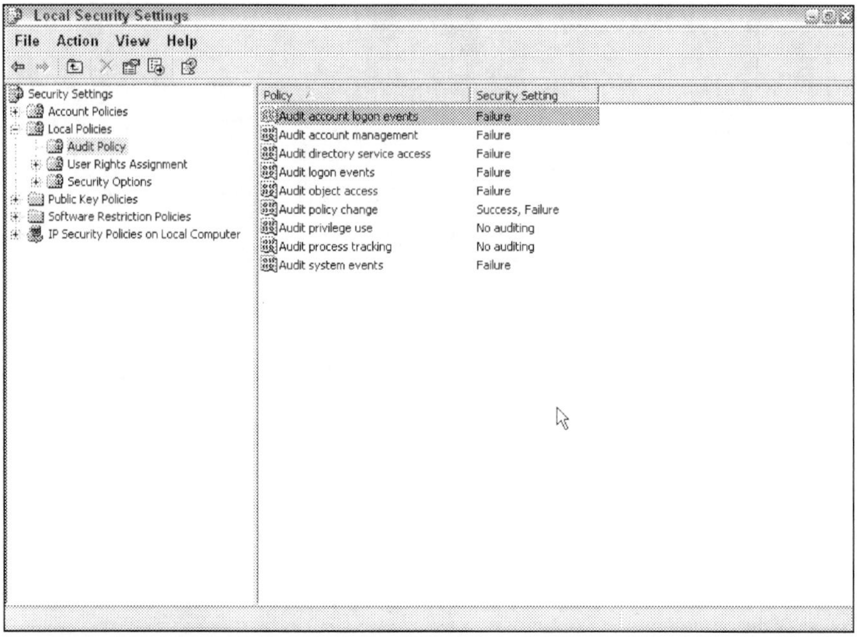

**Figure 6.43.** Set your audit access policies to audit certain failure events.

Each policy has three settings: Audit Success, Audit Failure, and No Auditing (no checkboxes selected). Recommended settings are:

- Audit account logon events: Failure
- Audit account management: Failure
- Audit directory service access: Failure
- Audit logon events: Failure
- Audit object access: Failure
- Audit policy change: Success, Failure
- Audit privilege use: No auditing
- Audit process tracking: No auditing
- Audit system events: Failure

Once you set these audits, you must log out and back in again to put them into effect.

---

### Auditing at home

If you are not on a corporate network and have otherwise protected yourself with a firewall, antivirus, and anti-spyware programs, setting up auditing sounds extreme. Who could possibly want to gain access to your system?

When my wife and I went on our honeymoon, I'd inadvertently left auditing enabled — I'd been writing a chapter on security measures and had been playing with logging security events. When we came back I took a stroll through the Event Logs. Sure enough, someone had tried to log on locally while we were gone.

After a little detective work, it turned out to be the boyfriend of a woman who was taking care of our cats in our absence. He had idly tried logging on to the computer while his girlfriend fed the cats. Moral of the story: You never know when an opportunity becomes irresistible to someone, so be prepared.

---

## Audit file access

File access is recommended only for particular files and not for entire folders or (gasp) entire drives. If you attempt to audit all events on all files, you will not only fill up your log file (and overwrite earlier entries when the log "rolls over" to the beginning) but you will quickly get bored digging through pages of information in search of the one single event.

If you want to audit file permissions, there are two basic requirements. First, you can only audit files and folders on NTFS partitions, and second, you must use NTFS file sharing rather than simple file sharing. FAT32 partitions won't work as they don't support the necessary file types, and simple file sharing sets a base level of access and default permissions without any auditing available.

You can turn on permission auditing by right-clicking the file and then clicking Properties. Click the Security tab and then click Advanced. Click the Auditing tab, click the Add button (see Figure 6.44), type the name of the group or user you wish to audit (only one object can be added at a time), and then click Check Names. If the object exists, the group or user will appear with an underscore. Click OK.

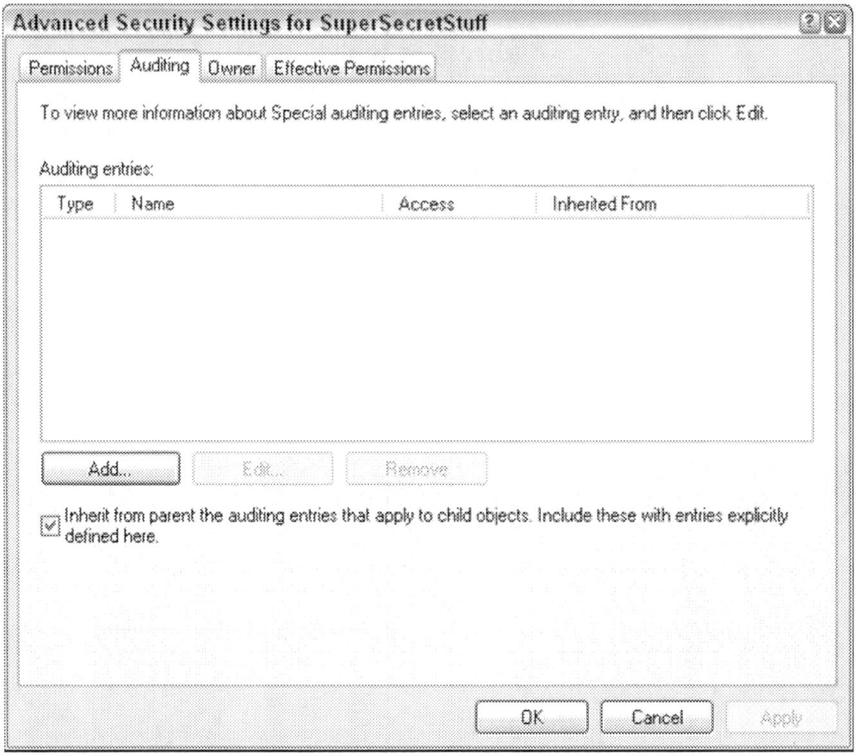

**Figure 6.44.** The Auditing tab is where you add groups, people, or computers that you want to watch.

The permissions can be audited for successful use or failed use (see Figure 6.45). For example, you may have set your accounting program's database file to full permission for yourself and deny permission to everyone else. You may want to audit failed read, write, execute, and delete permissions on the file. While it's conceivable that some of the other permissions may be attempted, you don't need to carry the paranoia too far, unless your company's policies regarding sensitive information require it. In that case, it's most likely that audits have been applied at a group policy level anyway. But it's always nice to know that you can audit so many things that you'll know when the file so much as sneezes without your permission.

## Review the Security log

The toughest part about auditing isn't enabling auditing, but poring through the event log in search of failed events or other indications of misbehavior occurring on your computer.

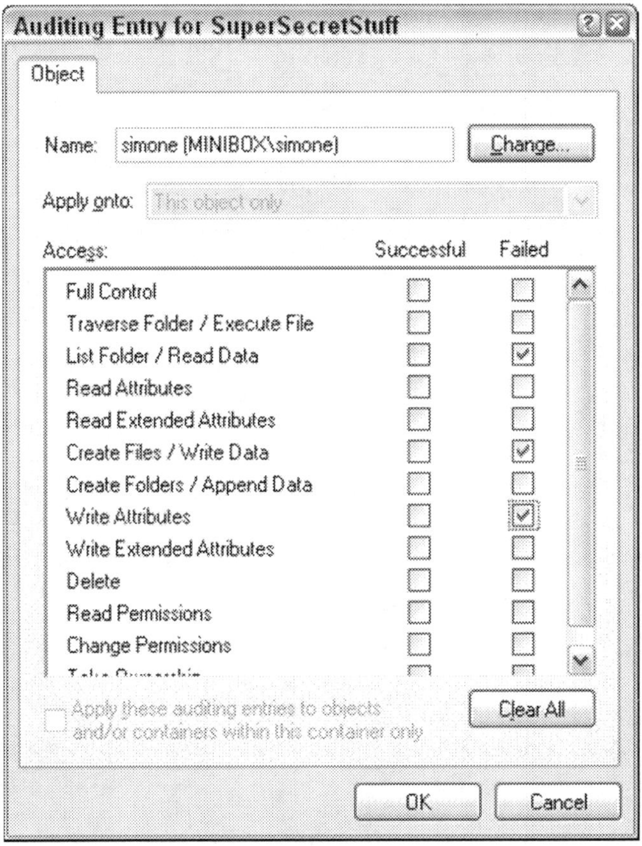

**Figure 6.45.** Select which file permissions you want to audit, whether successful ones or failed ones.

The tool used to view security-related events is, not surprisingly, the Event Viewer (see Figure 6.46). To open the Event Viewer, click Start, Administrative Tools, and then Event Viewer. You can use either an Event Viewer filter to show only the types of events you want to review, or you can use the Find command to look for specific event IDs that may have been logged to the Security log file. (More information on using the Event Viewer can be found in Chapter 11.) Some common access audit event IDs to look for are:

■ Event ID 529 : Unknown user name or bad password

■ Event ID 530 : Log on time restriction violation

■ Event ID 531 : Account disabled

■ Event ID 532 : Account expired

- Event ID 535 : Password expired
- Event ID 539 : Logon Failure: Account locked out
- Event ID 627 : NT AUTHORITY\ANONYMOUS is trying to change a password
- Event ID 644 : User account Locked out

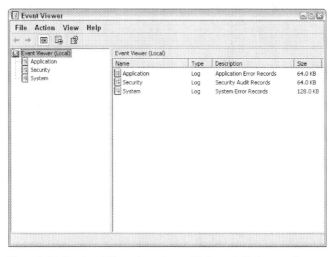

**Figure 6.46.** Use Event Viewer to review audited events that appear in the log files.

# Secure Internet Explorer

Microsoft's goal of bringing the Internet to everyone via Windows succeeded far more spectacularly than Bill Gates ever imagined. By integrating Internet protocols and applications directly into the operating system (of which Internet Explorer, or IE, is the most notorious example), not only was the Internet delivered to everyone's doorstep, but all the not-so-nice parts of it like hackers and spammers were brought right into everyone's living room, whether you wanted them or not. Ever since then, Microsoft has been fighting an ongoing battle between enabling cool multimedia and information technologies and stopping harmful exploits based on those same technologies.

---

**Hack**

Windows ships with a command-line VB Script log parser that you can use to automatically query for specific event IDs. Search for eventquery.vbs in the Help and Support Center for a listing of command syntax and usage. This is quicker than manually resetting filters in Event Viewer.

## Alternatives to Internet Explorer

Microsoft won the "browser wars" of the late '90s, relegating the Netscape browser (among others) to virtual obscurity. Yet Internet Explorer has slowly but steadily lost ground to other browsers, ones that do not present ongoing security headaches to users. These other browsers provide better security while at the same time taking up less disk space, loading faster, and having better features or extendibility than IE. Try one and see how you like it; you just may find it is a compelling reason to stop using IE.

- Mozilla (www.mozilla.org/products/mozilla1.x/) is a free Internet suite, featuring Web, e-mail, chat, newsgroup, and HTML applications all in one package. 11MB is still less than the typical IE bug fix rollup package.

- Firefox (www.mozilla.org/products/firefox/) is Mozilla's sleeker sibling. It's a free Web browser but a powerful, extensible one. At just under 5MB, it's a great way to try another non-Microsoft browser and help break your IE addiction.

- Opera (www.opera.com) is a blazingly fast browser and page-rendering engine and is popular with many people for its configurable user interface. It's shareware, $39 to buy, and weighs in at just under 4MB. Lightweight and speedy are positives in anyone's book.

The Web browser is the most commonly used framework for accessing the Internet, and as such many security invasions attempt to pry open cracks in the framework. IE is commonly cited as the poster child for insecure applications, though security flaws often arise from deeper in the operating system; IE is merely the most visible and accessible portion to the bad guys.

If you haven't already done so, go install firewall software, antivirus software, and anti-spyware software. These should be done before you go out onto the Internet unprotected. See the relevant sections earlier in this chapter for more details. Make sure you have run the Automatic Updates service and checked either the Windows Update or Microsoft Update Web sites for the latest fixes for your system. Then turn off any services you do not need running on your computer to help reduce the attack surface available to bad guys. See Chapter 11 for information on Windows XP services that you can set to manual or disable completely.

Service Pack 2 enhanced IE security by including numerous hotfixes, roll-ups, and feature additions to Internet Explorer. Some of IE's settings have been tightened up so that Web sites can't sneak ActiveX controls onto your computer. A pop-up blocker has been included to stop sneaky Web page scripts from generating an often-endless succession of new windows. And administrators have greater control over IE's features using the ever-popular Group Policy Editor.

## Control file downloads

Malicious programmers are sneaky. They know how to hide bad software inside a tasty, tempting wrapper. Before SP2, Internet Explorer allowed programmers to create dialog boxes that looked like Authenticode authorizations, informing users that they were downloading a "safe" program. People would click the OK button, and within a few seconds a malicious program would be downloaded, installed, and working its mischief. For example, some types of malicious software known as "root kits" would install themselves using holes in IE's security model, and the kit would provide instant Administrator access to the computer without the user's knowledge.

With SP2, the bad guys aren't able to create misleading Windows dialog boxes that can lead unsuspecting users to install malicious software. If a file is an executable file, IE pops up a security warning asking if you want to run the file or save it to your hard drive (see Figure 6.47).

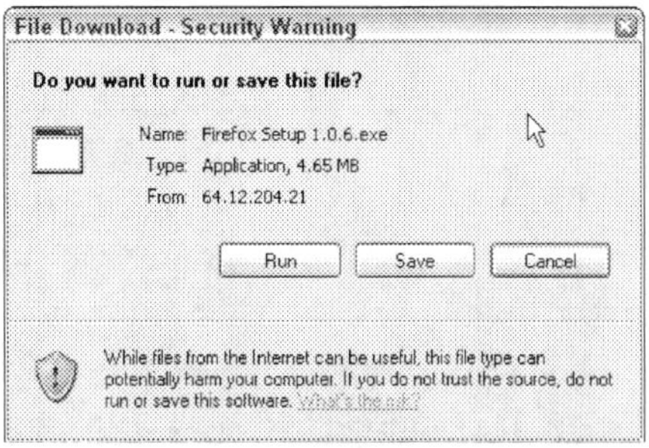

Once you download the file, you can click the Run button on the Download Complete dialog box to launch the executable, or you can run the file at a later time.

No matter which option you choose, IE checks the executable for signed credentials or to see if the credentials have been revoked. If the shield icon in the lower left is red, it means the program is not signed. If the icon is yellow, it means that it is signed but you should use caution anyway. As with any download, just because it's on a Web site that looks nice, that doesn't mean the application is nice, too. Think carefully about what this application is supposed to do and if you really need to install it on your computer.

**Figure 6.47.** If it's an executable file, IE asks if you want to run it or save it to your hard drive.

> **Bright Idea**
> You should always save files to a single download directory on your computer, run a virus scanner on it, and then decide whether to open it or run it. Not only is it safer but the original file is still on your computer should you need to reinstall it.

# Limit installation of Web page controls

With earlier versions of IE, when you visited a page that required some form of plug-in to work, IE would allow the Web page to push the software down onto your computer if you clicked a button. This was most common with "multimedia" plug-ins that were supposed to provide rich Web content like an audio file player, but the bad guys quickly turned this into a way to sneak bad programs onto your computer.

The most common form of abuse is in the form of malicious ActiveX controls. ActiveX controls make interactive Web pages look and behave like computer programs and provide methods for exchanging data between Internet Explorer and applications on a computer. The Windows Update, Office Update, and Microsoft Update Web sites use ActiveX controls to scan your system and determine which patches are needed.

Unfortunately, due to the integration of IE into the operating system, a clever ActiveX control could gain access to information within your browser or on your computer. Also unfortunately, you cannot download and separately install an ActiveX control; it must be loaded when the Web page is loaded in order for the page to work properly.

There are two security methods available for limiting installation of malicious Web page controls. The first is available in SP2 through the information bar. This IE-only feature stops Web pages from attempting to install anything to your computer. If it is marked as an ActiveX control, you are presented with a message in the information bar (see Figure 6.48) that lets you know what type of control (signed or unsigned) you are encountering and lets you decide whether to install it on your computer. If it is signed you have the opportunity to examine and further research the certificate to see if it is a legitimate control. If it is unsigned, IE won't install it even if you want it to.

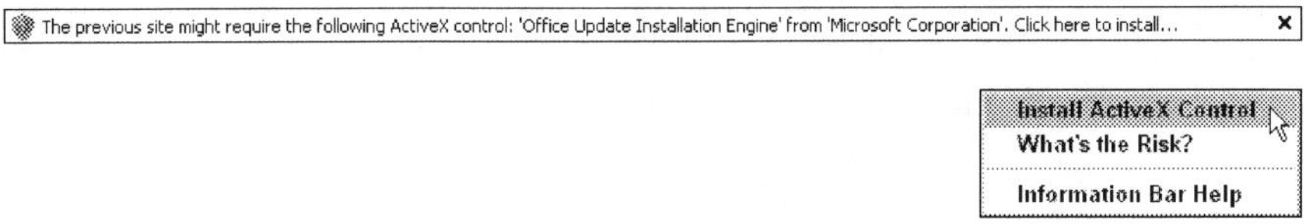

---

The previous site might require the following ActiveX control: 'Office Update Installation Engine' from 'Microsoft Corporation'. Click here to install...          ✕

> **Install ActiveX Control**
> What's the Risk?
>
> Information Bar Help

**Figure 6.48.** The Information Bar blocks installation of code, and you can decide whether to install or investigate the code.

---

## Are you in the zone?

From its early days Internet Explorer has used the concept of zones to define specific groups of browser security settings. The four zones — Internet, local intranet, trusted, and restricted sites — came with predefined but editable settings that allowed varying degrees of downloading and executing Web page code, and users could place Web sites into the different zones depending on their needs for active content.

In the real world, zones proved unwieldy. Unless you worked for a very large corporation with a not-very-busy IT department, most places did not use IE's security zones to restrict content delivery. It was far easier to filter requests at the proxy server or firewall and deny content using a hardware solution than to restrict it at the desktop. For most home and SOHO users, it's better to rely on ActiveX blockers and pop-up blockers than to configure individual Web sites for membership in a specific zone.

---

The second form of control is provided by your antivirus program's real-time scanning or anti-spyware scanning utilities. These block programs as they're being downloaded, check to see if they are on the "forbidden list," and offer you options as to how you'd like to deal with unknown code.

When the content is other than an ActiveX control, the information bar stops the site from downloading files to your computer. You can still choose to override the block and install the content, because it's more difficult (but not impossible) for non-ActiveX controls to wreak havoc on your computer.

## Stop pop-ups

The first time it happens, you wonder what you did wrong. You click on a link, and new windows start spawning like bugs on road kill. You get so many windows your taskbar is jammed with little icons and you can't tell what each window is. You must manually close down each window — and surprise, some windows can't be closed; others spawn new windows as they die. Eventually you throw the Big Red Switch, hoping that nothing bad has happened and your computer won't be DOA when it reboots.

Welcome to the wonderful world of pop-ups.

Back in the early days of HTML, the language gurus thought it would be helpful to generate new windows from within an existing window, ones that would show helpful content such as on-the-fly word definitions or useful parenthetical explanations. The ability is still used as it was intended, such as calculating shipping expenses or showing the remaining balance on a financial account.

But the bad guys were motivated by money. In the early days of Web advertising, advertisers paid fractions of a penny for each "impression" or visit to a Web site. It didn't take long for the bad guys to figure out that all they had to do was spawn tens or hundreds of windows that opened up onto the specified site; multiply that by tens or thousands of innocent surfers, and the bad guys could make some good money for not much work.

While advertisers have gotten smarter (now they typically pay by the click-through or the click-to-purchase ratio, not by impressions), the unwanted presence of pop-ups still plagues surfers who just want to read about Siberian tigers and not view pop-up ads about hair growth formula.

IE is one of the last browsers on the market to adopt pop-up blocker technology. However, it works well, is easily if modestly configurable, and will keep sites from spawning virtual acres of new windows on your desktop. One key feature is that you can set it so that if you click on a link that spawns a pop-up, that window will appear rather than be blocked.

The pop-up blocker is activated automatically when you install SP2. To see the blocker and edit its settings, click Tools, Pop-up Blocker, and then Pop-up Blocker Settings.

There are three pop-up filter settings (see Figure 6.49) for IE:

- **High.** Pop-up blocker stops all new windows, including ones generated by your own clicks. To override the block, press Ctrl and then click a link.

- **Medium (default).** This setting blocks most pop-ups unless you requested the pop-up by clicking a link.

- **Low.** IE allows most pop-ups except those that are generated by arriving at a Web site (the never-ending chain of spawned windows).

You can have IE play a sound when a pop-up is blocked, have the information bar display a warning, or both. You can also add exception sites, such as financial institutions, to the Allowed sites list, which lets you have a high security setting but still visit sites you know you can trust.

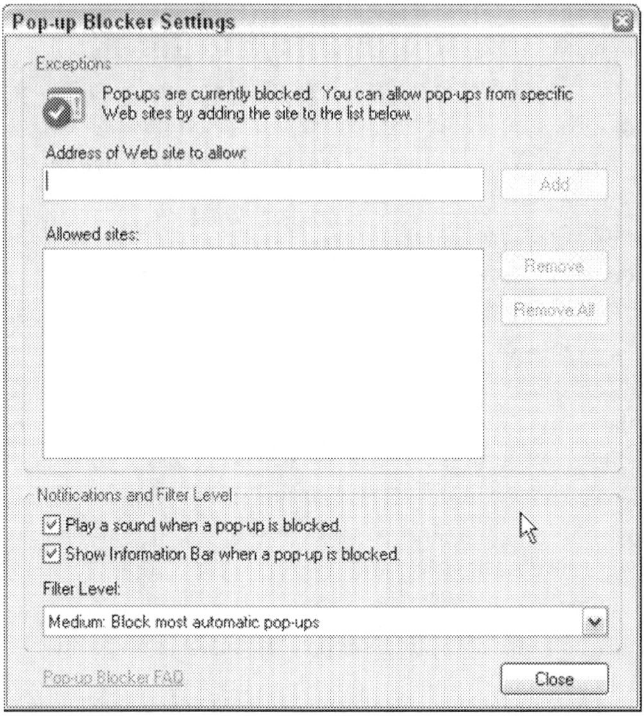

**Figure 6.49.** You can add sites to the exception list so that pop-ups work properly.

# Disable Web site scripting

Scripting is a necessary evil in the online world. Without scripting, most Web sites would be static, without menus that display when you move a cursor over them or images that change depending on what content you want to view. Clicking through static link after static link gets old very quickly, and scripting makes the usability that much nicer.

The down side of running Web page scripts is that the bad guys who are so clever at writing bad code can also write scripts on a Web page that perform undesirable behavior.

Microsoft lets you disable scripting, though it's an all-or-nothing approach. It either allows scripting or it doesn't with your Web sites. The one slight benefit is that you can set IE to Prompt, where it will ask you if you want to run each script it encounters; unfortunately, there is no easy way to identify what type of script it is, so you have to guess just what it is that you're allowing.

To disable scripting, click Tools, Internet Options, and then Security (see Figure 6.50).

**Internet Options**

General | **Security** | Privacy | Content | Connections | Programs | Advanced

Select a Web content zone to specify its security settings.

Internet | Local intranet | Trusted sites | Restricted sites

**Internet**
This zone contains all Web sites you haven't placed in other zones

Sites...

*Security level for this zone*

**Custom**
Custom settings.
- To change the settings, click Custom Level.
- To use the recommended settings, click Default Level.

Custom Level.. | Default Level

OK | Cancel | Apply

**Figure 6.50.** The Security tab lets you control scripting options for each zone.

Make sure the Internet zone is selected and then click Custom Level. Scroll down to the Scripting category, and set Active Scripting to Disable (see Figure 6.51).

## Put the crunch on cookies

Cookies are small text files that help Web servers keep track of data that is generated between the browser and the Web site. Cookies are used in most Web shopping carts, as trackers for your participation on Web forums and bulletin boards, and to remember specific Web page settings such as color

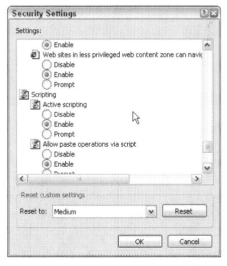

**Security Settings**

Settings:

○ Enable
🔒 Web sites in less privileged web content zone can navi(
  ○ Disable
  ◉ Enable
  ○ Prompt
🗿 Scripting
  🗿 Active scripting
    ○ Disable
    ◉ Enable
    ○ Prompt
  🗿 Allow paste operations via script
    ○ Disable
    ◉ Enable
    ○ Prompt

*Reset custom settings*

Reset to: Medium | Reset

OK | Cancel

**Figure 6.51.** The Disable Active Scripting option is near the end of the Security Settings list.

---

### The great cookie controversy

There is a climate of fear surrounding cookies, most of it fueled by tabloid-style gossip. Many reputable Web sites use cookies only for graphics enhancement ("Welcome back, Mike!") or shopping cart applications. But most people don't understand the benefits of first-party cookies, and recoil in fear when a Web site calls them by name. Personally I have no problems accepting first-party cookies from sites I do business with, and if I have any questions I review the site's privacy policy before accepting the cookies.

Third-party cookies, on the other hand, I refuse to accept for any reason. It's as if you are browsing in a library, followed by someone with a clipboard, who interrupts you and says, "I see you glanced through the magazine section. Would you be interested in three magazine subscriptions for $18?" It's nobody else's business where I browse or what for, and if I choose to check out a book from the library I'll do business with the library, not the clipboard-toting marketroid.

If you use the policy of deny first, accept later, you should be fine with any cookies whether first- or third-party. You can always delete the cookie later should you change your mind.

---

scheme or personal preferences. Sometimes cookies contain personal information, such as account numbers, though this is increasingly rare. These are referred to as first-party cookies, because they originate from the Web site you are currently viewing. They are not generally considered invasive.

Cookies can also be used to track aggregate browsing data, not just data related to a specific Web site. Cookies are used by many advertising-related servers to keep track of sites you visit and ads you view. Given time, these cookies can be used to create a profile of your viewing habits and which Web sites you frequent. These are called third-party cookies, because they are created for use by Web sites you are not currently viewing. They are generally considered invasive, because most of the time you don't know what data they are collecting, or how that data will be used.

Cookies are managed by clicking Tools, Internet Options, and then the Privacy tab (see Figure 6.52). The slider lets you select between six different levels of protection, from blocking all cookies to allowing all cookies. For most people, either Medium High or perhaps Medium will work best: Those allow most first-party cookies to be placed on your computer while rejecting third-party cookies.

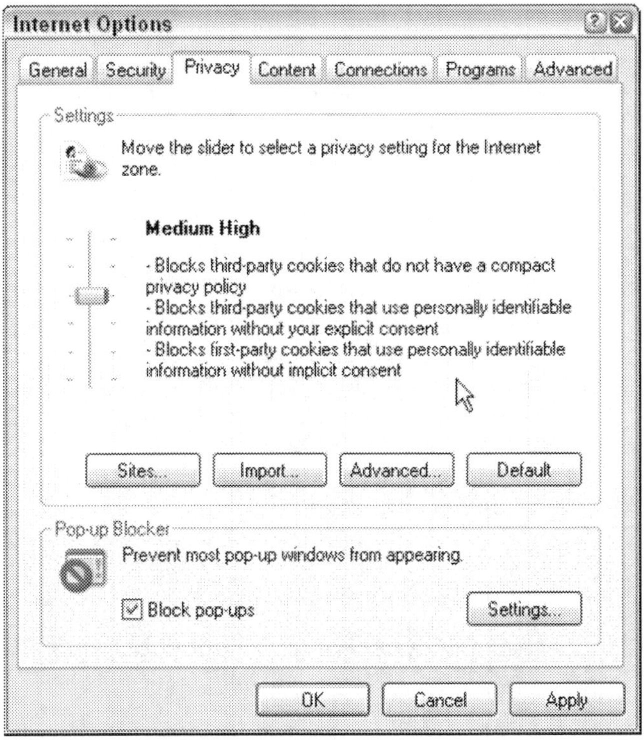

**Figure 6.52.** The slider lets you balance how first-party and third-party cookies are handled.

If IE's choices on how to handle first-party and third-party cookies isn't quite to your liking, it's a straightforward process to change how cookies are handled. Click the Advanced tab, select Override automatic cookie handling (see Figure 6.53), and then select how you want first-party, third-party, or session cookies handled. Your choices are Allow, Block, and Prompt. A decent basic choice is to Prompt for first-party cookies, Block all third-party cookies, and Always allow session cookies (which are automatically deleted when you close your browser). Notice that when you override automatic cookie handling, the slider on the Privacy tab goes away, to be replaced by a notice that you have enabled custom cookie handling.

**Figure 6.53.** Don't like IE's cookie-handling choices? Configure your own!

**Watch Out!**

Web browsers treat website.com and username.website.com as separate sites with respect to cookies. You will need to add exceptions for each one if need be — and the wildcard character (*) won't work here.

Even with all this configurability, you may want to tighten down IE to just this side of maximum. Block all cookies, first- and third-party, and then enter the exceptions for sites that you know you want to interact with, such as your bank. Exceptions are added on the Privacy tab. Click the Sites button, type the URL for the Web site you specifically want to block or allow and then click the appropriate button (see Figure 6.54).

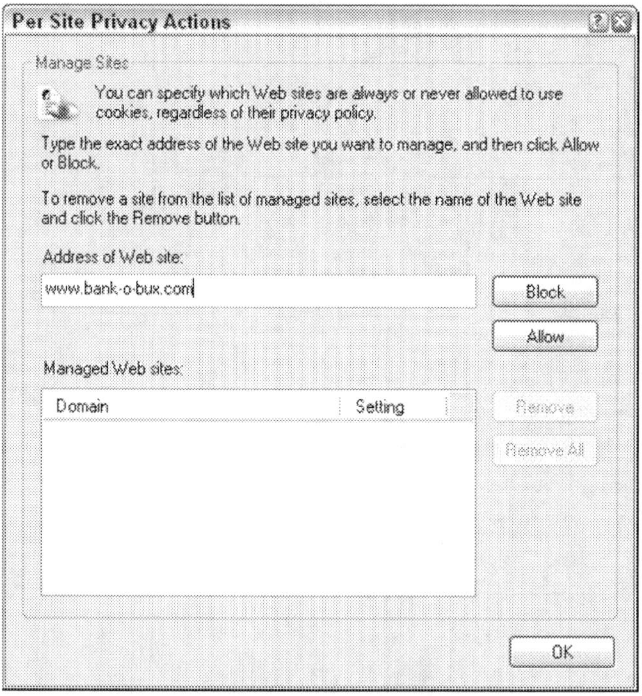

**Per Site Privacy Actions**

Manage Sites

You can specify which Web sites are always or never allowed to use cookies, regardless of their privacy policy.

Type the exact address of the Web site you want to manage, and then click Allow or Block.

To remove a site from the list of managed sites, select the name of the Web site and click the Remove button.

Address of Web site:

www.bank-o-bux.com | Block |

| Allow |

Managed Web sites:

| Domain | Setting | Remove |
|--------|---------|--------|
|        |         | Remove All |

| OK |

**Figure 6.54.** You can set exceptions to allow only trusted sites to set cookies, or to always deny cookies from untrusted ones.

You may be displeased to know that even with all your work to keep unwanted cookies from your machine, some Web sites refuse entrance, telling you that you *must* enable cookies to use the company's Web site. This attitude is tolerable from my bank, because I do business with them; it is not tolerable when I am looking for information about a product from a company's Web site. Get in the habit of sending an e-mail to the Webmaster of such sites, letting them know you took your dollars elsewhere (whether you did or not). Use your faux e-mail address as mentioned in the section on Outlook later in this chapter, in case they "accidentally" take your complaint as your permission to contact you personally with additional sales and marketing information.

## Review saved password settings

Cookies can maintain logon information and sometimes log you onto Web sites automatically, but IE also uses some code to remember user name and password pairs for you. It will fill in blanks for fields marked "Name" and "Password" on the assumption that you want to use the same ones you used the last time you visited. Most of the time the values automatically filled in are correct.

---

### Phishers: Bottom feeders of the Internet

Phishing is a despicable scam that uses real-looking e-mails and Web sites to trick you into revealing personal and financial information. The phishers then use the information for identity theft or to drain your bank account of your savings.

The scam usually comes in two parts: one, an unsolicited e-mail that looks like it came from a financial organization such as your bank, eBay, PayPal, or Visa. The e-mail notifies you of potential fraudulent activity on your account and to please click the link and log on to verify recent purchases.

The second part is a fake Web site designed to look like the real thing. The link from the official-looking e-mail uses HTML trickery to take you to the crook's Web site, not the official one, and they hope you fill in the Web form with your account number, password, or Social Security information.

There are two ways to beat the phishers. First, never, ever click links in e-mail requesting you to verify or confirm financial information. Second, download and install SpoofStick from www.corestreet.com/spoofstick. It's compatible with IE and Firefox, and it flashes a warning in big red letters if the URL you think you're at and the actual URL don't match.

For more information on phishing, archives of e-mails and spoofed sites, and resources to use before and after you have been phished, visit www.antiphishing.org.

But some sites have password rotation policies and you need to delete the old password. Or you asked IE to remember the information for your financial site, and then decided maybe that wasn't good information to have stored on your laptop in case your laptop grows legs and walks off.

Unfortunately, within IE, password management is both obscured and awkward to use. To manage your passwords, click Tools, Internet Options, click the Content tab, and then click the AutoComplete button (see Figure 6.55).

**Figure 6.55.** Password management is hidden in the AutoComplete section of the Content tab.

Select Use AutoComplete for user names and passwords on forms, and select Prompt me to save passwords (see Figure 6.56). Click the Clear Passwords button to delete all stored passwords. To delete a single password, you cannot do it within IE; you must first navigate to the Web page where the user name and password are entered. Then select the user name or password that IE suggests and press Delete.

Turn off password AutoComplete by deselecting User names and passwords on forms. You now must enter all user name and password information manually.

To be fair to Microsoft, it has always envisioned a world where the Active Directory would handle user names and passwords for resources internal to a business, while Passport would handle names and passwords for Internet accounts or other ones outside a business. IE was not really designed to handle or manage passwords, because authentication

**Figure 6.56.** Passwords are "managed" on an all-or-nothing basis.

would be handled by services external to it. But this technological dream has yet to come true, and most Web sites still use their own user name and password authentication mechanism. IE has yet to play catch-up to this "retro" technology.

## Set content filtering

The Content Advisor is the part of Internet Explorer that attempts to limit what information is presented in a browser. Most parents are interested in monitoring or restricting the sites their children can visit. The Content Advisor theoretically prevents access based on Web site ratings; however, Web site owners voluntarily rate themselves and most Web sites are not rated, so this set of controls is of dubious value.

The Content Advisor is found at Tools, Internet Options, Content. Click the Enable button.

The Ratings tab (see Figure 6.57) has a slider you can use to adjust the rating level for each of four categories: Language, Nudity, Sex, and Violence. The ratings go from zero to four, with zero as no content and four being unrestricted content.

**Content Advisor**

Ratings | Approved Sites | General | Advanced

Select a category to view the rating levels:

- **RSACi**
  - Language
  - Nudity
  - Sex
  - Violence

Adjust the slider to specify what users are allowed to see:

Level 0:  No violence

Description

No aggressive violence; no natural or accidental violence.

To view the Internet page for this rating service, click More Info.

More Info...

OK     Cancel     Apply

**Figure 6.57.** The Content Advisor lets you set different levels for content toleration.

The Approved Sites tab lets you add exceptions to the content filtering so that you or others can allow or deny sites regardless of filter settings.

The General tab (see Figure 6.58) has a collection of miscellaneous but important options, such as allowing users to view unrated sites (which is nearly all of them), setting an administrator password so your kids can't sneak in and change the filter settings when you're not looking, and buttons that let you visit various ratings organizations. The Advanced tab lets you import and manage other ratings settings for your computer.

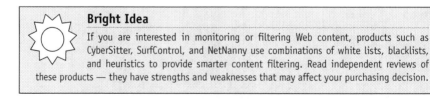

**Bright Idea**

If you are interested in monitoring or filtering Web content, products such as CyberSitter, SurfControl, and NetNanny use combinations of white lists, blacklists, and heuristics to provide smarter content filtering. Read independent reviews of these products — they have strengths and weaknesses that may affect your purchasing decision.

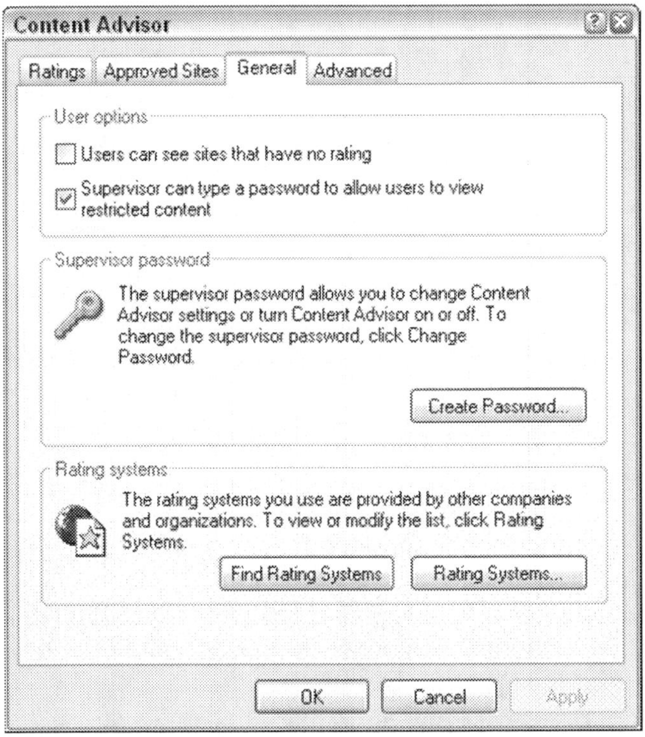

**Figure 6.58.** The General tab lets you set a parental password to lock your content settings.

# Secure Outlook Express

Outlook Express (OE) is the sad sibling of Internet Explorer. Sad, because much of its maligned reputation derives from IE's near-fatal character flaws. OE shares much of the same underlying technology as IE, and flaws reported in IE often extend to OE as well. For example (and it's a big example), the developers chose not to build OE to run within a least-privilege context. Instead, it has the same access rights and permissions as the user who is logged on. Because many people log on with local administrator rights, this means that OE's scripting language has unrestricted access to system and application objects — a recipe for disaster, as an unending stream of virus writers, skr1pt, k1dd33s, and haX0rZ, among others, remind us on a daily basis.

With Outlook Express there are two primary security concerns: stopping bad things from getting into the computer through the e-mail system, and limiting the damage that can be done if something nasty does get through.

---

### Why spam?

Why in the world would junk e-mail end up with the name of spam? Just what does a canned, cured meat product have to do with junk mail anyway?

The slang term "spam" originated as a reference taken from a Monty Python sketch, where ordinary conversation was continually interrupted and eventually drowned out by a group of noisy, boisterous Vikings singing only the word "Spam!" (You had to be there.)

Spamming came to mean flooding regular communication channels with nonsense or off-topic messages. Unsolicited commercial e-mail, due to its flooding barrage of sales pitches and come-ons, fits the spam appellation nicely.

---

You can stop some bad things from getting through with a robust antivirus program (discussed earlier in this chapter) which is designed to scan all incoming and outgoing e-mail for viruses, scripts, or other harmful attachments and content, and delete or quarantine it.

Other things worth stopping are e-mail with questionable or undesirable content. Millions of unsolicited commercial e-mail (UCE) messages, also known as spam, are routed through corporate and private e-mail servers, slowing down network services and clogging in-boxes everywhere. Spam filters are used to scan e-mail, evaluate the content, and then flag or dispose of spam so that it does not consume more of a user's time and hard drive space than it already does.

## Configure spam filtering

You can block spam from a particular sender. Click Message and then Block Sender. You can edit or remove this sender from the Blocked Sender list; click Tools, Message Rules, and then Blocked Senders list. Within this list you can add or remove individual e-mail addresses or entire domains (see Figure 6.59); however, wildcards or partial domains are not allowed.

Given the state of spam-fighting technology today, this is not an effective filter. It offers you too little in the way of controlling spam and doesn't have any learning features that improve its spam-fighting capabilities.

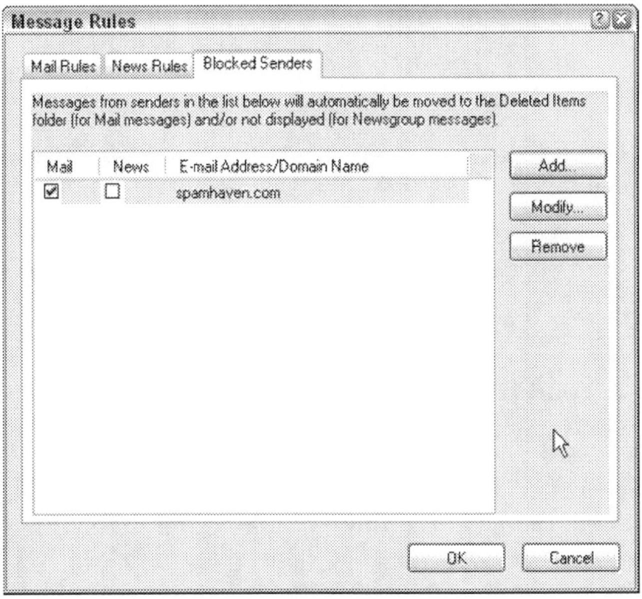

**Figure 6.59.** Configure your spam blocking "options" here.

Fortunately many antivirus programs include spam filtering as part of the services they provide, and many ISPs are also flagging spam for you. You can also download and install separate antispam proxies like SpamNet (www. cloudmark.com, $39.95 for 12 months) and Qurb (www.qurb.com, $29.95).

## Working with blocked attachments

Despite antivirus and antispam tools, bad things can still sneak into your system in the form of attachments. OE uses attachment blocking to keep users from opening or saving attachments that *may* be dangerous. For example, an executable file gets attached to an e-mail message. The attachment makes it past the virus scanner and the spam filter, but because it still could do something nasty when it is run, OE won't give users access to that attachment.

With Outlook Express it's an all-or-nothing approach. Either all potentially harmful attachments are blocked, or all attachments get in and it's up to you to make smart decisions about which ones to open. You don't even have the choice of saving the file and running a virus scanner on it; if you choose to block potentially harmful attachments, OE won't let you have access to the attachment, period.

The switch for turning attachment blocking off is found at Tools, Options, and then click the Security tab (see Figure 6.60).

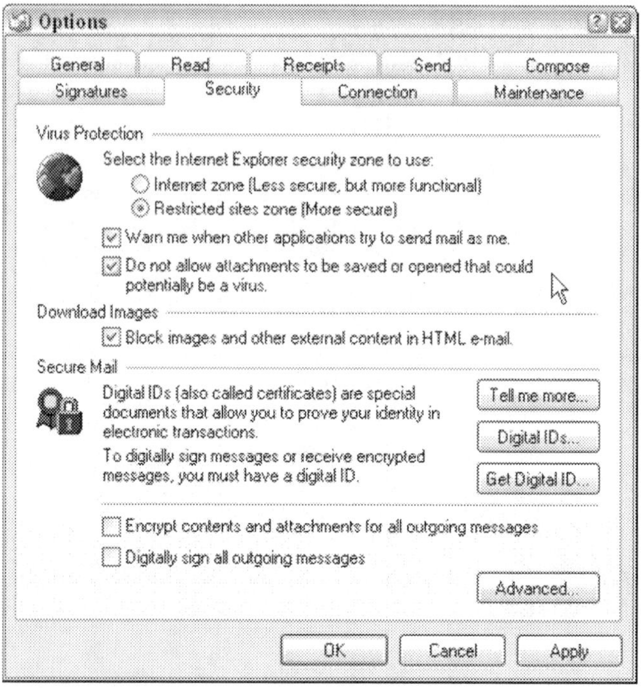

**Figure 6.60.** All attachments are evil, according to Microsoft.

Under Virus Protection, deselect Do not allow attachments to be saved or opened that could potentially be a virus. You now have access to blocked documents, though you may need to close and reopen OE for the new setting to take effect.

## Spam prevention tactics

Keeping spam out of your in box is a trying task even in the best of times. Here are some tactics you can employ to reduce the amount of spam you receive.

- Use bcc: instead of To: or cc:. Many people forward images or Internet humor to long lists of friends. Then they forward it, and they forward it, and somewhere along the line the bad guys get a nice long e-mail full of addresses waiting to be harvested. The blind carbon copy option (bcc:) hides e-mail addresses so they can't be snagged.

- Don't post your e-mail address on any Internet discussion forums. Most forum software contains special links that other posters can use to contact you. When you post your e-mail in the clear, harvesting bots pull your address off the Web pages and add it to the list.

- Carefully screen which newsletters you sign up for, and the relevant Web site's privacy policy. Amazon.com is a safe newsletter source; Phred's Midnight Discount Software is not.

- Sign up for a free e-mail account and use that for non-personal or questionable e-mail. I call it a "faux" e-mail account, because it's a real address but it is used as a dumping ground for all those questionable address requests. Services like Google, Yahoo, and Hotmail offer free e-mail accounts; sign up for one and use that address whenever a Web site asks you for your e-mail account. Use your main address for your friends, family, and close business associates; use the faux address for everything else.

## Block Web images

The HTML rendering engine provides mail clients with the ability to display HTML content as if it was a Web page in your message. Sounds great, right? The trouble is, this "feature" provides a tracking ability for spammers. When you open up an HTML e-mail with an image inside it, the image request is sent to a Web server. The Web server logs your request, thus validating to spammers that they have found a "live" e-mail address. In the spammer world, verified live addresses are valuable tender, and you've just guaranteed that you'll receive a whole lot more spam in the very near future.

By blocking Web images in your e-mail, you stop this behavior before it starts. Once you have verified the e-mail is from a legitimate source, you can click an image placeholder to retrieve the necessary images.

Click Tools, Options, and then click the Security tab. Under Download images, make sure you select Block images and other external content in HTML e-mail.

## Disable e-mail scripting

Similar to image blocking, the HTML rendering engine is heir to the same weakness as IE: The bad guys can write code that exploits security holes. This ability can be quickly disabled without significantly impairing the message's content or OE's functionality.

To turn off HTML rendering, click Tools, Options, and then click the Read tab (see Figure 6.61). Select Read all messages in plain text. Click OK.

**Bright Idea!**

Some messages launch malicious scripts just by being viewed in the preview pane. To turn off the preview pane, click View, Layout, and then deselect Show preview pane.

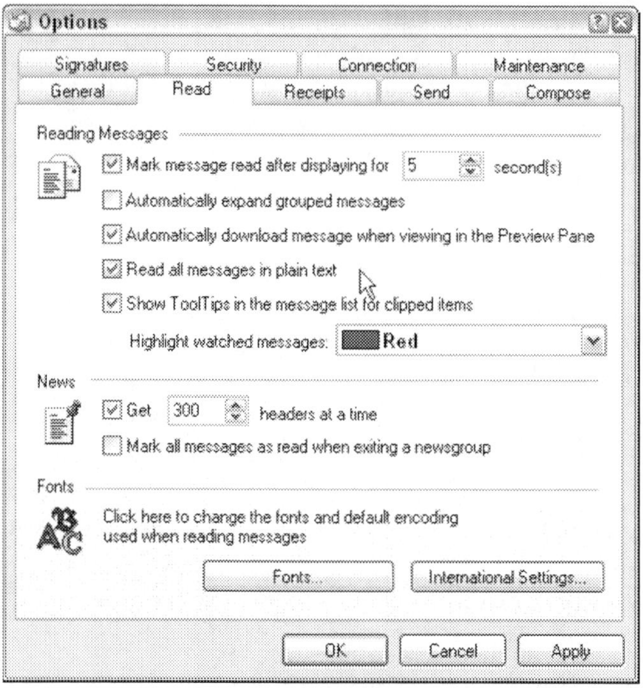

**Figure 6.61.** Messages are safer when viewed as text rather than HTML.

If you decide the message is safe and you want to view it in HTML, open the message. Click View and then Message in HTML. The message is back to its rich content view. This setting is not persistent; when you close the message, it goes back to plain text.

# Trip to nowhere: .NET Passport

Microsoft's .NET Passport service was intended to be *the* Internet identification database. Users with a Passport account could whip through merchant Web sites like a socialite through the velvet ropes outside a nightclub. Merchants would be assured that Passport holders actually had money (or at least a big credit limit) to buy things, and that the personal information such as the shipping address was valid.

A few large merchant sites signed up for Passport, notably eBay. Despite Microsoft claims of growth and consumer demand, the Passport service slowly faded into obscurity. Customers were understandably reluctant to entrust personal information with Microsoft; its security track record plus its strong-arm business tactics combined to create a distinctly negative impression of both the safety of the data plus questions as to how that data would be used.

Today, little is left of .NET Passport except for the initial pestering reminders in the notification area. Once you install Windows XP and connect to the Internet, reminder balloons insist that to do anything useful on the Web, you need a Passport (see Figure 6.62).

**Figure 6.62.** Anyone who's anyone has a .NET Passport!

As of this writing, to the best of my knowledge only three things require a Passport: MSN Messenger (or Windows Messenger, if you're chatting on an intranet), any Microsoft-controlled Web site such as MSN, Hotmail, or MSN Money, and IE when it connects to a Microsoft Extranet portal such as a beta test site or Partner site. You can still find information, brief as it is, about Passport at www.passport.net.

If you don't already have a Passport — and despite the balloon language, you don't require one — and you haven't used MSN Messenger to get one, you can fire up another wizard (see Figure 6.63) that will walk you through the process of getting one.

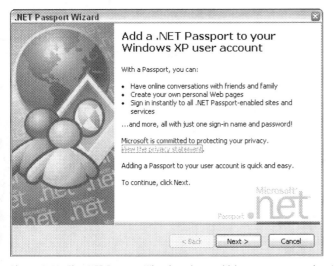

**Figure 6.63.** The .NET Passport Wizard awaits to whisk you away to nowhere!

Click Start, Run, type nusrmgr.cpl, and then press Enter. You can also click Start, Control Panel, and double-click User Manager. Click your user name. Click Set up my account to use a .NET Passport. The wizard starts, and you're well on your way to nowhere.

# Designate a digital certificate Recovery Agent

Digital certificates provide a "chain of trust" to help establish that something holding the certificate is what it says it is. In the case of Web sites, the business operating the site applies to a certificate authority (CA) with sufficient credentials to prove they are indeed a business, at a particular address, and so forth.

In the case of users, digital certificates are less common, especially among home or SOHO users. It's not often there's a need to establish trustworthy credentials, such as signing an e-mail with your certificate, to establish that it did in fact come from you. Because digital certificates are a complex issue more suited to large corporations or government agencies, they won't be covered in detail here. But there is a situation where managing digital certificates is useful to all users, and that is the case of encrypted files and folders.

The encrypted file system (EFS) is covered in Chapter 5. An encrypted file creates a personal digital certificate that is kept within Internet Explorer's certificate store. This certificate is like the master passkey to all your encrypted files: Even though each file has its own encryption key, your certificate can unlock the files. Conversely, if your certificate is lost, or if you forget your account password, you cannot unlock the files and the data is gone.

(Technically, this is not absolutely true; with enough time, energy, and computing power, the exponentially large number of encryption combinations can be tested against the file and one of them will eventually work. But don't count on that happening.)

If all you're trying to do is read your encrypted files while logged onto another computer, follow the certificate export and import procedure in Chapter 5. If you are looking to provide insurance in case your account is lost or your password forgotten, this procedure will help.

By designating a Recovery Agent, you can export your certificate in such a way that you can use it to recover encrypted files even if your Windows XP installation has been damaged or you forget your password.

# Export a recovery certificate

First, if you haven't done so already, encrypt a file or folder with EFS as described in Chapter 5. This automatically generates a certificate and places it in the Windows Certificate store.

Next, decide if you want to be a recovery agent for every file on the computer, or only for your own files. If the former, then you need to log on as someone with local administrator rights; if the latter, log on as yourself, but with rights to run MMC snap-ins. The procedure is otherwise the same.

Click Start, Run, type MMC, and then press Enter. Click File, Add/ Remove Snap-in, and then click Add. Select Certificates and then click Add. If you are logged on as Administrator or with administrator rights, select This snap-in will always manage certificates for my user account (see Figure 6.64) and then click Finish. If you are logged on as a user, the Certificates snap-in automatically loads. Click Close and then click OK.

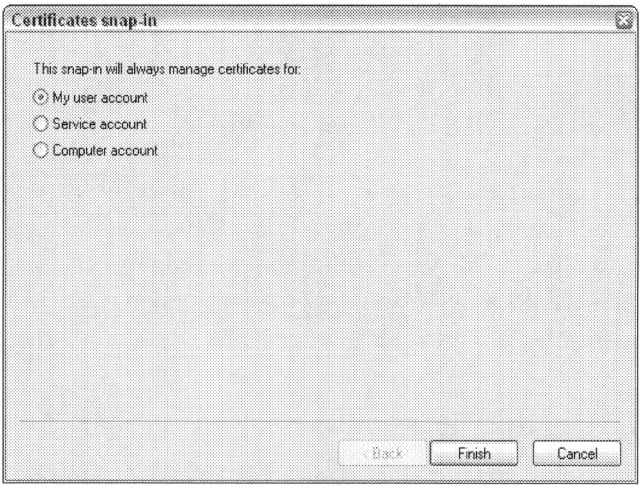

**Figure 6.64.** Each Certificates snap-in can manage only one type of account.

Browse to Certificates – Current User\Personal\Certificates. Right-click the user certificate, click All Tasks, and then click Export. The Certificate Export Wizard starts. Click Next.

Select Yes, export the private key. Click Next. Select Personal Information Exchange – PKCS #12 and make sure all the options are not selected (see Figure 6.65). Click Next. Type and confirm a password; do not forget this password or your private key and files that depend on it are locked away forever. Click Next. Browse to a removable media location, or to a secure storage area elsewhere on your network. This is the key to the kingdom; don't treat it lightly. Click Next. Click Finish. If the export was successful, click OK.

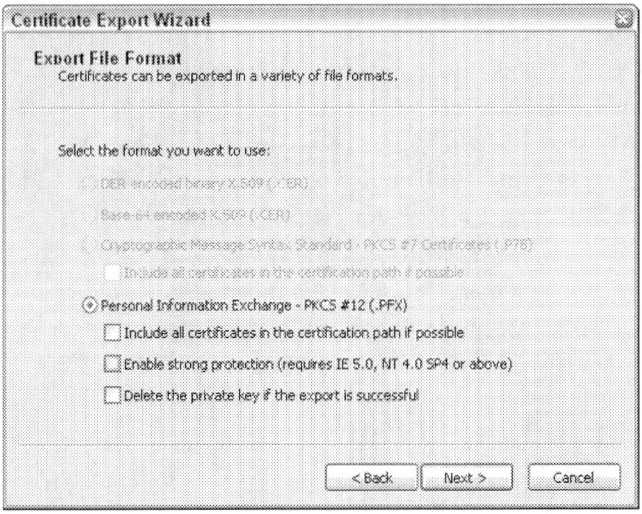

**Figure 6.65.** Lower the encryption options before exporting your certificate.

For the paranoid, once you have exported the encrypted certificate, you can then remove the certificate from the certificate store.

You should include a text file with your certificate (on a floppy disk or on a CD) that says, "EFS Recovery Disk for %username% on %computername%." Otherwise in a few days you'll have no idea who the .pfx file is for, or on what machine.

## Import a recovery certificate

Importing a certificate is a bit easier than exporting it. Create an MMC console with the Certificate snap-in loaded for your user account. Browse to Certificates – Current User\Personal\Certificates. Right-click the user certificate, click All Tasks, and then click Import. The Certificate Import Wizard starts. Click Next. Browse to the location where you are storing your encrypted certificate. You may need to change the file type filter to Personal Information Exchange to see the certificate. Select the certificate and then click Open.

Click Next, and then type the password you used to encrypt the certificate. Select Mark this key as exportable and then click Next. Make sure Place all certificates in the following store: (Personal) is selected and then click

Next. Click Finish. If the import was successful, click OK. The certificate should appear in the Certificate snap-in (see Figure 6.66). You should be able to access your encrypted documents.

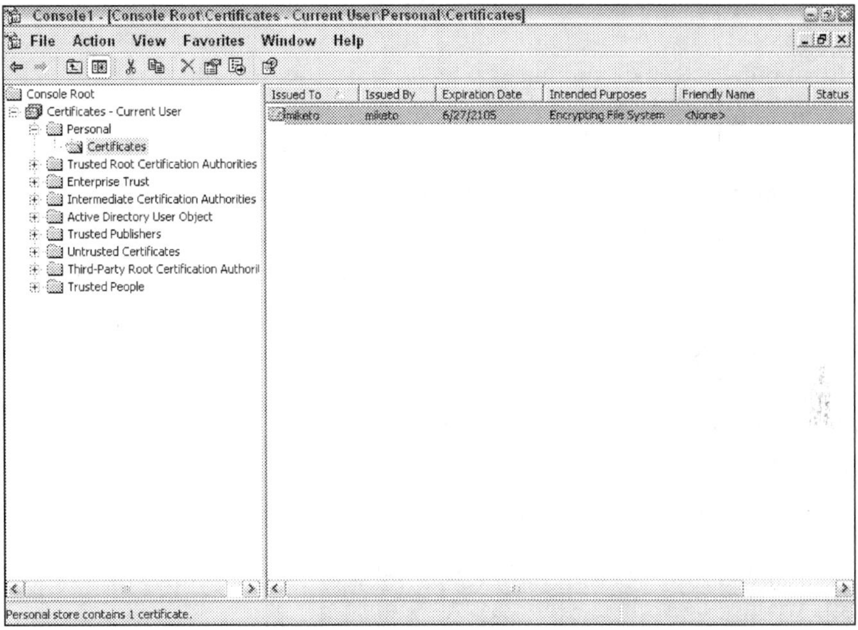

**Figure 6.66.** A successful import puts your certificate back into your personal store.

# For more information

Security is an ever-changing process. New attacks are created, new fixes and countermeasures developed. You can find out more information about how to secure your system with the help of the professionals who do it for a living.

Windows XP Security Guide v. 2, is an industrial-strength, enterprise-capable guide for securing Windows XP as a standalone computer and as a member of a domain. It contains invaluable descriptions of individual policies, VB scripts to handle common security tasks, and command-line "hacks" that you can run as part of a log on script to automate many one-time chores, such as rolling out a new administrative template. You can find the guide at www.microsoft.com/downloads/details.aspx?FamilyId=2D3E25BC-F434-4CC6-A5A7-09A8A229F118.

NIST (National Institute of Standards and Technology) Special Publication 800-68, Guidance for Securing Microsoft Windows XP System for IT Professionals (Draft), is likewise thorough and incredibly helpful. It

---

### Alternatives to Microsoft Windows

In a book about Windows it's unusual to find recommendations for non-Windows software. But if you feel like you're chasing your tail with respect to Windows security and you're interested to see what else is out there, you have two major operating systems to choose from.

- **Linux**. Linux is a free UNIX variant that is available in many distributions, or distros, that combine different features for specific markets or functions. Popular ones include Debian, Novell's SuSE, Mandriva (formerly Mandrake), and Ubuntu (a Debian variant). See Chapter 2 for information on Linux distros.

- **Mac OS X**. Apple Corporation's Mac OS X core relies on FreeBSD, a UNIX variant. The user interface is familiar to Mac users the world over, combining the best of both worlds. The downside: You must buy a Mac, which is the only hardware platform capable of running OS X.

---

contains a "real-world" view of how to secure Windows XP. You can find it at csrc.nist.gov/checklists/repository/1001.html.

Security bulletins with breaking news are available from Microsoft at www.microsoft.com/security, and you can sign up for vulnerability warnings for numerous products issued by CERT at www.cert.org. Your antivirus vendor may have a mailing list so you can sign up for alert bulletins; you should take advantage of one if it is offered.

## Just the facts

- "Security" is a process with many layers; there is no one thing that makes computers perfectly secure.

- Security Center provides monitoring functions but little else.

- Improve your security by installing third-party firewall, antivirus, and anti-spyware programs.

- Internet Explorer and Outlook Express require some persistence on your part to make them more secure.

- At the end of the day, the best security prevention device is you.

# Mastering Multimedia with Windows XP

**Chapter 7**

One of the most often used components of Microsoft Windows XP is the Windows Media Player. The player has greatly evolved over the years into a solid multimedia player/center for your music, video, and other multimedia outlets.

If you are using Windows XP Service Pack 2, you are using Windows Media Player 10, the second release in the Windows Media Player 9 series. This chapter will detail all the latest features and possibilities available with this release.

## Enjoy music with Windows Media Player

Listening to music on your PC has greatly improved from the days when you were limited to sticking an audio CD in the player and hoping it didn't skip. Windows XP Service Pack 2 ships with Windows Media Player 10, a complete audio player with an impressive range of features.

With competition from Real Player and Apple's iTunes, Microsoft had to come out with a legitimate response to these established products. Microsoft revamped the Media Player to look like full-fledged stand-alone product and not your typical operation system application. This "new look" takes the Windows Media Player well beyond your traditional music player — it now supports a number of media files (both music and video), creates catalogs and playlists, and even allows you to buy and download digital music and then sync to multimedia devices.

If you are a user who simply used Windows Media Player to listen to CDs, you'll be pleased by the quality of playback in the newest version as well as by the album information that is provided, such as track listings (if you have an active Internet connection), and by the ability to turn your CD into a collection of mp3 files for future use. For more advanced users, Microsoft's magazine-like Guide lets you keep up with what's current in today's music and movies, not to mention the imbedded link to XM Satellite Radio for XM subscribers.

## Recent versions of Windows Media Player

Microsoft has released several versions of Windows Media Player in a relatively short time span. In fact, if you're the type of person who doesn't update operating systems regularly, you may be several versions behind. Windows XP originally shipped with Windows Media Player XP (version 8), which cleaned up earlier versions found in Windows Me and integrated the now standard My Music and My Video folders.

Windows Media Player 9 followed afterwards and continued on the same path as the previous release, with greatly improved codecs. (A codec translates audio signals. It's short for coder/decoder.) By this time, Windows Media Player had escaped the shadow of its earlier days and was coming in to its own as virtual media empire. The problem was that you would actually need to sit down and actually learn how to use it, even though you just wanted to listen to a CD.

Let's fast forward to the present and Windows Media Player 10. Originally planned for the fabled Windows Longhorn release, the folks at the Windows Client team decided that the new features of this release couldn't wait for Longhorn. Microsoft released the Windows Media Player 10 as a stand-alone application (approximately 2 years before Longhorn is scheduled to ship).

If you've recently bought a computer, odds are that you have Windows XP Service Pack 2 right out of the box and are using Windows Media Player 10. If you are still running Media Player 9, you really should update to version 10; the performance and new features alone make this the obvious choice of the Media Player line. It is available for download at the Microsoft Web site or by using the Check for update feature in the Help menu of your current Windows Media Player.

---

### Windows Media Player 10 Mobile

Our lives are becoming increasingly mobile, and Microsoft has begun to address this with its portable music offerings. When you think of music on the go, it's easy to think of the obvious choices, past and present: Walkman, Discman, iPod, and satellite radio services, just to name a few.

Microsoft has gone beyond the obvious and gives you a new option for watching music and video on the go: Windows Media Player 10 Mobile.

Currently available for Windows Mobile 2003 Second Edition devices, Windows Media Player 10 Mobile ships with the Dell Axim X50 handheld and with the Audiovox SMT-5600 Smartphone. A number of HP iPaq models and the Dell Axim X30 can upgrade to Windows Media Player 10 Mobile. However, this version cannot be downloaded from Microsoft; for the handheld upgrade, you must update your ROM. For information on upgrading to Windows Media Player 10 Mobile, please visit the support sites for Dell or for Hewlett-Packard at http://welcome.hp.com/country/us/en/support.html.

Windows Media Player 10 Mobile enjoys many of the same features that your PC version contains, including playlists, a more convivial music library, all-in-one video and audio features, and even synchronization with your PC.

---

For those seeking the ultimate in multimedia experience, Microsoft recently released the Windows XP Media Center Edition, which gives users the total multimedia experience. You can read more about this in the introduction to this book, or later in this chapter in the section "Enjoy the digital experience."

# Get started with the Windows Media Player

There are a number of ways to start using the Windows Media Player. For example, if you want to listen to an audio CD, simply insert it into your CD-ROM drive and wait for it to load. If you haven't already set Windows Media Player as your default player, a screen appears proposing a number of suggested actions (see Figure 7.1). Select the option to play the CD; if you

are certain that this will always be
your response to this window, select
the Always do the selected action
check box.

When the Media Player appears
(see Figure 7.2), you can also select
any media files (CD, mp3, a wide
array of Windows files — video, TV
show, picture, audio, or Media —
or even MIDI files) using the standard Open file dialog box (Ctrl+O
or Open from the File menu). You
can select these files, either individually or using your standard Ctrl+A
(select all) or Ctrl (multiple selection) shortcuts.

**Figure 7.1.** The Select Task Action dialog box.

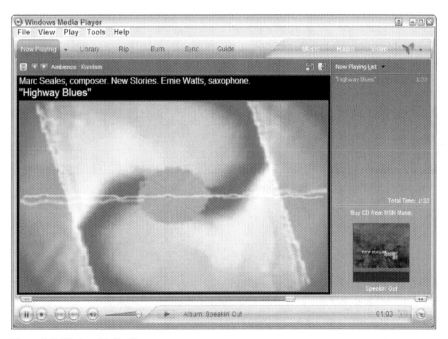

**Figure 7.2.** Windows Media Player.

**Watch Out!**

Depending on the quality of your CD-ROM drive and the type of CD you are attempting to play (standard musical CD, CD-RW, or DVD-RW), Windows may take a little bit of time to load the CD. Don't be surprised by this; it's normal.

The Now Playing tab also features a Quick Access panel (see Figure 7.3), which you can access by clicking the arrow next to the tab.

This panel will let you pick from any available CDs you have on your drive, playlists, musical albums/genres that you may have defined, or even all music/video files and

**Figure 7.3.** The Quick Access panel.

then load them into the Windows Media Player. You'll find out more about organizing your choices in the section "Using the Windows Media Player Library," later in this chapter.

Windows Media Player will then play your CD or your selected media files; sit back and enjoy!

Once your musical selection is playing, you'll notice a number of things going on in the Windows Media Player interface:

1. The Now Playing tab is the selected tab by default.

2. The Visualization screen will take up most of the actual Windows Media player interface; this screen can be rather psychedelic in nature and tends to make you forget what else is going on in the program. It doesn't serve any real purpose other than to look good.

3. If you have an active Internet connection, the album title as well as its track listing (title and length in minutes) appears on the right side of the Windows Media Player under the Now Playing List. A thumbnail of the album cover appears beneath the track listing along with a link to MSN Music, where it can be purchased.

**Inside Scoop**

To minimize CD lag (the time required for the Windows Media Player to read your CD, consider "ripping" the CD to audio files for use with the player. This is discussed in the section "Rip CDs," later in this chapter.

# Navigate the Windows Media Player

One of the biggest downsides to using the Windows Media Player (regardless of version) is the very presumptive nature of its interface. Why presumptive? The interface is intuitive — once you are familiar with it. For the first time user, the interface presumes that the user can get around easily. Even experienced computer users probably won't be familiar with terms like Rip, Burn, or Sync.

I'll point out the highlights of the interface in Figure 7.4.

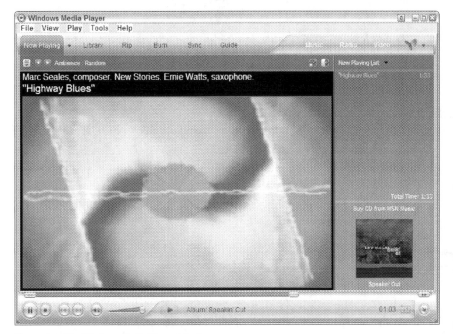

**Figure 7.4.** The Windows Media Player interface.

The Now Playing List displays the current selected tracks, the length of the song, and the album cover (if applicable). The bottom panel contains your standard music/video playback buttons, such as play, stop, next track, previous track, mute, and volume control. The current status is also displayed (stopped, playing, or paused). Two small buttons above the panel can be used to rewind or fast play the current track. Two other buttons on the bottom panel allow you to turn on the shuffle feature (next to the time elapsed timer) and to display the Windows Media Player in Skin mode (in the bottom right corner).

Adjacent to the Now Playing List is a panel that features a drop-down menu called the Now Playing Options menu, visualization buttons, the title of the

---

**Inside Scoop**

When adjusting the volume of the Windows Media Player, keep in mind that you may actually have three ways of adjusting the sound: the Windows Media Player itself, the Windows volume control in the Audio properties, and the volume control on any external speakers or headphones you may be using. For example, the Windows Media Player may be on full volume but you might not hear anything if your Audio properties volume is set low.

---

current visualizations, and options to either view the Windows Media Player as a full screen or to maximize/restore the Video and Visualization pane.

The Now Playing Options menu is an unusual menu for a number of reasons. First, it's quite easy to miss, especially if you are already playing music and are enthralled by the visualization. Second, it is a rather minute button compared to the rest of the Windows Media Player interface; yet it contains some options and features that are key components of the product. Third, it's primarily a mélange of the View and Tool menus, which are already available at the top of the screen whether or not you opt to view the Menu Bar.

Let's take a closer look at the Now Playing Options menu (see Figure 7.5).

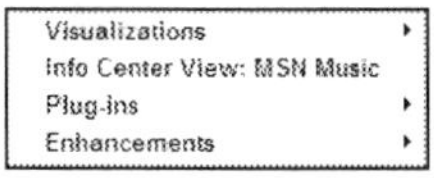

As if things weren't already strange enough, you'll find that the Options menu appears twice in the submenus — both pointing to the same location! (The Options menu also appears in the Tools menu.) The Visualizations submenu, which we will discuss in greater detail in the next section, allows you to pick or download your desired visualization for your multimedia experience. The Info Center View: MSN item opens up the Info Center in your Now Playing area of the Windows Media Player. The Info Center View provides information relevant to your musical selections.

| Visualizations | ▶ |
| Info Center View: MSN Music | |
| Plug-ins | ▶ |
| Enhancements | ▶ |

**Figure 7.5.** The Now Playing Options menu.

The Now Playing Options menu also allows you to select any previously installed Windows Media Player plug-ins. You may also opt to download new plug-ins using the Download Plug-ins command; once you select it, Windows Media Player opens an Internet browser in a new window and goes to the Microsoft download page. The Microsoft Web site provides plug-ins for

---

**Watch Out!**

You must have an active Internet connection in order for the Info Center to work. If you are currently connected to the Internet, make sure that you have not selected Work Offline from the File menu. Windows Media Player provides a link that allows you to connect to the Info Center and the online store. If you're working offline and try to access the Info Center, the Info Center won't appear, but you will get instructions on how to activate it.

audio effects, DVD decoders, MP3 creation, and so on. The Options submenu displays the exact same Options tab as in the Visualizations submenu.

The final submenu in the Now Playing Options menu allows you select an enhancement. Enhancements are a set of controls that allow you to custom set eight advanced parameters as SRS Wow Effects, Graphic Equalizer, Video Settings, Color Chooser, Crossfading and Auto Volume Leveling, Media Link for E-mail, Play Speed Settings, and Quiet Mode. The selected enhancement appears in the lower half of the Now Playing area. Each enhancement features a number of options unique to that particular enhancement. However, there are two unique elements to each enhancement: previous/next buttons and a close button to hide the enhancement window.

## Use visualizations

The Windows Media Player features a number of visualizations, which are display patterns, organized by category, that react to an audio signal as if they're "dancing to the beat" of your musical selection. Is there a significant value to visualizations? Your mileage may vary. This feature serves a purely entertainment function; there is no tangible enhancement to the product by using them.

If you are using the standard full mode, a chosen visualization is displayed in the main Now Playing area. In this mode, there are three ways of selecting your desired visualization:

1. From the View menu and selecting the Visualizations submenu.

2. By selecting the Now Playing Options menu and selecting the Visualizations submenu.

3. By right-clicking the Now Playing area and selecting the Visualizations submenu.

Visualizations are separated into different categories or collections (see Figure 7.6). Using the first two options listed above, you can download additional visualizations and set parameters for some of your visualizations using the Options window. However, please note that the Options are specifically for plug-ins and not the entirety of visualizations. Some of these visualizations can be customized or even removed. If you are interested in obtaining additional visualizations, you can download them using the Download Visualizations command in the Now Playing Options menu and the View

**Figure 7.6.** Visualization options.

**Watch Out!**

If you are using Windows Media Player in Skin mode, your selected visualization must be supported by the skin you are using in order for it to be displayed.

menu; if you are in the Options window, you can click the Look for plug-ins on the Internet link that opens a Microsoft download site on another page.

If you are using the Windows Media Player in mini-player mode, you can view visualizations in the Video and Visualization window (see Figure 7.7).

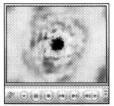

**Figure 7.7.** Visualizations in mini-player mode.

## Use skins

Like many other current software packages, the Windows Media Player allows you to use skins to enhance your multimedia adventure. Find the default interface a bit austere or boring? Apply one of the five standard skins to the Windows Media Player and completely change the look and feel of the program. Of course, if you're not impressed with any of those, you can opt to download skins in the Skin Chooser. If you're looking to find something a little more cutting-edge or non-Microsoft, use a search engine such as Google to find some original skins that may be more to your liking.

Perhaps you're the type of user that never really played around with the Windows Media Player interface. Think of a skin as a "glove" that you put over the Windows Media Player. Just like a fine leather glove, your Windows Media Player skin accentuates certain features. The downside to using skins is that you have to re-adjust to a whole new interface. The default interface discussed earlier in this chapter — menu items, buttons, and so on — may not apply or, at the very least, not occur in the same place in a skin.

To apply a skin, you must first select the Skin Chooser from the View menu. If you select the Skin Mode before you select your skin, the Windows Media Player will switch to 9SeriesDefault, the default skin (see Figure 7.8).

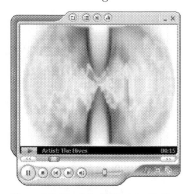

**Figure 7.8.** The default Windows Media Player skin.

**Watch Out!**

Not all skins provide complete product functionality; the features available for a given skin depend on the author of the skin. For example, some skins might not allow DVD playback.

Once you are in the Skin Chooser window (see Figure 7.9), you can select from one of five pre-installed skins. By clicking on the skin name, the main panel displays desired skin, as well as information pertaining to the skin, such as title, author, and copyright. If you are satisfied with your selection, click the Apply Skin button to validate your selection. You may also opt to delete an existing skin by clicking the corresponding button.

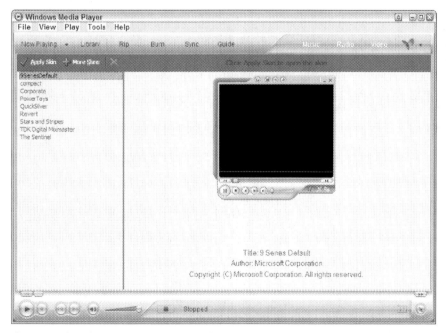

**Figure 7.9.** The default Windows Media Player skin.

If you click the More Skins button, a new browser window appears allowing you to download skins from the Microsoft Web site.

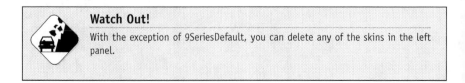

**Watch Out!**

With the exception of 9SeriesDefault, you can delete any of the skins in the left panel.

# Use the Windows Media Player Library

One of the Windows Media Player's strongest features is the highly-evolved and well-organized library and playlist features. What's the difference between a library and a playlist? They do sound somewhat similar. The library is an actual database that stores information concerning your media files on your computer or network. The playlist is literally a list that you can create (or have created automatically) of various media files that you would like to listen to or watch. You use the library to create a playlist.

Let's jump right in. You start simply by clicking Library from the Windows Media Player interface.

The Library page appears, greatly modifying the Windows Media Player interface that you've grown accustomed to (see Figure 7.10).

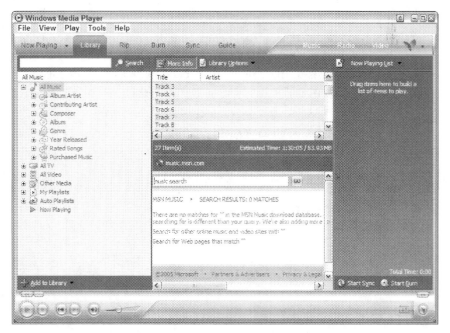

**Figure 7.10.** The Library page.

What's nice about the Library page is that the panels contain just about everything you need to create a playlist in a relatively well-organized package. Unfortunately, well-organized doesn't necessarily translate to "user-friendly." The Library is cluttered with too much information. For example, the numerous examples of genres make the pane difficult to navigate. Fortunately, you may or may not use all of the information on this page depending on how robust your media collection is.

**Inside Scoop**

The Contents pane is labeled with the name of the selected category. For example, if you are in the All Music category, All Music will appear as the title pane, as shown in Figure 7.10.

On the left side is the Contents panel; this resizable panel contains an expandable/collapsible menu that categorizes all of the media on your system. The menu features seven different media categories: All Music, All TV, All Video, Other Media, My Playlists, Auto Playlists, and Now Playing. The first three categories, as well as the Auto Playlists category, contain subcategories relevant to each category. For example, the All TV category contains subcategories such as Series or Actors. The Auto Playlists category is slightly different: it features playlists that have automatically been created. You can categorize a media file as a favorite or as new; if you dislike a song, you can file it under Songs I dislike, or Media Player can file the song for you if you rate the song with a certain number of stars (right-click the song title and apply a number of stars in the Rate menu). The Other Media category contains non-Windows Media Player native formats, such as WAV files. My Playlists lists any previous song that you may have saved on your machine.

There is an All Pictures category in your Windows Media Player library that appears if you have installed a device that can view pictures and it has been synchronized. (If you have installed a device to your computer — such as a handheld computer — you can sync it with Windows Media Player.) Similarly, categories are created in the Contents panel once the content has been synched to the device. The category name will use the name of the device.

If you have purchased any media from Microsoft's online stores, the corresponding files will appear in the Purchased Music/Purchased Videos subcategories of the All Music/All Videos categories.

## Create your own playlist

If you've come through the previous section unscathed, the good news for you is that you've got through the confusing part. Now is the time to create your own playlist, which you can eventually sync to another device or burn to CD with just the touch of a button.

Before we do that, look through your categories in the Contents pane and take a look at what you have in the archives. When you are ready to make your selection, click the Add to Library button (see Figure 7.11) and select one of the seven available options:

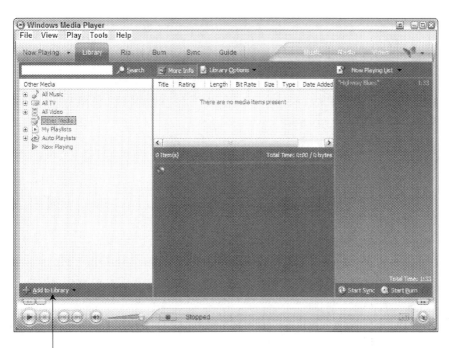

Add to Library button

**Figure 7.11.** The Add to Library button.

■ **By searching computer.** This option can be a time-consuming option depending on the size of your hard drive and the number of media files on your machine. If you select this option, you can specify which drives and/or folders to search. If you have an Internet connection, you also have the option of updating the media information, which can go by quickly (if only new media files are updated) or can be dreadfully slow (if all library files are updated and you have a record collection that rivals that of any music publisher). There are two advanced options that allow you to search music that has previously been removed from the library or to add volume leveling values for files. Be careful — this latter option can be time-consuming. It is not checked by default.

■ **By monitoring folders.** This option is a safe option for home users. Once you click this option, click Add to add folders to search. If you use this option, Windows scans certain directories (these directories are easily added or removed) for any file activity — added files, deleted files, renamed files, moved files, and so on — and then updates the Windows Media Player Library accordingly. In order to keep your network running smoothly and to avoid needlessly draining system resources, do not add network folders to your list of scanned categories. If you are a home user, you can avoid resource depletion by selecting a reasonable number of directories.

- **Add Currently Playing Item.** This option allows you to add the item currently playing to the playlist.

- **Add Currently Playing Playlist.** Similar to the option above, this option allows you to add the content of the current playlist to the new playlist.

- **Add Folder.** This option lets you select an entire folder for addition to your playlist. All supported files within the folder are added to the playlist.

- **Add File or Playlists.** This option allows you to manually select the media files or playlists to which you want to listen. As when opening files in the Now Playing panel, you can use keyboard shortcuts such as Ctrl+A (select all) or hold the Ctrl key for multiple selections.

- **Add URL.** Simply add the URL of the media file to which you want to listen.

Alternately, you may also drag and drop files from your desktop into the Windows Media Player library page. Once you use any of the above options, the selected files should now appear in the playlist.

# Enjoy the digital experience

Windows Media Player 10 focuses on the total multimedia experience. It is a fully integrated music and video software package that includes DVDs and high-definition playback. It has even added an interactive guide featuring music and video clips on demand, the latest music and movie releases, music downloads, and viewer's choice features. Let's not forget the online music stores, subscription-based satellite radio services, as well as free Internet-based radio services, all of which you can access from Media Player.

However, keep in mind that you need a broadband Internet connection to really take advantage of all Media Player has to offer. If you're still using a 56k connection to connect to the Internet, downloads can be extremely slow — plus, downloads from Microsoft Web sites are particularly long, due to the heavy traffic on those sites. If you haven't made the move to high-speed Internet, contact your local phone company, cable company, or Internet service provider to see what is available in your neighborhood.

## The Windows Media Center Edition

Microsoft recently released the Windows Media Center Edition 2005, which is the end-all be-all of the Microsoft multimedia experience. Built on Windows XP Service Pack 2, this is a standalone release that can only be bought as a unit; there are no upgrades available.

One of the biggest features of the Windows Media Center is that you can literally plug your computer in to your standard television or even a High Definition Television (HDTV). Like many home theatre systems, you can set this up relatively quickly using the remote control that comes with the unit. Unlike other home theatre systems, you can store all your multimedia files in a single location, burn or back up CDs and photos, or burn home videos onto a CD or DVD.

Microsoft really gives DVR-technologies and other competitors such as TiVo a run for their money with its new PVR (Personal Video Recording) system. You can record up to three live television shows simultaneously. If you're not sure what's on, use the Electronic Program Guide (EPG) to browse that day's programming.

For more information on the Windows Media Center Edition 2005 and any of its new features, please visit www.microsoft.com/windowsxp/mediacenter/default.mspx.

A lot of the above features are compatible with other media players, such as Real Player, but regardless of what software you end up using, be careful not to become too enthralled by all the features — you'll quickly forget your work and spend your day downloading.

Microsoft can certainly boast one of the world's largest online music collections. With a veritable music warehouse, you can find anything you're looking for, download it, and enjoy it using Windows Media Player 10 or a portable music player.

From either the Microsoft Web site or the Windows Media Player 10, you can select from one of eight boutiques selling a wide variety of goods and services (in the United States alone!). If you're using the Windows Media Player, you also have access to other specialized media outlets, such as CourtTV, MLB.com, or CinemaNow (see Figure 7.12).

**Figure 7.12.** Choose an online store.

If that's not enough, Microsoft and XM satellite radio have partnered to bring you satellite radio via the Windows Media Player. If you're already a subscriber, you can enter your e-mail and password and enjoy the same quality satellite broadcasts that you enjoy using your XM unit.

If you're not interested in signing up for a subscription-based service, the Windows Media Player offers thousands of free Web-streaming radio

---

## PlaysForSure

When deciding on a portable music player (including digital media receivers, car stereos, DVD and home theatre systems, Windows-based handhelds, or even portable media devices, just look for the logo: PlaysForSure.

The PlaysForSure logo is your guarantee that your musical device will play Windows Media Audio (WMA) files.

## What is satellite radio?

Satellite radio is one of the latest crazes in music technology. The satellite-based services provide a large number of unique music channels (each satellite service has its own radio stations) as well as national and international news stations, sporting events, concerts, and more. The most appealing aspects of satellite radio is that it is 100 percent commercial free. The music stations follow a format but are not restricted to the commercially-based playlist to which terrestrial stations are bound.

Satellite radio is not currently regulated by the Federal Communications Commission (FCC), which means that its stations aren't subject to restrictions on content that land-based stations are.

stations — you'll find local, national, and Internet-based stations. To listen to the radio using the Windows Media Player, click the Radio tab on the right side of the screen. The MSN Radio screen appears with easy-to-follow instructions for choosing your desired radio station (see Figure 7.13).

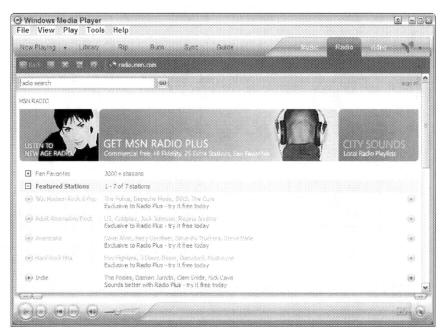

**Figure 7.13.** The MSN Radio screen.

**Watch Out!**

To use the MSN Radio feature, you will need to have a valid Microsoft passport, which is essentially a single e-mail address to use all of Microsoft's features on the Microsoft Passport Network. For more information on the Microsoft passport, please visit https://accountservices.passport.net/ppnetworkhome.srf?lc=1033.

# Windows Digital Rights Management

Microsoft now uses the Windows Digital Rights Management (WDRM) system for handling your subscription-based multimedia files. This system is also known as Janus. What sets this apart from other competitors, such as iTunes, is that it allows you to obtain a license for a song, for example, and then synchronize that song to another device without hassle. Once the license is expired, the file will cease to function. Unlike other programs, where you either cannot use the file on other devices, or you must re-register the file each time (with a limited number of registrations), the WDRM allows you to accomplish this easily. When a user opens a WDRM-protected file, he will be asked to activate the license by validating it (clicking a button). Once the license is activated, the user can listen to media file on that machine for the duration of the subscription. The file will not play on any other machine, including hand-held music devices, because it is not registered for those machines.

# Use PowerToys

Windows Media Player now supports the use of PowerToys — this is essentially a set of enhancements or "toys" that you can use with Windows Media Player for XP.

What benefits do the PowerToys bring to the Windows Media Player? The most valuable benefit of this component of the Windows Media Bonus Pack is the tray control. This new icon can be set into startup or launched on demand to perform basic functions such as volume and mute control, advance track, and play and pause with a single mouse click. A Most Recently Used List feature is also available to clear your list history as desired.

**Watch Out!**

It is important to keep in mind that PowerToys are not supported by Microsoft. In other words, they do not offer technical support or handle any incidents caused by PowerToys.

**Hack**

If you have a particularly large playlist (in excess of 4000 entries), split the playlist into two different files before you import them into Excel.

The next feature is the Media Library Management Wizard; however, it is only available if you are using Windows Media Player 7 or 8. Please note that this feature is not available if you are using the Windows Media Player Series 9 (which also includes Windows Media Player 10 for some reason), because an advanced library management feature is already available in this release. Quite frankly, since most XP users are already on Windows XP Service Pack 2, there is no real reason not to use Windows Media Player 10.

The bonus pack also includes a Playlist Import to Excel PowerToy that lets you import your playlist into Excel 2002 or later. Once you import the playlist into Excel, you can sort your data as desired and then export it to HTML. The HTML format is an easy-to-read file format that most people can open easily. For example, it is common for people to share their music playlists online; HTML format is perfect for this type of activity.

The PowerToy Skin feature gives you more flexibility in managing the library. To use this feature, install it and then select the feature in the same way you would select any other skin (see the section "Use skins," earlier in this chapter). In order for the skin to work, it must be able to read and write to the library. (In other words, it must be able to access the Media Library.) If it cannot, an error message will appear. To correct this, go to the Options submenu in the Tools menu and click the Media Library tab. Click Full Access under Access rights of other applications and click OK. Once you do this, all skins will be able to access (read/write) the Media Library.

The final feature of the PowerToys bonus pack is the Windows Media Player Skin Importer. This feature allows you to import Winamp skins (a Windows Media Player competitor that is also worth trying out) and to then install them as Windows Media Player skins.

For more information on any of these features or on how to use them, please see www.microsoft.com/windows/windowsmedia/download/bppowertoys.aspx.

## Use the Windows Media Bonus Pack

Similar to the PowerToys described above, the Windows Media Bonus Pack is an expanded package that was designed as a "thank you" to users of the

**Watch Out!**
It is important to keep in mind that PowerToys are not supported by Microsoft, even though they are released on an official Microsoft release, Windows Media Bonus Pack.

Windows XP digital media players. As with PowerToys, you must be using Windows XP in order to use the Windows Media Bonus Pack.

The Windows Media Bonus Pack features a number of interesting features that will certainly interest fans of the Windows Media Player. One of the best features in this little gem is the "light" version of the MP3 converter that is bundled with Plus! for Windows XP (the more robust, paid version). This tool helps you conserve disk space by converting bulky MP3 files to Windows Media Audio (WMA) files. Unlike MP3 files, Microsoft's audio format allows you to weigh quality versus size issues to determine the best sound quality using the least amount of disk space. For more information on Plus! for Windows, please visit www.microsoft.com/plus.

The bonus pack also includes a copy of the PowerToys for Windows Media Player XP (see above), a new batch of high-quality visualizations that go far beyond the original batch standard to Windows Media Player 10, a new series of skins, and finally, the Windows Movie Maker Creativity Kit. This kit lets you spice up your home movies with sound effects, music, clips, and other multimedia enhancements. For more information on the Windows Media Bonus Pack, please visit www.microsoft.com/windows/windowsmedia/download/bonuspack.aspx.

## Use TV tuner cards

Windows Media Player supports playback of DVR-recorded television shows as well as the direct transmission of television shows using a TV tuner card. The new Windows XP Media Center Edition also features television playback as well as program recording. The advantage to using the Media Center is that most of these machines come equipped with a single tuner that can pick up cable, satellite, or antenna signals.

If you're not quite ready to replace your PC just so you can watch television on it, you can still use a number of analog tuner cards with your standard Windows XP machine.

## Enjoy WMV HD

With the boom in high-definition television, it was only a matter of time before Microsoft used its operating system and multimedia software to offer the same technology for watching DVDs. In fact, many movie studios are

**Watch Out!**

If your Windows XP Media Center Edition PC does not come with an on-board TV tuner, you can upgrade. The Microsoft Web site features a list of partners who sell compatible tuner cards at http://welcome.hp.com/country/us/en/support.html.

distributing Windows Media High Definition Video (WMV HD) versions with their regular DVD releases.

To enjoy movies up to six times higher quality than standard DVDs, you may have to upgrade your current media configuration or buy a machine running Microsoft XP Media Center Edition.

For more information on Windows Media High Definition Video and to see if your machine is compatible, please visit www.microsoft.com/windows/windowsmedia/content_provider/film/AboutHDVideo.aspx.

# Go further with Windows Media Player

As I noted at the beginning of the chapter, the value of Windows Media Player 10 goes far beyond simply listening to your CDs and audio files. Today's player lets you rip CDs (taking a CD and turning each track into a distinct audio file), burn CDs (make copies), or even sync to external devices.

## Rip CDs

Another nice feature in recent Windows Media Player versions is the CD ripping functions. Depending on the CD, you should be able to rip CD-RW discs. If your disc uses next generation anti-pirating technology, you will not be able to rip the disc. To start, simply click the Rip tab in the menu bar on the left side of the page. If you have a valid audio CD in your CD-ROM drive, each individual track of the album appears along with relevant information (see Figure 7.14).

By default, all tracks are selected for ripping. Each track features information on the artist, composer, length, genre, style, and data provider. The rip status is blank but will change to Ripping, Pending, or Ripped once you start the process by clicking Rip Music.

If you want more information on this particular album, click the Find Album Info at the top-right of the panel. This page displays more information about the album, including cover art and the track listing. If you click Finish, your main page will be updated if necessary. If you wish to hear a sample of the album or even an entire track, or find out what other fans of the group enjoy, click View Album Info. If you have a Microsoft Passport, you can leave your own rating for each track.

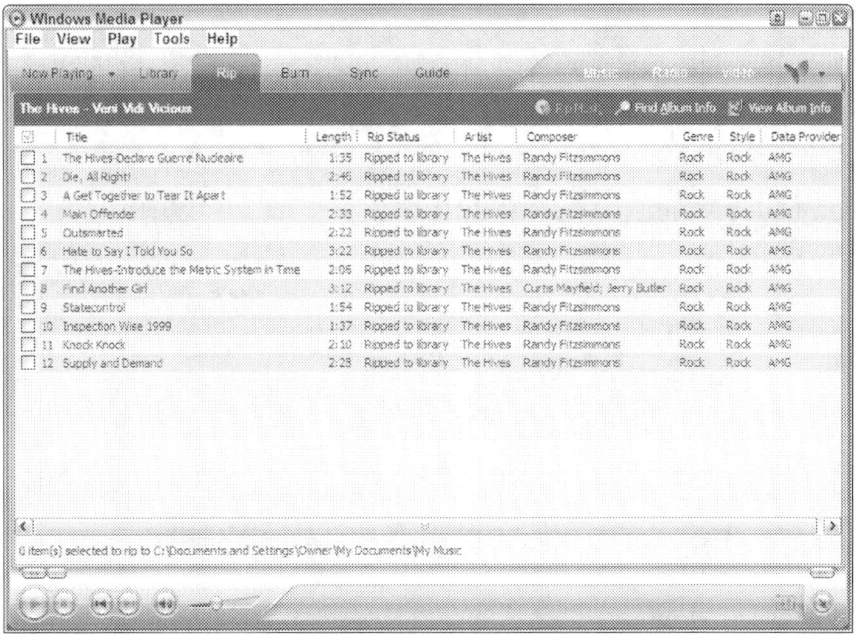

**Figure 7.14.** The Rip page.

Once your CD is ripped, the WMA files will appear in your My Music folder under the name of the group; the files are under the name of the album title. In the event that the music database couldn't find information on your artist or CD, the files will appear under unknown artist or unknown album.

It's important that you look through the Rip Music tab of the Options dialog box (see Figure 7.15). Click Tools and the Options to open it. Unfortunately, the Windows Media Player does not highlight the Rip Music tab; frankly, it's surprising that they didn't add a Settings link on the main Rip page. The options include typical settings, such as ripped music location and file nomenclature information. More importantly, the Options page lets you select output format. This is where the Windows Media Player is a bit weak — you can rip to mp3 or three variants of the Windows Media Audio (WMA). Real Audio, on the other hand, lets you also rip to AAC, Wave, and Real Audio. There is a link that directs to mp3 formats (click Learn more about MP3 formats), but it also includes other information, such as combined voice

---

**Watch Out!**

You cannot rip DVDs using the Windows Media Player. Remember that you're not supposed to be doing this anyway!

**Watch Out!**

A high-speed Internet connection is required to try out the WMA versus mp3 audio demonstration on the Compare Windows Media Audio to other formats link.

and music content. Check out the Compare Windows Media Audio to other formats link for comparisons between WMA files and mp3.

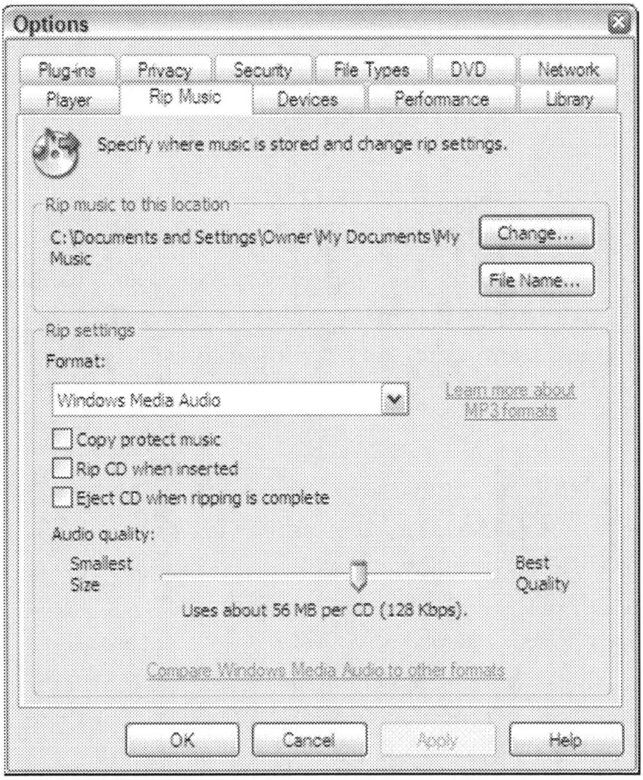

**Figure 7.15.** The Options dialog box.

Perhaps even more important than the format selection is the audio quality. Windows Media Player allows you to select Kbps rate for ripping CDs. The higher the rate, the higher the quality, and obviously, the higher the file size in MB. If you are ripping an album to mp3 for use on your computer or a device with a large storage space, it's best to rip at the highest rate possible. If you are using an older device with lower storage space, it would be a good idea to use 128 Kbps (default rate). Unless absolutely necessary, you should avoid ripping at any speed inferior to 128 Kbps.

---

### The future of CD ripping

Ripping CDs is convenient, and there certainly are valid reasons for doing so, but it is something that is becoming increasingly difficult to do within the context of current legislation.

More and more music publishers are using next-generation copyright systems that either limit or outright prevent ripping CDs to individual audio files. In some cases, you may believe you successfully ripped a CD, but once you listen to it on your computer or other device, you realize that you don't have a ripped audio track at all, but rather white noise.

---

Overall, the Windows Media Player has a decently integrated CD ripper; it's certainly not the best on the block, but it should suffice when you want simply to rip a standard music CD for listening on your Axim handheld. As stated above, it's difficult to tell how the future of music ripping will play out in the coming years, so this feature shouldn't be your sole reason to use or reject the Windows Media Player.

## Burn CDs

Not surprisingly, the Windows Media Player also lets you burn CDs, not just rip them. This can be practical for making backups of valued CDs or imports that are hard to replace. However, it should not be used for illegal copying.

When using the Burn feature in the Windows Media Player, it's important to remember the context within which you're working — if you're hoping to burn some data files, this is not the program for you. In fact, there is no real reason to use the Burn feature of the Windows Media Player for any reason other than that it's there. It will get the job done for burning a playlist or an audio CD, and yes, you can create a data CD, but the process gets so confusing that it's better to go someplace easier. You'd be better off to try another software package that offers a complete burning tool. In that case, don't run to a Windows Media Player competitor; Real Player, for example, has the same drawbacks when burning data CDs.

To start burning CDs in Windows Media Player, simply click the Burn tab from the menu bar on the left side of the page. The Burn page appears with the Burn List on the left pane and the current CD player contents detailed in the right pane (see Figure 7.16).

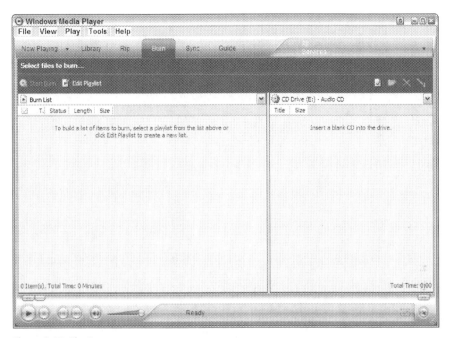

**Figure 7.16.** The Burn page.

From the left pane, you can use the drop-down menu to select a playlist or use the Edit Playlist option to create a new one (and not to edit an existing playlist). If you select the Edit Playlist option (simply by clicking the Edit Playlist button), you can select an item from the Library and add it to the burn list (see Figure 7.17). For example, you can mix and match songs available in various categories. If you do not use the Edit Playlist option, you can select any of the available categories.

---

### Burn Baby Burn

There are a number of decent shareware programs out there that can do the same things as the Windows Media Player burn feature and then some. A quick Google search will yield a number of fine examples.

If you're more comfortable with buying software, try the highly-rated Nero. This program is the real deal, though it is intended for advanced users.

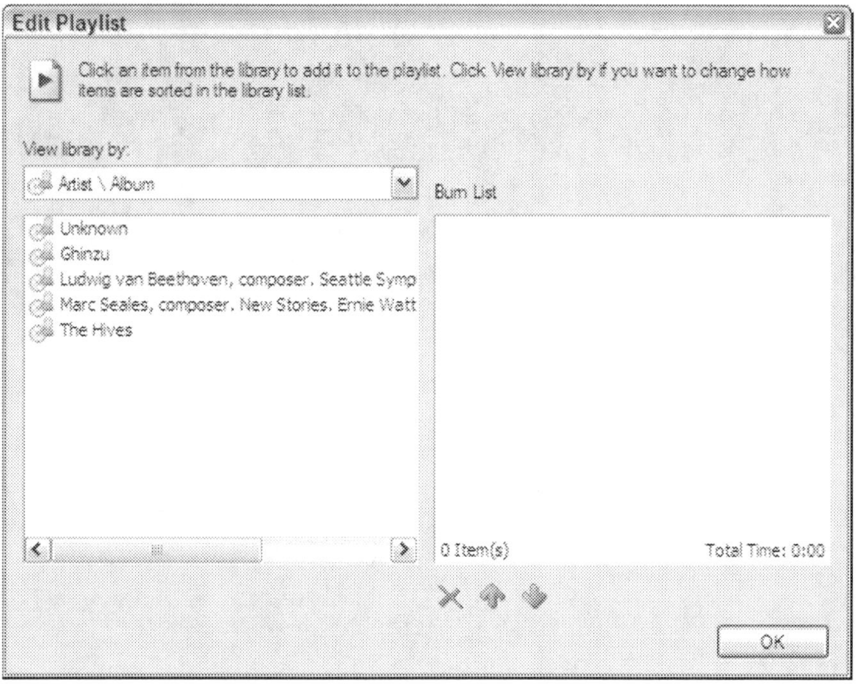

**Figure 7.17.** Selecting a new playlist in the Edit Playlist window.

The right panel of the Burn page lets you select the type of CD you wish to create (see Figure 7.18). Before you do this, make sure you have a valid CD-RW disc in your CD-ROM drive; otherwise, you will not be able to select files as desired.

One nice feature of the Burn page, as compared to the Rip page, is that you can go directly to the options. What's odd is that the options for the Burn are not in the Options page, but in a separate window called Display properties and settings, represented by the left-most icon (with the check-mark) on the right side of the window. Click it to open the properties dialog box (see Figure 7.19).

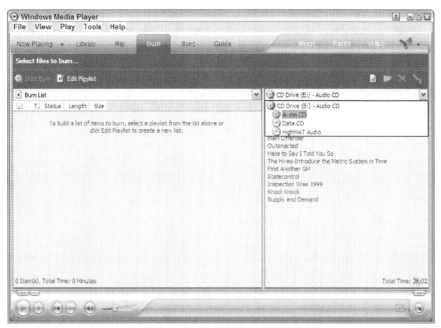

**Figure 7.18.** Choosing the type of CD.

**Figure 7.19.** The Recording tab of the CD Properties dialog box.

This dialog box features Recording options, but more importantly, quality settings similar to the ones mentioned in the "Rip CDs" section, but only for data CDs. The Recording options allow selecting a drive to store the "image" file that is created when burning CDs. This file may require up to 1GB in free disk space. This is also where you can set the write speed. It's best to select a mid-level speed — not the fastest, which can causer errors; nor the slowest, because you'll wait an eternity — when deciding on an appropriate speed. Turning your attention to the Quality tab (see Figure 7.20), you can set parameters for burning CDs and volume settings. For data CDs, you can let Windows optimize the quality automatically or manually set it — selecting either a smaller file size (lower quality) or higher quality (larger file size). For musical files, you can select whether to activate volume leveling. This feature levels the volume during the recording process so as not to distort the sound quality. Recording your music at a high volume with this option deselected causes a distorted playback even at a low volume.

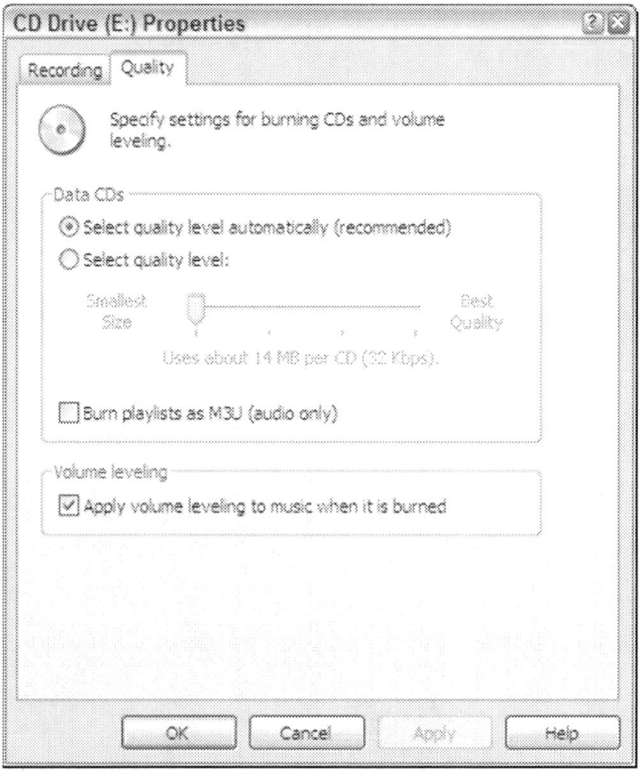

**Figure 7.20.** The Quality tab of the CD Properties dialog box.

Once you have selected your files, you can click the Start Burn button to start the process. The length of the CD burning depends on the size of the disc as well as the quality settings you may have set earlier in the Display properties and settings page.

# Multimedia without Windows Media Player

It's true that the Windows Media Player is your portal to the Windows XP multimedia experience. However, there are still some aspects that you might have forgotten about that don't necessarily involve music or video. Fortunately, Windows XP hasn't forgotten about them!

## Scanners

Windows XP, like its predecessors, uses the Intel standard, Plug and Play, which lets you install a device and lets the computer find and install the necessary drivers. This is still very much the case with scanners.

Scanners have taken many shapes and added new features over the years; in fact, scanners often act as photocopiers and fax machines in what are called "all-in-ones."

Once you have installed your scanner, you can view it in the Control Panel under the Scanners and Cameras heading.

Once you have scanned a document, you can use the Windows Picture and Fax viewer to preview it. See Chapter 9 for more about faxing. That said, it is preferable that you use any of the proprietary or third-party software that shipped with your scanner.

## Digital cameras

Most of the information for scanners also applies to digital cameras; both devices are most likely plug-and-play devices that are connected to the computer using a USB cable.

However, the folks at Microsoft offer a lot more options for digital cameras than they do for scanners. Unfortunately, most of these options and features are pretty low-key, so they're easy to miss. Plus, most digital cameras come with some sort of proprietary or third-party software that the camera

---

**Hack**

If your camera or scanner is not plug-and-play compatible, you may have to do things the hard way and add the device using the Device manager. See Chapter 4 for more about the Device manager. For more information on installing your device, please consult the documentation that came with the device.

manufacturer recommends using. Windows XP, in many ways, doesn't stand much of a chance from the start.

Nevertheless, it's important to know what you can do with Windows XP for creating photo albums, screensavers, or sending photos over e-mail.

Windows XP offers a low-tech way to create a photo album for your digital photos. In the My Pictures folder, create a new folder, right-click it, and then choose Properties. In the folder properties dialog box, select Photo Album from the Customize tab. The latest four photos in the album will appear as thumbnails in the folder icon (similar to ripped music folders displaying album art in My Music). Photo albums are best used with a smaller collection of photos. If you wish to incorporate a large number of files, you should use Pictures instead of Photo Album in the Customized tab.

If you'd like to have a customized screensaver on your machine, Windows XP lets you scroll through your pictures and take a literal stroll down memory lane. In the Display page (accessible from the Control Panel or by right-clicking the desktop and selecting Properties), click the Screen Saver tab and then select My Pictures Slideshow from the drop-down list (see Figure 7.21).

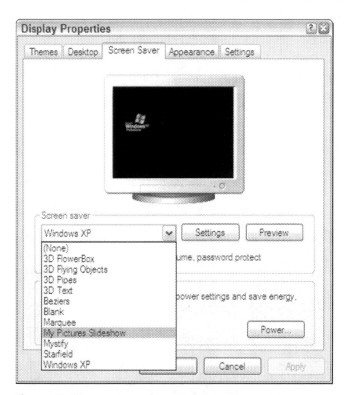

**Figure 7.21.** Choose your own pictures to use as a screen saver.

**Watch Out!**

By selecting My Pictures Slideshow, Windows XP will scroll through all photos and folders in the My Pictures directory. If you have any sensitive or non-work appropriate photos, you may wish to click Settings in the Screen Saver tab and select the desired folder to be used in the Slideshow.

As noted above, Windows XP will scroll through all folders and photos by default. It may be a good idea to create a folder in the My Pictures directory called "slideshow" and put a copy of the desired photos in this folder. In the Screen Saver settings, select this folder from the collapsible menu and you can rest assured that no other photos will display!

In the My Pictures folders, you can also do a number of things with your photos; again, these features are so nondescript that it's easy to just gloss over them. For example, if you click a photo, you can e-mail it to a friend by clicking E-mail this file in the File and Folder Tasks menu on the left of the folder. A menu appears asking if the picture should be resized. Once you've validated your selection, the default e-mail program opens with a new e-mail ready to go; simply add the recipient and send! From the same menu, you can also publish the files to your Web site. Click Publish this file to the Web and simply follow the steps and your photo will be online in no time!

Finally, you can also order prints of your digital photos. In the Picture Tasks menu (located just above File and Folder tasks), click Order prints online. A wizard walks you through the steps; select the photos you wish to order and then select one of three service providers: Fujifilm, Shutterfly and Kodak EasyShare Gallery (formerly known as Ofoto). Once you have made your choice, simply follow the instructions of the service provider and you'll have your photos in your mailbox in just a few days.

## Video cameras

You can use digital video cameras with Windows XP, specifically with Movie Maker 2, which we will discuss in the next section. Before you use Windows XP to realize your next film, make sure that you have the necessary cables.

Digital video cameras tend to be FireWire (IEEE 1394) devices that require a special cable and adapter. Make sure that your machine supports this standard and make sure that you have the correct cable (there are several types of adapter pins at the ends of the cable — in other words, the ends can be of different sizes).

**Watch Out!**

As you add more and more peripheral devices, such as digital cameras, handhelds, and video cameras, it's important to make sure that you have enough USB ports to get the job done. Most likely, you'll need to buy an adapter because most machines (especially laptops) only have three or four USB slots.

# Use Windows Movie Maker 2

Don't be confused by the title; if you're using Windows XP Service Pack 2, you also have Windows Movie Maker installed. Unfortunately, the wording in the About menu is so confusing that it's easy to think you're using version 5.1 Service Pack 2. At the bottom of the menu is a brief mention that you're using Movie Maker 2.1.

The Windows Movie Maker (see Figure 7.22) is a "home studio" for assembling and editing movies that you can eventually share on CD/DVD or put online for download. Overall, this is a very solid application that is a lot cheaper (read: free) and easier than buying a professional software package. However, though it's not overly complicated, Movie Maker isn't a beginner's tool, and it can be seem intimidating. Microsoft realizes this and has put together a pretty extensive support system that includes newsgroups, documentation, and books on the product. For more information, please visit www.microsoft.com/windowsxp/using/moviemaker/default.mspx.

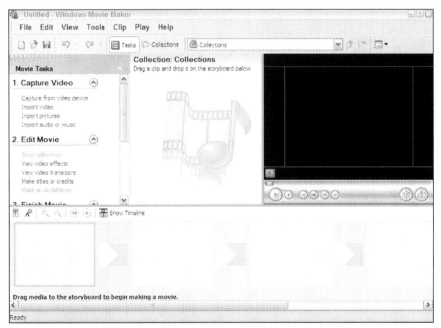

**Figure 7.22.** Movie Maker 2.1.

# Before you make a movie

The first thing you'll need to do to make your Movie Maker 2 experience a positive one is to know your hardware and know video basics. Movie Maker 2 requires a pretty powerful machine; if you're running the bare minimum requirements necessary to run Windows XP Service Pack 2, you may have a difficult time with this software. Please refer to the Microsoft Web site at www.microsoft.com/windowsxp/downloads/updates/moviemaker2.mspx for information on minimal requirements.

In addition to the usual requirements, such as enough memory, disk space, and processor speed, you'll need to make sure you have a FireWire (IEEE 1394) card for actually capturing the video. If you have a recent machine, most likely you have a single FireWire adapter. If you don't have a FireWire adapter, you will need an analog video capture card to capture video from your digital video camera. However, it doesn't make much sense to use an analog video capture card in this day and age; your video quality will decrease versus the FireWire adapter. If you are using an analog video camera or other devices, such as a Web cam, you will need to use an analog video capture card. A FireWire adapter is not an option in this case.

Take the time to read the documentation that came with your digital video camera. Knowing all of the features of your hardware will help you to make better movies, which will make using Movie Maker 2 easier. The Microsoft Web site listed above features a number of helpful articles on how to take good footage; being mindful of any lighting or sound issues. The better footage you have, the less editing you'll have to do in Movie Maker 2.

Finally, make sure you are using the most current version of Movie Maker. If you are running Windows XP Service Pack 2, you are using Movie Maker 2.1. If you are running Windows XP without Service Pack 2, run Windows Update to get the latest service pack and Microsoft Movie Maker 2.1.

# Make a movie

Once you're ready to go, shoot your film! Once you're finished, you'll hook up your video camera to your computer in one of the ways prescribed above. Be sure to set your video camera to Play (not just Camera on); otherwise, the

---

**Watch Out!**

FireWire (IEEE 1394) cables don't come for free; make sure that your machine has an adapter and then see what kind of cable you will need. Some cables have 4 or 6 pins; don't waste time having to run back to the store because you didn't properly verify the appropriate cable.

Movie Maker 2 software will not recognize the device when you begin to import your video. Once your camera is on Play, or when you click Capture from video device under the Capture Video menu on the left side of the screen, the Video Capture Wizard appears (see Figure 7.23).

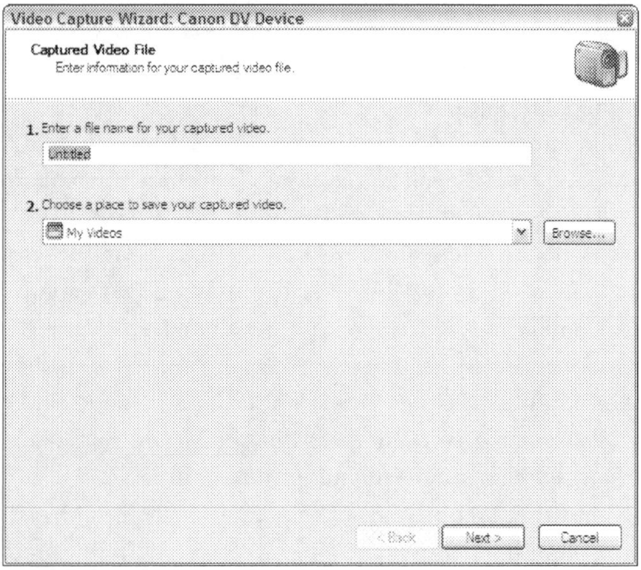

**Figure 7.23.** The first screen of the Video Capture Wizard.

The Video Capture Wizard walks you through all of the necessary steps. First, you will need to give your movie a title and select a location to save the file (My Videos by default). The next page allows you set video settings depending on the equipment you are using (see Figure 7.24).

For example, you may opt for best quality if you are planning on storing and leaving the movie on your computer. You can also select a digital device format, which is ideal if you plan on putting your movie on DVD-ROM or another media device. Finally, you can select another option from a drop-down menu; this menu has a number of varying formats (see Figure 7.25). The bottom of the screen features two distinct areas; on the left is information concerning the file type, bit rate, display size, and frames per second. On the right, you will find information indicating how much space is used (in MB) per minute of film footage. There is also a reminder of how much disk space remains on the selected drive.

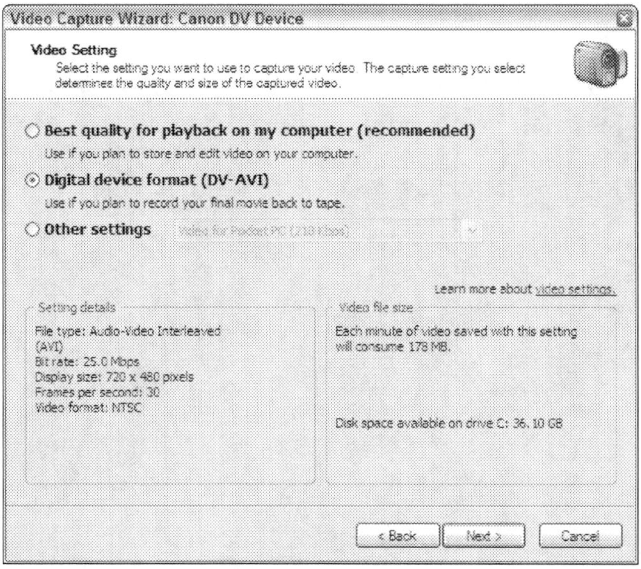

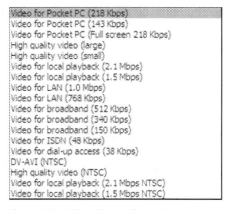

**Figure 7.24.** Choosing video quality settings.

**Figure 7.25.** Other video quality settings.

The next screen lets you select how you want to download the movie (see Figure 7.26). If you are certain that you wish to capture everything that you've put on tape, then use the automatic option. If you'd like to cut and paste what you'd like to capture, use the manual option. The latter option lets you watch your video and select when to start or stop the capture. You may also opt to view the preview; in other words, watch the film as it is saved to your disk. The video is then imported in to the storyboard.

Microsoft Movie Maker 2, in addition to a pretty robust documentation and article set, offers tips for making your movie right in the program! At the bottom of the Movie Tasks panel, there are four different help files full of tips on how to make your movie a successful one (see Figure 7.27).

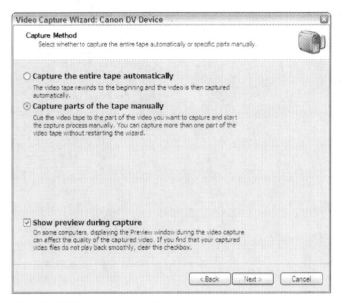

**Figure 7.26.** Choosing capture settings.

**Figure 7.27.** Tips on capturing video.

**Watch Out!**

Depending on how long your video is and the output quality/destination, these files can become exceedingly big. If you're down to only a few gigabytes on your machine, you may want to buy another hard disk or free up space on your current hard drive.

# Just the facts

- Windows XP Service Pack 2 provides Windows Media Player 10, a complete all-in-one media player.

- Windows Media Player 10 allows you to rip musical CDs as well as burn music and data CDs.

- PowerToys are available for download to further enhance your multimedia experience.

- Windows Media Player 10 can work with digital cameras, scanners, and digital video recorders to maximize your multimedia experience.

- MovieMaker 2 lets you be the director of your own digital videos.

# Networking with
# Windows XP

PART III

GET THE SCOOP ON...
Configuring wired, wireless, and dial-up Internet connections
▪ Sharing your connection with others ▪ Configuring
browsing and searching ▪ Discovering the finer
points of e-mail and chat

# Networking and the Internet

*Chapter 8*

**N**etworks are the lifeblood of computing. Without networking you can't send e-mail, search for bargains on books, read movie reviews, or find out the weather at your vacation destination. Networks make rapid information access possible, and Windows XP's tools help make network configuration easy.

This chapter focuses on the basics of getting connected, whether you are on a broadband connection or dialing in from somewhere on the road. The networking information in this chapter is useful for standalone or SOHO installations; connecting to domains or Active Directory is covered in Chapter 10. The information for applications such as Internet Explorer and Outlook Express is useful for both types of connections.

## Understanding networking basics

Networking has almost gotten to the point where you can just plug devices together and get access to the Internet. Most of this magic happened not to make your life easier, but to make the IT worker's life easier. The average IT worker got tired of running around to each computer working on device drivers, network protocols, and application configurations just so someone could read e-mail. Since these people are pretty smart, they figured out ways to simplify the connections and communications between computers and people.

There are numerous components that work together to make networking happen. The following sections will help you understand the different components and help you wade through the jargon that can often seem overwhelming.

## Physical connections

In the prehistoric days of the '80s, standalone computers communicated by "sneakernet." If you wanted to exchange data, you copied some files onto a floppy disk and walked the disk over to someone else's desk. Then as the prices of network adapters dropped, businesses began connecting computers together using off-the-shelf hardware.

Today it's rare to find a computer that isn't network-enabled out of the box. Many computers have network adapters built into them, while others have dedicated network adapter cards installed. The most common connection types today are:

- **Ethernet.** Ethernet connections are used for wiring a computer into a network. The plug is wider than a phone plug and has eight wires.

- **Wi-Fi.** This term refers to the 802.11 wireless protocols, including the a, b, and g flavors. 802.11g is becoming the default connection type, though a and b are still found in many Wi-Fi hotspots such as Internet cafés.

- **Dialup.** A computer uses a modem to connect to another computer. The modem cable is a standard phone cable with four wires.

There are other connection methods, such as ISDN (a precursor to DSL) and satellite, but these are rare.

Your computer then connects to others, usually with the help of a router or hub. These have ports on them that are used to connect computers, one per port. Routers and hubs connect computers in the same building, such as your home, or on the same floor of a business. When you connect two or more computers together in this manner you have created a LAN, or Local Area Network.

The next step is to connect your own network with the Internet. This is usually done through a gateway, cable modem, or DSL modem. These

---

**Watch Out!**

Patch cables connect computers to wall jacks or routers and gateways. You almost always will use patch cables to connect your computers. Crossover cables are used to connect routers to modems or two computers directly. Keep your crossover cables clearly labeled and separate from patch cables.

---

## Other choices for your ISP

Internet service to your home or business is comprised of two parts: the equipment and wires that transmit the signal, and the Internet services that run over the wires. Many people will sign up for a package deal where the cable or telco provides both, without knowing that there are other options.

Thanks to deregulation you don't have to use your cable company or telephone company as your Internet service provider (ISP). There are many providers in your area that can be your ISP, frequently offering faster service or more service options for less money.

A good review site for cable and DSL providers is www.broadband reports.com. You can also find tools to measure download speed and test your broadband connection. A visit to the site is highly recommended.

---

devices provide the necessary translation services between your LAN and the protocols used for long-distance communication.

# Networking protocol

All networks use a protocol, or agreed-upon form of communication, so that each device can send and receive information from other devices on the network. The protocol of the Internet is TCP/IP (Transmission Control Protocol / Internet Protocol) which, among other things, assigns a unique address to each device so that data information can be routed appropriately.

While TCP/IP is the most common, it is not the only protocol available. Novell had a protocol called IPX/SPX that was used for Novell LANs. Apple Macintosh computers have a protocol called AppleTalk that they can use to communicate. The granddaddy of all computer systems, IBM, had its own called DLC. For various reasons these never became as popular as TCP/IP, and except for older businesses or dedicated Mac shops you probably won't find these protocols in use.

### Bright Idea
Ever hear of a LAN party? Set up a temporary network using a router and have everyone bring over their computers. Connect them together and then play cooperative or competitive games. It's a great way to socialize and have fun at the same time.

## A quick history of TCP/IP

TCP/IP was initially developed in the late '60s by DARPA, a United States defense agency tasked with developing a communication system that could survive a nuclear attack. The new system was designed to route around damage so that messages could still be exchanged between stations.

The defense communication system eventually formed links to various scientific and research organizations involved in defense contracting work. They used it as a means of exchanging data and test results. Scientists being scientists, they quickly built upon the foundation of the early protocols and improved and expanded its capabilities.

While the military kept its own private network, the research institutions created their own inter-organization network, dubbed the Internet. While anyone could set up his own private TCP/IP network, people quickly realized the benefit was in connecting together a network of networks. Today TCP/IP is the default networking protocol around the world, used by everyone from consumers to businesses.

And, as if to prove the saying that everything old is new again, research agencies have funded and built Internet2. It is a private network designed to connect research institutions at very high speeds for exchanging huge quantities of data. As of this writing, normal mortals do not have access to Internet2 from the Internet.

## Available services

"The Internet" is not a single service but a collection of different services. Each service has its own access point, or port, that it uses to communicate with the same service on another computer. Some common services and their ports are:

- **HTTP, port 80.** HyperText Transfer Protocol is the Web's most prominent service. Every time you browse a Web site you are using HTTP. Its twin, Secure HTTP or HTTPS, runs over port 443 and is the one used when you connect to secure Web pages at your bank or on merchant Web sites.

- **FTP, ports 20 and 21.** File Transfer Protocol is one of the oldest services available, developed to transfer files between computers. It uses one port for data and one for command and control sequences.

- **POP3, port 110, and SMTP, port 25.** Post Office Protocol version 3 and Simple Mail Transfer Protocol are used to receive and send e-mail, respectively. When you send e-mail using Outlook Express (or any other client), you are using both services.

- **Telnet, port 23.** This terminal application, once pervasive, is hardly used in Microsoft products or by Microsoft administrators. It is more commonly used in UNIX and Linux networks by administrators to monitor and manage other machines and services. It is often used by bad guys to break into computer systems.

- **NNTP, port 119.** The Network News Transfer Protocol is also known as Usenet or newsgroups. Like a vast public marketplace, anyone can read or post to nearly every newsgroup. There are over 35,000 newsgroups in various languages around the world on every topic imaginable, including computer troubleshooting, hobbies, music, sports, and news of the day.

You can view a list of services and the common port assignments at www.iana.org/assignments/port-numbers.

The most common are Web browsing and e-mail, but others such as instant messaging and file transfer are almost as popular. Depending on your ISP and your service contract, these services may be limited. For example, you may not be allowed to run a Web server or e-mail server out of your home without upgrading to a business subscription. In other cases, "bandwidth throttles" may be used to restrict some services, such as file torrents or P2P file sharing, so that the ISP's other customers don't experience network slowdowns.

## Putting it all together

The most effective configuration for both homes and small businesses is to have a router connected to a cable or DSL modem, and every computer connects to that router. Depending on the router, it may have a firewall built in; otherwise there should also be a hardware firewall between the router and the modem. Wireless computers connect to a wireless gateway or wireless router.

**Hack**

Nearly all Internet services can be accessed by using telnet to connect to that service's port. You can check and read e-mail using telnet — though with the advances in e-mail clients, it's much easier to use the client.

Most gateways and routers provide network address translation, or NAT, which lets you use "private" addresses on your LAN while connecting to the Internet with a "public" address. The gateway or router's firewall may also provide the ability to automatically open a port for any outbound services you initiate, such as uploading a file to a server. Inbound services such as running a Web server require you to open a port in the firewall specifically for those services.

Making it all work together is almost automatic. You may still need to configure some aspects of your networking; that's what the rest of this chapter is about.

## Configure broadband connections

In a way, configuring your network adapter is automatic. When you install a new adapter on a desktop system or add a wireless adapter to your laptop, Windows detects the new hardware and configures the basics of your connection for you. If you performed a new installation of Windows (see Chapter 2), you already configured your adapter with the necessary information and your connection is up and running. Or if you used the Files and Settings Transfer Wizard, you moved your connection information from one computer to your current one.

But even with the mostly-automatic process, your connection details depend on what is needed by your ISP. If you are using static IP addressing you need the following information:

- **IP address.** The IP address is the unique address for every device on the Internet. Your address will look like 124.103.225.250, four sets of numbers separated by periods.

- **Subnet mask.** This number is used to subdivide address spaces. The most common subnet mask is 255.255.255.0, but use the one your ISP gives you.

- **Default gateway.** This is the point where your piece of the network puzzle connects to the Internet. If you don't have this address, your computers can talk to each other but that's about it.

- **DNS server addresses.** These computers do nothing but translate people-friendly names like www.miketoot.com into computer-friendly

---

## A quick tutorial on DHCP

In the early days of networking, each computer was manually configured with its IP address and other unique connection information. This was easy when only a few devices were on the network, but as workstations became commonplace, it was a huge burden to configure this information manually.

Dynamic Host Configuration Protocol (DHCP) is a service that makes networking much easier than it used to be. When your computer first boots up, it sends out a broadcast to find a DHCP server. The DHCP server sends back an IP address and subnet mask along with the default gateway and DNS server addresses it has available.

With networking and addressing information centrally administered, it makes it much easier to change configuration information, such as adding a new DNS server and pointing workstations to that server.

---

IP addresses like 64.255.238.206. Without DNS servers, your Web browser can't find anything unless you know the exact IP address for a Web server.

That's a lot of information for static IP addressing, and it's why many ISPs use dynamic addressing. Dynamic addressing is also simpler to configure on a computer, as you just tell the network adapter to go find a DHCP server and get the necessary configuration information automatically.

# Configure cable or DSL connections

If your computer connects directly to your ISP without a router between you and the modem, use the following procedure. Click Start, Run, type ncpa.cpl, and then click OK. You can also click Start, Control Panel, Network and Internet Connections, and then Network Connections (see Figure 8.1). Right-click Local Area Network and then click Properties. Highlight Internet Protocol (TCP/IP) and then click Properties.

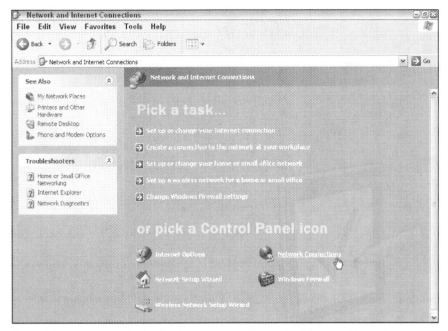

**Figure 8.1.** All your network-related tasks are accessed through the Network and Internet Connections dialog box.

With dynamic IP addressing, you don't need to do anything; leave Obtain an IP address automatically and Obtain DNS server addresses automatically selected (see Figure 8.2). If you're using static IP addresses, select Use the following IP address and Use the following DNS server addresses. Type the information into the appropriate field. When you're done, click OK. Make sure that Internet Protocol (TCP/IP) has a check next to it and then click OK.

If your ISP has provided you with specific information or specific directions on how to set up your network connection, follow the directions in the order given to you.

In situations where you have a router or gateway on your home network, you will most likely set it up so that its external or public interface uses the configuration information your ISP gives you. Each router or gateway has a separate configuration procedure, but fortunately most of them are easy to follow (see Figure 8.3).

---

**Bright Idea**

In the Local Area Connection Properties dialog box, select Show icon in notification area when connected and Notify me when this connection has limited or no connectivity. These indicators show you the status of your connection and answer the question "Is anything happening right now?"

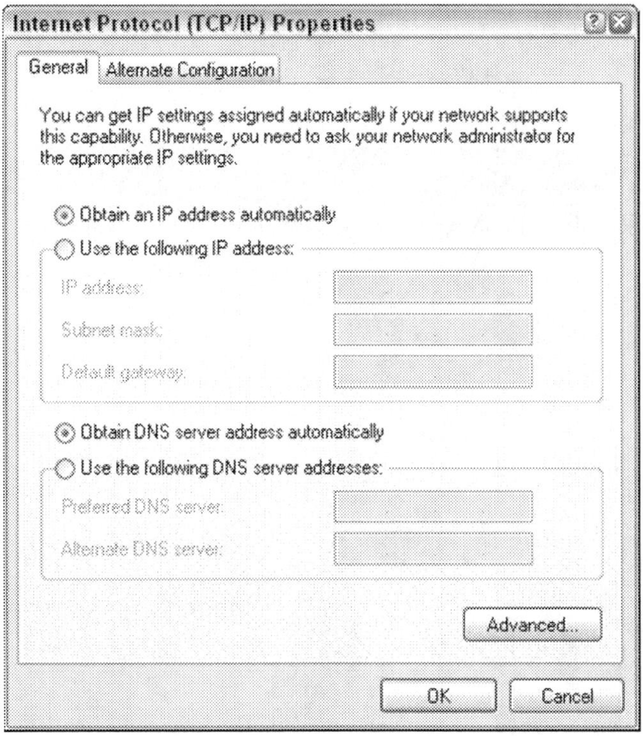

**Figure 8.2.** The TCP/IP Properties dialog box contains many of your adapter's configuration settings.

## Avoiding the Network Setup Wizard

Given that networking is integral to how Windows XP operates, you'd think that Microsoft would make its Networking Setup Wizard easier to use. Somehow this wizard made it out of Redmond without being reviewed by the usability group. Even the most common setup options are awkwardly worded and use geek speak — and if you were a geek, you wouldn't need the wizard. Contrary to the wizard's assurances, it does not actually configure file sharing or printer sharing for you; it only makes sure the protocols are installed and enabled. You still need to configure them separately.

The one time the wizard may be of help is if networking and file sharing isn't functioning properly. In that case the wizard falls into the "it couldn't hurt" category. Otherwise, you save time and button presses by using the directions in this chapter rather than following the wizard.

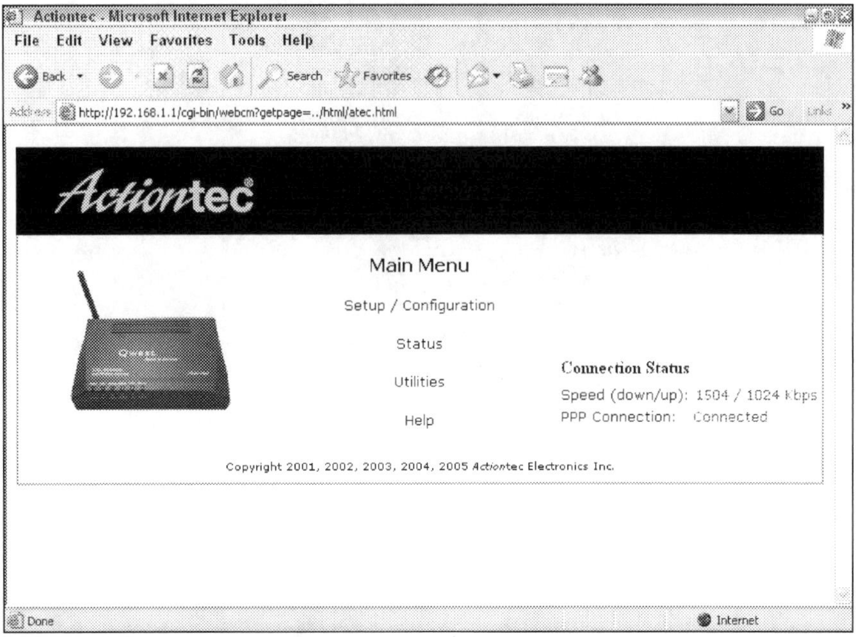

**Figure 8.3.** Your cable modem or DSL modem has its own configuration options; make sure it matches your ISP's configuration information.

When you configure an external interface with your addressing information, you can then use the router to provide network address translation and act as a DHCP server. This lets your computers obtain addressing information automatically and lets the router handle the networking details.

In these situations your ISP may have suggestions or information on how to best configure your router. Check their Web site or give a call to the technical support folks; my experience with small ISPs has been that they are very helpful answering setup questions and making my network run as smoothly as possible.

## Configure PPPoE connections

Some broadband providers use a connection type called PPPoE, or Point-to-Point Protocol over Ethernet. Instead of being "always on," the broadband connection becomes active only when you make an outbound request such as browsing a Web site or checking e-mail. This helps the ISP provision bandwidth and IP addresses more efficiently for its customers, at the expense of a short delay while your computer logs on to the ISP's network. If you want to run a server or provide access to inbound connections, you'll need one that provides a static IP address, rather than uses PPPoE.

## Get rid of QoS!

By default Microsoft installs and enables the QoS (Quality of Service) packet scheduler. In theory it's a good idea; the type of packet and the type of service changes the priority level, so services like streaming media, which are sensitive to dropped packets, can receive higher priority than a file transfer using FTP. The trouble is, if you are connected to a QoS-enabled network (which admittedly is very few networks out there), 20 percent of your bandwidth is being "reserved" without your permission. You can deselect the protocol or even uninstall it on each adapter, but Windows still reserves a full 20 percent of your network bandwidth for QoS even if it isn't enabled on your adapter.

To turn it off, open the Group Policy Editor (gpedit.msc) and browse to Computer Configuration\Administrative Templates\Network\QoS Packet Scheduler. Double-click Limit Reservable Bandwidth. Enable this setting, change the bandwidth limit to 0 percent, and then click OK. This change takes effect immediately.

You can configure either your computer, if it's connected directly, or your router to use PPPoE. Frequently an ISP provides you with a setup disk that runs a wizard on your computer and configures your connection for you, leaving you to fill in only your user name and password. Your router will need to be configured according to the ISP's instructions.

Even if your ISP provides you with a setup disk, you don't have to rely on your ISP's software. In fact, this is one time when it's better to use Microsoft's built-in software than using some other add-on to handle your networking. In most cases you will get better performance, and fewer crashes, by using Microsoft's own configuration tools than by running a PPPoE setup wizard. Naturally, if you have problems and call your ISP, they'll make you install the software they sent to you. It's up to you how to handle things at that point; but if you prefer to set things up for yourself, here's how to add a PPPoE connection.

Click Start, Run, type ncpa.cpl, and then click OK. Or you can click Control Panel, Network and Internet Connections, and then Network Connections. In the left pane click Create a new connection.

The New Connection Wizard appears. Click Next. Select Connect to the Internet and then click Next. Select Set up my connection manually and then click Next (see Figure 8.4).

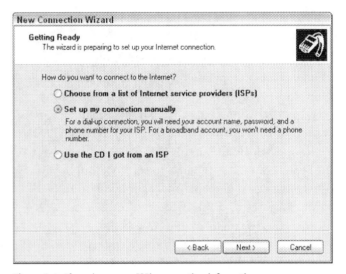

**Figure 8.4.** If you have your ISP's connection information, you can configure your Internet connection manually.

Select Connect using a broadband connection that requires a user name and password and then click Next (see Figure 8.5). In the Connection Name dialog box, you create a name for the connection. Type a name and then click Next.

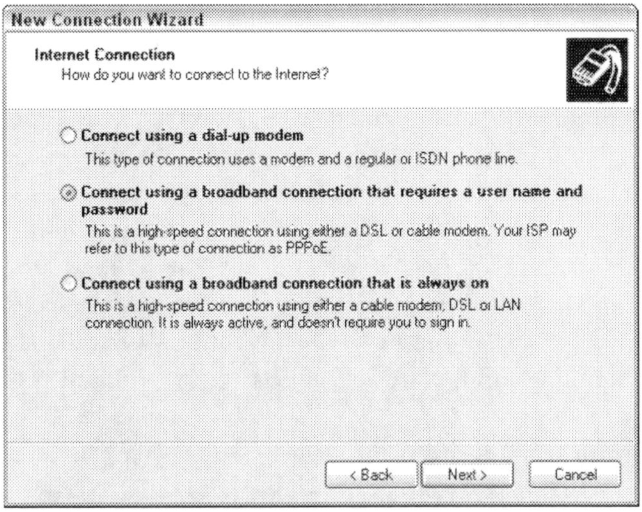

**Figure 8.5.** If your ISP uses PPPoE connections, selecting this option lets you enter a user name and password.

The Internet Account Information dialog box appears (see Figure 8.6). Type the user name and password for your ISP account. On most accounts you can leave both boxes checked that set this connection as the default, and for this connection to be used by everyone who uses this computer. This is distinct from logging on to the computer or checking e-mail; the ISP account is typically separate from users on that account, so everyone can use the same ISP account and not risk getting each other's mail. Click Next.

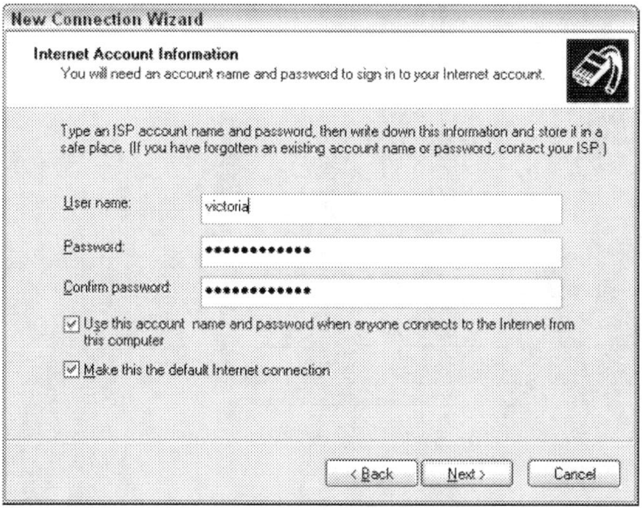

**Figure 8.6.** Enter your name and password in the fields provided.

The Completion dialog box appears; select Add a shortcut to this connection on my desktop and then click Finish. The Connection dialog box appears and you can start your connection by clicking Connect (see Figure 8.7).

If you want to fully automate your connection, there are two more things you must do. First, open the Network Connections dialog box, right-click your PPPoE connection, click Properties, and then click the Options tab. Deselect Prompt for name and password and then click OK. This will automatically connect to your ISP without bringing up the Connection dialog box.

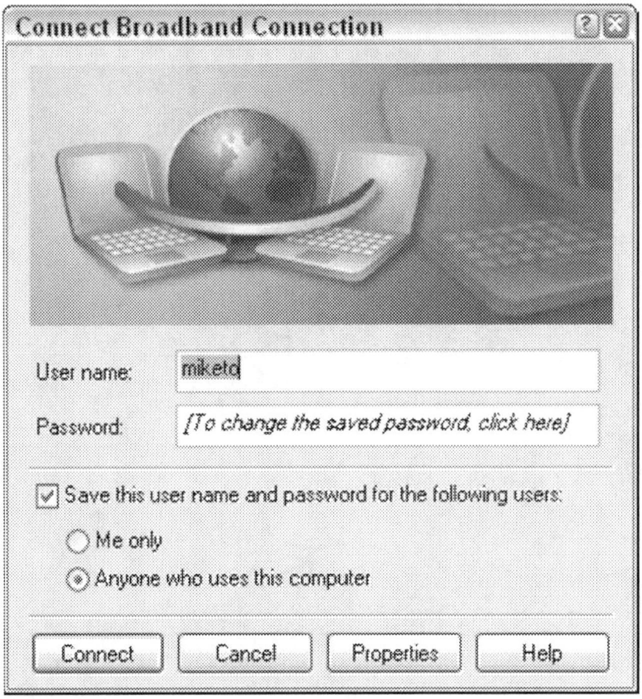

**Figure 8.7.** The Connect dialog box lets you start your PPPoE connection without wading through numerous menus.

Second, click Start, Control Panel, Network and Internet Connections, and then click Set up or change your Internet connection. You can also start Internet Explorer, click Tools, Internet Options, and then click the Connections tab (see Figure 8.8).

Select Always dial my default connection. If your new PPPoE connection isn't listed, select it in the Dial-up and Virtual Private Network settings list and then click Set Default. Click OK. Your connection will now be dialed anytime you want to connect to the Internet, such as surfing the Internet or checking your e-mail.

## Configure wireless connections

Wireless connections are The Big Thing in networking. It's like traveling first class: Once you try it, going back to wired connections seems like a giant step backward. Even though speeds are not comparable to wired connections (and LAN gamers are sensitive to network speeds), for sheer convenience they can't be beat.

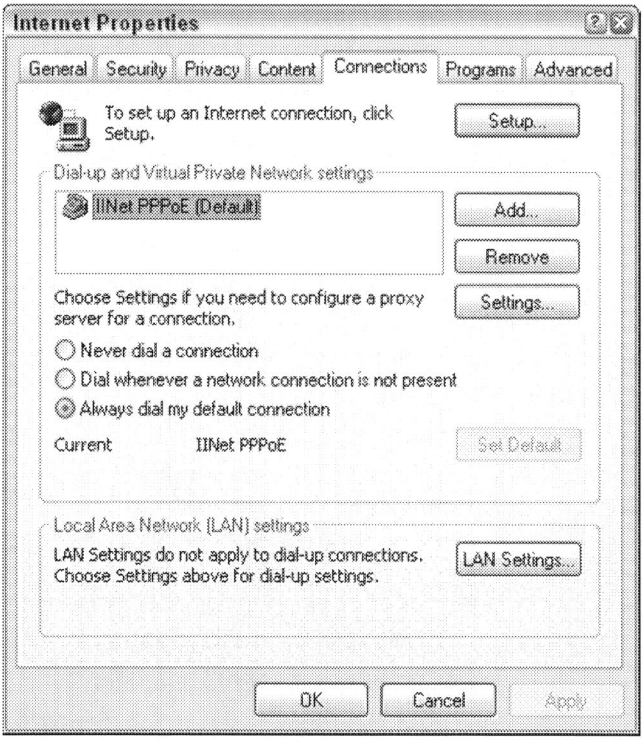

**Figure 8.8.** The Internet Properties dialog box sets dialing preferences for your PPPoE connections.

Most laptops sold today come with a wireless adapter built in, as well as a physical connection for wired networks. You can add wireless adapters to desktop computers, digital video recorders, gaming platforms — just about anything can be wired up for wireless.

## Types of wireless protocols

Like everything else in the computer world, the types of wireless protocols have changed and improved over time. The ones currently available are:

- **802.11a.** This protocol was one of the earliest that was adopted for home and SOHO use. It transmits on the 5 GHz band, with a theoretical throughput of 54 Mbps (actual throughput closer to 20). The higher frequency means shorter available range.

- **802.11b.** This is another older protocol that transmits on the 2.4 GHz band rather than the 5 GHz band. Actual throughput is around 6 Mbps, though theoretically it can reach 11 Mbps. It has longer range and is more popular than 802.11a.

- **802.11g.** This is the most common newer protocol that transmits on the 2.4 GHz band. It has a theoretical throughput of 54 Mbps and nearly 25 Mbps throughput in the real world. It is backwards-compatible with 802.11b.

Some wireless manufacturers have proprietary extensions to the above protocols that purport to give you speed boosts — but only if all your wireless equipment is from them (Netgear's RangeMax comes to mind). Almost all new adapters support b/g, and some support a/b/g. Another protocol on the horizon but not yet finalized is 802.11n, which may support real-world throughput of 100 Mbps and possibly longer range than existing protocols. If you are looking to go wireless, make sure your access point and your wireless network adapters support the same protocols. If you plan to be hanging out in coffee houses writing your Great American Novel, look for a b/g or a/b/g adapter so you are practically guaranteed a connection.

## Wireless security concerns

Wireless connections have an obvious advantage over wired network connections: You aren't restricted to where you can plug into the network, just connect to an access point and away you go. The big downside of wireless is that it's far less secure than wired connections. Anyone with a wireless adapter in range of an unsecured access point can connect to your network and surf the Internet or worse yet, use various tools to see what's on your network and what's available on your computers.

Your wireless access point can be particularly breach-prone because it conceivably is a single point of failure. Once it authorizes access, that person is inside your network. There are some simple things you can do to help secure your access point and your network.

- Use encryption. Whether WEP or WPA, configure your access point to use it and configure all your wireless devices to use the same encryption method. It's far too easy to sniff packets transmitted without encryption, or "in the clear." Use encryption!

- Turn off remote administration and use HTTPS. Unless you have a compelling reason for doing otherwise, you should always require a wired connection to your access point and use HTTPS for your administrative connections. There is rarely, if ever, any need to work on your access point from across the Internet, and especially not "in the clear."

- Use MAC filtering. If you have a small number of wireless devices, you can use MAC filtering in your access point so that only connections from those devices are allowed to connect. See Chapter 14 for information on using ipconfig to locate your adapter's MAC address.

- Turn off SSID broadcasts. You don't need to broadcast the Service Set Identifier (SSID) to the world; just configure your computers with the SSID and reduce your exposure.

Before installing wireless networking, do a realistic threat assessment of the area and people around your home or business. If you are in a single-family residence in the middle of nowhere, the chances of anyone hacking into your network over your wireless access point are slim. Conversely, if you are in a high-rise or in the middle of a business park, the chances of someone poking around in your network are significantly higher. Be smart about security and look at everything with a balanced eye to see what additional security measures may be needed.

## Set up wireless security

Wireless connections are configured in much the same way as regular network connections. The hardware is automatically detected by Windows XP and the basics are set up for you. You can then edit the connection if you want to use a static IP address.

In order to make a connection secure, you need four pieces of information: the type of network (infrastructure or ad hoc), the SSID, the type of encryption (WEP or WPA), and the encryption key. Fortunately, in Service Pack 2, Microsoft included a Wireless Network Setup Wizard. The wizard does a decent job of configuring the necessary information for you — though you can always poke around in the necessary dialog boxes if you want to.

Before you start working on your wireless adapters you need to configure your wireless access point with the above information. You will almost always be using a wireless infrastructure, rather than ad hoc, and the SSID can be anything you want as long as you change the default SSID from "default," "Linksys," or other obvious name to a non-obvious one.

 **Inside Scoop**

Download the latest firmware for your router, the latest drivers for your adapters, and then follow the manufacturer's instructions to upgrade to the latest code. If any problems arise, the first thing tech support will ask you to do is to upgrade, so you might as well do it now.

**Watch Out!**

I once spent two hours configuring and reconfiguring wireless router settings, baffled and frustrated with its failure to let anything connect. Turns out I'd overlooked a configuration setting that turned on and off wireless connectivity. Sometimes it's the basics that trip you up the hardest.

For encryption you have a choice to make. Nearly all access points support WEP (Wired Equivalent Privacy) and most support WPA (Wi-Fi Protected Access). If you have the choice between WEP and WPA and all your wireless adapters support it, use WPA. It has two big benefits.

First, WPA is much more secure than WEP. WEP was an early security protocol that was subsequently revealed to have significant weaknesses in it. In 2005, the FBI gave a demonstration where they broke WEP encryption in three minutes using publicly available hacking tools. WEP is good for stopping casual snooping, but it's not considered secure enough for even partially sensitive information.

The second reason to use WPA over WEP is that it's much easier to configure. Most access points have the ability to generate lengthy alphanumeric keys, which you then must manually copy and paste into your adapter's setup field. It's easy to accidentally mistype or incompletely copy the WEP keys into your adapter's configuration. WPA, on the other hand, uses PSK (Pre-Shared Key), which lets you use a passphrase to generate the necessary key and then use the same passphrase to configure your wireless adapters. This method is much easier to use for the average home or SOHO user and is less prone to configuration errors. Passphrases can be up to 1024 characters, so you could use "Given half a chance, we'd move to Italy or New Zealand in a heartbeat" as your passphrase.

To set up a wireless connection with your adapter, click Start, Control Panel, Network and Internet Connections, and then click Wireless Network Setup Wizard (see Figure 8.9). Click Next.

Type the SSID into the field. The SSID is case sensitive, so it should exactly match the one on your access point. Select Manually assign a network key. If all your devices support WPA and your access point is configured for it, select Use WPA encryption instead of WEP (see Figure 8.10). Click Next.

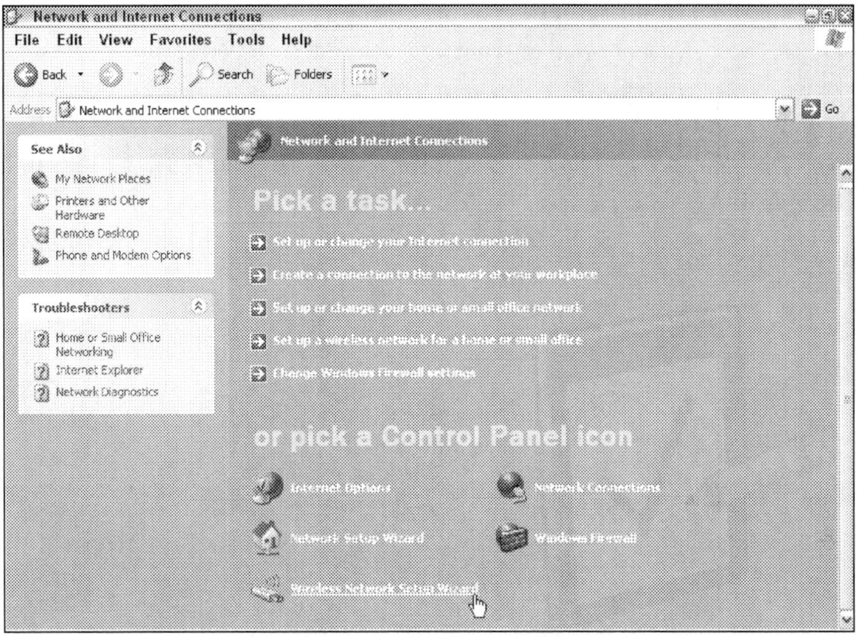

**Figure 8.9.** The Wireless Network Setup Wizard is launched from the foot of the Network and Internet Connections dialog box.

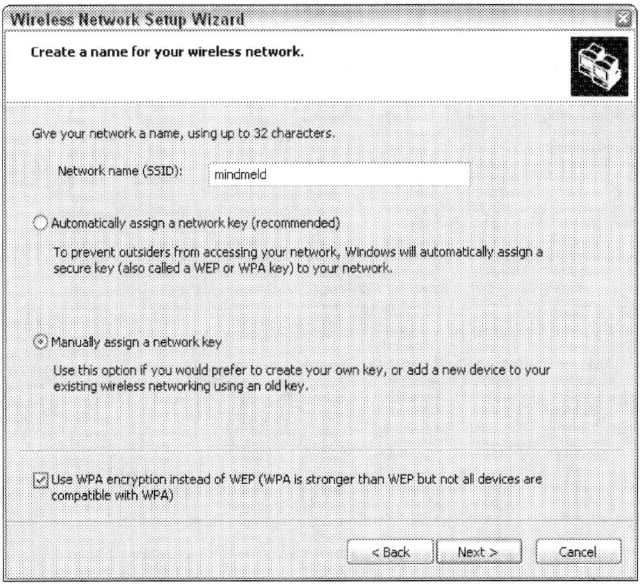

**Figure 8.10.** If possible, use WPA encryption instead of WEP. Even Microsoft thinks you should.

Type your passphrase in both boxes, or copy and paste your WEP key into both boxes. If no one is looking over your shoulder, deselect Hide characters as I type; you can make sure you've entered your keys correctly. Click Next. You can choose to export your encrypted passphrase or WEP key onto a USB drive (a great timesaver for USB-enabled devices) or choose to set up each device manually (see Figure 8.11). Click Next.

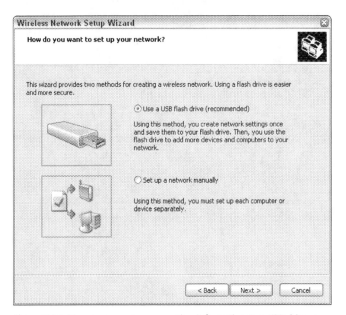

**Figure 8.11.** You can save your connection information to a USB drive, or set up your network computers manually.

If you selected to burn the files to a USB drive, you can take the drive to your other Windows XP computers. When you plug in the drive, a script file automatically runs and configures your wireless adapter for you. In theory you can use a USB drive to configure an access point (letting you use XP to do all your network configuration), but there are only a few access points that have a USB port and support the Network Smart Key feature. Most other devices probably don't support this feature (just try to do it to a Playstation 2), so you may still have to manually configure other wireless devices in your home or office. Click Next.

The wizard now lets you "print" your settings and delete the configuration information from the USB drive. Both are good ideas. By deleting the USB information you keep others from sneaking off with your drive and configuring their own computer for your network. And "printing" the file — in

---

### The connection software shuffle

Some laptops and wireless adapters come with their own software for configuring wireless connections and connecting to access points. My IBM laptop has its own software, while my wife's Toshiba laptop uses the basic Windows XP software. I prefer using IBM's software, but I'm nerdy enough to appreciate the control it gives me over my settings.

If you have adapter-specific software, you don't have to use it to configure your settings. You can switch between the two easily. Open the Network Connections control panel (ncpa.cpl), right-click your wireless network connection, click Properties, and then click the Wireless Networks tab. Select Use Windows to configure my wireless settings if you want to use XP's software, or deselect it if you want to use your adapter's software. The change is effective immediately, so you can try each one out to see which one you like best.

---

reality, opening it in Notepad — lets you save or print out the configuration information for the next time you configure a wireless device. I guarantee you, in six months you will forget what the passphrase was and how it was capitalized. Keep the information in a safe place, such as an administrator notebook that's kept under lock and key.

## Connecting to a wireless network

After setting up your home network and configuring your wireless adapter for the proper connection, connecting to it should be automatic. You will see a message in the notification area letting you know that you are connected to your access point. Hover your mouse over the icon in the notification area and you will get the name of your access point, the connection speed, and the signal strength (see Figure 8.12).

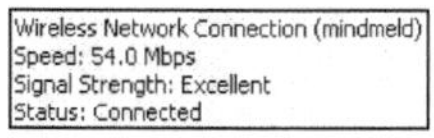

```
Wireless Network Connection (mindmeld)
Speed: 54.0 Mbps
Signal Strength: Excellent
Status: Connected
```

**Figure 8.12.** You can always check the wireless connection status with a simple mouse hover.

But if you are traveling and want to connect to a wireless hot spot, you need to configure your adapter for a new connection. Double-click the wireless network connection icon in the notification area, or click Start, Run, type ncpa.cpl, and then press Enter. Right-click your wireless network connection and then click View all wireless networks. You should see your access point listed (see Figure 8.13), along with others that your wireless adapter detects.

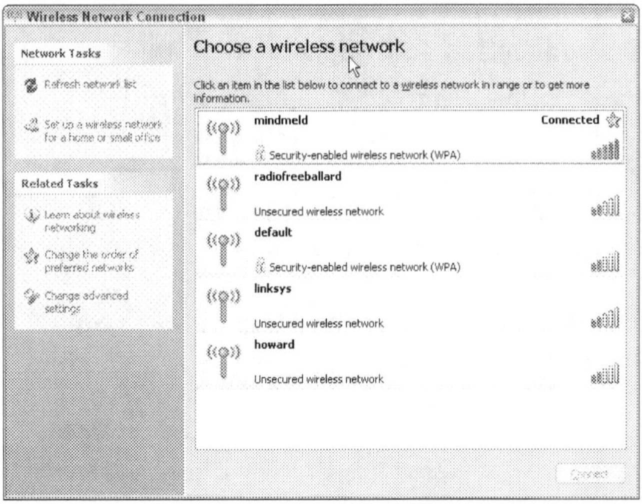

**Figure 8.13.** Your access point, and that of a neighbor or two, is listed in the connection dialog box.

The Wireless Network Connection list shows you any access points and the SSID being broadcast by the access point, gives you an indication as to what kind of encryption is being used, and shows a visual indicator of signal strength. You can refresh the list by clicking the link; sometimes access points with weaker signals are caught with the next refresh.

If you have previously configured any of the connections, you can select it and connect to it immediately. If not, use the Wireless Network Setup Wizard to create a new connection.

## Troubleshooting your Wi-Fi connection

Despite its popularity, sometimes Wi-Fi creates more problems as it solves. One of the biggest problems is reception. 802.11b and 802.11g operate in the 2.4 GHz spectrum, which is the same one used by many brands of cordless telephones. Metal objects such as pipes in the walls or the metal skeletons of high-rise office buildings can make access points inaccessible, even when they're only ten feet away.

Speaking of spectrum, Wi-Fi uses different channels within the 2.4 GHz band. Channel 6 is the default channel on most routers; make sure that your router and your wireless devices are configured for the same channel.

Problems with WEP keys have the potential to drive you mad. If you used your access point to generate the keys, you'll have to copy and paste them into a text file for later import. Forget about typing them in by hand; you'll make mistakes and go blind at the same time. If your computer pauses for an abnormally long time when trying to connect to your router and the signal strength is excellent, chances are it's a key-related problem.

Other problems can be related to obtaining a network address. Your laptop may be configured for DHCP, but for various reasons the DHCP server on your network either isn't getting your request or the new address is not being passed through the access point. You can try assigning a static IP address for your wireless device and then troubleshoot where the DHCP request is failing. See Chapter 13 for more on network troubleshooting.

# Configure dial-up connections

Many people use dial-up connections for their Internet surfing. If you're on the road and use one of the big providers for your Internet access (AOL, Earthlink, MSN), there is almost always a local-call dialup number you can use to get access to your e-mail. Oftentimes the big services have special dial-up software that contains all the local numbers; you select a city, click Connect, and the software does the rest.

On the other hand, if you aren't using pre-configured software to connect to your ISP, you must configure Windows XP for a new dialup connection.

The easiest way is to run through the New Connection Wizard and configure a new dialup setting. Click Start, Run, type ncpa.cpl, and then press Enter. You can also click Start, Control Panel, Network and Internet Connections, and then Network Connections. Click Create a new connection. The New Connection Wizard appears. Click Next.

Select Connect to the Internet and then click Next. Select Set up my connection manually and then click Next. Select Connect using a dial-up modem and then click Next (see Figure 8.14). Type a name for your connection, such as "Seattle Dial-up" and then click Next. Type the number including area code; you can use dashes to separate the numbers or parentheses around the area code. Click Next.

At this point you can type your ISP account name and password (see Figure 8.15), but it's not required; the connection will prompt you for your account name and password when you activate the connection and you can enter the necessary information at that time.

> **Watch Out!**
> Never, *ever* save your user name and password for dialup connections on a laptop. If someone steals your laptop, they have the same automatic ability to log on to a network as you. In security parlance, this is A Very Bad Thing.

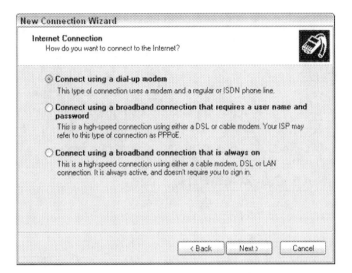

**Figure 8.14.** Dialup connections are easily configured using the wizard.

**Figure 8.15.** Enter the ISP account name and password.

You can choose to use this connection for anyone who uses the computer and make this dialup connection the default. If you only have dialup, go ahead and select both. If you're a road warrior dialing in from the road, you don't need to select either box. Click Next. The wizard completes, and you can choose to add a shortcut to your desktop.

---

### Get a router!

One of the biggest weaknesses of using your Windows XP computer as the choke point is that when you shut down your XP system for the night, no one else can connect to the Internet. You must either log out and leave your machine running, or keep playing endless games of FreeCell while your daughter keeps chatting on MSN Messenger or your son is killing orcs in an online game. If you like your sleep, look into getting a router instead of using Windows XP as a router. You'll be happier and have fewer bags under your eyes.

---

# Configure Internet Connection Sharing

Internet Connection Sharing (ICS) is a means of using your Windows XP machine as a router for other machines on your network. First introduced in Windows 98 Second Edition, it was envisioned as an inexpensive way to connect multiple computers to the Internet without requiring each machine to have its own dialup connection. At the time, hardware such as routers was fairly expensive, while network adapters were more affordable. With routers and firewalls so inexpensive, ICS is less important and probably less used than it used to be. It's most effective with broadband connections to your ISP. Dialup connections to your ISP will be painful when more than one person is accessing the Internet at a time.

In order to use ICS, your Windows XP computer must have two network adapters properly installed and configured (or one network adapter and one modem). One is dedicated to your outbound connection to your ISP, and one is connected to your home network. The adapter connected to your ISP will need to use the addressing information they provide; the one connecting to your home network can use either dynamic addressing (assuming a DHCP server is on your network) or static addressing.

There are two ways to configure ICS: the easy way, and the hard way. Your choice depends on what connections you have already configured on your computer and whether your computer is the first one on the network.

## Configure ICS the easy way

If you have a working connection to your ISP on one adapter and a working network on your other adapter (other computers can see yours in My

Network Places or Network Neighborhood), ICS is easy to configure. Click Start, Run, type ncpa.cpl, and then press Enter. Or you can click Start, Control Panel, Network and Internet Connections, and then Network Connections. Right-click your ISP connection and then click Properties.

Click the Advanced tab (see Figure 8.16). Select Allow other network users to connect through this computer's Internet connection. Click OK. This takes effect immediately. This quite possibly may be the simplest network configuration option anywhere in Windows XP.

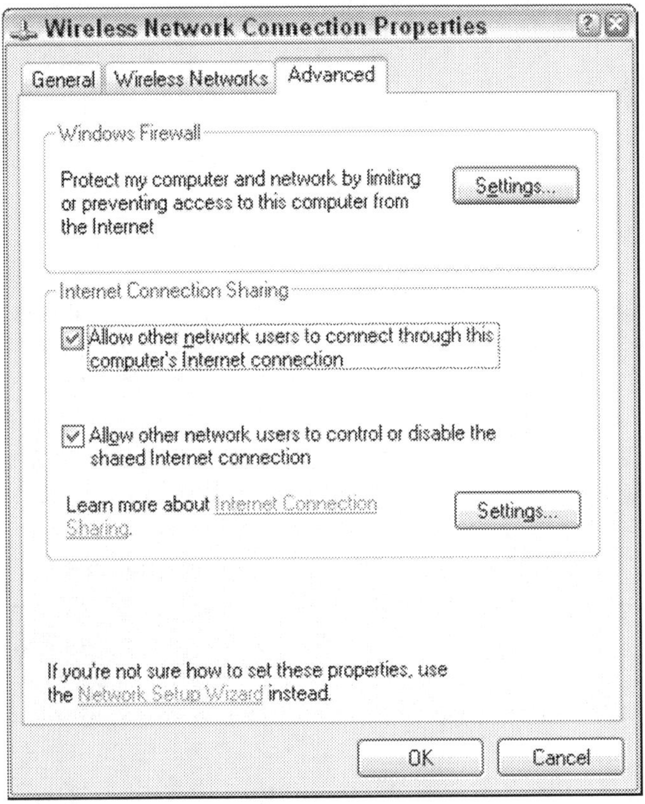

**Figure 8.16.** Enabling ICS is as simple as checking a box.

> **Bright Idea**
>
> Rename your network connections so you know which is which; "MyISP" and "HomeNet" are simple, easy to understand, and don't take up a lot of space in any balloon messages that appear in the notification area. Right-click the connection, click Rename, and then rename your connection.

# Configure ICS the hard way

There may be cases where you are starting from scratch: Your Windows XP computer is the first one on the network and you want to configure the others with the proper information after you get XP up and running. If you know you want to share your Internet connection, there is a more complicated way to configure ICS so that everyone communicates across your computer.

When you use this method, not only is your ICS computer acting as a router to the Internet, but it also sets itself up as a bare-bones DHCP server, handing out addresses to other computers on your network. The rudimentary DHCP server is not configurable, and you can't change the address space from the default of 192.168.0.2 through 192.168.0.254. Your computer also provides basic DNS proxy services, passing along DNS requests to the DNS server addresses provided by your ISP.

Click Start, Run, type ncpa.cpl, and press Enter. Or you can click Start, Control Panel, Network and Internet Connections, and then Network Connections. Click Set up a home or small office network. The Network Setup Wizard appears. Click Next. Read the information on the Before you continue dialog box, review the checklist (see Figure 8.17), and perform any needed steps or install any needed hardware.

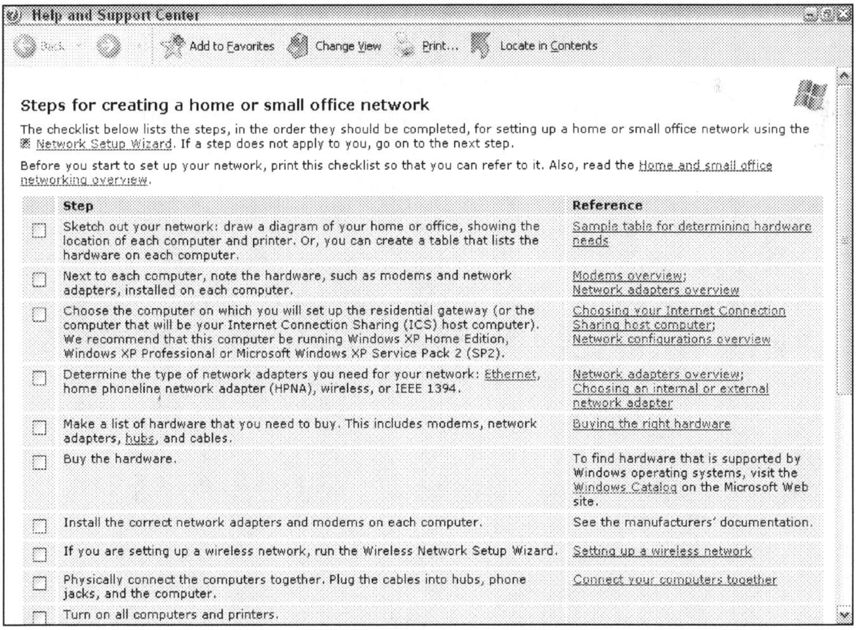

**Figure 8.17.** Review the checklist for the steps needed to prepare your network for ICS.

When everything is ready for setting up ICS, click Next. If Windows detects a router on your network, it gives you the choice of using that as your shared connection. Select Yes if you have one; otherwise, select No and then click Next. Select This computer connects directly to the Internet (see Figure 8.18). Click Next.

**Figure 8.18.** Select the configuration that best describes your network.

On the Select your Internet connection dialog box, select the adapter that connects to your ISP. Click Next. You can add a description that will show up in Network Neighborhood, but it is not needed. You can also change the name for your computer; if your ISP requires that your computer have a specific name, put that name here. Otherwise you can rename your computer if you want. Click Next.

You now have the opportunity to give your workgroup a name. It must be fifteen characters or less, without using spaces or punctuation. It is not case sensitive; in fact, Microsoft will capitalize all the letters for you. Click Next.

The File and printer sharing dialog box (see Figure 8.19) is a bit confusing. It does not create any file shares or any shared printers. Instead, it uses your selection to install and enable the File and Printer Sharing service on adapter. You will still need to manually share any printers that are attached to other computers on your network. Since file and printer sharing is almost always needed on workgroup computers, select Turn on file and printer sharing. Click Next.

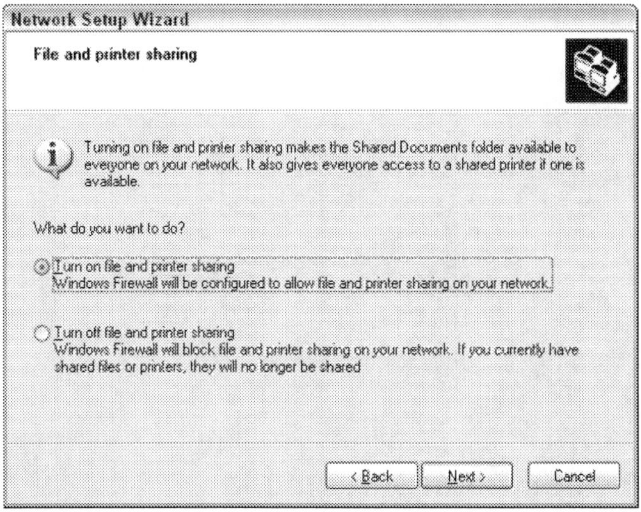

**Figure 8.19.** File and printer sharing is only enabled, not configured, when you get to this point in the configuration process.

A review dialog box appears, showing you the selections you've made so far. If you need to make changes, click the Back button as needed. When you have reviewed your settings, click Next. Your computer is configured with the appropriate settings.

When it is finished, you now have the option to create a Network Setup Disk (see Figure 8.20). This disk lets you configure the other computers on your network so they connect to your ICS computer for their network services. If your other computers are all Windows XP computers, you don't need a setup disk. The other options are holdovers from the Windows 9x era, and you probably don't need them. If you do, go ahead and create a setup disk and run it on the other machines.

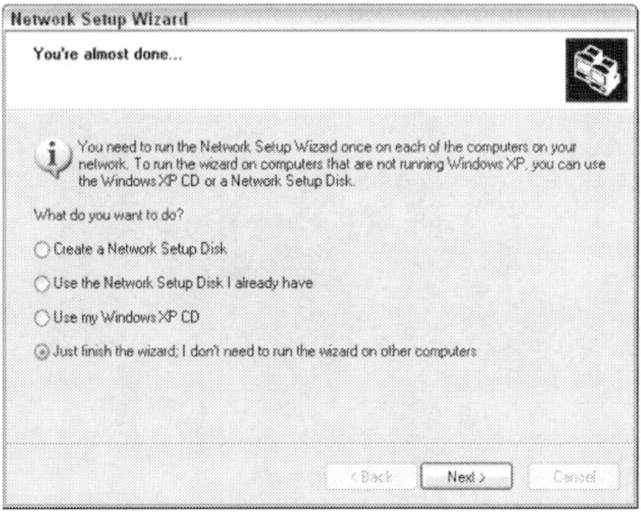

**Figure 8.20.** You can make a Network Setup Disk or manually configure the other computers on your network.

# Change Internet Explorer's behavior

Internet Explorer (IE) is, for better or worse, Microsoft's onramp to the Internet. Everything Internet-related runs through IE, or parts of IE, some of which are sunk deeply into Windows XP. There are good and bad points about this design decision; from an outsider's view, it means that flaws in IE can have unintended consequences, such as giving the bad guys access to financial information stored on your computer.

On the other hand, it's often easier for people new to the Internet to get started quickly, and most things on the Internet will work in IE without requiring additional tweaks or downloads.

This section won't tell you how to browse your favorite Web sites. What it will show you are ways to improve your experience with IE, either through changes you can make locally or with downloads that help turbo charge common Internet functions.

## Manage and edit Favorites and Links

Your Web favorites can be as sloppy or as organized as you like. IE doesn't force you to impose any organization on them. But if you get tired of reading through row after row of links, this may help you out.

Most people add links to Web pages by clicking Favorites, Add to Favorites, and then either clicking OK or taking an additional couple steps to create a new folder to store the link. Both Favorites and Links are stored

---

## Confidence game

As noted in Chapter 6, Internet Explorer isn't the most secure browser on the planet. Microsoft has clearly felt the heat from free browsers such as Firefox (www.getfirefox.com) and Mozilla (www.mozilla.org) and shareware browsers such as Opera (www.opera.com), which do not share the security flaws of IE. A major new release, IE version 7, is planned for sometime before Vista ships (the next version of Windows). Best guess at the time of this writing is the end of 2005, though this will probably prove optimistic. The new release is promised to be a "security release," focusing on closing security holes such as phishing, and reducing the gap between Web standards and IE's implementation of those standards. The downside is that it will be available only for Windows XP with SP2.

Microsoft has sung this song before: promising how good things are going to be in the next release in an attempt to build consumer confidence. History has shown otherwise; despite the last set of security revisions, there are just too many problems inherent with opening the operating system wholesale to the Internet via Internet Explorer.

If you want to improve the security of your current system, as well as get improved speed and flexibility, I strongly suggest looking into one of the browser alternatives just mentioned and not bet on the next version of IE fixing your problems.

---

in Documents and Settings\%username%\Favorites. Because the favorites are stored as separate "files" on the hard drive, you can create folders as complex or as deep as you care to go.

Another way to add items to either your Favorites or Links list is by dragging and dropping the URL from your browser into the respective folder. You can also right-click in the folder, click New, click Shortcut, and then enter the URL (see Figure 8.21). This works with any Internet resource, including FTP sites and shares or files on local servers.

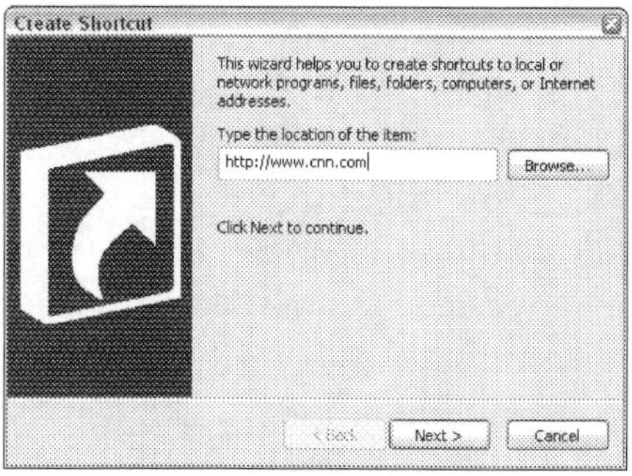

**Figure 8.21.** Links to Internet resources can be added into any folder as a shortcut.

---

### You say Favorites, I say Bookmarks

From the We Name Things Differently Because We Can Dept. comes Microsoft's contribution to customer confusion. Despite everyone else in the world calling them bookmarks, Microsoft renamed bookmarks to Favorites in IE and built a special toolbar called "Links" that connect to Web pages just like bookmarks. The difference between Links and Favorites is that Links are really your Favorites and your Favorites are ordinary links. Got that?

---

The Links toolbar is like your most popular resources that you always visit. When you put a link on the Links toolbar, you can jump to the resource with a single mouse click; you don't have to click Favorites and then wade through your collection of folders to find your site. This is convenient for resources that you visit several times a day, such as news Web sites or daily sales figures.

Because the Links bar doesn't grow vertically, you are limited to the number of Links that are visible on the screen at any one time, though you can scroll to links by clicking the double chevron (see Figure 8.22). In addition, the Links toolbar takes up screen real estate and for power users can be redundant. The next section has information on editing or hiding the Links toolbar and cleaning up your IE experience.

**Figure 8.22.** Your links may be hidden but are accessible with a single click on the double chevron.

## Set up offline caching

A somewhat unheralded feature of Internet Explorer is the ability to cache Web resources on your computer and make them available when you are not connected to the Internet. When you mark the resource as available offline, IE makes a copy of the resource on your hard drive and then looks to the cache copy when you're not connected to the Internet. You can tell IE to refresh the cache when you are connected so you are assured of having the most recent copy available; you can also tell IE how many levels of links you want copied to your hard drive. The difference between two and three links deep can be an exponentially large number, so it is strongly recommended you surf the site for a bit to determine how many links you absolutely need to have cached locally.

**Watch Out!**
I'm not kidding here. Don't try deep-caching sites bursting with content, such as msn.com or cnn.com. The best plan is to be selective and synchronize single pages, not layers of Web sites, unless you know for certain the site is not very deep.

You can set offline status either for new links or ones you have already added to your Favorites. To cache a link, click Favorites, Add to Favorites, select Make available offline, and then click Customize. The Offline Favorite Wizard appears. You can get rid of the introductory message by selecting In the future do not show this introduction screen. Click Next.

You have the choice of whether to cache deeper links and how many levels deep you want to go. Select whether you want to cache downlevel links, and then select how many levels deeper you want to go (see Figure 8.23). Click Next.

**Figure 8.23.** Do not go too deeply or you will bloat your hard drive in no time flat.

The synchronization page appears. If you plan to manually synchronize the resource, select Only when I select Synchronize from the Tools menu and then click Next.

If you want IE to automatically synchronize the resource for you, select I would like to create a new schedule, and then click Next. IE can synchronize at most only once a day, or any interval greater than one day, at a time of your choosing (see Figure 8.24). You can name your schedule and select whether to go online to synch up, which can be useful if you are on dialup and want to have your resources updated while you sleep. Once you have set up the schedule to your liking, click Next.

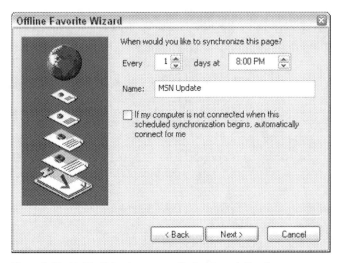

**Figure 8.24.** At this dialog box you are limited to updating the resource only once a day.

Once you've created (or bypassed) a synchronizing schedule, the password dialog box appears; if the resource requires a user name and password you can fill them in here. Otherwise click Finish. You are returned to the Add Favorites dialog box; now that you have customized the link you must click OK to add it to your list of favorites. Once it's added to your Favorites, you can right-click the link and change its offline availability status, or you can synchronize it on demand — this is true of links you manually synchronize, and ones for which you've created a synchronization schedule.

While caching is useful, you may need to fine-tune the link's behavior once it's added to your favorites. Select the resource and a Properties button appears, along with a Make available offline check box. The Properties button brings up a dialog box similar to a File Properties dialog box but with two new tabs: Schedule and Download. The Schedule tab gives you access to other options, though you have to hunt for them. Select your synchronization schedule, click Edit, and then click Schedule (see Figure 8.25).

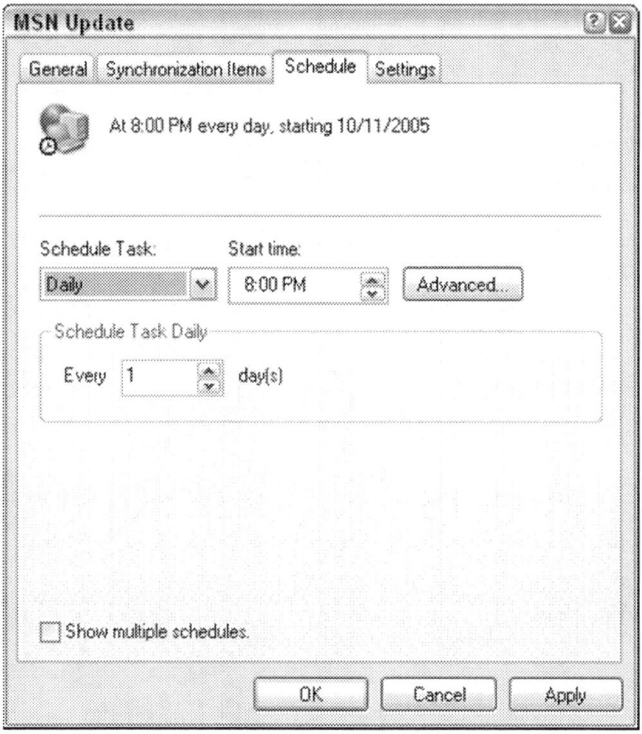

**Figure 8.25.** Though the controls are deeply hidden, you can set very granular synchronization schedules for your resources.

More scheduling options are available under the Schedule Task dropdown list, and in combination with the Advanced button you can synchronize your resource nearly every second of every day. This is a set of controls fit for the most finicky user; if you use them, let me know how it works. And no, I don't know why Microsoft didn't put the Schedule dialog box contents on the Schedule tab.

Back in the synchronization properties dialog box, the Settings tab (see Figure 8.26) lets you configure the wake-up capabilities. If your computer is in Sleep mode, the task scheduler will wake up at the appropriate time to run the synchronization. You can also set power management options so that you can minimize battery drain if you are unplugged.

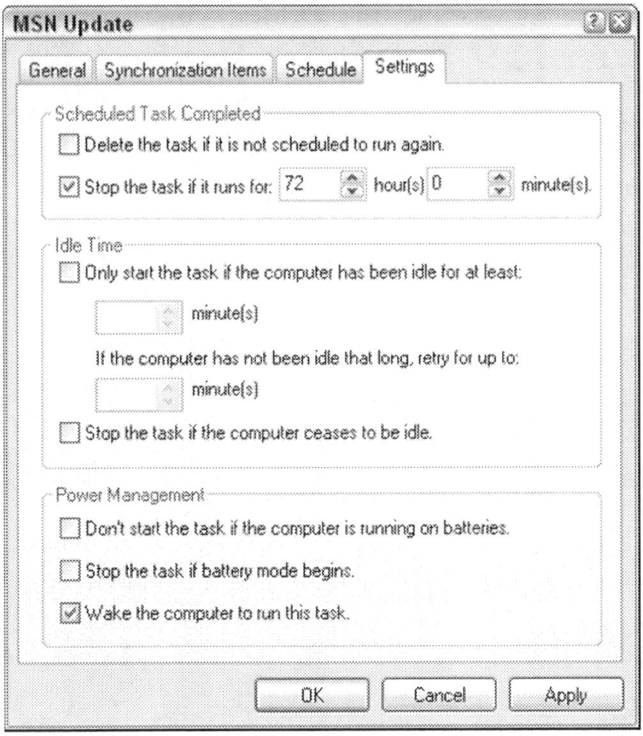

**Figure 8.26.** You can set your computer to wake up at a predetermined time and synchronize your resources.

Once you have set options for your synchronization task, click OK. You are back on the resource's main Properties page. The other tab of interest is the Download tab. On this tab you can change the deep linking limit, and you can also place a limit on how much disk space the particular resource should consume. To help place limits on what is downloaded, click the Advanced button (see Figure 8.27). You can select what items are downloaded; if your resource is important for its content rather than its dancing icons, you don't need to download ActiveX controls or Java applets. Even images may be optional, depending on what information is important to

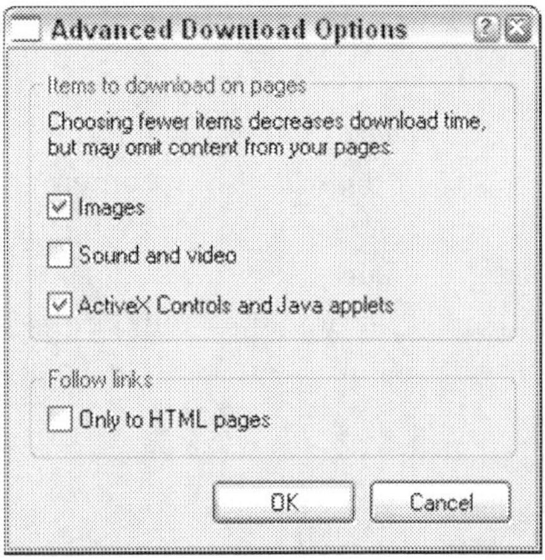

**Figure 8.27.** You can instruct IE not to download bandwidth- and space-hogging elements on synchronized Web pages.

you. Select the items you want downloaded and click OK until you get back out to the Organize Favorites dialog box. Click close.

## Hide, edit, or install toolbars

Internet Explorer has several toolbars that you can show to best reflect your browsing habits. To hide or show the various toolbars, click View, Toolbars, and then select Standard, Links, or Address. A check mark appears in the menu when the toolbar is visible.

You can edit which buttons you want visible and the text associated with the buttons on the Standard Toolbar. To edit it, unlock the toolbar by selecting View, Toolbars, and then Lock the toolbars. Click View, Toolbars, and then Customize. The Customize Toolbar dialog box appears (see Figure 8.28).

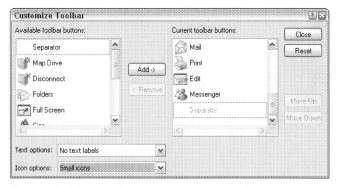

**Figure 8.28.** Edit your toolbar appearance and text to give you the information you need, and no more.

You can add, remove, or change the order of buttons on your standard toolbar. Select a button from the list on the left, click Add, and then use the Move Up and Move Down buttons to change the order. A separator icon is available so you can group buttons more effectively and make them more pleasing to the eye. To remove a button, select it from the list on the right and then click Remove.

You can also choose whether to use large or small icons in your toolbar to help clean up the real estate. Once you are familiar with each button's purpose, you can also use only selective text or even remove the text associated with each button. Play around with these settings to see what looks best for you in IE's toolbar. If things get too mixed up, the Reset button acts as a "panic button" and restores the defaults so you can start again with a clean slate. When you are finished, click the Close button.

---

## Internet Explorer keyboard shortcuts

There are a number of shortcuts you can use to speed up Internet Explorer. While some folks prefer to mouse for everything, there are times when using the keyboard is faster than reaching for the mouse or typing out entire links. Some favorite shortcuts are:

- Alt+D jumps to the address bar and highlights the contents. You can start typing a new URL and replace the old one.

- Ctrl+Enter automatically adds "http://www" and ".com" to a URL. This is a great shortcut if you know a company name such as "Microsoft."

- Backspace is the same as clicking the Back button.

- Shift+Click opens a URL in a new window. It is the same as right-clicking a link and then clicking Open in new window.

- F4 opens the URL drop-down list. Use the up- and down-arrow keys to quickly select a previously-visited URL.

- F11 switches IE between full screen and standard mode. If you really want to clear your browser of space-eating features, use this key.

---

While the Standard Buttons toolbar is the only one that can be edited, all the toolbars can be repositioned. When the toolbars are unlocked, move the mouse over the dotted handles on the left of each toolbar. Click and drag a toolbar to a new location. The other toolbars adjust to match your new ordering. In order to save real estate, I move my Address toolbar into the same row as the menu toolbar; the Links toolbar I hide from view and just use the Favorites list (see Figure 8.29).

**Figure 8.29.** Hide or rearrange your toolbars to suit your browsing needs.

# Change search engines

When you type in a phrase or saying into the Address URL, Internet Explorer helpfully goes off to a search engine in an attempt to find useful Web resources for you. Unsurprisingly, IE's default search engine is search.msn.com. It's easy to change the default, and along the way you can get rid of the animated Search Companions if you want.

In the Standard Buttons toolbar, click the Search button. The Search Companion appears (see Figure 8.30). Click Change preferences and then Change Internet search behavior. A number of engines are available to choose from; select one and then click OK. The change is effective immediately.

To get rid of the charming animated doggie, click Change preferences and then select Without an animated screen character. If you want something else, you can switch between Rover, Merlin, Courtney, and Earl (see Figure 8.31) by clicking With a different character and then clicking Back and Next to move between the animated characters. You're probably best off saving the processor cycles for actually running the search rather than making Courtney fly her plane.

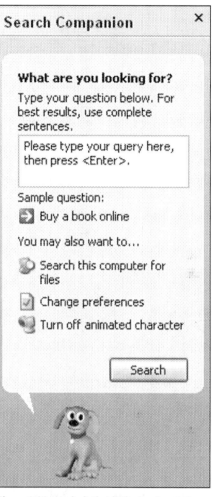

**Figure 8.30.** Aw, isn't that little doggie cute?

**Figure 8.31.** And to think someone at Microsoft was paid to write the code for these guys.

The Search Companion is Microsoft's attempt to make searching more friendly, without requiring knowledge of query syntax. It also lists tasks that may be useful to you in your search. If you prefer greater flexibility over your searches you can try using the Search Assistant. Click Change Internet search behavior and then select With classic Internet search. Click OK. You must close the Search window and restart Internet Explorer for your change to take effect.

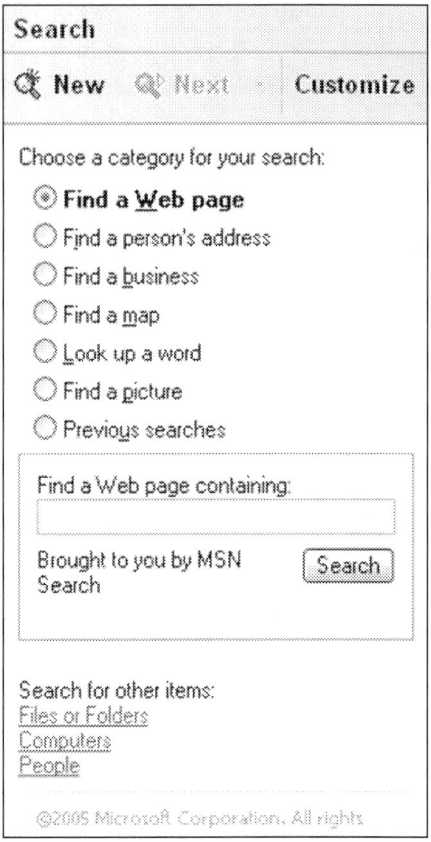

With the Search Assistant, you can select a category before launching your search (see Figure 8.32). Each category represents a search using a different search engine; for example, looking up a word runs a search at Dictionary.com.

Click Customize to see the list of search engines available for each task (see Figure 8.33). If you want, you can select which search cate-

**Figure 8.32.** The Search Assistant lets you search by category.

gories are shown in the Search Assistant by selecting the check box next to the category name. The one big down side is that you cannot add your own search engines to the Search Assistant. Believe it or not, but most of the search engines listed in IE have business partnerships with Microsoft, so unless you can convince Microsoft to do business with your favorite niche search engine, you probably won't see it listed in the categories anytime soon.

Finally, the Search Assistant lets you change the search behavior of the Address toolbar. Click Autosearch settings, and the Customize Autosearch Settings dialog box appears. You can have the Address bar search run on a different engine than the Search Assistant (the Search Companion and the Address search share the same search setting). This can be convenient if you have casual searches that you want to run via the Address bar, but you can run against a different engine that gives you results more appropriate to specific searches. The Customize dialog box also lets you turn off Address bar searches, jump to the "most likely site," display the results, or display the results and go to the most likely site.

Bottom line: If you prefer to use task-focused searches, use the Search Companion. If you prefer content-focused searches, use the Search Assistant.

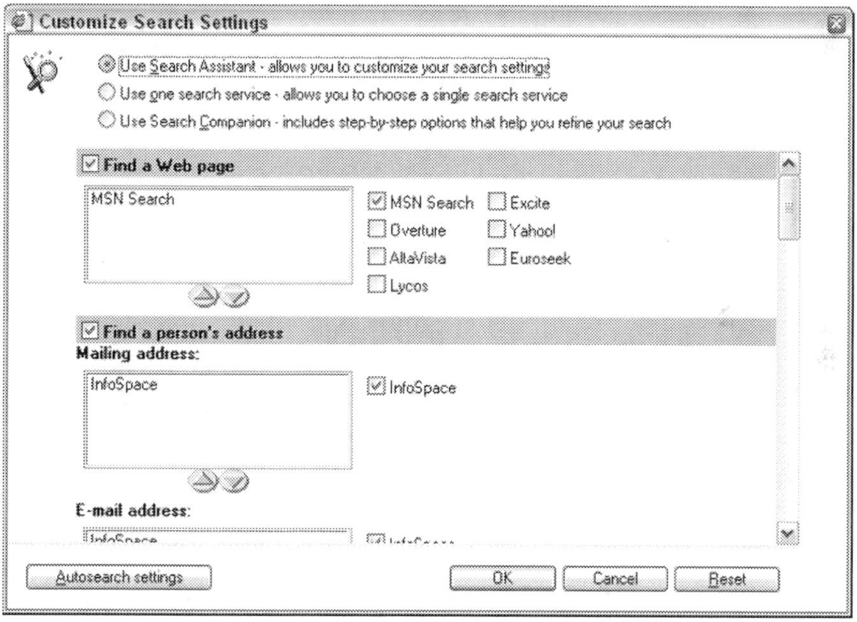

**Figure 8.33.** Customize the list of available search engines.

# Work with MSN and Google toolbars

But wait! The quest for the ultimate search tool is not over! Both the Microsoft Network and Google offer downloadable toolbars that improve your search capability at their online sites. They also offer tools to search the content on your own computer, including documents, text files, even e-mail from various e-mail programs including Outlook Express.

## MSN Search Toolbar with Windows Desktop Search

The MSN Search Toolbar with Windows Desktop Search (WDS) lets you search the Web and your computer without having to open a search page. You can download the latest version at toolbar.msn.com.

WDS creates a complete index of the files and folders on your computer so that you can find files almost instantly. You can search the contents of nearly everything on your computer: e-mail messages, appointments, documents, and multimedia files, and more.

One benefit of the MSN toolbars is that they provide a cleaner access point into the desktop search engine. Rather than have to choose between the Search Companion, the Search Assistant, and the Address bar search capability, you are given three different ways to get into the same search engine. They are:

- **MSN Search Toolbar.** This IE toolbar gives you access to the underlying search engine, plus creates one-click buttons for access to MyMSN, MSN Messenger, and MSNBC.com. If your Internet existence is linked to everything Microsoft, this toolbar will seem like heaven. It also adds tools to IE like a pop-up blocker, tabbed browsing, and search term highlighting.

- **MSN Search Toolbar for Microsoft Office Outlook.** You can add a similar search bar into Outlook, giving you direct search capability for your e-mail and personal folders.

- **MSN Search Deskbar.** The Deskbar is dockable, riding either on your desktop or on your taskbar. It's similar to having the Address toolbar visible; you can type a search term into the Deskbar and be taken to the Search window.

**Inside Scoop**

Adobe PDF files are extremely popular, especially as instruction manuals for downloadable software. It pays to visit www.adobe.com and download the PDF plug-in so the MSN Search engine can index these documents as well.

**Watch Out!**

E-mail messages will be indexed only when Outlook or Outlook Express is running. If you have a large personal store (PST file), you may want to leave Outlook running while you go to lunch.

With Toolbars in these three places, you can start your search and find your files, documents, and Internet content faster than by using separate search tools. To do this, WDS creates and maintains a desktop index of your computer. The index contains additional searchable information like the time a file was created and its file type. The index is updated every time you add or change a file or message.

When you first install MSN Search Toolbar, WDS indexes the file locations you chose in the MSN Search Toolbar Customization Wizard. If you did not complete the wizard, Desktop Search indexes your My Documents folder and e-mail messages by default. You can easily change which files are indexed. When the initial index is complete, you're ready to search your computer. The time required for WDS to create the index depends on how much data you have on your computer. If you have many files on your computer, indexing could take a few hours.

After installing the toolbars, open Internet Explorer. The new toolbar is visible, along with the new tabbed browsing capability. You can change the toolbar search properties by clicking the Change MSN Search Toolbar options button that looks like a pair of pliers and a screwdriver.

Click Desktop Search (see Figure 8.34). This is where you can choose the basic list of what to include in the desktop index: e-mail and all hard drives, e-mail and My Documents, or a custom mix that you define. The Advanced section lets you choose what documents to index, selected by extension. This is one of the more awkward dialog boxes because the index list is a long text box that you cannot scroll. Editing out particular files, such as .vbs if you're not a programmer, will take some time.

Most of the other toolbar settings are self-explanatory, such as the check boxes to select which buttons appear on the toolbar. However, one downside is that it does not come with any desktop-resident help files — you must have Internet access to use the help files at toolbar.msn.com. This can be a problem especially if you work with advanced query syntax for your searches. You may want to save a copy of the syntax page to your computer for future reference. Don't forget to index it.

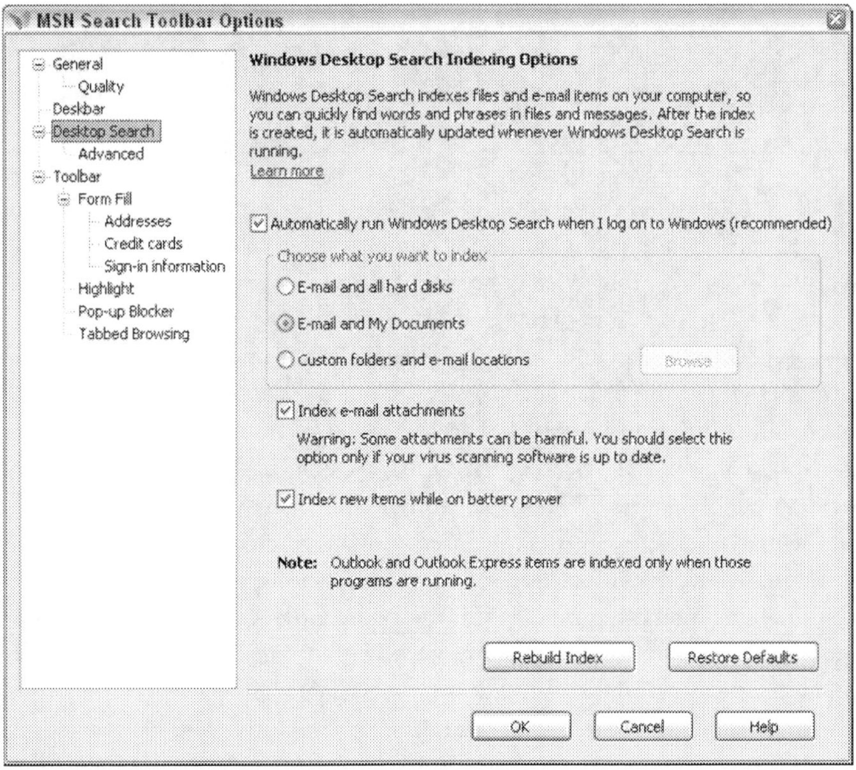

**Figure 8.34.** The MSN Search options are capable of basic searching on your computer.

There are also third-party plug-ins that provide greater search extensibility for the toolbar. You can find a list of them at addins.msn.com.

## Google Toolbar and Google Desktop Search

The search site Google takes a slightly different approach than MSN to enhancing your desktop. Instead of putting all the tools into one package, you can choose which tools to download and install separately. Google offers both a search toolbar and a desktop search tool. These tools are available along with the Google Deskbar, the Gmail notifier, and the Picassa photo organizer at www.google.com/downloads. You can download them a la carte or as one single download.

### Hack

You can change the MSN Search Toolbar to use another search engine, but you need to know the search query format for that engine. To use Google, the query string would be "www.google.com/search?q=$w".

## Google Earth

Google Earth is one of the coolest desktop add-ons ever. The idea is simple: It's a globe that sits inside your PC. It combines satellite imagery, maps, and the Google search engine to bring an entire world's worth of images and information to your desktop.

You can point and zoom to anyplace on the planet that you want to explore. Tilt and rotate the view to see 3-D terrain and buildings. Save and share your searches and favorites with your own personalized annotations. It's totally cool.

You can find Google Earth at earth.google.com.

The Google Toolbar provides a quick link to the Google search engine; a pop-up blocker; Web page highlighting; AutoLink to find addresses, package tracking, and ISBN book listings; AutoFill (similar to the now-defunct Microsoft Wallet); a word translator; and spell-check engine.

After you install the toolbar, you can move it around IE's menu area and hide it using the View, Toolbars menu. The Google toolbar's options can be set by clicking the Google button and then clicking Options, or by clicking the Options button that has several colored spheres on it.

The Browsing tab (see Figure 8.35) lets you manage navigation and productivity options, including translation and spell check functions. A simple check box enables each option and displays an icon on the toolbar; if you don't use an option very often, you don't need to have it active and taking up real estate on the toolbar.

Almost all of the options have further settings you can configure; the AutoFill option gives you the ability to save your name, address, and encrypted credit card information for filling in purchase information on Web forms.

The Search tab gives you some more options on your searching, such as remembering your last search or opening a new window for your search results. It's also easy to select a different Google search engine; you can search country-specific Google sites (all ninety of them). You can also add buttons for category-specific searches such as images, groups, and the ever-popular "I Feel Lucky" button.

The More tab lets you add even more options to the Google toolbar, such as adding the Options button or adding a Web page to your account at blogger.com.

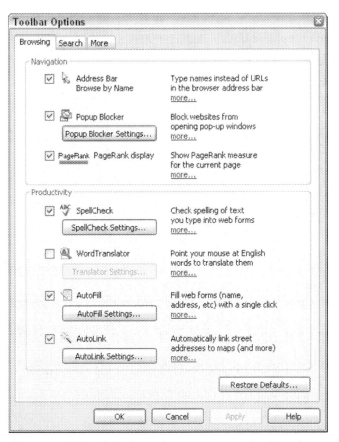

**Figure 8.35.** The Google Toolbar options are more comprehensive and flexible than the MSN toolbar's.

On every tab you have access to a "panic button," a Reset Defaults button that restores the original out-of-the-box settings. This can be helpful if the changes get too overwhelming and you want to have a cleaner, meaner toolbar in IE.

Google Desktop Search (GDS) works similarly to Windows Desktop Search, but they differ both in what they can index and how they search. GDS indexes more e-mail clients, including Thunderbird and Netscape Mail, natively searches PDF files, and can index your AOL Instant Messenger

**Bright Idea**

Google also makes a toolbar for Firefox. Google's Web site will suggest the appropriate toolbar depending which browser you use. As of this writing Microsoft has no plans for a Firefox-compatible toolbar. Google Desktop Search works no matter which browser is installed.

chat logs. If you are not Microsoft-centric on your desktop, GDS offers you the ability to extend your search into other products — a feature that Microsoft is reluctant to support.

GDS indexes your hard drives by default, rather than only a subset. This can be a blessing or a curse; the indexing process takes longer than WDS both due to the indexing scope and because GDS only runs its index while your computer is idle — WDS does its indexing while you work, so you will often see system slowdowns as the initial index is created. With both products, if you have a lot of material to index, it's best to leave your computer on for the night and let the respective products create the master index.

When you install GDS, a search bar will be added to your taskbar. You can configure it to be a floating window on your desktop, and you can select whether its primary search will be on the Web or on the desktop search engine.

To set GDS options, click the drop-down arrow in the search bar, click More, and then click Preferences. The GDS options page (see Figure 8.36) uses the same style as Google's online Preferences page, with many of the same settings available, such as number of results to display per page. It also lets you exclude local files and directories or specific Web sites you don't wish to include in your search results.

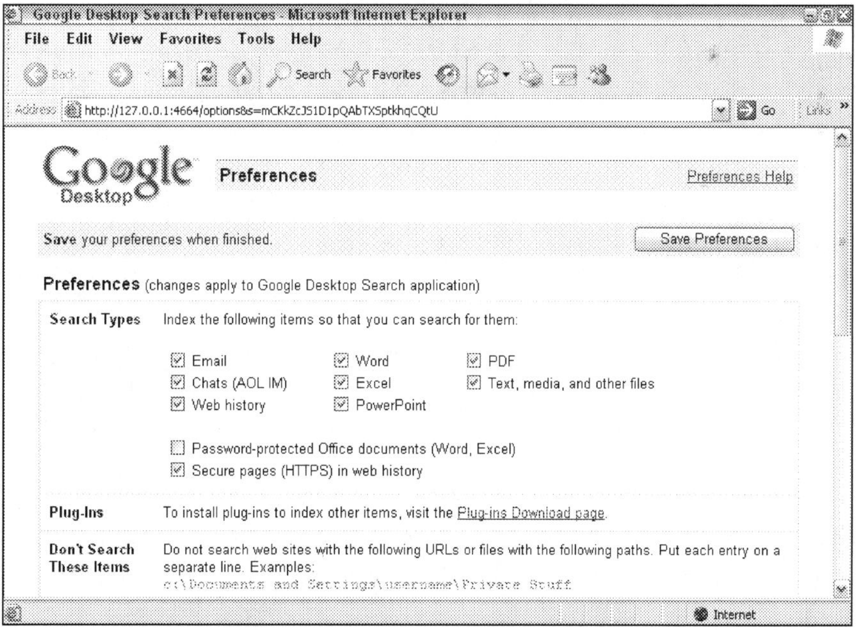

**Figure 8.36.** GDS search options are straightforward and get the job done.

The most interesting setting is the Google Integration setting. You can choose whether to display the local search results as part of the Web results; in other words, if this box is selected, whenever you run a "Web" search, it also returns any hits from your local index. This integration is done locally, so that your personal results are not uploaded or shared with Google. By way of contrast, Windows Desktop Search requires that you run two separate searches: one on the Web and one against your local index. If you're a searchophile and you like to save time, GDS is the way to go.

Finally, there are many more plug-ins for GDS than for Windows Desktop Search. You can find the plug-ins (I especially appreciate the one for ZIP, JAR, and RAR files) at desktop.google.com/plug-ins.html.

## Get a handle on ActiveX and Java

An Achilles heel for Internet Explorer has been its extensibility for Web content. Microsoft promoted ActiveX as bridging the gap between server-side and desktop-resident Web extensions. The ActiveX controls could be or do anything, from multimedia to custom data-handling applications for use within a business. ActiveX was available only for Windows systems, and IE was the sandbox for loading and running these extensions.

At about the same time, Sun Microsystems' Java language was developed for the same reasons, with the added goal of being portable so it could run on anything, from Windows to Macintosh to Linux systems. Because it had to be portable, a separate virtual machine was used for running Java code. A Java Virtual Machine was needed for each platform, written in language suitable for the operating system. But the Java code itself was platform-neutral.

This turned out to be a problem for Microsoft. Because ActiveX controls were written to the Windows platform, malicious coders wrote code that took advantage of holes in IE and Windows. Despite installing various security controls and levels of permission, malicious controls could still be downloaded and installed by unwary end users.

With Java, it was not as easy to write malicious code. There were more security layers to break through, and the JVM sandbox didn't easily divulge information about the underlying operating system; this made it difficult — though not impossible — to write malicious Java applets.

As a user it's important to understand what has been loaded onto your machine and how to unload it if necessary. ActiveX and Java applets are managed within Internet Explorer though the doorway is somewhat obscure.

## Sun and Microsoft: The Java Wars

Sun wrote it; Microsoft embraced and extended it. Lawsuits were filed, sabers were rattled. In the end they kissed and made up. Yet the future of Java on Windows is uncertain.

Early in Java's development, Microsoft obtained a license to create and distribute its own Java Virtual Machine on the Windows platform, ostensibly to optimize the JVM for Windows performance while conforming to the Java specification. In the process, Microsoft's extensions were not portable to other platforms, breaking Java applications that otherwise ran on Sun's virtual machine.

This incompatibility caused a major rift between the two companies, with Microsoft at one point pulling its VM (it dropped the "J" as part of its legal maneuvering) from Windows XP Service Pack 1. This angered many users and other companies who relied on Windows as a near-ubiquitous application development platform, who believed Microsoft should act Hippocratically and, at the very least, do no harm.

Eventually Sun and Microsoft mended their fences and announced a new partnership, with the Java wars behind them. Yet Microsoft's deprecation of Java in favor of .NET leaves little doubt that it tolerates Java but has few plans to improve Java support in Windows.

With Internet Explorer open, click Tools and then Internet Options. On the General tab, click Settings and then View Objects. The Downloaded Program Files window appears. You can also browse to this folder in Windows\Downloaded Program Files. Your ActiveX and Java applets are listed here (see Figure 8.37), with a custom view that includes the installation status, size, and version number.

If you right-click an object you can update it, remove it, or view its properties. If you remove an object without knowing what it does, you could break an application that you need on your computer. The Properties dialog box has a number of nerd-specific bits of information, including the GUID (Global Unique Identifier) and program dependencies. If you are comfortable with rooting around, you can usually find out what the object is for and determine whether it is safe to remove.

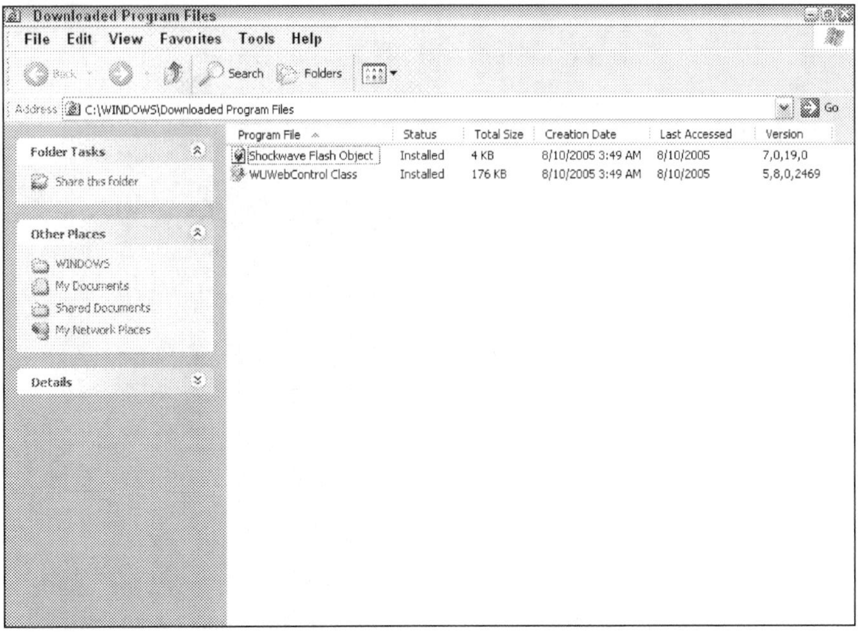

**Figure 8.37.** ActiveX and Java applets, including ones for Windows Update and Microsoft Update, are hidden deep within IE.

The object's status may be reported as damaged, or the version may be older than a newer one you know is available (most often seen with Sun's Java Runtime Environment). You can update the control by right-clicking the object and then clicking Update; IE will go to the originating Web site, check for a new version, and then download and install it if one is available.

Now, to confuse the issue further: ActiveX controls and Java applets are not the only things IE is hiding from you. It also has browser helper objects (BHO) that embrace, extend, and enhance IE — at least, that's what it says here in Microsoft's marketing materials. With Service Pack 2, IE has a new section devoted to managing BHOs.

In classic Microsoft fashion you can get to the BHO manager in two different ways: click Tools and then Manage Add-ons, or click Tools, Internet Options, Programs, and then Manage Add-ons.

The Manage Add-ons dialog box (see Figure 8.38) defaults to showing which add-ons are currently loaded by Internet Explorer. Most, if not all, of the objects listed will be enabled. You can update or disable an object by selecting it, selecting the appropriate setting, or clicking the Update ActiveX button. If an object is disabled, it could be from a failure of the associated program, a service that is set to manual or disabled, or an administrator who configured a policy that prevents running the object.

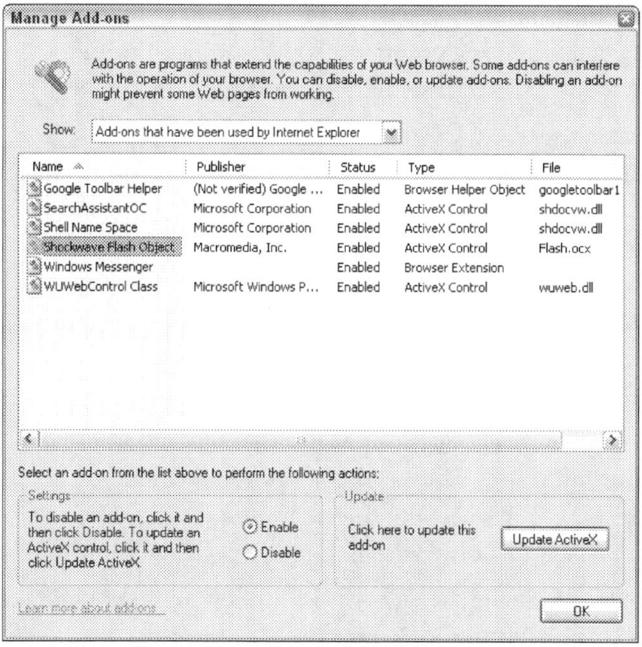

**Figure 8.38.** Browser add-ons, whether BHOs, ActiveX controls, or Java applets, can be enabled, disabled, or updated here.

This dialog box also lets you view a list of add-ons that have been used by Internet Explorer. Select this option from the Show list, and you will see a much longer list. Many of these are ones that are called on demand, such as the Acrobat Reader helper object that launches Adobe Reader when you click a PDF link in IE.

Note that you cannot remove an object using this dialog box; in most cases there is an associated program that should be uninstalled, or an ActiveX or Java applet that must be removed from the Downloaded Program Files directory.

## Make things happen faster

Internet Explorer isn't the fastest browser available, especially when it becomes loaded down with add-ons and helper objects. There are some things you can do to help improve IE's load time and browsing time, though some of these may not work on your system depending on your configuration and how much latitude you have been given by your IT department.

- Move the temp folder to a different drive. Much like moving the Windows swap file to a different hard drive, moving the IE temp file to a different drive will result in a speed improvement. Click Tools, Internet Options, and on the General tab click Settings. Click the Move button and browse to a new hard drive and create a new folder for your IE temp files.

- Reduce the cache size. On the same dialog box, you can reduce the size of the IE cache, which limits the number of objects it sorts through to determine if any of the cached pages have changed. Use the slider to set the size, or type in a number in megabytes and then click OK.

- Change the frequency IE checks for new pages. IE defaults to checking "automatically" for new pages, which means that during a browsing session it will not check for updates to pages it has in its cache. This is usually the fastest for pages with somewhat static content. But if you browse pages with primarily static content, you can set the option to Never and IE will use only its cached version. You can always hit the Refresh button to check a Web site for changes.

- Disable default browser check. Click Tools, Internet Options, and then the Programs tab. Unless you are in the habit of installing and uninstalling browsers, you can deselect the Internet Explorer should check to see whether it is the default browser option.

- Disable unneeded multimedia. Click Tools, Internet Options, and then the Advanced tab. The Multimedia section has a number of settings you can disable, such as Automatic Image Resizing, Play animations, sounds, and videos in Web pages. If you want to view any of these you can always right-click the object placeholder and click Show.

## Surf anonymously with proxy servers

Internet browsing is thought by most people to be anonymous. The truth is that you leave footprints all over the Internet, and with a little sleuthing your tracks can be retraced. Normally it takes a system administrator to read firewall logs or server logs, so not just anyone can snoop around the system. On the other hand, depending on your views of liberty and personal freedom, anonymous browsing should be possible — after all, it's nobody else's business which books you decide to check out of the public library.

Anonymous surfing has been possible for some time, either through companies that provide security-oriented services, or through the use of proxy servers, which provide nearly-anonymous browsing across the Internet. With either service, you direct your Web browser to servers which in turn forward your requests to the destination Web site. These servers act as intermediaries, concealing your TCP/IP address and browser information from the destination sites. In spy-versus-spy terms, they act as "cut outs," such that anyone attempting to trace your tracks backwards will hit the intermediary and be stopped cold.

> **Watch Out!**
>
> Most businesses take a very dim view of employees using encrypted, anonymous communications through the corporate firewall because doing so represents a potential leak for confidential information. Save your anonymous surfing for your home connection.

Anonymous surfing is achieved in two ways: by running client software on your computer that acts as a mini-proxy, or by connecting directly using your existing browser in a session that may or may not be encrypted.

Two Web sites that offer anonymous surfing software and other secure services are GhostSurf at www.tenebril.com and Anonymizer at www. anonymizer.com. Anonymizer charges $29.95 per year for its Anonymous Surfing product; however, it has a free portal you can use for simple anonymous surfing. The portal will not display some sites that use a lot of scripting, but this limitation is removed with a subscription. GhostSurf Standard Edition charges $19.95 per year, does not have a free portal, but does offer a free fifteen-day trial. Both products route all traffic through their own private proxy servers and claim that no data is cached, nor are logs kept, of Internet traffic.

If you don't want to pay a yearly fee, you can use open anonymous proxy servers that are available on the Internet. These servers provide the same service, but with a significant downside: They are often very slow or unavailable, so you have to be willing to reconfigure your browser for a new proxy server if your connections aren't going through.

Three sites that list open proxies are www.proxy4free.com, www.public proxyservers.com, and www.atomintersoft.com. You can reconfigure Internet Explorer to connect through a proxy. There are three types of proxies: transparent, which does not conceal any information about your browser or session; anonymous, which conceals your own IP address but does indicate you are using a proxy; and high anonymity, which hides everything. Any of these may use encrypted (HTTPS) sessions.

To configure Internet Explorer for a proxy server, go to one of the open proxy lists. Find a proxy server that has the type of session you want, including encryption; that has a high percentage of uptime; and that has a low response time, usually listed in milliseconds. Write down the IP address and port number; this will often look like nnn.nnn.nnn.nnn:pppp, where the port number follows the IP address after the colon.

Open Internet Explorer. Click Tools, Internet Options, and then the Connection tab. Click the LAN Settings button.

Select Use a proxy server for your LAN (see Figure 8.39). Type the proxy server's IP address and port number in the appropriate boxes. Select Bypass proxy server for local addresses, and click OK twice. You can now surf Web sites using the proxy server. Remember that this will slow down your browsing by quite a bit, so be patient.

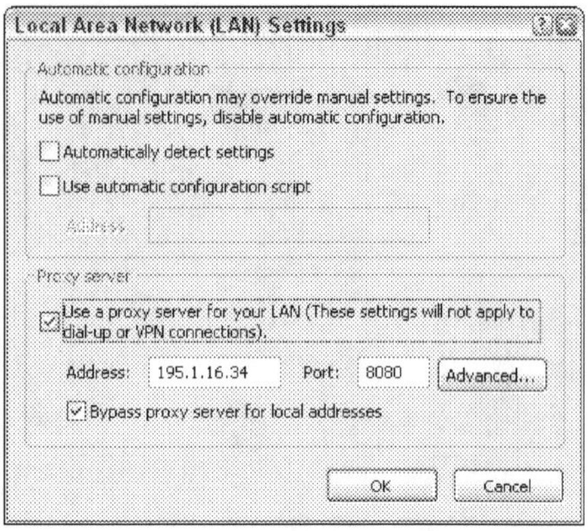

If configuring and re-configuring IE for anonymous surfing isn't your idea of a good time, you can use a popular shareware tool to handle the dirty work for you. Invisible Browsing (www.amplusnet. com/products/invisiblebrowsing/ overview.htm) lists open anonymous proxy servers and automatically reconfigures IE for you. It also has an auto-change feature, rotating your connection to different proxies at a specific interval. It has a free evaluation download, and costs $19.95 to register. If you plan on doing a lot of proxy surfing, either this solution or one of the private surfing products should help you out.

**Figure 8.39.** IE's proxy settings can be pointed at an open proxy server for anonymous browsing.

---

### Pros and cons of open proxy servers

Open proxy servers inhabit a gray area in Internet behavior and possibly in legal considerations. Some servers are open and anonymous by choice; they have been set up by benevolent administrators to provide a service to Net citizens. Other servers are open by oversight (or neglect) and are being used without the knowledge and consent of the owners. In those cases, people using the server as a proxy may run afoul of local laws pertaining to access to systems. Sometimes it's not easy to tell if a server is open by choice or by oversight. If you aren't sure, don't use the server.

Also, some servers are run by less-than-benevolent people who can monitor all your communications through the server. These types of servers make it dangerous to engage in commercial transactions, such as logging on to your bank or purchasing over the Internet, as you expose your user name, password, and credit card information to a sniffer.

In general, when using open proxies, be wary of where and how you surf. Read the FAQ on proxy servers at www.stayinvisible.com/ index.pl/proxy_servers_faq.

# Sanitize Internet Explorer

Browsing the Internet generates a lot of information that is stored on your local computer. Cookies are the most notorious (see Chapter 6), but other surfing information is stored as well. You can clean up Internet Explorer (and, by extension, much of Windows XP) by knowing what data is stored and how to remove it.

Sanitizing IE can't be done manually all at once, though there are products available on the Internet that will perform all the sanitizing steps at one time. You can do a decent job by doing the following.

Click Tools and then Internet options (see Figure 8.40). On the General tab, there are three buttons that help clean up your Internet surfing. The Delete Cookies button deletes all the cookies on your computer, so this is an all-or-nothing policy. If you want to edit cookies individually, click the Privacy tab and then the Sites button. You can select individual cookies or groups of cookies in the Managed Web Sites list, and then delete them using the Remove button.

**Figure 8.40.** Cleaning out cookies, browser files, and browser history can be done from the Internet Options General tab.

On the General tab, the Delete
Files button will remove all cached
files in your Temporary Internet
Files folder except any cookie files
(see Figure 8.41). You can also
delete all offline files here, including ones that you have cached
using the Offline Files feature.

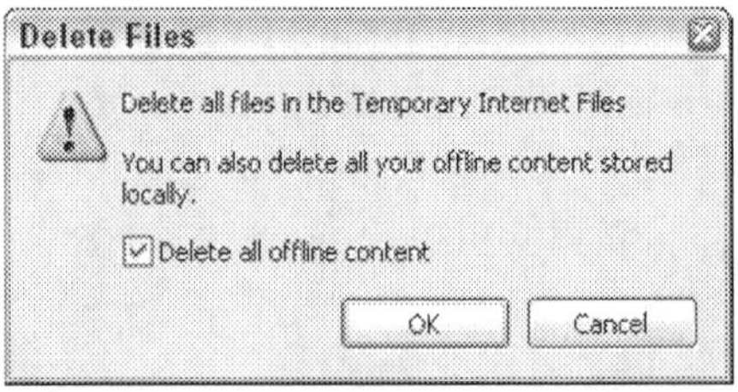

**Delete Files**

Delete all files in the Temporary Internet Files

You can also delete all your offline content stored
locally.

☑ Delete all offline content

OK    Cancel

**Figure 8.41.** Clear out the trash!

The third button on the General tab is the Clear History button. By
default IE maintains a twenty-day history of where you surfed, and any material older than twenty days is automatically deleted. If you want, you can
delete the history files by clicking the button. You can also set a shorter expi-
ration period; setting it to zero will clear your history when you close IE.

Next, click the Content tab and then click the AutoComplete button.
AutoComplete maintains its own separate history of what you have entered
onto Web forms and what passwords you have used with different Web sites.
To clear out the AutoComplete information, click the appropriate buttons.
Unfortunately you don't have the ability to choose which passwords to retain
and which to delete; again, it's an all-or-nothing exercise. You also can't view
or export any saved passwords, so if you hit the button you will lose passwords to infrequently-visited sites.

If you use certificates, you can clear your SSL cache by clicking the Clear
SSL State button.

Finally, click the Advanced tab, scroll down the list, and then select
Empty Temporary Internet Files folder when browser is closed (see Figure
8.42). This will take the place of clicking the Delete Files button.

The TweakUI Powertoys (see Chapter 3) can also be used to help sanitize
both IE and Windows XP. Open TweakUI and browse to the Explorer item.
In the checklist on the right, select Clear document history on exit (see
Figure 8.43). This will clear the My Recent Documents folder and some
most-recently-used lists in Windows applications. It will also clear out the
Run dialog box.

---

**Hack**

If you need to view but not edit saved passwords for Web forms, the freeware utility
Protected Storage PassView at www.nirsoft.net/utils/pspv.html will show you the
matched user name and password pairs for a particular Web site.

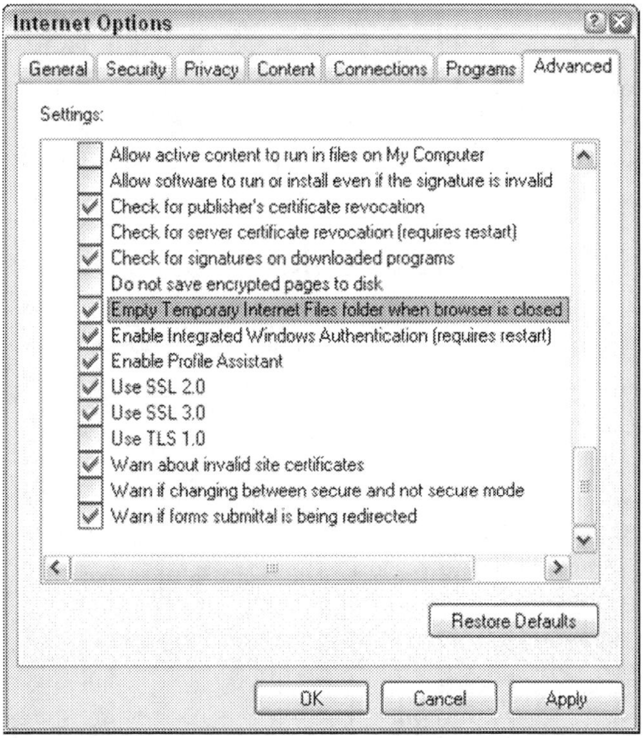

**Figure 8.42.** Instruct IE to empty the trash every time it closes.

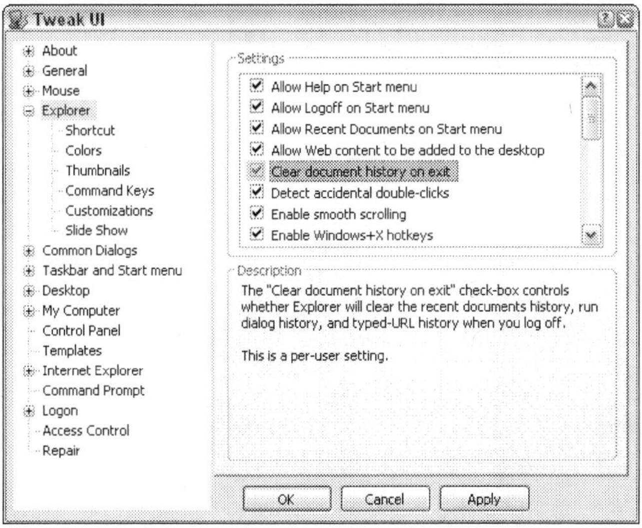

**Figure 8.43.** Cover your tracks by clearing out the My Recent Documents links.

Next, you can deselect Maintain document history; this will prevent the tracking of document history at all. If you use the Clear document history, you may want to leave this enabled so you still have a useful history while logged on, but clear the history when you log out. You can also deselect Maintain network history to delete any network URLs or shared resources you accessed while logged on.

# Become an Outlook Express expert

Outlook Express (OE) is perhaps the world's most notorious e-mail client (see Chapter 6 on securing OE from various bad things). That doesn't mean it's a bad one; in fact, for a basic e-mail client it's pretty decent. It just takes a bit of effort to secure it from potential threats.

If you prefer working with Microsoft products, OE is one of two choices you have, the other being Microsoft Office Outlook. OE has one big advantage: It's free and comes with the operating system — no need to download any new client or pay for one with more features than you'll ever use like the other Outlook.

Before you use OE, contact your ISP and set up an e-mail account with them. You will be given some information for setting up your e-mail client that includes your e-mail address and your e-mail server addresses. Most ISPs have a configuration page or document that you can download from their Web site and print out. Many of them have one that walks you through the OE dialog boxes step-by-step. If they have specific information that varies from this book, use their information instead.

## Set up e-mail accounts

Click Start and then E-mail. If you haven't set up an e-mail account yet, Outlook Express opens the Internet Connection Wizard for you. Type the name you want to appear in the "From" section of your e-mail and then click Next. Type your e-mail address that you will use with your ISP; often it's yourname@ispname.com, but use the one you've set up with them. Click next. The E-mail Server Names dialog box appears (see Figure 8.44).

**Inside Scoop**

Most ISPs provide more than one e-mail address with an account. You can use "familyname" as your ISP account name and then have separate e-mails such as "mothername@ispname.com" and "daughtername@ispname.com" with each account. Check with your ISP for details.

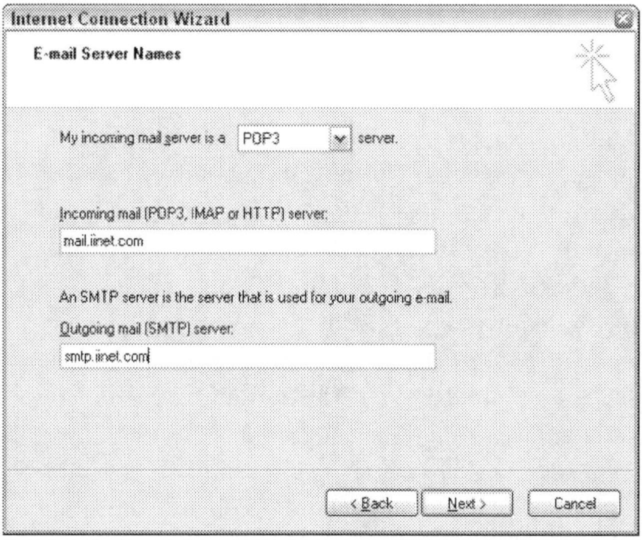

**Figure 8.44.** Your e-mail server addresses are only slightly more important than your own e-mail address.

Select the type of incoming mail server from the drop-down list box. In most cases this will be a POP3 server. Type the incoming and outgoing mail server addresses in the appropriate boxes. Many times an ISP makes it easy by using the same name, such as mail.ispname.com. Use the addresses they give you. Click Next.

The Internet Mail Logon dialog box appears. Type the account name you set up with your ISP and the password. You can select whether to remember your password, or to have OE prompt you every time you connect to enter your password. Click Next. To save the settings, click Finish. Congratulations, you have e-mail!

# Use advanced features

Outlook Express may not have all the glitz and glamour of its much larger namesake, Outlook. But it does have some big-time features in it that few people know or use on a daily basis. With a few of these you can move beyond merely reading and sending e-mail and become a true Outlook Express master.

## Create distribution lists

Distribution lists are collections of e-mail addresses into useful categories. Most people associate distribution lists with e-mail servers such as Exchange,

---

### Identities: Who are you?

Outlook Express has been around since the prehistoric days of Windows 95, which didn't support "user accounts" that had separate access rights and security privileges. This meant that everyone shared the same e-mail client. In order to keep people's accounts, mail, and address books separate, Microsoft added "identities" to OE so that users could switch between them and keep information separate.

With Windows XP identities aren't needed because user data and e-mail are kept separate, so there is no danger of Mom's stock trade confirmations being read by her daughter. The only reason for identity support is that if you were using identities with Windows 9x or ME, you can import an identity's e-mail into the appropriate user account. Click File Import, Messages, Microsoft Outlook Express 6, and then select the identity to import.

---

where the address book contains entries such as DevAll or LunchBunch. When you are selecting addresses for the To: field, you can select a distribution list, and the e-mail will automatically go to all the members of the list.

You can create your own distribution lists in Outlook Express for quickly sending e-mail to numerous addresses. Click the Addresses button or click Tools and then Address Book. The Address Book opens. Click New and then New Group.

Type a name for the group, such as Sailing Buddies or Cat-Herders (see Figure 8.45). From here you can select group members from your address book, create a new address book contact and then add the person to your group, or add a name and e-mail address without creating a new contact. When you are done, click OK.

### E-mail paranoia: Return receipts and bcc:'s

For the cover-your-assets crowd, Outlook Express has return receipts and blind carbon copies, or bcc:'s, to help you survive in today's bureaucrat-eat-bureaucrat world. OE's return receipts are automatically generated when the message is read by the recipient. This can be useful if you are under the gun to deliver a report and want to confirm whether it was received in time.

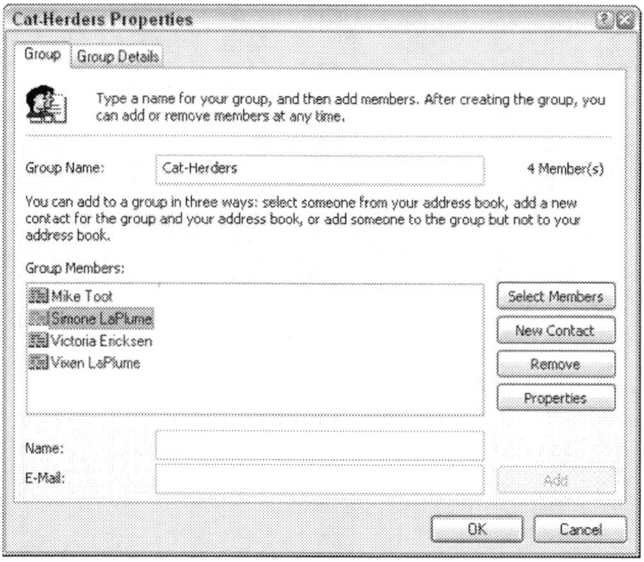

**Figure 8.45.** Create groups for faster addressing of e-mail.

There are two ways to request read receipts. First, in an e-mail you are about to send, click Tools and then Request Read Receipt (see Figure 8.46). Your message will generate a receipt when it is read or marked as read, which is not always the same thing.

**Figure 8.46.** You can add a Request Read Receipt on the spur of the moment.

Second, you can configure OE to always generate a read receipt for all e-mail. In the main OE window click Tools, Options, and then the Receipts tab. Select Request a read receipt for all sent messages. Whenever you create a new message, the Request Read Receipt option is checked, and you can uncheck it if you don't absolutely need a read receipt for that message (see Figure 8.47).

But just because you request a receipt doesn't mean you'll get one. On the Receipts tab there are options that determine how OE will handle read receipt requests. It can always send a receipt, ask whether to send a receipt, or never send a receipt. The default is to notify when one is requested, and you can then decide whether to send a read receipt. Just remember that if you can request a read receipt, so can anyone else; and if you decide to toss all read receipts into a black hole, so can anyone else.

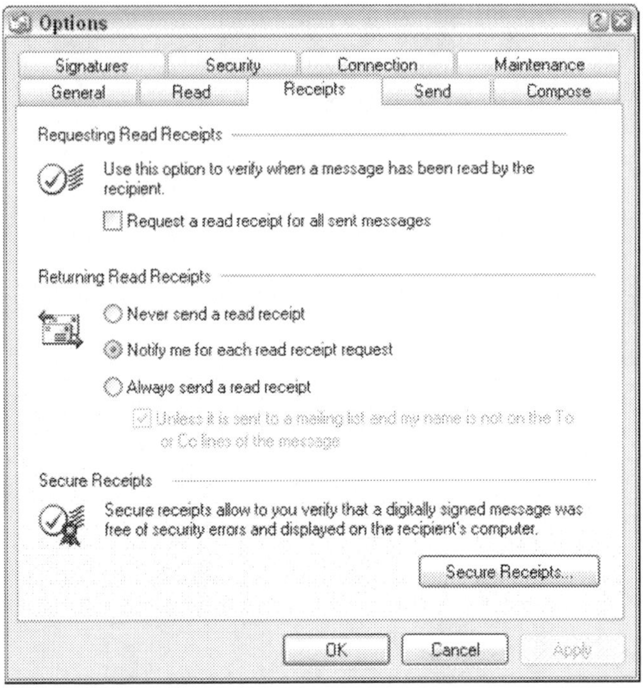

**Figure 8.47.** Receipts can be requested but may not be sent, depending on the options you select.

Bcc:, or blind carbon copy, is a third address field you can use with your messages. It is a way of sending a copy of the message without alerting the others in your To: and CC: fields. I use it on a regular basis when I send out updates or humor e-mails to my friends, many of whom don't know each other. Rather than share a list of my friends with everyone else, I use the Bcc: field. More conspiratorially-minded individuals use the bcc: to notify the boss that something is afoot without alerting the main recipient of the message. No matter how (or if) you use it, it is there should you need it.

Create a new message. Click View and then click All Headers (see Figure 8.48). The Bcc: line is available in your message, and will be there for all new messages. If you don't want the real estate taken up by the additional header, you can always add addresses to the Bcc: line using the Address Book, which has a button specifically for blind carbon copies.

---

**Watch Out!**

Most, but not all, of today's e-mail clients support return receipts; many HTML or server-based e-mail programs like Hotmail do not. If you don't get a receipt, consider whether you sent it to someone who may not have the receipt feature available.

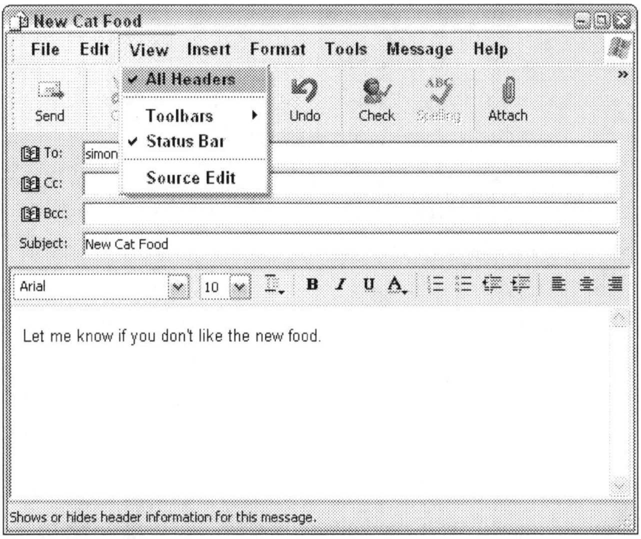

**Figure 8.48.** Add the bcc: option if you want to send e-mail to large groups without sharing their addresses with everyone else on the list.

## View e-mail headers

E-mail headers are a part of every message sent across the Internet. As each message passes through a mail server, it adds a few lines of information that identify the server, the time the message passed through it, and any specific message handling information. These lines are normally hidden from view, since most of us don't care what path the message took to get from outbox to inbox.

But there are occasions where this information is needed, especially when there is a mail delivery failure, or worse yet, a spammer at work. Then mail headers are like footprints that can help track down where things went wrong.

To view the message header, open the e-mail message. Click File, Properties, and then the Details tab (see Figure 8.49). All the message header information is there in all its glory.

**Figure 8.49.** Message header information can be informative if you take the time to look through it.

# Manage e-mail with message rules

Many people view e-mail as *the* mission-critical application, both for conducting business and for personal communications. Over time people quickly build up a steady stream of incoming e-mail: business documents, pictures from friends, electronic newsletters, and of course spam. While Outlook Express has some ability to handle spam, it's the other types of e-mail that can sometimes be disorganized and overwhelming.

Fortunately OE (and most other mail clients) has the ability to automatically sort and organize your e-mail for you. This lets you determine what is important and what can be dealt with at a later time.

First, create folders for your e-mail. Right-click Local Folders and then click New Folder. Type a name that is meaningful to you, such as project names or ones based on topics. You can create nested folders if you want, so that projects are broken down by milestones or subject matter. Click OK.

Next, create some message rules to route your mail to the folders you just created. Click Tools, Message Rules, and then Mail. The New Mail Rule dialog box appears (see Figure 8.50).

**Figure 8.50.** Your message rule will act on specific conditions that occur in your e-mail.

---

### Effective rule-making

Outlook Express doesn't have a very sophisticated rule-processing engine, certainly not on the scale of its big brother Outlook. But it is effective for many people and can do most of what you want within its conditions and actions. Some tips for effective rule-making are:

- Keep rules simple. Don't try to create complex sets of conditions and actions within a single rule; use single conditions and actions within a rule. This is much easier to troubleshoot or edit later.

- Use negative rules. You can create conditions that apply to messages that *don't* have specific words or people associated with them. This is simpler than creating rules with all possible words or people associated with them.

- Create rules from e-mail. You can quickly create a rule from a message by selecting the message and then clicking Message ➪ Create Rule From Message. This opens the New Mail Rule dialog box with OE's best guess as to what conditions and actions should be applied. You can then edit the rule to fine-tune its behavior.

- Processing order matters. Rules are processed in the order listed. If mail isn't being processed the way you think it should, try changing the order of some of the rules.

---

Scroll through the conditions list and select one or more conditions that you want to look for. Do the same thing for the actions that you want OE to take when the conditions are met. When you click a condition or an action, an underlined value appears in the Rule Description field. Click the value to bring up an additional dialog box where you can enter the information needed to process the rule. Fill in the conditions, click OK to return to the rule dialog box, and then click OK again. Your rule is added to the Message Rules dialog box where you can modify or delete a rule, or change the order in which it is processed.

## Set up and subscribe to newsgroups

Newsgroups are the vast, untamed wilderness — or, as some might quip, the pale white underbelly — of the Internet. There are two kinds of newsgroups: private ones that may be run by a business and are usually moderated

(Microsoft has numerous newsgroups available) and public ones that are available through your ISP and may or may not be moderated.

Private ones tend to be topic-specific or product-specific and the content is related to those products. The public ones are like a gargantuan public bulletin board with every conceivable topic available for browsing. This means that there is a lot of mature language and adult content available, so if you have concerns about children wandering out onto newsgroups, you can arrange with your ISP not to allow newsgroup connections with your account.

Setting up a newsgroup connection is similar to creating an e-mail account. Click Tools, Accounts, Add, and then News (see Figure 8.51). The Internet Connection Wizard walks you through the process, and if you have already set up an e-mail account, it will fill in a number of newsgroup fields with the default settings from your e-mail account.

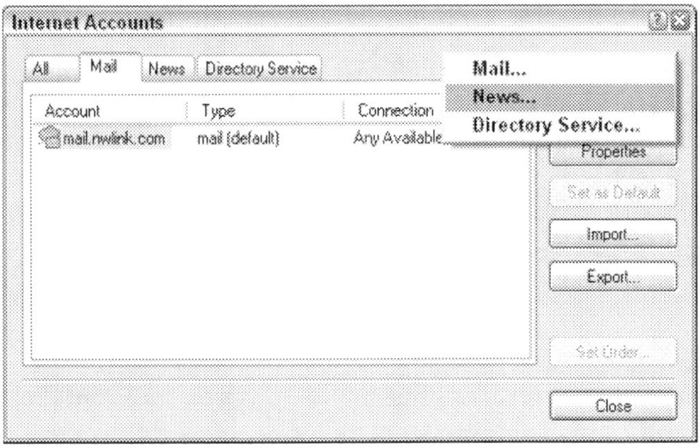

**Figure 8.51.** Newsgroups are another account type that you can add to Outlook Express.

Type your display name and then click Next. Type your e-mail address and then click Next.

On the Internet News Server Name dialog box, type in the server address. Many ISPs configure this as news.ispname.com, but use the name

---

**Watch Out!**

Spammers harvest e-mail addresses from public newsgroups. Don't post a message with your e-mail address in it; use disguising methods such as inserting a nonsense phrase in the middle of your address, such as "youre-mailDONOTSPAM@ ispname.com".

you have been provided. There is also a check box to select whether your news server requires you to log on. If so, you will be taken to a dialog box similar to the one you used to log on with your account name. Click Next and then click Finish. When you are done, OE asks if you want to download newsgroups for your new account. If this is a public newsgroup server, go get some coffee; there are over 50,000 newsgroups and depending on how many your ISP subscribes to and whether you are on dia-up, downloading a list may take quite a bit of time (see Figure 8.52).

To read newsgroup messages you need to subscribe to a newsgroup. Right-click the account and then click Newsgroups. The Newsgroup Subscriptions dialog box appears (see Figure 8.53).

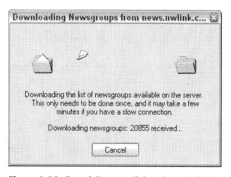

**Downloading Newsgroups from news.nwlink.c...**

Downloading the list of newsgroups available on the server. This only needs to be done once, and it may take a few minutes if you have a slow connection.

Downloading newsgroups: 20855 received..

[ Cancel ]

**Figure 8.52.** Especially over dialup, it can take some time downloading just the names of all the newsgroups available.

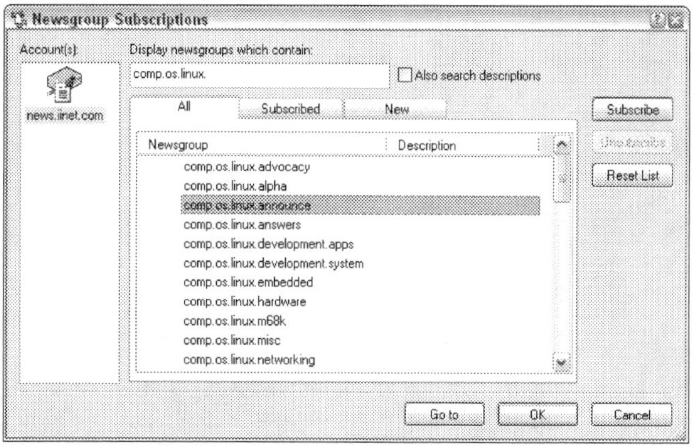

**Newsgroup Subscriptions**

Account(s):        Display newsgroups which contain:

news.iinet.com      comp.os.linux.                      ☐ Also search descriptions

                    All      Subscribed      New              Subscribe

Newsgroup                    Description                      Unsubscribe

    comp.os.linux.advocacy
    comp.os.linux.alpha                                      Reset List
    comp.os.linux.announce
    comp.os.linux.answers
    comp.os.linux.development.apps
    comp.os.linux.development.system
    comp.os.linux.embedded
    comp.os.linux.hardware
    comp.os.linux.m68k
    comp.os.linux.misc
    comp.os.linux.networking

                              Go to      OK      Cancel

**Figure 8.53.** The huge collection of newsgroups can be winnowed down by being selective in your subscriptions.

The listing is a fully-expanded, hierarchical one; you can take time to scroll through the thousands of names in the list or you can type all or part of a word or phrase in the Display newsgroups which contain field. This will narrow down the newsgroup list to ones that match your filter. When you have found a newsgroup that sounds interesting, click the Subscribe button. An icon appears next to the newsgroup name, and the newsgroup appears on the Subscribed tab. When you are done subscribing to newsgroups, click OK.

By default OE will synchronize new messages to the newsgroup, both message headers and content. Unfortunately, the first time you subscribe to an account, it will download both the headers and the content of all new messages in a newsgroup. If the group has a lot of traffic, this could be a problem, especially over dialup. Make sure the synchronization settings grab only the information you need. Click the Settings button and choose the option you want: Don't Synchronize, All Messages, New Messages Only, or Headers Only (see Figure 8.54).

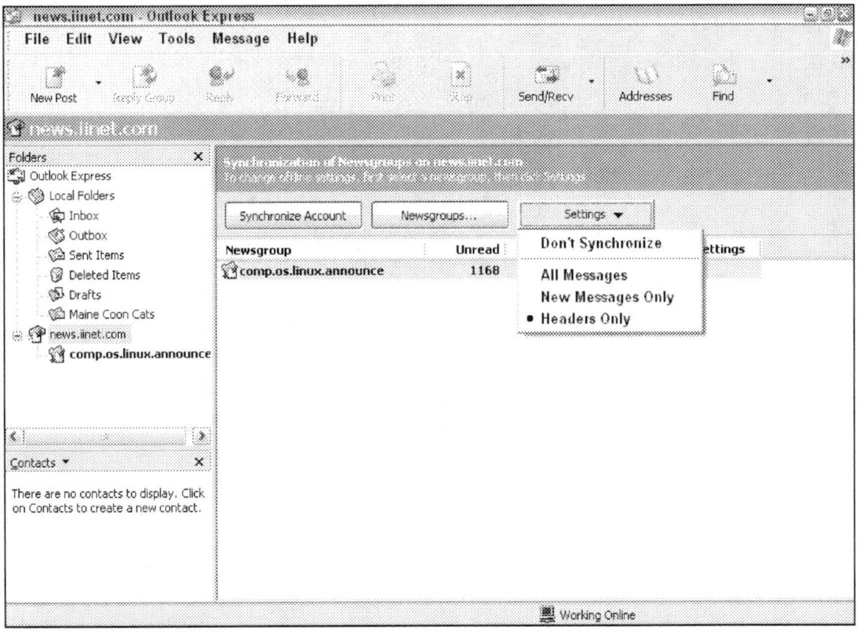

**Figure 8.54.** Synchronize headers only until you have a feel for the newsgroup's content.

The other setting you should know about controls the number of headers that are downloaded at one time. Click Tools, Options, and then the Read tab (see Figure 8.55). In the News section you can select to download only a certain number of headers at one time. By default OE downloads only 300 headers; deselect this option to download all headers since the last time you synchronized the newsgroup. You can also mark all messages as read when exiting the newsgroup. By default, any newsgroup message you haven't read is left marked as unread, but if you are a casual newsgroup reader you can select this box and all messages will be marked as read and eligible for cleanup.

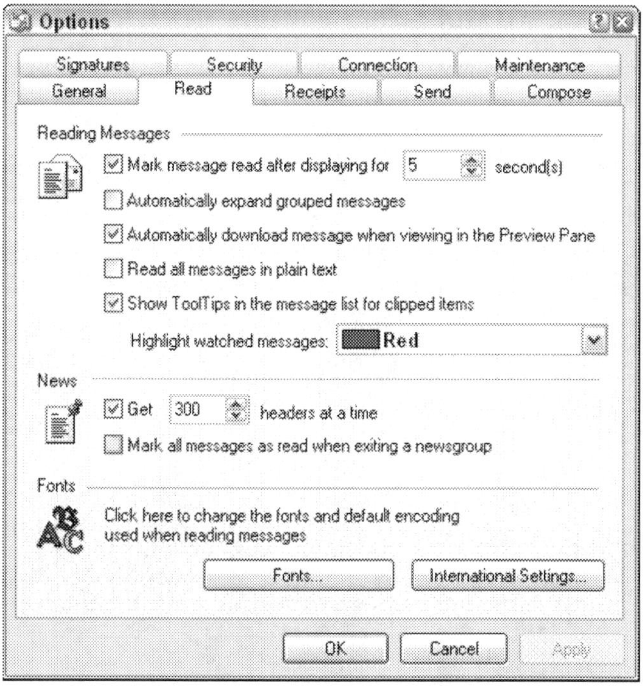

**Figure 8.55.** You can control how many headers to download, or whether to mark groups as read when you exit OE.

## Reclaim wasted space

Even if you prune your folders, delete old messages, and empty trash, the index files still have the messages and folders stored within the message base; the files and folders were merely hidden by Outlook Express when you "deleted" them. Over time, the message base consumes a lot of space on your hard drive. You can reclaim much of this space by compacting the message base.

Click Tools, Options, and then the Maintenance tab. Click Clean Up Now. OE reports on the amount of wasted space in the message base for both e-mail and for newsgroups. Click the Compact button to reclaim this space. The other three buttons are specifically for newsgroup message handling, so if you need to clean up your newsgroups or reset message folders, you can do that here.

# Back up your messages and address book

With the importance of e-mail to the average user's life, you'd think Microsoft would make backing up your mail client's files easy. Not so. Outlook Express' message base and address book files are scattered over several different sections of your hard drive.

Your messages are stored in Documents and Settings\%username%\ Local Settings\Application Data\Identities\{GUID number}\Microsoft\Outlook Express. Your contacts are stored in Documents and Settings\%username%\ Application Data\Microsoft\Address Book. Your settings, account information, preferences, and e-mail rules are stored in the Registry at HKEY_CURRENT_ USER\Identities\{GUID number}. Ancillary account information, such as any LDAP servers you are using for identification, are stored in the Registry at HKEY_CURRENT_USER\Software\Microsoft\Internet Account Manager. As you can see, it's nearly impossible to remember where all this information is stored or how to back it up.

If you want to back everything up manually, you can use the Windows Backup program (see Chapter 12) to copy the message base files and address book files, and use the Registry to export the keys to .reg files (see Chapter 11) and then back up those keys as well.

If you don't relish the thought of digging around in the registry every time you want to make a simple backup of your e-mail information, there are a couple utilities available that automate the process. Genie-Soft's Outlook

---

### Why I hate Outlook Express

Microsoft makes it very, very difficult to switch to another e-mail client. You can export your address book as a text file in comma separated value format, which most other clients can import. But you cannot do the same with your message base — you can only export to Microsoft Outlook or export to an Exchange server.

Even knowing where all the various files are stored and all the gotchas involved, I once lost all my e-mail *and* my address book due to a perfect sequence of inability to export the message base, inattention on my part, and a DVD burner that made a copy (or so I thought) of my data but actually made a nice coaster instead.

As a result I've switched over to Mozilla Thunderbird (www.mozilla. org/products/thunderbird) which makes it much easier to manage and back up my e-mail and address book, and I haven't looked back.

Express Backup (www.genie-soft.com/products/oeb/features.html) is a $29.95 shareware application that has a lot of really cool features including the ability to view individual messages from a backup file and synchronize between existing e-mail and e-mail in your backup.

You can also download Outlook Express Quick Backup at www.oehelp. com/OEBackup/Default.aspx. It is freeware, not as fully-featured as Outlook Express Backup, but it will let you export your message base along with your address book and settings.

# Get your chat on with Windows Messenger

Cross a telephone with a typewriter and you get Internet chat. One of the most popular applications on the Internet today is the chat application. There are several chat services available, and they largely use different protocols, do not talk with one another, and have different strengths and features that appeal to different groups.

But chat programs are not just about chatting. Nearly all chat clients can transfer files, use Webcams and headsets for video and audio conferencing, and Windows Messenger has the additional ability of sharing a whiteboard space and sharing a desktop application with another person.

Microsoft actually makes two chat clients available: Windows Messenger, which ships as part of Windows XP, and MSN Messenger, a free download from MSN.com (see Figure 8.56). Functionally the primary difference between them is that Windows Messenger integrates with Microsoft Exchange, enabling intra-corporate chats without having to go out to Microsoft and back in through the corporate firewall. Visually MSN Messenger is much flashier, with tabs that take you to MSN services, smilies, nudges, and rotating banner ads at the bottom of the window. Whichever one you use comes down to personal taste and which interface looks best to you.

## Set up the chat service

To set up Windows Messenger (WM) click Start, All Programs, and then Windows Messenger. You can also double-click the WM icon in the notification area. Choose Click here to sign in. WM is one of the few remaining Microsoft services that requires a .NET Passport. (See Chapter 6 for more on .NET Passport.) If you haven't added one already, when you start WM for the first time the .NET Passport Wizard appears, ready to walk you through the process of getting your very own Passport. Click Next.

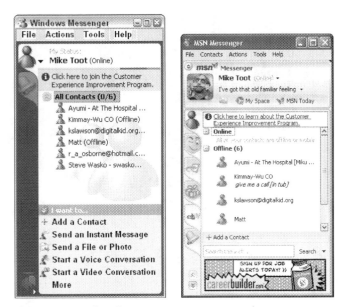

**Figure 8.56.** Two chat clients, one common purpose: to let you procrastinate more effectively.

## Universal Chat: Gaim and Trillian

MSN Messenger is not the only chat game in town. Other chat services are available such as Yahoo Chat, AIM (AOL Instant Messenger), and IRC (Internet Relay Chat). If you wanted to chat on those systems you needed a wholly separate client — until now.

Two popular multi-service chat clients are Gaim (gaim.sourceforge. net) and Trillian (www.ceruleanstudios.com). Both are free; Gaim is open-source and multi-platform, while Trillian is Windows only and offers a Pro version for $25.00. Gaim is quirky but offers straight-ahead chat on multiple services with no frills. Trillian has boatloads of eye candy, is skinnable, and does your laundry if you ask it nicely. Its interface may prove too distracting to the easily-distractable.

Both connect to MSN Messenger as well as the other services. If you want to work with only one user interface but multiple chat services, either of these clients will work well.

Part of the Passport sign-up process requires a valid e-mail address for the account verification e-mail. Select whether you have an existing e-mail address, or whether you want to sign up for a Hotmail account. Click Next. If you have already activated your Passport account, select Yes, sign in with my Passport Network Credentials; otherwise, select No, sign up now. Click Next.

You must enter your e-mail address and Passport account's password (see Figure 8.57). Most users will want to associate the Passport account with the Windows XP user name; leave the box selected. Click Next. When the wizard is finished, click Finish. At the first log on, you may be prompted to install a newer version of Windows Messenger. Select yes, and then click OK. After updating you will need to restart your computer.

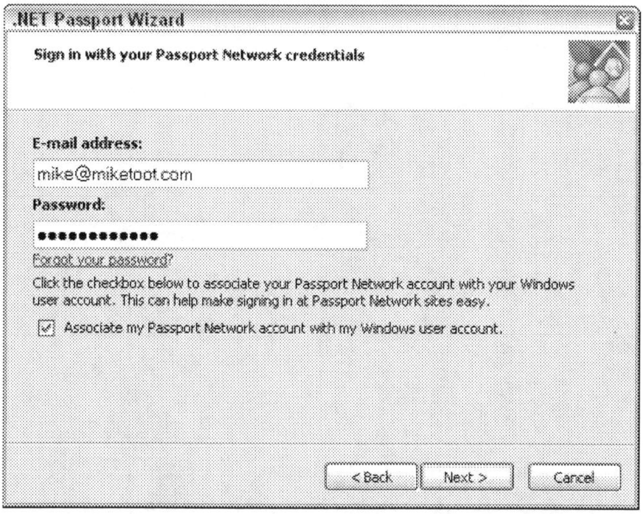

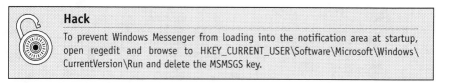

**Figure 8.57.** Use your e-mail address and Passport network credentials to log on.

By default WM logs on to the Messenger chat service whenever you log on, though it does not necessarily contact the WM servers and log you on to the chat client. You can change the startup behavior by clicking Tools, Options, and then Preferences (see Figure 8.58). Deselect Run this program when Windows starts.

**Hack**

To prevent Windows Messenger from loading into the notification area at startup, open regedit and browse to HKEY_CURRENT_USER\Software\Microsoft\Windows\CurrentVersion\Run and delete the MSMSGS key.

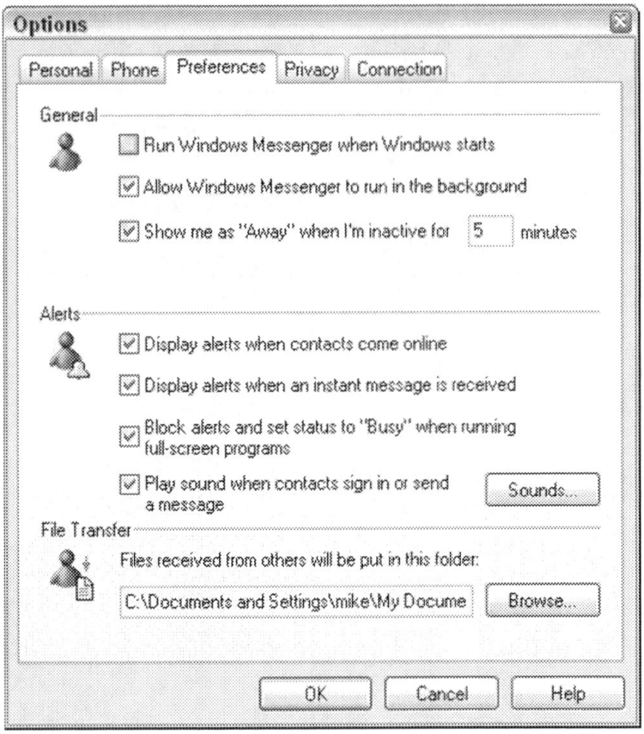

**Figure 8.58.** Turn off the "boss monitor" by turning off the autostart feature of Windows Messenger.

## Chat with friends

In order to chat you need to add contacts to Windows Messenger. Click Add a Contact to start a wizard. You can add a contact using her e-mail address or sign-in name, or you can search for the user. The search function is anemic, so don't bother; add people in using their e-mail or Messenger contact name. Click Next.

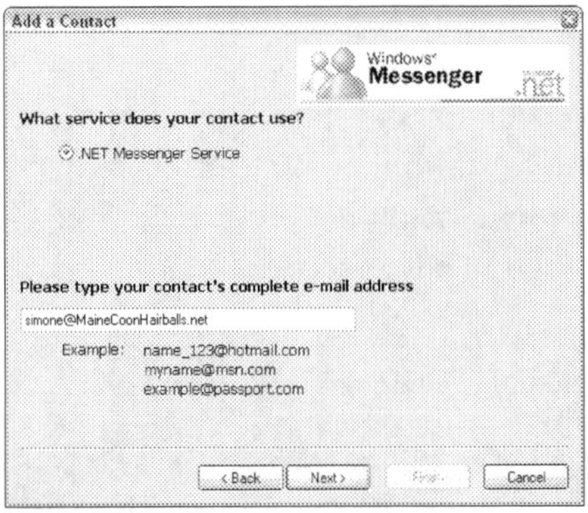

Type in the person's e-mail address and then click Next (see Figure 8.59). If Messenger didn't find them in the database, it kindly offers to send them an e-mail, inviting them to join the Microsoft group mind. You now have two options: Next, which lets you continue adding new contacts, or Finish, which closes the wizard.

**Figure 8.59.** Adding a person using her e-mail address is the easiest way to get started.

**Bright Idea**

You can have up to five people chatting at once in the same conversation. Click Actions and then Invite Someone to this Conversation. You can choose other online friends to join your chat.

When one of your contacts is online you can start a chat session with her by double-clicking her name. You can also select her and then click Send an Instant Message, or right-click her and then click Send an Instant Message. A chat window appears; click in the window and start typing. Press the Enter key to send the message. And that's it!

## The hidden gems of Windows Messenger

Windows Messenger started out as a quickie text utility but it quickly matured into a multimedia communications application. There are many things you can do with WM:

- If you have a sound card with a microphone jack, you can plug a headset into your sound card and have live audio chat sessions with other similarly-equipped Messenger friends. Start off by having a text chat session, and then click Start a Voice Conversation. If this is the first time you have run the voice chat, you will run through quick tuning wizard to adjust audio levels.

- Similarly, if you have a Webcam you can have live video feeds between chat partners. Most Webcam software integrates with WM and will have its own tuning and picture adjustment software. Even on broadband you won't get live-television-quality video feeds, but you can still wave at friends and laugh at their new tattoos.

- File exchanges are available so you can swap large files without worrying about e-mail server attachment limits. This is a great way to share large PowerPoint files or get program fixes from technical support.

- Application sharing lets you share Word, Excel, or any other Windows application with someone else. You both can edit and change the document in real time, or you can walk people through a new application you've written without having to package it up and distribute it to them.

- Finally, a whiteboard is available for drawing, editing, and changing images on the fly. It's useful but not often used; watching someone draw or edit is about as exciting as it sounds.

## Wherefore art thou, NetMeeting?

NetMeeting was Microsoft's answer to collaborative conferencing. It had many of the features currently built into Windows Messenger, including a whiteboard application and application sharing. However, the early versions were limited by bandwidth and server horsepower. Internet companies sprung up to offer low-cost virtual conferencing facilities, and by the time NetMeeting caught up, its technology ended up in other applications like WM. More powerful desktop sharing is available in Remote Desktop, or in corporate environments Terminal Services, so NetMeeting's popularity has waned.

You can still find NetMeeting on your computer and use it for conferencing without requiring a beefy server on the back end. Type Start, Run, type conf, and then press Enter. Its chief benefit is that you can have more than one person whiteboarding or application sharing, which is WM's limit.

# Just the facts

- Networking isn't complex, and there are many ways to get connected to the Internet.

- Internet Explorer can be reconfigured to better reflect your surfing habits.

- Search engines are available for improving your ability to manage information, both on your desktop and on the Internet.

- E-mail can be best managed with a few message rules and a bit of common sense.

- Chat applications can do more than just chat; they can enable multimedia conversations with others.

GET THE SCOOP ON...
Sharing and managing your printers ▪ Using your computer
to send and receive faxes ▪ Installing Internet Information
Services ▪ Using remote desktop access

# Working with Network Services

## Chapter 9

**W**indows XP is designed to be a good network citizen. It supports multiple users, can be managed remotely, and can provide network services to others. This flexibility means that you do not always need a server version of Windows in order to enjoy services commonly associated with servers. While you probably don't want to use Windows XP to provide services for more than ten other computers, you can provide these and other services for small or SOHO networks.

The types of services available range from traditional file and print services to Web servers and FTP servers. You can also interoperate with non-Microsoft computers or technology. This chapter shows you how to work with the grab-bag of network technologies and open up your Windows XP desktop to a more powerful capability.

## Share and manage printers

Sharing printers and sharing files (see Chapter 5) make up the Dynamic Duo of networking. These two services were the big reason — to some, the only reason — for installing networks into small businesses. It's much more cost-effective to share printing hardware than to attach a dedicated printer to every computer. For example, you can share a photo printer, a laser printer, and a color printer with others on the network. While everyone can dream up reasons why they *need* a dedicated color laser printer, the printing technology built into

## Microsoft printing terminology

Microsoft has different names for the technology used to make information on the screen appear on pieces of paper. This should save you time if you're on the phone with Microsoft Support about a print job gone awry.

- **Print device.** This is the actual hardware at the far end of the cable. Everybody but Microsoft calls them "printers."

- **Printer driver.** This is device-specific software that controls the print device with printing codes, form feed, or duplexing commands, or anything specific to the device itself. This is usually provided by the hardware manufacturer, though many drivers are shipped with Windows XP for convenience.

- **Printer.** This is the Windows software that receives print jobs from other applications, manages print queues, and provides overall print device management. It works together with the printer driver to create printable documents.

To keep things simple, the term "printer" will be used throughout the chapter except where a more specific term is needed for clarity.

---

the Windows family makes it easy to share, control, and manage shared printers on your network.

## Install a printer

Between USB, Plug and Play, the Add a New Printer Wizard, and the device driver library on your hard drive, Windows XP is able to get you up and running with all but the newest or oldest printers.

Printers come in two varieties: ones attached to the computer you are working on, and ones located elsewhere on your network (standalone or attached to another computer). They are referred to as local and remote printers. The process for connecting to them and setting them up is similar. If you upgraded from an earlier version of Windows, or if you had your printer connected during a clean install, your printer is most likely set up and configured already. But if you add a new printer you can follow this procedure. To install a local printer you must be logged on as an account with local administrator rights.

**Watch Out!**

Make sure you read the printer's installation directions before plugging it in. Some USB printers require that you install the drivers and related software before connecting the device. If you do not follow the directions, you will descend into version control madness. Read and follow the directions!

Your printer may come with a disk that has the necessary drivers as well as applications that enhance or take advantage of your printer's features. Run the disk's setup program and follow its instructions, and in most cases it will configure Windows XP for you — you will never need to use the wizard.

Connect the USB, parallel, or serial cable to your computer. If Plug and Play detects your printer, it will install the necessary drivers automatically. If not, click Start, Printers and Faxes, and then Add a Printer. The Add a New Printer Wizard starts. Click Next. Select Local Printer and select Automatically detect and install my Plug and Play printer (see Figure 9.1). Click Next. Your printer will probably be detected; follow the remainder of the instructions on the wizard.

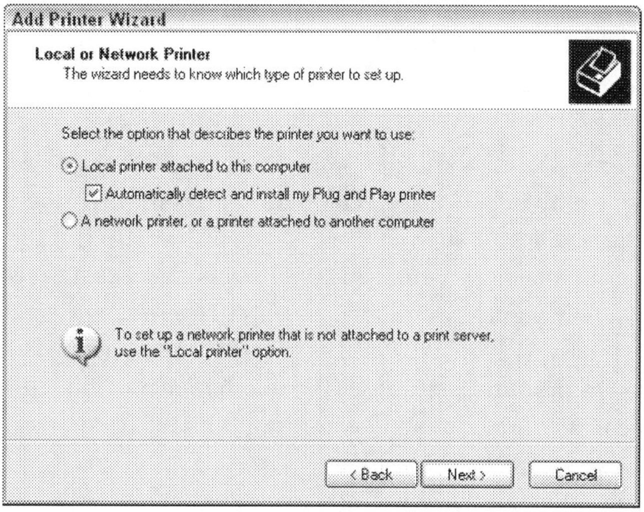

**Add Printer Wizard**

**Local or Network Printer**
The wizard needs to know which type of printer to set up.

Select the option that describes the printer you want to use:

◉ Local printer attached to this computer

   ☑ Automatically detect and install my Plug and Play printer

○ A network printer, or a printer attached to another computer

ⓘ To set up a network printer that is not attached to a print server, use the "Local printer" option.

[ < Back ]  [ Next > ]  [ Cancel ]

**Figure 9.1.** Detect printers attached to your computer with the "local printer" option.

However, if your printer doesn't support Plug and Play, the wizard will tell you it cannot detect the printer and you must manually install it. Click Next.

Select the port from the drop-down list (parallel printers use LPT, serial printers use COM) and then click Next. The Install Printer Software dialog box appears, with a list of manufacturers on the left and a list of printer models for each manufacturer on the right (see Figure 9.2). Select a manufacturer and the printer model from the list and then click Next. Alternatively, if you have a driver disk for your printer, click Have Disk and then browse for the INF file for your printer on the disk.

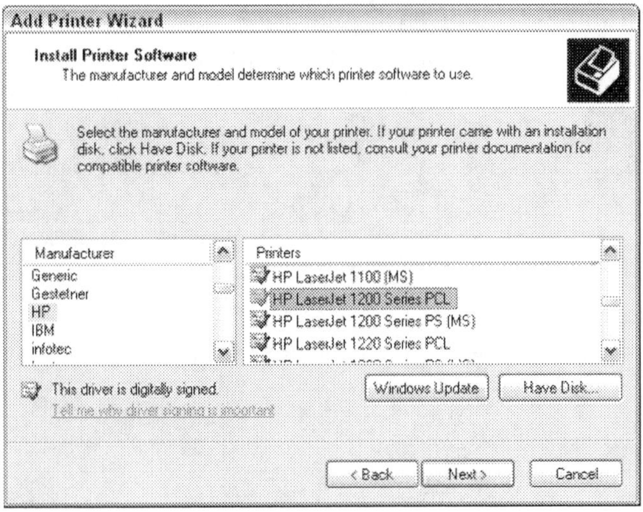

**Figure 9.2.** Select your printer manufacturer and model.

The Name Your Printer dialog box appears. You can accept the default or give it a name that is meaningful to you. Select whether you want this printer to be the default and then click Next.

In the Printer Sharing dialog box you can choose whether to share this printer with other computers on your network. When you share the printer, it means that your computer will act as a print server and it must be turned on in order for others to print to the printer. Give it a share name that others will recognize; the name should be 15 letters or less, without any punctuation or spaces in the name. Click Next.

The Location and Comment dialog box lets you add information about the printer that will be visible in Network Neighborhood or Active Directory's

---

**Hack**

Older printers often emulated the Hewlett-Packard Printer Control Language, or PCL. You should be able to use an HP LaserJet Series II driver and get satisfactory results with your older hardware.

Global Catalog. In a home or SOHO environment this probably isn't needed, but in larger companies it's a good idea to put the room or office number into the name so the printer can be located for maintenance and troubleshooting purposes.

Finally, the Print Test Page appears. You can send a single-page print job to the printer that prints out the share name, location, and printer driver information. In larger businesses this page can be a handy reference so keep the test page with your network binder. Click Next. The Add Printer Wizard confirms your settings (see Figure 9.3); click Back to change any of the settings, or Cancel if you change your mind about adding the printer. Otherwise click Finish. The printer icon is added to the Printers and Faxes window, and you can select it as a printer from within any of your applications.

**Figure 9.3.** Confirm your settings, or click Back to change them.

Remote or networked printers are installed in the same manner. In the Add a New Printer Wizard, at the Local or Network Printer dialog box, select A network printer, or one attached to another computer and then click Next.

In the Specify a Printer dialog box (see Figure 9.4), you can browse for a printer, and then type in the share name or type in the URL. The easiest is to type in the share and then click Next.

## Psycho printer

Most print devices today have settings for print quality, paper size, printer trays, duplexing, and other whiz-bang features. You probably want to print your resumé on the good paper at high dots per inch, your draft documents at low quality, and duplexed on the cheap paper. With Windows you can create different printers (Windows printing software plus appropriate device driver) that print to the same print device but with different settings. That way, when you print a document, select the appropriate printer from the print dialog box, and it will automatically have the correct settings for paper, print quality, and paper tray already configured. It seems like you're doing the impossible, but you're not; you're just leveraging the different facets of your printer's personality.

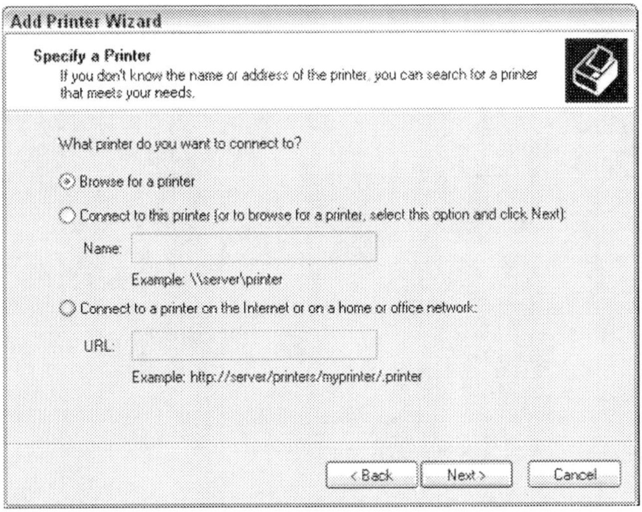

**Figure 9.4.** You have a choice of detection methods for network printers.

From here the dialog boxes are the same as for a locally-attached printer. You can print a test page to confirm your new printer works correctly.

**Inside Scoop**

If your printer has an Ethernet port or connects to a network through an HP JetDirect connection, you may need to install the software that came with your printer. The Add a New Printer Wizard may not be able to detect the printer without the software.

# Improving upon shared printers

If you decide to share a printer, there are features you can enable that will help others on your network with their printing and print jobs. Sharing printers can be done whether you are running simple file sharing or NTFS file sharing. Right-click the printer and then click Sharing. When you do this for the first time on a standalone or workgroup computer, you may see the caution dialog box, warning you about the risks of file sharing. You can run the Network Setup Wizard as described in Chapter 8, or you can click the "I understand the risks" link and proceed with sharing your printer. A confirmation dialog box appears, asking if you want to run the wizard regardless (see Figure 9.5).

You can run the wizard just to be safe. Or select Just enable printer sharing and then click OK. Select Share this printer and accept the default name or give it an informative share name (see Figure 9.6). Click OK. The printer is now shared and will appear in the Network Neighborhood.

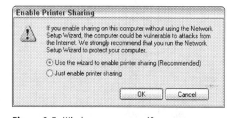

**Figure 9.5.** Windows warns you if you are exposing your computer to dangerous activity such as letting people print documents on your printer.

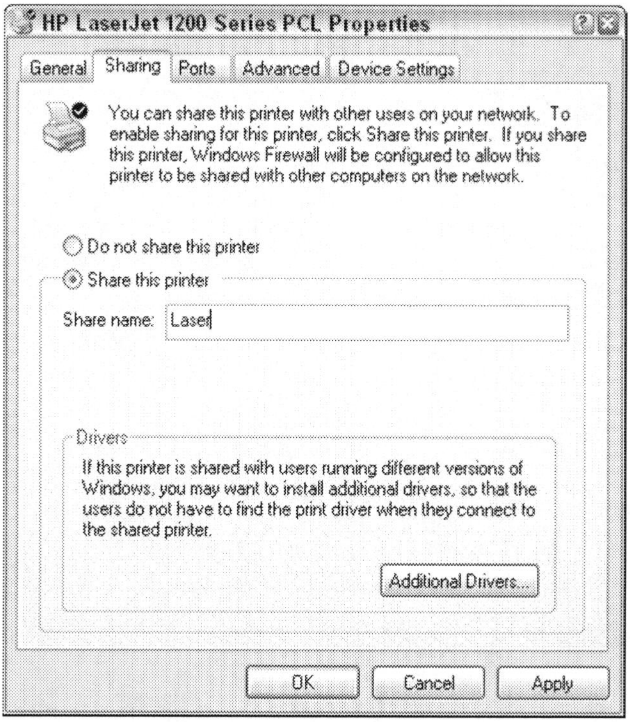

**Figure 9.6.** When you share the printer, use a simple name like "Laser".

You can configure shared printers to use separator pages for print jobs. Open the Printers and Faxes dialog box, right-click a printer, click Properties, and then click the Advanced tab (see Figure 9.7).

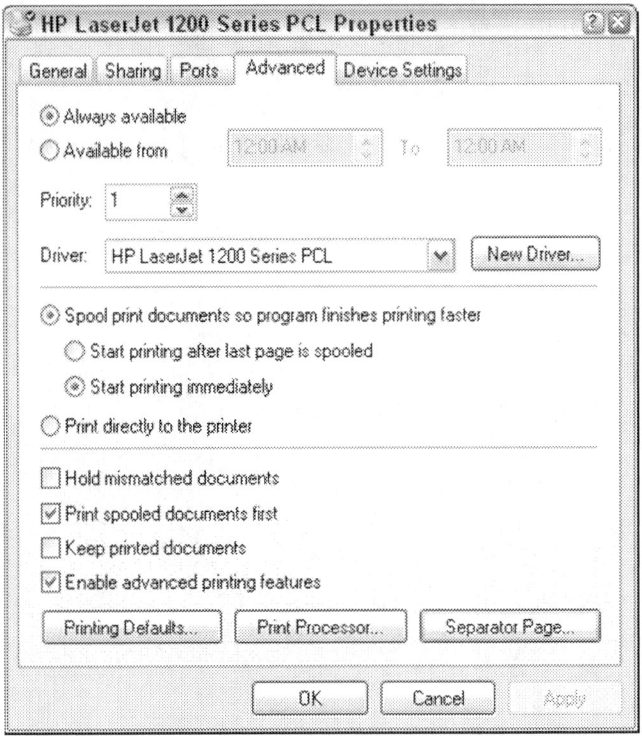

**Figure 9.7.** Separator pages are great for tracking numerous print jobs, or if many people use the same printer.

Click Separator Page and then click Browse. The Windows\system32 directory has four separator pages you can use:

- **pcl.sep** uses Hewlett-Packard's Printer Control Language to print out a page with the user name, print job number, date, and time.

- **pscript.sep** prints out the print job using PostScript but does not print out a separator page.

- **sysprint.sep** switches the printer to PostScript and then prints a separator page with user name, job number, date, and time.

- **sysprtj.sep** does the same but uses Japanese fonts if they are available.

Select a separator page file and click Open. Click OK twice. Your print jobs will now use a separator page.

**Hack**

If you have the time and the inclination, you can create your own separator pages. They are text files with an SEP extension, and they use various "@" codes to format and display information. Search the Help and Support Center for "create custom separator page" to see a code list.

If you are sharing a printer, Windows XP lets you copy printer drivers for non-XP Windows operating systems onto your system. When a non-XP system connects to the printer, it will automatically download and install the necessary driver from XP so you don't always have to go hunting for device driver disks for that other system.

To install other drivers, right-click the printer, click Properties, click Sharing, and then click Additional Drivers (see Figure 9.8). Select the drivers you want to have available and click OK. Browse to the driver disk or to the set of downloaded files from the manufacturer and then click OK. Your drivers are now available for non-Windows XP systems. Windows Update will not update these driver files for you; if the manufacturer issues new device drivers for non-XP systems, you must update them using this same process.

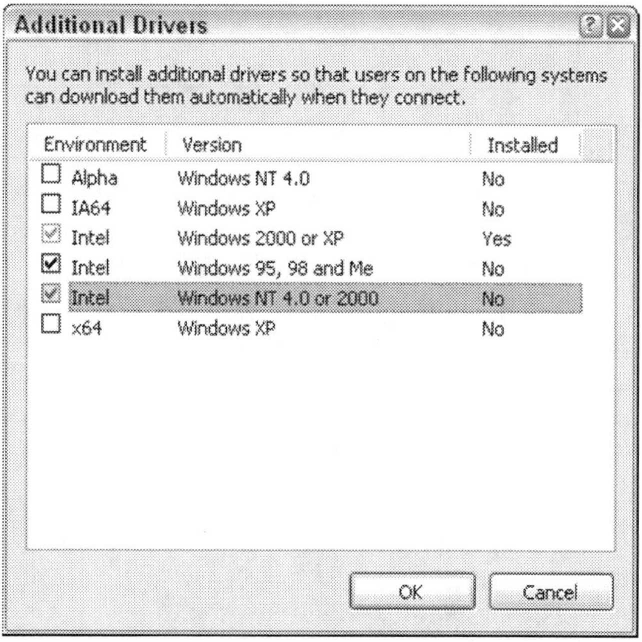

**Additional Drivers** [?][X]

You can install additional drivers so that users on the following systems can download them automatically when they connect.

| Environment | Version | Installed |
|---|---|---|
| ☐ Alpha | Windows NT 4.0 | No |
| ☐ IA64 | Windows XP | No |
| ☑ Intel | Windows 2000 or XP | Yes |
| ☑ Intel | Windows 95, 98 and Me | No |
| ☑ Intel | Windows NT 4.0 or 2000 | No |
| ☐ x64 | Windows XP | No |

[ OK ]   [ Cancel ]

**Figure 9.8.** You can set up shared printers to automatically download printer drivers to other computers on your network.

---

## Networked versus shared printers

A printer directly attached to a network is a wonderful addition to a home or SOHO environment because it is always available, doesn't require a print server such as your computer, and can handle most normal-sized print jobs without breaking a sweat. Each computer on the network manages its own print queue, so printing multiple print jobs is slower than with a dedicated print server.

A shared printer server is best for larger businesses or organizations. It provides greater print job management and more resources for creating and spooling print jobs. The computer acting as the print server doesn't need to be robust; any computer with a slower CPU will work just fine. The two major requirements for a decent print server are enough disk space to hold all the spooled print jobs and enough RAM to work with the largest print job.

Both a networked printer and one connected to a print server benefit by adding more RAM to the printer. When you purchase your printer, you should seriously consider adding more RAM than the default it ships with. You will be pleased by how fast your print jobs, especially graphics-intensive ones, fly through the printer.

---

## Manage print jobs

In general, users manage their own print jobs. When a print job is sent to the printer, it is put into a print queue where it can be paused, restarted, or removed from the queue.

You can show the print queue (see Figure 9.9) by double-clicking the printer icon in the Printers and Faxes window or by double-clicking the printer icon in the notification area.

Documents in the queue can be managed by selecting a document, clicking Document, and then selecting one of the following menu items:

- **Pause** a print job. You can pause a print job that's in the queue by right-clicking it and then clicking Pause. If the job is already printing, Pause only stops the portion of the job that is still being spooled; if it's already in the printer's buffer, the printer will continue to print. When a job is paused, other jobs will move ahead of it in the queue automatically.

- **Resume** a print job. Right-click a paused print job and then click Resume. The remainder of the document in the spooler will be sent to the printer. If some of it has already been printed, you will need to collate the pages together yourself.

■ **Restart** a print job. If you have paused printing and want to start the print job over from the beginning, right-click the print job and then click Restart.

■ **Cancel** a print job. If a job has yet to print, this removes the print job from the queue altogether. Right-click the print job and then click Cancel. You can also select the print job and then press Delete. If the print job is already printing, any part of the job still in the spooler will be deleted while the remainder in the printer's buffer will continue to print.

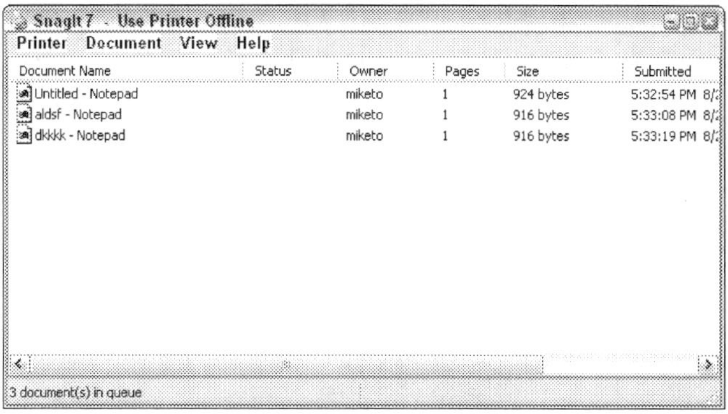

**Figure 9.9.** The print queue lists what jobs are printing, pending, or paused.

If you need to manage the entire queue, not just individual documents, click Printer and then click one of the following menu items:

■ **Pause printing all print jobs.** You can also pause all print jobs by right-clicking the printer in the Printers and Faxes window and then clicking Pause Printing. All print jobs in the queue are paused, though any print jobs in the printer's buffer will continue to print.

■ **Cancel all print jobs.** You can also cancel all jobs by right-clicking the printer icon in the Printers and Faxes window and then click Cancel All Documents. Any print jobs in the printer's buffer will continue to print.

Print jobs can be re-ordered in the print queue by dragging them higher in the queue. This is handy if you discover you're running late for a meeting and need a particular printout now, not five minutes from now.

If you need to stop printing immediately, such as to clear an ongoing paper jam or replace a toner cartridge, you should take the printer offline at the printer's own control panel. The printer status will change to offline and

---

### Print me! Print me!

There are more ways to print documents in Windows than just about any other function. It's as if Microsoft's holiday bonus depended on the number of ways printing could be enabled within XP. The different ways available are:

Within an application, click File and then Print. This is the classic method for any application that works with documents. It brings up the Print dialog box where you can select the number of copies, choose a different printer, or adjust paper size.

Click the Print icon in an application. This skips the print dialog box and sends the job to the printer using the default printer settings.

On the desktop, in the Start menu, or in Windows Explorer right-click a document and then click Print. This opens the application that created the document and then sends the print job directly to the printer.

Drag and drop a document onto a printer icon or into a printer queue. This option behaves similarly to the right-click-and-print method.

---

all print jobs will be paused. However, if you use the BRS (big red switch) to shut off the printer, any print jobs that were in progress will need to be restarted: Any information that had been spooled to the printer's buffer was lost when you shut off the printer.

While the printer is offline, you can still send print jobs to the printer queue and they will be held and spooled until the printer is back online. This is a handy trick to use if you are on the road with a laptop; set your printer to offline status, print as usual, then when you reconnect to your network change the printer status to online, and your print jobs will complete. This is much handier than keeping a list of documents you want to print out at a later date.

## Advanced printer management techniques

Depending on your office situation you may want to use some advanced printer management techniques. These let you define global settings such as providing notification for print job completion or error conditions, to setting user permissions and hours of use. These latter are convenient if you don't want everyone printing to the expensive color laser printer for everyday print jobs.

You can control the global settings for all printers installed on a computer by right-clicking anywhere in the Printers and Faxes dialog box and then clicking Server Properties. The most useful of these are on the Advanced tab (see Figure 9.10).

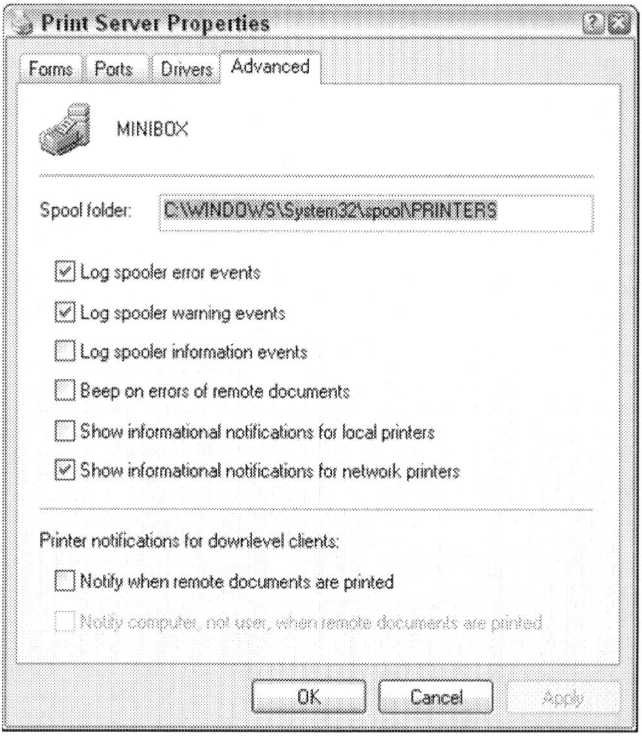

**Print Server Properties**

Forms | Ports | Drivers | Advanced

MINIBOX

Spool folder: C:\WINDOWS\System32\spool\PRINTERS

☑ Log spooler error events

☑ Log spooler warning events

☐ Log spooler information events

☐ Beep on errors of remote documents

☐ Show informational notifications for local printers

☑ Show informational notifications for network printers

Printer notifications for downlevel clients:

☐ Notify when remote documents are printed

☐ Notify computer, not user, when remote documents are printed

OK | Cancel | Apply

**Figure 9.10.** Print server properties can help you monitor and manage your printers, whether locally attached or remote.

The first option available is the spool folder. By default it is in the Windows\system32\spool\printers folder. You can move the folder to another hard drive in case the default drive is full or to improve print spooling performance. You can also set error logging options so that errors will appear in the System log for troubleshooting purposes.

If you want to be notified when a remote printer is having a bad day, select the Beep on errors of remote documents option. The next two options generate informational messages near the notification area.

The Printer notification for downlevel clients section relies on the Alerter service which is enabled in pre-XP versions of Windows but is disabled in XP. It pops up a dialog box in the middle of the screen letting you know your print job is complete. If you are printing a number of documents, you receive a message for each one and must close them individually. These are not enabled by default; unless you have a good reason for enabling them (and generating additional network traffic), leave them off.

There are advanced options you can set on a per-printer basis that give you greater control over who can use your printers, when they are available, and how they are managed. For example, you probably don't want everyone printing to the boss' printer and walking into her office at all hours to reclaim a print job. The down side is that these advanced options come at a price: You must be using Windows XP Professional, and you must be using NTFS file sharing (see Chapter 5 to enable NTFS file sharing). Windows XP Home Edition does not have the support for these additional settings because they are more commonly used in domain-based networks.

There are four permission types available for each printer. They are:

- **Print.** Users with this permission can print documents, control their own documents' properties, and pause, resume, restart, and cancel their own print jobs. By default, the Print permission is assigned to all members of the Everyone group.

- **Manage Printers.** This permission allows users to share printers, change printer properties, add, delete, or install new print drivers, change permissions for other users, and pause or cancel all print jobs. The user can pause and restart the printer, change spooler settings, share a printer, adjust printer permissions, and change printer properties. By default, members of the Administrators and Power Users groups have full access, which means that members of those groups have all three permission types assigned to them.

- **Manage Documents.** This allows users to pause, restart, move, or remove all documents that are in the print queue. However, the user cannot send documents to the printer or control the printer status. By default, the Manage Documents permission is assigned to members of the Creator Owner group.

- **Deny.** All of the preceding permissions are denied for the printer. When access is denied, the user cannot use the printer, manage the printer, or adjust any of the permissions.

The procedure for setting advanced permissions is the same as setting permissions for files and folders (see Chapter 5). To set permissions for a specific printer, right-click the printer for which you want to set permissions, click Properties, and then click the Security tab (see Figure 9.11).

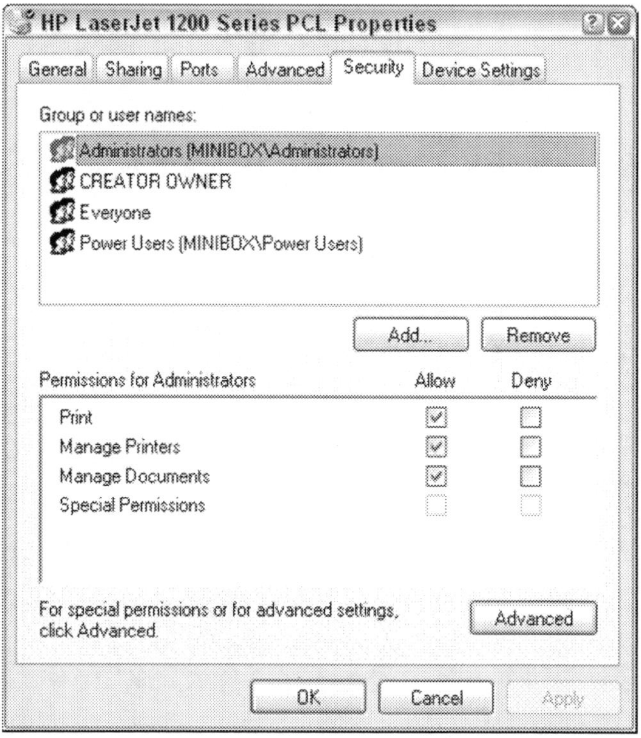

**Figure 9.11.** General permission categories can be set for individuals or groups.

On the Security tab, click Add, click Look For, select the types of users you want to add, and then click OK. Click Look In, browse for the location you want to search, and then click OK.

In the Name box, type the name of the user or group you want to set permissions for, separating each name with a semicolon. Click Check Names. Recognized names are underlined. Once all the names you want are listed in the Name box, click OK.

Click the Advanced button. On the Permissions tab, click the Allow or Deny check box for each permission you want to allow or deny (see Figure 9.12). Click OK until you get back out to the Printers and Faxes dialog box. These changes take effect immediately.

The other management tool you can use on printers is setting the hours of use. This is quite a bit easier than setting permissions and may be the better way to manage printer use. To set the hours of use, right-click the printer, click Properties, and then click Advanced. Select Available from, and then enter the hours when you want the printer available (see Figure 9.13). It's a good way to keep employees from printing out 400-page game guides after work, or (conversely) keeping your kids from doing the same after they get home from school but before you get home from work.

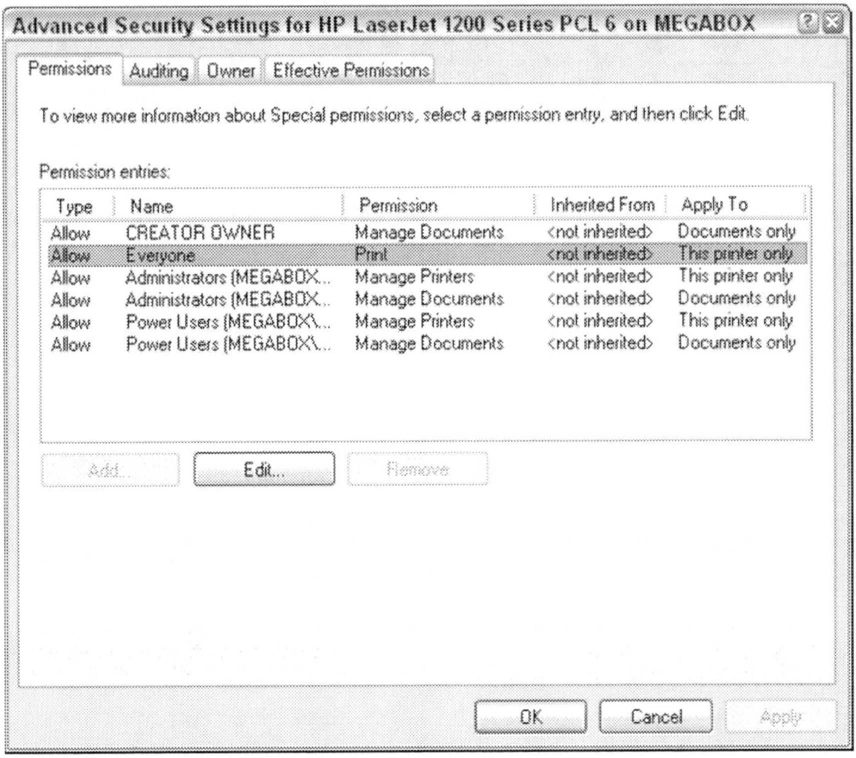

**Figure 9.12.** Set advanced permissions for users or groups in order to determine who can print, manage, or be excluded from using the printer.

The final gadget to help manage printers is the Priority setting. Since you can make different software print queues have different priority, even when they go to the same print device, this is an easy way to make sure the boss' reports pop to the top of the print queue. The priority values range from 1, the lowest, to 99, the highest. The setting takes effect with the next print job you send through the queue.

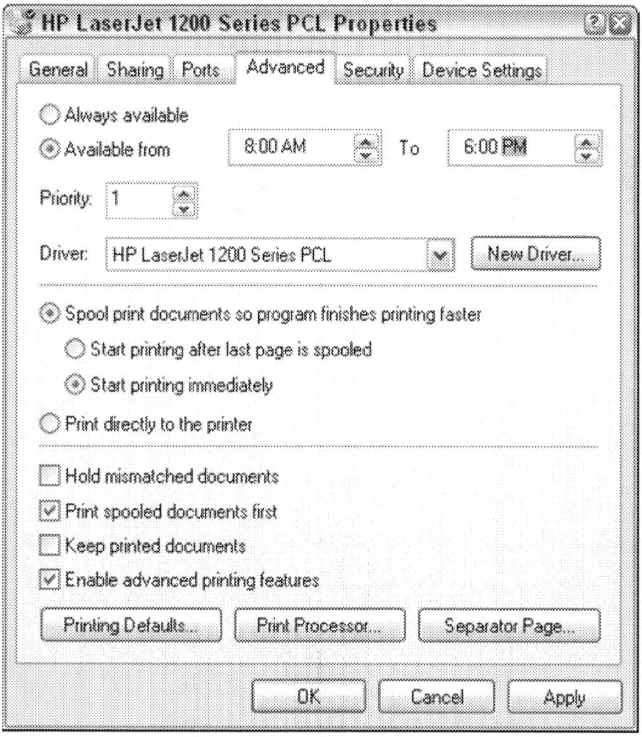

**Figure 9.13.** Set the hours you want the printer available to groups or individuals to help prevent print job abuse.

# Send and receive faxes

If you have a modem on your computer, you can set up Windows XP to send and receive faxes. This is especially handy if you have a laptop computer; you can run your office, complete with sending and receiving faxes, without having a roomful of separate devices connected to a phone line.

Interestingly, with a clean installation on a modem-enabled computer, Windows XP does not install fax capability by default. You must go through the installation process manually. Fortunately this is a straightforward task and doesn't require that you have the original Windows XP disk available, as older versions of the fax service did.

You may still have an older version of the fax software on your computer, especially if you performed an upgrade installation from Windows 9x, Me, or Windows 2000. The new fax service will copy most, if not all, of your older settings and make them available to you.

---

## Multiple versions of fax software

You may already have non-Microsoft fax software installed on your computer, especially if you work for a company that has special fax setups for employees. In my experience fax programs do not coexist peacefully. If you decide to use the Windows XP version, I recommend uninstalling the other software, rebooting, and then installing the Windows XP version. Check with the other software company to see if they have recommendations or cautionary tales about working with Windows XP, and follow any directions they may have to help remove the other software.

---

To install the fax service, click Start, Printers and Faxes, and then Set up faxing. You can also right-click anywhere in the window, and then click Set Up Faxing. You can also install it by clicking Start, Control Panel, Add/Remove Programs, Add/Remove Windows Components, selecting Fax Service, and then clicking Next. All three methods launch the automatic setup of the fax service and install a new service, appropriately called Fax, in the Services window. You may need to insert the Windows XP CD to install files that are not present.

## Configure the fax service

The first time you send a fax, the Fax Configuration Wizard appears and walks you through the steps needed to finish configuring the fax. Open the Printers and Faxes window and then click Send a fax. The Fax Configuration Wizard appears. Click Next. Fill in the necessary information in the fields provided (see Figure 9.14). Click Next.

On the Select Device dialog box, if you have more than one fax, you can choose which fax to use (see Figure 9.15). This allows you to configure different faxes for sending and receiving if you so choose. Enable Send lets you send faxes, while Enable Receive lets your computer act as an incoming fax device.

With Enable Receive, you can choose to have Windows XP automatically answer after the specified number of rings, or you can manually instruct XP to receive the fax. Windows XP doesn't include auto-detect capability, so your choice depends on whether you will have a dedicated fax line and whether your computer is on all the time. If you use one phone line for both voice and fax calls (a common setup for homes or SOHO environments), select Manual answer. That way you won't have XP picking up the phone for a fax when you're racing to pick up an important business call. Click Next.

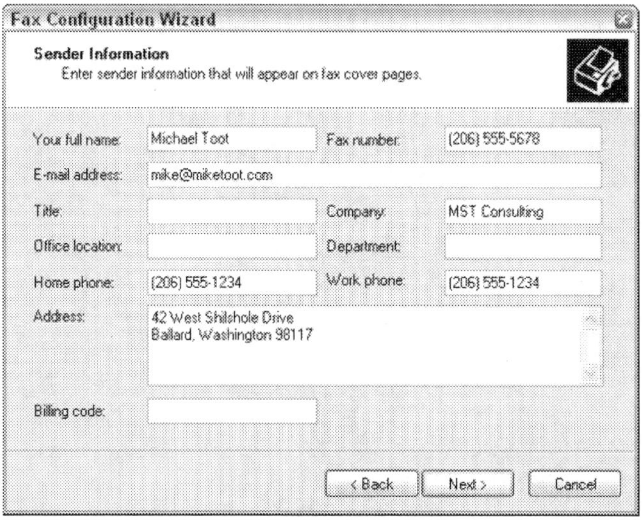

**Figure 9.14.** The information in this dialog box is used to complete the fax cover page.

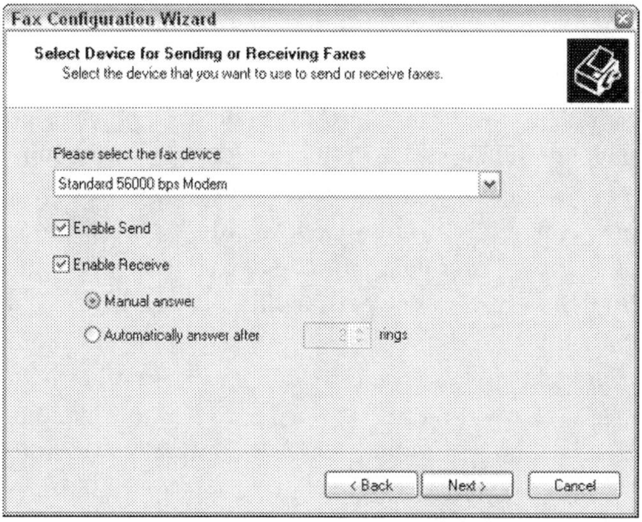

**Figure 9.15.** Your fax modem can send faxes, receive faxes, or both.

The Transmitting Subscriber Identification (TSID) dialog box lets you enter information that is displayed on the recipient's fax machine when you call them. Though Microsoft doesn't tell you in the dialog box, the field is limited to twenty characters. Common practice is to put your fax number in this field (see Figure 9.16). Click Next. The Called Subscriber Identification (CSID) dialog box is the information sent back to a fax machine when they call you. Again, the field is limited to twenty characters, and common practice is to put your fax number in this field. Click Next.

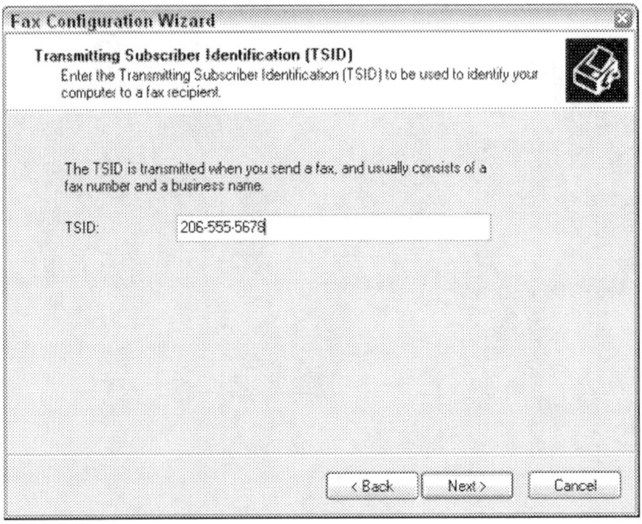

**Figure 9.16.** Use your fax number in the TSID field, and again in the CSID field in the next dialog box.

The Routing Options dialog box (see Figure 9.17) doesn't so much route your faxes as it does generate additional copies that you can use. All inbound and outbound faxes are already stored in the Fax Console; the Routing Options dialog box gives you the opportunity to either print out a hard copy on any printer that is set up on your computer, or save another electronic copy on your hard drive. Since I run a one-person office, I keep the faxes in the digital realm and then if I need them as a hard copy, I print them out later. But if you have several people who receive faxes, you can print them out as they arrive instead. That way they don't need to log on to your computer to see if any faxes are waiting for them. Select the options you want to use and then click Next. The completion dialog box appears confirming your choices. Click Back to change any of them, or click Finish. Your fax is now configured and the Send a Fax Wizard appears.

## Send a fax

If you've already completed the Fax Configuration Wizard, the Send a Fax Wizard appears. The wizard helps you configure a cover page and attach any documents that you want, and then sends the fax to the desired recipients.

## The Windows super-secret fax folders

Notice how many folders start with "My"? There are My Documents, My Music, My Videos, My Received Files... the list grows with every new Microsoft toy. You'd think Windows would create a My Faxes folder — but it doesn't.

Faxes are stored in a completely non-intuitive place: Documents and Settings\All Users\Application Data\Microsoft\Windows NT\MSFax. Notice that this data is not associated with My Documents, and so is not a part of roaming profiles or any redirected folders. What this means to you is that, unless you know about this secret, non-obvious folder, you probably don't have it listed as one of the folders to automatically back up.

You have two options to make backup easier: Configure the fax service to save another copy in a more convenient location ("My Faxes" located under My Documents, maybe?) or configure the service to move the archive to another location. To move the archive, open the Printers and Faxes window, right-click the Fax icon, click Properties, click the Archives tab, and then change the sent and received folders to something more to your liking — and easier to back up.

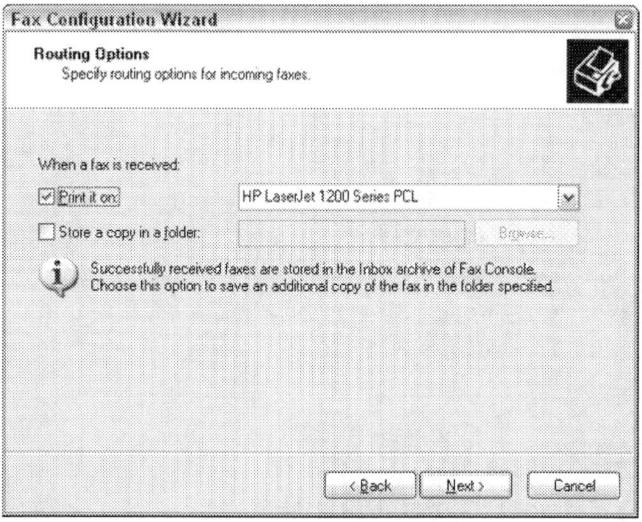

**Figure 9.17.** You can route the fax to your printer or store it in yet another place on your hard drive.

Otherwise, to send a document by fax, in any Windows application click File and then Print, select Fax from the drop-down list of printers, and then click Print. The Send a Fax Wizard appears. Click Next.

The Recipient information dialog box appears (see Figure 9.18). Type in the names of recipients and fax numbers, and add any dialing rules (for example, if you need to add country codes for a fax). You can also click the Address Book button and quickly add names and numbers of recipients for your fax. Click Next.

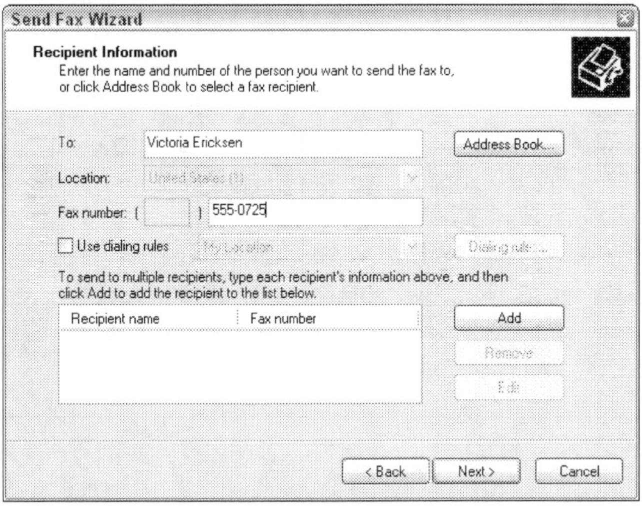

**Send Fax Wizard**

**Recipient Information**
Enter the name and number of the person you want to send the fax to, or click Address Book to select a fax recipient.

| | | |
|---|---|---|
| To: | Victoria Ericksen | Address Book... |
| Location: | United States (1) | |
| Fax number: [ | ] 555-0725 | |

☐ Use dialing rules    My Location    Dialing rules...

To send to multiple recipients, type each recipient's information above, and then click Add to add the recipient to the list below.

| Recipient name | Fax number | Add |
|---|---|---|
| | | Remove |
| | | Edit |

[ < Back ] [ Next > ] [ Cancel ]

**Figure 9.18.** For convenience, you can send the same fax to multiple recipients at multiple numbers.

On the Preparing the Cover Page dialog box (see Figure 9.19) you can choose between four different styles of cover page, small images of which appear to the right when you select a style from the drop-down list. Click the Sender Information button to edit your information, such as when you want to send a personal fax instead of one with your business information on it. Type a subject line and any notes you want to appear in the cover page's body. Click Next.

**Inside Scoop**

If Outlook is installed, Fax will use the Outlook Address book to store and retrieve address information. Otherwise, the Windows Address Book is used, which fortunately is also used by Outlook Express.

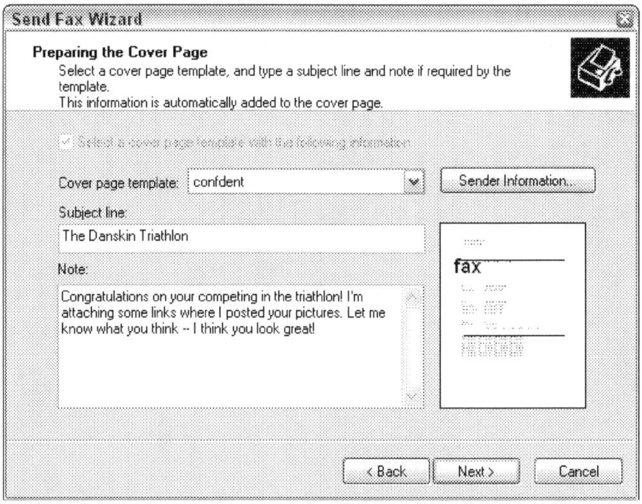

**Figure 9.19.** Your cover page will have your contact information, subject line, and notes attached to it.

The Schedule dialog box appears (see Figure 9.20). From here you can set a fax delay so that the fax is sent when rates are low, or you can accept the defaults and have the fax sent immediately. The Priority section lets you prioritize faxes in your fax queue, so if you have other "Normal" priority faxes pending, you can assign a fax "High" priority and it will pop to the top of the queue. Click Next.

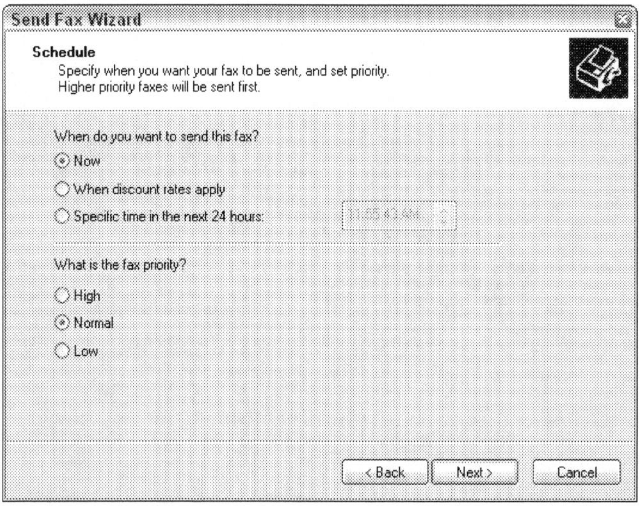

**Figure 9.20.** Schedule and prioritize your fax.

The Completing the Send Fax Wizard dialog box appears to confirm your choices (see Figure 9.21). Click the Preview Fax button to see how your cover page will look. Click Finish to send the fax.

**Figure 9.21.** Preview your fax cover page, confirm your settings, and then send it off!

The Fax Monitor dialog box appears while your fax is sent (see Figure 9.22). Click the More button to see the details of your fax's progress.

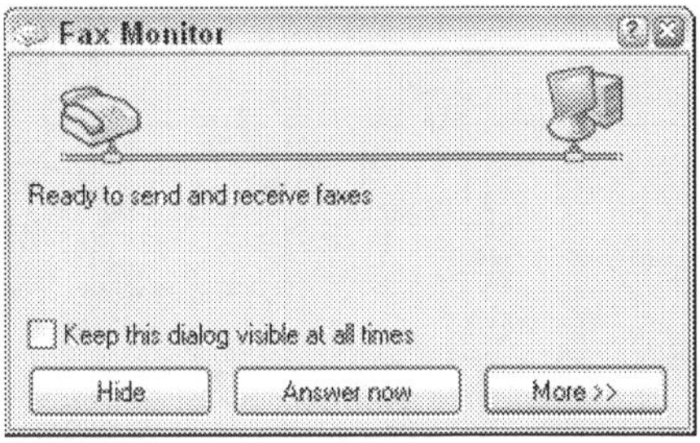

## Receive and review faxes

If you have configured the fax service for manual answer, when the modem detects an incoming call, it

**Figure 9.22.** Keep track of your fax while it's being sent.

will pop up a notification asking if you want to answer the call as a fax call. Click the notification to "pick up" the fax. Windows XP will then process the incoming fax. If you have configured automatic answering, your incoming fax will be received.

In each case, when the fax is complete, another notification will appear showing you the sender's TSID. Click that notification to open the Fax Console. You can also open the Fax Console at any time by clicking Start, All Programs, Accessories, Communications, Fax, and then Fax Console.

**Inside Scoop**

Once the fax service is installed, try using your word processing program's fax wizard rather than the Send a Fax Wizard. See which you like better and which generates better cover pages.

The Fax Console (see Figure 9.23) is where you can view faxes you've received, faxes you've sent, incoming faxes, and faxes waiting in the outbound queue. Faxes are stored as TIFF files, and you can view these images using the Windows Picture and Fax viewer. Double-click a fax to open it in the viewer. You can print out a fax by selecting it, clicking File, Print, and then OK.

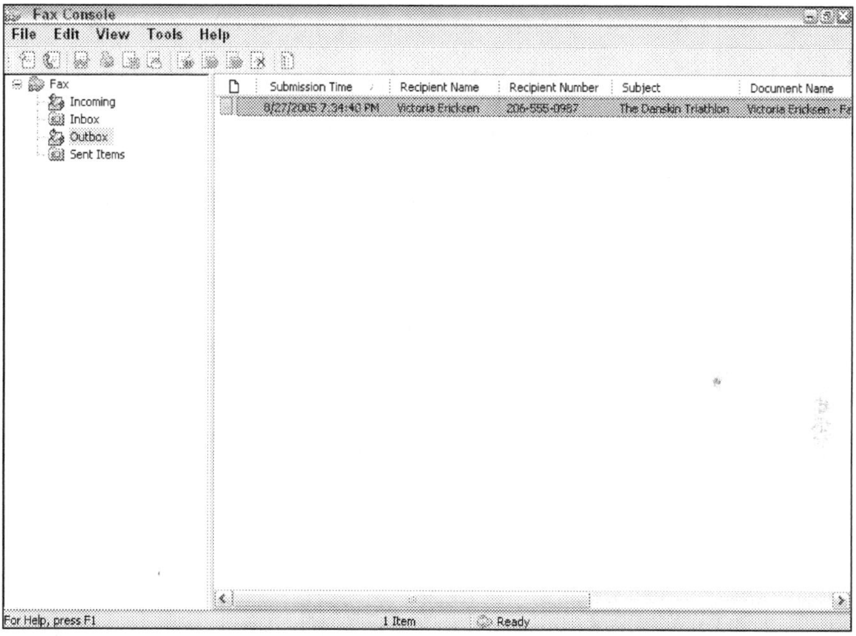

**Figure 9.23.** The Fax Console is your fax clearinghouse for sent and received faxes.

## Create new fax cover pages

The four cover pages that ship with the fax service leave something to be desired. On the bright side, Microsoft includes a Fax Cover Page Editor that lets you create your own cover pages. On the dark side, the Cover Page Editor uses a closed format so you can't import any fax cover pages you created with Microsoft Word's Fax Wizard or any of Office's fax templates.

**Bright Idea**

Save yourself time wading through menus and create a shortcut to the Fax Console. Right-click and drag the console onto the desktop and click Copy Here, or drag it to the Start Menu's upper left section, pinning it for quick access.

To open the Cover Page Editor, click Start, All Programs, Accessories, Communications, Fax, and then Fax Cover Page Editor. You can also launch the editor by opening the Fax Console, clicking Tools, and then Personal Cover Pages. The Personal Cover Pages dialog box appears where you can open or modify an existing cover page. The easiest way to create a new cover page is to open a copy of an existing cover page and then edit it as necessary. If you need to find the original files, the four basic cover pages are stored in Documents and Settings\All Users\Application Data\Microsoft\Windows NT\MSFax\Common Coverpages.

Click Copy, select one of the four existing cover pages you want to modify (confdent.cov is a good choice), click Open, select the cover page in the dialog box, and then click Open (see Figure 9.24).

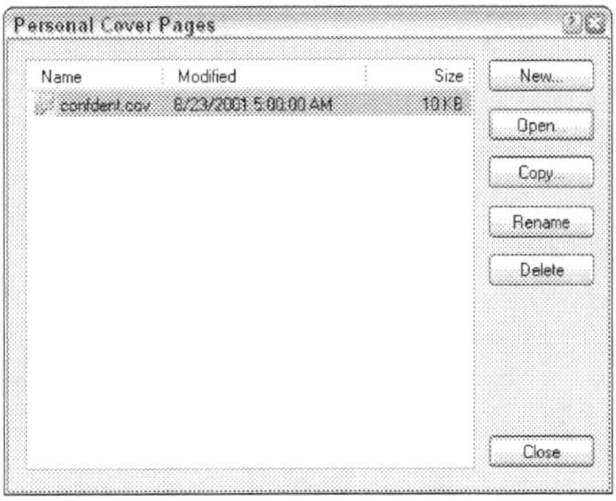

The Fax Cover Page Editor opens with your selected cover page available to edit (see Figure 9.25). All page elements are surrounded by dotted lines. Click once on an element to select it; click and drag one of the black handles to resize the element. To move the element on the page, move the mouse cursor until a four-way arrow appears; click and drag the element to move it about the page. To delete an element, select it and then press Delete.

**Figure 9.24.** Copy an existing cover page into this dialog box and then open it for editing.

Graphics, such as company logos, can be added using copy and paste. All graphics can be resized, though it will look better to use a larger graphic and size it downward than use a smaller graphic and enlarge it.

You can dynamically generate information on your cover page by using fields; the good thing is that you don't have to worry about weird formatting syntax. Because a cover page is supposed to be only a brief, informative document, the only data field available to you is Recipient, Sender, or Message. It can be inserted by clicking Insert and then clicking the specific field you want added to the cover page.

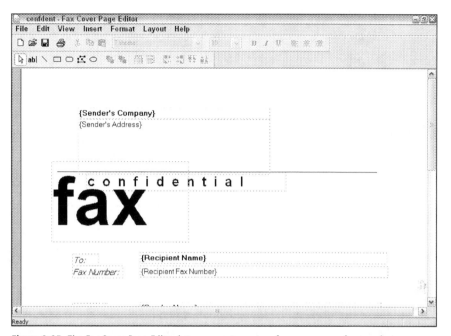

**Figure 9.25.** The Fax Cover Page Editor lets you create custom fax cover pages for your faxes.

## Cheaper fax solutions

Modems are inexpensive and are standard equipment on most laptops. But if you have more than a few desktops, buying hardware and setting up fax capability for those computers on a single phone line can be a nightmare. There are other fax options available to help with this situation.

Two inexpensive fax services are MyFax (www.myfax.com) and eFax (www.efax.com). These services let you send and receive faxes using your e-mail client. You let others know your assigned fax number, and when a fax is sent to you it appears in your e-mail inbox.

For small businesses, a better option is Microsoft Small Business Server. Both the Standard and Premium Editions come with the Shared Fax Service. Desktops can send faxes over the network to the fax server which then handles delivery. Incoming faxes can be automatically routed to Microsoft Exchange inboxes. For more information on Small Business Server visit www.microsoft.com/sbs.

When you are done creating your new cover page, click File, Save As, and then save your new fax. The default location for edited faxes is %username%\My Documents\Fax\Personal Coverpages. Close the editor, and you are returned to the Personal Cover Pages list, where your new cover page is listed.

# Install and configure a Web server

Web servers are the workhorses of the Internet. They are the first point of contact between people and information of all kinds. Web servers can be portals to Web applications, database front ends, message boards, e-commerce sites, or just a list of personal pictures and links that you find interesting. Behind the scenes, Web servers are doing all the heavy lifting.

Though Windows XP is a desktop operating system, you can run Microsoft's Internet Information Server (IIS) on it. Normally you don't want to run industrial-strength services on a desktop for two reasons: First, desktop hardware isn't designed for server loads and requirements; and second, your desktop applications introduce potential stability and security holes that would keep the server from running smoothly. But it can be handy to run a server, especially if you are developing a prototype Web site and want to see how it works before you deploy it on the actual Web server.

With those limitations in mind, Microsoft built in two significant restrictions to the desktop version of IIS: You can have only ten concurrent connections, and you can have only one Web site running on your server. These limitations shouldn't be a problem; when you create a prototype you are designing the look and feel, or testing basic Web site functionality, and not testing capacity or server stability.

If you intend to run IIS on your desktop and make it a public Web site, there are several things you must do.

- Assign a static IP address to your computer. This allows others to use DNS to locate your new Web site. You may need to contact your ISP and change your account from dynamic to static addressing in order to do this.

- Convert any FAT partitions that will hold your Web files to NTFS. This lets you use XP's permissions and security to prevent unauthorized access to your Web site and its files.

- Obtain a domain name, and have it point to your static IP address. Your ISP can usually handle the necessary paperwork and get you set up with this.

## What's not here

This section does not teach you how to create Web pages, work with graphics, or explain the nuances of Web server configuration. There are entire shelves of books devoted to these subjects, and the topics are worth more space than the brief discussion here. Good books to consider are *Teach Yourself VISUALLY HTML*, ISBN 0-7645-7984-3, by Sherry Kinkoph and *Mastering Windows Server 2003*, ISBN (0-7821-4130-7) by Mark Minasi et al., both from Wiley Publishing.

You can also subscribe to one of the better newsletters available for IIS. Visit www.iisfaq.com and sign up to receive information and troubleshooting tips for IIS. The Web site has plenty of resources and real-world advice on IIS as well, so even if you are determined to run IIS on Windows XP, you may find some suggestions for making IIS a decent desktop performer.

- Make sure your firewall allows inbound HTTP requests. This may involve creating an addition to its routing table so that HTTP requests are routed directly to your machine.

- Invest in, and install, antivirus software.

- Prepare to be connected all the time. You don't need to invest in an uninterrupted power supply (UPS), but you will need to leave your computer on so that the public can find your Web server.

- Buy a good book on securing and running a Web server. Read it. Work with your Web server prior to making it accessible to the public. You will be glad you did!

Installing IIS is easy. Click Start, Run, type appwiz.cpl, and then press Enter. Click Add/Remove Windows Components. Scroll down the list to Internet Information Services (IIS) and click Details (see Figure 9.26). In the Internet Information Services (IIS) details dialog box, deselect SMTP Service and click OK. If you will be using Microsoft FrontPage to create and

**Watch Out!**

If you are a business employee, DO NOT run a Web server without asking permission from your IT department first, even if it is intended for internal audiences only. You could unknowingly create network problems, and — trust me — you don't want the IT department mad at you.

edit Web pages, select FrontPage 2000 Server Extensions. Click Next. The necessary files are copied onto your hard drive; you may need to insert your Windows XP CD-ROM. When the service is configured and started, click Finish.

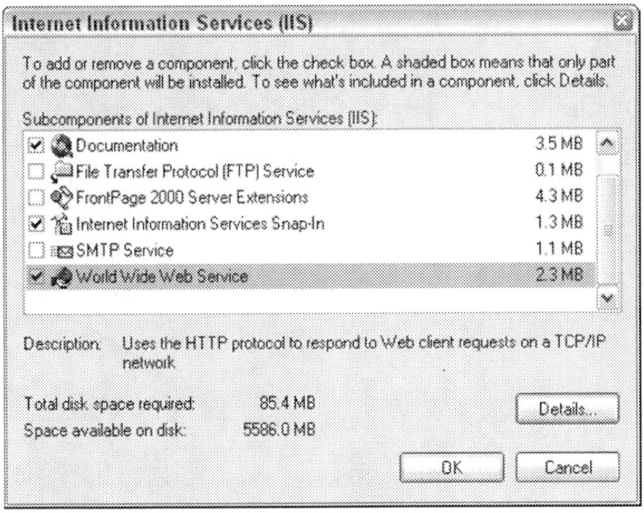

**Figure 9.26.** While you can install many components for IIS, start with only the basics.

A basic Web site is now running on your computer. Open Internet Explorer. In IE's address bar type localhost and then press Enter.

Two windows appear. One displays a large Windows XP graphic and contains introduction text to IIS. The other is the online documentation (see Figure 9.27), which is well worth your time to review and use to get familiar with your Web server.

Web server management is done with the Internet Information Services snap-in. Click Start, All Programs, Administrative Tools, and then Internet Information Services. The IIS snap-in appears. Browse to %computername%\ Web Sites\Default Web Site. Right-click Default Web Site and click Properties (see Figure 9.28).

---

**Hack**

You can manage other IIS servers remotely by installing the IIS snap-in on Windows XP and clicking Action and then Connect. Type in the computer name or browse to it. Select Connect As, and enter the name and password for an account with administration privileges.

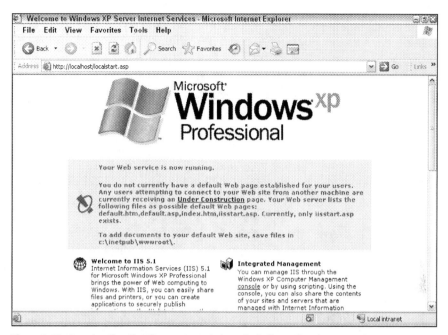

**Figure 9.27.** Browsing "localhost" opens two windows, including online documentation.

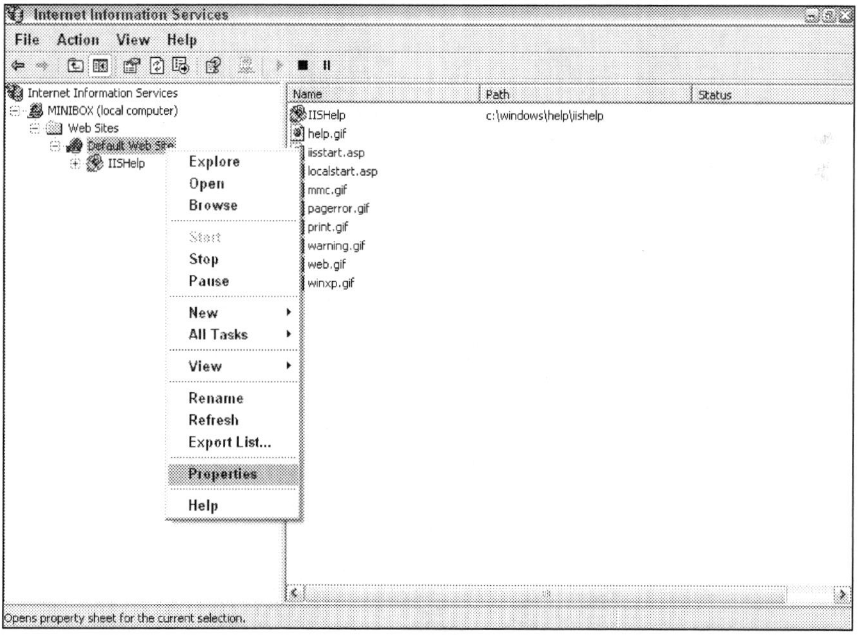

**Figure 9.28.** All Web site management is done with the Internet Information Services snap-in.

The Web Site tab allows you to change the name from Default Web Site to something useful. This name is for your benefit only; it's not visible to browsers to your Web site. You can leave the IP Address set to (All Unassigned), which means your IIS will respond to all Web site requests.

Click the Home Directory tab (see Figure 9.29). This is where you point to where your Web site's files will be kept on a hard drive. The default is set up on the same drive where Windows is installed, usually c:\inetpub\wwwroot, and you may want to change this to another partition or hard drive for security and ease-of-backup reasons. When you are done, click OK to close the dialog box and return to the snap-in.

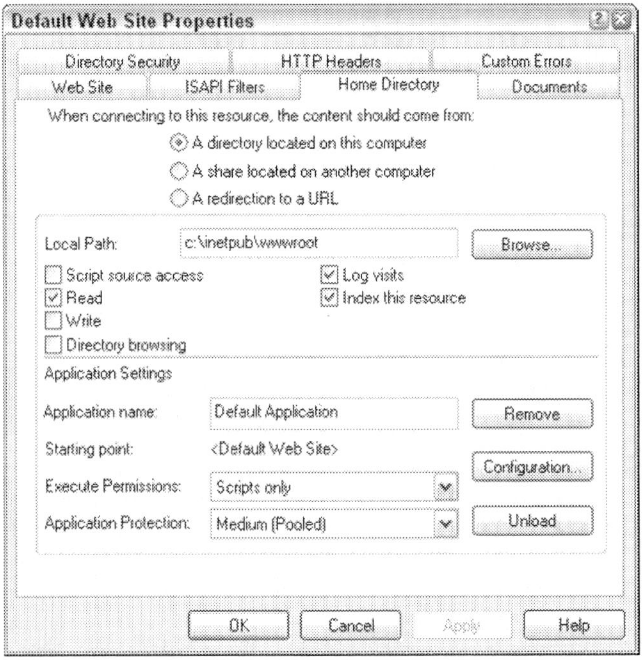

**Figure 9.29.** All Web site management options are available on the Web site's Properties dialog box.

Back in the snap-in, you can view a file listing of what files are on your Web server. The files and folders that make up your Web site are listed in the left pane, under your Web site's name. You cannot edit them from this window, but you can delete them if they are no longer needed.

Finally, as a Web server administrator, you may need to pause, stop, or restart your Web site. For example, if you are updating files, you don't want anyone attempting to connect to a page when the contents are changing mid-stream. Select your Web site and then click one of the appropriate buttons in the snap-in's toolbar (see Figure 9.30). This setting is persistent over reboots.

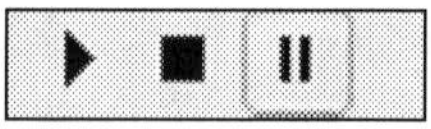

**Figure 9.30.** Start, stop, or pause your Web site.

Note that this only pauses or stops the server from serving up pages for the Web site; it does not stop the IIS itself. If you need to stop the server completely, click Start and then Run, type services.msc, and then press Enter. Scroll down the list to World Wide Web Publishing (see Figure 9.31) and then click the appropriate button in the toolbar. This setting is also persistent over reboots.

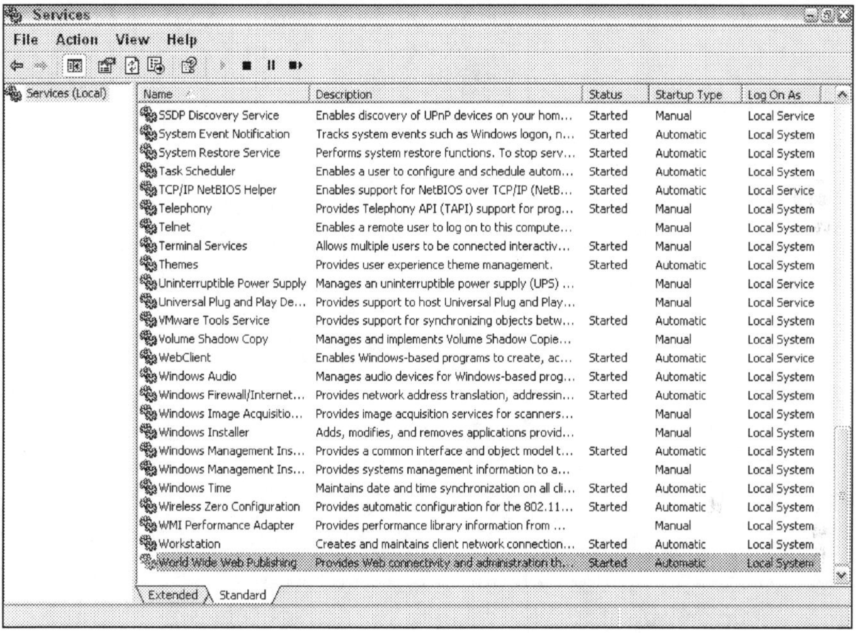

**Figure 9.31.** Start, stop, or pause your Web server.

## Rethinking IIS on the desktop

IIS has a long history of security holes, server exploits, and other hackable nastiness. Not only should you think twice about having a desktop run a Web server that is accessible to the public, you should think thrice about running IIS as your Web server. The version that ships with XP is version 5.0, a far less stable version than 6.0 which had major improvements in security and usability. Version 6.0 is only available on Windows Server 2003, and is not available as a separate upgrade to Windows XP.

*(continued)*

*(continued)*

But if you are determined to run a public Web server on your desktop, make sure you run Windows Update after installing IIS to get the latest in security patches and hotfixes *before* you make your server available to the public. Then visit www.microsoft.com/technet/security/tools/locktool.mspx for an IIS Lockdown Wizard that helps secure your server. Subscribe to Microsoft's security bulletins so you can be informed with any late-breaking security notifications. And then hope no bad guys target your server.

The moral of the story is: If you can have someone else host your Web services, do it.

# Using Remote Desktop

Remote Desktop is a fantastic tool that allows you to view and control another computer's entire desktop and have access to all its programs, much as if you were sitting in front of its screen and keyboard. It works similarly to commercial programs such as Symantec's PCAnywhere or Laplink Software's Laplink Gold. You can run applications, work with files, print to printers, or do most anything to the remote PC. You don't have to be running Windows XP on the remote computer; Windows XP comes with client software that you can install on any version of Windows back to Windows 95.

The benefits of Remote Desktop multiply the more you use it. You can use it to access your office computer when you are on the road, or when you are at home and need to retrieve a report that was e-mailed to your work address. You can also use Remote Desktop as a help-desk tool. If people keep asking you to figure out what's wrong with their computer, you can connect to their desktop and work with it without leaving your own desk.

One good feature of Remote Desktop is that it is not enabled by default, and you must specifically add the names of people who will be allowed access. Otherwise it would be a gaping security hole, and even Microsoft thinks that giving anyone remote access to your computer isn't a good idea.

**Hack**

Install the Remote Desktop software on another computer by inserting the Windows XP CD and then clicking Perform Additional Tasks and Remote Desktop Connection. The wizard walks you through installation and setup on the new computer.

To use Remote Desktop, you first set up the remote computer so that you can connect to it remotely. Log on as a user with administrator privileges on the computer. Click Start, right-click My Computer, click Properties, and then click the Remote tab (see Figure 9.32).

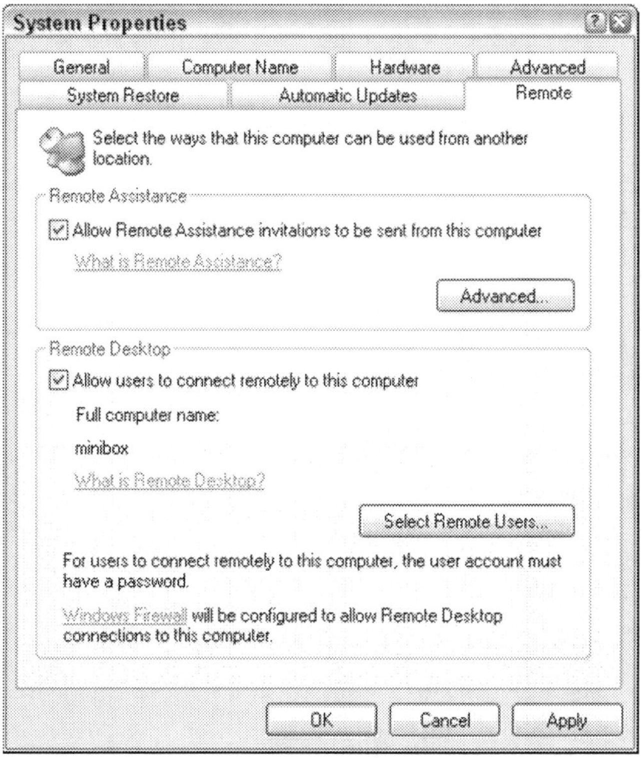

**Figure 9.32.** Enable Remote Desktop with one click.

Click Select Remote Users. Click Add. Type in the domain and name for people you want to give access to the computer; click Examples to see the different ways you can grant access to people or computers. Click Check Names to verify the names you've added. When you're done, click OK three times to return to the Windows desktop. You also need Terminal Services running. Click Start, Run, type services.msc, and then press Enter. Scroll down the list to Terminal Services. If it is not set to automatically start up, double-click it, select Automatic from the drop-down list (see Figure 9.33), click Start if the service is not running, and then click OK.

To connect to the remote computer, log on to your Windows XP computer. Click Start, All Programs, Accessories, Communications, and then Remote Desktop Connection. Click the Options button (see Figure 9.34).

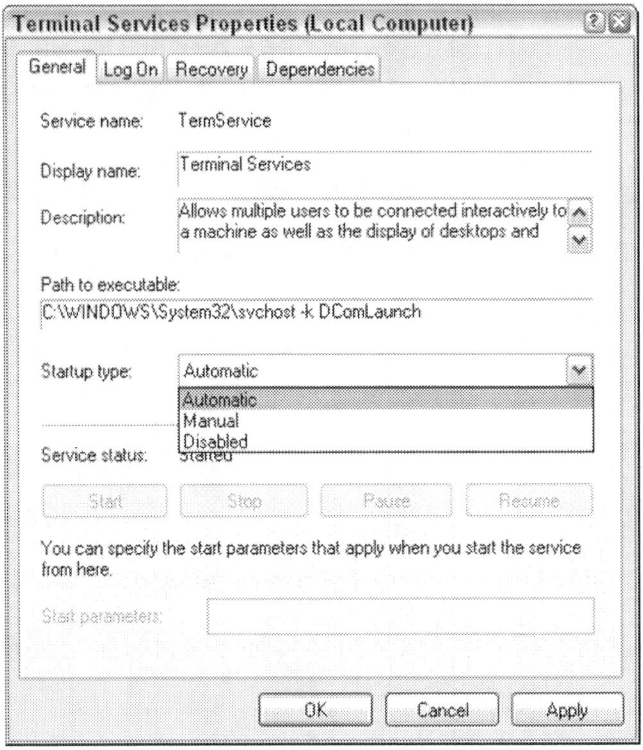

**Figure 9.33.** You must have Terminal Services running in order to gain remote access to your desktop.

Select the remote computer name from the drop-down list box. Type the user name and password for the account that you granted permission on the remote computer. If you are a member of a domain, enter the domain so the log on credentials can be verified. You can click any of the other tabs and adjust settings for your remote session, such as connection speed, desktop size, and various desktop effects. Click Connect. The remote desktop appears.

You can copy and paste information between the remote session and your local computer, or if both desktops are visible at the same time, you can drag and drop documents between them. To end the session, you can either click the Close button on the remote session's tab, or click Start and then Disconnect.

**Inside Scoop**

If you can't connect to a computer, your firewall is probably blocking inbound requests. Remote Desktop listens on port 3389, so you may need to explicitly open that port to allow incoming requests.

**Figure 9.34.** Log on and configure remote options from the Remote Desktop Connection dialog box.

Note that if someone is connected to the computer when you attempt to log on, they will be notified that you are connecting and they will be logged off. If Fast User Switching is turned off, they won't even get a message — they'll be disconnected automatically.

Turnabout is fair play; if you are logged on remotely and someone else logs on to the remote computer, you will be disconnected. So while XP claims to be a fully-featured multi-user system, it doesn't allow two people to have an active session at the same time.

# Using Remote Assistance

Remote Assistance is a specialized version of Remote Desktop. It uses the Terminal Services capability but it does not allow you to automatically log on, even if you have an account on the machine. Instead, an invitation is sent out from one user, asking another user to connect to the machine. Both users must accept before the connection starts. Also, both users must have appropriate access through their respective firewalls.

To request help using Remote Assistance, click Start, right-click My Computer, click Properties, and then click the Remote tab (see Figure 9.35). Select Allow Remote Assistance invitations to be sent from this computer. If you want, you can set limits on how long the invitation is valid, and whether the remote computer can control your desktop. (You may want them to see your desktop but talk you through a troubleshooting session over the phone, rather than giving them control.) Click the Advanced button, and you can set either of these parameters for your remote session. Click OK twice.

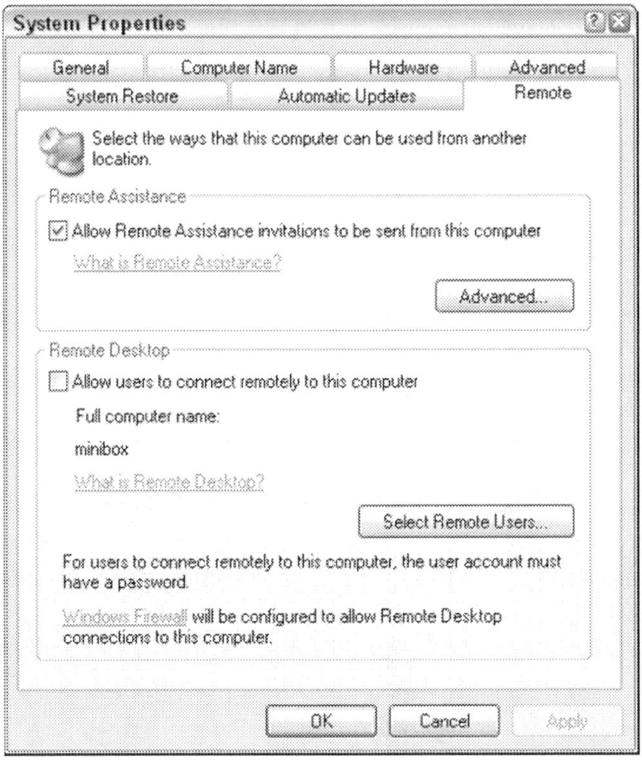

**Figure 9.35.** Remote Assistance is controlled by a simple on-off switch.

To send a request, click Start, Help and Support, and then Invite a friend to connect to your computer with Remote Assistance. Click Invite someone to help you. You are given a choice for your call for help (see Figure 9.36). You can use Windows Messenger or you can use Outlook Express.

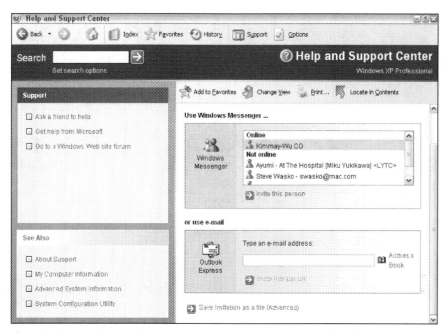

**Figure 9.36.** You can send an instant message or an e-mail asking for remote assistance.

If you have a .NET Passport account, you can sign in with Windows Messenger. Click Sign in, and a list of your contacts appears. Select your contact, and then click Invite this person. If they accept, a notification appears asking if you want them to view your screen and chat with you. Click Yes. Your buddy now has access to your computer and can assist you with your call for help.

If you would rather use e-mail, you can use Outlook Express to send the appropriate request. Type a friend's e-mail address into the To: box, or you can open the Address Book and select a name. Click Invite this person. Type the name you want to appear in the invitation, and a message describing the problem. Click Continue. You can set how long you want the invitation to

---

**Bright Idea**

Windows Messenger (but not MSN Messenger) lets you send a request directly without wading through the Help and Support screen. Open Windows Messenger and click Actions and then Ask for Remote Assistance. Select the helper's name and click OK. The rest proceeds as normal.

remain active and whether you want your friend to use a password to connect to your computer (see Figure 9.37). This means that, somehow, you
need to send her the password or let her know which one to use. Click Send
Invitation.

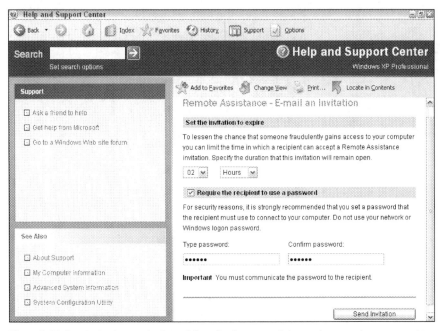

**Figure 9.37.** Your invitation can be "open" for a fixed amount of time and can require a password to
gain access to your computer.

An e-mail message is sent to your friend with an invitation link and an
attached file which has encoded information about the session that is used
by Windows XP to initiate the Remote Assistance connection. The rest proceeds similarly to the Windows Messenger method.

If you revisit the Help and Support link (see Figure 9.38), you will see
that Windows tracks your remote assistance invitations and lets you expire,
resend, or delete the invitation.

The other person doesn't automatically have control of your computer
when he connects, even if you have granted remote control privileges. The
remote helper must click the Take Control button on his screen, and then
you must give explicit permission for him to share control. When this happens, you both can use the mouse and keyboard to control your computer;
for this reason, you shouldn't use your mouse or keyboard at the same time.
Use Windows Messenger (or a telephone call) to coordinate desktop actions.

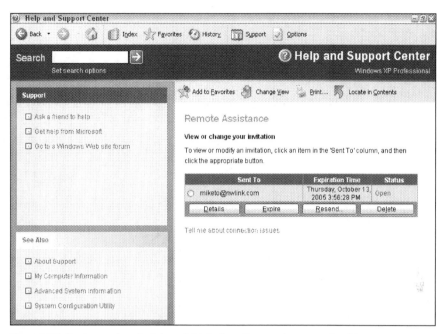

**Figure 9.38.** Track your pleas for help and delete them if you no longer need assistance.

At any time, if you get nervous about the way things are going, or if you'd just rather not share your desktop, press the Esc key and the remote control is terminated. The other person can still see your desktop but must ask permission again to regain shared control.

If you're the person who is being asked for help and you receive an e-mail request for assistance, open the attached file to initiate the session.

# Just the facts

- Your printers can be set up with different settings to handle different print jobs.

- The Fax Service is one of the least talked about, and most useful, capabilities of Windows XP, especially if you have a laptop.

- You can run a Web server on Windows XP, though it's recommended more for internal development than for use as a public server.

- The Remote Desktop ability lets you connect with work PCs from home, or vice versa.

- Remote Assistance is an easy way to help others fix desktop problems or to have others help you.

GET THE SCOOP ON...
Windows domains ▪ Working with objects ▪ Working with
domains ▪ Using logon scripts ▪ Using IntelliMirror ▪
Searching for users and printers ▪ Understanding
the global catalog

# Integrating with Active Directory

T his chapter introduces the Active Directory, which is an essential part of Windows NT technology. You'll find that the Active Directory has less to do with Windows XP than it does Windows 2000 or 2003. The Active Directory is a central point for manageability, security, and interoperability.

Part of this manageability is the IntelliMirror feature; using this feature in either Windows XP or Windows 2000/ 2003, you can intelligently manage user accounts and profiles, both of which are controlled by the Active Directory.

## Set up a Windows domain

It is important to understand exactly what a domain is before trying to work with the Active Directory. A domain is essentially a group of machines that have a similar group of user accounts and security policies through a shared database. The database for this domain is stored in what is called the Active Directory. Though the domain must follow common rules and procedures, it still has a unique name. Following this logic, an Active Directory domain is a group of computers defined by the Administrator of the Windows network. In Windows XP Professional, the Active Directory is managed using the Microsoft Management Console.

Windows domains are set up using Windows 2000 or 2003 Server. This is not possible in Windows XP because Windows XP cannot be a domain controller; however, you can work

**Watch Out!**
The majority of this chapter deals with concepts and features that are only available on Windows 2000 or 2003 and can be used in conjunction with Windows XP Professional addition. If you do not use Windows 2000/2003 or are using the Home edition, this chapter might not be for you.

with domains — for example, join a domain — in Windows XP Professional. The Active Directory is available only in domains containing Windows 2000 or 2003 domain controllers.

For more information on setting up a Windows domain, check out Microsoft's Windows 2003 Web site at www.microsoft.com/windowsserver2003/default.mspx.

# About Active Directory objects

The Active Directory is a database of object information; it lists every resource included in it — users, domains, or printers, for example. In basic Windows parlance, the term "objects" refers to users, computers, or groups. In Active Directory, these objects are controlled by a schema, or set of rules. The Active Directory generates a portion of the values, or attributes, necessary upon creation of an object. For example, if you are creating a user in the Microsoft Management Console (MMC), the Active Directory creates the globally unique identifier, or GUID, but it is up to the administrator to give a name to the user. These values, or attributes, will change depending on the nature of the object in the Active Directory; values are required to fill your object with data.

To create a user, for example, open the Control Panel and select Administrative Tools and then Computer Management. Under System Tools, expand Local Users and Groups and then right-click Users. Select New User from the menu that appears; the New User dialog box appears (see Figure 10.1), and you can enter the requested information to add a new user.

To work with these objects, such as the user created above or any other resource, you can use the Active Directory Users and Computers tool in Windows 2000 or 2003. This tool is for Domain or Enterprise administrators to handle standard object tasks, such as creating new objects or changing properties. You can also apply policy templates to these objects. (A Domain or Enterprise administrator is the system-wide administrator that has full control over the Active Directory configuration — your company may use a different name for this administrator.)

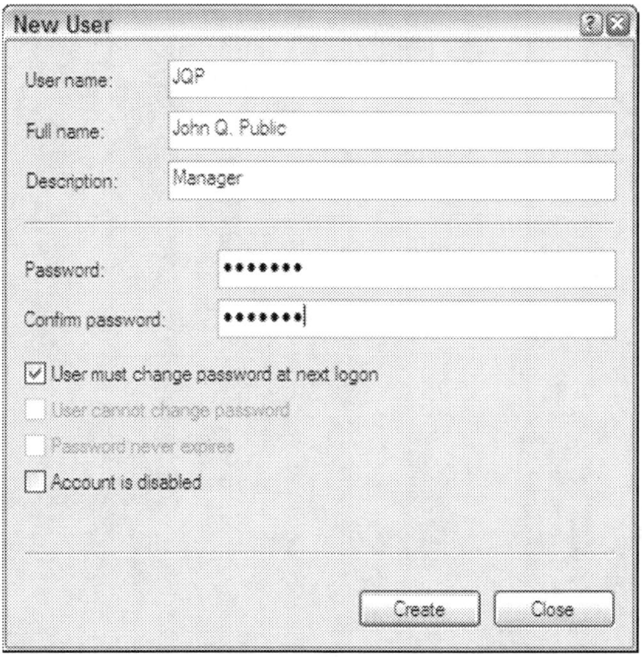

**Figure 10.1.** The New User dialog box.

For more information on using the Active Directory Users and Computers tool or on defining Active Directory objects, please refer to Windows 2000 or Windows 2003 documentation.

# Configure Windows XP for use with a domain

Windows XP Professional edition is designed to work with domains and workgroups; if you are running the Home version, you can configure your machine to work with a workgroup, but domains are not an option.

To configure your machine to work with a domain, double-click the My Computer icon to open it and then click View system information in the System Tasks pane. The System Properties dialog box appears; click the Computer Name tab (see Figure 10.2).

**Hack**

If you're tired of having to use the Control Panel or right-clicking My Computer to access the System Properties window, press the Windows logo key plus the Break key.

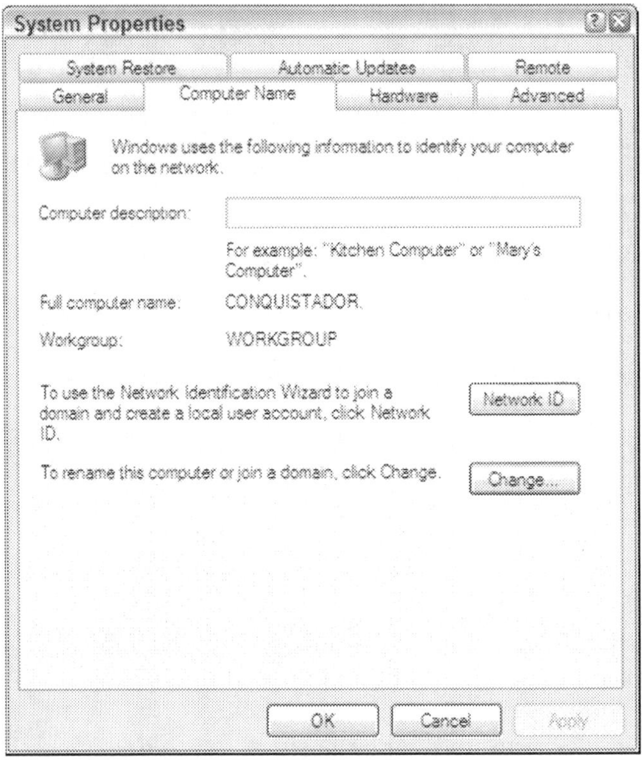

**Figure 10.2.** The System Properties dialog box.

If a name hasn't already been selected, add a name for your machine and validate using the Apply button. Having a name is important for finding your machine on the network, especially in My Network Places, which is where you can store shortcuts to FTP sites, network computers, or even to Web sites (see Figure 10.3).

Depending on whether or not you have TCP/IP installed, your desired computer name can be up to 63 characters long. If your machine does not have TCP/IP installed, you are limited to a paltry 15 characters. However, if you are using Windows 2000 domain controllers, the administrator will need to allow longer names in the Active Directory domain account (for names over 15 characters).

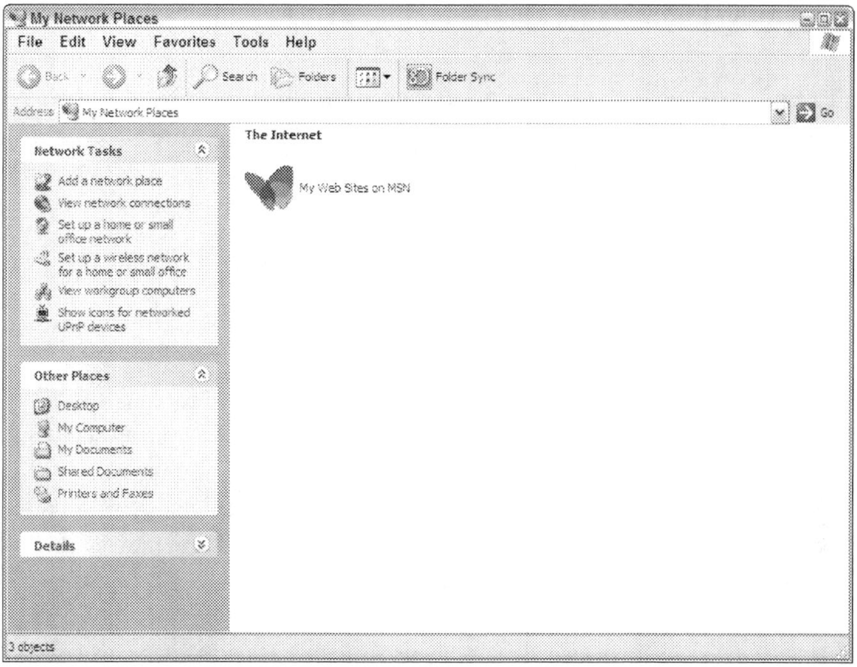

**Figure 10.3.** My Network Places.

If you wish to change the name of your machine, simply click the Change button in the System Properties dialog box (see Figure 10.2) and keep the above rules in mind. The Computer Name Changes dialog box appears (see Figure 10.4); this is how you will also join a domain. Before you attempt to join a domain, make sure you have everything you need to join a domain — the sidebar that follows will help you make sure.

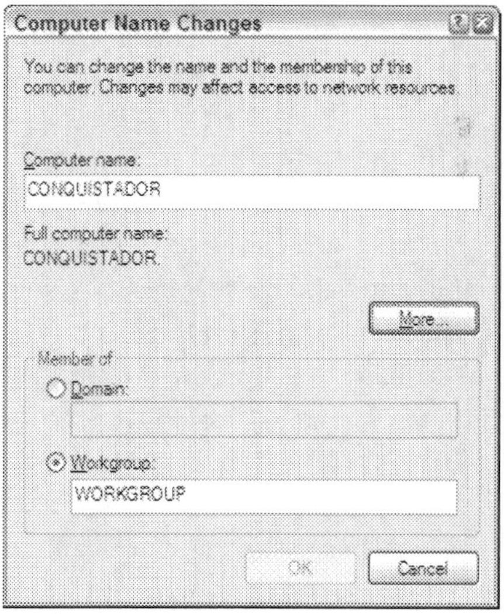

Once you enter the name of the domain at the bottom of the Computer Name Changes dialog

**Figure 10.4.** The Computer Name Changes dialog box.

---

### Get the gear

Before you attempt to join a domain, you should make sure your machine has all the necessary hardware and other bits and pieces to make this a success. If you are using an office machine, odds are that your system administrator has already taken care of this for you.

If you are the administrator, this info will seem second nature to you; if you are a home user (or even a guru who may be a little rusty), this quick crash course or refresher will help you through a relatively easy procedure.

If you are going to join a domain, you are going to need to have a network card (or at least wireless network capabilities), a working IP address (get it from a DHCP server or your system administrator), a LAN connection, a fully working DNS server, a permanent connection to the domain controller, and local admin rights. Also, having the domain name and the proper logon and password will also help you achieve this goal.

Most of these things cannot be bought at your local electronics store; however, these are all basic components of a properly functioning server. If you are a regular user and have any questions, be sure to contact your system administrator.

---

box (in the Member of area — see Figure 10.4), one of two situations will occur: If everything in the sidebar above is present and functioning, a logon/password dialog box will appear asking you to enter your details. (You can use any valid user name here; however, it's best to choose a user who has administrator rights on the machine). On the other hand, if there is a problem, a dialog box appears indicating the problem and a detailed explanation of the problem and how to best resolve it (see Figure 10.5).

If you click the More button on the Computer Name Changes dialog box (see Figure 10.4), the DNS Suffix and NetBIOS Computer Name window appears. There is no need to manually enter a Primary DNS Suffix. Simply leave it blank; it will automatically be set to the DNS suffix of the domain.

## Use the Network ID feature

Perhaps you are new to networking and worried about entering the wrong thing and dooming your machine for eternity. That's understandable — the Network Identification Wizard is here to help you!

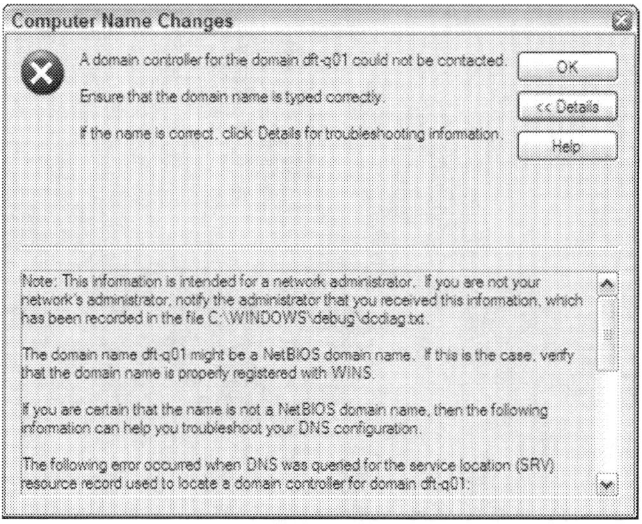

**Figure 10.5.** The Error message with detailed description.

Back in the Computer Name window of the System Properties window (see Figure 10.2), there is the Network ID button (just above the Change button) that allows you to join a domain and create a local account. Click this button, and the wizard begins.

The Network ID Wizard (see Figure 10.6) starts by asking you a simple question: Is the machine part of a business network used to connect to other computers at work or is it a home-based computer, not part of a business network? If you select the latter option, the response is swift: Click Finish to complete the procedure and the machine will restart. Why? This is because your computer already has been configured as a workgroup with a default name of WORKGROUP.

On the other hand, if you selected the former option, as shown in Figure 10.6, you are not getting away so easily. The wizard then wants to know what kind of network you are connecting to, specifically whether your network uses a domain. If you select "without domain," the wizard tells you that you will be assigned to a workgroup and not a domain. The wizard will now let you select the name of your workgroup (though it is still WORKGROUP by default, as shown in Figure 10.7). You will then need to click Next and then Finish and restart your machine.

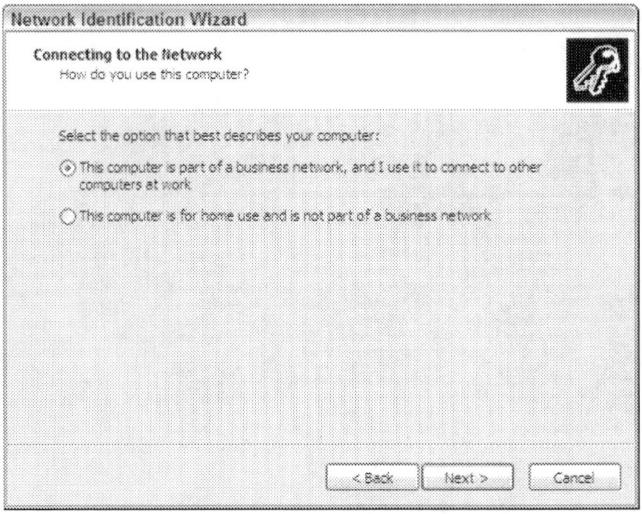

**Figure 10.6.** The Network Identification Wizard.

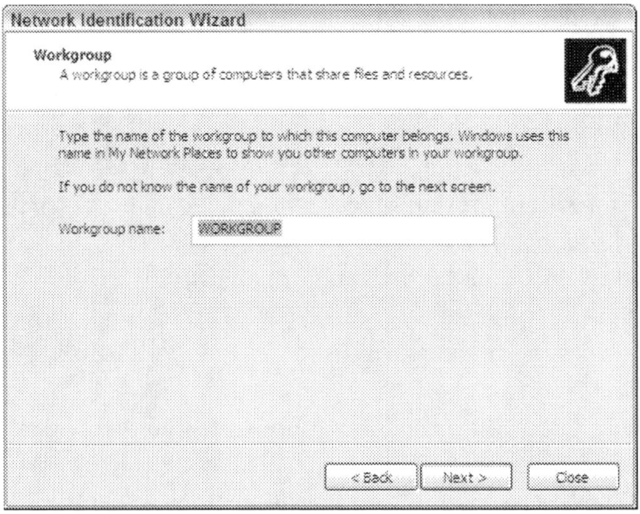

**Figure 10.7.** The Network Identification Wizard Workgroup window.

If you told the wizard that you are indeed using a domain, the next screen will provide a list of necessary information before you can connect to a Windows network. The next screen solicits user account and domain information. This is where you will finally enter your user name, password, and the domain. The wizard will then look for your computer on the domain. If it cannot find it, it will ask you for your computer name and computer domain again.

## Rename your computer or join a domain

Back in the Computer Name tab (see Figure 10.2) of the System Properties dialog box, there is the Change button (just below the Network ID button) that allows you to rename your computer or join a domain. Once you click the Change button, the Computer Names Changes dialog box appears (see Figure 10.8).

You can rename the computer at the top of the dialog box. You can also add a new domain or workgroup or update an existing one at the bottom of the dialog box. If you click More, you can add a primary DNS number for your computer. You may also notice that you can opt to change the primary DNS number when the domain membership changes. Please note that you are unable to update your NetBIOS name here.

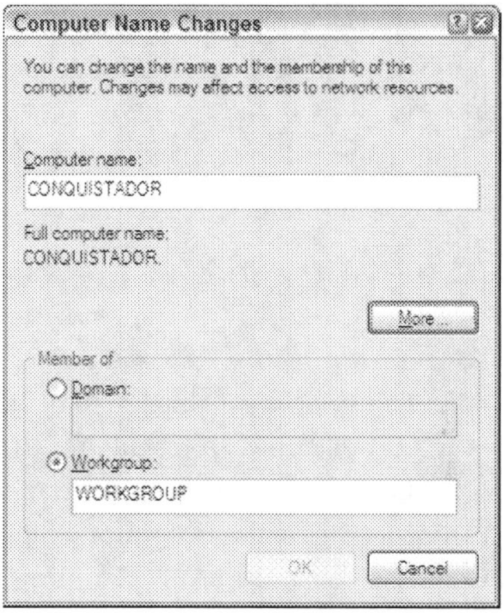

**Figure 10.8.** The Computer Names Changes dialog box.

# Create and deploy logon scripts

Logon scripts are locally stored scripts that tell Windows XP what to do when starting up. These scripts can contain any valid command line instruction. Usually in the form of a batch file, logon scripts can be added to user accounts and run automatically each time the user logs on to Windows XP. Like many other features discussed in this book, this is only for the Windows XP Professional edition.

## Write logon scripts

Writing logon scripts is similar to writing a regular program, though not as involved. For example, you can use a logon script to map a drive. In other words, the drive \\domain-2\home1 could be assigned the drive letter "H."

**Watch Out!**

Don't be fooled! Logon scripts can also be executable files or procedures (like VBScript or Java). They can also be command (.cmd) files.

Using a standard text editor, simply use the necessary (and valid) instruction or command. For example, in the case above, you would write: net use H: \\domain-2\home1. You can name the file as desired; just remember to give it a .bat extension and to save it in the appropriate location (\System32\ Repl\Import\Scripts folder). Please note that this location is not created when Windows XP is installed; this location must be created in the System32 directory.

This drive will be recognized as drive H, assuming you perform the following steps.

## Set logon scripts for a user

To set logon scripts, you will need to access the Computer Management MMC. To do this, open the Control Panel and then open Administrative Tools. The Computer Management MMC is accessible by double-clicking it in the Administrative Tools menu.

In the Computer Management MMC, you can click the Users subfolder in the Local Users and Groups folder to view the available users on your machine (see Figure 10.9). You must be the administrator or belong to the administrators group to do this.

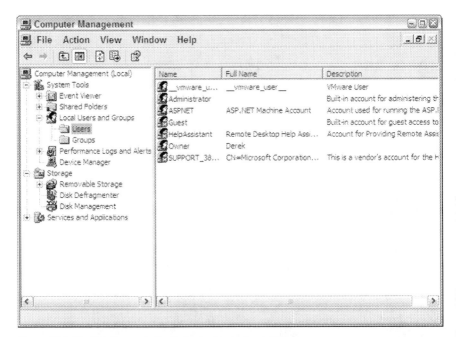

**Figure 10.9.** The list of users in the Computer Management MMC.

By right-clicking on the desired user account and selecting Properties, you can quickly assign a logon script to the user. In the Profile tab, simply add the name of your logon script (see Figure 10.10). Please note that the name of the script may change; if you are not the administrator, please see your administrator if you do not know the name of the script.

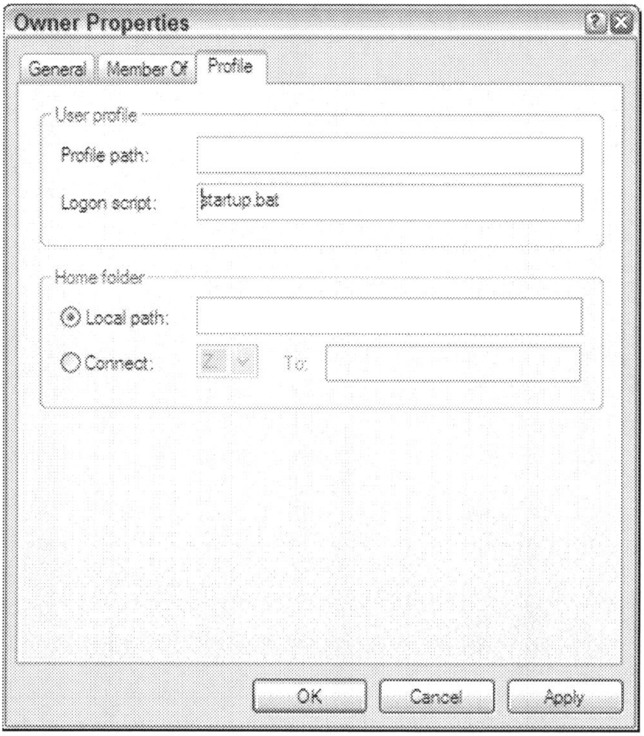

**Figure 10.10.** The Profile tab.

Once you have assigned your script, validate it by clicking OK. The logon script will be run when the user logs on to the machine locally, but not on the domain.

Of course, we aren't quite finished with the logon script just yet. These scripts are stored in the \System32\Repl\Import\Scripts folder, which must be shared. To share this folder, right-click it and select either Sharing or Security from the menu that appears. Or, click Properties from the menu that appears, and then click the Sharing tab in the folder's properties dialog box (see Figure 10.11). In the Network sharing and security section, select the Share this folder on the network check box and enter "netlogon" as the Share name. Click OK when you are finished.

**Watch Out!**

You can share and apply "netlogon" to any folder that is accessible during logon. However, it must be applied before any logon script will work.

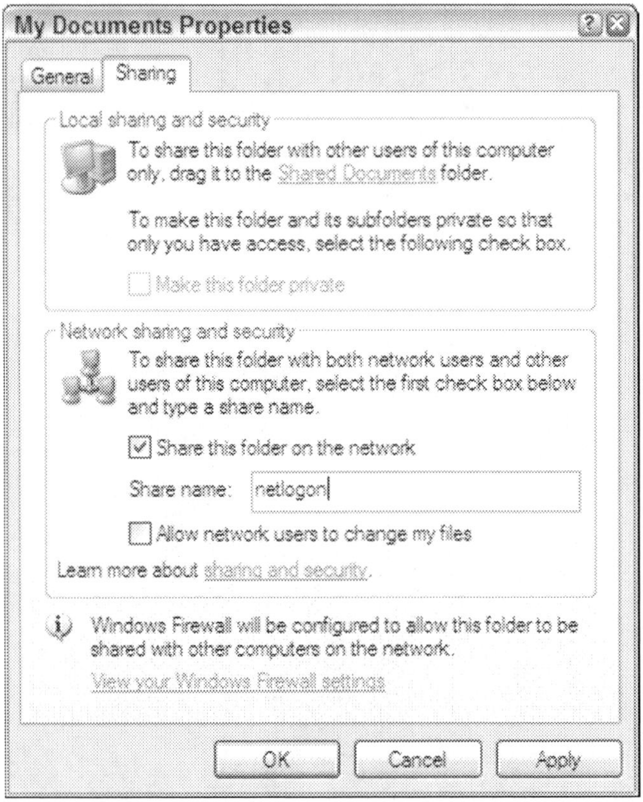

---

**My Documents Properties**

General | Sharing

┌ Local sharing and security ──────────────

To share this folder with other users of this computer only, drag it to the Shared Documents folder.

To make this folder and its subfolders private so that only you have access, select the following check box.

☐ Make this folder private

┌ Network sharing and security ──────────────

To share this folder with both network users and other users of this computer, select the first check box below and type a share name.

☑ Share this folder on the network

Share name: netlogon|

☐ Allow network users to change my files

Learn more about sharing and security.

ⓘ Windows Firewall will be configured to allow this folder to be shared with other computers on the network.

View your Windows Firewall settings

[ OK ]  [ Cancel ]  [ Apply ]

**Figure 10.11.** Sharing a folder in the folder's properties dialog box.

# Install programs using IntelliMirror

Back when Windows 2000 was released, Microsoft added IntelliMirror as a management system that was designed to lower the cost of desktop environment management and to increase productivity. This management system was brought along for the Windows XP ride, but not surprisingly, for the Professional version only.

IntelliMirror's benefits are basically divided into three different categories that can be used independently or in combination: User Data Management, User Settings Management, and Software Installation and Maintenance.

It's the latter feature that interests us in this section. Software Installation and Maintenance handles basic tasks associated with installation: installation, repairing, configuring, product updates, and removing the software from your machine.

What makes this unique is that instead of handling a single user installation or repair, IntelliMirror works in terms of groups of users and computers. It's essentially the Group Policy settings on a desktop level; IntelliMirror might dictate what software is available to a given user account regardless of what machine he is logged on. In a similar fashion, you might want to determine how applications are repaired or updated — for example, either by user or by computer. Using IntelliMirror, there are two types of applications: assigned applications and published applications.

## Use assigned applications

An assigned application is similar to those Windows update alert messages. How so? Let's say that the head of a documentation department decides that his technical writers should all use Microsoft Word on their machines.

The manager will work with the administrator (you) to make the application an assigned application. From now on, when any of the 15 technical writers logs on, he will find a Microsoft Word icon, perhaps named "Install me," in his Start menus. The writer now has two choices: Click the icon and install the application, or disregard the file and delete it.

There's no point in a technical writer trying to be clever. If his manager or administrator wants Word installed, it will be installed because it is an assigned application. Every time a writer logs on to his account, the icon will appear until he installs the software. In other words, you can run but you can't hide — this is not an optional installation. An alternate installation option for the writer is to open an associated file (Word, in this case), and the software will install prior to opening the file. In the event that the technical writer decides to delete the assigned application from his machine, the application is removed; however, it is replaced with the original icon on the desktop inviting him to re-install the application.

**Inside Scoop**

The technical writer doesn't need to worry about disk space; the icon on the desktop installs the bare minimum of files on his machine at this point. It's essentially an icon and file associations for the registry.

## Assign an assigned application

Open the MMC by clicking Start, Run, typing mmc in the text box, and then clicking OK. Open any MSC file that has the software installation included. (Files read in the MMC have an .msc extension; for example, the Computer Management file is called "compmgmt.msc.") If you do not have a file with software installation included, you can create one by clicking Add/Remove Snap-in (Ctrl+M) from the File menu. Click Add in the Add/Remove Snap-in dialog box and select Group Policy Object Editor from the drop-down list. Click Add, Finish, and then Close. Go to the Extensions tab of the Add/Remove Snap-in dialog box and select Group Policy Object Editor from the drop-down list. Make sure the two software installation add-in files are checked and then click OK.

With the Software Installation snap-in selected in the console tree of a MMC, create a new package by right-clicking the Details pane and then selecting New and Package from the menu that appears. Select a Windows Installer from the Open dialog box. In the Deploy Software dialog box, check Assigned and click OK to validate your selection.

## Use published applications

Published applications are slightly more "democratic" than their assignment counterparts. Unlike the former, which are required one-click installations, published applications are voluntarily installed using the Add/Remove Programs window from the Control Panel. The application is simply available to those following the Group Policy object; it is not actually installed, simply made available.

For example, suppose the same documentation manager thought it would be useful for the team to use Microsoft Picture It! The next time a technical writer logs on to his accounts, he will notice that that software application is available for installation using the Add/Remove Programs window. If the team member doesn't install it, either because he didn't want it, or because he didn't notice it, he can ignore it or he can install the software by clicking on a file associated with the software. The primary difference between assigned and published applications is that everyone must install assigned applications — published applications can be made available to specific users without requiring everyone to install it.

## Assign a published application

The procedure for assigning a published application is nearly identical to assigning an assigned application. The only difference is that in the Deploy

Software dialog box, you, as the administrator, check Published and validate your selection.

## Set software installation defaults

Like most aspects of this section, defaults are managed through the Software Installation snap-in discussed earlier. Clicking on the Properties feature of the Software Installation snap-in, take a look at the General tab. In this tab you can determine the default package location, which is the central application distribution point. This is also the right place to set whether to publish or assign new packages. For optimal control of each application package, you can use the Display the Deploy Software dialog box and the Advanced windows to determine how much control to have over a given package.

Finally, you can set whether the Installation user interface options should be set to Basic or Maximum. The answer depends on how transparent the process should be for all users. In the Basic interface, only progress bars and errors are displayed. Maximum, as you may have guessed, is a little "richer" and features the entire interface supported by the application. If you are an administrator or a user who is comfortable with Windows XP or the application, you should use the Maximum interface. If you are a beginner or quite simply not interested in any details beyond the progress and any errors, you should use the Basic interface.

## Upgrade an application

Both assigned and published applications can be updated from the server. When a team member from the documentation teams logs on to an account, any new applications or updates are installed on the machine.

For the administrator, it's back to the Properties option in the Software Installation snap-in, only this time you will work with Upgrades tab. You will need to set the current Group Policy object as the source of the upgradeable package or find the relevant group policy.

All other assigned or published packages for the Group Policy appear in Package to upgrade. The administrator will select which package to upgrade. He then must decide if the upgrade means first uninstalling the application and then re-installing with the upgrade or whether to process the upgrade over the existing application.

**Watch Out!**
In this case, there's no point in uninstalling the application unless it's a different software package. Upgrading from the current version guarantees that your settings and files are not written over.

Finally, you can decide whether or not the upgrade should be optional or mandatory by choosing something somewhere. If you are working with a team of users, it's better to make it mandatory so that you are guaranteed that everyone is using the same version.

## Remove a managed application

Managed applications — applications that are either assigned or published — can easily be removed in just a few simple steps.

Perhaps as administrator you decide that the software is no longer necessary for the team. Back in the Software Installation MMC, the administrator must right-click All Tasks from the left side of the window and then select Remove. The Remove Software dialog box offers you to removal options, both of which are discussed in the next paragraph.

As administrator you can let team members continue to use the software; however it will no longer be available if the team member has not yet installed it (assigned application), or if he removed it (published application). You can also have the software removed immediately from a user's machine. In this case, "immediately" means the next time the user reboots or logs on.

# Search for users or printers

Searching for users, printers, or computers in the Active Directory is as simple as your standard search performed on a workgroup machine. This is helpful if you have just been set up on a domain at work and you have been told to print to network printer.

From the Start menu, select the Search feature. The last green arrow is for searching printers, computers, or people in the directory. If you do not have an Active Directory, your search page will only propose searching computers or people.

The search assistant will ask you to check which group you are looking for. If you opt for printers, select it and then enter a name, location, or model (for example, Brother 1040). By default, Windows XP will search the entire directory for your printer. Any results are returned at the bottom of the window.

This is the same principle for people; enter a name or a description for a user, contact, or group, and Windows XP will search the entire directory (unless you choose to limit your search parameters). You can also find shared folders by entering a name or a keyword. Windows XP will search the entire directory and return any results at the bottom of the window.

**Watch Out!**

Don't overload your system with global catalogs because they can consume a great deal of system resources. One per domain per machine should be ample.

# Understanding the global catalog

The global catalog is primarily a Windows 2000/2003 concern, but it does affect the Active Directory. It is essentially a domain controller with a replica of all objects in the Active Directory; however, it only stores a few features of each object. The features "kept" in these replicas are features that are most likely to be used in a search and those needed to find a complete clone of the Active Directory object.

This is all done automatically based on a base model created by Microsoft. Obviously, this is the type of feature that is only accessible to administrators, so it's not surprising that they can modify or add properties based on their requirements.

For information on configuring the global catalog on your Windows 2000/2003 server, please consult the Microsoft documentation.

# Just the facts

- The Windows Active Directory is primarily a Windows 2000 or 2003 feature; however, its influence and use extends to Microsoft Windows XP Professional edition.

- The Microsoft Management Console (MMC) is the tool designed to management the Active Domain and its objects.

- You can use logon scripts to configure a user's environment or, from the Administrator's perspective, influence a user's environment without getting too close.

- IntelliMirror is a great feature of the Active Directory that allows you to assign or publish software for members of your team.

- Use the Search feature to look up computers, printers, or network users in exactly the same way that you would to look up files when you are not on a domain.

# Manage the Hardware Environment

PART IV

GET THE SCOOP ON...

Using System Information and Device Manager to manage
your computer ▪ Displaying information about programs
and processes with Task Manager ▪ Reviewing system
errors in Event Viewer ▪ Managing computer services
for optimal performance

# Working with Windows Internals

**Chapter 11**

T here is an inverse relationship between how easy technology is to use and the underlying complexity that makes it work. The telephone system is one example; everyone knows how to use a phone, but just try to explain the call switching, inter-carrier exchanges, or even the billing systems to someone.

Windows is no different; it is much easier to use Windows XP than DOS or even earlier versions of Windows, but the underlying technology is exponentially more complex.

This chapter gives you a glimpse into the workings of Windows XP, providing information on the services and components that make everything happen, from the Services Manager to the Registry Editor and back again.

## Display system information

There is a lot going on under the hood of Windows XP. The operating system has to keep track of all the hardware devices that are added and removed, all the device drivers and what versions to use, and even individual settings for those drivers that change depending on who is logged on to the computer.

The System Information utility is a one-stop center for information on your hardware, software, and some of the registry and domain settings that are affecting your computer.

Most of the time this utility will help out people troubleshooting your computer, but it also proves useful if you aren't quite sure which version of modem you have or what version of drivers are being used with it.

Launch the System Information utility by clicking Start, Run, typing msinfo32, and then pressing Enter. You can also dig deeply into the menu structure and launch it by clicking Start, All Programs, Accessories, System Tools, and then System Information. It may take a few moments for System Information to collect and display the information, since it queries hardware and software — and there is a lot of it to query.

When the dialog box appears (see Figure 11.1), you can browse through the different categories much like using Windows Explorer. The most useful categories are the System Summary page, where you can determine what version BIOS your system is using without having to watch carefully at boot time, and Hardware Resources\Conflicts\Sharing, which lets you determine if any devices are vying for the same system resource and perhaps causing you trouble.

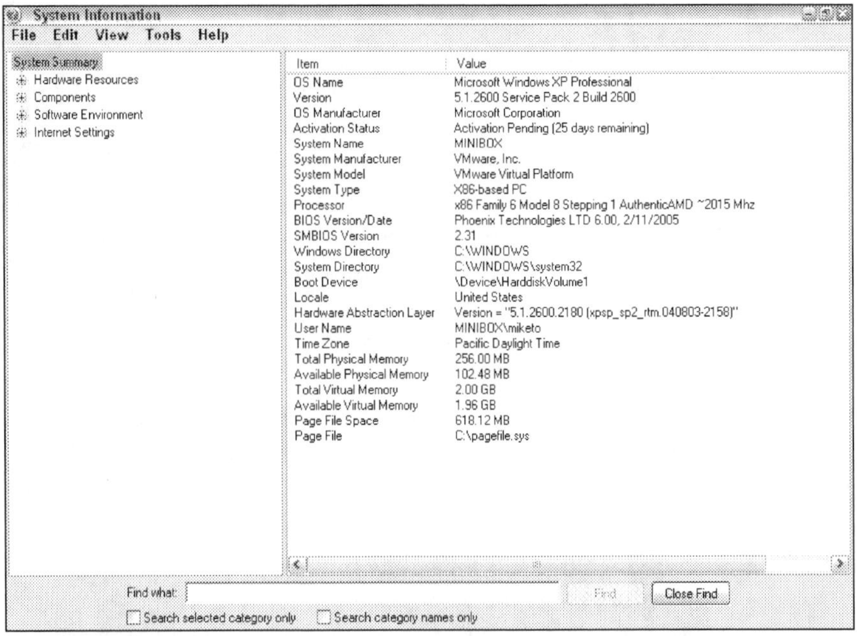

**Figure 11.1.** The System Information utility has more information on Windows than you may have thought existed.

At the bottom of the dialog box is a search function which lets you look for particular system devices or manufacturer names. Type a name and then click Find.

Five "hidden" system-related tools are located within System Information; click Tools to see the list. Among the tools are Net Diagnostics (see Figure 11.2). You can also reach this tool by clicking Start, Help and Support Center, Use Tools to view your computer information and diagnose problems, and then Network Diagnostics. The Net Diagnostics program will run tests to help isolate where potential communications problems arise: your network adapter, your local network, or network-based services.

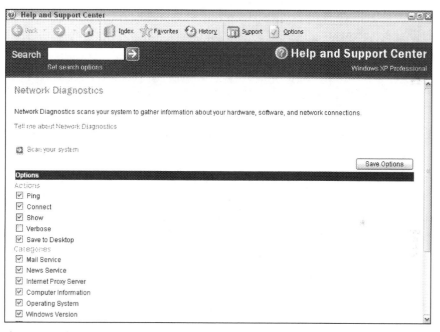

**Figure 11.2.** The Net Diagnostics tool can be configured to test specific network functions and collate the data for troubleshooting.

The System Restore utility is most often used after installing new hardware or software that renders Windows XP unstable — it allows you to get back to a working system. You can get to the utility many ways, though the most common is by clicking Start, All Programs, Accessories, System Tools, and then System Restore. System Restore lets you "turn back the clock" and restore your system to its state at an earlier date. This utility is covered in more detail in Chapter 12.

The File Signature Verification Utility lets you determine if any unsigned device drivers or files are in use on your system. This can be useful, though many of the latest driver updates are not signed even though they are "final" ones from the publisher.

A fairly useful troubleshooting tool is the DirectX Diagnostic Tool (see Figure 11.3). This tool lets you run tests on audio, video, and online play components of the DirectX component suite. DirectX versions back around 5 and 6 were often prone to driver conflicts and instability, but with 9.0c most stability issues have been resolved. In all likelihood, if you're looking to squeeze the last bit of performance out of your games, you'll adjust your settings in your video adapter's settings, not mess around with DirectX.

| 🔵 DirectX Diagnostic Tool | | | | | | | 🗕🗖❌ |
|---|---|---|---|---|---|---|---|
| System | DirectX Files | Display | Sound | Music | Input | Network | More Help |

This tool reports detailed information about the DirectX components and drivers installed on your system. It lets you test functionality, diagnose problems, and change your system configuration to work best.

If you know what area is causing the problem, click the appropriate tab above. Otherwise, you can use the "Next Page" button below to visit each page in sequence.

The "More Help" page lists some other tools that may help with the problem you are experiencing.

┌─ System Information ─────────────────────────────────────────────────────────

              Current Date/Time: Thursday, October 13, 2005, 17:11:50
              Computer Name: MINIBOX
              Operating System: Microsoft Windows XP Professional (5.1, Build 2600)
              Language: English (Regional Setting: English)
              System Manufacturer: VMware, Inc.
              System Model: VMware Virtual Platform
              BIOS: PhoenixBIOS 4.0 Release 6.0
              Processor: AMD Athlon(TM) XP2400+, MMX, 3DNow, ~2.0GHz
              Memory: 256MB RAM
              Page file: 130MB used, 487MB available
              DirectX Version: DirectX 9.0c (4.09.0000.0904)

☑ Check for WHQL digital signatures

                    DxDiag 5.03.2600.2180 Unicode  Copyright © 1998-2003 Microsoft Corporation.  All rights reserved.

| Help | | Next Page | Save All Information... | Exit |

**Figure 11.3.** DirectX Diagnostic Tool tests all portions of your multimedia system, including audio and video.

**Watch Out!**

If you work for a business you should not run the Net Diagnostics tool unless you have been instructed to by your IT department. The tool generates traffic on the network that can trigger intrusion detection alarms. A false alarm will make IT angry. Do not make IT angry.

The last tool on the list, Dr. Watson (see Figure 11.4), is a holdover from the 16-bit Windows days. It is an error debugger that dumps information from memory directly into a file. Unless you are a programmer, or are instructed to load Dr. Watson prior to duplicating the error, you probably won't use the good Doctor.

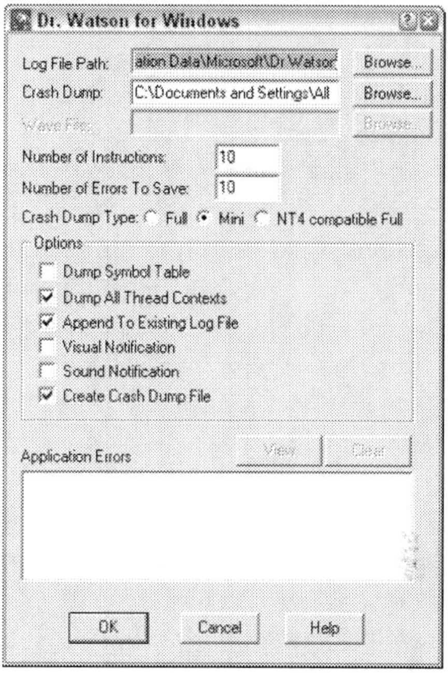

The tool that yields perhaps the most valuable information is the Net Diagnostics tool. Instead of running multiple command-line utilities that can test your network (see Chapter 13), Net Diagnostics already has the command-line switches configured for you. The results are presented in summary categories that can be expanded by clicking the plus sign next to each category. In Verbose mode you can see the actual results from the command-line tools. You can also save the results for troubleshooting purposes, such as sending it to your ISP.

**Figure 11.4.** Just like a real specialist, Dr. Watson's information is often understood best by other trained professionals.

# Work with Device Manager

Device Manager is like a kindergarten teacher with thirty students: Most of the time the students obey the teacher and are well-behaved, but when disruption breaks out it affects the whole class. Behind the desktop, Device Manager is keeping track of all the hardware and device drivers, trying to keep conflicts to a minimum and isolating components that don't quite fit in the scheme of things.

In the days of Windows 95, Device Manager was one of the first stops for conducting any hardware troubleshooting. Older hardware used interrupt request (IRQ) or input/output (I/O) settings that could only be changed using jumpers. If a conflict with other hardware popped up, users had to open the computer and either move tiny switches or replace pin jumpers — which often meant finding the hardware manual, or calling tech support, or ... you get the idea.

Hardware and software manufacturers worked together to make hardware that could be changed using software interfaces. Plug and Play, FireWire, and Universal Serial Bus (USB) were all ways to make adding and removing hardware simpler, with fewer conflicts. Today nearly all hardware lets the operating system change its settings so that conflicts are minimized.

However, conflicts still happen. If you constantly add and remove new hardware, you are likely to run into a case where the device isn't working, or another one stops working. This happens when Windows runs out of the assignable resources that are being requested by the new hardware.

To check the status of all your hardware, click Start, Run, type devmgmt.msc, and then press Enter. You can also right-click My Computer, click Hardware, and then click Device Manager (see Figure 11.5). Another way to launch Device Manager is by opening the Control Panel, clicking Performance Options, and then clicking System.

A yellow exclamation point next to a device means there is a configuration problem and the device is not functioning. Any devices with a red X next to a device means the hardware has been disabled. Right-click the device and then click Properties. The Device Status dialog box will give you some information about the device, such as any error codes. You can do a search for the error codes in the Help and Support Center, which often has recommendations on how to resolve the issue.

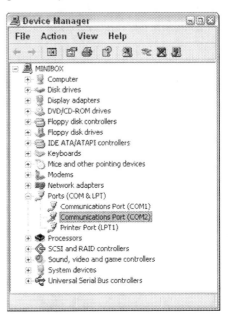

**Figure 11.5.** Device Manager alerts you to hardware conflicts that should be resolved.

The most common reason to see a yellow exclamation point is a conflict with another device's resources. Sometimes you have to give Device Manager a little help and pick an IRQ or I/O region that is not in use, and then the device will work. Click the Resources tab (see Figure 11.6) and then click Set Configuration Manually. Deselect Use automatic settings. You can now select a conflicting resource in the Resource Settings window, click Change Setting, and then use the up and down arrows to select a different setting. The Conflict Information field will let you know if another device is using the resource.

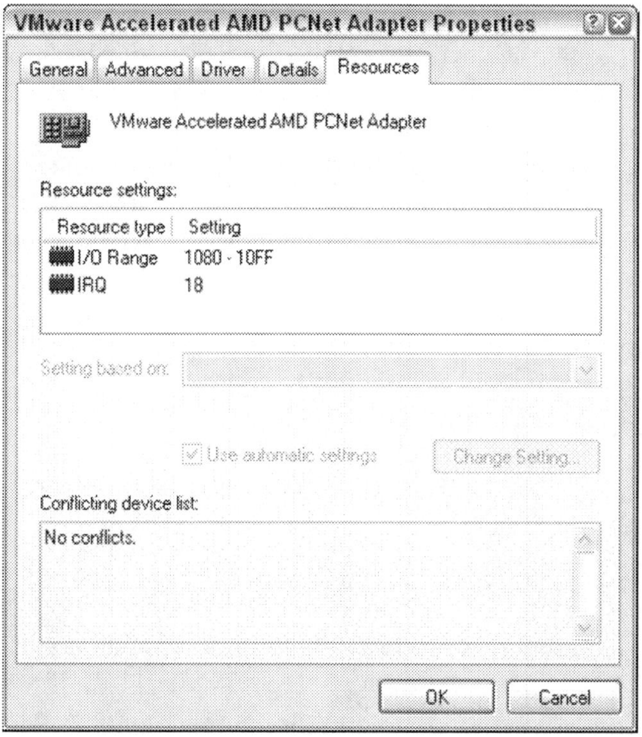

**Figure 11.6.** Device Manager alerts you to hardware conflicts that should be resolved.

In some cases you may need to either disable some of your infrequently-used hardware (such as an infrared port), create different hardware profiles for laptops, or if you just can't get everything to work together, perform a new installation with all your desired hardware connected to the computer. This will let Windows start over with a clean slate and try to assign different combinations of resources so that all your hardware can work together.

# Work with Task Manager

If Device Manager is like a kindergarten teacher, Task Manager is like a traffic cop. It monitors the various processes running on Windows, lets you see which ones are misbehaving, and lets you shut down processes that are not

**Inside Scoop**

With any hardware conflicts it always pays to make a visit to the manufacturer's Web site for the latest device drivers and to check the FAQs and support forums. There may be suggestions for different hardware settings that will avoid conflicts.

responding or are consuming all of Windows' resources. Open Task Manager by clicking Start, Run, typing taskmgr.exe, and then pressing Enter. You can also bring it up by pressing Ctrl+Alt+Delete (once, if connected to a workgroup, twice if connected to a domain) and then clicking Task Manager.

The five tabs give you different views into Windows. The Applications tab shows you user-mode programs that are running on your computer — in other words, programs you have started and currently have running. The Processes view shows you the different processes, both kernel-mode being used by the operating system and user-mode processes such as Task Manager itself (see Figure 11.7).

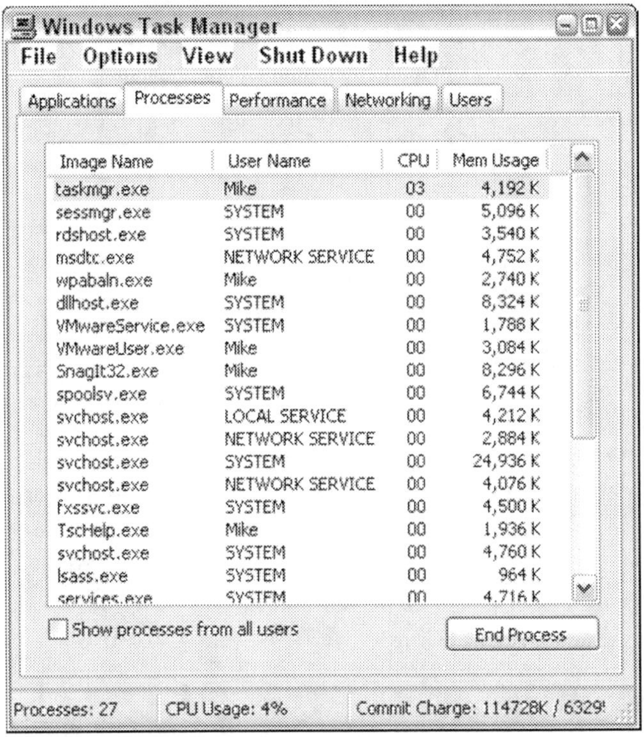

**Figure 11.7.** The Processes view shows you what is currently running and how much resources are being consumed.

The Performance view (see Figure 11.8) displays the work being done by your processor (or processors, if you have a dual-processor motherboard), RAM, and page file usage.

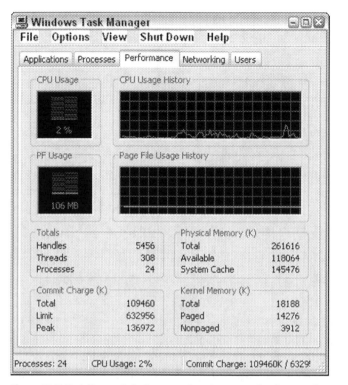

**Figure 11.8.** Task Manager's Performance view shows you what is currently running and how much resources are being consumed.

If you have a lot of data moving on and off your computer, the Networking view lets you monitor which adapters are being used, and how much. Finally, you can see which users are connected to your computer with the Users view. For example you can obtain a listing of those working with shared files on your computer.

Task Manager will remember the last tab you selected and open to that one the next time you restart it. You can also change the refresh rate by clicking View and then Update speed. Leaving it at Normal, which updates at roughly once every two seconds, will give you plenty of information without overloading Windows with refresh requests.

**Bright Idea**

Add a shortcut to Task Manager in your startup group, or add it to the All Users startup group, so that it launches when you log on. It doesn't consume many resources and you always have an indicator of your system's health where you can see it.

## Deep in the heart of processes

Task Manager is a great general tool, but the more you know about Windows, you wonder which processes are linked to other processes, and sometimes you want to end a process in spite of Windows telling you that you're not allowed to bump it off.

A freeware program called Process Explorer is available from www.sysinternals.com. It lets you end any process (whether you *should* end it is another question entirely) that you wish, displays a tree view of processes and associated DLLs, and does all this with an interface that is like Task Manager on steroids. If you are a tinkerer who really likes to get under the hood, Process Explorer is well worth checking out.

Your viewing preferences can also be changed under the Options menu. The two I prefer are Minimize on use and Hide when minimized. This puts Task Manager in the notification area, so if something is going wrong I can bring it up quickly with the mouse.

The most useful tab is the Processes tab, where you can end a process that is consuming all system resources, or that has stopped responding. An application that isn't responding will be displayed on the Applications tab; an out-of-control process will display 99% CPU on the Processes tab. Select a process and then click End Process. Windows will attempt to end the process, and display an End Process dialog box. You can wait for the process to time out or you can click End.

Some processes are so fundamental to Windows that you cannot end them using Task Manager. If your computer is completely out of control and Task Manager can't end your woes, it's time for the BRS (big red switch). Restart your computer. You can either try to duplicate the circumstances for purposes of filing a bug report with Microsoft, or you can try *not* to duplicate the circumstances in hopes of avoiding another system lock-up.

## Work with Event Viewer

Continuing with the theme of utilities-as-people, Event Viewer is like the town gossip — not a thing happens without Event Viewer seeing it. If a service is failing to start, an application is running out of disk space, or someone is trying to hack into the administrator account, you will find clues to all these happenings in the event logs.

Event Viewer (see Figure 11.9) is the utility used to view the three different categories of events. To open Event Viewer, click Start, Run, type eventvwr.msc, and then press Enter. You can also click Start, Administrative Tools, and then Event Viewer.

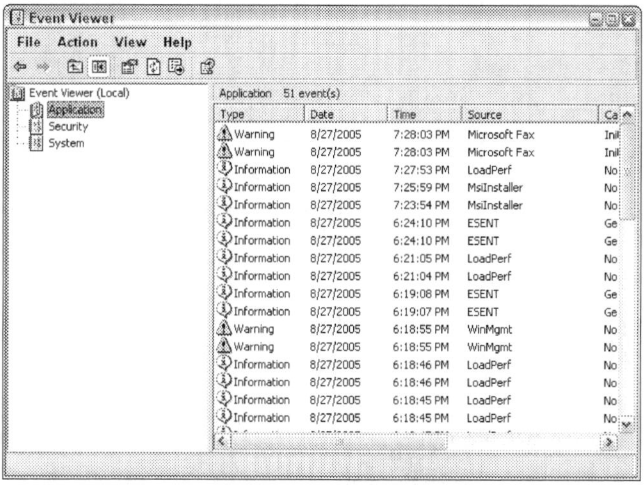

**Figure 11.9.** Important clues to your computer's health are found in Event Viewer.

The three categories of logged events are:

▪ **Application.** The application log contains events logged by applications or programs. For example, a database program might record a file error in the application log.

▪ **Security.** The security log records events such as valid and invalid log on attempts, as well as events related to resource use such as creating, opening, or deleting files or other objects. An administrator can specify what events are recorded in the security log. For example, if you have enabled log on auditing, attempts to log on to the system are recorded in the security log.

▪ **System.** The system log contains events logged by Windows XP system components. For example, the failure of a driver or other system component to load during startup is recorded in the system log. The event types logged by system components are predetermined by Windows XP.

Application and system logs contain three types of events: errors, displayed with a red X, indicate a significant problem, such as loss of data or loss of functionality; warnings, displayed with a yellow exclamation point, are

**Inside Scoop**

Sometimes it's difficult to find information on particular event IDs. If Microsoft doesn't have information, take a look at www.eventid.net. It has links to other sites with information, as well as postings by others who have encountered the event in question.

events that are not necessarily significant, but may indicate future problems; and information, displayed with a blue I, describes the successful operation of an application, driver, or service.

The logs can sometimes be helpful in determining what failed and why. The System log contains events that usually have an Event ID associated with them, and by searching the Help and Support Center, you can often find out more information about the problem and if any hotfix has been issued for it.

Application events are somewhat different. The application manufacturer is responsible for writing an application that properly logs its events into the file. There may not be an event ID associated with it, or if there is, you will have to search the manufacturer's support forums to find it. The data may be relevant only to the original programmers. Or in many cases the application writes its own error log into its home directory or other location. The bottom line: An application may crash but sometimes it won't show up in the Event Viewer.

The Security log contains different events: success audits, displayed with a yellow key, and failure audits, displayed with a yellow lock. Out of the box Windows does not log many events to the Security log, not even log on failures that you might see during a brute-force password attack. Audit events must be enabled separately. Fortunately, most of them can be quickly enabled by using the Group Policy Editor; see Chapter 6 for more information on auditing security events.

Each event log can have a number of its properties changed from the default. Right-click a log in the left pane and then click Properties (see Figure 11.10). The default settings should be fine for nearly all cases except where you are running a Web server or checking particular error conditions; then you may want to point the log file to a different location, increase its size, or change the overwrite behavior for older events.

On the Properties dialog box, click the Filter tab (see Figure 11.11). From here you can pick a component's events, view by event ID, or review the log from a particular date and time. This is exceptionally handy, especially when you want to find out when a hardware component first began throwing errors, or how often and at what time account lockouts started happening. As a final note, you can export any Event Viewer listing into a separate file, so you can configure a filter to show only relevant events and then save the results into a file for future use. In Event Viewer, click Action, Export List, select the format (comma delimited is most useful for importing into Excel), type the filename, and then click Save.

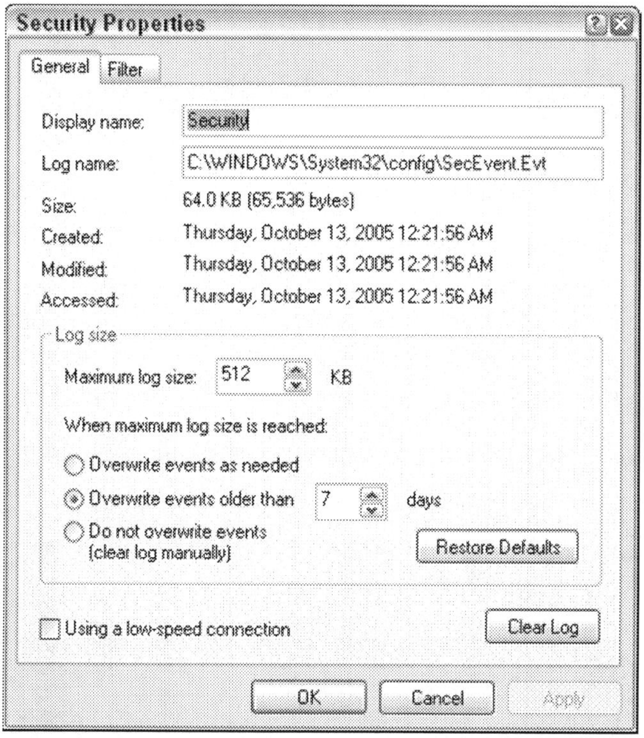

**Figure 11.10.** Each log file, in this case the Security log, can be configured for size and overwrite behavior when the log becomes full.

# Remote log viewing

If you have local administrator rights on other computers, you can use Event Viewer to connect to other event logs and view the contents remotely. Make sure Event Viewer (local) is selected in the left pane, click Action, Connect to another computer, and then browse for the computer. If it is available you will be asked to log on with your credentials. Once approved you can view the event logs as needed.

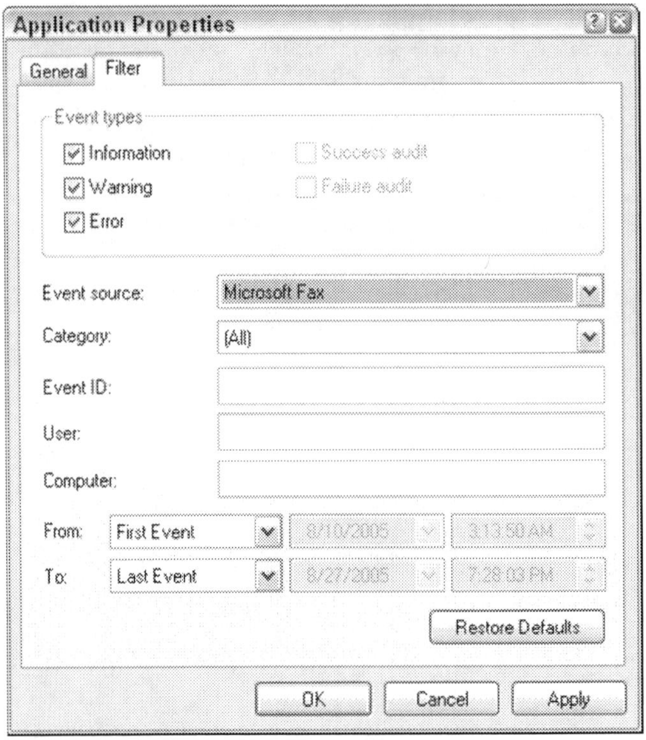

**Figure 11.11.** The Filter tab makes it much easier to find specific error conditions or errors generated by the same component.

# Perform system surgery with RegEdit

Throughout the book references have been made to the Windows Registry (see Figure 11.12). The registry is a centralized listing of every setting Windows and its applications require for proper operation. It's a configuration file gone monstrously, horribly wrong. With Linux each subsystem and application has its own text configuration file, stored where it can easily be found. Windows requires that all settings be placed into the registry, using naming conventions that, at best, were created by a committee of insane Scrabble players.

Windows XP and Windows applications make changes to the registry, though you don't know it. Whenever you change a setting in Control Panel, or change your default font choice in a word processing application, values are created or edited in the registry. This ensures that the proper keys are edited and the correct values assigned.

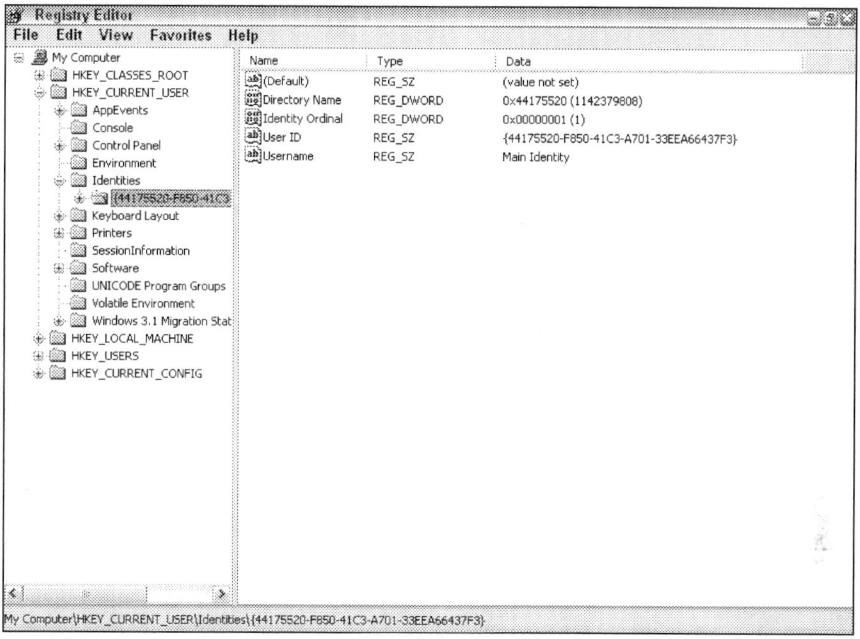

**Figure 11.12.** Windows Registry looks like Windows Explorer, but its contents are much scarier to work with.

To get started performing your own surgery on the registry, click Start, Run, type regedit, and then press Enter.

The registry has five main collections of settings, called hives, which control different aspects of operation. These hives are:

- **HKEY_CLASSES_ROOT.** This is a mega-glossary for Windows. It contains information on file types, objects, and how to handle them.

- **HKEY_CURRENT_USER.** Contains information on the currently-logged-on person. Technically, it's actually just pointers to a subset of information from HKEY_USERS; any changes made here appear in both places.

- **HKEY_LOCAL_MACHINE.** All the information about your computer is contained here. It doesn't include information specific to particular users.

- **HKEY_USERS.** This is the master hive for all user-related information, whether logged on or not. When you log on, your information is copied from here to HKEY_CURRENT_USER.

- **HKEY_CURRENT_CONFIG.** Contains pointers to other keys in other hives.

Click a plus sign next to a registry hive, or double-click it. In each hive are keys that contain data in a particular format. The keys — Microsoft's term for "settings" — are determined by programmers, while the values are data that the program can use. For example, a key could be called "DefaultInstallation" and have a value of "C:\Program Files\SoftwareInstalledHere." Values also have a particular data type, such as string, binary, and DWORD or double word length, referring to programming data types rather than English sentences jammed together.

When editing the registry you must know three things:

1. The registry key's exact name and location

2. The value's data type

3. The value or permissible values for the key

There are many places you can find suggestions of keys to edit for results that aren't otherwise available through Windows. If you are looking primarily for user interface changes, then install TweakUI (covered in Chapter 3), which has numerous settings you can edit without hacking into the registry. There are Web sites available with tweaks, some good, some indeterminate; with all edits, do some research first before changing registry values. One site that usually has good information is www.tweakxp.com. You can search different categories to find out if someone has figured out how to change a setting you're interested in.

As every reference will tell you, if you make the wrong changes you can render your system inoperable.

Before editing the registry you should make a backup of part or all of it. The two easiest ways are to create a system restore point and to export the current registry key and its value. To find out how to create system restore points see Chapter 12. To export a registry key, open regedit and browse to the key you are about to change. Select the key (or, if you're especially paranoid, the parent key), click File, Export, type a name for your exported key (see Figure 11.13), browse to a location where you'd like to save the key, and then click Save.

**Watch Out!**

Making the wrong registry changes can render your system inoperable. I'm not kidding. Do not use regedit if you do not want to assume this risk — use TweakUI or other third-party tools to change registry settings for you.

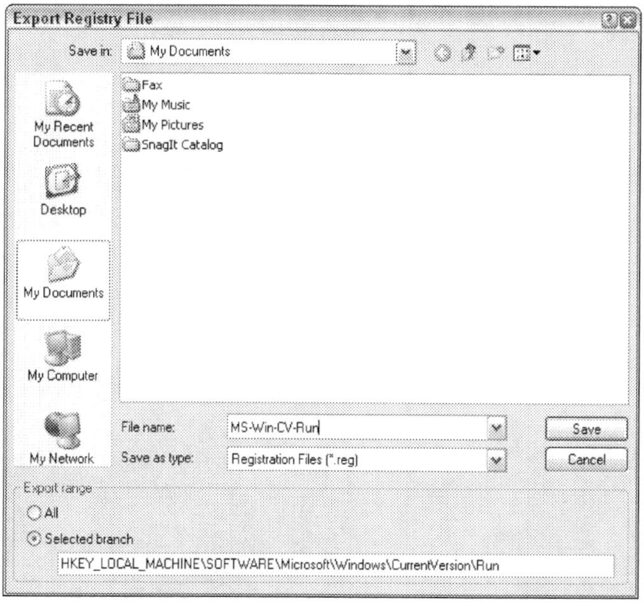

**Figure 11.13.** Give your exported key a useful name so you can import it to the proper location without guessing.

To edit a registry key, double-click the key. An edit dialog box appears (see Figure 11.14). Select the base if necessary, type the new value in the box provided, and then click OK.

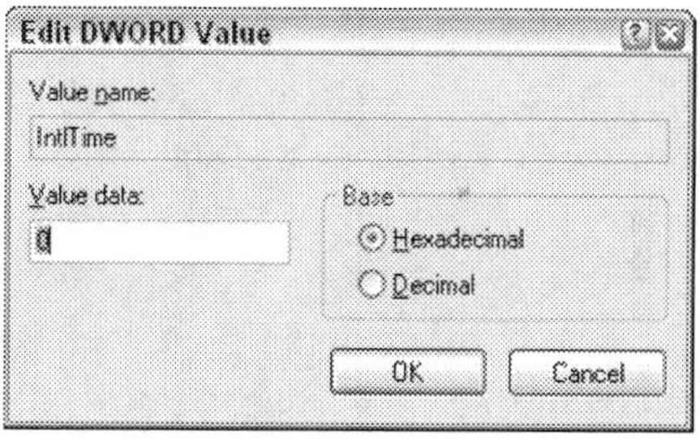

Sometimes you need to create a new registry key, especially when you're tapping into undocumented settings that curious users have discovered. To create a new key, right-click anywhere in the right pane, click New, and then click Key. Type the key name you want to create and then click OK.

**Figure 11.14.** DWORD values can be entered in decimal or hex format; the dialog box automatically converts between them if needed.

You can then enter a value for the key by right-clicking it, clicking New, and then clicking the data type for your new value. Enter in the data and click OK (see Figure 11.15).

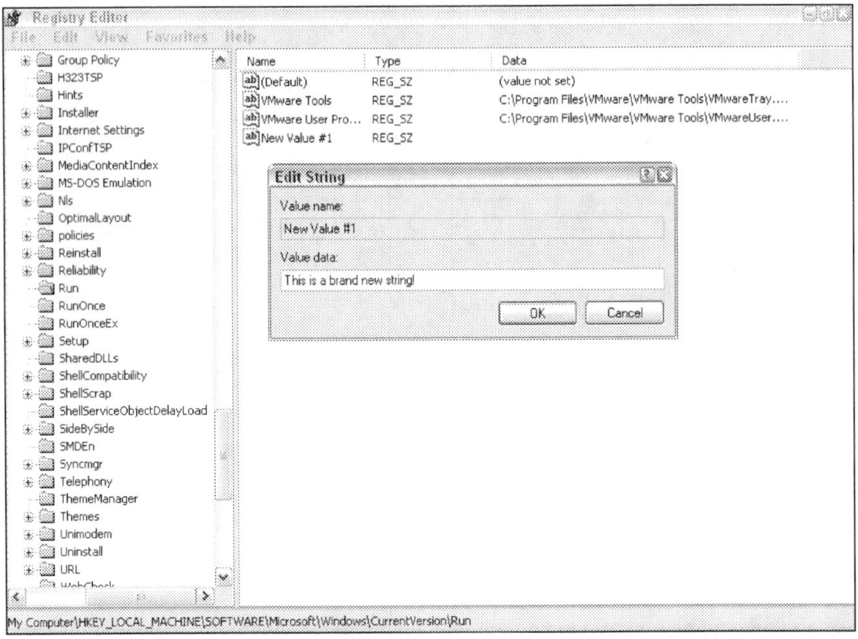

**Figure 11.15.** New key values are easy to add.

Depending on the component, service, or application you are working with, your registry change may take effect immediately or it may require you to restart the service or application. Some keys require a reboot of Windows itself.

In some cases there are exported registry key files available, usually ending in .reg, that contain the necessary keys and values. Importing the keys can be quicker than slogging through the registry, plus you are assured that the syntax and values are correct. To import a registry key (such as an example of the above, or one you backed up and want to restore), open regedit, click File, Import, select the file, and then click Open (see Figure 11.16). You should get an information dialog box stating the file was successfully imported into the registry.

A quicker import method is to double-click the .reg file. Windows will ask if you are sure you want to import the data; if you are, click Yes. The data is then imported.

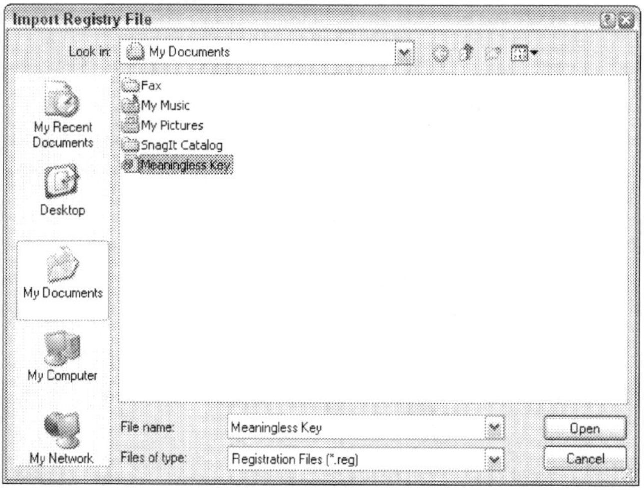

**Figure 11.16.** Importing keys is faster and easier than hand-typing the data.

## Tracking down the elusive registry

With all the effort Microsoft put into creating a monolithic settings repository, logic states that it should also be a single file on the hard drive. However, the registry is actually several files, some of which may not be on the local hard drive! The two "real" registry hives are HKEY_USERS and HKEY_LOCAL_MACHINE — the other hives contain pointers to those two hives.

HKEY_LOCAL_MACHINE has five subkeys: Hardware, SAM [security account manager], Security, Software, and System. All but Hardware are located at Windows\system32\config using the appropriate name in all capitals and without an extension (example: SAM). Hardware is dynamically generated at boot time and doesn't exist as a file on disk.

HKEY_USERS is a collection of pointers to user profiles which are stored at Documents and Settings\%username%\ntuser.dat.

These files can only be backed up by registry-aware utilities, including Windows Backup; you cannot manually copy them to another location. The only exception is ntuser.dat files for anyone other than the logged-on user; you can back those up or manually copy them.

# Start and stop services

At the most basic level, services are programs that need to run whether or not a user is logged on to the system. An example is the Print Spooler service that lets others send print jobs to the printer queue on your computer without your being logged on. Some services start after you log on, such as video card helper applications; there's no sense in having them consume resources when no one is logged on to the computer, so they load when a user logs on.

The Services snap-in (see Figure 11.17) is used to see which services are available, which are running, and whether they are set to start up or are disabled. To see the snap-in, click Start, Run, type services.msc, and then press Enter. You can also see the snap-in by clicking Start, Administrative Tools, and then Services.

In this window you can start, pause, stop, or restart a service. Highlight the service and then click the appropriate toolbar button. Pausing or restarting services may be needed if the service seems "stuck," as sometimes happens with print queues.

Somewhat more useful to know is the service's startup type. You can see the startup type listed in the Services snap-in, but it may not be set to the correct type for your computer. Double-click a service to open the service properties dialog box (see Figure 11.18).

| Name | Description | Status | Startup Type | Log On As |
|---|---|---|---|---|
| Alerter | Notifies selected users and comput... | | Disabled | Local Service |
| Application Layer Gateway Service | Provides support for 3rd party pro... | Started | Manual | Local Service |
| Application Management | Provides software installation servi... | | Manual | Local System |
| Automatic Updates | Enables the download and installati... | Started | Automatic | Local System |
| Background Intelligent Transfer ... | Transfers files in the background u... | | Manual | Local System |
| ClipBook | Enables ClipBook Viewer to store in... | | Disabled | Local System |
| COM+ Event System | Supports System Event Notificatio... | Started | Manual | Local System |
| COM+ System Application | Manages the configuration and tra... | | Manual | Local System |
| Computer Browser | Maintains an updated list of compu... | | Automatic | Local System |
| Cryptographic Services | Provides three management servic... | Started | Automatic | Local System |
| DCOM Server Process Launcher | Provides launch functionality for D... | Started | Automatic | Local System |
| DHCP Client | Manages network configuration by... | Started | Automatic | Local System |
| Distributed Link Tracking Client | Maintains links between NTFS files ... | Started | Automatic | Local System |
| Distributed Transaction Coordin... | Coordinates transactions that spa... | | Manual | Network S... |
| DNS Client | Resolves and caches Domain Name... | Started | Automatic | Network S... |
| Error Reporting Service | Allows error reporting for services ... | Started | Automatic | Local System |
| Event Log | Enables event log messages issued... | Started | Automatic | Local System |
| Fast User Switching Compatibility | Provides management for applicati... | Started | Manual | Local System |
| Fax | Enables you to send and receive f... | Started | Automatic | Local System |
| Help and Support | Enables Help and Support Center t... | Started | Automatic | Local System |
| HTTP SSL | This service implements the secure... | | Manual | Local System |
| Human Interface Device Access | Enables generic input access to Hu... | | Disabled | Local System |
| IMAPI CD-Burning COM Service | Manages CD recording using Imag... | | Manual | Local System |
| Indexing Service | Indexes contents and properties o... | | Manual | Local System |
| IPSEC Services | Manages IP security policy and sta... | Started | Automatic | Local System |
| Logical Disk Manager | Detects and monitors new hard dis | Started | Automatic | Local System |

**Figure 11.17.** The Services snap-in is a lengthy listing of what is currently running under the hood of your computer.

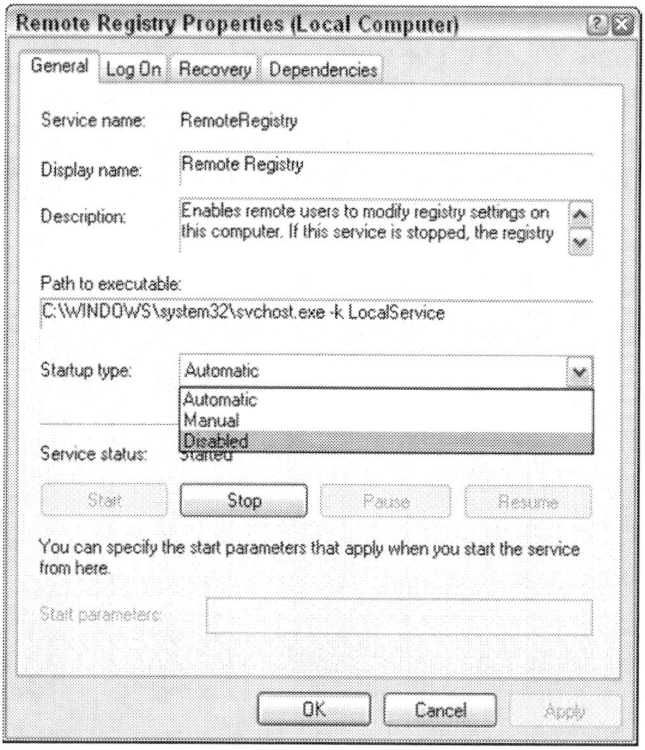

**Figure 11.18.** You can change the startup type for each service depending on what you want running at boot time.

The most useful setting in this dialog box is the Startup type. The drop-down list box lets you set how you want the service to behave when the system reboots. The choices are:

■ **Automatic.** The service starts when the computer boots up. This is the setting for must-have services, or for services that would severely limit functionality if they weren't available.

■ **Manual.** The service will start if it is called by an application, though this is not always the case. Windows Installation, in particular, seems to have problems when in Manual mode.

■ **Disabled.** The service is not available and cannot be started. You must change the status to manual or automatic before you can start the service.

To change a service's status, select the status from the drop-down list and then click OK. The startup type changes in the Services snap-in to the new startup type.

## What are all these services for?

The services listed in the services snap-in don't always tell you what they are for, and some are downright cryptic. A common phrase is "If this service is disabled, any services that explicitly depend on it will fail to start." Not much help when you don't know what a service does in the first place.

Fortunately there is a Web site dedicated to enumerating the Windows XP services and telling you what they do. Visit The Elder Geek's Web site at www.theeldergeek.com/services_guide.htm for guidance on what you can safely set to manual or even disable. Turning off services is one of the easiest, non-intrusive ways to reduce potential attack surface.

If you have an account with local administration rights on another computer, you can connect to it and manage its services remotely. This can be extremely useful, especially when working to clear a print queue as mentioned previously. In the snap-in's left pane, right-click Services and then click Connect to another computer. You can then type in the computer name or browse the network. You will be asked for log on credentials; provide them, and you are now connected to the Services manager on the other computer.

# Work with Scheduled Tasks

Scheduled Tasks, which shows up in the Services list as Task Scheduler, is a familiar program from the Windows 9x days. Its purpose in life is to run services or applications when it's told to, as often as it's told to. Most operating systems have similar utilities or services so that things like system maintenance or periodic update checks can run.

**Hack**

Services can be started and stopped at the command line. Type net start "service name" or net stop "service name" and then press Enter. "Service name" is the name found in the Services snap-in, such as Windows Image Acquisition. The quotes are needed if the service name contains spaces.

To set up a new scheduled task, click Start, All Programs, Accessories, System Tools, and then Scheduled Tasks. The Scheduled Tasks window appears. Click Add Scheduled Task. The Scheduled Task Wizard appears (see Figure 11.19). Click Next.

A list of programs is shown to you, but these are not all the programs that are installed or available. Disk Defragmenter, for example, is not shown in the list. You can choose an application or you can browse for one. When you have selected an application, click Next.

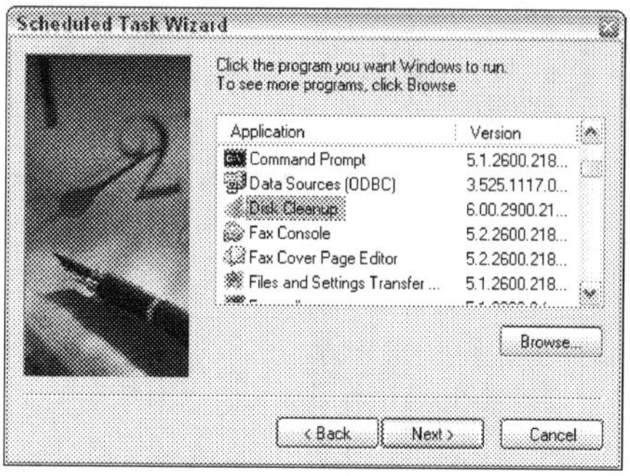

**Figure 11.19.** You can choose an application from the list or browse to the one you want to run.

Type a name for the task in the space provided. Select how often you want the task to run — daily, weekly, or even one time only. Click Next. Depending on your previous choice, you are given a selection of days, dates, and times for your task to run (see Figure 11.20). Click Next.

You now must enter the machine name and user account for your application. It defaults to using the current machine and user logged on, which for nearly all cases is sufficient. Type and confirm your password. Click Next.

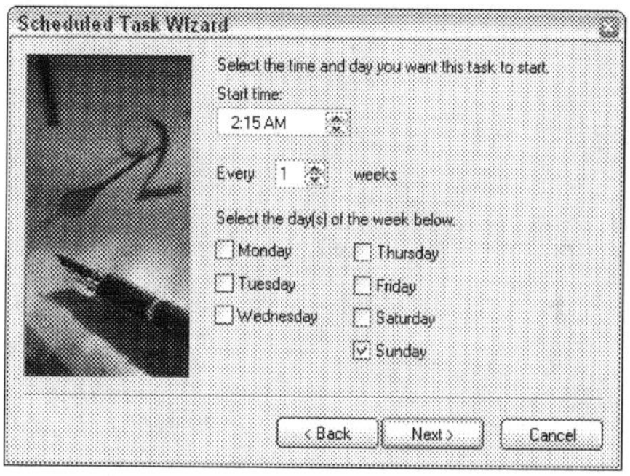

The final dialog box lets you review your settings; click Back to change any of them. You can also select to open the advanced properties dialog box for a task when the

**Figure 11.20.** Set the days and times you want your task to run.

wizard is done. Click Finish. Your task appears in the Scheduled Tasks window.

Double-clicking your new task opens the Task Properties dialog box, where you can fine-tune or adjust any settings without having to delete and re-create your task.

---

### When tasks won't run

When you create a task, you should run it before relying on Task Scheduler to do the work for you. If it doesn't run, check the following:

- Use the correct command-line options. Many Windows applications use command-line options, also called switches, at startup to control how they run. Some applications have switches to fully automate them, others don't. Check the documentation (or search the Help and Support Center) for the options your program uses. Double-click the task and add the options to the end of the Run box.

- The task isn't running. You may have specified the task to run under another user's account. If that user logs on, then Fast User Switching is in effect, the task is running under his name, not yours.

- The task didn't run when scheduled. Your computer may have been turned off, in hibernation mode, or low on battery power. Check the Event Log to see if the task is listed as a Missed Task, and try running it manually.

---

## Just the facts

- System Information and Device Manager contain anything worth knowing about your computer's hardware and its operation.

- Task Manager can be your first indication that something is going wrong with your computer.

- It's worth checking your Event Viewer logs to see if something is failing, or is about to.

- Determine which services are truly necessary on your computer, and set the others to manual or disabled.

# Working with Hard Drives

**W**indows XP, like earlier versions of Windows, offers a number of system tools to keep your computer — hardware and software — running smoothly. This chapter illustrates how you can manage your hard drives and make them into more than simple storage space: spanning, extending, and quotas are all discussed in this chapter.

This chapter will also detail the use of backup devices or UPS, to protect your data as well as how to properly back up your data. Finally, I will show you how to maximize your screen space by using multiple monitors for a single computer.

## Improve system performance

Managing your machine's performance is a job unto itself; in fact, it's almost like being a parent. If you'd like a better analogy, maintaining your machine is similar to taking care of your car: Both must be cleaned, regularly maintained, inspected, checked for aging parts, and so on.

Fortunately, keeping on top of your system performance is largely a routine, automated task nowadays. There are a number of excellent programs that monitor your system and repair errors, including Norton SystemWorks or McAfee Office. However, let's not discount Microsoft XP's offering. While it's hard to say if the tools have actually improved over the years, it's safe to say the amount of available tools has certainly increased.

In addition to the standard offering of a character map, disk cleanup, and disk defragmenter, the System Tools menu (see Figure 12.1) has been expanded to add:

- Backup (XP Pro only)
- Files and Settings Transfer Wizard
- Scheduled Tasks
- Security Center
- System Information
- System Restore
- Activate Windows (XP Pro only)

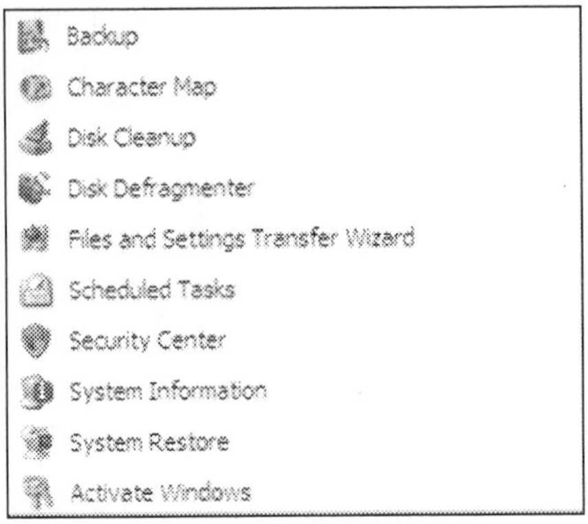

| Backup |
| Character Map |
| Disk Cleanup |
| Disk Defragmenter |
| Files and Settings Transfer Wizard |
| Scheduled Tasks |
| Security Center |
| System Information |
| System Restore |
| Activate Windows |

**Figure 12.1.** The System Tools menu.

If you've decided to use the tools on hand, you have about half the items you'll need to keep your machine running smoothly. What is most surprising about Microsoft XP's system tools is that despite years of security breaches and worm/virus scares, Microsoft hasn't thought to integrate a virus or adware package into the system tools. Although most new computers feature trial antivirus software, you are still forced to go to a third-party for this ultimate system tool. Let's review the tools that are available for Microsoft Windows XP (Home and Professional).

## Character Map

The Character Map doesn't do much in the way of improving system performance, but it is a helpful little utility that may prove invaluable for out-of-the-ordinary characters such as foreign currency symbols, math symbols; for drawings; for different characters from languages such as Arabic or Japanese; or for accents for Spanish or French words. The Character Map lets you simply select and copy the character to the clipboard, and it provides the ASCII code as well.

**Inside Scoop**

Use ASCII codes to quickly apply foreign language accents or other special characters. You can insert an ASCII code into your document by pressing the Alt key and entering a three digit numeric code.

# Disk Cleanup

The Disk Cleanup feature lets you clean up temporary files, Internet files, Web Client files, Office Setup files, or the Recycle Bin in any combination. Unfortunately, this has always been one of the weaker links in the Windows operating system. Notoriously slow, it can take a long time to scan your system for files and if you are running a similar third-party program, the Disk Cleanup feature seems even slower (and stops working on occasion). This is especially the case if Norton CleanSweep is installed.

There are some positives to this utility, though. Using the More Options tab (see Figure 12.2) allows you to lighten your hard drive by uninstalling little-used applications or even Windows XP components right then and there — click Clean up, and the Add or Remove Programs window appears.

**Figure 12.2.** The More Options tab of the Disk Cleanup dialog box.

# Disk Defragmenter

The Disk Defragmenter is a valuable tool that analyzes your hard drives to check for file fragmentation. If this number is too high versus the percentage of free space, the Disk Defragmenter will defragment your hard drive. The utility provides a very detailed report on the status of your hard drive and individual files.

You should run this utility fairly regularly, depending on how often you use your machine. A good sign that your machine is fragmented is when your machine and applications run markedly slower for no apparent reason.

# Backup

The Backup feature, like many Microsoft utilities, is a bare-boned utility. Like many other Windows applications, the Backup feature is used with the help of a wizard. If you're a seasoned veteran you may opt to use the Advanced mode, discussed later in this section. The Windows Backup utility is fine, but it's not Microsoft's specialty or a flagship product or feature. This is another situation where it may be best to use more specialized, third-party software or, quite simply, a removable USB drive that has proprietary software and is designed to easily perform system backups.

How often should you back up? It depends on how much you use your computer as well as the sensitivity of your data. Your average home user should back up at the very minimum once a month. Your computer configuration and layout can greatly change over a short period of time — you may have a new operating system, new applications, new documents, and so on. You certainly do not want to be in the position of losing your hard drive and then finding that your last backup was from six months ago and does not have any of your files or applications on it. If possible, try to schedule a system backup once a week.

Sensitive data/files are another matter. If you have sensitive data on your computer, not only should it be backed up on a daily basis, but you should also consider encrypting this data, especially if you use a laptop or a computer that is frequently accessed by other users. (For more on encryption, see Chapter 5.) Get in the habit of using a thumb drive to back up important files, such as the My Documents folder.

---

**Watch Out!**

If you must defragment a drive, it is best to do it when you have downtime. For example, good times would be late in the evening (letting it run during the night) or on the weekend. Depending on the size of your hard drive and the fragmentation rate, this procedure can take a long time — in some cases, well over an hour.

## Okay, I can't take it anymore! What is a thumb drive? What is a removable drive?

It's true; this chapter tends to refer to these little gadgets quite a bit.

Not so long ago, computer-friendly people faced a dilemma: how to store or transport data with the least amount of risk.

At the time, the options were a 5.25" floppy disk (literally, a floppy disk) or a 3.5" diskette. Iomega brought out the Zip disk which could hold 100MB of data in an oversize blue drive. That led to the upgraded version, called a Jazz drive which could hold 1GB. These eventually faded away as hard drives held more data, making these storage device sizes (especially Zip) obsolete. Iomega lost its luster (perhaps in part to the literal size of the disks, the price, or the legendary click of death — a familiar term for the clicking noise that Iomega drives would make before breaking).

Finally, a legitimate solution to data storage for the ever increasing hard drive arrived. External hard drives, connected to your computer using a SCSI bus and SCSI cable, hit the market. These drives were the founding fathers of our current external drives, which are now connected via an IEEE 1394, or FireWire, connector or even using USB. Plug and play was finally something more than a mouse or a keyboard! These external drives are great for enhancing your data storage capacity, but they're also great if you are often on the road and often need to use the same files over several computers. Finally, many of these drives are designed to be a backup system where you can perform a one-touch system backup.

This is also the time that companies such as SanDisk put out the cruzer mini thumb drive. These devices are named for exactly the reason you think — they are literally the size of a thumb and easily plug into an open USB port. Despite the size, they offer storage sizes from 128MB to 4GB. Despite the ever increasing storage size, these drives have come down in price. These devices are excellent for transferring files or backing up mail folders, applications, or even entertainment files.

**Watch Out!**

Remember that the Windows XP Backup utility is only available for Windows XP Professional.

The Wizard mode (which is the default mode until you deselect the checkbox) is straightforward. It asks you if you want to either back up or restore files and settings. If this is the first time you use the Backup feature, you must select Backup and then select which files to back up (see Figure 12.3). The options are wide ranging: your personal My Documents folder and settings, all My Documents folders and settings on the machine, the entire machine, or selected information that you choose.

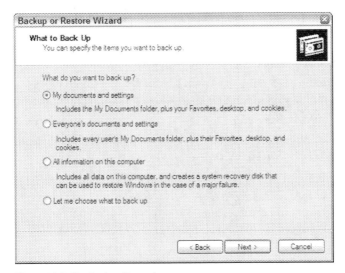

**Figure 12.3.** The Backup file options.

Once you decide which information to back up, you must decide where you want to store it and then choose a filename. It's best to store the backup on a removable device, such as a thumb drive, a removable USB hard drive, or a floppy disk. You could even save it to your disk and then burn it to a CD-R. Keep a copy on your hard drive, but it's always good to have a second or third source (like one listed above) to make sure you are safe. Validate your selection and you're almost done — you can either Finish or go the Advanced screen that is found on the Completing the Backup or Restore Wizard, which allows you to select one of five backup types, each of them followed by a brief description.

The five backup types are as follows:

- **Normal.** Selected files are backed up and marked as such.

- **Copy.** Selected files are backed up, but are not marked as backed up.

- **Incremental.** Backs up files that were created or modified since the last backup.

- **Differential.** Backs up files that were created or modified since the last backup, but does not mark these files as backed up.

- **Daily.** Backs up files created or modified today.

If you clicked Advanced, in the next wizard screen you can ask the Backup utility to verify backup data once finished, to use hardware compression (if available), or to disable volume shadow copy. Don't worry; a brief description appears after each option to help make the right choice. The next wizard screen allows you to decide to append or replace the backup if your data already contains backups. Select when to start the backup and click Finish.

The Restore feature, which is found on the second page of the Backup or Restore Wizard, works in a similar fashion; select a backup file to restore and follow each step of the wizard. Unfortunately, things can become slightly confusing if you use the Restore feature in the Advanced mode instead of the Wizard mode (see Figure 12.4). The operations in Advanced mode are not particularly difficult, especially if you've already used the Backup utility before; however, the nomenclature is a little strange.

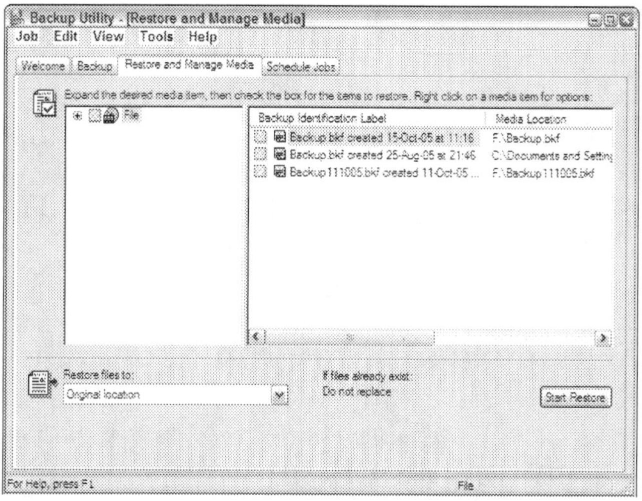

**Figure 12.4.** The Restore feature in the Advanced mode.

The Welcome tab of the Advanced Mode window proposes three different functions: Backup Wizard, Restore Wizard, and Automated System Recovery Wizard (see Figure 12.5). These wizards are similar to the easier Wizard mode. One wonders why they opted to use the term "wizard" or even the same concept in an advanced feature. This is another example of unusual nomenclature that Microsoft uses.

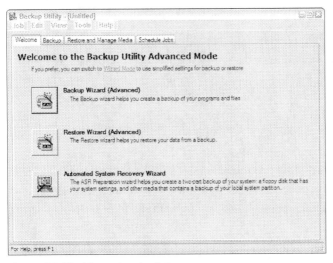

**Figure 12.5.** The Advanced mode window.

The Backup tab of the Advanced mode lets you choose files and folders to back up. Simply select the corresponding check boxes, enter a backup name, and click the Start Backup button.

The Restore and Manage Media tab of the Advanced mode looks similar to the Restore window in that you select the desired backup file; select the restore directory and then click the Start Restore button.

The Schedule Jobs tab in the Advanced mode allows you to select a date from a calendar and schedule a backup. Once you select a date and click Add Job, the Backup Wizard (Advanced) appears.

If you feel that you are in over your head with the Advanced mode and decide not to use its backup functions, you can go back to the Wizard mode from the Tools menu.

The Tools menu also allows you to select any of the tasks listed in the Welcome tab of the Advanced mode window or set a variety of preferences in the Options menu. The Options menu lets you set parameters for restoring, backup type, backup logs, and excluding files.

# Create automated system recovery disks

This feature is the sort of the new and improved version of the Emergency Repair Disk utility in Windows NT. It is only available in Windows XP Professional. I'm not very sure why it's called Automated — everything is done manually — except that it automatically selects the system files to back up. This feature is really a skeleton backup; it only backs up system files. Your data files are not backed up, so it's important to use the regular Backup utility often.

The Automated System Recovery feature creates a two-part backup of your machine; essential system files and settings are stored on a floppy and your disk is backed up as a backup file to another media. The floppy drive acts as a "recovery disk." If you do not have a traditional floppy drive, you will not be able to use this option.

This process is done from the Advanced Window of the Backup utility (as discussed in the section "Backup," earlier in this chapter). In the Welcome tab, simply click the Automated System Recovery Wizard button.

The first step is to back up your system by giving it a name and selecting a location for it (see Figure 12.6). By default, Windows XP chooses a Normal backup, which uses select files and settings. You can manually modify which files should be included in the file; however, keep in mind that the more you select, the longer it will take to back up. You can program your backup, if desired, or you can just run it. Once you complete this and run the backup, you will be asked to insert a floppy disk. If, like many modern systems, you do not have a floppy drive, you will instead be asked to close the window and you are finished.

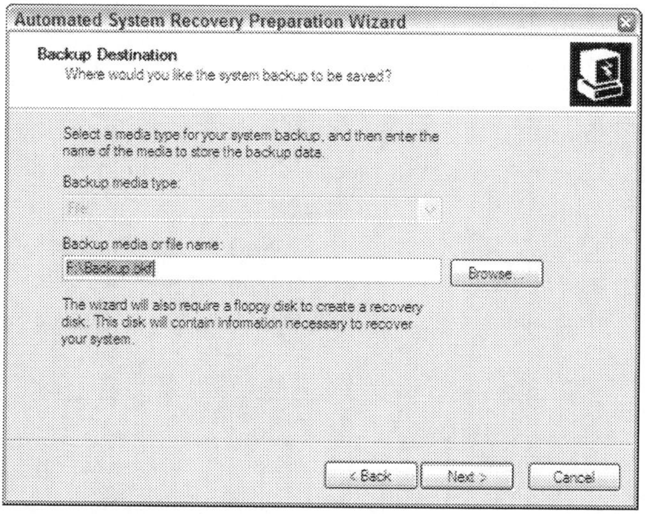

**Figure 12.6.** Choosing a location for your backup.

**Watch Out!**

This is a very simplistic, bare-boned method to backing up your machine. It provides a skeleton backup of your machine in case of disk failure. Files, such as those in the My Documents folder, are not backed up in this process.

Curiously enough, Microsoft did not add this basic utility to Windows XP Home edition. However, hope is not lost if your machine shipped with the Home edition — there is a way around this problem. Microsoft provides system restore points, which takes a snapshot of your computer and uses it to restore your computer to an earlier point in time.

## Files and Settings Transfer Wizard

The Files and Settings Transfer Wizard is a helpful utility available for both XP Home and Professional. Its purpose is to help you transfer files and settings from an old computer to a new computer.

The utility lets you transfer a number of settings including Internet Explorer and Outlook Express settings as well as desktop and display settings and Internet dialup connections.

Microsoft recommends using a direct cable connection or a network for transferring files. In fact, Windows even offers you a help topic on the main page of the wizard so that you can brush up on connecting computers (see Figure 12.7). However, if you are not comfortable with networking or dealing with cables, then you can easily (and without hassle) transfer files and data using removable media — such as a thumb drive — or by storing data in a folder on your hard drive and then burning the data to CD.

What is the rationale for this? Why not just directly transfer data between two machines via a cable? One reason for this is that using one of the suggestions listed above means that you now have a backup of these files. Should your computer crash or a file corrupt, you have an accessible replacement, which is especially important if you use a laptop and are on the road.

Once you start the wizard, you must first select if you are the "new" or "old" computer (see Figure 12.8). In other words, are you transferring the files and settings or receiving them? Choose Old computer. Selecting it and moving on to the next menu lets you decide on one of four transfer methods.

**Watch Out!**

In order to use this utility, you must be running Windows 95 or later (Windows 98, Windows 98SE, Windows ME, Windows NT 4.0, Windows 2000, Windows XP, and Windows Server 2003) on the old machine.

**Figure 12.7.** The first page of the Files and Settings Transfer Wizard.

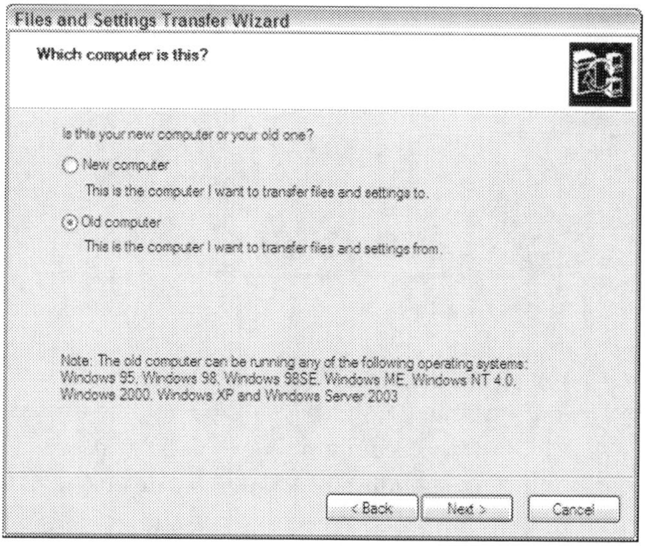

**Figure 12.8.** Specify a computer in the Files and Settings Transfer Wizard.

You may transfer files via these methods, as shown in Figure 12.9:

- **Direct cable.** This is what it sounds like using a PC to PC serial cable. The first page of the wizard provides a help topic on this option.

- **Home or small office network.** This option is only available if you have a home or small office network. If not, it is dimmed.

- **Floppy drive or other removable media.** This option allows you to use any removable media such as thumb drives, USB/FireWire drives, or even floppy disks. Given the propensity of floppy drives to go wobbly (corrupt), try using one of the removable media types. CD-ROM or DVD-ROM drives cannot be used here.

- **Other.** This option lets you save settings and files to a hard drive or network drive. This option is good if you use a network drive as a backup or an archive. It's also a good option if you wish to save it to your desktop and then burn it to CD-RW.

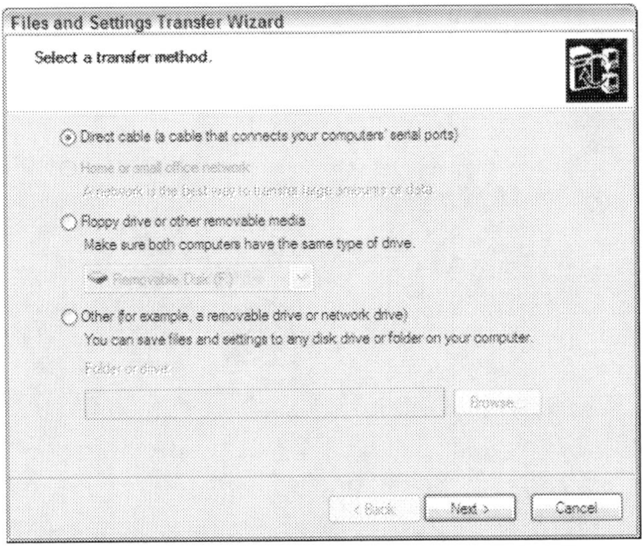

Files and Settings Transfer Wizard

Select a transfer method.

- ⊙ Direct cable (a cable that connects your computers' serial ports)
  - Home or small office network
  - A network is the best way to transfer large amounts of data.
- ○ Floppy drive or other removable media
  - Make sure both computers have the same type of drive.
    - 💾 Removable Disk (F:) ⌄
- ○ Other (for example, a removable drive or network drive)
  - You can save files and settings to any disk drive or folder on your computer.
  - Folder or drive:
    - [                    ]  [ Browse... ]

[ < Back ]  [ Next > ]  [ Cancel ]

**Figure 12.9.** Transfer methods in the Files and Settings Transfer Wizard.

The next window lets you choose between saving settings, files, or both. Depending on your selection, a box on the right side of the window displays the specific file types as well as which program settings will be transferred. Of course, you can select the corresponding check box on this page and customize your list. In this event, the next screen lets you add, modify, or remove items.

**Watch Out!**

If you decide to use the third option, the removable media must be plugged in and turned on in order for it to appear in the drop-down list. If you plug in the drive after the wizard is open, the drive will not appear as an option. You will need to quit the utility and start over.

Once you move on to the next page, the wizard may remind you (if necessary) to install certain software programs on your new machine. The old computer then saves and compresses your files and settings.

Importing the settings to the new computer is quite similar; go back to the wizard, select New computer (see Figure 12.8), and then get ready for an odd question. The wizard reminds you that it also needs to be run on the old computer (see Figure 12.10). It offers to create a wizard disk to use on the old machine or use the wizard on the Windows XP CD. Eh? Option four on this page — I don't need the Wizard Disk. I have already collected my files and settings from my old computer — ideally will be the right option for you. If not, you should cancel and go back and collect the files and settings. Of course, Windows does give you other options: create a wizard disk on a floppy or removable drive; create a wizard disk using the wizard on the Windows XP CD; or use the wizard disk you already have. Once you click Next, the wizard asks you where to look for the files and then go! The wizard will then import your settings to the new computer.

**Files and Settings Transfer Wizard**

Do you have a Windows XP CD?

You will also need to run this wizard on your old computer. You can either create a wizard disk to use on your old computer, or use the wizard from the Windows XP CD.

To create a Wizard Disk, insert a blank, formatted disk into this computer's disk drive. Make sure the old computer has the same type of drive.

○ I want to create a Wizard Disk in the following drive:

    Removable Disk (F:)

○ I already have a Wizard Disk.

    I will use the wizard from the Windows XP CD.

⊙ I don't need the Wizard Disk. I have already collected my files and settings from my old computer.

    [ < Back ]  [ Next > ]  [ Cancel ]

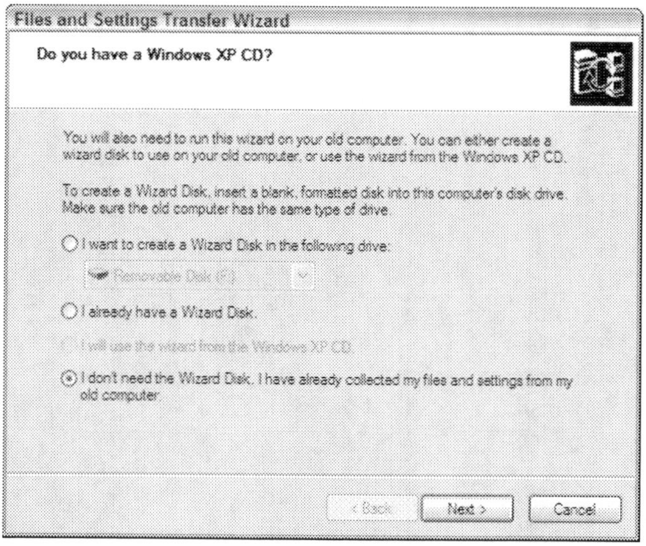

**Figure 12.10.** The wizard reminds you that it also needs to be run on the old computer.

## Watch Out!

Unfortunately, this utility is an all-or-nothing utility; even though there is a Back button, it is dimmed. Should you need to go back to a previous screen your only option is the Cancel button.

# Scheduled Tasks

The Scheduled Tasks utility (see Figure 12.11) lists various bits of information for programmed third-party tasks. These may include programmed antivirus software tasks or firewall-related tasks that often occur unnoticed. This is a very helpful utility, especially if you are someone who is busy and would otherwise forget to manually run important tasks like anti-virus or adware. It is also helpful for people who are not regularly on the computer and would not think to perform such tasks.

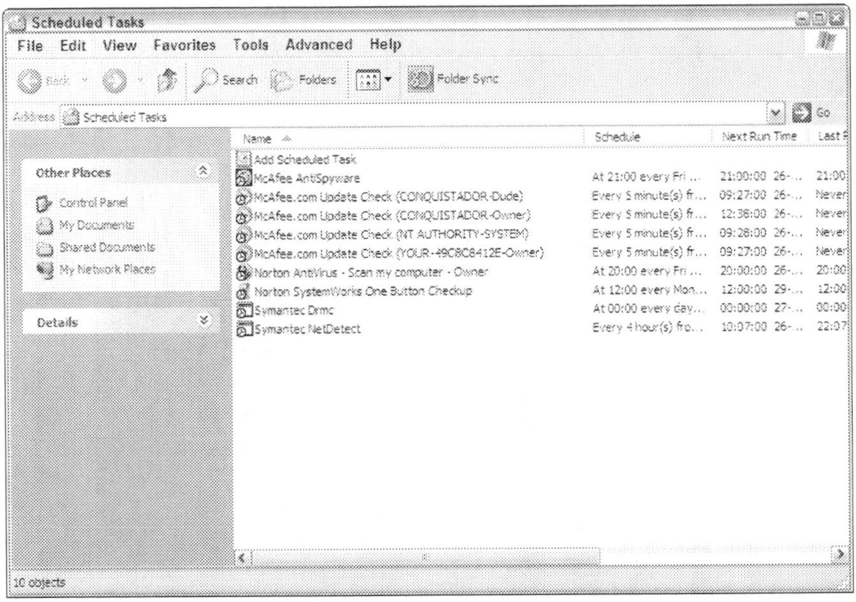

**Figure 12.11.** The Scheduled Tasks window.

Select Add Scheduled Task button to open a wizard (see Figure 12.12) that lets you choose a task for Windows to run. You can then select an application from the list of programs, or you can use Browse to pick the desired program.

Once you've picked your program, you must decide the frequency (see Figure 12.13). Microsoft XP offers seven options, varying from

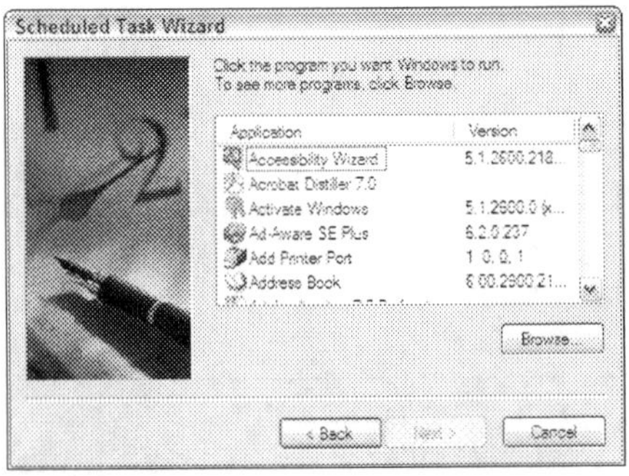

**Figure 12.12.** Choose the program you want Windows to run in the Scheduled Task Wizard.

**Watch Out!**

Keep in mind your computer's usual activity when you program a task. For example, if you want to schedule a system-wide maintenance, set it for Friday evening when you're likely to have more system resources available. If you run too many tasks at the same time during prime working hours, your system may slow down.

daily to monthly to when you log on. The wizard lets you set the time and the frequency with a specified-start date. In the next screen of the wizard, select a user name and add the appropriate password (twice). Once you've done that, the wizard confirms the details all over again.

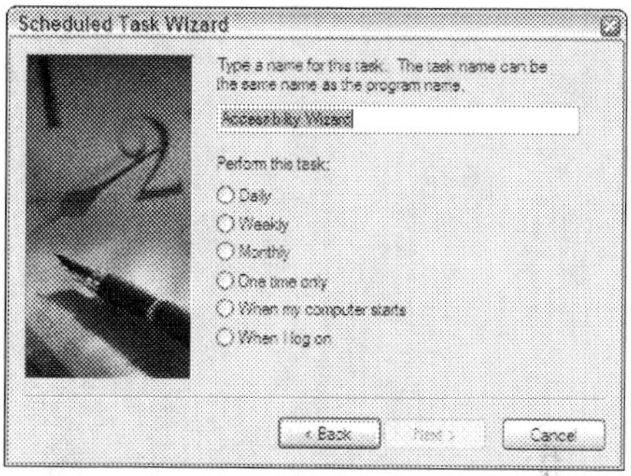

**Figure 12.13.** Choose a frequency in the Scheduled Task Wizard.

# Security Center

The Security Center (see Figure 12.14), which is also available in the Control Panel, is the central location for working with security settings, including Virus Protection and the Windows Firewall (which is now included in Windows XP Service Pack 2). For complete information on the Security Center, please refer to Chapter 6.

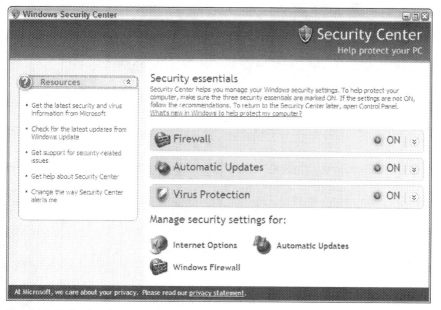

**Figure 12.14.** The Security Center window.

## System Information

The System Information window (see Figure 12.15) is largely informational and doesn't necessarily contribute to improved system performance, but it is still an invaluable system tool. It is helpful if you need to verify your computer's stats in comparison with the minimum requirements for a software program.

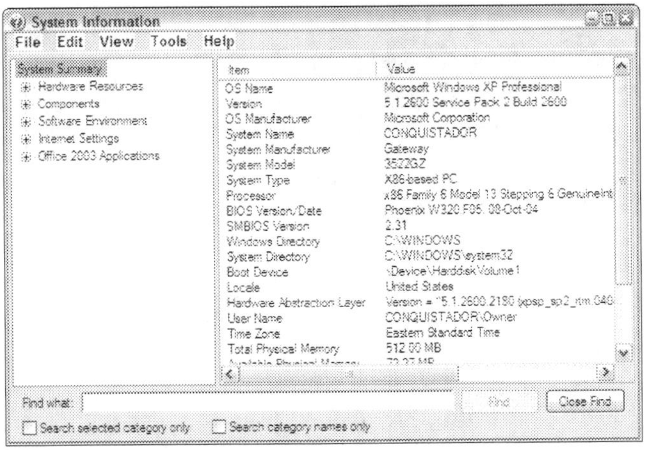

**Figure 12.15.** The System Information window.

This window contains summary information for hardware resources, components, software environment, Internet settings, and Office applications. You can also perform a search for a particular item in the submenus.

The System Information window also features a number of diagnostic utilities that can be run from the Tools menu. These tools include:

- **Net Diagnostics.** This utility scans your machine and provides information about your hardware, software, and network.

- **System Restore.** This launches the System Restore utility detailed in the next section.

- **File Signature Verification Utility.** This utility verifies the authenticity of digitally signed files on your machine.

- **DirectX Diagnostic Tool.** This utility lets you verify and test DirectX components on your machine.

- **Dr. Watson.** This utility checks for crash dumps to analyze problems when they occur.

# System Restore

The System Restore utility (see Figure 12.16) is a helpful utility that lets you re-create your machine based on earlier restore points. These points, called system checkpoints, are created automatically, but you can also opt to manually create a system checkpoint.

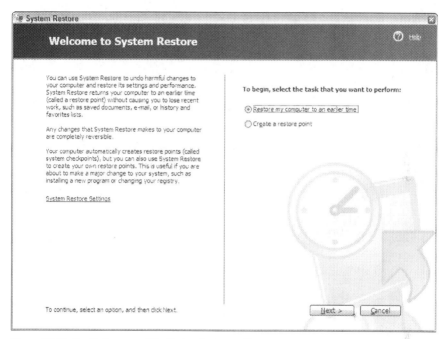

**Figure 12.16.** The first screen of the System Restore utility.

The System Restore feature is available for both Home and Professional editions of Windows XP. Barring any external or third-party backup solutions, this is as close as a Home edition user will get to actually performing a back up using a Windows utility.

This is a "lite" version of a backup; the feature acts like a camera and "freezes" a shot of your computer at a desired point in time. Should you suffer catastrophic hard disk failure, you can recall an existing restore point without the risk of losing important files or documents, favorites, history files, or e-mail.

Windows XP will automatically create a restore point for you if you install a System Restore-compatible application, if you use Windows Update, if an existing restore point is restored, or if an unassigned driver is installed.

One positive aspect of this utility is that it is very easy to roll back any changes made (such as system settings or software installations) if you restore your machine based on a restore point.

The utility is, like most others, presented in a wizard format that allows you to either create a restore point or implement one. On the left pane of the window, there is a System Restore Settings link that is a bit confusing; users may be tempted to skip over it since it looks like an online help topic in a window that looks otherwise pretty straightforward. However, clicking it actually opens up a Settings window where you can opt whether or not to activate the System Restore feature on all drives (see Figure 12.17).

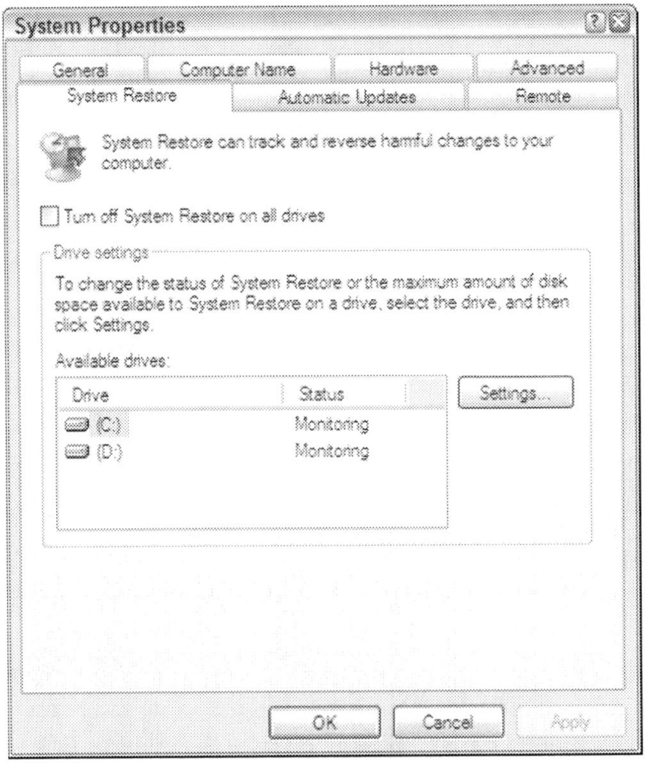

**Figure 12.17.** Choose System Restore settings.

If you decide to create a restore point, simply follow the steps of the wizard and provide a description and that's it. However, it's important to keep in mind that this restore point cannot be changed once generated. If you decide to restore your system based on an earlier restore point, simply pick out the date on the calendar and the restore point from the list on the right (see Figure 12.18).

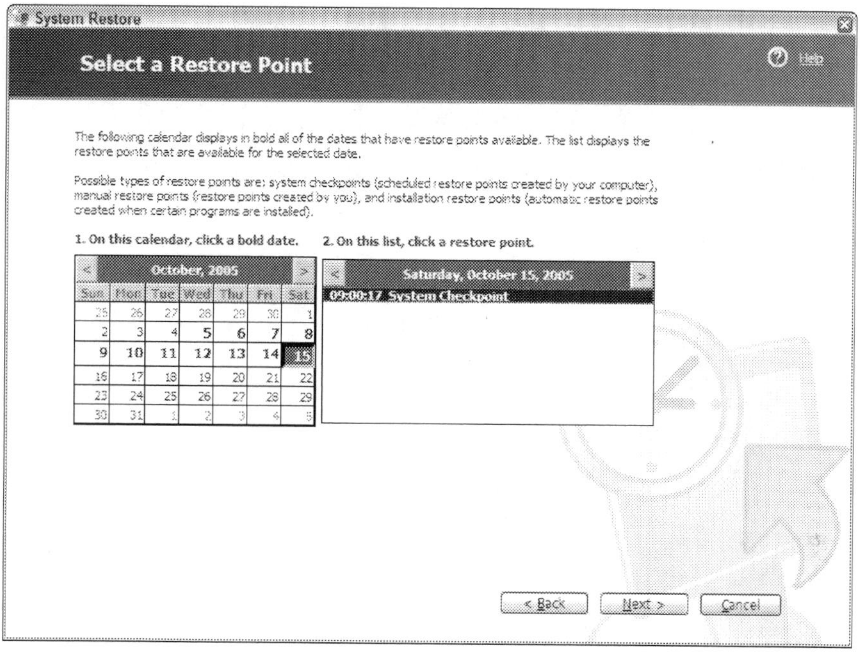

**Figure 12.18.** Choose a System Restore date.

Even though it says you will not lose your work, Microsoft tells you (rightly so) to save your work and close applications before starting the system restore.

# Activate Windows

The Activate Windows utility is only available for Windows XP Pro. Theoretically, your Windows XP operating system should already have been activated. If not, this is where you would do so. To run Windows, you must activate the operating system within the first 30 days in order to use it. If this period expires without activation, the operating system will lock down and only the Activate Windows utility will work.

---

**Hack**

Yes, it hardly seems fair that only Windows XP Professional edition users are having fun. Here's a little secret: Deep inside the Windows XP Home edition CD-ROM is a little file called NTBACKUP.MSI. It is in the <disk drive>: \Valueadd\msft\ntbackup directory. For more information, a quick Google search will reveal all you need to know about this little gem! Enjoy!

---

**Watch Out!**
Do not confuse activation and registration. Activation is an anonymous process that is required in order to use the Windows XP operating system. Registration requires more personal information, is optional, and guarantees product support and updates.

## The bottom line

Windows has increased its offering of utilities that make your system run smoother and take advantage of your powerful processor. Unfortunately, most of them are still nothing to get excited about. Another problem is that some essential features, such as Backup, are only available in the Windows XP Professional edition and not the Home edition. One big change that suggests that Microsoft will re-consider their tool and utility offering is the integrated Windows Firewall. See Chapter 6 for more on that utility.

All things being equal, it is still better to use third-party system performance software such as Norton SystemWorks or McAfee Office. These tools are somewhat pricey — Norton System lists for about $70 on many sites — but worth looking in to. The primary advantages of these applications are that they fully integrate into your system, they consistently monitor your machine, and they run well in the background. Finally, an automatic update feature lets you quickly update your software with updated patches or updated virus definitions as long as you are connected to an active Internet connection. Conversely, Windows system tools seem to wait to be found and don't "play well with the other kids on the playground." The tools do their job, but they simply aren't powerful enough to cover features offered by Norton or McAfee.

## Create new partitions

Hard drives are decreasing in physical size but ever increasing in data size. For serious hard drive hogs — users running multiple operating systems on a home machine, or gamers, or developers who need extra space for their projects — this is great news, especially as the price of drives decreases proportionately with the decrease in size.

There are, however, some drawbacks. Once these disks become fragmented, it takes forever and a day to defragment them. It's also no picnic to reformat a disk. One way to deal with these types of problems is to partition your hard drive; in other words, divide your disk into several drives.

This is a huge benefit if you wish to keep data separate on your hard drive. For example, if you use your machine for both home and professional

**Watch Out!**

If you have a large hard drive, you should consider partitioning the drive. Larger drives take longer to defragment and experienced decreased performance as the drive is filled.

purposes, you might keep personal information on one partition and professional information on a second partition. If you decide to make your machine a dual boot machine (in other words, run two different operating systems on your machine), running Linux on your machine side by side with Windows, for example, creating a second partition (essentially dividing the disk in two or more sections) helps you achieve this. You can also reformat a single partition without losing the content of an entire disk each time you format the partition. You may want to partition your hard drive if you decide to run more than one operating system (in the example above), or if you have a large hard drive (to increase performance), or if you plan on doing any type of testing or development that would require frequent reformatting.

Unfortunately, creating a partition can be a confusing task using the Microsoft Windows XP method. This is area where Windows XP unfortunately falls short; creating and managing a partition is much better handled using Norton PartitionMagic.

There are two ways of using Windows XP to create a new disk partition: via the command line (prompt) or using the Windows interface.

## Use the command line

If you are logged on as an administrator or at least belong to the administrator group, you can create a new partition using the command line (see Figure 12.19).

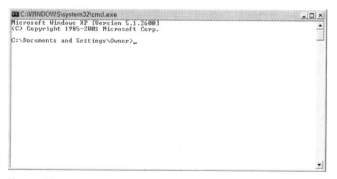

**Figure 12.19.** The Windows Command line.

## How low should I go?

How to partition your hard drive is not always an easy or obvious answer. First, you must decide if your disk is reasonably worth partitioning. Frankly, it may not be worth partitioning a hard disk that is less than 40GB.

Remember, the primary partition will still "host" your operating system and its files, which will eat up a large chunk of drive space. So, cutting a 20GB drive into two 10GB partitions might not be a wise idea — one partition will be dedicated to the operating system and everything that comes with it (My Documents, My Music, and so on), while the other partition will be limited to the remaining 10GB for your applications and files. This space will fill up very quickly, especially if you store a lot of audio or video files.

Determine the size of your partition based on how you plan to use your machine. If you intend to install a second operating system, you'll most likely want to halve the disk, depending on the secondary operating system's requirements. Remember that you can create multiple partitions, so make the sizes reasonable and not random numbers. Never make a drive too small, because you never know when you may unexpectedly need more. 30%/70% or 25%/75% would be reasonable partition examples.

However, this is the more complicated of the two Windows XP options; if you're looking for something simpler, by all means, use the Windows interface, which is covered in the next section.

Creating a partition is done through the use of the Diskpart utility. The Diskpart utility lets you handle objects, for example, and disk partitions through the use of scripts from a command line.

The details surrounding the inner working of this command interpreter are beyond the scope of this book but are detailed by Microsoft at www.microsoft.com/technet/prodtechnol/windowsserver2003/library/ServerHelp/ca099518-dde5-4eac-a1f1-38eff6e3e509.mspx.

**Watch Out!**

If you are used to using other versions of the Windows operating system, such as Windows 2000 Server, please note that the Diskpart utility is not the same as the Diskpar utility found in Windows 2000 Server.

## Use the Windows interface

The Windows interface is the easier of the two methods for creating a new partition, especially if you're not a Windows XP power user.

This is done through the use of the Computer Management console, which is one of the pre-installed Microsoft Management Consoles (MMC). For more information on using a MMC, please refer to Chapter 4.

In the Disk Management part of the console, you can see a "sketch" of the drives available on your machine, including CD-ROM drives and external/USB drives (see Figure 12.20).

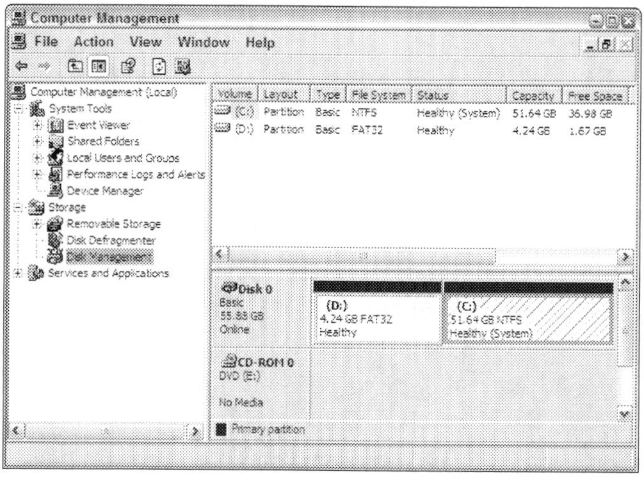

**Figure 12.20.** The Disk Management window.

By right-clicking the desired drive, you can format it, delete partitions, change drive letters, and so on.

## The bottom line

Creating a new partition can be a cumbersome task in Windows XP. Frankly, it seemed much easier when home computing was in its infancy, before Windows. If you are an advanced Windows XP user, use the Windows options that are presented above. It's important to attentively read all available instructions in this book or in the Microsoft Windows XP before attempting to create a partition. Should you inadvertently format your hard drive, there is no undo feature to bring it back.

If you're lacking in confidence when it comes to delicate maneuvers such as this, invest in a third-party application designed for managing disks, drives, and volumes. Norton PartitionMagic is a perfect example of such an application; it uses a wizard format to walk you through hard drive and partition management. For more information on Norton PartitionMagic, please visit www.symantec.com/partitionmagic.

# Create dynamic disks

Dynamic disks are actual physical disks that can only be accessed using Windows 2000 and Windows XP Professional. If you are working on a machine that has Windows XP Home installed, you will not be able to access your dynamic disks, only basic disks such as your hard drive.

Unlike basic disks, dynamic disks can be used to create volumes that span multiple disks or to create fault tolerant volumes. Fault tolerant hardware or software guarantees data integrity in case of hardware failure.

## Before you consider a dynamic disk

There are a couple of hard and fast rules that Windows XP Professional requires you to follow before you can even consider using a dynamic disk over a basic disk.

You cannot install Windows XP Professional on a dynamic disk; however, you can extend the volume in order to do so. Extending a volume is simply incorporating unused disk space into the volume without losing or compromising data.

Dynamic disks cannot be used on portable computers (laptops), on USB or FireWire (IEEE 1394) disks or other removable disks, or disks using SCSI busses. In other words, you need to use a desktop computer with a standard hard drive.

If you are using a dual-boot machine (a machine that has more than one operating system; the desired OS is selected as the machine boots up), the secondary operating system must not be MS-DOS, Windows 95/98, Windows Me (Millennium Edition), Windows NT 4.0, or Windows XP Home. The secondary operating system could be Windows XP Professional or something else, such as Linux Red Hat, Debian, or a UNIX operating system.

## Convert a basic disk to a dynamic disk

"Creating a dynamic disk" basically means converting a basic disk to a dynamic one. Assuming your system meets the criteria listed above, it's a straightforward process. Remember, however, that this is a definitive process. What does this mean? It means you cannot convert your disk back to a basic disk unless you delete every volume on the disk. In other words, the entire hard disk — for example, the data on all drive letters (such as C, D, and F) associated with the disk — will be erased.

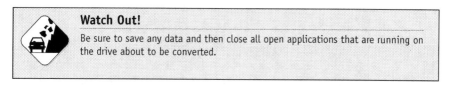

**Watch Out!**

Be sure to save any data and then close all open applications that are running on the drive about to be converted.

In the Disk Management window (see Figure 12.21) of the Computer Management console (which is found in the Administrative Tools page of the Control Panel), right-click the disk on the right side of the window (the disk has a small icon next to it).

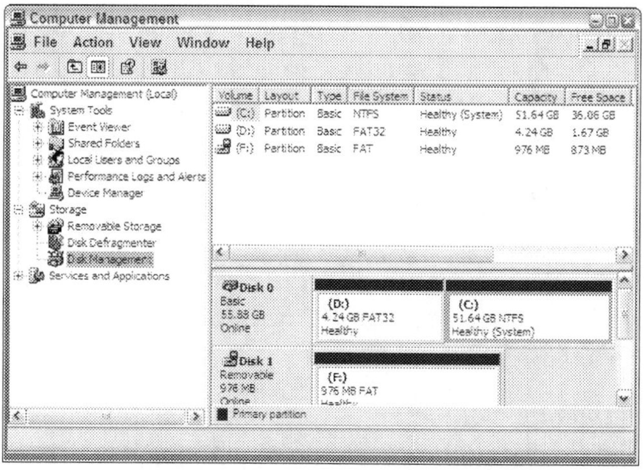

**Figure 12.21.** The Disk Management window.

Select the Convert to Dynamic Disk command from the menu that appears, and you will be asked to select a basic disk(s) for conversion (see Figure 12.22). The mini-wizard will ask you to confirm your selection twice before converting your basic disk to a dynamic disk and confirm that you understand the file systems on the disks will be dismounted. Once you do this, it's as simple as clicking OK. However, do realize that if you convert to Dynamic Disk, you will not be able to mount any other operating systems from any other volume on the disk.

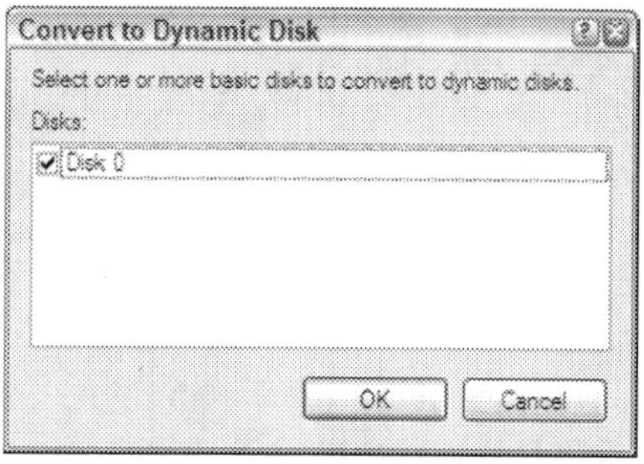

**Figure 12.22.** Select a basic disk to convert to a dynamic disk.

**Inside Scoop**

Creating a dynamic disk is not a perfect science; it is possible that you may encounter an error. One common error I found was a missing or corrupt hal.dll file. To combat this problem, use the Recovery console on the Windows XP installation CD; select the Recovery console to try and repair the current Windows installation. Press Enter when it asks for your administrator password. At the prompt, type bootcfg/list and then type bootcfg/rebuild. Select Y (Yes) and add a name. Once you validate, you can reboot and select this new operating system, and Windows will load.

So, what is the benefit of creating a dynamic disk or converting a basic disk to a dynamic disk? It's a great feature for spanning hard drives and creating a combined logical drive. In other words, if you have some smaller hard drives, say 5GB each, around the house, you can create a dynamic drive of 20GB using the four drives. Keep in mind that Windows XP Professional will allow you to "combine" up to 32 hard drives.

## Work with dynamic disks

Now that you've got your disk converted to a dynamic disk, there is still quite a bit you can do, as I will demonstrate below! You can create or extend a simple or a spanned volume. If the dynamic disk isn't working out for you, you can even delete it (in most cases).

### Create a simple or spanned volume

This is similar to the first step necessary for converting a basic disk to a dynamic disk. You may want to keep a simple volume if you do not plan on installing a second operating system, plan on doing any type of development or testing, or if you have a modest hard drive capacity. Spanned disks are ideal if you have multiple hard drives installed on your machine, all of which have modest capacity, and you'd like to string them together to make one large virtual disk.

Back in the Disk Management window of the Computer Management console (which, as discussed earlier, is in the Administrative Tools page of the Control Panel), right-click the disk on the right side of the window (with the icon next to it) and select New Volume from the menu that appears.

The wizard (see Figure 12.23) lets you decide between creating a simple (one disk), or a spanned (multiple disk) volume. If you opt for the former, select the disks you want to use to install a simple volume from the Selected dynamic disks menu. If you opt for the latter, make sure the desired disks appear in the All available dynamic disks area.

**Figure 12.23.** The New Volume Wizard.

You can then select a size and a drive letter, if desired, before moving on to the formatting options. Whether you choose to format the partition is up to you. Formatting the partition is ideal if you want to start fresh with a "new" drive. For example, if you decided to span three 10GB hard drives to make a "single" 30GB hard drive, you may want to format it before trying to install a complete installation of Windows XP Professional.

## Extend a simple or spanned volume

Once a volume is created on a dynamic disk, you may want to extend it. If you are working with a simple volume, you can extend it to include unused space on that disk or another disk without having to lose any of your data. To do this, the simple volume must be either unformatted or formatted as a NTFS drive (and not FAT32). Why would you want to extend a volume? Let's say you have two drives — one is 25GB and the other is 50GB. On the smaller drive, the capacity is reached and you require 5GB to complete a software installation. You can extend this drive by "borrowing" from the larger disk without losing data on either drive. Certain conditions must be met to do this; see below for details.

Of course, not all volumes can be extended. For example, if you are running the boot volume on a simple volume, you cannot extend it. Also, the simple volume must have been created after the conversion from basic to dynamic disk. If it was created prior to the conversion, the volume cannot be extended.

Extending a spanned volume is essentially the same, including the use of unformatted or NTFS formatted volumes.

For both types of volumes, this is done similar to the creation procedure. However, in the size box, you can now enter a new volume size and then validate.

## Use RAID disks with Windows XP

Unfortunately, Microsoft XP does not provide software support for hardware RAID (Redundant Array of Independent Disks) configurations. RAID is a commonly-used way to standardize and categorize disks. It is similar to a spanned disk; the difference is that spanned disks are not fault-tolerant and RAID is fault-tolerant. In other words, RAID guarantees the integrity of your data in case of hardware failure; spanned disks do not. However, if you are using Windows XP Professional, you have the alternate workaround of using dynamic disks as discussed earlier in this chapter.

## Understanding disk quotas

Windows XP Home and Professional allow the use of disk quotas. Disk quotas are limits assigned to a given user account limiting the amount of disk space the user can use. Disk quotas allocate resources among different users. You can assign 20 percent amount of disk space to 4 users, for example. Quotas can be both a blessing and a curse; a blessing if you are a fair administrator with a realistic sense of how to divide disk space when faced with the realities of your machine's hardware. They can be a curse if you are a non-administrator user and you find yourself locked out.

---

### The next best thing!

So you cannot really use a true RAID disk on Windows XP Professional (or Home for that matter). There are still some fun RAID-related things you can do with your XP box. For example, you can create a RAID-5 volume on a remote Windows 2000 machine.

To do this, it is assumed that you will first know how, and be able, to access a remote computer using the Computer Management module.

In the Disk Management module (not to be confused with the Computer Management module above), select a part of the dynamic disk where you will create a new RAID-5 volume. You can then set it up the same way you set up a dynamic disk (detailed earlier in this chapter) and once you're finished, simply disconnect from the Disk Management module.

**Watch Out!**

The minimum disk quota should be 2MB, which is the amount of space required for user policies on Windows XP. Any less than this and the user will not be able to use Windows properly.

Using disk quotas can be a good way of regulating your disk resources among various users. For example, if you're in college and your roommates use your computer, it's a great way to prevent the gamer from using up all your disk space with a 6 CD game that eats up 4GB on your machine. If the gamer has a quota of 1GB, the game can't be installed.

Remember, only the administrator or computer owner can set these quotas. Keep in mind that with this privilege comes responsibility. How so? It's important to be realistic when setting quotas. As the computer administrator, don't shortchange yourself on the disk quota — you need some of the space you've allotted to other accounts. Also, it's important to decide whether all accounts will have quotas or just specific ones. If all accounts are subject to disk quotas and have received a certain amount of disk space, what will you do if you need to add more accounts later? You may be forced to divvy up the pie again.

Disk quotas are set using the My Computer window. There are two distinct ways to modify default disk quotas (and this may sound familiar): using the command line or the Windows interface. As in previous examples, the Windows interface is the easier option for most users.

## Set up disk quotas

If you right-click a volume from the My Computer page and then click Properties, you will see a tab called Quota (see Figure 12.24). This tab will not be visible if you're not part of the administrators group or if your disk is formatted at FAT32. Only NTFS formatted volumes can have disk quotas.

Most likely, the status is set to Disk quotas are disabled. This is easily changed by checking the Enable quota management check box. This window allows you to deny disk space to users exceeding quota limit. Before you enable this option, keep in mind that one day the user that goes over the account allocation and is locked out may be you!

Surprisingly enough, you can opt to enable quota management yet decide to not limit disk usage for new users. It seems odd that Windows would allow you to not limit disk usage for new users, yet still allow denial of disk space to previous users in excess of their limit.

**Inside Scoop**

Don't forget to delete a user's account or disk quota when you are sure that the account will not be used again. Freeing up unnecessary disk space provides more space for other users.

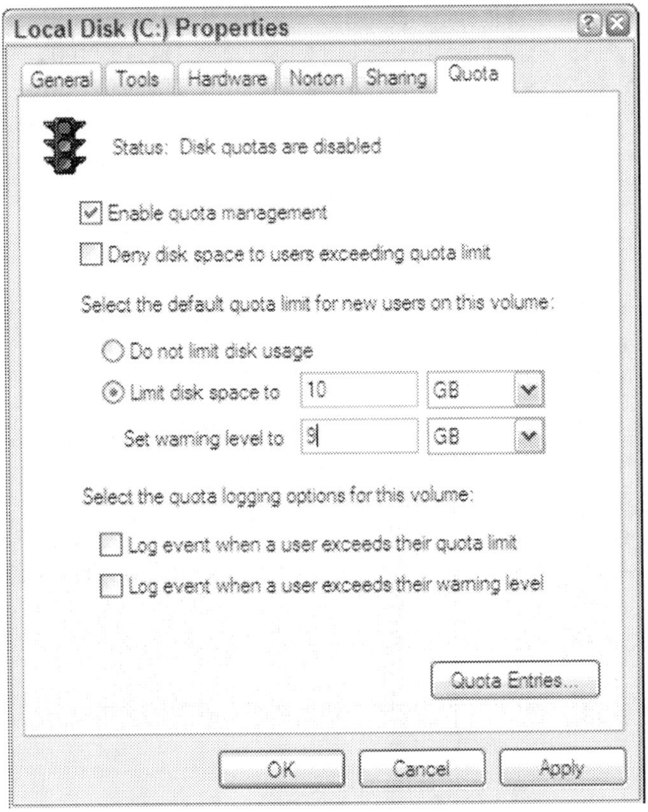

**Local Disk (C:) Properties**

General | Tools | Hardware | Norton | Sharing | Quota

Status: Disk quotas are disabled

☑ Enable quota management

☐ Deny disk space to users exceeding quota limit

Select the default quota limit for new users on this volume:

○ Do not limit disk usage

⦿ Limit disk space to | 10 | GB ▼

Set warning level to | 9| | GB ▼

Select the quota logging options for this volume:

☐ Log event when a user exceeds their quota limit

☐ Log event when a user exceeds their warning level

Quota Entries...

OK | Cancel | Apply

**Figure 12.24.** The Quota tab of the selected volume in My Computer.

The limits can be set up to 1 Exabyte (you read that right — 1,000 terabytes or 1,000,000 gigabytes) with a corresponding warning level set at your discretion that will gently remind users that they are nearing the quota limit. Windows XP also logs any time a user exceeds a quota or warning level.

There is one more important feature on this tab — the Quota Entries window (see Figure 12.25). Click the Quota Entries button to open it.

**Watch Out!**

Don't forget that you can set disk quotas for removable drives (USB or FireWire) but not for thumb drives.

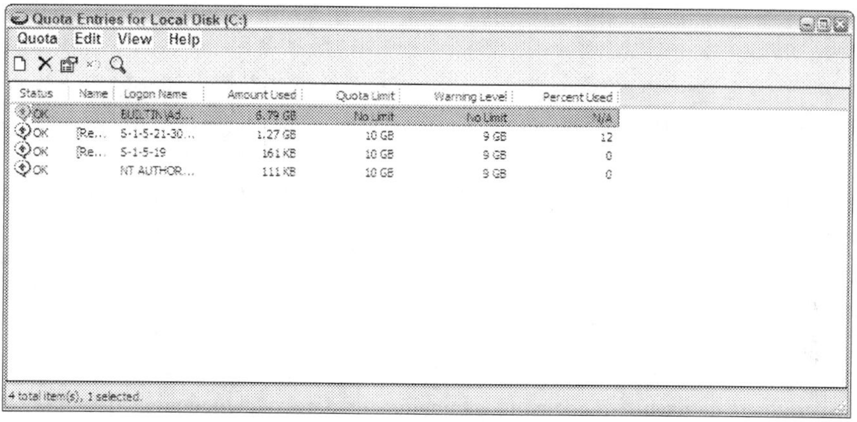

| Status | Name | Logon Name | Amount Used | Quota Limit | Warning Level | Percent Used |
|---|---|---|---|---|---|---|
| OK |  | BUILTIN\Ad... | 6.79 GB | No Limit | No Limit | N/A |
| OK | [Re... | S-1-5-21-30... | 1.27 GB | 10 GB | 9 GB | 12 |
| OK | [Re... | S-1-5-19 | 161 KB | 10 GB | 9 GB | 0 |
| OK |  | NT AUTHOR... | 111 KB | 10 GB | 9 GB | 0 |

Quota Entries for Local Disk (C:)
Quota  Edit  View  Help

4 total item(s), 1 selected.

**Figure 12.25.** The Quota Entries window.

You can easily add a new entry from the Quota menu or by clicking the blank page icon (first icon on the left). In the text box, add the user as directed (for a sample of proper nomenclature, click the Examples link above the text box). Use the Check Names box to validate your selection if necessary. The Advanced button provides the Select Users menu that can help you locate users in a given location. Click OK to finalize your choices.

Once the new entry appears in the Quota Entries window, double-clicking it (or right-clicking it and selecting Properties) opens the Quota tab (see Figure 12.24), where you can set a disk limit or warning level (or to not limit usage). The quota used and amount remaining also appear on this page.

The Quota Entries dialog box also allows you to export quota settings by right-clicking an entry and selecting Export from the menu. Simply save the settings as desired.

## Assign default quotas via the command line

From the command line, you can assign or modify default quota values for a user. Access the command prompt by choosing Start ⇨ All Programs ⇨ Accessories ⇨ Command Prompt, or by choosing Start ⇨ Run and then typing cmd in the Run dialog box.

Again, make sure the volume is NTFS; FAT32 volumes cannot take advantage of the disk quota feature. From the command line, simply type:

```
fsutil quota modify [volumepathname] [threshold] [limit]
[username]
```

The first value, volumepathname, is simply the drive letter where you wish to set the quota. The second value is the warning level limit in bytes (not megabytes or gigabytes, but plain old bytes). The limit is just that, the limit. It, too, is measures in bytes. The final value is the user name, which must respect the domain\user name format in order to work.

The fsutil value is a versatile command that is very helpful when in managing disk quotas. Consult the Windows XP online help (using "fsutil" as a search term) for more information on the use of this command, which includes disabling, tracking, enforcing, and querying disk quotas.

## Assign default quotas via the Windows interface

As stated earlier in this section, this is done through the Quota tab of the selected volume in My Computer. The Limit disk space to field is the appropriate place to assign or modify default quotas.

## Configure a UPS

Windows XP Home and Professional editions both allow the use of Uninterruptible Power Supplies (UPS). A UPS is a device that sits between your machine and the electrical socket. In the event of a power outage, the UPS guarantees a continuity of power for a limited amount of time.

The UPS also protects your machine against potentially fatal enemies such as power surges. At the very minimum, if you cannot afford a UPS device for your home system, or you think it will not provide enough value to justify the cost, make sure you have a quality surge protector to protect your machine. Personal experience makes this bear repeating: At the very minimum, buy a proper surge protector for your computer equipment — make

---

**Inside Scoop**

If you've decided that disk quotas are not helping out, simply open the Quota tab in the My Computer volume and deselect the Enable quota management option. This may be the case if you are the lone user, or you find that you have to constantly readjust your quota limits.

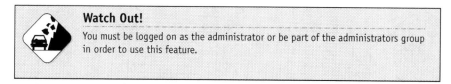

**Watch Out!**

You must be logged on as the administrator or be part of the administrators group in order to use this feature.

sure it says surge protector, not all multiple socket plugs actually protect against surges or brownouts.

One last thing, please consult the product documentation for your UPS device before attempting installation.

Once you have installed your UPS, you can manage its properties in the Power Options menu in the Control Panel. The Power Options Properties dialog box has a UPS tab (see Figure 12.26) that features device status (as well as device estimates) and details about the device, such as the manufacturer or model.

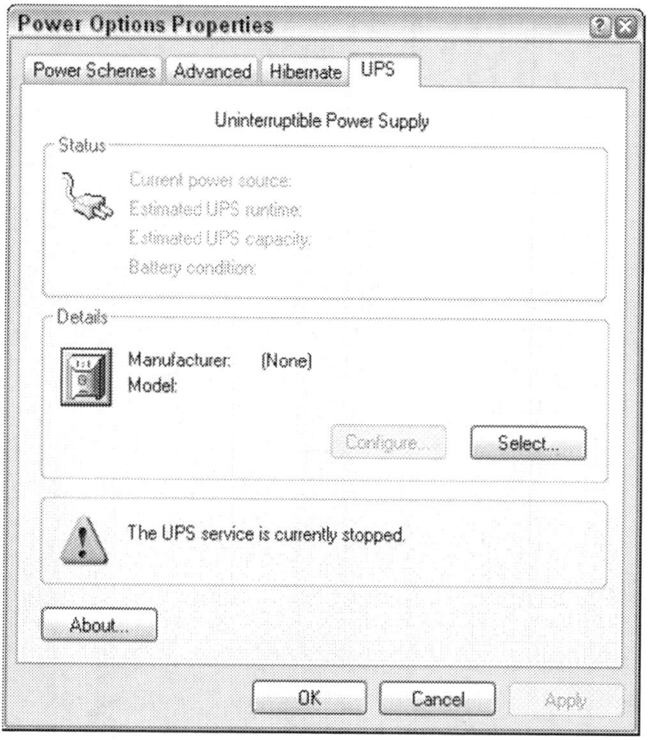

**Power Options Properties**

| Power Schemes | Advanced | Hibernate | **UPS** |

Uninterruptible Power Supply

Status

Current power source:
Estimated UPS runtime:
Estimated UPS capacity:
Battery condition:

Details

Manufacturer:     (None)
Model:

Configure...     Select...

⚠ The UPS service is currently stopped.

About...

OK     Cancel     Apply

**Figure 12.26.** The UPS tab of the Power Options Properties dialog box.

**Watch Out!**

Do not, at any time, attempt to change these settings before consulting the user documentation provided with your UPS device. The warning even appears at the top of the Power Options page with a large warning icon. Heed it.

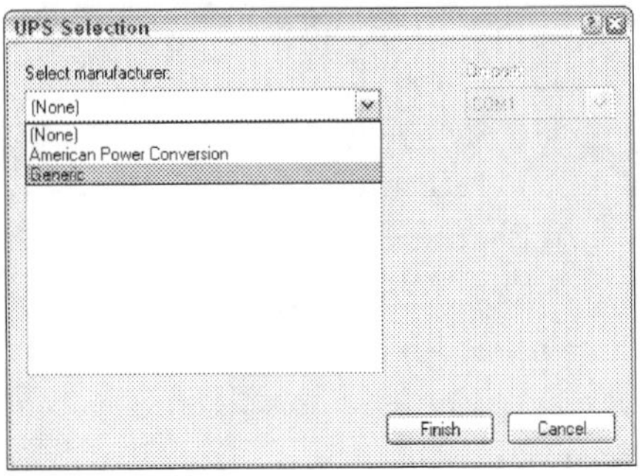

To configure your UPS device, simply go to the Power Options Properties dialog box, click the UPS tab, and then click Select in the Details section. The UPS Selection window appears. None appears by default: Select Generic (see Figure 12.27). Once Generic appears as the selected manufacturer, click Custom in the Select model area. Select the port where

**Figure 12.27.** Select Generic in the UPS Selection window.

the UPS is installed. Once you go on to the next page, you can configure the signal polarities for your device and then click Finish.

Once installed, it may be a good idea to test your device. However, do not test it on the key computer in your network. Try it on the weakest link of your computer collection. If you only have a single machine, you're not in luck: You can only test on your main computer. There is always the potential of shorting out your machine.

To test, simply unplug the UPS device and wait until the UPS battery is almost flat; then plug it back in (this will simulate a power outage). If all is right with the world, everything will be working normally.

If you wish to remove the device, go back to the Power Options Properties dialog box and click Select and then select None from the list of manufacturers. The device is now safe to remove from your machine.

# Work with dual monitors

If you work in Information Technology or in the graphic arts, you can certainly appreciate the need for dual monitors. Windows XP Home and Professional editions continue the Windows tradition of allowing such a configuration. In fact, you can connect up to 10 monitors for a single field of vision.

In this setup, a single monitor is designated as the primary display. This is the monitor hooked up to the first video out port. If you have a laptop, you have a feature called Dualview, which is essentially the same as what's described above, with the exception that you cannot select your primary display. The primary display is always the LCD display.

The monitors are set in the Display panel either in the Control Panel or by right-clicking Properties on the desktop and then clicking the Settings tab (see Figure 12.28).

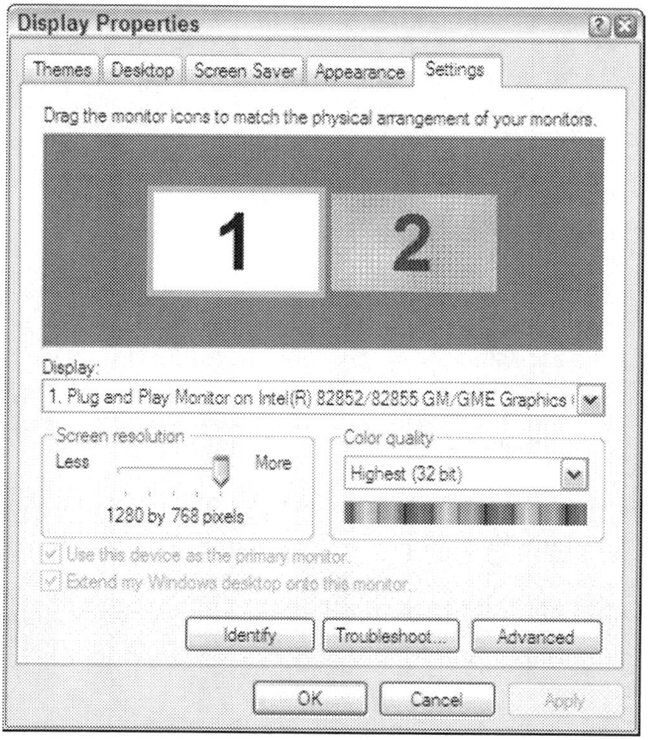

**Display Properties**

Themes | Desktop | Screen Saver | Appearance | Settings

Drag the monitor icons to match the physical arrangement of your monitors.

**1** **2**

Display:

1. Plug and Play Monitor on Intel(R) 82852/82855 GM/GME Graphics

Screen resolution
Less ———————— More
1280 by 768 pixels

Color quality
Highest (32 bit)

☑ Use this device as the primary monitor.
☑ Extend my Windows desktop onto this monitor.

Identify | Troubleshoot... | Advanced

OK | Cancel | Apply

**Figure 12.28.** The Display Properties window.

The list of available monitors (displays) appears in a drop-down list in the middle of the window. To find which display is currently active, click the Identify button. The monitor icons appear illustrating which monitor is number one, number two, and so on. Displays appear in a preview area toward the top of the page. You can arrange the monitors depending on how you want to drag items across your screens. If you'd like to move desktop

**Watch Out!**

Visit the Microsoft Web site at http://support.microsoft.com/default.aspx?scid=kb;en-us;307397 and make sure your display adapter is compatible with the multiple monitor feature.

items from top to bottom, place the second display below display number one. If you wish to move items from left to right, place the second display next to the right of the first display. Once you have orchestrated the positioning of the multiple monitors, you are set to go.

## Just the facts

- No matter how often you use your computer, it is essential that you back up your data and system files. Windows XP offers some on-board tools to help get this done.

- Windows XP helps you maximize hard drive space by allowing you to extend or span disk drives.

- Keep track of your users and disk usage by using Windows XP's disk quota feature.

- Windows XP works with UPS devices to protect your machine and data in case of power outage.

- The dual monitor feature allows you to connect several monitors to a single computer, making your work area larger. This is an excellent feature for graphic artists or anyone else who spends his day working in front of a single monitor.

GET THE SCOOP ON...
Efficient laptop power management ▪ Connecting to
your home or office using VPN ▪ Working with
copies of your important files

# Managing Portable Computers

*Chapter 13*

Laptop computers are a popular option for people who don't have room for a full desktop system (like students) or people whose work requires portability and access to important documents. While other chapters have material that is useful to laptop users — such as faxing in Chapter 9 — this chapter contains information that is most likely to be used by laptop users.

Of primary interest are hardware profiles, managing battery life, and improving remote connectivity and usefulness while on the road. Windows XP gives you tools to manage your power consumption, to connect to your home office through the corporate firewall, and to automatically take your files with you while leaving a copy on the network.

## Working with hardware profiles

Windows XP has a built-in hardware profile manager you can use to manage different hardware configurations. This is most applicable to laptop users, where you may have a docking station at work with different hardware attached, and perhaps a second docking station (or no docking station) at home.

For example, at one job I had a docking station complete with its own network adapter, external monitor, keyboard, mouse, and speakers. In the morning I'd connect my laptop to the station, turn on the laptop, and use the peripherals. When I left for the night, I'd undock the station, take the laptop home, and then connect to my home network to continue working. This meant that I used different sets of network adapters, monitors, mouse devices, and speakers depending on where I was connected.

Hardware profiles kept everything neat and orderly, as far as the operation of Windows XP was concerned. Windows knew which resources were available and how to use them efficiently, without having to guess whether a device was connected or not.

Setting up different profiles is easy to do. Connect all your hardware that you use at one location. This includes things like scanners, wireless mice and keyboards, and even joysticks or game controllers. If you haven't set up your hardware, see Chapter 1 for information on installing or upgrading hardware on your computer. Then click Start, right-click My Computer, click Properties, click Hardware, and then click Hardware Profiles (see Figure 13.1).

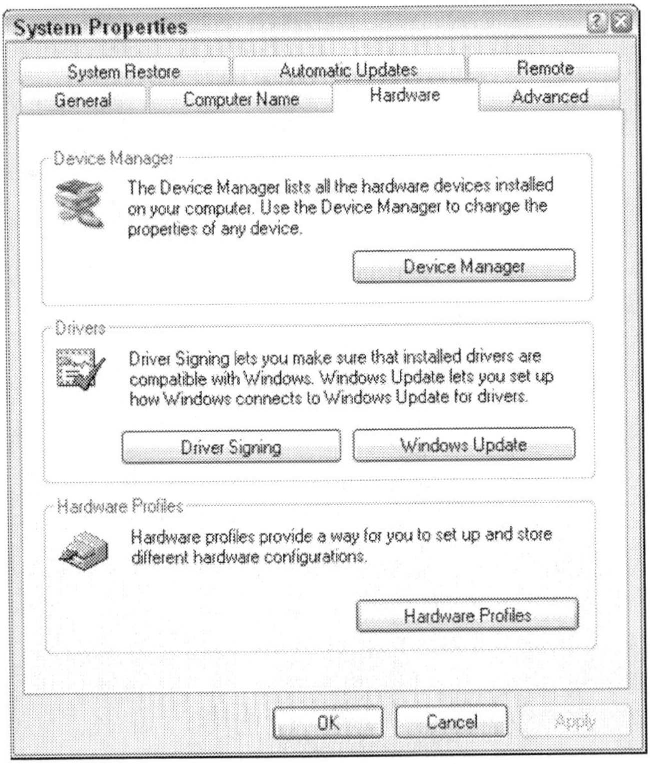

**Figure 13.1.** The Hardware Profile manager is one of the easier-to-use management utilities for your computer.

By default, the current profile is named Profile 1. Click the Rename button and change the name to something easy to remember, like "Docked" (see Figure 13.2). Then click Copy, rename your current profile, and then click OK. Select whether to wait for a profile selection or to automatically boot the first one after a specified time elapses. If you want to change the display order, select a profile and then click the up or down arrows to move the profile higher or lower in the list. When you are done with configuring your profiles, click OK twice.

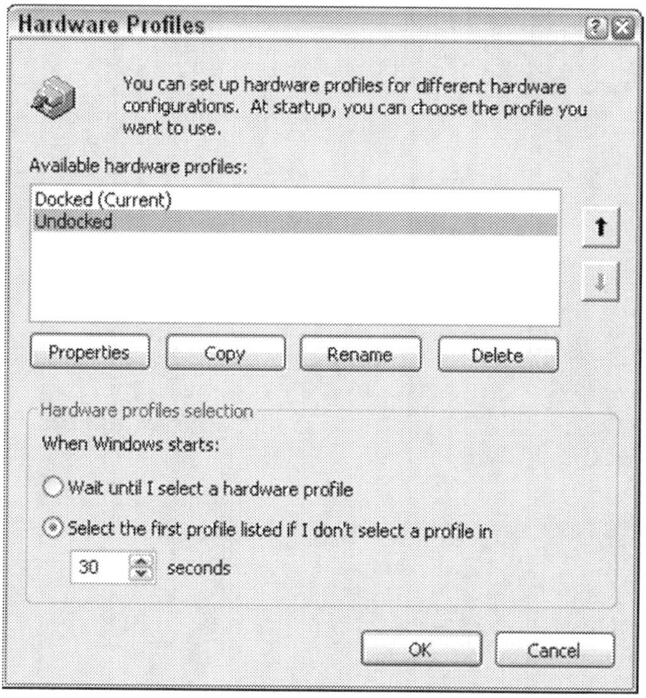

**Figure 13.2.** Rename, create, delete, and re-order profiles to match your needs.

To use the new profile, shut down your computer and remove devices you don't want (or won't have available) in the new profile. Turn on your computer; at boot time select the new profile (see Figure 13.3).

After Windows finishes booting, use Device Manager to disable any hardware that is not available; see Chapter 11 for information on enabling and disabling hardware. In Device Manager, select "Do not use this device in the current hardware profile" and then click OK (see Figure 13.4).

Note that the hardware profiles apply to any user who uses the computer. This means that all users potentially can access all the hardware available in a particular profile. It's not as serious as it sounds, though, because you can control access to programs using user profiles or special user accounts. See Chapter 4 for information on managing user accounts, Chapter 6 for file permissions, and Chapter 10 for managing permissions in a domain.

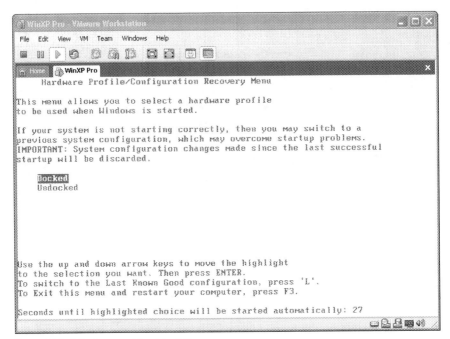

**Figure 13.3.** Select your profile at boot time.

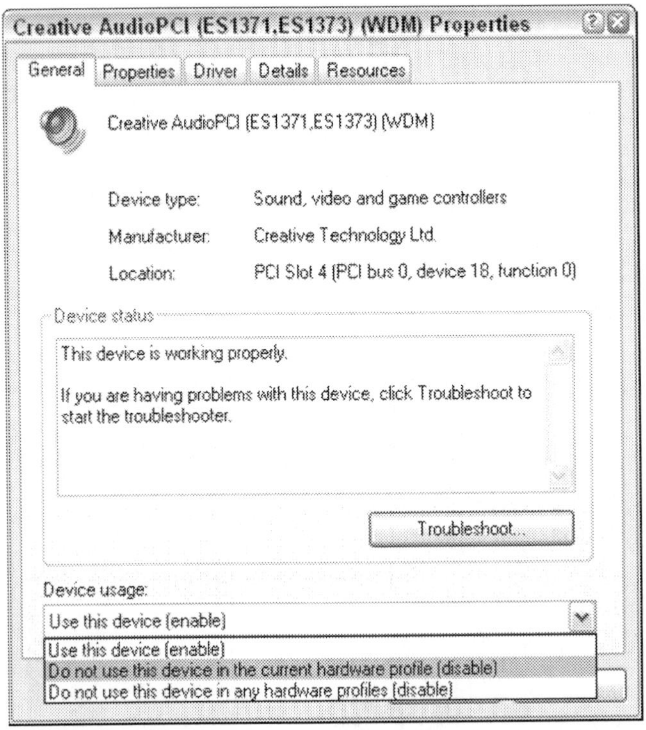

**Figure 13.4.** Disable the hardware that is not connected in this profile.

# Explore power management options

If you are a student or business traveler, you know that lugging a power supply around can be a hassle. It's much easier to just pull out your laptop and start typing. The downside, of course, is battery life; no matter what the laptop's marketing literature said, the battery seems to last far less than was promised in the glossy brochure.

One of Windows XP's smarter capabilities is its power management. You can use existing power profiles, or create your own, to set hardware options for how quickly your hardware drains the battery.

To view the power options utility, click Start, Run, type powercfg.cpl, and then press Enter. Or click Start, Control Panel, Performance and Maintenance, and then Power Options.

The Power Schemes drop-down list (see Figure 13.5) has several preconfigured schemes you can apply, from Always On to Home/Office Desktop to Portable/Laptop. Each of these changes settings in the Settings area, where you can set time intervals depending on whether you are plugged in or on battery power.

You can change any of the settings for an existing profile and then click OK, or you can click the Save As button and save your profile with a different name. This lets you configure settings that match how your system is being used, so you can maximize your laptop's battery life.

The four options in the Portable/Laptop scheme and their functions are:

- **Turn off monitor.** Cuts power to the display. This can result in a fair amount of battery life extension, especially if you have your laptop's brightness setting at its highest level.

- **Turn off hard disks.** Your laptop powers down the hard drive so that it doesn't continually draw current as it waits for Windows XP to request a file from the drive.

- **System standby.** Puts your system into "sleep" mode, where a key press or mouse movement can wake your computer up again in just a few seconds. A trickle of power is kept flowing to the BIOS, but everything else, including the processor, is shut off, resulting in huge power savings. If you want your computer to wake up on an incoming phone call or fax call, the computer should be in this mode.

- **System hibernates.** If Hibernation is enabled on the Hibernate tab, this option puts the computer into suspended animation so that only pressing the power button can wake it up again. No power is consumed in this mode.

**Inside Scoop**

Many laptops come with power management utilities that increase your ability to manage power consumption. I'll cover the basic Windows XP functions, but it is worth your time to explore your laptop's own management utilities.

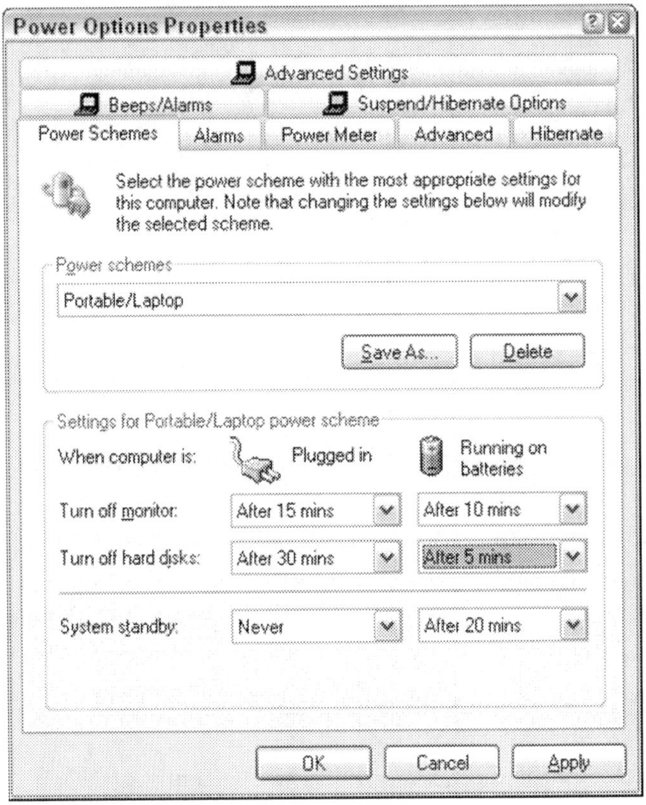

---

**Power Options Properties**

| Advanced Settings |
| Beeps/Alarms | Suspend/Hibernate Options |

Power Schemes | Alarms | Power Meter | Advanced | Hibernate

Select the power scheme with the most appropriate settings for this computer. Note that changing the settings below will modify the selected scheme.

Power schemes

Portable/Laptop ▾

[ Save As... ] [ Delete ]

Settings for Portable/Laptop power scheme

| When computer is: | Plugged in | Running on batteries |
|---|---|---|
| Turn off monitor: | After 15 mins ▾ | After 10 mins ▾ |
| Turn off hard disks: | After 30 mins ▾ | After 5 mins ▾ |
| System standby: | Never ▾ | After 20 mins ▾ |

[ OK ] [ Cancel ] [ Apply ]

**Figure 13.5.** Feel the power! Take command of your laptop's energy consumption habits.

The Portable/Laptop default settings are a bit too long for my work habits. Keeping the monitor on for twenty minutes without any activity is wasteful; the same thing is true for the hard drive. I like setting the monitor to switch off after ten minutes, the hard drive to power down after five, and have the system go into standby at twenty minutes. My work habits are such that if I'm unplugged, I'm working diligently in order to get a lot done with the battery power I have left; I don't walk off for an hour to do something else. Edit the settings to reflect your work habits.

---

### The hidden power vampire

Your wireless connection is not controlled by Windows' power management capabilities. Wireless adapters consume quite a bit of energy and will drain your battery quickly if you are uploading or downloading files for a significant amount of time.

Some wireless adapters come with software that lets you configure power use profiles so you can set the power consumption level depending on desired network performance or wireless connection type. Check with your adapter manufacturer to see if your adapter supports power use profiles.

---

Another balancing act to consider is monitor shutdown versus screen saver with password setting (see Chapter 3). For security reasons it's usually a good idea to password protect your laptop so that when the screen saver runs, you need a password to return to the desktop. I usually set my screen saver to start after fifteen minutes of no activity. This means the screen blanks at ten, the password kicks in at fifteen, and the system powers down at twenty. This progressive series of system shutdowns and protection works well for me, but your needs may be different. Feel free to play with these settings, too.

The other tabs on the Power Options Properties dialog box are fairly straightforward, with two exceptions. The Hibernate tab (see Figure 13.6) lets you control whether your computer can go into hibernation mode.

When you enable hibernation, Windows creates a file on your hard drive that is the same size as the amount of RAM on your computer. When your system enters hibernation, it creates an exact copy of your RAM in the file on your hard drive. When your laptop comes out of hibernation it copies the file from your hard drive directly into memory. This is much faster than waiting for your system to boot up, authenticate against a server, and configure all the services needed to run your laptop. It also consumes less energy restoring the hibernation file, so your battery life is extended a bit by skipping the standard boot procedure.

One down side to hibernation is that the hibernation file can be quite large, depending on the amount of RAM you have installed on your laptop. If your laptop is running out of disk space and you find that you don't use hibernation mode, you can disable hibernation on this tab and reclaim some space on your hard drive.

**Figure 13.6.** Before you enable hibernation, you can verify how much additional space it will consume on your hard drive.

Another down side is that some services and activities don't work when you come back out of hibernation. If you are connected to a Web server for a transaction and you go into hibernation, the session won't be available when you come back. Likewise, if you were connected to a wireless access point, go into hibernation, then come out of hibernation at a different access point, your wireless connection won't be available. In these cases you'll need to either re-establish the connection, or reboot the system so it starts "clean" without any services in a frozen or pending state.

Because of these downsides I disable hibernation and rely on standard shutdown and boot processes. I'm not in the habit of starting and stopping my work sessions; when I sit down to work, I'm there for the duration. If you dash from meeting to meeting, or class to class, then hibernation may be perfectly acceptable for you.

## The system BIOS and power management

All newer systems, including laptops, support two different methods of power management: ACPI (Advanced Configuration and Power Interface) and APM (Advanced Power Management). These features are controlled by the system's BIOS (Basic Input / Output System) and allow operating system software to define what happens when shutdown, hibernation, and wakeup events are triggered.

While the BIOS has its own power management settings, the Windows settings are supposed to supersede the ones set in your BIOS. If you have conflicts, such as your laptop "hangs" at the power off screen or doesn't suspend properly, there may be a conflict or a bug with the BIOS. Visit your laptop manufacturer's Web site and see if an updated BIOS is available (see Chapter 1 for warnings and cautions about working with the BIOS), and visit Microsoft's Knowledgebase at support.microsoft.com/search/ for recommendations on power management settings that may overcome the conflict.

The second tab with helpful power management options is the Advanced tab (see Figure 13.7). This tab lets you configure your laptop's behavior when certain "shut down" activities happen, such as closing the laptop lid or pressing the power button. Note that if you disabled hibernation on the Hibernate tab, you will not find hibernation listed as an option in the drop-down lists.

Finally, you can require a password for when your computer comes out of standby. This is helpful if you want to be extra-secure with your laptop, but is not terribly helpful if you use the auto-answer fax option; with the latter, you'd have to be available to type a password in order to pick up the fax, which defeats the whole idea of auto-answer.

**Watch Out!**

Most laptops support using a BIOS or boot time password. If you enable hibernation, try a dry run with it to see if the boot time password is needed when coming out of hibernation. If so, you may need to reset it for any auto-answer features you want to use.

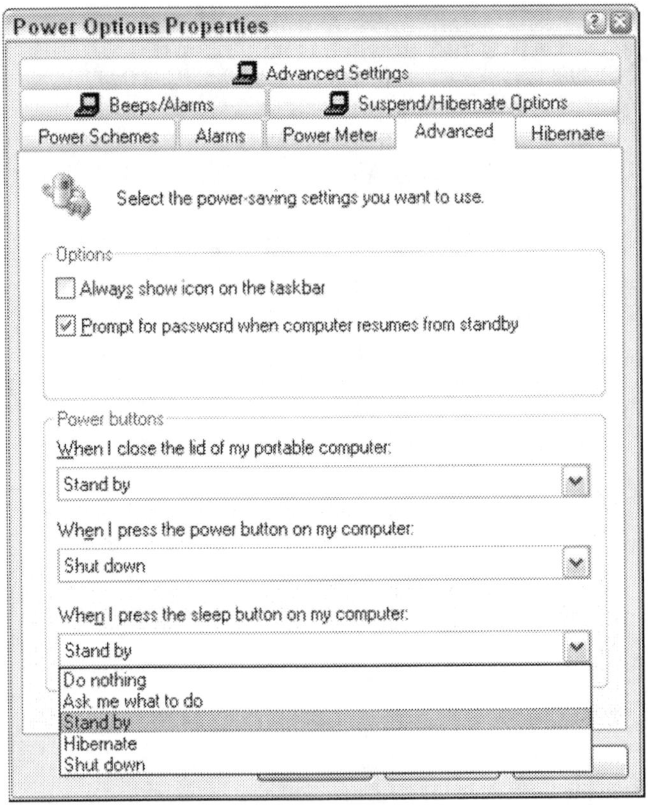

**Power Options Properties**

Advanced Settings

Beeps/Alarms          Suspend/Hibernate Options

Power Schemes    Alarms    Power Meter    Advanced    Hibernate

Select the power-saving settings you want to use.

Options

☐ Always show icon on the taskbar

☑ Prompt for password when computer resumes from standby

Power buttons

When I close the lid of my portable computer:

| Stand by | ⌄ |

When I press the power button on my computer:

| Shut down | ⌄ |

When I press the sleep button on my computer:

| Stand by | ⌄ |

Do nothing
Ask me what to do
Stand by
Hibernate
Shut down

Figure 13.7. Configure your laptop's behavior to various shut down activities.

# Set up a VPN connection

Virtual Private Networks, or VPN for short, are ways of connecting remote computers to office networks so that your remote computer behaves as if you are on the LAN. This gives you maximum flexibility for working with files, printers, or network applications like Exchange, while maintaining a degree of security.

Other ways of gaining access to your office while you are on the road include browser-based Web applications, Terminal Services, and Remote Desktop Connections. Web applications give you access to information and data without requiring any software, other than a browser, on your computer, while Terminal Services lets you run a specialized client that presents you with a full "desktop" that actually resides on a network server. Remote Desktop, discussed in Chapter 9, gives you direct access to a specific computer on the network.

**Inside Scoop**

If you are using a third-party VPN solution, do not attempt to configure Microsoft's VPN solution for a VPN connection. Consult with your IT department because there are probably very specific connection requirements needed for a successful configuration.

With the exception of Remote Desktop, these other methods of remote access are usually found in larger businesses as they require significant amounts of hardware, specialized software, and dedicated IT specialists to keep the whole system running.

VPN is often the cheapest and easiest way to give employees access to internal resources while on the road. As a laptop user you may find that a VPN client is all that is needed. It sits between your operating system and a network adapter, and as such does not consume large quantities of hard drive space or processing cycles.

## Configure a VPN server

In order to use VPN you must prepare your network so it can receive incoming connections. Your hardware or software firewall must be configured to forward TCP port 1727 to your network's VPN server. The wizard configures the Windows Firewall to accept incoming connections so you don't have to create any exceptions. But if you are running a third-party firewall, you need to add an exception for the VPN connection.

Your VPN server must also have a fixed IP address, not a dynamically assigned one. If you want to set up Windows XP as a VPN server you need to change a network adapter to use a fixed address. See Chapter 2 for information on networks and configuring your adapter. You should also know that Windows XP accepts only one VPN connection at a time, so you are not able to provide VPN services for an entire branch office with a single copy of Windows XP.

To set up a VPN server, click Start, Run, type ncpa.cpl, and press Enter. Click Create a new connection. The New Connection Wizard starts; click Next. Select Set up an advanced connection and click Next (see Figure 13.8).

Select Accept incoming connections and then click Next. Do not select anything in the Devices for Incoming Connections box; click Next. Select Allow virtual private connections and click Next.

In the User Permissions dialog box select which users you want to grant access to your network through your computer and then click Next (see Figure 13.9).

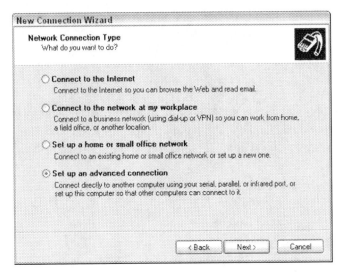

**Figure 13.8.** VPN connections are considered an advanced connection type.

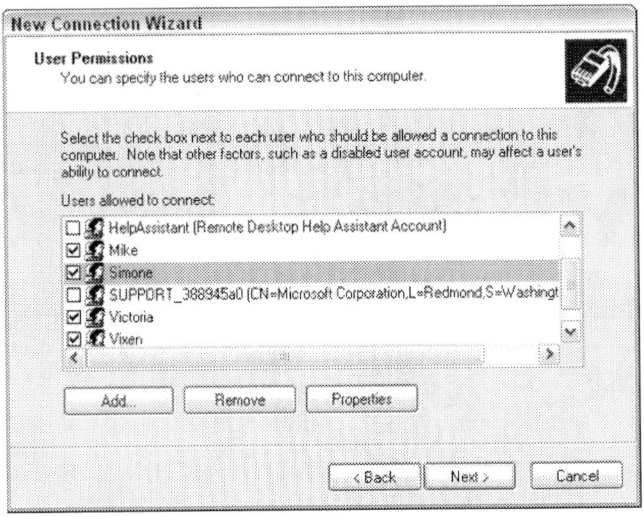

**Figure 13.9.** Select the users you want to grant access to your computer from a remote location.

In the Networking Software dialog box, select Internet Protocol (TCP/IP) and click Properties. Select Allow callers to access my local area network (see Figure 13.10). You can use DHCP to dynamically assign the computer a network address, specify an address range that incoming computers can use, or let the incoming computer specify its own address (usually using a static IP address reserved for just such connections). When you specify a range, it turns your Windows XP computer into a mini-DHCP server, so you must make sure the range you assign isn't preassigned or reserved elsewhere on your network. Click OK, click Next, and then click Finish.

Your Windows XP computer is now set up as a VPN server and the connection icon appears in the Network Connections window. You can change any of its settings by right-clicking the connection and then clicking Properties, for example if you want to add or remove users who can connect to your network remotely.

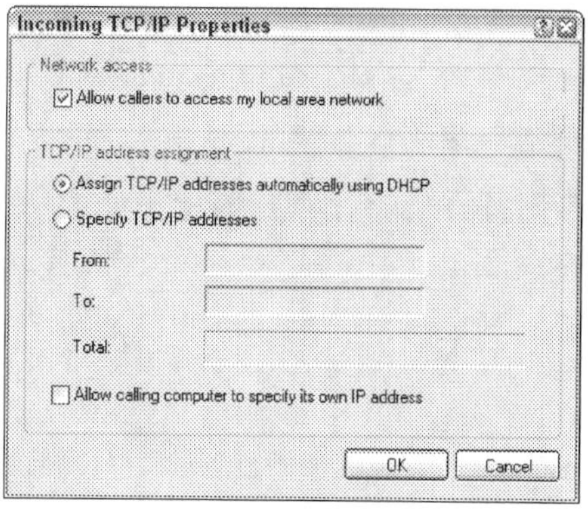

**Figure 13.10.** Your network can assign the VPN computer an address, or you can choose other ways to give it an address.

---

## The perils of virtual networking

VPNs can quickly run afoul of your network, and troubleshooting VPN connections can be extremely frustrating. Some examples of what can trip up newcomers to networking:

- Windows defaults to using Point-to-Point Tunneling Protocol (PPTP) for VPN connections, but it can be configured to use Layer Two Tunneling Protocol (L2TP) which requires using certificates and Internet Protocol Security (IPSec). The latter is more secure but is more difficult to set up. Stick with PPTP and avoid L2TP unless you have a networking background.

- Networks with multiple subnets will require you to configure routing tables so your VPN computer can reach other network resources. Again, don't try to configure routing tables unless you have a networking background.

- You can run into conflicts and potential security problems when you try to use a VPN for connection to your network, and a non-VPN connection for Internet access. Though it's slower, stick to using your VPN through your company network for combined VPN-and-Internet access.

If you have fewer than ten computers to manage, a better solution is Remote Desktop Connection or Web-based applications for your remote needs.

If you want to use Windows 2000 Server or Windows Server 2003 as a VPN server, please see their respective online help sections on configuring and managing a VPN server.

## Configure the VPN client

To set up your remote computer to act as a VPN client, click Start, Run, type ncpa.cpl, and press Enter. Click Create a new connection. The New Connection Wizard starts; click Next. Select Connect to the network at my workplace and then click Next. Select Virtual Private Network connection and click Next (see Figure 13.11). Type a name for your connection; it could be the server name or company name. Click Next.

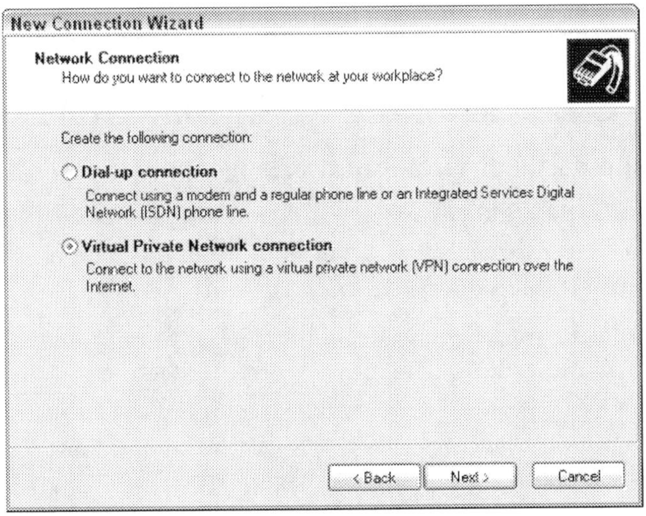

**Figure 13.11.** Connect to your VPN server using, you guessed it, a VPN connection.

In the VPN Server Selection dialog box, type the IP address of the VPN server you want to connect to, or if the server's host name is registered with the Domain Name Service (for example, servername.mycompany.com), type the server's full address. Click Next. You can add a VPN connection to your desktop by selecting the check box. This gives you a one-click stop for connecting remotely to your office. Otherwise click Finish.

When the wizard closes you are immediately given the opportunity to connect to the VPN server (see Figure 13.12).

Type your user name and password to connect to the server. You can also click the Properties button to change any of the settings. The ones most helpful for connecting are located on the Options tab (see Figure 13.13).

You can define whether to use the Windows logon domain as part of the security sequence (required if you are connecting to a domain rather than a workgroup), set the number of redial attempts, and the length of time to wait between attempts.

If you are having trouble connecting, check your firewalls to make sure they are allowing inbound connections on port 1727, and check to see whether you are using Windows logon information as part of the sequence.

**Figure 13.12.** The Connect dialog box prompts you for your user name and password to connect to the VPN server.

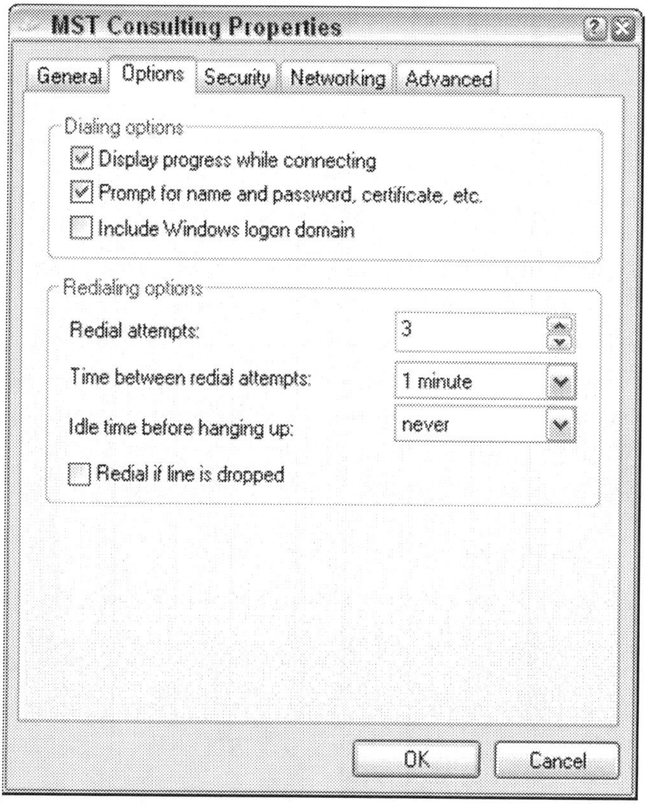

**Figure 13.13.** You can modify connection settings in the Options tab of the Properties dialog box.

# Configure Offline File Sharing

Offline File Sharing (OFS) allows you to take copies of your files with you when you leave the network, work with them while you are on the road, and then have your local copies synchronize with the originals when you reconnect to the network. A grown-up version of Briefcase, it provides more sophisticated synchronization options and flexibility than its older cousin. OFS is only available on Windows XP Professional edition, so if you are considering a new laptop purchase, you should opt for the Professional edition rather than Home edition.

There are two caveats to working with OFS, one technical, one human. The technical caveat: You cannot enable Fast User Switching and OFS at the same time. For laptop users this shouldn't be too much of a problem, because it's unlikely more than one person will be using your laptop at the same time.

The human caveat is that you should be careful which network folder you want to synchronize with. OFS compares date-time stamps to see which is the newest version and copies that version over the older one. This can be a problem if others make changes to your network versions that are newer than changes made to your local version. There goes your hard work! When you choose a network directory for synchronizing, either make sure it's one that others don't have access to, or make your own copy of other shared documents that you can synchronize with.

To set up OFS, first create a share on the network (see Chapter 5). Next, open Windows Explorer or any other folder, and then click Tools, Folder Options, and Offline Files (see Figure 13.14).

Select Enable Offline Files. You can also select when you want Windows XP to synchronize with the network — when you log on, when you log off, or both. You definitely want to synchronize when you log off, and if you are a road warrior who does a lot of work on the road, you want to synchronize when you log on.

---

**Bright Idea**

If you need more sophisticated version-control systems for managing documents and changes to them, consider using Windows SharePoint Services. It's a browser-based document management system with links into Microsoft Office and is a part of Microsoft Windows Server 2003.

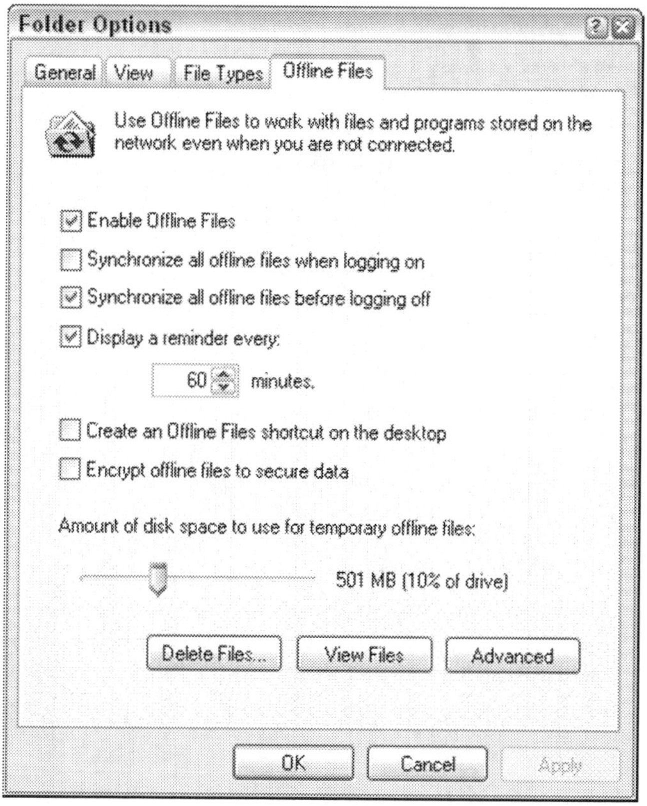

**Figure 13.14.** Offline files can be synchronized when you log on, log off, or both.

You can also set how much disk space your offline files will take up. You are much better off synchronizing only documents or data files, not program files or multimedia and music files. These latter examples can take a long time to synchronize, even over a network connection, and if you're trying to synchronize these files over a dialup connection, good luck!

Once you have enabled OFS, you need to select which files or folders you want synchronized. Open Windows Explorer, browse to your network share, right-click the folder and files you want to synchronize, and then click Make available offline. The Offline Files Wizard starts. Click Next. Select Automatically synchronize the Offline Files. Click Next. You can select whether to receive offline reminders and whether to create a desktop shortcut to the offline files (see Figure 13.15). Click Finish. The files are synchronized for you.

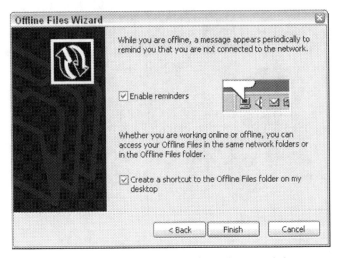

**Figure 13.15.** You can receive offline reminders and create a desktop shortcut.

When you log off, Windows synchronizes the files with the network share. When you log back on and the network is not available, you can view your files three ways:

- Double-click the Offline Files icon on your desktop (if you selected that option)

- Open My Network Places and browse to the "share" (which is now a locally-cached copy of the files)

- Open Windows Explorer, click Tools, Folder Options, Offline Files, and then View Files

When you reconnect to the network, your files are compared with the ones on the network share and the newest ones are copied in whichever direction is appropriate. If new files were added to the share while you were off the network, you will get a copy added to your offline cache.

If you need to change your synchronization options, click Tools, Synchronize, select a synchronized folder or file, and then click Setup.

There are many settings you can adjust to meet your needs in the Synchronization Settings dialog box, such as synchronizing your files when the computer has been idle for a specified length of time. While the default settings will work for most people, if you need more granular control this is the place to do it. For example, if you want to synchronize your files on a schedule in addition to log on and log off, click the Schedule tab and set up a schedule. A more convenient way is to synchronize your files after your computer has been idle for a while. Click the On Idle tab (see Figure 13.16), click the Advanced button, and then set up how long you want your computer idle before synchronizing the files. Note you can set the computer not to synchronize if you are running on battery power.

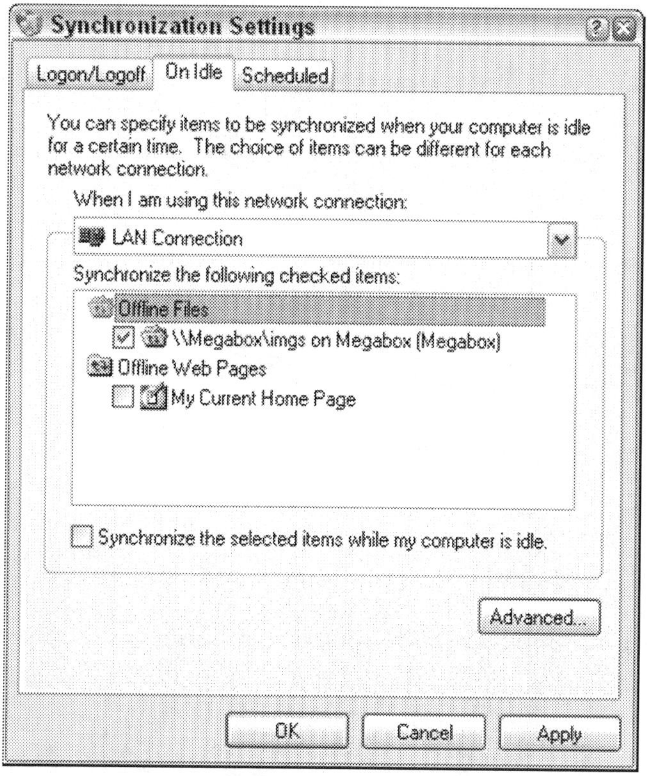

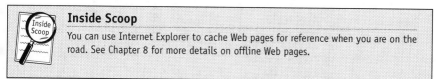

**Figure 13.16.** Your synchronization settings can be changed without re-creating the offline folder.

Finally, you can configure different synchronization behavior depending on what network connection you have active. If you are connected to a docking station, you can synchronize frequently; but if you connect remotely using a modem, you may choose not to synchronize your files as the transfer times may be horrendous for large files over slow lines.

**Inside Scoop**
You can use Internet Explorer to cache Web pages for reference when you are on the road. See Chapter 8 for more details on offline Web pages.

# Use ClearType on LCD screens

Laptop users, or desktop users with LCD screens, have complained for some time about font clarity. At some resolutions fonts are fine, while at other resolutions the fonts are terrible. The problem isn't with the fonts, but LCD technology. Liquid crystals in the display are larger than CRT display pixels, and they are squarish or rectangular in shape rather than round. This means that things displayed on an LCD screen sometimes look blurry because two or more crystals try to display only part of the image apiece.

One way you can improve clarity on laptop or LCD screens is to run the screen at its native resolution. All screens and monitors claim to support different screen resolutions, but only one is considered native. Usually this is 1024 × 768, but this resolution could be higher in the case of newer, pricier displays. Use the resolution that fills your LCD screen completely and doesn't show any signs of distortion or blurry features.

The other way to improve clarity is to try Microsoft's ClearType fonts that are available on Windows XP. ClearType fonts are designed especially for laptop and LCD screens, using clever dithering algorithms to help the fonts look cleaner and less blurry. ClearType isn't a panacea; it works better on some displays than others, but since it's free and takes only a moment to enable, give it a try and see if it helps improve font resolution on your screen.

To turn on ClearType fonts, right-click the desktop, click Properties, click Appearance, and then click Effects. Select Use the following method to smooth the edges of screen fonts, select ClearType from the drop-down list (see Figure 13.17), and then click OK twice. You should see a change in your fonts. If they are less visible, change ClearType back to Standard and click OK twice.

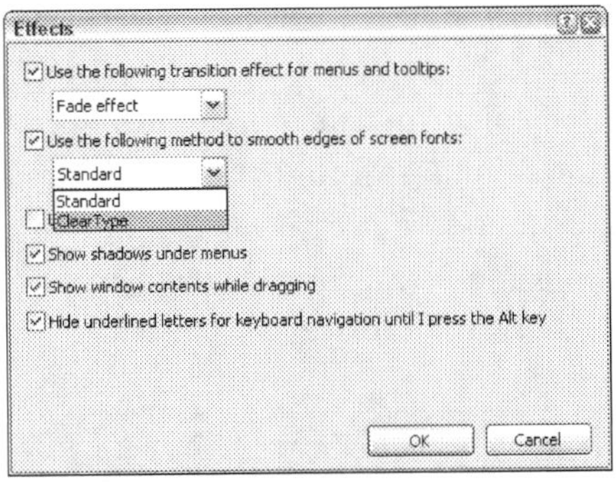

Microsoft also provides a PowerToy that helps "tune" ClearType fonts for your display panel. The ClearType Tuner is located at www.microsoft.com/typography. You can run through a Web-based version of the tuner, or you can download the tuner and install it on your computer and run through it later. The tuner displays

**Figure 13.17.** The ClearType setting is deeply buried but can be well worth the effort of finding it and using it on your laptop or LCD screen.

two different sets of fonts, and much like an eye exam, asks you to pick the one that's clearest. You can always revert back to not using ClearType if you decide you prefer the default display.

# Just the facts

- Use power management options to extend your laptop's battery life.

- Virtual Private Networks allow remote connections through a firewall or security appliance.

- VPNs can be tricky to set up and manage so you may want to explore other remote options such as Remote Desktop Connection.

- Offline File Sharing is an excellent way to take files with you and have them synch up with the originals on your network when you reconnect.

- ClearType fonts may improve font clarity on your laptop's screen.

GET THE SCOOP ON...

Using Help and Support Center for Windows troubleshooting ■
General troubleshooting tips ■ Tracking down network
problems wherever they occur

# Troubleshooting Windows XP

*Chapter 14*

S ome people run Windows XP and never have a problem, like my wife. Others, like me, repeatedly push the limits of what the operating system and installed applications can do and run into the occasional difficulty.

Windows XP is much more stable than earlier versions of Windows, is more robust, and can recover faster from crashes caused by poorly-written software or device drivers. But what really helps is the collection of powerful troubleshooting tools and utilities that are available. You can use them to help determine what is not working properly, and in many cases learn how to fix the problem.

## Using the Help and Support Center

Most online help isn't worth the electrons it's created with. However, the Windows Help and Support system (see Figure 14.1) provides surprisingly good tools and utilities for getting help with the operating system. When you are connected to a network, you also have links to the Microsoft Knowledge Base, so when you conduct a search, you can pull up relevant information from others who may have similar questions. To open the Help and Support Center (HSC), click Start and then Help and Support.

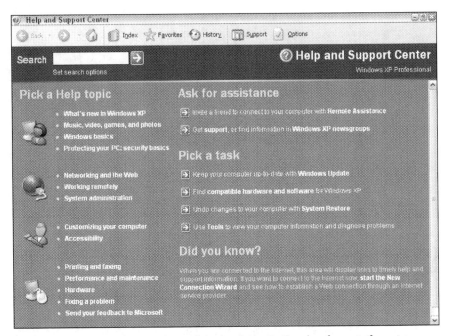

**Figure 14.1.** The Help and Support Center dialog box is the starting place for most of your troubleshooting tactics.

The Pick a Help topic section on the left lists tasks loosely grouped into four categories: user, networking, interface, and system tasks. Several of these, such as System administration and Fixing a problem, take you to pages with many links to other pages or support tools. Oftentimes the HSC offers a friendlier, browser-based interface than the underlying tool, which may use command-line options to work its magic. Because of this, the HSC is one of your first, best places to look for help.

The area on the right of the HSC main page has two sections: Ask for assistance, covered in Chapter 9, and Pick a task, which lists the most common computer-oriented tasks that users might look for. The Use Tools task jumps you to a list of tools and resources you might try to get your computer back to its top operating condition (see Figure 14.2).

At the top of the HSC page is the Search box. You can type in one or several search terms and then press the green arrow. Windows will run your search and return results, if any, on another Web page. If you want, you can change the search parameters. Click Set search options, which you'll find directly below the Search box (see Figure 14.3).

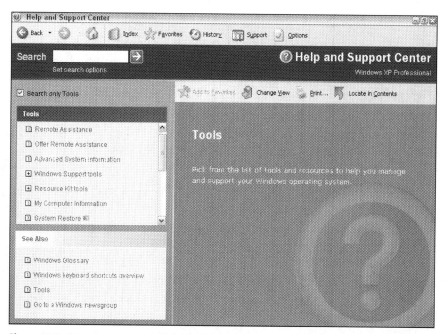

**Figure 14.2.** There are numerous tools in the Help and Support Center that can diagnose or pinpoint problems with your computer.

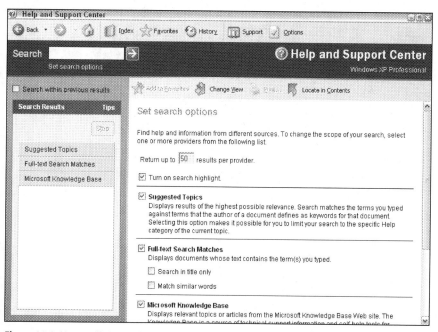

**Figure 14.3.** You can limit or refine your search options to improve the quality of the "hits" you receive.

The HSC Search has several options you can select to alter your results. The most useful ones I've found are the number of results returned; Windows defaults to only 15, but you can increase that to any number up to 999. Try 30 or even 50 as a good starting point. I also turn off the search highlight, because I don't need to see the search term in day-glo orange.

Another option that proves useful is the Microsoft Knowledge Base drop-down list box. You can search for terms against all Microsoft products, or pick a product to narrow your search. HSC defaults to searching against all products, but it's not likely you'll want to see results for printing problems that occurred in Windows NT 4.0 Workstation. Stop here and limit your search if you think your query is limited to a specific product such as Windows XP.

The HSC can be customized to some extent using the Options button located at the top of the HSC browser page. Click the Options button and then click an option in the left-hand pane. In addition to giving you a link to the Microsoft Knowledge Base search options, the options let you change the appearance of the HSC (see Figure 14.4) including the font size used for Help content and various text labels for the HSC buttons.

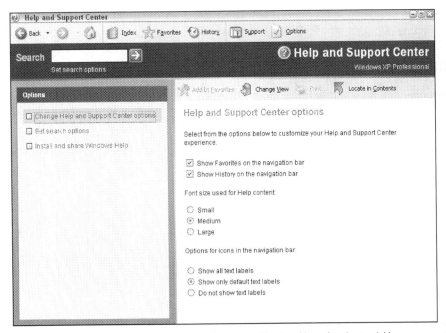

**Figure 14.4.** Your HSC can be customized so it is more readily viewable and understandable.

For more sophisticated users, such as system administrators, you can install and view the help files from other versions of XP-related technology, such as Windows Server 2003. Click Install and share Windows Help, and then select the appropriate option, whether it's installing the help files from a CD or switching to the other system's help file (see Figure 14.5).

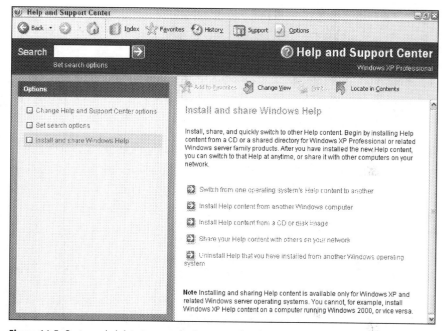

**Figure 14.5.** System administrators can further customize the HSC.

## Help is a click away

Many Windows dialog boxes have Help buttons that call up the appropriate Help page. But what do you do when no Help button is present? There are three ways to call up helpful information without resorting to the Help and Support Center.

First, you can right-click an object in a dialog box and then click What's This? A help balloon appears with information on the dialog box object. Second, click to place the cursor in a field or on a selectable object and then press F1. A help dialog box appears with information on the field, button, or check box.

*(continued)*

*(continued)*

> With the third method, click the question mark in the dialog box's upper right corner. The cursor changes to an arrow with a question mark; the next object you click will bring up the balloon help for that object. This will bring up information from the other two methods depending on what type of object you clicked.

If you perform the "help desk" functions for your coworkers, or administer a business and its servers, this option gives you the flexibility to do it all from your workstation.

## General Windows troubleshooting techniques

Throughout the book there have been suggestions and recommendations for shooting troubles related to specific areas. If the printer isn't printing, check the obvious (is the paper out?) and then proceed to more complicated solutions, such as pausing and restarting the printer queue.

But other times you are left scratching your head when your computer, normally well-behaved, decides to surprise you with a cryptic error message, a sudden inability to read files on your hard drive, or worst of all, a blue screen of death, also known as the BSOD (see Figure 14.6). It is times like these that you have to resort to playing detective and determine what failed, why, and whether it can be fixed quickly.

Generally speaking, with computers there are three types of errors:

- **Hardware.** The inside of a computer case is an unfriendly environment. High heat, poor ventilation, dust bunnies, and mysterious radiation from space aliens can all cause hardware to fail sooner or later. My experience has been that the importance of the failure is in direct proportion to the importance of the deadline you're trying to meet. Some hardware failure is obvious, such as a hard drive failing. Others, like bad memory, are insidious, and cause inconsistent, intermittent failures of all kinds.

- **Software.** This may come as a huge surprise, but software is bug-ridden. Your word processing application decides to crash to the desktop and take your report with it. Some software bugs are hardware-related, such as when buggy device drivers cause your video card to run only in 640 × 480 mode. This is really annoying when you just paid $500 for that killer LCD panel and expected it to work right out of the box.

■ **Human.** This may also be a surprise, but people can do the oddest things, like trying to delete the entire C: drive or move the operating system to the server because it would be safer there. There is an acronym that is used surreptitiously in technical support: PEBKAC, meaning "Problem Exists Between Keyboard and Chair." In other words, the human being driving the computer is causing the problem.

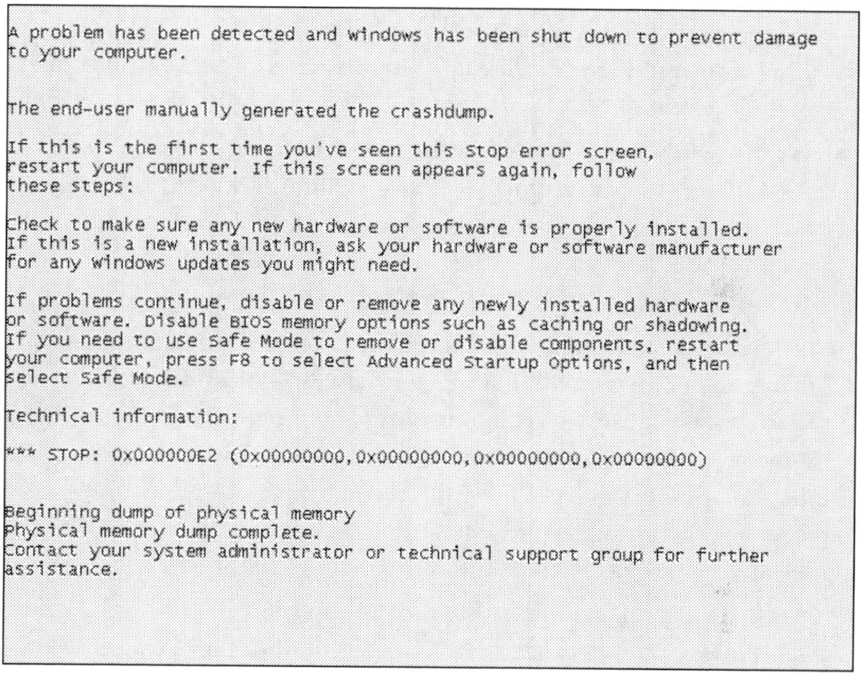

```
A problem has been detected and windows has been shut down to prevent damage
to your computer.

The end-user manually generated the crashdump.

If this is the first time you've seen this stop error screen,
restart your computer. If this screen appears again, follow
these steps:

Check to make sure any new hardware or software is properly installed.
If this is a new installation, ask your hardware or software manufacturer
for any windows updates you might need.

If problems continue, disable or remove any newly installed hardware
or software. Disable BIOS memory options such as caching or shadowing.
If you need to use Safe Mode to remove or disable components, restart
your computer, press F8 to select Advanced Startup Options, and then
select Safe Mode.

Technical information:

*** STOP: 0x000000E2 (0x00000000,0x00000000,0x00000000,0x00000000)


Beginning dump of physical memory
Physical memory dump complete.
Contact your system administrator or technical support group for further
assistance.
```

**Figure 14.6.** The legendary Blue Screen of Death. Few see it and live to tell the tale.

Of course, there can be combinations of these, such as when you accidentally spill your favorite beverage onto the keyboard, and now the "e" key doesn't work. When you are troubleshooting, it's important to take a step back and make some intelligent guesses as to where the problem lies.

There is no one path to figuring out how to solve the problem. The more time you spend working with computers, the more you will feel comfortable trying out different techniques to isolate and solve the problem.

There are some questions that anyone can use to help narrow down the problem's scope. The questions aren't a product of genius, just helpful starting points to get some useful information surrounding the problem. The more information you have, the likelier it is you will locate what's ailing your system.

- **What was being done just prior to the problem?** It's the rare bug that "just happens." Most problems occur as a result of specific steps that trigger the misbehavior. Think back over the previous few minutes: What were you trying to do, which buttons did you press, and which files were open? Determining the conditions for a crash is a big first step in troubleshooting the problem.

- **Can you repeat the problem?** Once you figured out the scenario, can you repeat it? Try doing the same series of steps and see if the same thing happens. A repeatable bug is much more likely to be fixable than an intermittent one.

- **Any new hardware, software, or Web widget installed recently?** More often than not, it's something new that is causing the problem: a new video card, a new game, a new multimedia plug-in that triggers the sudden onset of crashes and desktop woe. Even patches that were released to fix other problems can cause problems of their own.

- **Is the problem reported elsewhere?** Thanks to the Internet, it's easier than ever before to find out if someone else has a flaky video card or flaky drivers that are behaving similarly to your setup. Knowing that someone else is having the same problem is comforting; it's reassurance that it's not you, but a problem with the hardware or software. Most technical support specialists will tell you that you don't have to know the answer, you just need to know where to *find* the answer.

Check the manufacturer's Web site for updated drivers, application patches, FAQs, or forums where other users share their stories. Check independent forums as well, since some manufacturers take a dim view to any posts that imply their product is less than fantastically perfect.

The following techniques can be used as diagnostic or curative techniques, depending on what your sleuthing has uncovered.

- **Reboot.** As any long-time Windows user will tell you, the first fix-it technique is to reboot. If your computer is not locked up (not responding to any mouse or keyboard input), choose Shut Down from the Start menu, wait a minute, and then restart your computer. If your computer is locked up, hit the Big Red Switch, wait a minute, and then restart. You'll be amazed how often this clears up those random, intermittent problems.

- **Remove.** If you installed a new something — a program, a network adapter, a USB sound card — remove it. You may need to visit

Add/Remove Programs to really get things clean; some hardware installs lots of trial or helper applications without your permission, and you should remove those along with the mothership.

- **Reinstall.** Try reinstalling the software or re-seating the hardware (removing and then pushing the hardware back in its slot). Sometimes things just don't "take" the first time around. I've also had success fixing things by reinstalling Service Pack 2, even though Microsoft says you don't need to do this anymore. My guess is that this reinstalls corrupted files or fixes mangled registry keys.

- **Restore.** Roll back your system to an earlier state by using the System Restore feature. In theory this gets you back to a known good state. See Chapter 12 for details on using the System Restore feature. If you haven't been using it, or turned it off to save disk space, I bet you're wishing you hadn't turned it off right about now....

- **Report.** Some people have good luck reporting bugs to hardware and software vendors. You should try reporting the bug: You may get a fix with instructions on how to install it and a request to report back your results. For every 50 bugs I've reported, I've received one contact back from a technical support person. (I don't count automated "customer care" bots that fire off canned responses as a useful reply.) Despite my not-great record, I continue to report bugs in hopes that it helps out somehow.

When you troubleshoot your problem, remember to change only one thing at a time. If you adjust several settings and your system starts working, it's nearly impossible to determine which change, or set of changes, actually fixed the problem. And if you've ever tried home repair where you attempt to fix several things at once but succeed only in making things worse, you'll understand the wisdom of diagnosing and fixing only one bug at a time.

If these techniques fail, I use a two-hour repair policy. If I can't figure out or solve the problem in two hours, it's time to consider wiping the hard drive and reinstalling Windows and all the necessary service packs, applications, and miscellany. Reinstalling takes time, usually more than two hours, but there comes a point of diminishing returns in attempting to isolate and fix a bug yet I'm still sitting there with a nonfunctional computer. The best bet is to save all user data off the hard drive, format the drive, and then reinstall everything.

# Launch and use Safe Mode

Sometimes your computer is in a very bad way. It may not even boot up, or boot partway and hang. When that happens, the traditional reboot method doesn't work; your computer just hangs again and you're left hoping that you have a recent backup somewhere.

Windows XP has several boot options grouped under the general name of Safe Mode that let you boot your computer without loading device drivers that may be causing your computer to crash. If your computer works after you boot into safe mode, you have narrowed down the list of things that could be causing the crash — most likely it is device drivers from recently installed hardware (or recently updated software) that is causing the problem.

To start Windows in safe mode, you have to be quick on the draw. Between the time the BIOS messages and the Windows logo appear, you must press the F8 key. This is a fairly narrow window of time, and if you see the Windows logo, you've missed the opportunity. Reboot and try again.

If you pressed the F8 key at the right time, you will be asked which Windows installation you want to start. This screen appears even if you only have one Windows installation on the computer. Press F8.

The Safe Mode options (see Figure 14.7) are straightforward, though there are quite a few of them.

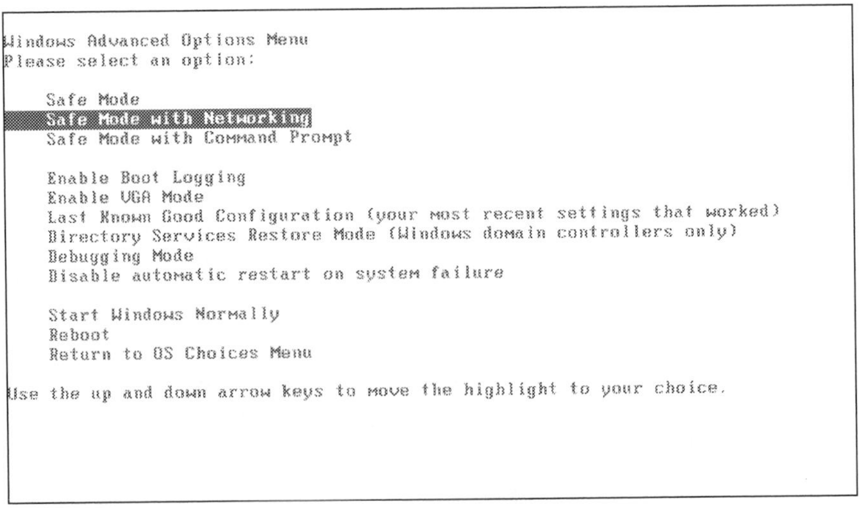

```
Windows Advanced Options Menu
Please select an option:

    Safe Mode
    Safe Mode with Networking
    Safe Mode with Command Prompt

    Enable Boot Logging
    Enable VGA Mode
    Last Known Good Configuration (your most recent settings that worked)
    Directory Services Restore Mode (Windows domain controllers only)
    Debugging Mode
    Disable automatic restart on system failure

    Start Windows Normally
    Reboot
    Return to OS Choices Menu

Use the up and down arrow keys to move the highlight to your choice.
```

**Figure 14.7.** The Safe Mode screen looks a lot like a command prompt, but it controls driver loading at boot time.

> **Bright Idea**
>
> This is a good time to remind you to make a backup of your important information. See Chapter 12 for information on automatically creating backups.

- **Safe Mode.** Starts using only basic files and drivers, such as a mouse, keyboard, hard drive, 640 × 480 8-bit video, and no network.

- **Safe Mode with Networking.** Same as above but adds network capability.

- **Safe Mode with Command Prompt.** Same as Safe Mode, but starts at a command prompt instead of the desktop.

- **Enable Boot Logging.** You can reboot with only this option enabled, or you can use it with other Safe Mode options. It logs all the drivers and services loaded during startup to windows\ntbtlog.txt. If your system hangs, enable boot logging and then look at the last few lines to see which drivers or devices failed.

- **Enable VGA Mode.** Starts your system normally but uses the basic VGA driver. Use this option when your new video card's software is causing your system to bomb.

- **Last Known Good Configuration.** Not nearly as useful as it sounds. When Windows shuts down properly, it writes out registry information to this setting as being "good." If things were going haywire, you decide to reboot, and you click Start and then Shut Down, just like you're supposed to do. When you do this, you overwrite the previously good settings with the bad ones from your current flaky desktop. In my years of troubleshooting I have not used this setting once. A friend of mine reports he has used "Last Known Good" successfully, but that if the user has reached the logon screen and then the crash occurs, it won't work. Once past the logon point, the "Last Known Good" function continues to save the bad registry information that may be causing the crash.

- **Directory Services Restore Mode.** This is only for servers running as domain controllers, not desktops. I have yet to hear a reasonable explanation why it's an option on Windows XP systems.

- **Debugging Mode.** Starts while sending debug information through a serial cable to another computer. Unless you are familiar with system-level programming, you will never use this option.

---

### Use the Recovery Console

The Recovery Console is an even more pared-down version of Windows, giving you only a bare-bones command prompt that lets you access the Windows directory and its subfolders — you don't have access to user files in the Documents and Settings folder. It's truly an option for the savvy troubleshooter, because any surgery you do at this level requires knowledge of the registry, Windows system files, and other lost-in-the-weeds details.

You can start the Recovery Console in two ways. The first is to boot from the Windows CD. At the welcome screen press R, press the number next to your operating system, type the administrator password, and then press Enter. You are dropped at a command prompt; type Help and then press Enter to see the limited subset of commands you can use.

The other way is to install the recovery console sometime after you install Windows but before everything goes sideways. Open a command prompt and browse to the Windows CD and then to the i386 directory. Type winnt32 /cmdcons and then press Enter. Follow the rest of the instructions above.

For more information on the recovery console, see the Microsoft article at http://support.microsoft.com/default.aspx?scid=kb;EN-US; 314058.

---

When you boot into safe mode (see Figure 14.8), you have most of the standard Windows utilities available to you, such as System Restore, Add/Remove Programs, and Device Manager. The easiest way to cure a system with the blues is to use System Restore (see Chapter 12).

On the other hand, the best way to remove misbehaving device drivers without losing all your other changes since the last system restore point was created is to boot into Safe Mode and then uninstall any software or device drivers related to the hardware. When you shut down the computer, open the case, remove the offending hardware, close the case, and then restart your computer. See Chapter 1 for important safety warnings and suggestions for adding and removing hardware.

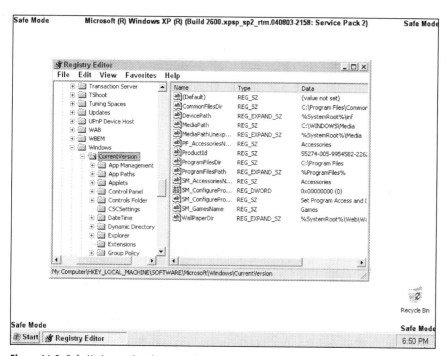

**Figure 14.8.** Safe Mode runs in a lower resolution and without any networking or autorun programs launched.

# Troubleshoot network problems

"Honey, the network's not working again!" I've heard this call for troubleshooting help a few times around my house, and in talking with my other technical friends, they hear it from their families too. One of the commonest calls for help is in figuring out why a computer that was surfing like a champ one day decides to sit for an eternity before returning a "Cannot find your-ispname.com" error message. My standard technique is to save all information in any open documents and then reboot the computer. Nine times out of ten, the network connection comes back, and everyone is happy. But the tenth time needs a little more work.

There are three overall approaches to troubleshooting network problems: Start outward and work in, start in and work outward, or take a best guess approach. I prefer a systematic approach, and in the case where the computer was working fine before, the likeliest culprits are, in order: the remote Web site, your ISP, and finally your own network or computer. This suggests working inward, but you can use whichever method works best for you.

The easiest test is to try to connect to the Web site with another computer on the same network. If it works, try again on the misbehaving computer. If it still doesn't work, focus your troubleshooting efforts on the non-connecting computer.

If both computers can't reach the first Web site, try another Web site. If they both fail again, it's most likely your ISP, or possibly your router, firewall, or hub that's experiencing technical difficulties. Try connecting to your ISP, and if that doesn't work, then it's your broadband provider, your modem, or your router that isn't moving traffic for you.

The three handiest tools in your diagnostic toolbox are ipconfig, ping, and tracert. These are all command-line tools, so in order to use them, open a command prompt by clicking Start, Run, typing cmd, and then pressing Enter.

If you worked with the Windows 9x utility winipcfg, you'll feel comfortable with ipconfig. It does the same thing as that older utility: reports the details of your computer's network configuration in one place so you can see if it matches what the configuration *should* be.

At a command prompt, type ipconfig and press Enter. Ipconfig returns the details about your adapter including its IP address, subnet mask, and local gateway. If you want to see more information, type ipconfig /all and press Enter. This returns information about the DNS servers, the adapter's MAC address, and details about all adapters installed on your system (see Figure 14.9).

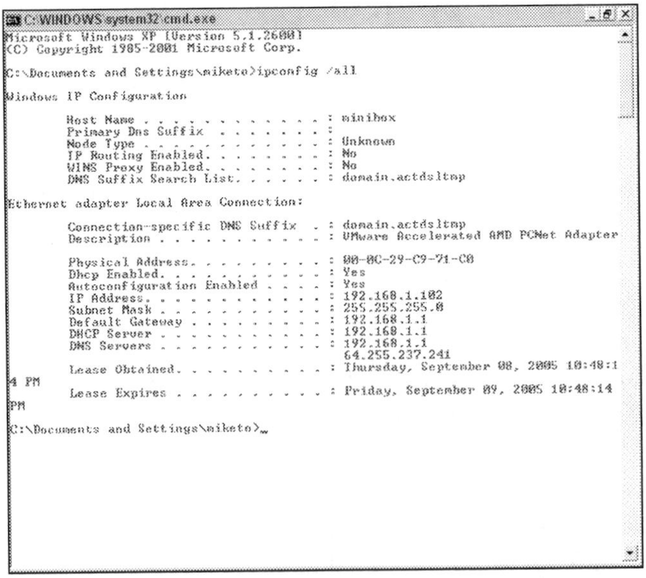

**Figure 14.9.** Ipconfig will give you plenty of information about your network adapter, which you can then confirm against what it should be.

Another handy feature of ipconfig is the ability to release and renew an IP address. Type ipconfig /release to delete the IP address; type ipconfig /renew to reassign an IP address to your adapter. This resets your adapter to use the information that is assigned to it from a DHCP server, or to read in new static IP address information that you have assigned in case the DHCP server is down.

Ping is a network utility that was supposedly named after the sound a sonar echo makes. Ping sends out a series of packets to a destination IP address, essentially asking, "Are you there?" The destination machine sends back a packet in reply. Ping reports on how many packets made it back, and how long it took.

At a command prompt, type ping followed by an IP address or a host name such as your-isp-name.com (see Figure 14.10).

**Figure 14.10.** Ping lets you check whether the destination is available and how long it takes to receive a reply.

Ping is a quick and easy way to tell if a network connection is working. If you are getting ping responses from over the network, then you know the network connection is doing its job. You can ping your own router or gateway to see if it's functioning, or ping your own adapter (type ping localhost to ping your own adapter). Anything that doesn't reply to a ping is not necessarily the culprit, but has been promoted to the suspects list.

**Inside Scoop**

Most larger Web sites do not reply to ping requests, so lack of a response doesn't always mean the server is unavailable. Hackers discovered you could flood a server with pings and keep it from responding to legitimate service requests. Large web site administrators use the ability to disable ping requests to prevent this.

The last helpful utility is tracert. In conjunction with ping it lets you know where a "break" in the system is happening. It asks for a reply from each router along the path to the destination. A very long reply time, upwards of one second, and timeout messages show a router that is not working, keeping your service request from reaching its destination.

Open a command prompt and type tracert followed by an IP address or a host name and then press Enter (see Figure 14.11).

```
C:\WINDOWS\system32\cmd.exe                                    _ 8 X
Microsoft Windows XP [Version 5.1.2600]
(C) Copyright 1985-2001 Microsoft Corp.

C:\Documents and Settings\miketo>tracert www.iinet.com

Tracing route to www.iinet.com [64.255.238.206]
over a maximum of 30 hops:

  1     *        *        *     Request timed out.
  2    31 ms    30 ms    30 ms  ipi.usw158.dsl-acs2.sea.iinet.com [209.20.158.1]

  3    31 ms    31 ms    31 ms  fe-0-0-0-1.acs-rtr01.seatwa0.iinet.com [207.202.
214.167]
  4     *        *        *     Request timed out.
  5     *        *        *     Request timed out.
  6     *        *        *     Request timed out.
  7     *        *        *     Request timed out.
  8     *        *        *     Request timed out.
  9     *       ^C
C:\Documents and Settings\miketo>
```

**Figure 14.11.** Tracert traces the route your packets take and reports back on the health of routers along the way.

Tracert prints out the IP address and reply time from each step, showing you where there may be problems. It's a quick way of determining if it's your ISP's equipment that's at fault or perhaps your own equipment.

Sometimes you will get a call from a family member, saying the network isn't working again. If you ask him if he downloaded anything or changed anything, he will look at you with wide, innocent eyes and tell you nothing has changed. It's times like that you know for sure something has changed and you are probably looking at the culprit. When troubleshooting bad network connections on the computer, look for:

- Loose or disconnected network cables at both the wall and on the computer

- The network connection accidentally set to Disabled

- New firewall or antivirus software that somehow appeared on the machine

- Changed or missing network connection settings

- New network connections that somehow appeared on the computer, such as a wireless connection to your neighbor's Wi-Fi access point

As you can probably tell by now, it's pretty rare for a computer's own networking capabilities to fail without some other intervening agent or cause. Network adapters can fail, but it's easy to run the Help and Support Center troubleshooter to diagnose potential problems. Click Start, Help and Support, click Use Tools to view your computer information and diagnose problems, click Network Diagnostics, and then click Scan your system.

# Just the facts

- The Windows Help and Support Center is a very good first resource to check when things go awry.

- Take a step back and determine what was happening when your computer began having problems.

- Network diagnostic tools are available to help you figure out who to blame.

# Index

## Numerics

802.11 wireless protocols, 335–336

## A

Access policy auditing, 248–250
Actions, 165–166
Activate Windows utility, 501–502
Active Desktop, 68
Active Directory (AD)
  complexity, 28–29
  defined, 28
  distribution folder sharing, 55
  domains, 439
  integrating with, 439–455
  objects, 440–441
  Users and Computers tool, 440
ActiveX controls
  defined, 257
  installation, limiting, 257–258
  listing, 369
  problem, 368
Ad-Aware SE, 226, 227
Add a New Printer Wizard, 399–402
Add a Port dialog box, 206, 207
Add or Remove Programs dialog
  box, 96, 97
Add Standalone Snap-in dialog
  box, 131
Add User Wizard, 114
Add/Remove Snap-in dialog box,
  131, 132
Address toolbar, 87, 88
Administrator accounts
  editing, 120–122
  permissions, 112
  user account modifications,
    121–122
Administrator Tools/Computer
  Management console, 75, 236
Advanced Attributes dialog box,
  168–169, 173
Advanced Download Options dialog
  box, 356

Advanced Privacy Settings dialog
  box, 263
Advanced Security Settings dialog
  box, 251–252
Advanced Settings dialog box, 208
Alert Settings dialog box, 200
Alt-Tab Replacement, 94
Anonymizer, 373
Anti-spyware software
  adding, 222–227
  CounterSpy, 226
  decision factors, 227
  installing, 226–227
  Microsoft Windows
    AntiSpyware, 222–226
  Spybot Search & Destroy,
    226, 227
Antitrust icon, 83–85
Antivirus partners, 220
Antivirus protection, 219
Antivirus software
  evaluations, 221
  functions, 219
  installing, 222
  real-time virus scan, 222
  types of, 221
Application Compatibility
  Toolkit, 107
Application log, 469–470
Applications
  assigned, 451–452
  best performance for, 101, 102
  DOS, running, 104–107
  managed, 454
  managing, with Task Manager,
    98–99
  old Windows, running, 104–107
  published, 452–453
  upgrading, 453–454
Archives. *See* Compressed archives
Assigned applications, 451–452
Attachment blocking, 271–272
Attachment Manager, 42

559